W9-BRS-620

CMRB-ZXEQ-1XV1-0PZ9-MX6W

IMPORTANT

HERE IS YOUR REGISTRATION CODE TO ACCESS MCGRAW-HILL
PREMIUM CONTENT AND MCGRAW-HILL ONLINE RESOURCES

For key premium online resources you need THIS CODE to
gain access. Once the code is entered, you will be able to
use the web resources for the length of your course.

Access is provided only if you have purchased a new book.

If the registration code is missing from this book, the registration screen on our
website, and within your WebCT or Blackboard course will tell you how to obtain
your new code. Your registration code can be used only once to establish
access. It is not transferable.

To gain access to these online resources

1. USE your web browser to go to: **www.mhhe.com/rickabaugh**

2. CLICK on "First Time User"

3. ENTER the Registration Code printed on the tear-off bookmark on the right

4. After you have entered your registration code, click on "Register"

5. FOLLOW the instructions to setup your personal UserID and Password

6. WRITE your UserID and Password down for future reference. Keep it in a safe place.

If your course is using WebCT or Blackboard, you'll be able to use this code to
access the McGraw-Hill content within your instructor's online course.

To gain access to the McGraw-Hill content in your instructor's WebCT or
Blackboard course simply log into the course with the user ID and Password
provided by your instructor. Enter the registration code exactly as it appears to
the right when prompted by the system. You will only need to use this code the
first time you click on McGraw-Hill content.

These instructions are specifically for student access. Instructors are not required
to register via the above instructions.

The McGraw-Hill Companies

Higher Education

Thank you, and welcome to your
McGraw-Hill Online Resources.

0-07-319581-2 t/a
Lips
A New Psychology of Women, 3/e

REGISTRATION CODE

REGISTRATION CODE

The McGraw-Hill Companies

McGraw Hill **Higher Education**

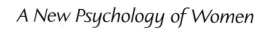
A New Psychology of Women

A New Psychology of Women
Gender, Culture, and Ethnicity
THIRD EDITION

Hilary M. Lips
Radford University

Boston   Burr Ridge, IL   Dubuque, IA   Madison, WI   New York
San Francisco   St. Louis   Bangkok   Bogotá   Caracas   Kuala Lumpur
Lisbon   London   Madrid   Mexico City   Milan   Montreal   New Delhi
Santiago   Seoul   Singapore   Sydney   Taipei   Toronto

*The **McGraw-Hill** Companies*

McGraw Hill **Higher Education**

A NEW PSYCHOLOGY OF WOMEN: GENDER, CULTURE, AND ETHNICITY
Published by McGraw-Hill, a business unit of The McGraw-Hill Companies, Inc., 1221 Avenue of
the Americas, New York, NY, 10020. Copyright © 2006, 2003, 1999 by The McGraw-Hill
Companies, Inc. All rights reserved. No part of this publication may be reproduced or distributed in
any form or by any means, or stored in a database or retrieval system, without the prior written
consent of The McGraw-Hill Companies, Inc., including, but not limited to, in any network or other
electronic storage or transmission, or broadcast for distance learning.

Some ancillaries, including electronic and print components, may not be available to customers
outside the United States.

This book is printed on acid-free paper.

1 2 3 4 5 6 7 8 9 0 FGR/FGR 0 9 8 7 6 5

ISBN 0-07-299785-0

Editor in Chief: *Emily Barrosse*
Publisher: *Stephen D. Rutter*
Senior Sponsoring Editor: *Michael Sugarman*
Marketing Manager: *Melissa Caughlin*
Developmental Editor: *Kirsten Stoller*
Senior Project Manager:
   Christina Thornton-Villagomez
Manuscript Editor: *Ginger Rodriguez*
Associate Designer: *Srdjan Savanovic*
Cover Designer: *Srdjan Savanovic*

Art Manager: *Robin Mouat*
Photo Research: *Alex Ambrose*
Cover Credit: *J. W. Stewart*
Lead Production Supervisor: *Randy Hurst*
Media: *Alex Rohrs*
Permissions editor:
   Marty Granahan/Hilary Lips
Compositor: *TBH Typecast, Inc.*
Printing: *Quebecor World Fairfield Inc.*

Credits: The credits section for this book begins on page C1 and is considered an extension of the
copyright page.

Library of Congress Cataloging-in-Publication Data

Lips, Hilary M.
   A new psychology of women : gender, culture, and ethnicity / Hilary M. Lips.—3rd ed.
     p. cm.
   Includes bibliographical references and index.
   ISBN 0-07-299785-0 (softcover: alk. paper)
   1. Women—Psychology—Cross-cultural studies. 2. Women—Identity—Cross-cultural
studies. 3. Women—Health and hygiene—Cross-cultural studies. 4. Sex role—Cross-cultural
studies. 5. Sexism—Cross-cultural studies. I. Title.
HQ1206.L549 2006
305.42—dc22
                      2004060967

The Internet addresses listed in the text were accurate at the time of publication. The inclusion of a
Web site does not indicate an endorsement by the authors of McGraw-Hill, and McGraw-Hill does
not guarantee the accuracy of the information presented at these sites.
www.mhhe.com

To Wayne,
whose partnership, support, and enthusiasm
have helped to make this and many other projects
more engaging, intricate, and joyful

About the Author

Hilary Lips was born in Canada and completed her undergraduate work at the University of Windsor. After earning her doctorate at Northwestern University, she taught at the University of Winnipeg for a number of years where she developed a course on the psychology of gender and helped to initiate the Women's Studies program. She has been a visiting scholar at the University of Arizona's Southwest Institute for Research on Women, the University of South Florida, The University of Costa Rica, and the Institute for Psychology of the Chinese Academy of Sciences. She is the author of a number of books and articles about the psychology of women and gender, including ***Women, Men, and Power*** (Mayfield, 1991) and ***Sex and Gender: An Introduction,*** **Fifth Edition** (McGraw-Hill, 2005). She recently spent time in New Zealand as a recipient of a Distinguished American Scholar award from the New Zealand-U.S. Educational Foundation. She now chairs the Psychology Department at Radford University, Virginia, where she is also the Director of the Center for Gender Studies.

Preface

It is becoming increasingly clear that the world is a small and interconnected place, and that those of us who live our lives in North America cannot afford to ignore the lives, experiences, and opinions of those whose lives are lived elsewhere. Psychology, like many other disciplines, is shifting its focus to include an awareness that our theories and research are not culture neutral—that what any one of us thinks we know about human beings in general is shaped and limited by our own culture and experience. This book is designed to place the study of the psychology of women in line with this shifting focus.

One of the scholars who reviewed the initial proposal for this book, after expressing the opinion that such a project was timely and important, went on to say, rather ominously, "She is trying to write the psychology of *all* women *everywhere*." Let me say at the outset that this impossible task is indeed *not* the one I would presume to set for myself. I cannot but write from my own perspective, my own cultural background, my own habits of thinking. In using a global, multicultural approach to writing about the psychology of women, I do not pretend to be neutral or "perspectiveless." My perspective is that of a feminist social psychologist, a middle-class White woman who grew up in Canada and now teaches and writes in the United States. I have tried to be sensitive to the limitations of this perspective, to seek out and include the voices and work of those whose backgrounds differ from mine, to provide some overview of the type and amount of the diversity that exists among women, and to illustrate some ways that the knowledge we create, learn, and transmit about women and gender is shaped by our culture.

Throughout the book, the primary aim is to provide some understanding of how gender-related expectations interact with other cultural assumptions and stereotypes, and with social and economic conditions, to affect women's experiences and behavior. A second goal is simply to provide information about the ways women's lives differ in different cultures.

An important focus of the book is research carried out by scholars outside the United States, or outside the mainstream within the United States. Each chapter includes discussions of findings by researchers in various countries, thus allowing readers to form an image of what issues are considered important *within* other cultures. By using this approach, I have tried to avoid, to the extent that it is possible, the type of comparative method that uses the experience of middle-class Americans as a yardstick against which everyone else's experience is judged.

Women, in particular, have much to gain by learning about the ways their difficulties and opportunities as women transcend, or do not transcend, cultural and ethnic group boundaries. In most (some would argue all) cultures, women are disadvantaged in some ways in relation to men. Around the world, men control more of the resources, hold more of the leadership positions, are more likely to visit violence on their partners, and wield more formal power than women. Thus women in different groups might well benefit from exchanging their perceptions of the obstacles they face and sharing their strategies for gaining power, and women worldwide are likely to gain strength by working together as they try to move toward better conditions for women. A prime example of such collective strength was the coming together of women from all over the world for the United Nations Congress on Women in Beijing in 1995.

But there is another benefit when women from different groups listen carefully to one another's voices. If we understand something more about our similarities and differences, we as women may be less likely to share in or tolerate the assumptions and practices that oppress women of other groups. Those of us who are European American may, for instance, begin to understand why African American women might feel excluded and invisible in a college course that treats the notion of employment as a choice women have traditionally been able to make. We may, as temporarily able-bodied (TAB) women, begin to see how women with disabilities are sometimes marginalized when issues of strength or sexuality are discussed. We may begin to see the connections between development aid and the literacy and reproductive control that give the women of rural India a chance to break out of and change patterns of dowry deaths, high infant and maternal mortality, and grinding poverty.

Women do not automatically understand one another or treat one another well just because they are women; barriers of race, class, and culture can, depending on the meaning they are given, prove insurmountable. Idella Parker, the African American woman that European American novelist Marjorie Kinnan Rawlings (1896–1953) called her "perfect maid," wrote later of the difficulties of this relationship. The two women were together in their maid–mistress relationship for many years. Parker may have been Rawlings's best and most loyal friend. At any rate, she was very fond of Rawlings, rescued her from many disastrous situations involving alcohol, and protected her reputation for years. Rawlings, for her part, often treated Parker more as a friend and confidante than a servant, and provided her with resources that were unusually generous. Yet, under the influence of racist attitudes, the power relationship between the two women was such that Parker finally had to leave. She was never allowed to sleep in Rawlings's house. (Neither was any other Black woman. On one occasion, Parker was forced to share her own bed with the African American writer Zora Neale Hurston, who was visiting Rawlings.) She was expected to place Rawlings's needs first under all circumstances. The scenario, with its complex mix of affection and subordination, is reminiscent of what used to be thought of as the ideal marriage relationship between a man and a woman: the wife protecting and supporting the husband at all costs, he controlling the agenda and rewarding her with extra privileges. We can learn something from this parallel: Where the subordination of women is concerned, men do not always stand alone as villains. Women, like men, have a lot to learn about other women.

Chapter 1 explores the reasons for taking a global, multicultural approach to the psychology of women. In Chapter 2 we apply this approach to the beliefs and findings about female–male differences around the world. Having examined the general framework, we turn in Chapters 3 and 4 to specific questions of how girls are socialized through childhood and adolescence: How are they taught to feel about their bodies, and what expectations are they led to develop about their identities, abilities, and accomplishments? Chapters 5, 6, and 7 focus on how these early messages are translated into later behavior in three areas: assertiveness and interpersonal power, communication, and the formation of close relationships. Chapter 8 connects these issues to the workplace and explores the research on equity and fairness with respect to women's employment. The social conditions and relationships that make up women's lives have an impact on their well-being; thus Chapters 9 and 10 examine physical and mental health. Chapter 11 looks at ways in which all of these issues develop and change for women as they make transitions from young adulthood to middle and old age. The last three chapters deal with particular topics that both strongly reflect and strongly affect women's experience in every culture: sexuality, violence against women, and power. Each chapter includes learning activities, suggestions for making social change, discussion questions, a list of key terms, and suggestions for additional reading and Web resources. In addition, to show the diversity of perspectives that has constructed our understanding of women's psychology, each chapter includes a profile of a woman who helped shape psychology.

In this, the third edition, I have updated the statistics in many areas, from healthcare, to divorce, from violence against women to women in political leadership, from poverty to occupational segregation. I have added new research on women's attitudes toward their bodies, their academic self-views, media portrayals of girls and women, the use of and response to self-disclosure and "troubles talk" by women and men, gender and expectations about career, earnings, and family, gender differences in coping with stress, violence within lesbian couples, factors that affect whether a woman who is sexually assaulted labels her experience "rape," and women's leadership. Developments in knowledge about hormone replacement therapy are discussed, as are new findings on attitudes toward affirmative action. There is a new material on the situation of women around the world: the struggle of Japanese women to keep their own names, the prevalence of child marriages in India and Ethiopia, changes in the legal status of same-sex marriage in the United States and elsewhere, the status of parental leave legislation around the world, the progress of Korean women in the political arena, rising lung cancer rates among women in many countries, the plight of juvenile prostitutes in Taiwan, the effectiveness of special "rape courts" in South Africa, the acceptance of women's rights as human rights in various countries. Discussions of diversity within U.S. culture have been expanded as well: coming-of-age issues for Latina women, the different ways African American and European American women are portrayed on television, the widening gap in breast cancer survival rates between African American and European American women. My ability to include such material has been enhanced by an increased focus on diversity among researchers and a growing sense among many writers and scholars that the world is an interdependent community—and that what happens anywhere is likely to be relevant to many of us.

I have many people to thank for help and support with this book. Radford University granted me a professional development leave when the first edition of this book was in its formative stages. During that precious year, Ellen Kimmel found me a home for one semester in the Department of Psychological and Social Foundations of Education at the University of Southern Florida. She and her colleagues supported and encouraged me as I shaped this project and others. I am grateful especially to Ellen and to Nancy Greenman at USF for their support, encouragement, and willingness to discuss ideas about gender and culture during the time I spent in Tampa. I am also grateful to Mirta Gonzalez Suarez at the Interdisciplinary Program for the Study of Gender at the University of Costa Rica. Mirta facilitated my stay as a Visiting Scholar at the University of Costa Rica, and she and her colleagues did their best to expose me to a variety of international perspectives on women and feminism during my one-semester stay there. My year ended with a one-month stay in China, where Zhang Kan and Gu Hongbin of the Institute for Psychology of the Chinese Academy of Sciences went far out of their way to help me learn about China and to understand some of the issues facing women in that country.

Many thanks are due to the reviewers, who helped me see some of my own biases, made helpful suggestions about material to include, and generally encouraged me to make this the best book possible. My thanks go out to these reviewers: for the first edition,

> Shawn Meghan Burn, California Polytechnic State University;
>
> Myra Heinrich, Mesa State College;
>
> Paulette J. Leonard, University of Central Arkansas;
>
> Laura Madson, New Mexico State University;
>
> Shirley M. Ogletree, Southwest Texas State University;
>
> Joan S. Rabin, Towson University;
>
> Vicki Ritts, Southern Illinois University at Edwardsville;
>
> Midge Wilson, DePaul University;
>
> Mary Wyly, Buffalo State College;
>
> and Carolyn Zerbe Enns, Cornell College;

for the second edition,

> Carla Golden, Ithaca College;
>
> Veanne Anderson, Indiana State University;
>
> Dorothy Bianco, Rhode Island College;
>
> and Joanne Marrow, CSU Sacramento;

and for the third edition,

> Carole R. Beal, University of Southern California;
>
> Joan C. Chrisler, Connecticut College;
>
> Betty J. Dorr, Fort Lewis College;
>
> Sandra R. Fiske, Onondaga Community College;
>
> Carla Golden, Ithaca College;
>
> and Carole A. Lawton, Indiana-Purdue University Fort Wayne.

The first edition of this book was developed under the guidance of sponsoring editor Franklin Graham. In the second edition, I benefited from the careful copyediting of Ginger

Rodriguez, the project manager, Christina Thornton-Villagomez, and the cheerful and supportive assistance of associate editor Katherine Bates. In developing this edition, I have appreciated the help and encouragement of Developmental Editor Kirsten Stoller and the assistance, once again, of copyeditor Ginger Rodriguez and project manager Christina Thornton-Villagomez. I have appreciated their help and their many useful suggestions. I extend my gratitude also to Pat Donat, who put together a carefully thought-out and meticulously correct revised Instructor's Manual for this edition. She has added numerous resources and suggestions that will help those who use the book.

Much of my energy and inspiration for writing about these topics comes from my students, particularly those who have taken my Psychology of Women class during my years at Radford University. I thank my students and colleagues at Radford for sharing ideas, for humor and friendship, for patience and support.

Finally, I thank Wayne Andrew, whose support has been unfailing and unflinching. I am grateful to him for uncountable instances of help and encouragement, for assistance in numerous concrete ways at every stage of this project, for many long days and late nights.

Contents

CHAPTER 1

Why a Global, Multicultural Psychology of Women

CHAPTER OUTLINE

In 1873, Amelia Edwards, a redoubtable Englishwoman, published an account of her travels through the Dolomites. The book, *Untrodden Peaks and Unfrequented Valleys,* documents her journey with another woman—on foot and on horseback—over terrain that was rough and uninviting to travelers, particularly women travelers. At a time when most English gentlewomen led sheltered, uneventful lives, Amelia Edwards craved and found adventure in her explorations. Not content with the vision of the world that she had inherited as a White Victorian woman of comfortable means, she traveled the globe with her women friends to gain and communicate new perspectives.

Edwards was an ardent advocate of women's rights. She correctly intuited that if women were to develop a sense of independence and strength, they needed to step out from the protective embrace of their families—even their country and culture—to undertake their own journeys and gather their own experiences. Amelia Edwards followed her own advice: She forged an exciting life as an adventurer, travel writer, and archaeologist. She journeyed to remote corners of the world, wrote well-received novels and travel books, and rose to prominence as a lecturer in Egyptology.

In 1921, Bessie Coleman, born not to privilege, but to poverty, earned her pilot's license. She had spent the early years of her life picking cotton and living in a three-room shack in east Texas—an unlikely start, perhaps, for the world's first African American female aviator. It was while she was working as a manicurist in Chicago that she began to dream of flying. When no one in that city would teach her, she raised the money to travel to France. There she studied at one of the best flight schools. In defiance of the restrictions associated with her race, class, and gender, she became a glamorous and daring pilot, drawing large crowds when she performed in air shows. She used her fame to encourage other African Americans to fly, and pointedly refused to perform in places where Blacks would not be admitted. She died tragically at the age of 34 when she fell from her plane as it nosedived toward the ground while preparing for a flying exhibition.

Bessie Coleman, who could barely write, left few records of her exploits or of her thoughts and feelings about her flying career. Because she was African American, mainstream newspapers of the day gave her little coverage. Her funeral was attended by 10,000 mourners, but after her death, her accomplishments faded into obscurity for many years. However, she has always been remembered by African American flyers, and in 1977 a group of African American women pilots established the Bessie Coleman Aviators Club. Finally, in 1996, her accomplishments were returned to prominence when she was featured on a U.S. postage stamp.

In 1992, at the age of 33, Rigoberta Menchú was awarded the Nobel Peace Prize, praised by the Nobel Committee for standing "as a uniquely potent symbol of a just struggle." A Mayan Indian of the Quiché people, Menchú grew up in Guatemala. Her mother was a midwife and healer, her father a community leader and organizer. As a child Menchú picked cotton and coffee beans, and later worked as a maid in Guatemala City. Before the age of 20, she was traveling with her father around the countryside, urging Native American peoples to resist the appropriation of their land and villages. The struggle proved to be a tragic one for her family: Her younger brother, father, and mother were killed because of their political activities.

Menchú was literally forced into the international arena by these events. She became an organizer of peasants, students, and workers. Soon she was wanted for "subversive activities" and fled to Mexico. She told the world about the conditions in Guatemala through her published autobiography and joined international efforts to protest human rights abuses by the Guatemalan government.

In 1992, Mae Jemison blasted off on the shuttle *Endeavour,* becoming the first African American woman to travel into space. As a child growing up on the south side of Chicago, she had watched the stars in awe, dreaming that someday she would visit them. Her route to the stars took her through a host of high school science projects, university training as a chemical engineer, training in choreography and dance, a medical degree, and a stint in the Peace Corps in Thailand. Through it all, she learned to think of her life as a journey, and not to limit herself because of anyone else's limited imagination.

Jemison, a modern-day explorer who now spends a good deal of her energy encouraging young women to expand their horizons, sees the world as a small and interconnected place. Viewed from space, the earth presents a face that inexorably calls forth a global perspective.

What if these four great women could meet? What would they say to one another? Would they feel a sense of kinship? How well would they understand one another? Would they be friends? They grew up in different times and places. One was relatively wealthy, two crushingly poor, one middle-class. One was a product of the British Empire at its height, a privileged citizen of a country that viewed itself as the center of civilization. One grew up in a rural Black American community, under conditions of strict racial segregation. One was raised in a poor family in a country where the stirrings of a class struggle were beginning to change lives. One grew up in a large U.S. city where formal racial segregation was illegal—but where informal segregation was rampant. What all four would have in common is their gender and their sense of courage. Would that be enough?

What kind of a "psychology of women" would address the lives and experiences of these four women? Surely the description of the anxieties and aspirations, identity development, and family relationships that characterized Amelia Edwards would, for instance, be quite different from those that characterized Bessie Coleman. Is "woman" a useful category of analysis here?

An examination of the psychology of women looks at the ways women's shared experience is distinct from that of men. One of the things women may have in common is the barriers they face. Different groups of women may vary in the ways they experience and interpret those barriers, in the strategies they adopt for overcoming them, in how successful they are at transcending them. For instance, the four women described here share certain barriers, despite the dramatic differences in their lives. All four faced cultures in which men were traditionally the travelers, the organizers, the great explorers and adventurers. Women, with fewer resources and surrounded by an ideology that expected them to be home centered and subordinate to men, were supposed to wait and worry while men traveled the world. These obstacles are different in degree, but perhaps not in kind, from those facing women of various backgrounds as we try to enlarge our perspective on the world. We have less money and fewer opportunities to travel than our male counterparts do. We are imbued with the notion that we need protection and should not wander about on our own. We are expected, in many instances, to be subordinate to and more home centered than men.

Perhaps we should pay special attention to one obstacle that sometimes bedeviled Amelia Edwards: the blinders imposed by her membership in a privileged class in a nation that viewed itself as the center of civilization. Edwards was known for her friendliness to those she met during her travels, but that friendliness could not always escape a hint of condescension. She was moved, on one occasion, to write that it was easy for her to regard the hoteliers of southern Italy "almost as equals" (Edwards, 1987, p. 220) because they came from old, well-bred families.

Each of us sees the world from our own necessarily limited vantage point. And what we see of those we encounter in our travels is often colored by our assumption that *our* way is normal, whereas theirs is exotic. White, middle-class, North American women, of whom I am one and who include many of the readers of this book, may be especially hindered by the habit of seeing the world through the eyes of privilege. One of my European American students, baffled by the list of possibilities on a questionnaire that asked for ethnic background, asked me in genuine puzzlement, "What do we check if we're just *normal*?"

Yet most of us do have one advantage over Amelia Edwards. We do not have to travel vast distances to encounter new perspectives or to meet people whose views of the world are quite different from our own. The world is a smaller place now than it was in the 19th century. Easier travel and immigration and the breakdown of legalized racial, ethnic, and religious segregation in most countries have made the populations of many nations increasingly diverse. We have more opportunities to learn from one another now than ever in the past— and none of us can afford the assumption that our own group is the one that is "normal."

Femininity and Masculinity Are Socially Constructed

Among the Hima people of western Uganda, fat is beautiful—at least for women. Men measure a woman's attractiveness by her obesity, and a young woman is prepared for marriage in ways guaranteed to fatten her up: the least possible activity and the most possible

BOX 1.1 MAKING CHANGE
Reaching across Boundaries

A first step in gaining a more multicultural, global perspective on the psychology of women is to listen to women whose backgrounds are different from one's own. One way to do this is to read what women from a variety of cultural or ethnic groups have written—and there are many suggestions for such reading at the end of each chapter. But what about conversation? Can you find ways to meet and talk with women who are located differently than you are with respect to ethnicity, race, nationality, social class, age, sexual orientation, physical ability? Try to get to know someone new who differs from you on one or more of these dimensions. Have some conversations in which you do most of the listening. If your campus has an international students' association, attend some of the events and talk with the women who are involved. What can you learn about the world and about women from such conversations? What can you learn about yourself? What social changes might occur if many people did this?

food. By the time of her marriage, a young woman may be so fat that she cannot walk, only waddle. At the wedding, onlookers will comment on how beautiful she is, noting with approval the cracks in her skin caused by the fat and the difficulty she has walking. Once married, a woman is kept fat by consuming surplus milk from the herd—often coerced to do so by her husband when she has long passed the point of satiation. The wife leads a life of leisure. She is assigned no heavy physical work, rarely leaves home, and spends her days in sexual liaisons with a variety of men approved by her husband. These sexual relationships cement economic ones: The obese, conspicuously consuming wife is both a symbol and an instrument of her husband's economic prosperity (Tiffany, 1982).

A similar pattern is seen in other West African countries. One report from Niger describes fat as a beauty ideal so prevalent that women take steroids to gain weight or pills to increase their appetite (Onishi, 2001). At one festival in that country, women of the Djerma ethnic group compete in a beauty contest for which they train by gorging on food and by drinking as much water as they can on the morning before the contest: The heaviest woman wins. In some parts of neighboring Nigeria, women go to fattening farms for a few weeks before their weddings, and there they are stuffed with food and massaged into a rounder shape. As is the case with the Hima women, in these countries a woman's corpulence is a status symbol for her husband. A fat wife is a sign that a man is wealthy and responsible—a good provider for his family.

In China, and in the Chinese American community in the United States, until the early part of this century it was common to tightly bind the feet of young girls. Small feet, "golden lilies," were considered a sign of beauty and refinement. Not only did binding keep the feet from growing to full size, it deformed them and prevented them from developing the normal strength and flexibility needed for walking—making it difficult or impossible for a woman to walk unassisted. These women were not necessarily being prepared for a life of leisure, however. The average young Chinese woman looked forward to

In China, the traditional practice of foot binding left women with deformed, atrophied feet. Now discontinued, the procedure was meant to guarantee that a woman's feet would be small and dainty, but it also guaranteed that she would hobble and be in constant pain.

an arranged marriage in which she would be expected to serve her mother-in-law and submit to her husband. Her life revolved around the necessity for obedience—as a daughter, to her parents; after marriage, to her husband; in widowhood, to her son (Pascoe, 1990).

These very different cultures have something in common: They include strong ideas about what it means to be feminine. And the notions of femininity have overlapping themes: the cultivation of beauty, restrictions on movement and other freedoms, subservience to husband. Parallel themes may be found in the United States today: for example, the use of drastic methods such as liposuction and breast augmentation surgery to shape women's bodies to cultural standards of beauty, the popularity of high-heeled shoes and short skirts even though these garments make it impossible for women to move comfortably, the tradition that a woman takes her husband's name at marriage. Cultures differ greatly in their details, but some general themes that define femininity are very similar across many cultures: Women should be beautiful (however that is defined), not strong, and under the authority of men.

Gender is the term used to encompass the social expectations associated with femininity and masculinity (Unger, 1979b). Finding that cultures also *differ* from one another in their rules and expectations for femininity (and for masculinity) is a good clue that gender is **"socially constructed."** In other words, each society, to some extent, makes up its own set of rules to define what it means to be a woman or a man, and people construct gender through their interactions by behaving in "appropriate" ways. Another clue that gender is socially constructed is the way the rules tend to change arbitrarily over time, even within a given culture. For example, in the United States, the current division of infant clothing into pink for girls and blue for boys is actually a reversal of an older rule. Before World War I, girls wore blue—a color that was supposedly delicate and dainty—and boys wore pink, the "stronger" color (Salmans, 1989, cited in Garber, 1992).

The rules for femininity and masculinity are grounded in the biological/anatomical distinctions between women and men (what we call **sex differences**), but go well beyond such distinctions. For example, one important sex difference is that women can become pregnant and men cannot. This biological distinction has been used in many cultures to create a set of "femininity" expectations for women that include being maternally inclined, nurturing, and close to the earth.

Being maternally inclined or nurturing are not obviously biological or anatomical qualities. Rather, they arise from social expectations that *build on* women's biological ability to bear children. But it is not at all clear that particular ways of acting or thinking necessarily go with being biologically female or male: Cultural notions of what behavioral, emotional, or even spiritual qualities are tied to biological femaleness or maleness vary widely across time and place. Qualities such as nurturance and inclination toward motherhood, then, appear to be aspects of gender, not of biological sex.

But just how easily can we separate biological sex from socially constructed gender? Biological differences between women and men are not absolute. As we will delve into in some detail in Chapter 3, the biological categories *female* and *male* overlap, and decisions about where to "draw the line" between them is often a social, not a biological, one. So even sex "is not a pure physical category" (Fausto-Sterling, 2000, p. 4). Also, even the physical, sexual body is, in some ways, shaped by the social environment: We "embody" gender as we develop within our social world. If we are female, for example, we are, in some circumstances, encouraged to become pregnant and may face disapproval or pity if we do not bear children. If we have an unplanned pregnancy, societal rules govern whether we will be able to decide for ourselves whether to carry it to term. The biological capacity to become pregnant is not independent of the social expectations surrounding femininity.

Thus, the distinction between sex and gender is at best a fuzzy one: The two overlap. Biology and environment work together so intimately that they are like two sides of the same coin, and it is virtually impossible to label a particular female–male difference as purely based in either biology or culture. In this book, *gender* is used as the more inclusive term when discussing female–male differences that may be caused by any combination of environment and biology. *Gender* is also used as a label for the system of expectations societies hold with respect to feminine and masculine roles. *Sex* is reserved for discussions of anatomy and the classification of individuals based on their anatomical category.

How Many Genders Are There?

History is dotted with examples of women who refused to live within the bounds of behavior that was prescribed for them by social expectations of femininity. For example, in 1778 Deborah Samson of Plymouth, Massachusetts, disguised herself as a young man, Robert

Shirtliffe, and enlisted for the term of the Revolutionary War. She served for three years and was wounded twice. However, her sexual identity went undetected until she contracted brain fever (Ellet, 1848). In the American Civil War, an estimated 400 women dressed as men, enlisted, and served as soldiers (Burgess, 1994). In England, as early as the 18th century, women acting as men in the military were common enough to raise the concerns of the courts. In cases such as this, the women were often fleeing poverty or severe restrictions on their lives and were seeking the privileges, opportunities, and economic security that could be obtained only by adopting male dress. Many of these women lived as men for their entire adult lives (Wheelwright, 1990).

These women transgressed the two-gender system by crossing over to the other gender. However, they had to be secretive about their choice. In some cultures, alternatives to the two-gender system are institutionalized, and individuals can make a relatively public choice to opt out of the female or male gender. Nothing puts the social construction of gender into such sharp relief as a look at societies in which gender is discussed not in terms of two categories (feminine or masculine), but in terms of three or more categories. For those of us who have grown up thinking of gender as a binary concept, it may be difficult to imagine a **third gender** or a society in which an individual's gender is considered fluid or changeable. However, in a number of cultures, gender "is understood in a psychological or psychospiritual sense much more than a physiological one" (Allen, 1986, p. 207). In such cultures, more than two genders exist.

When anthropologists encountered individuals in Native American societies who apparently had an "intermediate" gender status, accomplished by combining or mixing the attributes and behaviors of females and males, they tried to fit these individuals into their own Western understanding of gender. Thus they used terms such as *man-woman* and *half-man-halfwoman* to translate the Native American terms for such individuals: *nadle, winkte, heemaneh.* Yet it now appears that these translations were misleading. The Native American terms describe a distinct third gender—one that is not simply a mixture of masculine and feminine, but defined separately from them (Callender & Kochems, 1983; Fulton & Anderson, 1992). Such a person is neither a man dressing and acting like a woman, nor a woman dressing and acting like a man, but a man or woman who has adopted a third role that is neither feminine nor masculine. The man-woman in preconquest Native American societies did not fit neatly into the categories that academics from other societies felt (and still feel) comfortable with. These categories, such as **homosexual** (someone who is sexually attracted to members of her/his own sex) and **transvestite** (someone who enjoys dressing in the clothing of the other gender), do not always adequately describe the behavior of a man-woman. For example, not every individual who engaged in same-sex sexual relations would be considered a man-woman by the Native American community. Nor did every man-woman engage in same-sex sexual relations. These individuals were not simply cross-dressing (dressing in the clothing of the other gender) but were wearing clothing appropriate to their third-gender status: clothing that was a mixture of the items customarily worn by women and by men.

Some anthropologists now believe that by adopting a role that bridged the categories of female and male, individuals of the third gender became regarded as intermediaries for dangerous passages between categories. These third-gender individuals often presided over transformational events such as birth, marriage, and death and were highly valued by their communities as arbiters of continuity in a precarious world (Fulton & Anderson, 1992).

The idea of more than two genders is not limited to indigenous North American societies. In Samoa, for example, a third gender category of person is known as *fa'afafine,* meaning "the way of women." These are males who dress in women's clothing and are often included in female activities. These individuals do not "pass" for women, nor do they follow the rules that are understood to be in place for "proper" women; rather, they act as jesters who mock certain gender restrictions and can violate them with impunity. For instance, a Samoan girl may whisper some suggestive remark about a passing boy—perhaps a sexual comment about some feature of his anatomy—to a *fa'afafine.* The *fa'afafine,* not bound by the same restrictions of propriety as the girl, will then make a loud joke out of her comments, attracting the attention of the boy (Mageo, 1992).

In India, a group of men who adopt female dress and become a kind of third gender are called *hijras.* These individuals believe that their spiritual power stems from a renunciation of male sexuality, and they sometimes submit to castration to define their status. They count themselves as women in some situations; however, they do not follow the standards of modesty and restraint required of Indian women (Nanda, 1990).

In certain cultures, gender categories are viewed as somewhat fluid, rather than immutable. In the Samoan culture described above, *fa'afafine* can leave their role behind if they decide, as adults, that they want to be married men with families. Among the Zuni of the American Southwest, gender was thought to be established by specific ritual experiences. In Inuit mythology even sex was changeable; it was believed that a fetus could change its sex during the birth process (Saladin d'Anglure, 1988). Clearly, the notions of femininity and masculinity many of us are familiar with represent one way, not the only way, to think about gender.

The blurring of the binary, either–or notion of gender is not limited to small or preindustrial societies. Cross-dressing, although not exactly common, is a well-established institution in North America, Europe, and Asia. Besides such famous figures as Boy George and Dennis Rodman, there are many less well-known individuals, such as the Tiffany Club of Waltham, Massachusetts, a group of 350 transvestites, most of whom are male, middle-class, and married (Garber, 1992). A fascination with the theme of cross-dressing has been apparent in film (*Tootsie, Victor/Victoria, Yentl, Some Like It Hot, The Ballad of Little Jo, Mrs. Doubtfire, The Crying Game*) and literature (Virginia Woolf's novel *Orlando,* and David Henry Hwang's play *M. Butterfly*). However, the act of dressing as a member of the other sex has usually been treated as an aberration, a trick, or a joke. Western industrial societies have generally refused to accept or institutionalize a third gender category whose existence threatens the ability to categorize every person as female or male.

Actually, it is not necessary to cite cross-dressing or a formally identified third gender to question the notion that gender is a neat dichotomy that places all of us into one of two groups who either "act like women" or "act like men." What does a woman act like? Look like? Think like? For most people, the answers to those questions would be: "It depends on what kind of woman she is." Indeed, American researchers have found that respondents differentiate among many different "types" of women, some of whom appear to have little or nothing in common except for their biological sex. For example, respondents in one

BOX 1.2 LEARNING ACTIVITY
Gender Transgressions in the Movies

Movies have been a "safe" place for society to explore and transgress the boundaries of gender. The following movies feature persons who adopt aspects of gender that do not "match" their biological sex. Choose one of more of these movies to watch. Record your observations of how the characters learn and/or perform gender. Do these observations change your ideas about the flexibility or rigidity of gender categories?

Tootsie

Victor/Victoria

The Birdcage

The Crying Game

Switch

To Wong Fu, Thanks for Everything, Julie Newmar

Boys Don't Cry

Mrs. Doubtfire

The Adventures of Priscilla, Queen of the Desert

Orlando

Yentl

study described several distinct clusters of "types" of women: a progressive or nontraditional cluster, which included such types as the feminist, the intellectual, the career woman; a traditional or conservative cluster, which included types such as the housewife, the secretary, the conformist, and the maternal woman; and a cluster characterized by sexuality, including the vamp, the sex bomb, and the tart (Six & Eckes, 1991). To each different type of woman, respondents attributed different personal and behavioral qualities.

Before leaving the discussion of the many different ways in which gender can be conceptualized, we should note the possibility that, in certain cultures, gender may not be a particularly important category for organizing people into roles. Because we think of gender and its categories as important, we tend to assume that this emphasis is common to all cultures. Yet, as Nigerian anthropologist Oyeronke Oyewumi (1997; 1998) notes, this is not the case. She describes the Yoruba culture in her own country as being organized around relative age rather than gender. Yoruba pronouns do not indicate sex; instead, they indicate whether the person being spoken of is older or younger than the speaker. She argues that, when societies have been studied through the gendered perspective of European-based cultures, gender in these societies has in some ways been constructed by the scholars who have studied them.

Why, in our study of female psychology, should we even try to make a distinction between "gender" and "sex"—a distinction that may be fuzzy at best and misleading at worst? The main reason is to remind ourselves that much of the behavior we associate with women does not stem in any simple, predetermined way from simply being female. Femaleness is relevant, of course, in the sense that an individual's body provides possibilities and limits to such attributes as strength, size, voice quality, and reproductive capacity. Yet the behavior of each woman and girl is sharply influenced by her own society's notions of femininity—of what a woman is supposed to be like.

If Gender Is the Issue, Why Focus on Women?

Psychologists have discovered that in Western cultures, individuals explaining the actions of others tend to assume that those actions stem from internal dispositions—from the way the other person *is*. In contrast, one's explanations of one's own actions focus more strongly on *external* forces—outside pressures, extenuating circumstances, fear of punishment, hope of reward (Jones & Davis, 1965).

The same may be said of the way the members of one group tend to judge or explain the actions of members of another group. People attribute more homogeneity, or sameness, to members of another group than they do to their own. We expect the members of the other group to be more alike than members of our own group (Taylor, 1981). In effect, when we judge members of another group, we are assuming that "these people are the way they are," and thus we make fewer allowances for the effects of outside forces on them than we do for ourselves.

Even though all groups tend to make judgments in this way (for example, men may say "Women! They are so complicated, so emotional!"; women may say "Men are so insensitive; they are all only after one thing!"), the impact of these judgments is not the same for every group. The more powerful groups' judgments are given the most media time, prevail most often, receive a great deal of attention, and become accepted as the truth. This is true of women and men. Men are more visible as experts, hold more high-status positions, and generally are accorded more credibility, authority, and power than women. Thus, men's judgments about most matters, including women, have more impact than women's judgments.

A colleague recently described, with a mixture of irritation and humor, a formal debate she had witnessed in which two male scientists argued about the true nature of female orgasm. Each man had his own notion of the female sexual experience, and elaborated it at length, while a respectful audience listened and took notes.

"Why wouldn't they include a woman—or two women—in an event like this?" she asked in disbelief. "Who would expect two men to be able to provide a complete picture of female sexuality?"

Men have a long history of making pronouncements about women. Many of those pronouncements have as a theme that women are, by nature, a certain way. Here are some of the more sweeping ones that have survived the years and are still quoted:

"Frailty, thy name is woman!"—William Shakespeare, *Hamlet*

"Woman is the lesser man . . ."—Alfred Lord Tennyson, *Locksley Hall* (1842)

"In revenge and in love woman is more barbarous than man."—Friedrich Wilhelm Nietzsche, *Thus Spake Zarathustra* (1883)

"Girls are injured more than boys by school life; they take it more seriously, and at certain times and at a certain age are far more subject to harm. It is probably not an exaggeration to say that to the average cost of each girl's education through high school must be added one unborn child."—psychologist James Mckeen Cattell (1909, p. 91), explaining that higher education is bad for girls because intellectual work impairs their fertility

"The immediate outcome of [the] feminine mental type is woman's tact and aesthetic feeling, her instinctive insight, her enthusiasms, her sympathy, her natural wisdom and morality; but, on the other side, also her lack of clearness and logical consistency, her tendency to hasty generalization, her mixing of principles, her undervaluation of the abstract and of the absent, her lack of deliberation, her readiness to follow her feelings and emotions."—psychologist Hugo Munsterberg (1901, p. 159)

Women's pronouncements about men, or indeed, about women, have been less publicized. In fact, Elaine Partnow (1977) was moved to compile a two-volume set of quotations by women after finding that among the standard quotation collections such as Bartlett's and Oxford, women made up 1 percent or less of the sources.

Because men have had more power than women to define gender expectations, their tendency to judge the "other group" (women) as being more alike and less influenced by external forces than their own group (men) has had a big impact. Women, as the group whose opinions have received less attention, have been particularly affected by the tendency to view gender-related expectations as natural, rather than as socially constructed. Concepts such as feminine frailty, maternal instinct, female irrationality, all considered to be built in to female biology, abound, and have traditionally been used to explain restrictions on women's roles. Parallel or similar concepts for men have had less impact. Masculine-stereotyped qualities such as sexual insatiability and irresponsibility, aggressiveness, and reluctance to commit to a relationship are sometimes ascribed to male biology, but such attributes generally have not been used to justify the disqualification of men from positions of high status and responsibility. If anything, they have been used to excuse antisocial male behavior.

In essence, we know less about women than we should because the study of gender has been shaped, like the study of anything else, by power relations. Because, as a group, men have held more power than women, they have had the luxury of a privileged viewpoint: being able to ignore things that seem irrelevant to themselves and defining the truth in terms of their own experience. And the assumptions made by groups with the most power tend to carry the most weight. For example, the first psychologists to study achievement motivation focused on men—presumably because they assumed that male achievement was most important and that women were not interested in achievement. Thus John Atkinson's classic work on achievement motivation, *Motives in Fantasy, Action, and Society* (1958), mentions women in only a single footnote, and David McClelland's book *The Achieving Society* (1961) omits any mention of women. A study of the psychology of women reexamines such assumptions. It tries to redress the balance and provide a more complete picture by looking at women from women's perspective.

Should a Psychology of Women Be "Feminist"?

In at least one university I know, the psychology of women course came into being long before there were calls on campus to question the status quo with respect to women and gender. In the context of a women's college, the course was developed as a way to teach women their role, their proper place, in society. Women students who took this course could expect to learn the reasons why marriage worked best when husbands were in charge, why women were naturally suited to motherhood, why a woman's place was in the home. It was an approach that did not question traditional gender expectations and was not concerned with gender equality. Is this the kind of approach you hoped to encounter when you signed up for this course? If not, you may be relieved to know that most psychology of women courses no longer follow this model. Rather, they take a perspective that has been termed **feminist psychology.**

What exactly does this mean? Feminist psychology is characterized by a focus on understanding women's own experience, rather than on fitting women into traditional, often male-centered, views of human behavior and social relations. A feminist psychology of women is oriented toward questioning traditional assumptions about gender and toward empowering women. Feminist psychologists often try to understand gender-related behavior by looking at power inequalities between women and men. In addition, they are alert to cultural differences that affect women's psychology, acknowledging that there are many differences among women and that these differences too are often linked to power inequalities among groups.

Film and television star Sarah Jessica Parker has proclaimed, "I love referring to myself as a feminist. 'Feminist' is an exquisite word." (Stave, 2001, p. 40). Yet many people are uncomfortable with the term **feminist.** In one recent study, more than 77 percent of a sample of female college students did not label themselves as feminists even though many of them did support some or all of the goals of the feminist movement (Liss, O'Connor, Morosky, & Crawford, 2001).

Do people refuse the label *feminist* because they disagree with the ideas espoused by feminists? Actually, it appears that a reluctance to label oneself as feminist can often mask an agreement with such core aspects of feminist consciousness as a pro-woman stance and a rejection of traditional gender roles. Women and men who were young adults during the early 1970s—a time when feminism was experiencing a strong and visible resurgence as a social movement—are more likely than their younger or older counterparts to identify themselves as feminists (Schnittker, Freese, & Powell, 2003). However, among the latter (non-70s) groups, there was no difference between self-identified feminists and nonfeminists in their agreement with specific feminist positions. Similarly, a study of students in the United States and Russia revealed that there was little correlation, in either country, between feminist identification and beliefs about such issues as abortion, the sharing of household work between women and men, and providing women with time off work to care for families (Henderson-King & Zhermer, 2003).

Feminism comes in many different versions, but all of them share certain premises: the notion that inequalities between women and men should be challenged; that women's experiences and concerns are important; that women's ideas, behaviors, and feelings are worthy of study in their own right. These ideas seem eminently reasonable, so why do so

BOX 1.3 WOMEN SHAPING PSYCHOLOGY
Sandra W. Pyke

Sandra Pyke's doctoral studies in psychology at McGill University prepared her to be an academic psychologist and earned her a Ph.D. in 1964. However, they did not prepare her specifically for what was to be her most important role in psychology: leadership in the efforts to make psychology as a discipline responsive to and reflective of women's experiences and concerns.

Pyke's early career as a faculty member at York University in Canada included a focus on research and applied training. However, in 1972 she was a participant in an "underground symposium" titled *On Women, by Women* at the Canadian Psychological Association (CPA) convention. The symposium (and the reaction it caused) proved to be a catalyst for the formation of a new organization: the CPA's Interest Group on Women in Psychology—and Pyke became its first coordinator. Hoping to represent women's interests within the governance of the larger organization, Pyke soon sought and won election to the CPA board of directors. Eventually, in 1981–82, she served as president of CPA, one of only a few women to do so.

Sandra Pyke's university career was also focused on advancing the status of women. She served as coordinator of York University's undergraduate program in Women's Studies, where she provided

many women feel uncomfortable calling themselves feminists? Perhaps because, through the efforts of some opinion leaders, the label has been distorted and discredited. Feminists are sometimes described as man-haters, bitches, shrews, even "femiNazis"—unlovely, irritating women (Condon, 1999). Who would happily accept a label with such a meaning? But before turning her back on the label *feminist,* every woman should remember that such negative characterizations are likely to be applied to people who challenge existing power relations. British writer Dame Rebecca West is quoted as saying, "People call me a feminist whenever I express sentiments that differentiate me from a doormat" (quoted in Warner, 1992, p. 316).

BOX 1.3 WOMEN SHAPING PSYCHOLOGY (continued)
Sandra W. Pyke

mentorship and support for many students who were just starting to think about the role of gender in shaping their lives. She established a feminist counseling program. Later, as Dean of the Faculty of Graduate Studies (the first woman to hold this position at York), she presided over the establishment of the first Canadian doctoral program in Women's Studies.

In her research and writing, Sandra Pyke has consistently put feminist issues in the foreground, particularly with respect to education. She has studied and written about sexual harassment and discrimination in educational environments, the ways that gender affects the time it takes students to complete doctoral degrees, and other issues relevant to understanding the role played by gender in structuring the educational experiences of students. She has also written about how psychology as a discipline has responded to the increasing presence of women.

Pyke has been honored in various ways for her contributions to psychology, but perhaps the most notable distinction bestowed on her is the 1996 *CPA Award*

for Distinguished Contribution to Psychology as a Profession. The citation for that award notes that, throughout her career, she has "contribute[d] concentrically from the core of her convictions, to her sense of sisterhood among women, and ultimately to the collegial network of the professional world in which she has had such a notable impact" (Robinson, 1996).

Read More about Sandra Pyke

Robinson, B. (1996, Fall). CPA Award for Distinguished Contributions to Psychology as a Profession. *Psynopsis.* **http://www.cpa.ca/Psynopsis/awards.html**

Read What She Has Written

Pyke, S. W. (1996). Sexual harassment and sexual intimacy in learning environments. *Canadian Psychology, 37*(1), 13–22.
Pyke, S. W. (1992). The more things change . . . *Canadian Psychology, 33*(4), 713–720.
Pyke, S. W. (1997). Education and the "woman question." *Canadian Psychology, 38*(3), 154–163.

The early suffragists, the women who fought for and eventually won for women the right to vote, were also characterized as unlovely, irritating women. Looking back at their struggles, we may wonder what all the fuss was about—why was there so much resistance to something that now seems so reasonable, so normal? But if we had been there at the time, would we have been distancing ourselves from them, saying things like, "I'm not one of those suffragists, but I do support women's right to vote," just as many people now say, "I'm not a feminist, but I do believe that women and men should be equal"?

A psychology of women that does not shrink from the label *feminist* is positioned to question gender stereotypes and traditional power relations between women and men.

This book, like most of the new scholarship in the psychology of women, takes a feminist perspective.

Why a Multicultural, Global Approach?

Just as men's views on gender, and on women, have tended to overshadow women's views, so the voices of some groups of women have come through more strongly than those of others in the debates about women's psychology.

Because of the economic dominance of the United States in the world and sheer power of the American media, the voices of U.S. women often drown out those of their sisters in other countries. And in the United States and elsewhere, most of the women who are in a position to make their voices heard in public discussions about the status of women, what women are like, and the barriers faced by women are professionals: professors, lawyers, writers, politicians. In the United States, most of the women in these categories are of European American ancestry, were raised in middle-class families, and have lived a relatively privileged life. African American women who have attained doctorates are likely to have come from middle-class homes as well (Reid & Robinson, 1985).

The study of women's psychology has been shaped by these realities. Even though women's psychology is no longer considered the exclusive province of male experts, as an academic discipline it often focuses narrowly on the experiences of particular groups of women. Just as the power relations between men and women have tended to privilege men's viewpoints about human experience, so too the power relations among cultural and ethnic groups have tended to privilege White middle-class American women's viewpoints about women's experience. In our attempt to analyze and understand gender relations, women in this group often have inadvertently echoed the behavior of privileged men: We have tended to define the "truth" about women in terms of our own experience and to ignore or treat as "exceptions" the experiences of other groups of women. We have tended to speak of the experience of gender as if all women, regardless of race, ethnicity, class, or culture, experience it the same way. Distinctions among groups of women and among their social contexts have often been ignored. And public discussions about women's issues often focus narrowly on White, middle-class, Western women—as if such women were prototypical of women in general.

This is not a new insight. As long ago as 1851, Sojourner Truth, a Black woman who had been raised in slavery, is said to have publicly challenged the definition of *woman* that was being used in American debates about female suffrage. At a women's rights convention in Akron, Ohio, she rose to address the audience after a parade of male speakers had argued that women were too weak, too fragile, too inferior intellectually to be granted political equality with men. This is part of the speech that has been attributed to her:

> That man over there says that women need to be helped into carriages, and lifted over ditches, and to have the best place everywhere. Nobody ever helps me into carriages, or over mud puddles, or gives me any best place! And ain't I a woman? Look at me! Look at my arm. I have plowed and planted, and gathered into barns, and no man could head me! And ain't I a woman? I could work as much and eat as much as a man—when I could get it—and bear the lash as well! And ain't I a woman? I have borne thirteen children, and seen most of them sold off to

Sojourner Truth, a former slave who led hundreds of slaves to freedom on the Underground Railway, disputed the vision of femininity that portrayed women as weak and helpless.

slavery, and when I cried out with my mother's grief, none but Jesus heard me! And ain't I a woman? (quoted in Safire, 1992, p. 569)

Some scholars now dispute the text of this famous speech (Nordquist, 2004). However, the words handed down to us go to the heart of the issue of what womanhood is and who gets to define it. The questions now echo in the debates about women's psychology. In recent years, complaints have been raised that in the research literature on the psychology of women, the perspectives of women of color have been overlooked by White American women (Espín, 1995; Reid, 1988), that the perspectives of poor women have been neglected by middle-class women (Reid, 1993; Saris & Johnston-Robledo, 2000), that the perspectives of women with disabilities have been ignored by able-bodied women (Fine, 1991). It appears that in the research literature as well as in public debates, not only have we studied, written about, and spoken about women as if they all fit a particular mold, the mold has been a White, middle-class, "mainstream" American one.

With such a focus, how can we separate what goes with being female from what goes with being White, middle-class, and American? We cannot. As Oliva Espín argues, "there will not be valid theories of the psychology of women as long as . . . these theories are based on a very limited sector of the population. . . . this whole issue of inclusion is not about 'affirmative action' but rather about the nature of knowledge, both in the psychology of women and in the discipline of psychology as a whole. The theories and the research we now have are, for the most part, incomplete and faulty pieces of knowledge, no matter how elegant they may seem." (p. 73).

If we really want to understand gender, if we really want to understand the psychology of women, we must explore the experiences of a variety of groups. As psychologists Beverly Greene and Janis Sanchez-Hucles (1997) have argued, "all women share gender oppression but . . . they experience this oppression through their individual historical, social, political, economic, ecological and psychological realities. To understand any woman, therefore, one must incorporate an understanding of many different aspects of her, not merely gender." (p. 183). There is no single "woman's experience" but a complex set of similar issues and problems, faced differently and under different circumstances. Australian theorist Sneja Gunew (1991) notes that in trying to grasp the differing experiences of women from a variety of cultures,

> we should perhaps use the image of a kaleidoscope, where each turn produces different patterns and no single element dominates. Maybe a better image needs to be more prickly because these interactions need not always be harmonious. We need to recognize tensions and contradictions and learn from them. To facilitate this we need to undo our ignorance concerning the foreign, to learn these histories, languages, traditions, geographies. It is a way of discovering the world rather than forever rediscovering our place in the West. (pp. 34–35)

Stereotyping and Discrimination:
Universal Barriers for Women?

In Japan, girls have traditionally been taught from an early age that femininity involves modesty in speech. The appropriate and natural speaking style for females, they learn, involves softness of voice, reticence, extreme politeness, and covering the mouth when talking or laughing. So well do they absorb these lessons that as adult women, their speech is often characterized by deference and accommodation. For example, when one researcher studied the speaking style of popular television cooking show hosts in Japan, she found striking gender differences. The male host tended to give authoritative directives to his underlings, telling them "Add this to the bowl," or "Stir this now." The female host, on the other hand, was likely to phrase her directive in a more deferential way, such as "If you would now do me the favor of stirring this" (Smith, 1992).

Every cultural group has its own version of **gender stereotypes:** socially shared beliefs that certain qualities can be attributed to individuals based on their membership in the categories *female* or *male*—or occasionally, as discussed above, in some third or intermediate category. To an individual in a given culture, at a particular time, the stereotypes may seem natural and normal, or they may seem prisonlike in their rigidity. In either case, an individual who is immersed in them will find it difficult to imagine that the stereotypes are constructed and maintained largely by implicit social agreement, are fairly specific to time and place, and may be quite different elsewhere.

How Universal Are Gender Stereotypes?

Using the adjective checklist approach to measuring stereotypes that is standard in psychological studies, it appears at first glance that only minor variations in gender stereotypes exist among cultural groups. More than two decades ago, researchers found that American university students asked to categorize 300 adjectives as being typically associated with women or men agreed strongly on a cluster of 30 adjectives for women and 33 for men (Williams & Bennett, 1975). For instance, women were described as dependent, dreamy, emotional, excitable, fickle, gentle, sentimental, and weak; men were thought to be adventurous, aggressive, ambitious, boastful, confident, logical, loud, rational, and tough.

Researchers in Canada (Edwards & Williams, 1980) and Britain (Burns, 1977) found similar patterns, and a study of gender stereotyping in 30 countries showed considerable cross-cultural uniformity in the patterns of adjectives associated with women and men (Williams & Best, 1982). Studies of adults in 25 countries showed that six (out of a possible 300) items were associated with men in every country: adventurous, dominant, forceful, independent, masculine, and strong (Williams & Best, 1990). Only three were associated with women in every country: sentimental, submissive, and superstitious.

When Williams and Best (1990) scaled the items for affective meaning along the dimensions of *favorability, strength,* and *activity,* they found no cross-cultural consistency in how favorably the female- and male-associated traits were viewed. In some countries, such as Japan, South Africa, Nigeria, Malaysia, and Israel, the male stereotype was viewed more favorably than the female stereotype. However, in other countries, such as Italy, Peru, Australia, Scotland, and India, the female stereotype was most favorable. They did, however, find consistency across cultures on the other two dimensions: strength and activity. In all countries, the male stereotype items were stronger and more active, and the female stereotype items were weaker and more passive. These strength and activity differences were greater in countries that were socioeconomically less developed, where literacy was low, and where a low percentage of women attended university.

How can we make sense of the similarities and differences in gender stereotypes and ideologies across cultures? Some of the apparent similarity across cultures may be due to the fact that it was college students—a privileged group, in many cases not particularly representative of cultural attitudes and more influenced by Western thought than others in their culture—who completed the questionnaires in each culture. It may also be useful to remember that university students are more representative of their age group in some cultures than others, as countries vary widely in the percentage of the population that has the opportunity to attend university. Another factor contributing to the similarity across cultures may be the status difference between women and men that is common to most of them. In most cultures, men are accorded somewhat higher status than women—and researchers have shown that high-status people are usually judged to be more agentic, or self-oriented, whereas low-status people are judged to be more communal, or relationship oriented (Conway, Pizzamiglio, & Mount, 1996). This difference parallels stereotypical gender differences.

Judith Gibbons, Beverly Hamby, and Wanda Dennis (1997) point out that cultures vary in the domains in which women's and men's roles differ or in the settings in which such roles are relevant (e.g., marriage, family, employment, education, politics). If we ask about certain domains when we ask about gender stereotypes, we may find cultural differences but not if we ask about others. And in some cultures we may not know enough about these domains to ask the right questions. For example, in some cultures, the most important domain for gender differences may be agricultural work: who does the planting, harvesting, and so on. If a questionnaire about gender stereotypes fails to includes any questions about this domain, the researchers might find no evidence for gender stereotypes in that culture. Furthermore, some settings are simply irrelevant in some cultures. For example, as Gibbons and her colleagues (1997) note, it is no use asking whether "On a date, the boy should be expected to pay all expenses" in a setting such as Iran, where dating does not exist.

Another problem in comparing gender stereotypes across cultures is the way people in different groups interpret items on the questionnaire. Setting aside the problem of translation, which is a major one in cross-cultural research, even within a language the same terms may have different meanings for different ethnic groups. For example, Hope Landrine, Elizabeth Klonoff, and Alice Brown-Collins (1995) asked White women and women of color to rate themselves on a series of adjectives. The two groups did not differ on their self-ratings on these items. However, they apparently meant different things by at least some of the items. For instance, by "passive" the largest percentage of European American women said they meant "am laid-back/easy-going," while the largest percentage of women of color said they meant "don't say what I really think." And by "assertive" White women were more likely to mean "stand up for myself" while women of color were more likely to mean "say whatever's on my mind."

Judith Gibbons and her colleagues (1993) report another example of different meanings assigned to the same concept. In their research, adolescents from Guatemala, the Philippines, and the United States depicted the ideal woman as working in an office. However, further analysis revealed that "in the Philippines office work was associated with glamour, in the United States with routine and boredom, and in Guatemala with the betterment of the family."

Knowing how to interpret cross-cultural findings on gender stereotypes is also hindered by the lack of context provided for the responses on questionnaires. When a respondent declares that the adjective *sensitive* is more descriptive of females than of males, she is assumed to be making an abstract judgment. She is not supposed to be describing any

BOX 1.4 LEARNING ACTIVITY
Mapping the World of Women's Information Services

As you go through this book you may find yourself wondering about the situation of women around the world. Mapping the World of Women's Information Services, at Web address www.iiav.nl/mapping-the-world, is an online database of women's information centers and libraries. Become familiar with the resources at this Web site and you will find a wealth of information resources at your fingertips—it contains at least one center in almost every country in the world. The database, which is updated weekly, can be searched by name, country, subject, type of organization, and other key words. You will, for example, find information about the Jessie Street National Women's Library in Sydney, Australia, the Lesbian Herstory Archives in New York, the Archives of Women in Science and Engineering in Ames, Iowa, and the Zambia Women Artists Documentation Project. Visit this site and get a sense of the scope of the efforts of the women's movement worldwide.

Some of the information centers listed on this site collect oral histories of ordinary women in their regions. Does your own region or locality have anyplace where oral histories of women are recorded and kept? If so, visit this collection and listen to some of the recordings. What can psychologists learn from this type of data?

particular female, but rather a prototypical or average female. Nor is she describing particular behaviors or beliefs—just a vague, general tendency. If we examine gender stereotypes in a different way, by looking at the real-world expectations for women and men in important areas of behavior, a picture emerges of stronger cultural differences. Let us look, for example, at gender-related expectations in the realm of work.

In the United States, the notion of a woman as head of state—as president, or even vice president—is so problematic for so many people that the major parties seldom consider the possibility. A woman could not possibly be tough enough, authoritative enough, to succeed as president, according to the stereotype. A host of other countries, some of which have strong traditions of female subservience, have shown fewer qualms and have actually, at some point, installed a woman as a head of state. Some examples include Bolivia, Burundi, Canada, Dominica, the Philippines, Ireland, Finland, Pakistan, Haiti, India, Israel, Nicaragua, Britain, Poland, Iceland, Sri Lanka, Turkey, Bangladesh, and Norway.

In a similar vein, the people of the United States have shown more reluctance than certain other populations (for example, those of Canada, Norway, and the Netherlands) to allow the involvement of military women in combat. Testimony to a number of government commissions often stressed the notion that it is wrong and unnatural for women to engage in combat, that women are not *supposed* to be tough. Although Congress has now repealed most restrictions on women in combat some unease about women's military roles remains.

By contrast, certain cultures view women as the only ones strong enough to carry out particular jobs. The South Korean divers who go into the sea off the island of Cheju in search of pearls are all women—and the accepted cultural wisdom is that men are not tough enough for this highly skilled, dangerous job (Schoenberger, 1989).

Where Are Gender Stereotypes Most Traditional?

Across a wide range of cultures, many researchers find that girls hold fewer traditional gender attitudes than boys do. Is this a universal phenomenon? Almost, but not completely, according to a review by Gibbons, Hamby, and Dennis (1997). Researchers have found no gender differences in gender-role ideology in Malaysia, Pakistan, or Spain, and they have even found more liberal attitudes among men than women in samples from Brazil and Dublin.

Judith Gibbons, Deborah Stiles, and their colleagues have also demonstrated that, in societies as diverse as Mexico, Spain, Iceland, and the United States, adolescent daughters and sons of mothers who work outside the home hold less conservative gender role attitudes. Similarly, John Williams and Deborah Best have shown, in their 14-country study of gender ideology, that idealized gender roles are less differentiated in societies in which a higher percentage of women work outside the home and are university educated (Williams & Best, 1990). Gibbons, Stiles, and Shkodriani (1991) showed that adolescents from wealthier, more individualistic cultures report less traditional gender role attitudes than adolescents from poorer, more collectivist countries.

It appears, then, that flexibility in gender attitudes is linked in some ways to the perception of individual choice. Young women who see their mothers employed or well-educated are more able to imagine a wide variety of roles for themselves; young people growing up in cultures that value individuality and that have many resources are more likely to be flexible about gender expectations.

Components of Gender Stereotypes

The preceding examples give us some clues that stereotypes cannot be assessed simply by lists of traits; different components of gender stereotypes exist. An individual may be judged more or less feminine or masculine because of information about these various components: her personality traits, her occupation, her behaviors, her appearance. American research shows that people see these components as varying independently to some extent. For example, a person could have a very feminine appearance but not necessarily be in a feminine occupation or show a lot of feminine personality traits.

Information about one of the components can influence people's assumptions about the others, however. For a hypothetical person, Deaux and Lewis (1984) gave respondents a sex label (female or male) and information about specific role behaviors (feminine, masculine, mixed), and asked the respondents to estimate the likelihood that the person possessed particular feminine or masculine traits, pursued particular female- or male-associated occupations, and was heterosexual or homosexual. For example, respondents were given the following description: "A woman has been described in terms of the following characteristics and behaviors: source of emotional support, manages the house, takes care of children, responsible for decorating the house. Consider these characteristics carefully and think about what type of woman this would be." Respondents concluded that this woman was more likely to show feminine traits such as emotionality, gentleness, and understanding of others and to be in a feminine occupation such as occupational therapist or elementary school teacher than to show masculine traits or be in a masculine occupation. They also indicated a high probability that the woman was heterosexual. Obviously, a little bit of information can go a long way when people are constructing stereotype-based judgments of others.

The Impact of Stereotypes

Why should we worry about gender stereotypes—or any other kind of stereotypes? Do people's judgments of others really matter? It turns out that such judgments do matter. First, they may help shape the prescriptive beliefs about what women and men should be allowed to do, thus supporting gender inequality. They have an impact on the people being judged, often pressuring them to fulfill the stereotypes in order to make social interactions run smoothly. For example, women present themselves in a more or less stereotypically feminine manner, depending on how gender-traditional they think a male job interviewer's attitudes may be (von Baeyer, Sherk, & Zanna, 1981). Perhaps most importantly, through a process called **stereotype threat,** stereotypes create conditions that can affect people's performance (Steele, 1997).

Suppose a person is in a situation where she or he has to perform well, but where stereotypes about gender or racial group imply that the person will perform poorly. Research now suggests that, in such a situation, the person's performance will suffer. In a series of studies, researchers have shown that stereotype threat, an individual's awareness that he or she may be judged by or may self-fulfill negative stereotypes about gender or ethnic group, can have a dramatic negative effect on performance. In one study, women and men who had demonstrated high math ability were brought to the lab to complete a difficult math test. In one experimental condition, participants were told that the test was one on which gender differences in performance usually appeared. In a second condition, the test was described as not showing gender differences. When the test was described as likely to reveal gender differences—that is, when the stereotype threat was high—the women performed substantially worse than the men did. However, when the participants had been led to expect no gender differences, women performed at the same level as men. This occurred even though both conditions used the same math test (Spencer, Steele, & Quinn, 1999).

Stereotypes, then, have real consequences with respect to performance. They may also have consequences for life choices. People may tire of doing battle with negative stereotypes, of having to prove themselves continually in the face of negative expectations. Under such conditions, people show a tendency to "leave the field" psychologically: They disengage or "disidentify" with the domain in which the stereotype occurs and move away from that domain as a source of self-esteem or positive identity (Major, Spencer, Schmader, Wolfe, & Crocker, 1998).

Prejudice: Negative Evaluation of Women and Their Work

Is there **prejudice** against women—are women evaluated negatively just because they are women? The answer is complicated. Some American research suggests that women are stereotypically viewed as having more positive qualities than men and that people like women more than men (Eagly & Mladinic, 1994). In keeping with stereotypes of femininity, the ascribed positive qualities are communal ones: *helpful, gentle, kind, understanding.* Yet when it comes to the instrumental, competence-related qualities that people consider neces-sary for the accomplishment of high-quality work, women are often judged wanting—at least among the mainly White, middle-class respondents most of the studies use. People, especially, but not only, men, often express dubiousness about women as leaders (Boyce & Herd, 2003; Lips, 1993; Rudman & Kilianskii, 2000; Sczesny, 2003), frequently give higher ratings to work produced by men than to work produced by women (Bowen, Swim & Jacobs, 2000; Top, 1991), and show preference for men over women in hiring and promo-tion (Brown, 1998; Harvie, Marshal-McCaskey, & Johnston, 1998; Rudman, 1998). In many work environments, women are viewed with less respect than their male co-workers (e.g., Reskin, 1998; Zafarullah, 2000). All of these reactions are evidence of **sexism:** prejudiced attitudes and discriminatory behaviors toward women simply because they are women.

When women *do* exercise authority or behave in competent or directive ways, they may receive negative evaluations because they have violated the feminine stereotype. Competent, assertive women may be viewed as unfeminine (Lips, 2000; Rudman & Glick, 2001). Women who have a no-nonsense, autocratic, directive leadership style are judged more harshly than men with a similar style (Eagly, Makhijani, & Klonsky, 1992), and women who promote their own competence are judged less likable than men who do the same (Rudman, 1998). Moreover, women who act in such highly assertive, confident, or competent ways sometimes find that their ability to influence others, particularly males, is reduced (Carli, 2001). People respond with dislike, hostility, and rejection to such assertive women, presum-ably because these women are violating prescriptive norms for gender-appropriate behavior.

Suspicion or disapproval of competence or authority in women is not simply a North American phenomenon. For example, accounts from Russia, where women have struggled to gain political power, suggest that many Russian citizens do not view women as appro-priate business or political leaders. At a recent meeting sponsored by the World Economic Forum, Elena Panina, President of the Moscow Confederation of Industrialists and Busi-nessmen, argued that women in small businesses are often not taken seriously and confront a "where's your manager?" syndrome (World Economic Forum, 2003). At the same meet-ing, Irina Khakamada, a politician who is Deputy Chair of the State Duma of the Russian Federation, argued that the Russian media perpetuate an attitude among both women and men that governing is for men. "No women vote for me," she noted.

Although many people would not endorse such overtly sexist statements as "Men should be the decision makers," research in the United States and Canada shows that subtle sexism lingers on. **"Modern" sexism** is manifested in underlying negative atti-tudes about women and in resentment of and lack of support for social policies aimed at reducing gender inequalities. Scales measuring such subtle forms of sexism ask respondents to indicate their level of agreement with items such as "Women shouldn't push themselves where they are not wanted" (Neosexism Scale, Tougas, Brown, Beaton, & Joly, 1995) and "It is rare to see women treated in a sexist manner on television" (Modern Sexism Scale, Swim, Aikin, Hall, & Hunter, 1995). In general, North American studies using these scales show that men hold more of these attitudes than women do, and that modern sexism is associated with negative attitudes toward women, feminists, and affirmative action and a lower tendency to define a situation as sexual harassment. A similar pattern of results has been found in Sweden (Ekehammar, Akrami, & Araya, 2000).

Does sexism have to mean a dislike for women? Not necessarily. Researchers have found that there are two kinds of sexism: **hostile sexism** and **benevolent sexism** (Glick & Fiske, 2001). These complementary ideologies, which have been found to exist cross-culturally, are both correlated with gender inequality. Hostile sexism is the kind that people are most likely to recognize as sexism: "an antipathy toward women who are viewed as usurping men's power" (Glick & Fiske, 2001, p. 109). An example of such an attitude is the following item from the Ambivalent Sexism Inventory (Glick & Fiske, 1996): "Once a woman gets a man to commit to her, she usually tries to put him on a tight leash." Benevolent sexism, on the other hand, may seem, at first blush, to be a benign, positive attitude toward women. It is defined as "a subjectively favorable, chivalrous ideology that offers protection and affection to women who embrace conventional roles" (p. 109). An example from the same inventory is ""Many women have a quality of purity that few men possess." Women often do not recognize this attitude as sexism, not realizing the condescension that it implies or the rejection that will follow if they step outside conventional roles. Yet, benevolent sexism, by rewarding women only if they stay within traditional prescribed roles, is a barrier to gender equality. Glick and Fiske note that research with over 15,000 women and men in 19 countries shows that national averages on both benevolent and hostile sexism are correlated with gender inequality.

Sexism's Links with Other Forms of Prejudice

At an exclusive private golf course in Florida, any female golfer is denied access to the course on Saturday mornings. This practice fits seamlessly with other exclusionary practices that permeate the history of certain American country clubs: banning individuals from membership because of their race, ethnicity, or religion. For institutions that are in the habit of excluding people because they belong to a certain group, gender is simply one more category by which individuals can be ruled out.

Except for instances of categorical exclusions, however, it is rare to react to another person only on the basis of membership in one obvious category, such as gender. Rather, our initial reactions to others are affected by many discernible characteristics: race, ethnicity, age, physical attractiveness, height, weight, apparent social class, and occupation.

All of these characteristics are associated with stereotyping. A host of "isms," such as racism, ageism, classism, and beautyism, can interact with sexism. The interactions can be thought of as a "matrix of oppressions" (Kirk & Okazawa-Rey, 1998, p. 3). For example, in the United States, the forms of racism directed at African American women may differ from those directed at African American men, and sexism may be expressed toward and experienced by a woman differently as a function of her race. The interactions among different forms of oppression such as racism and sexism may be even more complex when comparisons are made across countries.

Professor and writer bell hooks describes how the racism and sexism expressed by her professors often combined to make graduate school in the United States a bitter experience for her. Professors would "forget" to call her name when reading the roll, avoid looking at her, and pretend they did not hear her when she spoke. In one class, "I, as well as other students, was subject to racist and sexist jokes. Any of us that he considered should not be in graduate school were the objects of particular scorn and ridicule. When we gave oral presentations, we were told our work was stupid, pathetic, and were not allowed to finish. If we resisted in any way, the situation worsened" (hooks, 1989, p. 57).

She notes that White students of both sexes and Black male students were also subjected to humiliation, insults, and condescension, but these other groups had some defenses that Black female students did not have. The White students were more likely to be from privileged backgrounds. For them, the humiliations of graduate school were something they could compartmentalize and treat as temporary. But

> [t]hose of us who were coming from underprivileged class backgrounds, who were black, often were able to attend college only because we had consistently defied those who had attempted to make us believe we were smart but not "smart enough"; guidance counselors who refused to tell us about certain colleges because they already knew we would not be accepted; parents who were not necessarily supportive of graduate work, etc. White students were not living daily in a world outside campus life where they also had to resist degradation, humiliation. To them, tolerating forms of exploitation and domination in graduate school did not evoke images of a lifetime spent tolerating abuse. (hooks, 1989, pp. 58–59)

Black male students, hooks suggests, are subjected to racial biases, but for a Black man in graduate school "his maleness may serve to mediate the extent to which he will be attacked, dominated, etc. . . . While many white scholars may be aware of a black male intellectual tradition, they rarely know about black female intellectuals. African-American intellectual traditions, like those of white people, have been male-dominated" (hooks, 1989, p. 60).

Psychotherapist and performing artist Nancy Wang (1995) describes the interaction of racism and sexism she has experienced as a Chinese American woman. She notes that Chinese culture prescribes that authority be granted to those older or more powerful than oneself, and that the dominant Anglo culture is thus seen to hold great authority. But what does it mean to accept such authority? She says,

> to give America's dominant culture this respect and obedience is also to accept the way in which the dominant culture perceives my value or lack of it. As a woman, too, I cannot be more than a second-class citizen, and in traditional Chinese families, daughters are considered far less valuable than sons. To act in accordance with Chinese traditions regarding obedience, I am to accept, to yield to the treatment rendered me. As a less-worthy family member, a less-worthy citizen, it means yielding to an onslaught of behaviors that attack my self-esteem, my assertiveness, my ability to act positively on my own behalf. (p. 103)

Wang notes that she learned at a young age that, in the United States, it was better to be White: "So I, and thousands of other Chinese American women, tried real hard to convince ourselves that we were white: we tried to paint our eyes big and round, we learned to be embarrassed by our parents . . ." (p. 98).

Racism interacts with sexism in every culture. For example, in India, a pervasive and long-standing caste system has organized ethnic groups into a hierarchy, with the Dalit people, originally referred to as "Untouchables" at the bottom. For Dalit women, who are often uneducated and paid even less than their male counterparts, the combination of racism and sexism is devastating. These women make up the majority of landless laborers and scavengers in India, and they are often forced into prostitution (Human Rights Watch, 1999). Ruth Manorama, head of the National Federation for Dalit Women, notes that "Dalit women are at the bottom in our community. Within the women's movement, Dalit issues have not been taken seriously. Within the Dalit movement, women have been ignored. Caste, class and gender need to be looked at together. . . . Women's labor is already undervalued; when she is a Dalit, it is nil. . . . The atrocities are also much more vulgar" (Human Rights Watch, 1999, IX).

In Eastern Europe, the Roma people (traditionally known as "Gypsies") have been victims of discrimination for many years. Roma women, however, have, as activist Sabin Xhemajli notes, "drawn the losing card. Their lifestyle is comparable to what it was five hundred years ago." (*Roma Rights,* 2000). Her colleague, Rozalija Iliae, agrees:

> Roma in Europe lack protection in the fields of education, employment, health care, housing, and the preservation of their culture, language, tradition, and personal identity. Romani women are the most vulnerable ones, and hardly anyone cares about our protection and education. . . . Patriarchy among the Roma has lasted for centuries. The whole ethnic group has additionally been marginalised in the wider society. Taken together, these factors have reduced the lives of Romani women to the biological reproduction and care of their children and the family. . . . Legal and customary norms on the position of women are very archaic and they deprive Romani women of their rights. Today, 96% of Romani women are unemployed and 80% of them are illiterate. (*Roma Rights,* 2000).

In Australia, where Blacks are the indigenous, Aboriginal people, their culture has frequently been described and "officially" defined by White anthropologists. Blacks are a smaller minority in Australia than in the United States, making it even more difficult for them to gather power. For Aboriginal women, in particular, the dominance of White society has meant invisibility and a loss of power. Colonization and the confinement to settlements undermined women's power, which, in Aboriginal religion and ritual, was intimately bound up with the land. Until recently, anthropologists ignored women's roles in these societies, assuming that males dominated all important aspects of social life. When the Australian anthropologist Diane Bell (1983) focused on the women of one Aboriginal community, she saw something quite different:

> Because my teachers were patient and dedicated to teaching me "straight," I learnt to see much through the eyes of Aboriginal women. What I saw was a strong, articulate and knowledgeable group of women who were substantially independent of their menfolk, in economic and ritual terms. Their lives were not ones of drudgery, deprivation, humiliation and exploitation because of their lack of penis and attendant phallic culture, nor was their self-image and identity bound up solely with their child-bearing and child-rearing functions. Instead I found the women to be extremely serious in the upholding, observance and transmission of their religious heritage. Religion permeated every aspect of their lives—lives which were nonetheless full of good

BOX 1.5 WOMEN SHAPING PSYCHOLOGY
Carolyn Robertson Payton (1925–2001)

When Carolyn Roberston Payton enrolled at the University of Wisconsin in 1945 to pursue a master's degree in psychology, her tuition and expenses were paid by her home state of Virginia. Why? Because Virginia held to a "separate but equal" educational policy, under which, rather than allowing the racial integration of its universities, the state covered the expenses of Black students who went elsewhere to obtain degrees that were not available to them at the Black state schools. Thus, Payton began her psychology career in a context in which racial issues loomed large. She soon found that, within psychology as well, race was a contentious issue. In her classes—where there were no other Black students—she encountered stereotypes about White intellectual superiority, and she confronted these stereotypes head-on by doing a thesis project in which she used the newly developed Wechsler-Bellevue Test of Intelligence to compare the performance of Blacks and Whites. This research convinced her that the test was a poor measure of Blacks' ability. Many years later, she revisited this issue while serving as a field supervisor for the standardization program of the Wechsler Adult Intelligence Scale. At that time, she ensured that Black participants, selected for age, gender, and socioeconomic status, were included in the development of norms for this test—one of the first times that this had been done for a well-known test.

Payton drew her fighting spirit from the support of her family and from her experience as an undergraduate student at Bennett College, a small historically Black women's college in Greensboro, North Carolina. At Bennett College, she said, she had developed her aspirations and acquired a sense of what she could do as a woman. This sense of her capabilities sustained her as she developed her career: completing a Ph.D. at Columbia University while joining the faculty at Howard University. At Howard, she taught child, abnormal, and experimental psychology, but she was lured away to become a field assessment officer for trainees in the Peace Corps in 1964. Within two years she had become the Peace Corps Director for the Eastern Caribbean region—one of only

BOX 1.5 WOMEN SHAPING PSYCHOLOGY *(continued)*
Carolyn Robertson Payton (1925–2001)

two women to hold a directorship. Eventually, in 1977, she became the first woman, the first African American, and the first psychologist to direct the United States Peace Corps, but within two years her refusal to back down on issues she considered critical led to her resignation from that position. She became director of the Howard University Counseling Service and later Dean of Counseling and Career Development. In these positions, she worked to incorporate training and supervision for graduate students in mental health fields and to raise awareness of the counseling and psychotherapeutic needs of culturally diverse groups.

Carolyn Payton was a significant force in opening up leadership roles for women and ethnic minorities in the American Psychological Association. She was one of the original members of APA's Task Force on the Psychology of Black Women and served on many of the organization's boards and committees, including the Committee on Women in Psychology and the Gay, Lesbian and Bisexual Concerns Committee. She received many honors, including the APA Distinguished Professional Contributions to Public Service Award in 1982 and the APA Award for Outstanding Lifetime Contribution to Psychology in 1997. A Leadership Citation that she received from the Committee on Women in Psychology in 1985 read, in part, "In recognition of her extraordinary influence on cross-cultural understanding in her work settings, in APA and interna-

tionally. She is an outstanding teacher, role model, and mentor for women and ethnic minorities . . . Her commitment to equality and justice for all oppressed peoples has made a precious difference in all our lives." (quoted in Keita & Muldrow, 1990). She was a tireless advocate for the inclusion of women and minorities in APA's decision-making bodies, and she worked hard to move psychology in the direction of increasing cross-cultural understanding. "It is my belief that we decided to study psychology because we saw it as a means of contributing to the human race," she argued, "Let us place our talents, our expertise, and our energy in the service of our conscience as well as our discipline" (Payton, 1984, p. 395).

Read More about Carolyn Robertson Payton

Keita, G. P. (2001, Summer). Carolyn Robertson Payton (1925–2001). *The Feminist Psychologist, 28*(3), 4–5.
Keita, G. P., & Muldrow, T. (1990). Carolyn Robertson Payton. In A. N. O'Connell & N. F. Russo (Eds.), *Women in psychology: A bio-bibliographic sourcebook* (pp. 266–274). New York: Greenwood Press.

Read What She Wrote

Payton, C. R. (1984). Who must do the hard things? *American Psychologist, 39*(4), 391–397.
Payton, C. R. (1985, March). Addressing the special needs of minority women. *New Directions for Student Services, 29,* 75–90.

humour and a sense of fun. Why then have Aboriginal women so often been cast as second-class citizens? (p. 231)

Although racism and sexism always interact, they do not always interact in exactly the same ways. For example, in Australia, Black women have been viewed stereotypically as subservient to Black men; in the United States, the stereotype of Black women offered by social scientists encompasses strength, self-reliance, and a strong achievement orientation (Epstein, 1973; Fleming, 1983a); a "Black matriarchy" theory has described African American women as more dominant, assertive, and self-reliant than African American men. This stereotype of African American women is not, however, offered by the social science literature as a *positive* one. Rather, it is sometimes used to accuse this community of women of "emasculating" their men. Patricia Collins (1991) argues that the image of the Black matriarch has been held up to all women as a symbol of the negative consequences of rejecting "appropriate" gender norms: "Aggressive and assertive women are penalized—they are abandoned by their men, end up impoverished, and are stigmatized as being unfeminine." (p. 75). What is particularly striking is that no matter how women are stereotyped—as weak and dependent or as strong and self-reliant—criticism is implied in the stereotype.

These examples are only some of many in which prejudices based on gender interact with those based on other social categories: race, ethnicity, age, (dis)ability, sexual orientation, social class, religion. Clearly, too, the interaction may differ across cultures. We cannot examine every possible combination; rather, the important fact to remember is that women's experiences of prejudice can differ enormously in quality, and those differences are related to culture, to time and place, and to the variety of ways societies construct and label particular social categories as salient.

Discrimination: Keeping Women Down and Out

In Iran, a woman's testimony carries only half the weight of a man's in court; family law places nearly all authority with respect to divorce, child custody, and other family matters in the hands of husbands and fathers; and the "blood money" paid by a murderer to avoid receiving the death penalty is half the amount if the victim was a woman than if the victim was male (Moore, 2001a).

In Saudi Arabia, women are not allowed to drive cars. When a group of 47 defiant women did drive in a demonstration during the Persian Gulf War of 1991, the reaction of the religious fundamentalists was swift and devastating. The women, who were mainly professors and students, became scapegoats for every problem faced by their embattled country. They lost their jobs, had their passports confiscated, and, along with their families, were harassed mercilessly (Sasson, 1992). Saudi women are not allowed to travel without the permission of their husbands or fathers, to appear in public without the flowing black *abaya* that covers them from head to toe, or even to enter cemeteries (because they might distract male mourners) (Slavin, 2001).

In the Ukraine, more than 70 percent of the unemployed are women. In an effort to flee poverty and hopelessness nearly half a million young Ukranian women have left the country and been smuggled into the West in the past decade. One-fifth of the women who are smuggled out have been forced into the sex trade (Kutova, 2000).

In the United States, women are not permitted to serve in direct ground combat positions with the Army or Marines. No women are allowed in the Navy's special forces. Yet having served in combat is an important credential for many leadership positions, even outside the military—leaving women disadvantaged in this respect (Wood, 2002).

In Japan, married women may not legally keep or use their birth names—unless their husbands abandon their own names and adopt their wives' names. Sociology professor Reiko Sekiguchi, who tried to continue to use her birth name after marriage, ran into problems when she insisted on signing that name to the claim forms for reimbursement from her university for research expenses and travel allowances. The reimbursement was denied, and Sekiguchi took the matter to court. She lost (Japanese court, 1993). Although it has, in recent years, become a more common practice for Japanese women to use their birth names for business and professional purposes, married couples are still legally required to have the same last name. Thus, even though many Japanese companies and government agencies now permit married women to use their birth names, about 98 percent of women are still officially registered as having their husbands' surname—a practice that can create confusion and inconvenience (Mutsuko, 2001).

In Taliban-controlled Afghanistan, a perverted version of Islamic law mandated that women were not allowed to attend school, work outside the home, receive medical treatment by male doctors, wear makeup, show any part of their bodies, or wear shoes that make noise. Houses with women had to have all windows painted black. Parents were not allowed to teach their daughters to read. Women were forbidden to interact with men who were not relatives and had to be escorted by a male relative whenever they left the house. Outside of the house, they had to wear a *burqa,* a black, tentlike garment that covers them from head to toe and makes it difficult to see. Burqas cost about 3-months' salary; thus many women could not afford to buy them and were literally imprisoned in their houses. Women who violated these rules risked being severely beaten or even killed (Schulz & Schulz, 1999).

In the Bangladeshi village of Chatakchara, the local court ordered the stoning death of a young woman because she had remarried after a divorce. Her new husband was spared. Writer Taslima Nasrin, who has focused attention on such events in her newspaper columns and novels, became the subject of a *fatwa,* or death sentence, initiated by Bangladesh's Council of Soldiers of Islam (Nasrin, 1993).

The problem of sexism goes beyond stereotyping, beyond the way women are perceived. It extends to the ways women are treated. **Sex discrimination,** the differential treatment of individuals because they are female or male, has a long history and is visited frequently on women all over the world, but it takes different forms in different places. In many instances, it is not as obvious as the direct prohibitions listed above. Rather, it takes more subtle forms: disparaging women and girls in small ways, discouraging girls and women from engaging in particular occupations, promoting women more slowly through the ranks than men, rewarding women's accomplishments less well than men's, providing fewer resources for girls' and women's education and advancement than for boys' and men's, maintaining an environment that is safer, or simply easier, for males than for females.

TABLE 1.1 Women around the World: Some examples of the similarities and differences in the life contexts of women in different parts of the world

Country	Women per 100 men*	Women's life expectancy at birth (years)**	Literacy rate for adult women**	Female enrollment level in post-secondary education[1]***	Fertility rate (number of children per woman)**	Women as a percent of the labor force**
Algeria	98	72	57	—	3.1	28
Ethiopia	99	43	31	1	5.7	41
Chile	102	79	95.6	36	2.2	34
Costa Rica	98	80	95.6	18	2.5	31
Haiti	103	55	47.8	—	4.4	43
Afghanistan	94	43	—	—	6.8	36
India	93	63	45.4	8	3.1	32
Japan	104	85	99	44	1.4	41
Italy	106	82	98	57	1.2	39
United Kingdom	103	80	99	67	1.7	44
Canada	102	82	99	69	1.6	46
United States	104	80	99	83	2.1	46

Sources (Accessed April 13, 2004)
* CIA World Factbook: http://www.reference-guides.com/cia_world_factbook
** World Bank: http://devdata.worldbank.org/genderstats/
***United Nations Development Program: http://hdr.undp.org/reports/global/2003/indicator/index_indicators .html

1. The number of students enrolled in postsecondary education, regardless of age, as a percentage of the population of official school age for that level.

Even subtle forms of sex discrimination have an impact, however. Women notice them and are bothered by them, at least some of the time, according to research in the United States. Women university students report experiencing nearly twice as many sexist events (directed against themselves or against women in general) as male students do (Swim, Cohen, & Hyers, 1998). The events reported by these students were often comments about women's lack of particular abilities, remarks imputing stereotypical traits, such as passivity, to women, or assertions that women should restrict themselves to certain arenas (e.g., that they should stay at home or should not go into politics). The events also included unwelcome and objectifying sexual comments, unwanted touching, and street harassment. Women students in another study reported that each week they experienced one to two sexist events significant enough to have an impact on them (Swim, Hyers,

Cohen, & Ferguson, 2001). According to the women's self-reports, these events, which included such things as expressions of prejudice, demeaning and degrading comments, and being treated as sex objects, caused them to feel uncomfortable, angry, and depressed and lowered their self-esteem. Ninety-nine percent of the adult women in yet another sample reported that they had experienced sexist events such as being forced to listen to sexist or sexually degrading jokes, being sexually harassed or called sexist names, or being treated with a lack of respect because of being female (Klonoff & Landrine, 1995). More than half of this sample said that they had been picked on, hit, shoved, or threatened because of being female; 40 percent said they had been denied a raise or promotion because they were women, and over 19 percent reported they had filed a lawsuit or grievance or taken other serious action in response to sexist discrimination. In this sample, women of color reported significantly more sexist discrimination than White women did.

Even when they do not respond publicly, women are not complacent about sexist events. In one study, Janet Swim and Laurie Hyers (1999) brought participants to their lab to work on a task that required group discussion and decision making. During the discussion, male confederates made several scripted comments that were sexist. The researchers monitored the female participants' behavior in response to these comments. Later, they administered a questionnaire to measure self-esteem and asked the women to review a tape of the session and record their feelings. Although fewer than half of the women responded publicly to the sexist comments, most women later said they found the remarks objectionable, viewed the person making the remark as prejudiced, and felt anger toward him. Also, women who held traditional gender-role attitudes showed lower self-esteem after hearing sexist remarks.

Within any culture certain types of discrimination may go unnoticed because they appear "natural." One of the advantages of comparing gender relations across cultural and ethnic groups is that we begin to see that various discriminatory practices are not natural, that particular stereotypes and gender attitudes are not an inevitable aspect of human societies. In the chapters ahead we will examine not only a number of particular areas where women and men are treated differently, but also the psychology of discrimination itself and the impact of prejudice, discrimination, and resistance on women's psychology.

SUMMARY

As the examples in this chapter illustrate, women in many groups are linked by common issues and problems related to the gender hierarchy that places men above women in terms of power and status. They are often stereotyped in ways that imply incompetence, trained from girlhood to accept subservient roles, taught that their worth depends on such qualities as beauty and fertility, and victimized by discrimination in the realm of employment. The details of these issues vary a great deal across groups. The ways women in different groups conceptualize and respond to these issues may vary widely as well.

We have seen that one of the reasons differences exist among cultural and ethnic groups in their ideas about and treatment of women is that femininity and masculinity are socially constructed. Many of the qualities associated with women and men are not a direct result of female or male physiology and anatomy, but of social expectations and cultural norms. The importance of cultural norms in defining gender is most clear when we examine societies in which gender is viewed, not as a binary, female–male distinction, but as a plurality of three or more genders.

Although women have been studied for many years, much of the study has been done from male perspectives. Men, who have traditionally had higher status as experts, have had more power than women to define gender expectations. This situation has produced a distorted view of women's psychology: a view shaped by power relations. To provide a more complete view of women's psychology, and one less weighted in the direction of the traditional stereotypes associated with gender hierarchy, it is now important to make women a central focus of study and to take women's own perspectives seriously. Thus, a feminist approach to the psychology of women has developed. Such an approach makes women's experiences and perspectives a central concern, questions traditional assumptions about gender, and is oriented toward empowering women.

Even within a feminist psychology of women, there has been a strong tendency, rooted in differences among groups of women in power and status, to develop theories and research that do not address the experiences of all women. Rather, there has been a tendency to focus most strongly on White, middle-class, North American women. It is now clear that this focus is far too narrow. We cannot develop good, clear theories and research about the psychology of women without considering the experiences of women in many different groups in many different times and places.

One of the first issues to consider in an examination of the psychology of women is gender stereotypes. Research shows that gender stereotypes can be found in all parts of the world and in virtually all groups; however, the content of the stereotypes differs somewhat across cultures and ethnic groups. The stereotypes have an impact: helping to keep individuals in conformity with societal gender expectations, affecting performance, often promoting gender inequality.

Women and their work are often evaluated in sexist ways. Such prejudicial reactions are not always blatant, but are sometimes manifested in subtle ways—ways that have been labeled modern sexism. And sexism is no longer thought to be a simple phenomenon. Rather, it has at least two aspects: hostile sexism and benevolent sexism. Each of these aspects has been linked to gender inequality across cultures. Furthermore, sexism interacts with other forms of prejudice, such as racism, classism, ageism, and heterosexism. Such interactions also differ across cultures.

There is ample evidence that women in all parts of the world face discrimination. The particular forms of discrimination faced by women in different times and places varies. However, even the subtle forms of discrimination are noticed by women, causing reactions that range from disappointment to anger.

As students of the psychology of women, we are interested in the thoughts, feelings, and behaviors of women from all groups; we are fascinated by both similarities and differences. In the chapters that follow, as we study the processes of female psychology within different cultural contexts, our agenda is not to discern some grand set of rules that will neatly subsume and explain all the variations. Rather, it is to gain a better appreciation of the various patterns of the human kaleidoscope.

KEY TERMS

gender	feminist psychology	modern sexism
social construction	feminist	hostile sexism
sex differences	gender stereotypes	benevolent sexism
third gender	stereotype threat	sex discrimination
homosexual	prejudice	
transvestite	sexism	

DISCUSSION QUESTIONS

What does it mean to say gender is socially constructed? Can you identify some ways you participate in constructing gender when you interact with your friends?

Why is it important, in studying the psychology of women, to study women in a variety of cultures and contexts? Has the material in this chapter about women in various cultures changed your ideas about what it means to be feminine? If so, how?

What does it mean to take a feminist approach to the psychology of women? What does such an approach entail? Do you consider yourself a feminist? Why or why not?

How universal are gender stereotypes? What are the issues that make it difficult to give a definite answer to this question?

FOR ADDITIONAL READING

Edwards, Amelia. (1987). *Untrodden peaks and unfrequented valleys.* Boston: Beacon Press. Edwards describes her challenging journey through the then-uncharted Dolomite Alps. (Originally published in 1873.)

Espín, Oliva M. (1997). *Latina realities: Essays on healing, migration, and sexuality.* Boulder, CO: Westvew Press. This psychologist, herself an immigrant and a widely traveled and experienced teacher, therapist and scholar, poses questions and explores answers about the psychological experiences of Latinas.

Menchú, Rigoberta. (1984). *I, Rigoberta Menchú, an Indian woman in Guatemala* (Elizabeth Burgos-Debray, Ed.; Ann Wright, Trans.). London: Verso. This autobiography recounts the Nobel Peace Prize–winning author's life in Guatemala, her involvement in the revolutionary struggle there, the deaths of her family members, and her own deepening commitment to social change. The autobiography continues in Menchú's 1998 book, *Crossing the borders: An autobiography* (London: Verso).

Rich, Doris L. (1993). *Queen Bess: Daredevil aviator.* Washington, DC: Smithsonian Institution Press. This book tells the story of Bessie Coleman's life and her exploits as a pilot.

Shah, Sonia (Ed.) (1997). *Dragon ladies: Asian American feminists breathe fire.* Boston: South End Press. In a series of pungent articles, Asian American feminists address such questions as identity, violence, raising children, globalization, and poverty.

Tinling, Marion. (1989).*Women into the unknown: A sourcebook on women explorers and travelers.* New York: Greenwood Press. This is a fascinating collection of stories about women who transcended their geographical boundaries in order to attain a more global perspective.

WEB RESOURCES

Association for Women in Psychology. This is the site of the original feminist psychology organization in the United States. Here you can learn about the history of the organization, upcoming conferences, and regional groups and caucuses. **www.awpsych.org**

WWWomen. This site bills itself as the premier search engine for women online. It is a good place to start when you want to learn about women in different parts of the world. Click on "Diversity among women" to obtain a long list of links to information about women in virtually every country and culture. **www.wwwomen.com**

CHAPTER 2

Female—Male Comparisons: The Meaning and Significance of Difference

CHAPTER OUTLINE

An old Chinese proverb has it that "Women have long hair and short intelligence" (Chang, 1991). The French educational philosopher François Fénelon declared in the 17th century that science education for girls was inappropriate and that girls should be taught to have "a prudishness about science almost as fastidious as that which inspires a horror of vice" (Peiffer, 1991). American flyer Charles Lindbergh, disgruntled by his discovery in 1938 that women were flying in the USSR air force, carped to his diary, "I do not see how it can work very well. After all, there is a God-made difference between men and women that even the Soviet Union can't eradicate" (quoted in Roberts, 1994, p. 78). When Hungarians Susan and Judith Polgar, who eventually became two of the youngest players to achieve top-level rankings in chess, first tried to gain admittance to championship-level tournaments in the 1980s, male players were incredulous. Chess, long thought to be a "man's game," was deemed foreign and unsuited to women. As world chess champion Garry Kasparov commented, "Through the millennia, men have learned to fight this kind of fight better. Chess looks very peaceful, but it is in fact a violent game. And because of the tradition, today it happens to fit man's nature better" (quoted in Weber, 1996, p. B10). Clearly, some pervasive beliefs exist about differences between women's and men's abilities and behaviors.

And *why* might women behave, think, or perform differently from men? Opposing opinions have been held stubbornly and proclaimed loudly across boundaries of time and place— often in ignorance, or in defiance, of researchers' findings. The Spanish theorist Juan Huarte argued in the 16th century that the testicles maintained the heat and dryness of spirit necessary for intelligence—an obvious reason for male intellectual superiority (see Shields, 1975). Christian theological tracts in the Middle Ages noted that men were active and women were passive, that women were inferior to men by virtue of the curse laid upon them at the Fall of Adam and Eve, and that the meaning of sex differences lay in the parallel relations between woman and the soul, man and God (Maclean, 1980). Shiite Muslim ideology holds that women have innate physical and moral weaknesses: emotionality, a relative lack of reason, and a dangerous sexuality (Friedl, 1993). In Hindu mythology, all animating power is female; the female gender is associated with shakti, or power, and is thus linked with energy, authority, and creativity, whereas the male principle is passive and weak (Gold, 1993). Orthodox Hinduism, however, postulates an ideal for women that is based on silence, subservience, self-effacement, and sacrifice; no less an authority than Gandhi stated that women were naturally superior to men in the courage of self-sacrifice (Liddle & Joshi, 1986).

It is our task in this chapter to examine the processes and findings of research into whether, how, and why the behavior and experience of women may differ from those of men. Do women and men have different mental abilities? Do they have different tendencies to be aggressive, nurturing, or dominant? Such questions have been scrutinized by researchers for years. Their findings can help us to evaluate the stereotypes. Yet we cannot review these studies without also taking a step back and asking why everyone is so interested in female–male differences. Ever since beginning to consider women, psychology as a discipline has been preoccupied with the differences between women and men. Has the research been propelled by a desire to justify women's subordination? To shore up the notion that women and men are best assigned to different kinds of work? To show that women and men are not really very different? Or simply to get at the real truth about the nature of women and men? And just how has the research been shaped by the attitudes and cultural surroundings of the researchers themselves? By the end of this chapter, it will have become evident that this very emphasis on differences has had strong implications for psychology's approach to understanding women, men, and gender. Whether or not this emphasis has been useful or appropriate has been the subject of heated debate among feminist psychologists. Ultimately, we will be asking whether the question of female–male differences is the right question.

A Brief History of the Research

Scholarship on female–male differences was for many years a study of "revealed truths." The philosopher Aristotle disseminated the notion that *male* and *female* were related opposites: the male–female duality was aligned with such other dualities as odd–even, right–left, straight–curved, light–darkness, good–evil, completion–incompletion. This notion of polarized dualities in which one was superior to the other was echoed in European writings for centuries. Some statements about sex differences in early writings became accepted as authoritative, and subsequent writers who wanted to "prove" that certain differences existed simply cited these authoritative statements. Collections of such statements, or "commonplaces," could be found in major treatises on sex differences, such as the French jurist André Tiraqueau's 1513 essay on marriage law. They included such nuggets of accepted wisdom as the notion that women are more open to lust, less trustworthy, and less perfectible than men. Because these "commonplaces" were attributed to recognized authorities or "experts," and because they fit the intellectual outlook on sex differences that was current at the time, they were accepted and quoted as true. For example, medieval theologians such as Alexander of Hales and Thomas Aquinas cited Aristotle as an authority and built upon his ideas to demonstrate that a woman is an incomplete or imperfect man

(Maclean, 1980). These ideas in turn were used to rationalize the need for women, as inferiors, to be subordinate to men in many contexts, particularly marriage. Thus the English writer of an 18th-century treatise on marriage could, with perfect confidence, advise wives: "You shall not be mistress of yourself, nor have any desire satisfied, but what is approved of by your husband" (Fleetwood, 1705, cited in Nadelhaft, 1982, p. 566).

For many years, Western scientists were so sure about the differences between the genders that they paid scant research attention to them. In many cases, when researchers did focus on gender comparisons, their purpose was to explain differences that they assumed to exist rather than to test for the existence of differences. Thus, in the 19th century, Franz Joseph Gall and his students measured male and female brains in order to demonstrate that female brains had more areas devoted to "tender" feminine traits. Other investigators concentrated on showing that female brains were smaller—a perfect explanation for women's assumed mental inferiority. When later forced to acknowledge that women's smaller bodies accounted for smaller brain size, and that when brain size was measured as a ratio of body size, women's brains were larger than those of men, researchers simply shifted ground and started searching for the *part* of the brain that was larger in men than in women (Shields, 1975).

In fact, during the 19th century, most of the enterprise of looking for sex differences could be characterized as a search for proof of women's inferiority. When differences were found, they were interpreted in ways consistent with the notion that women were less skilled, less moral, or weaker than men. For example, in 1887, George Romanes reported research results showing that women could read faster and more accurately than men (Romanes, cited in Caplan & Caplan, 1999). This finding was *not* interpreted to show that women were better readers than men or that they were smarter than men in this particular domain. Rather, it was explained this way: People who read well tend to be good liars—women are better liars than men (Caplan & Caplan, 1999)!

This interpretation reflects the attitudes toward women and men that were prevalent at the time. Clearly, prevailing social attitudes affect the way scientists conceptualize, carry out, and interpret research. Research questions or interpretations that support these prevailing attitudes are easy to perceive as properly conducted, legitimate, fair, and objective. However, research that challenges these attitudes is more likely to be viewed as illegitimate, biased, or improperly done. In particular, research that could lead to a questioning of hierarchical power arrangements may be viewed as "political," whereas research that seems to support these arrangements is more likely to be viewed as objective and unbiased.

It was an American woman, Helen Thompson, who as a graduate student in psychology at the turn of the century first used the Western scientific method to ask the question, "What psychological differences actually exist between women and men?" She administered a huge battery of tests to 25 female and 25 male University of Chicago undergraduate students: tests for motor skills, reaction times, sensory abilities, ability to hit a target, rapidity of finger movement, pain threshold, ability to discriminate heat and cold—tests that were thought to reveal differences in the ways women and men process information. She found a striking lack of gender differences, providing some of the first scientific evidence to counter the notion of vast intellectual differences between women and men (Thompson [Woolley], 1903).

As the field of psychology unfolded during the 20th century, its Western practitioners and scholars showed a strong tendency to assume that female–male psychological differences were "natural" and intractable. The differences were ascribed to biologically based differences between female and male personalities. In developing his theory of evolution, Charles Darwin had argued that women were less evolved than men. This argument was taken up by the educator Edward Clarke, who argued that women's brains were relatively undeveloped and unsuited to the intellectual rigors of higher education. Sigmund Freud traced the differences back to sexual anatomy and "penis envy." Edward Thorndike, an early-20th-century American psychologist, favored the notion of maternal instinct, arguing that women were biologically predisposed toward motherhood.

The American psychologist Naomi Weisstein (1971) helped to provoke a turning point in this approach with a blistering critique of the discipline's unwillingness to examine the impact of social and environmental forces in the construction of female–male differences. Thereafter the discipline began to incorporate social and environmental variables more strongly into gender-related research, with some critics even suggesting that a criterion for feminist research is the starting assumption that "there are no significant differences between women and men not attributable to differences in socialization, current reinforcement, and social expectations" (Kahn & Jean, 1983, p. 662).

Research into female–male differences continues to flourish in Western psychology. Researchers are still engaged in the search for the differences between female and male brains (e.g., Cahill, 2003; Swaab, Chung, Kruijver, Hofman, & Hestiantoro, 2003). Others look for evidence that women are different from men in their behavior: perhaps more person centered, more caring, less power oriented, more relationship oriented (e.g., Belenky, Clinchy, Goldberger, & Tarule, 1986; Gilligan & Attanucci, 1994). Still others seek to demonstrate that gender differences in most areas are small and unimportant (e.g., Hyde & Kling, 2001). As we will note, researchers' own implicit beliefs, as well as the current social or scientific acceptability of particular viewpoints, continue to affect the questions that are asked about gender differences and the interpretations of the answers.

Approaches to Knowledge:
Issues of Method, Evidence, and Truth

Feminist Issues and Influences in Psychological Research

One thing that is obvious from our brief history of psychological research on women and female–male differences is that what we "know" about these topics is shaped by how we ask research questions and interpret the findings. For decades, psychologists "knew" women were inferior to men—but the reason they knew it was that their research flowed from and reflected societal assumptions about gender. In the past several decades, feminist psychologists have turned a critical eye on the research process, asking, "Are there ways of approaching research that would produce less biased outcomes and that would be less detrimental and more empowering for women?"

BOX 2.1 WOMEN SHAPING PSYCHOLOGY

Helen Bradford Thompson Woolley

At the turn of the last century, psychology graduate student Helen Bradford Thompson conducted a pioneering psychology experiment to test the differences between women and men in "mental traits." This research, which became her doctoral thesis, showed few of the expected differences between the sexes. For years afterward, the results of her research, published as two books by the University of Chicago Press, helped to undermine gender stereotypes.

Helen Thompson was awarded her Ph.D. summa cum laude from the University of Chicago in 1900. She then accepted a fellowship to travel and study in Berlin and Paris for a year, returning to the United States to take up a position as an instructor at Mt. Holyoke College in 1901. The following year, at the relatively early age of 28, she was promoted to professor of psychology and director of the Psychological Laboratory. A brilliant career seemed assured: Her former mentors at the University of Chicago even speculated that she might be offered a regular faculty position at that high-profile institution—something virtually unheard of for a woman.

Personal factors intervened in Thompson's career, however. In 1902 she married Paul Woolley and moved with him to the Philippines, where he had been offered a job. Over the next four years, she moved four more times to accommodate his career: first to Bangkok, then back to Chicago, to Nebraska, and finally to Cincinnati. During this time, she bore the first of two daughters and tried valiantly to maintain a professional life. As historian Rosalind Rosenberg (1982) notes, "For most women, the many

Feminist criticisms of traditional research approaches have focused on two broad and complex issues: (1) the researcher–participant relationship, and (2) the notion of objectivity. On the first point, feminists have examined the implicit power relations between researchers and their "subjects." Researchers are often from privileged groups; additionally, they are granted high social status because of their education and professional credentials. The people they are studying are often lower in social and educational status. Researchers (and the insti-

BOX 2.1 WOMEN SHAPING PSYCHOLOGY (*continued*)
Helen Bradford Thompson Woolley

moves and domestic responsibilities that burdened Helen Thompson Woolley would have killed all professional ambition. Blaming failure on either their own inadequacies or the unavoidable obligations of domestic life, they would have abandoned their youthful hopes of professional success. Woolley shared these feelings of inadequacy and fatalism about her domestic world and often felt isolated, but she was not defeated." (p. 82).

In Cincinnati, she forged a network of supportive women friends and built a professional life for herself as a child development specialist, reformer, and suffrage leader. She worked very hard to link her scientific work to a commitment to social reform, concerning herself not only with women's equality, but also with child labor and other child development issues. By her colleagues, she was hailed as an expert in mental testing and an innovator in interdisciplinary approaches to the study of children, and she became associate director of the Merrill-Palmer School in 1922.

In 1924, the Woolleys separated—a blow to Helen, even though she and her husband had lived rather separate lives. The next year, at the age of 50, she moved to New York to accept a prestigious position as director of the new Institute of Child Welfare Research and professor of education at Teachers College, Columbia University. A successful first year setting up the Institute buoyed her somewhat, but the trauma of her separation, health problems, and the lack of her supportive network of women friends took a heavy toll on her. Emotionally drained and unable to work, she took a two-year leave of absence. However, she never regained her capacity for effective work, and was forced to resign her position in 1930. She spent the remainder of her life living with her daughter Eleanor.

Read More about Helen Bradford Thompson Woolley

Rosenberg, Rosalind (1982). *Beyond separate spheres: The intellectual roots of modern feminism.* New Haven, CT: Yale University Press. (See especially Chapter 3: "The new psychology and the new woman").

Read What She Wrote

[Woolley], Helen Bradford Thompson. (1903). *The mental traits of sex: An experimental investigation of the normal mind in men and women.* Chicago: University of Chicago Press.
Woolley, Helen T. (1914). The psychology of sex. *Psychological Bulletin, 11,* 353–379.

tutions in which they work) define what questions are worthy of study, what kinds of information count as "data," and how such data should be interpreted (Morrow, 2000).

Such decisions traditionally have not taken into account the perspectives of the other set of participants in the research process: the people whose behaviors, thoughts, and feelings are being investigated. Furthermore, there has been an effort to minimize any personal relationship between researcher and research participant: The participant is merely a "subject"—

someone who is studied. Such an approach can be dehumanizing and exploitative. Feminists are alert to this possibility because of the long tradition in which male psychologists studied women through a masculinist lens without giving significant weight to women's own perspectives. In a similar vein, psychological researchers have often studied people of color, poor people, old people, and persons with disabilities as if these individuals were simply "specimens" to be examined rather than persons with important perspectives and potentially valuable insights.

Many feminist researchers have argued that one important function of research ought to be to disrupt the traditional power relationship between researcher and "subject" and give voice to research participants:

> Giving voice to participants implicitly recognizes that some people are denied a voice and a place in psychology, and the field, as well as groups of people, suffer for it. Listening to people's voices means hearing what they have to say on their own terms rather than testing preconceived hypotheses using preformed categories and the idiom of the researcher. It means taking seriously life experiences and conditions and people's attempts to make meaning from them, elevating and examining everyday practices as well as everyday language and thinking. Giving participants voice means sharing the right to name categories and codirect the process of data collection. (Rabinowitz & Martin, 2001, pp. 36–37)

With respect to objectivity, the conventional viewpoint has been that objective research meets certain criteria: The researcher is separate from and independent of his/her "subject"; the behavior or phenomenon under study is separate from its context; and the research is neutral, value free, and apolitical (Hubbard, 1988; Morrow, 2000). In such a definition of good science, the researcher's own viewpoints, assumptions, and feelings are invisible: They are assumed not to have an impact on the research. However, feminists and others have argued that they *do* have an impact, and should, for this reason, be acknowledged:

> Myths of objectivity and separateness between researcher and researched have perpetuated the practice of nondisclosure by the researcher. Although the orienting assumptions and worldviews of investigators have potent effects on the paradigms and methodologies used to "discover" information, objectivity remains a mask behind which the investigator can avoid being known. Thus, the person of the researcher remains safely outside the realm of criticism. (Morrow, 2000, p. 24)

Feminist analysts have also noted that the traditional practice of **context-stripping** (studying and discussing the behavior, thought, or feelings of a person or group as if they were separate from the context in which they are normally embedded) produces a distorted vision of human experience. When researchers study people's behavior without taking the social context into account, the only way they can explain that behavior is with reference to intrapsychic qualities: qualities internal to the persons being studied (Morrow, 2000). Within this framework, for instance, if researchers found women to be more depressed than men, their explanation would tend to focus on some deficiency in women that caused the depression. Research that took social context into account, on the other hand, would consider the ways in which the differing social contexts in which women and men function might produce gender differences in depression.

In light of these criticisms, some feminists have proposed that the practice of psychological research should have certain important characteristics. First, it should treat participants in a respectful, careful, and nonexploitative manner and "centralize . . . instead of marginalizing the experiences of those who have traditionally been silenced" (Morrow, 2000, p. 25). Second, it should be reflexive (Crawford & Kimmel, 1999; Rabinowitz & Martin, 2001). **Reflexivity** in research means that, as researchers, we try to be aware of and to reflect on the ways "our identities—as individuals in Western society, members of particular ethnic or religious groups, gendered beings, and feminists—influence our work and, in turn, how our work influences these aspects of the self" (Crawford & Kimmel, 1999, p. 3). Third, it should not depend on a single method or let the method drive the inquiry (Crawford & Kimmel, 1999; Rabinowitz & Martin, 2001). Rather, it should use a range of methods, choose those that fit best with the question being asked, and always be aware of the consequences of choosing a particular method. Finally, many have argued that research that is done from a feminist perspective has an activist dimension: It incorporates an orientation to the possibility of social change, of transforming gender relations (Crawford & Kimmel, 1999; Morrow, 2000). Many researchers who identify as feminists "want to do research that will change the world" (Crawford & Kimmel, 1999, p. 6). It is useful to keep these goals in mind as we turn to a discussion of some philosophical approaches that provide the underpinnings of our research assumptions.

Doing Science: Logical Positivism, Essentialism, and Social Constructionism

Years ago, in many countries, opponents of women's suffrage scoffed at the notion that extending the vote to women would make any difference. "Women will vote with their husbands" was the commonly accepted wisdom. "The result will be no change at all." This was an argument in the absence of evidence, as women did not yet have the vote and no one could know for certain what they would do with it. Ever since women won the vote, researchers have been gathering that evidence, keeping close track of female voting behavior to see whether it followed the predictions of the cynics. The data they have accumulated suggests that the predictions were wrong. A "gender gap" in voting behavior has been found in many countries (International Institute for Democracy and Electoral Assistance, 2004). The 1996 and 2000 presidential elections in the United States showed large gaps between candidates favored by women and those favored by men (Center for American Women and Politics, 2003). By collecting appropriate evidence, researchers have been able to show that the scoffers were wrong—and they have been able to discern a clearer picture of how women make political choices.

The search for knowledge in Western psychology, as in many other disciplines, has been dominated by the scientific method, a method whereby ideas are tested against observations. If I have the idea that men have more mathematical ability than women, the scientific method would require that I test this notion by gathering comparative data about the mathematical performance of women and men under similar conditions. The data would serve as a check on my idea: How does my belief stand up against reality? Helen Thompson used the scientific method to test the prevailing ideas about ability differences between the sexes.

In dealing with stereotypes and strong, unsubstantiated opinions, such a method has obvious advantages: Put them to the test by gathering evidence. It is indeed useful to have solid facts at one's command when facing a tough decision, a wide-ranging discussion of issues, or a hostile debate. Little wonder, then, that the scientific approach has won such favor.

But just how far can we go with this approach? Can we always agree on what counts as evidence? Are some facts better than others? If we gather enough facts, and do it with enough care, can we arrive at the "pure truth" of a situation?

These are questions that have bedeviled scientists for years. It used to be commonly accepted that reality or truth could be discovered through the careful application of the scientific method, a philosophy of knowledge that is called **logical positivism.** This approach assumes that reality is independent of the knower and can be discerned "objectively" under the proper conditions. In the realm of research on female–male differences, a logical positivist approach might be characterized in this way: "We must do the best, most careful, scientific research, find out what the differences really are—and once we've found them we'll always know." For people who take a logical positivist approach, "the truth is out there," and they just have to do good enough research to find it.

In the realm of gender, there is another philosophical approach that has shaped (and continues to shape) research, **essentialism.** Essentialism might be characterized as "the truth is in there." It refers to a view that gender (along with other characteristics, such as sexual orientation) is something that lies within the individual—a quality that belongs to that person. For someone who takes an essentialist view about gender, women *are* a certain way and men *are* a certain way, and in some respects, they simply differ. In other words, there are things about women that make them different from men, and things about men that make them different from women. This kind of framework has been used for centuries by researchers whose mindset predisposed them to prove women inferior to men. In recent years, however, essentialism has also been used by feminist researchers to look in new ways at gender differences and to claim positive value for the qualities traditionally attributed to women. Feminist essentialists have argued that, yes, women and men are different—and women are better. This approach has been popular. As Susan Morrow (2000) notes,

> Essentialist perspectives often resonate powerfully with women, in part because those perspectives give women validation for previously undervalued qualities such as nurturance, emotionality, and relationality. Now, instead of being "wrong" (codependent, histrionic, or some other "feminine" disorder), we are valued for the same female virtues that male scientists of yore said made us unfit for higher education, nontraditional work, or the professions. (p. 27)

Critics of the essentialist perspective (e.g., Bohan, 1992) have argued that it is politically dangerous to emphasize gender differences because, in a climate of greater male than female power and status, gender differences can easily be interpreted as women's deficiencies. They have also noted that essentialism emphasizes the universality of feminine qualities and thus ignores the diversity of women's experience. However, perhaps the most important criticism is that essentialism treats gender as *real.* And, as psychologists and other scholars have become increasingly aware, in many ways, observers create their own realities.

BOX 2.2 LEARNING ACTIVITY
Locating Yourself

Feminist psychologists and others have argued that science is never objective and value free, that researchers, and all of us, bring personal perspectives, biases, and blind spots to the enterprise of trying to understand the world. This argument suggests that we should think about the ways in which our own perspective, our own "location" in the matrix of gender, race, class, nationality, and other dimensions, affects our perceptions of the world. Where are you in this matrix? Write a paragraph about your location. How does it affect the perspectives you bring to understanding women whose location differs greatly from your own? How might it limit your understanding?

In our personal lives we know that our expectations can shape our relationships, our successes and failures, the impressions we form of other people—our social reality. For example, it is difficult for me to "discover" what another person is *really* like, independent of my expectations. My expectations influence the way I perceive that person and how I interact with that person, which in turn influences the way that person perceives and behaves toward me. Together, we construct a mutual social reality—and each of us might be very different with other people. What I know as a "fact" about that person is not something I have gathered by objectively observing a reality independent of myself. More accurately, it could be described as a construction: a hypothesis about reality that is completely tied to my own social interactions with the person.

A similar process can be said to happen in science. Researchers hold expectations and implicit beliefs that affect the way they search for knowledge. Those expectations and beliefs, which are not only individual but are also shaped by social, cultural, and historical consensus, color their perceptions of the reality they observe. They do not discover independently existing facts through objective observation; rather, they construct knowledge that is influenced by the social context of their inquiry. "What is produced by such knowledge-seeking . . . is not a free-standing and revealed truth, but a best guess, based on selective vision, using limited tools, shaped by the contextual forces surrounding the search. It is not Truth; it is a historically and contextually situated understanding, a social construction" (Bohan, 1992, p. 8). This perspective on knowledge, called **social constructionism,** suggests that we will never find one true answer, for every time and every place, to the question of what women and men are like and whether and how women and men differ on a particular dimension. The answer changes as a function of the investigator, the social context, and the people being studied. It also suggests that the qualities we attribute to women and men are not "possessed" by them, but created by them in their interactions with other people. A social constructionist would say that individuals don't *have* a gender —they *do* gender. And they do it differently, depending on where, when, and with whom they are interacting.

A social constuctionist approach has now moderated the logical positivism once favored by many psychologists. As noted by social psychologist Alice Eagly (1994), "it would be startling to find a modern social scientist who would fail to agree that science is socially constructed or who would maintain that science is objective or value-free" (p. 162). Social constructionism has also provided an important balance to the essentialist approach to gender differences: emphasizing the contexts in which gender differences are observed instead of the differences themselves.

What Is Good Scientific Evidence?

Even though we are aware that knowledge is socially constructed and that "facts" are really "best guesses," we still engage in gathering and evaluating evidence. Just as we do not stop trying to get to know another person just because we are aware we will never know her or him with complete and objective accuracy, we do not stop trying to understand gender just because we are aware that we can never settle comfortably on "The Truth" with respect to gender differences. No evidence about human behavior is pure and uncontaminated by the social context and the researcher's point of view, but we can take certain precautions to eliminate obvious biases of sexism, racism, heterosexism, and other "isms" in the way research questions are framed and investigated and the results interpreted. In fact, guidelines are available to help scientists conduct research that is nonsexist (Hyde, 1994; McHugh, Koeske, & Frieze, 1986; Stark-Adamec & Kimball, 1984).

Framing the Research Question For many years, researchers studied the effects of maternal deprivation on children, asking, Does it harm children to be raised without sufficient contact with their mothers? The term *maternal deprivation* became familiar in scientific and popular literature. Its use often struck guilt into the hearts of mothers who left their children in the care of others for several hours each day in order to go out to work. By contrast, the term *paternal deprivation* was seldom used. The reason, perhaps, is that researchers did not think to question fathers' long daily absence from their families. Researchers' questions were influenced by their acceptance of the status quo.

In a similar vein, psychologists have spent years questioning how and why women may form a lesbian identity (see Kitzinger, 1987, for a review), but until relatively recently, they have asked few research questions about the formation of a heterosexual identity. Why? Perhaps because the formation of a heterosexual identity was considered normal, thus needing no explanation. When a special issue of the journal *Feminism & Psychology* was devoted to "heterosexuality and feminism," a host of new and interesting questions were raised (Wilkinson & Kitzinger, 1992). How do women construct a heterosexual identity? What factors are important in this process? How important is this identity to the women who label themselves in this way? Such questions had long been ignored because of the assumption that heterosexuality simply unfolded naturally.

The questions that researchers ask must, of course, limit the answers they find. Thus it is important to examine the assumptions that underlie the way questions are chosen. As researchers or consumers of research, we must continually ask ourselves why we are curious about some matters while we take others for granted.

Research Design: Samples and Methods In the social sciences, gathering evidence involves choosing samples of individuals to study, deciding on the type of information to be gathered from these individuals (e.g., in-depth interviews, behavioral observation, questionnaires), and in many cases selecting groups that can be compared with each other.

A basic principle of the scientific approach is that the sample of individuals to be studied should be as representative as possible of the population the researcher is interested in. However, for many years, psychologists have made general conclusions about human behavior based on research that relied mainly on North American college undergraduates as respondents—a practice that has imperiled the validity of their conclusions (Sears, 1986). Moreover, the database of participants has been rather homogeneous with respect to race, ethnicity, and class. This narrow database means that frequently the conclusions of the researchers cannot really be interpreted as statements about human behavior, because, as Graham (1992) drily noted, "In contemporary society, most of the population is not White and middle class" (p. 638).

With respect to research on women, the same pattern of problems applies. Investigators must be cautious in making general statements about women on the basis of research that has sampled only women of a particular age, race, class, or nationality. For example, in a review of articles on Latinas, Ginorio and Martínez (1998) note that few psychology research articles devote attention to the "interplay between gender and ethno-race in the phenomenon under study" (p. 55) and that few pay attention to the differences among populations of Latinas, such as country/culture of origin, language fluency, level of acculturation, and so on. These omissions make it difficult or impossible to gather useful information about particular groups of women and to transcend stereotypes.

Even when aware of the need for a diverse sample, a researcher may find it difficult to obtain information from respondents from a group to which he or she does not belong. For example, Celia Kitzinger (1987), in her study of the social construction of lesbian identity, found that it was difficult to include Black, working-class, and Jewish women in her sample:

> The politically conscious black lesbians . . . refused to be interviewed by a white woman, and radical working-class women declined to cooperate with the work of a hierarchical academic system from whose benefits they are systematically excluded. My own obvious whiteness and middle-classness (and self-definition as non-Jewish) severely limited the extent to which I could be perceived as an "insider" by some women . . . [T]heir absence is an important loss: the various different identity constructions of white middle-class gentile women are not invalidated or made untrue by my inability to tap the constructions of politically engaged black, working-class, or Jewish lesbians, but they are revealed as a limited and partial selection of the many different visions of the world and of themselves that lesbians as a whole have constructed. (p. 87)

Besides issues of ethnic, racial, and other types of diversity, researchers must consider other issues when deciding how representative their sample is. It seems obvious, for instance, that someone who wishes to study the ways women cope with stress should not choose a sample that is limited to women who are seeking help at a counseling clinic.

The kind of information that researchers collect can strongly influence their conclusions. For example, when female college students respond to closed-ended questions about the potential conflict between their future family roles and a possible scientific career, they may indicate that they see little difficulty (Lips, 1992); when similar questions are posed in an open-ended way, giving the students a chance to answer in their own words, they may express much more anxiety (Lips & Asquith, 1995). It is often necessary to collect information in several different ways to get a clear picture of how respondents are thinking, feeling, or behaving.

Through measurement, science is constructing reality rather than simply discovering it: When researchers create categories and ways of counting people, those categories become "real." In other words, scientists, by measuring something, are actually constructing the very reality they are trying to measure. For example, many years ago, Alfred Kinsey and his colleagues (1948), in a groundbreaking survey study of human sexual behavior, created a set of categories for measuring self-reported sexual attraction to women and men. The research team asked people to place themselves on a 0 to 6 rating scale, on which 0 meant 100 percent heterosexual and 6 meant 100 percent homosexual. Today, "Kinsey's categories have taken on a life of their own. Not only do sophisticated gays and lesbians occasionally refer to themselves by a Kinsey number (such as in a personal ad that might begin, 'tall, muscular Kinsey 6 seeks . . .'), but many scientific studies use the Kinsey scale to define their study population" (Fausto-Sterling, 2000, p. 10).

Group Comparisons   Social scientists often wish to compare the responses of different groups, in order to be able to make statements such as "Women are more _____ than men" or "Middle-class women are more likely than lower-class women to _____" or "Postmenopausal women experience more _____ than premenopausal women do." It should be immediately obvious that such comparisons are fraught with difficulty.

In the first place, they imply that the two groups being compared have been sampled in ways that are equally representative. This assumption may not be justified. For instance, if I choose to compare the attitude-scale responses of female and male university students, using a sample of psychology majors, it is likely that I am getting a more representative sample of female than male university students. Why? Because more females than males choose to major in psychology, so the males in my study will represent a more selective sample than the females.

Second, when the responses of two groups are compared, there is an assumption that the measures and manipulations used in the study were equivalent for the two groups. What if I try to measure how males and females resist conformity pressures by giving a sample of North American students a quiz about football, and then comparing the reactions of women and men to having their answers challenged? If the women turn out to be more likely than men to change their quiz answers in response to challenge, would that mean women conform to pressure more readily than men do? Or what if I try to study gender differences in level of sexual desire by comparing the responses of women and men to a stranger who approaches them at a party and offers to have sex with them? If the men turn out to be more agreeable than the women to this suggestion, should I conclude that men have stronger sexual desires than women do?

The answer to both questions is no. In both examples, the measure used has different meanings for women and men. In the first, history and social context make it likely that the women will know less about football and be less invested in that knowledge than the men are. So the women will feel less secure in their knowledge and also less threatened at the idea of being wrong, predisposing them to conform more than the men on this topic. A different topic might yield very different results.

In the second example, history and social context also lead to responses that differ between the women and men, regardless of their respective levels of sexual desire. The women have probably learned, for many reasons, to be more wary of strangers offering sex, and the effect of sex with a stranger on one's reputation is still different for women and men.

A statement comparing two groups may also suggest that the two groups are operating under equivalent conditions. Consider, for example, a researcher who wishes to compare the behavior of female and male business executives. Female and male executives do not have the same working conditions in at least one very important way: Women are very much a minority at the top levels of business; men are members of the majority. Any statement comparing their behavior must take this difference in their social environment into consideration before easily concluding that women and men "do things differently" in the executive suite simply because of their gender.

Similar cautions must be employed when comparing different groups of women. For example, imagine a study in which African American and European American women attending a predominantly White university complete a questionnaire about their fears for the future. What does it mean if the African American women produce less "fearful" responses than their European American counterparts? This finding is difficult to interpret, because the relatively few African American women who choose to attend this university are unlikely to be as representative of African American women in general as the European American respondents are of European American women in general.

Why make comparisons at all if it is so problematic? Indeed, some researchers avoid comparisons and focus instead on careful, in-depth case studies of individuals' experiences. This **idiographic** approach is valuable for the detail it provides and for the new possibilities for understanding human beings that it can unearth. For example, Rosario Ceballo (1994) studied the life of an African American social worker, using an oral history approach to investigate the themes that had been important to this woman as she constructed her identity, formed relationships, and committed herself to her work over her long life. Lykes (1994) investigated the impact of exile and a return from exile on the self-understanding of one refugee Maya woman of Guatemala. She did this not only through extensive interviewing, but within the context of a 10-year friendship with her informant. In both cases, the authors were able to discern themes in their respondents' experience that may well have gone unnoticed in larger studies.

Yet a **nomothetic** approach, which combines the responses of similar individuals in order to make summary statements about groups and/or compare one group with another, is valuable for discerning patterns and evaluating beliefs and stereotypes about particular groups. For example, a stereotype flourished for years in the medical literature that said pregnant women were emotionally very vulnerable and unstable. The stereotype probably grew out of numerous case studies of women who sought help for emotional difficulties during pregnancy—not necessarily a representative sample of pregnant women. However, when research compared the emotionality of pregnant women with that of other women, or with that of their husbands, it showed little evidence for the stereotype that emotionality was associated with pregnancy (Lips, 1982, 1985).

It is sometimes the presence of the comparison that challenges a stereotype. For example, the finding that 24 percent of a sample of pregnant women agreed with the statement "I sometimes feel as if I am going to have a nervous breakdown" might be taken as supporting the emotional instability stereotype—unless, as was the case in the study in question, it was balanced by the finding that the comparison group (female college students) showed an agreement rate of 57 percent with the same item (Barclay & Barclay, 1976).

Interpreting the Results: What Is a Difference?   For researchers studying gender differences, a finding of "no difference" is often interpreted as "no result." Most differences research is designed to reveal a difference. If the difference fails to appear, researchers cannot be sure whether it means that there is no difference or that their sample was not large enough or their measures not sensitive enough. Just as it is easier to demonstrate the existence of ghosts by gathering anecdotes from people who claim to have seen them than it is to prove their nonexistence by gathering testimonials from people who have never seen them, it is easier to demonstrate a difference than the absence of difference.

Compounding the problem is the fact that "no difference" findings are often rejected for publication because they are considered less interesting and less definitive than demonstrations of differences. Thus the whole enterprise of investigating group differences is biased in favor of demonstrating—rather than debunking—differences.

When differences are shown, the tendency is to interpret them in a good–bad, normal–abnormal, or hierarchical way. In the case of gender, male behavior has often been considered normative; when women's behavior differs, it is often described as less adequate, or it at least requires an explanation. The very labels we use to describe behavioral differences reveal this bias. Consider, for example, the terms used to describe findings that in some perceptual tests men zero in on particular items whereas women pay more attention to the whole context. Reports of such findings say "Men are field-independent, women are field-dependent"—instead of "Men lack context awareness, women are context sensitive." When the difference is described in the latter way, it makes women appear superior; when it is described in the previous way, men seem superior.

When a gender difference is reported in the scientific literature, it is usually phrased something like this: "The mean (average) score for men differed significantly from the mean score for women." A focus on differences between sample means is the most common way of expressing differences between groups. Usually, it is understood to indicate "The average man scores differently on this test from the average woman." Yet this focus can be deceptive. To understand what a mean difference actually implies, it is necessary to know the distribution of scores for the two groups. Two groups with very different distributions of scores can achieve the same means, and two groups with different mean scores can have a high degree of overlap in the distributions of their scores, as shown in Figure 2.1.

Sometimes, a focus on mean differences makes very little sense. Such a difference should not be used to infer that most, or all, women differ from most, or all, men on some general factor. The apparent difference between the group means may be based on a factor that does not affect all members of the groups; in fact, it may affect only a small minority of one group. For instance, more males than females are color-blind. On a test of color vision, a researcher might therefore report that the mean score for females was higher than the mean score for males. It would be misleading to interpret this finding as "Men see color less well than women," since most men *do* see color as well as women do. The difference is confined to a subset of individuals and is more appropriately described in terms

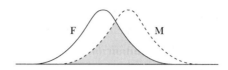

Distribution of hypothetical puzzle solution times, graphed separately for females and males, showing overlap between the distributions.

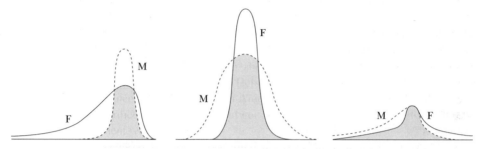

Examples of different ways in which males and females could achieve identical averages in puzzle solution times.

Source: Adapted from H. M. Lips. (1997). *Sex and Gender: An Introduction* (3rd ed.). Mountain View, CA: Mayfield.

Figure 2.1

of relative frequency: "There are more color-blind individuals among males than among females." It would be most informative, however, to show a distribution of the scores—which would show one group of males scoring very low and another group whose scores overlapped significantly with those of the females (Favreau, 1991, 1993).

Interpreting the Results: Why Is There a Difference? A final problem in interpreting the findings of gender differences research lies in explaining why a difference occurred. Often, the research includes no data collection that could answer the *why* question, and researchers simply speculate on the reasons females and males differ in the particular behavior. Since the social experience of the two genders differs in dramatic and subtle ways on many dimensions and they are also biologically different, the scope for such speculation is extremely broad. One error that researchers sometimes make is to fall back on biological explanations when they cannot think of any social or environmental reason that males and females may differ on a particular dimension—even when the biological mechanisms that might be involved are not apparent. Somehow, it sounds more scientific to say something like "We don't know how it happens, so it must be hormones" than to say "We don't know how it happens, so it must be some subtle form of social conditioning." The point is, if we don't know how or why a difference happens there is no "must be" about it!

In the absence of clear data about the *why* question, scientists' own worldviews help shape their interpretations of research findings about gender differences or similarities. One psychologist (Halpern, 2000) relates a discussion she had with a colleague when she pointed out to him that girls achieve better grades than boys in school, but males obtain higher scores on certain tests of cognitive abilities. Her colleague interpreted these findings to mean that schools must be biased against boys. Not necessarily, she argued. The same findings could be interpreted to mean that the tests of cognitive abilities are biased against girls.

Alternative Approaches to Knowledge

While Western science stresses the importance of "real" physical evidence to the accumulation of knowledge, other perspectives stress the importance of different factors. Some perspectives (espoused, for example, by Eastern philosophers and many artists and writers) emphasize intuition, insight, and wisdom that cannot be transferred easily from one individual to another, but must be won through individual practices such as meditation, observation, and reflection.

Other approaches assume the existence of dimensions outside observable, tangible reality. They consider these dimensions when interpreting observable events such as health and illness, behaviors, and feelings. For example, traditional Chinese medicine postulates that channels of energy flow through the body and must be kept in balance in order to promote good health. These channels cannot be seen in the body, but the practice of acupuncture and other aspects of Chinese medicine are based on their existence. Similarly, the discipline of hatha yoga rests, in part, on the idea that an energy called *kundalini,* or serpent power, rests at the base of the spine and can be awakened by proper concentration and breathing exercises. As the yoga practitioner reaches more advanced levels of discipline, the kundalini moves up the spine through a series of chakras, leading to higher levels of consciousness (Vishnudevananda, 1970). Neither the kundalini nor the chakras can be seen or measured by scientific instruments; however, they and their effects are certainly experienced as real by practitioners.

Another example: Members of some Native American cultures assume that

> a person is composed of a physical body, a psychological component, and a spiritual being with a connectedness to the earth and to other spirits/souls. . . . the spiritual being has definite relationships with the earth, with other spirits (living and dead), and with powers both animate and inanimate. These powers take the form of animals, deities, elements of nature, objects, one's relatives . . . such relationships are real, powerful, crucial, and *as* important as the tangible, physical world is to the Western medical mind." (Perrone, Stockel, & Krueger, 1989, p. 11)

For the average Westerner, schooled in the notion that the only reality (and thus the only *evidence*) is physical, observable reality, such concepts can be difficult to grasp and to take seriously. Yet Western physics now postulates the existence of large amounts of matter (called *dark matter*) that cannot be seen or observed through any method yet discovered. So Western science is not absolute in its reliance on observable reality. Additionally, it should be noted that scientific reliance on tangible evidence becomes less firm when a particular theory or idea "fits" accepted notions—as can be seen in the history of the study of sex differences.

BOX 2.3 MAKING CHANGE
Toward Female-Friendly Science and Technology

Women have stayed away from many scientific and technological fields because of stereotypes that said women were intellectually unsuited to these fields and because their experiences in these fields have often been isolating and unwelcoming. Women within these fields have organized to try to change the stereotypes and the environment for women. You can participate in this change by joining one of these organizations—student members are welcome. Better still, if your campus or geographic region does not have a chapter, investigate the possibility of starting one.

Association for Women in Science: **www.awis.org**

Association for Women in Computing: **www.awc-hq.org**

Association for Women in Mathematics: **www.awm-math.org**

Society of Women Engineers: **www.swe.org**

Gender Differences and Similarities in Cognitive Abilities or Styles

Physicist Fumiko Yonezawa directs a lab that brings in millions of yen in grants at Japan's Keio University. Yet she is an unlikely scientist. Her mother, forbidden by her own father to attend college, bucked Japanese custom by beginning to teach geometry to Yonezawa when she was still in kindergarten. Most parents, Yonezawa asserts, would not have steered a daughter in this direction: "Parents say girls are not good at mathematics, and they don't want to spend a lot of money educating their girls in science . . . I think it will take generations to correct that" (Koppel, 1993).

The debate over gender differences in **cognitive abilities** (abilities related to thinking, learning, and remembering) has been long and acrimonious. For years, women in the United States and elsewhere were denied access to higher education because of assumptions about their unfitness (relative to men) to undertake serious intellectual work. Experts argued that if women spent too much time thinking, their overstressed brains would rob energy from their bodies, leaving them weakened and possibly unable to bear children (Rosenberg, 1982). When women finally *were* allowed into colleges and universities, experts switched their objections from concern for the women to concern for the institutions. One historian, for example, noted that coeducation exerted "debilitating, feminizing, corrupting influences" on American colleges (Rudolph, 1962, p. 324). To reduce such influences, female students were sometimes subjected to severe restrictions. For example, when Martha Lewis breached the barriers to women in 1849 by enrolling in the Teacher Training School in Saint John, New Brunswick, Canada, she was ordered to enter the lecture room 10 minutes before the male students and leave 5 minutes before the end of class, sit alone at the back of the room, and wear a black veil at all times (*Herstory,* 1995).

American psychologists of the 1880s and 1890s such as Mary Calkins, Christine Ladd-Franklin, and Margaret Washburn were denied official status in graduate programs simply because they were women (Furumoto & Scarborough, 1986). Mary Calkins eventually became the first woman to serve as president of the American Psychological Association and also the first to preside over the American Philosophical Association. Washburn, the first woman to receive a Ph.D. in psychology, was the second woman president of the American Psychological Association, and also the second woman to be elected to the National Academy of Sciences. Clearly, these were very talented women; yet, because of prevailing attitudes about women's intellectual inferiority, they had to fight to be accepted into graduate study. Calkins was, in fact, denied a Ph.D., even though she had completed all the requirements and was recommended by her professors—because Harvard refused to award a Ph.D. to a woman.

For African American and other minority women, the situation was especially grim. The first African American woman to receive a medical degree in the United States, Dr. Rebecca Lee, graduated from the Boston Female Medical College in 1864, 14 years after Elizabeth Blackwell became the first European American woman to receive an M.D., despite the expressed reluctance of the faculty to recommend a Black woman (Walsh, 1977). It was 1933 (more than three decades after the first doctoral degree in psychology was granted to a White woman) before the first African American woman, Ruth Howard, was awarded a Ph.D. in psychology.

Women would-be scientists faced similar difficulties around the world. Women in 19th-century Russia found the universities closed to them and were forced to travel to Western Europe to study science (Koblitz, 1988). German mathematician Emmy Noether (1882–1935), the founder of abstract algebra, attended college before it was legal for women to obtain degrees, lectured under someone else's name because she had been forbidden to teach, and submitted her articles for publication through a friend. Gerty Cori, who won a Nobel prize in 1947 for her biochemical research, was educated in her Czechoslovakian homeland under a system in which girls were not taught Latin, mathematics, physics, or chemistry—all subjects that she needed in order to pursue her chosen career in medicine (McGrayne, 1993). In Brazil, women had few opportunities to enter higher education until well into the 20th century. The first Brazilian woman to obtain a doctorate in science, Elza Gomide, was granted her degree in 1950 (Silva, 1988). The English physicist and inventor Hertha Ayrton in 1902 became the first woman to be nominated to the Royal Society in London (Mason, 1991). Her nomination was rejected, however, because as a married woman she had no legal status, and thus could not be a fellow of a chartered society!

Reading the words hurled at women who dared to invade the realm of science indicates that the controversy had as much to do with power as with presumed differences. When Harriot Hunt, the first woman to practice medicine successfully in the United States, launched her career in 1835, one medical journal wondered in print whether she "knew the difference between the sternum and the spinal column" (Walsh, 1977, p. 2). As women physicians grew in numbers, an editorial in the *British Medical and Surgical Journal* in 1853 noted nervously that it was no longer possible to laugh away the "serious inroads made by female physicians in obstetrical business, one of the essential branches of income to a majority of well-established practitioners" (cited in Walsh, 1977). When Gerty Cori's husband and research partner, Carl, was offered a prestigious job at the University of Rochester in 1930, it was on condition that he stop collaborating with his wife. He refused (McGrayne, 1993).

When women did get into scientific fields, their contributions were often ignored or lost to history. An interesting example for psychologists is the well-known photograph of the early-20th-century Russian physiologist Ivan Pavlov, famous for his classical conditioning experiments, with his research group. The original photograph includes two women who were part of the research group. They are missing in the version of the picture that is commonly reproduced—literally cut out of the picture (Herzenberg, Meschel, & Altena, 1991).

Research on Cognitive Differences

Is there any evidence that women and men think differently? And what kind of evidence would be convincing? One thing we do know is that there are no simple answers. As cognitive psychologist Diane Halpern (2000) argues,

> It seems likely that our abilities are influenced by age, birth order, cultural background, socio-economic status, sex role orientation, learning histories, and so forth, in addition to the simple fact that we were born either female or male. In reality, these variables work together in their effect on cognitive abilities. It is possible, for example, that wealthy females who are firstborn tend to develop excellent verbal ability, whereas lower-middle-class females who are second- or thirdborn don't tend to develop these same excellent abilities (perhaps because firstborn wealthy females are talked to and read to more often). . . . A host of sociodemographic (e.g., age, place of residence), psychological (e.g., motivational), biological (e.g., health status), and life history (e.g., level of education) variables operate in conjunction with sex to determine the level of each cognitive ability that an individual obtains. (p. 73)

For many years, psychologists have focused on gender differences in three areas of cognitive performance: verbal, quantitative, and visual–spatial. In 1974, Eleanor Maccoby and Carol Jacklin's landmark study of male–female differences, which consolidated the hundreds of studies then available, concluded that reliable gender differences had been demonstrated in these three areas of cognitive performance (verbal, quantitative, and visual–spatial), plus aggression. Although their approach received some criticism, it set the stage and provided the framework for much of the research on gender differences that has occurred since the publication of their book. In this chapter, we focus in turn on each of the four differences they identified.

Remembering that research findings are in certain ways constructed by the research community, it is important to note that the framework established by Maccoby and Jacklin's (1974) findings has had an enormous influence on the ways in which questions about gender differences have been organized and asked. As Halpern (2000) points out, ". . . the categories that scientists create to conceptualize research findings and to guide future research also constrain the results. It is possible that a different system of categorizing cognitive abilities would show a different pattern of sex differences" (p. 91). And remember the Yoruba—the Nigerian culture described in Chapter 1 for whom age rather than gender is a primary organizing factor? Would they have framed research on cognitive abilities in terms of female–male comparisons at all? Probably not. As we examine the findings about gender differences and similarities in the four areas Maccoby and Jacklin identified, we must keep in mind that, by focusing on gender comparisons, and by focusing on them in particular ways, the research community creates a body of knowledge and a climate in which such gender comparisons are considered important.

Current research supports, in a limited way, some, but not all, of the differences first listed by Maccoby and Jacklin (1974). The newer conclusions are based on a research strategy called **meta-analysis,** which employs statistical methods to combine the findings of a large number of different studies of the same behavior in order to evaluate the overall pattern. It is a useful tool because it can provide information about the average size of the "effect" of gender with respect to a particular behavior. Using the means and standard deviations reported for females and males in each study, the researcher calculates the effect size for that study. There are two common measures of **effect size:** (1) the proportion of variation in the mixed (female + male) population that can be accounted for by gender differences, and (2) the distance, in standard deviation units, between the means for females and males. Once the researcher has determined the effect size for each study in the collection, the average effect size can be calculated across all the studies in order to draw conclusions about the robustness and importance of the difference in question.

Some caveats: Information about "average effect size" carries some of the same limitations as single-study findings of mean differences. It reveals nothing about whether the effect is caused by differences that distinguish all members of the two groups, or only a small subset of individuals (Favreau, 1993; Feingold, 1995). Furthermore, there may be many studies that are not included in a meta-analysis because they were not published, and thus not available to the person compiling the meta-analysis. This is especially problematic because unpublished studies are particularly likely to be those that have not found significant differences between the groups. Finally, and perhaps most importantly, the studies included in most meta-analyses are based on a narrow range of participants (usually young, North American students) and are not reflective of the population at large—although this limitation tends to be obscured by the combination of many studies into a single analysis (Halpern, 1995). Thus, meta-analysis, like any other research method, does not provide a perfectly clear picture of group differences.

Verbal Performance   Maccoby and Jacklin (1974) reported that females performed better than males on tests of verbal skills. The difference was consistent, but small. Their conclusion was reinforced by Hyde's (1981) meta-analysis of these studies, which showed that gender accounted for an average of only 1 percent of the variance in verbal performance scores. At the low end of the distribution of verbal performance, the differences are more dramatic; for example, boys are 3 to 4 times more likely than girls to be stutterers (Skinner & Shelton, 1985), and 5 to 10 times more likely than girls to be dyslexic (Vandenberg, 1987).

When differences between males and females are found on tests of verbal performance, they almost always show females performing better. Gender differences in verbal performance appear earlier than other cognitive differences. Girls reportedly have larger vocabularies and generate longer utterances at earlier ages than boys do (Shucard, Shucard, & Thomas, 1987), and they maintain superior verbal performance through elementary school (Martin & Hoover, 1987). However, some confusion in the literature is caused by the fact that verbal ability is not a single, unitary ability, but a collection of related abilities, such as word fluency, grammar, spelling, reading, writing, and oral comprehension (Halpern, 2000). A meta-analysis of 165 studies found no overall gender differences across all types of verbal tests (Hyde & Linn, 1988). When researchers examined tests of specific verbal skills separately, they found no gender differences in vocabulary, reading comprehension, essay writing, or the SAT-Verbal; small gender differences favoring females in anagrams and general/mixed verbal abilities; a small difference favoring males in analogies, and a moderate difference favoring females in speech production.

An examination of gender differences among children in performance on verbal tests showed that such differences had declined sharply since 1947 (Feingold, 1988). However, this conclusion may reflect a change in samples, criteria for publication, or changes in measurement over this time period (Halpern, 2000). For example, studies that find no significant differences are more likely to be published now (and thus included in meta-analyses) than they were several decades ago. Thus, the evidence that gender differences in verbal abilities are decreasing is difficult to interpret, and some reviewers have concluded that the differences have been relatively stable over the last several decades (Hedges & Nowell, 1995).

Studies in a variety of settings continue to report gender differences in verbal performance. A study of high school students in Japan and the United States reported higher average scores by girls than boys in both countries on a word fluency test (Mann, Sasanuma, Sakuma, & Masaki, 1990). A study of cognitive performance among high school students in China showed girls performing at higher levels than boys on word knowledge and word span tasks (Huang, 1993). Hines (1990) reported a large female advantage of more than one standard deviation on tests of associational fluency (generating synonyms). On the other hand, males have scored higher than females on the SAT-Verbal since the early 1970s. This may be because low-ability males do not take the test and because the SAT-V was heavily weighted with analogies—the only verbal test on which males tend to outscore females (Halpern, 2000). Analogy items have recently been removed from the SAT-V (Pringle, 2003).

It appears that consistent gender differences turn up on some types of verbal tasks, but that many types of verbal performance show no differences. The largest differences occur at the low end of the distribution; gender differences are much smaller within the average range of verbal abilities.

Quantitative Performance   Numerous reports state that girls obtain higher school *grades* in mathematics than boys do (Kimball, 1989). Meta-analyses done in the early 1980s, however, showed that between 1 percent and 5 percent of the variance in mathematics *test performance* was associated with gender, with males achieving higher scores than females (Hyde, 1981). More recent meta-analyses indicate a smaller gender gap (Friedman, 1989; Hyde, Fennema, and Lamon, 1990); however, as for verbal performance, it is difficult to know whether the gender gap is actually decreasing or whether the smaller differences are the result of changes in samples, publication criteria, or other factors. These meta-analyses show that gender differences in mathematics performance are found to be greater among White Americans than in Black, Hispanic, Asian American, Canadian, and Australian samples. Smaller gender differences are also found in samples from lower socioeconomic groups than from higher ones (Fischbein, 1990). International studies continue to find somewhat higher mathematics test performance by male than female students in many countries (Mau & Lynn, 2000; Randhawa & Gupta, 2000; Wang, 2001).

Female and male students seem to think of themselves differently with respect to mathematics too. A study of Norwegian students at several levels showed that the males had higher academic self-concept, performance expectations, intrinsic motivation, and motivation to "look good" in mathematics than girls did (Skaalvik & Skaalvik, 2004). Studies of university students show that women are less likely than men to imagine strong future possibilities for themselves in the realms of mathematics and science (Lips, 2004).

A strong predictor of scores on mathematics tests is the number of mathematics courses taken (Jones, 1984), and this background variable tends to be confounded with gender. When data are adjusted to take into account the number of mathematics courses completed, gender differences in performance are greatly reduced, although they do not disappear (Meece, Eccles-Parsons, Kaczala, Goff, & Futterman, 1982).

Most studies show no gender differences in performance on general mathematics achievement tests until early adolescence. In one study of more than 5,000 students aged 13 and 17, no differences were found among the 13-year-olds, but among the 17-year-olds the boys significantly outperformed the girls (Jones, 1984). Differences do appear earlier in some subareas of mathematical competence, however. Girls show a small advantage in computation in elementary and middle school. As early as first grade, some studies have found boys performing better than girls on mathematical problem solving (Lummis & Stevenson, 1990). In the latter study, first-grade boys outscored girls in problem solving by equivalent amounts in the United States, Japan, and Taiwan. Japanese girls achieved higher average scores on problem solving than American boys did; however, the gap in problem-solving performance between Japanese boys and Japanese girls was as great as that between American boys and American girls. A follow-up study of these students and some of their fellow students when they were in 11th grade showed a similar pattern of national differences: American students received the lowest scores in mathematics: Only 14.4 percent of the Chinese and 8 percent of the Japanese students scored below the average score of the American students (Stevenson, Chen, & Lee, 1993). Also, by 11th grade, the gender difference in mathematics performance had increased in all three cultures and was greater among the Chinese and Japanese than among American students. Among these 11th-grade students, culture was associated with more variation in mathematics test performance than gender was. Girls from both Taiwan and Japan scored higher than U.S. boys on the test (Evans, Schweingruber, & Stevenson, 2002).

In the United States, much of the controversy about gender differences in mathematical performance has swirled around test scores on the SAT-Math, a standardized test of mathematical reasoning. On this test, there has been a lingering tendency for males to score higher (by 40 to 50 points) than females over the past quarter century (College Entrance Examination Board, 1997; Halpern, 1994). The test, given great weight by college admissions offices in the United States, tends to produce larger gender differences in performance than other tests (Hyde et al., 1990).

Attention was drawn to gender differences on the SAT-M by Benbow and Stanley (1980, 1982, 1983; Benbow, 1988), who examined scores on the SAT-M for about 50,000 seventh- and eighth-grade students. The sample was not chosen to be representative of seventh- and eighth-graders; rather, it comprised high-ability students who had been iden-

TABLE 2.1   Number of People Graduating with Bachelor's Degrees per 100 Persons of the Theoretical Age of Graduation, by Sex

Country	Percent graduating from university, 1989		Percent graduating from university, 1996	
	Women	Men	Women	Men
Australia	21.1	18.9	43.3	28.9
Austria	5.5	7.6	9.6	11.4
Denmark	14.4	11.5	33.0	23.1
Italy	8.7	9.1	13.8	11.4
New Zealand	15.5	16.6	35.4	26.2
Norway	31.7	18.1	34.8	20.2
Spain	21.0	14.6	31.0	21.5
Switzerland	5.3	10.1	7.2	11.5
United States	29.2	25.2	38.9	30.6

The belief that women were not capable of serious intellectual work kept them out of higher education for some time. In some countries, they are still less likely than men to receive a university education. However, as this table shows, more women than men now graduate from university in a number of nations.

Source: (Digest of Education Statistics, 2000)

tified by the Johns Hopkins National Talent Search because they scored in the top 3 percent in the nation. Among this very select sample, Benbow and Stanley found a 30-point mean difference favoring boys. They also found that at the top end of the distribution, the higher the score, the greater the ratio of boys to girls who attained it. Among students who scored above 500, the ratio of boys to girls was 2.1 to 1; among those scoring about 600, the ratio was 4.1 to 1; among those scoring over 700, 13 to 1 (Benbow & Stanley, 1983). Thus, the differences appear largest when considering the most highly gifted students.

If Benbow and Stanley had relied on a test other than the SAT-M, they might have found smaller gender differences in performance. Even putting skepticism about the SAT-M aside, however, there are reasons to be cautious in interpreting the results of this research. The information provided by Benbow and Stanley's research is based on an extremely select sample, and it should not be used to draw inferences about general gender differences in mathematical performance or about the suitability of women and men for mathematical and scientific careers (Rossi, 1983). The girls and boys in their sample were much more mathematically talented than average and, as voluntary participants in the Talent Search, were to some extent self-selected (and parent selected) for motivation and interest. In this sample, already limited to the top 3 percent of scorers, only about 7 of every 1,000 boys and 5 of every 10,000 girls scored over 700. The finding of large differences in the proportions of males and females at these levels is relevant to such a small segment of the population that it has little practical significance. In fact, even among these extremely mathematically talented children, factors other than ability obviously weighed heavily in the choice of career. Follow-up data showed that the majority of this highly gifted sample did *not* pursue mathematics or science as a career: Of the 47 percent who went to graduate school, 42 percent of the men and 22 percent of the women chose scientific or mathematical fields (Benbow, 1988).

Being mathematically talented has different implications for women and men. A subsequent report on the status of Benbow and Stanley's participants at the age of 33—20 years after their participation—indicated that, although the vast majority of them obtained college degrees, these mathematically talented males and females pursued different educational and career paths: About 44 percent of the males and 22 percent of the females earned bachelor's degrees in mathematics or inorganic sciences (engineering, computer science, physical sciences). At the master's degree level, about 16 percent of the males and 8 percent of the females earned degrees in these areas, and at the doctoral level, 5.5 percent of males and 1.3 percent of the females (Benbow, Lubinski, Shea, & Eftekhari-Sanjini, 2000). In terms of occupation, males were far more likely than females to become mathematicians, computer scientists, or engineers; females were far more likely than males to become homemakers or health care workers. More than 15 percent of the women were homemakers at the time of the follow-up. Clearly, there is more than mathematical ability at work in producing these different patterns for women and men. All the study participants—boys and girls—tested in the top 3 percent of mathematics ability when they were in seventh or eighth grade and thus would have had the necessary ability to pursue careers in mathematics or inorganic sciences.

One main reason for administering standardized tests of mathematical and other abilities is to predict success in college. Research indicates, however, that SAT-M scores do a poorer job of prediction for females than for males. Using a sample of 47,000 university students, researchers compared the admitting SAT-M scores of females and males who had obtained the identical grades in the same university courses and found that females who were performing at the same level as males in college had scored an average of 33 points *lower* than the males on the SAT-M (Wainer & Steinberg, 1992). More recently, a College Board study of students at 23 U.S. universities has shown that there is a tendency for the SAT-M to err in opposite directions for women and men with respect to predicting their college performance: tending to underpredict women's and overpredict men's performance (Kobrin, Camara, & Milewski, 2002). Added to reports that the SAT-M tends to produce larger gender differences than other tests, such findings may shake our confidence in the validity of this widely used test for predicting college-level performance.

Is it universally true that females are missing from the highest levels of mathematical performance? Stanley (1990) noted that of 144 winners of the U.S.A. Mathematical Olympiad (a prestigious mathematics competition for high school students) since 1972, only 2 were female. In 1998, Melanie Wood became the first female member ever to be a part of the U.S. team to the International Mathematical Olympiad—where she won a silver medal (she repeated this feat in 1999) (Shulman, 2000). Although 10 to 16 percent of participants in the U.S.A. Mathematical Olympiad have been girls in recent years, there have been no girls on the six-person team sent to the international competition since then. On the other hand, in 2001, when high school student Mariangela Lisanti won first place the Intel Science Talent Search with a quantitative physics project, she became the third female in a row to win this award (Intel Science Talent Search Awards, 2001).

At the international level, there has also been a clear shortage of female mathematics contestants; for example, in 1988 there were only four female participants (from a total of 49 countries) in the International Mathematical Olympiad. Japan's team included a girl in 1996, and she won a gold medal. Teams from Canada, South Africa, and the United Kingdom have sometimes included girls in recent years, but the majority of participants continue to be male. The proportion of female participants is always less than 10 percent, and it is rare for a country to have more than one girl in its team of six (Webb, 2001). In the 2001 Olympiad, there were only 16 girls among the 242 award winners. Yet one country stands out in contrast. For four years in a row, the Chinese team included a girl, and these four Chinese girls were extremely successful, winning three silver medals and one gold. China's success in this instance suggests that the absence of women from the highest-achieving groups in mathematics is not inevitable. This conclusion is supported by at least one study of Chinese high school students, which showed no gender differences in mathematical thinking and reasoning tasks (Huang, 1993).

Visual–Spatial Performance   Visual–spatial performance reflects a broad range of abilities that enable us to "imagine what an irregular figure would look like if it were rotated in space or . . . to discern the relationship between shapes and objects" (Halpern, 2000, p. 98). Like the other areas of cognitive ability discussed, visual–spatial ability is not a unitary ability, but a constellation of several different abilities.

Gender differences in various types of visual–spatial performance have been reported since Herbert Witkin's (1949) early research demonstrated better performance by men than women on the Rod and Frame Test. On this task, a participant sitting in a darkened room must adjust a luminous tilted rod suspended inside a tilted frame to true vertical. Because the room is dark, the participant has no visual context cues outside the rod and frame, only cues relating to his or her own body position and gravity. People unable to adjust the rod to a vertical position were labeled "field dependent" by Witkin. Such individuals were, according to Witkin, unable to overcome the effect of the environmental context (in this case, the frame) in perceiving a particular aspect of their world.

Eventually, Witkin went on to develop an elaborate theory about how performance on this task was an indicator of an important personality variable: the degree of "psychological differentiation" between self and environment (Witkin et al., 1954). Field independence indicated a reliance on strong internal frames of reference and the ability to resist environmental influences. Field dependence was associated with a tendency to submit to authority, to need support from the environment, to deny internal feelings, and to have difficulty with impulse control—all, according to Witkin and his colleagues, signs of arrested emotional development.

The characterization of field dependence (more likely among women) and independence (more likely among men) fit neatly with the gender stereotypes of post–World War II America. Both the perceptual and the personality aspects of the research were used to justify the exclusion of women from industrial jobs after the war (Haaken, 1988).

Does Witkin's notion of field dependence and independence, and the greater value placed upon the latter, sound familiar? It should, for it carries echoes of the two perspectives on science discussed earlier in this chapter. Positivist science requires a "field independent" (or "context-unaware") approach, one that isolates the phenomenon under study from the surrounding context. Social constructionism requires the opposite: a sensitivity to context, a "dependence" on the surrounding field for clues to understanding. Given the views of science, of gender, and of society that prevailed at the time of Witkin's research, it is not surprising that his extrapolation from perceptual tasks to personality gained such easy acceptance.

Current research on visual–spatial performance focuses on specific skills rather than on such global orientations as field dependence. Gender differences favoring males on many tests are still reported consistently (Halpern, 2000; Weiss, Kemmler, Deisenhammer, Fleischhacker, & Delazer, 2003). But a recent cross-cultural review noted that in contrast to the reliable gender differences in variability in spatial performance found in the United States, no consistent gender differences in variability in spatial abilities appear across countries (Feingold, 1994a).

Linn and Petersen (1985) conducted meta-analyses of the studies that employed particular tests of spatial abilities. They concluded that at least three different types of spatial abilities can be distinguished in these tests: **spatial visualization, spatial perception,** and **mental rotation.** Spatial visualization, which involves complicated, multistep mental manipulations of spatial information, is often measured using the Embedded Figures Test, which requires analytical ability: Respondents must find a "hidden" figure embedded in a complex background. Linn and Petersen's meta-analysis showed no reliable gender differences in performance on this type of task, a conclusion echoed 10 years later in a meta-analysis by Voyer, Voyer, and Bryden (1995).

Spatial perception, which involves determining spatial relationships with respect to one's own body orientation, is the ability measured by the Rod and Frame Test. Linn and Petersen found that gender differences on this type of task, with males scoring higher, begin as early as age 8. The differences become larger (two-thirds of a standard deviation) in samples of respondents over the age of 18. Voyer and colleagues (1995) also reported significant gender differences on this type of task.

Mental rotation ability is traditionally measured by displaying a picture or object and asking questions that require you to "rotate" that picture or object in your mind, to visualize it from another angle. Scores are based on speed rather than accuracy, since most people can mentally rotate an object accurately, given sufficient time. Males reliably obtain higher scores than females on this type of task, with the size of the effect varying from one quarter of a standard deviation to an entire standard deviation (Linn & Petersen, 1985; Voyer, Voyer, & Bryden, 1995). Such mental rotation tests tend to produce the largest male–female differences in performance. Recent research has replicated the finding of male–female differences in mental rotation performance—but only when using traditional paper-and-pencil measures. When performance is tested in a virtual environment, no differences are found (Parsons, Larson, Kratz, Thiebaux, Bluestein, Buckwalter, & Rizzo, 2004).

A fourth type of visual–spatial ability, **spatiotemporal ability,** involves judgments about moving visual displays. In tests of this ability, respondents are asked to make "time of arrival" judgments about a moving object. Some researchers have found that females are less accurate than males in such judgments (Schiff & Oldak, 1990; Smith & McPhee, 1987). However, the body of research on this type of spatial performance is still small relative to those discussed above.

Finally, a fifth type of visual–spatial ability, **generation and maintenance of a spatial image,** is one that enables participants to generate an image from memory and then use the information about the image to perform a task (Halpern, 2000). For example, think of your bedroom at home. Is the reading lamp on the left side or the right side of the bed? To answer the question, you must generate a visual image of your bedroom and then hold that image in your memory while answering a question about the way it looks. Some evidence suggests that males are faster, but not more accurate, than females on this type of task (Loring-Meier & Halpern, 1999).

There has been some tendency to use these differences as explanations for women's underrepresentation in such fields as engineering and architecture. But the gender differences in certain spatial skills, though reliable, are not sufficient to explain the huge gender differences in participation rates in engineering, where men continue to outnumber women by more than 9 to 1 in the United States. This conclusion is reinforced by an examination of the engineering field in Russia, where, as in North America, adolescent girls score somewhat lower than boys on spatial tests (Kova & Majerova, 1974), but a high proportion of engineers and scientists are women.

Finally, although researchers have demonstrated some differences between women and men in cognitive performance, it is important to remember that, in general, such differences have not been found in very many areas. In fact, despite the focus on differences, "Males and females are overwhelmingly alike in their cognitive abilities." (Halpern, 2000, p. 128)

Explanations for Gender Differences in Cognitive Performance

Most biological explanations for cognitive gender differences emphasize the influence of sex hormones, either on the structure or the functioning of the brain. For example, researchers have attempted to link hormones to cognition by showing that among normal women, performance on some cognitive tasks varies along with the menstrual cycle. These researchers have found a cyclic variation in which performance on some visual–spatial tasks improves when estrogen and progesterone are low, and verbal fluency, speech articulation, and manual dexterity improve when these hormones are at high levels (Hampson, 1990a, 1990b; Hampson & Kimura, 1988). Men too show fluctuations in cognitive performance in concert with changing hormone levels throughout the day: Spatial performance is lower early in the morning, when testosterone levels are low (Moffat & Hampson, 1996). Other researchers have pointed to sex differences in handedness (the extent to which an individual is right- or left-handed) as an indication that females and males differ in brain organization, arguing that such differences may affect performance differences (e.g., Casey & Brabeck, 1989; Coren & Halpern, 1991). Some of these issues will be discussed in more detail in Chapter 3, when we look at sexual differentiation. At this point, however, it is important to note that hormones may, through action on the brain,

Whereas middle-class European Americans value technical intelligence as a distinct and important skill, some African groups emphasize that children's intelligence includes both capability and social responsibility.

play a role in some aspects of cognition. The levels of these hormones vary a great deal among individuals of the same sex and even, over time, within the same individual.

It is important to remember that cognitive performance does not occur (and cannot be tested) in a cultural vacuum: The values placed on various skills and the practice that is encouraged for such skills are bound to color both the efforts of the people being studied and the observations of researchers. The undeniable impact of culture and the social environment on cognition has been noted by many researchers (see Rogoff & Chavajay, 1995, for a review). For example, cultures differ in what they label *intelligence*. Whereas middle-class European Americans value technical intelligence as a distinct and important skill, some African groups emphasize that children's intelligence includes *both* capability *and* social responsibility. In Western schools it may be considered cheating to rely on a classmate for help; in some other cultures, the refusal to accept a classmate's help may be viewed as foolish or egotistical. Villagers in Uganda think of intelligence as manifested by being slow and careful; more Westernized groups in Uganda associate intelligence with speed. Such cultural values are transmitted through parents, teachers, peers, and other socializing agents. Not surprisingly, then, cultural and environmental explanations for cognitive gender differences emphasize such factors as training, practice, and encouragement. Here again, there may be differences not only between females and males but among same-gender individuals and over time for the same individual.

Studies in North America suggest that boys receive higher levels of encouragement and support from teachers and parents for mathematical performance than girls do. For example, in some studies teachers have been found to pay more attention to boys and direct more questions to them (Sadker & Sadker, 1985), and to be more likely to encourage boys than girls to "try harder" when they fail (Dweck, 1999). Some parents expect sons to have and credit them with more mathematical talent than they do daughters (Entwisle & Baker, 1983; Yee & Eccles, 1988), and they tend to give toys to boys that facilitate practice in quantitative and spatial skills (Miller, 1987). These differences in the way girls and boys are treated are likely based on the stereotype that males are better at math. As we saw in Chapter 1, such a stereotype can have an impact on performance through stereotype threat.

Even within the United States, intergroup differences based on culture are evident. Chinese American girls perform as well as Chinese American boys in high-level mathematics, including the SAT-M, whereas a gender gap exists in European American students' performance. One study designed to explore the reasons for this discrepancy examined the family interactions of mother–father–daughter triads from the two cultural groups as the fifth- and sixth-grade girls tried to solve a spatial rotation puzzle (Huntsinger & Jose, 1995). These researchers found that the ratio of encouraging comments to discouraging comments from Chinese American parents to their daughters was 15 to 1, whereas for the European American parents the ratio was 6 to 1. They also noted that for the European American but not the Chinese American parents, comments from mothers and fathers about their own and the other parent's mathematical abilities reflected gender stereotypes. Fathers said things such as "Don't listen to your mother" or "Even Mommy can do this"; mothers made comments such as "Your dad is a math brain," "Math isn't my area," and "I hate this. I hate math!" (p. 493). As a group, European American mothers liked mathematics less and rated it as more difficult than Chinese American mothers or fathers or European American fathers did. These and other findings of this research program support the notion that cultural differences in interaction patterns and parental behaviors are linked to daughters' mathematics achievement.

Some international gaps in math achievement are more striking than the average gender gap within countries. For example, one study comparing mathematics performance among elementary school children in the United States, China, and Japan found that by the fifth grade, the top U.S. class scored, on average, below the lowest Japanese class and the second-lowest Chinese class (Lummis & Stevenson, 1990). Although the gender gap in elementary school mathematics performance has been found to be about the same size in Japan as in the United States, Japanese girls perform better than American boys (Stevenson, Lee, & Stigler, 1986). In high school, the gap between countries increases, as does the gender gap. Among the 11th-grade students studied, the gender gap in the United States is slightly (and nonsignificantly) larger than the gap between Chinese and American students (Stevenson, Chen, & Lee, 1993). The gap between countries may be attributable to differing amounts of formal school training and parental help and expectations. The gap between the genders may reflect, in the other countries as in the United States, a differing emphasis on mathematics and science for girls and boys. Indeed, when 11th-grade students in the United States, Taiwan, and Japan are asked about their preferred academic subjects, boys show preferences for science, math, and sports, whereas girls say they prefer language arts, music, and art (Evans, Schweingruber, & Stevenson, 2002). These researchers conclude that cultures can affect these gendered preferences through socialization and schooling practices.

Findings among less industrialized cultures also suggest a link between socialization and cognitive performance. John Berry (1966) demonstrated that northern Canadian Inuit outscored members of the African Temne people on every spatial test, and that gender differences in performance were not present in the Inuit sample. The results may reflect the differing lifestyles of the Inuit and Temne groups. Among the Inuit, both women and men traveled long distances from home to hunt—activities that might well develop spatial skills. Among the Temne, only the males tended to travel long distances from home, and the two sexes led rather segregated lives.

Research on more than 1,000 children from Quechua-speaking Indian families in Peru shows that gender plays a minor role in comparison to other demographic and socialization factors in determining cognitive performance (Stevenson, Chen, & Booth, 1990). The children, who lived in the shantytowns of Lima and in remote villages of the Peruvian highlands or the tropical rain forest, were tested for reading and mathematics achievement, as well as a number of cognitive tasks such as concept formation and auditory memory. The study examined gender differences relative to other variables: schooling versus nonschooling, amount of schooling, location, and chrononological age. Gender differences never accounted for more than 5 percent of the variance in the children's test scores; however a combination of the other background variables typically accounted for more than 20 percent of the variance. Gender differences were greatest for nonschooled and first-grade children and tended to decrease with increasing years of schooling, a result the researchers suggest is due to the sharing of common experiences that occurs in school. The differences that were observed tended to favor boys, and the researchers argue that this pattern is related to the privileged status of boys in Andean cultures. In support of this interpretation, they noted that fathers participated in cognitive activities more often with boys than girls, that boys were expected to use money earlier, to stay alone for a whole day, to be able to take a half-day trip, and to attain higher-status jobs and positions in the community than girls. Girls, by contrast, were expected to learn more practical activities to be able to take care of their siblings at a younger age than boys. Stevenson and his colleagues argue that "The smallness of the gender effects found in the various tests become even more impressive in view of these indications that parents provided boys with greater opportunities for cognitive stimulation than they provided girls" (p. 550).

The debate about whether the patterns of gender differences and similarities are due to biological or environmental variables has grown more complex with each passing year, and it seems unlikely to be resolvable. Diane Halpern and Mary LeMay (2000) suggest that, rather than the nature–nurture split, a better way to think about the "why" question is though a **psychobiosocial model.** Their model is rooted in the idea that some variables are *both* biological and social, and so cannot be readily classified as either biological or environmental. For example, learning, they argue, is an event that occurs in a social context

---

BOX 2.4 LEARNING ACTIVITY
Women Inventors

As this chapter notes, women have often been discouraged from entering science and technology fields. Yet women have made many scientific discoveries and are responsible for a number of important inventions. Can you name five inventions by women? That is the question that you will be asked as you start your visit to this Canadian Web site: **www.inventivewomen.com**.

   Even if you cannot answer the question, watch the opening graphics of the site to see an amazing list of the things women have invented. Then click on the *Inventive Women Library* and follow some of the links to individual women inventors. Read the stories of several of these inventors and write down your reactions. What kinds of difficulties did they have? How much of their difficulty was related to discrimination based on gender? What kinds of resources did they use to overcome difficulties? What difference do you think the social environment makes to the success of women as inventors?

---

and is affected by social variables (such as encouragement, opportunities, prior learning experiences), but it also has a biological basis. Specific learning experiences affect the brain, causing changes in such things as cell size and connections. With respect to learning, then, the line between social and biological events is blurred.

Gender Differences and Similarities in Aggression

In recent decades, the entertainment industry has "discovered" female aggression. From Glenn Close's enraged "other woman" in *Fatal Attraction,* to Sharon Stone's seductive predator in *Basic Instinct,* to Demi Moore's calculating power seeker in *Disclosure,* to Zhang Zi Yi's vengeful princess skilled in martial arts in *Crouching Tiger, Hidden Dragon,* to Uma Thurman's vengeance-oriented spitfire in *Kill Bill,* the implication is that women can be dangerous. But the media fascination with dangerous women seems based on their novelty, their deviance.

   The stereotype that men are more aggressive than women has held for decades (White & Kowalski, 1994) and across many cultures (Williams & Best, 1982). It is widely believed that women are reluctant aggressors, handling aggressive feelings badly and expressing them only under special conditions. Women, according to social myth, are "nonaggressive, 'sneaky' in their expression of aggression, unable to express anger, prone to outbursts of 'fury,' psychologically distressed if they are aggressive, aggressive in defense of their children, and motivated to aggress by jealousy" (White & Kowalski, 1994, p. 489).

   Maccoby and Jacklin (1974) concluded that the existence of gender differences in aggression was well established by research. A meta-analysis a decade later (Hyde,

1984) showed that gender accounted for an average of 5 percent of the variance in aggression found in the combined-sex population of 75 studies, with the male mean being about one-half a standard deviation higher than the female mean. Differences were largest and most consistent for physical aggression. Other reviewers, however, have challenged the blanket conclusion that men are more aggressive than women (Bjorkqvist, 1994; Eagly & Steffen, 1986; Frodi, Macaulay, & Thome, 1977; Hyde & Linn, 1986; White, 1983).

Any conclusion based on a large number of studies is only as good as those studies. The studies on which the conclusion of greater male aggressiveness is based have a number of limitations. They are more likely to measure physical aggression than other types, they use situations for which women have learned that aggression (or female aggression) is inappropriate, they do not examine situations in which women are likely to aggress, and they may base their conclusions on the extremely aggressive behavior of a few males. What researchers have observed may be a difference in *style* of aggression rather than level of aggressiveness (Bjorkqvist, 1994). Researchers who have studied **relational aggression,** which involves harming others by manipulating and damaging their peer relationships, find that this type of aggression is more typical of girls than boys (Crick & Grotpeter, 1995). Parents and teachers may not notice relational aggression because it is done secretly and in small groups; thus girls maintain their image of being unaggressive and nice while still inflicting harm on their peers (Simmons, 2002).

Furthermore, aggression may be as much a product of the situation as something that is "built-in" to males more than females. For example, Maccoby (1998), in summarizing studies on children's aggressive behavior, argues that boys' aggressiveness is not a personality trait, but a product of a particular situation: "a characteristic of male-male play—better seen as a property of male dyads or groups than of individuals" (p. 37).

A different body of research might produce different conclusions about gender similarities and differences in aggression. When girls and women are provoked, or when they are rewarded for aggression, they are as likely as their male counterparts to behave aggressively (Frodi et al., 1977). Studies now report women to be at least as aggressive as men in intimate relationships; women are as likely as men to say that they have aggressed physically against a spouse or dating partner (Archer, 2000; Archer & Ray, 1989; Bookwala, Frieze, Smith, & Ryan, 1992; White & Koss, 1991)—although violence against women by men in such relationships tends to be much more severe and cause more injury (Archer, 2000; Holtzworth-Munroe & Stuart, 1994). Cross-cultural research reveals a wide range of aggressive behaviors performed by women (Burbank, 1987). For example, one study of Mexican American girls in gangs in California illustrates that when group norms favor female aggression, girls are quite likely to engage in violent behavior (M. G. Harris, 1994). It appears that earlier, confident conclusions of greater male aggressiveness may have been overstated. Women may have as much potential to be aggressive as men do, but "because of opportunities, resources, and socialization pressures, the situations in which women will display aggressive behaviors appear to be more circumscribed" (White & Kowalski, 1994, p. 492).

Some researchers argue that the stereotype of women as nonaggressive serves a societal function: to keep women weak, fearful of male aggression, and thus dependent on men. Feminist sociologist Martha McCaughey (1997) notes that "The presumed inability to fight in part defines heterosexual femininity" (p. 7) and that "aggression is one way that we culturally tell men and women apart. The construction and regulation of a naturalized heterosexual femininity hinges on the taboo of aggression, and often what challenges femininity is labeled 'aggressive'. . . . Cultural ideals of manhood and womanhood include a cultural, political, aesthetic, and legal acceptance of men's aggression and a deep skepticism, fear and prohibition of women's" (p. 3).

McCaughey argues that, furthermore, the stereotype of feminine nonaggression becomes embodied, affecting the way women feel in their bodies as well as the kinds of movements and postures that women habitually use. Training to move, sit, and stand modestly, to make gestures of deference rather than challenge, and to avoid certain physical tasks helps women build gender into our bodies—and into our consciousness. Feminine socialization, then, becomes not just a state of mind, but a "state of the body" (p. 39). Physical change, she says, is intimately connected with change in consciousness, and she suggests that one way to challenge the system of gender relations would be to change the sense of physical superiority that boys have over girls and that men have over women by teaching girls and women to be effectively aggressive. Her own training in self-defense and her research on the women's self-defense movement convinced her that "self-defense transforms the way it feels to inhabit a female body. It changes what it means to be a woman" (p. 2), and she suggests that "training for physical combat could help girls in the twenty-first century as much as raising their self-esteem" (p. 13).

Explaining Differences and Similarities: Can Biology and Environment Be Separated?

Even though the gender differences discussed in this chapter have been the targets of thousands of studies for many years, controversy still lurks about whether they are "real." By real, in this case, most people mean solid, unchanging, reliable—and for many people interested in gender, that might be translated as "biologically based."

There are problems with these assumptions. In the first place, as we have seen in the discussion of social constructionism above, "facts" may be less solid, more ephemeral, than they appear. They can vary with the biases of the observer, the social context of the research, the climate of acceptability for certain approaches or findings in the discipline. A gender difference that appears real in one era, such as the much-ballyhooed male–female difference in brain size mentioned earlier in this chapter, may seem to vanish or appear ludicrous in another.

In the second place, the equation of *real* with *biological* implies the acceptance of two mistaken assumptions: that biologically based differences are necessarily set and immutable (i.e., essential), and that it is possible to discern the separate effects of biology and environment. In regard to the first assumption, many researchers have noted that biological differences can be changed by environmental variables. For instance, experiences can and do influence the structure and function of brain cells and the morphology of the brain (Ungerleider, 1995).

As for the second assumption, recognition is growing that the effects of biology and environment cannot be separated. The nature–nurture question "How much of the difference can be explained by biology, and how much by environment?" has obsessed psychologists for decades. Yet it has become increasingly clear that neither culture nor biology acts alone in shaping behavior: They *always* interact—and they interact at each stage of development. Genes are the DNA codes that carry the potential for the emergence of particular traits. Having the genetic code for a particular trait, however, does not mean an individual will actually have that trait. The expression of genes into the actual physical appearance, or the physical, personality, or behavioral traits of the individual, depends on the effect of environmental triggers at every stage of development. Furthermore, the effects of the interaction between genes and environment are cumulative, so that each stage of the individual's development is influenced by the previous stage.

A particular set of genes may affect behavior by influencing physical appearance, which affects the selection and impact of experiences during the individual's development, which may in turn affect the individual's biology (for instance, brain development, muscle development, health), which may again affect the person's experience, and so on (Bouchard, Lykken, McGue, Segal, & Tellegen, 1990). For example, a particular girl may carry the genetic potential to be taller than average. This potential will be expressed only in the presence of proper environmental conditions, such as good nutrition at critical developmental times. If her potential to be extra tall *is* expressed, the fact that she outgrows her girlfriends when she is a young teenager may have important social consequences. Depending on her culture, she may be made to feel awkward and unfeminine or regal and striking. These self-perceptions will affect the way she presents herself physically. Does she stoop and try to shrink, or does she walk tall and carry herself proudly? Her behavior in this regard may affect other aspects of her physical self as diverse as digestion, her development of muscular strength, her tendency toward backaches in later life. Clearly, these consequences are not direct results of either her genetic potential or her environment, but rather of a cumulative series of interactions between the two. The whole thing is a "double-sided process" (Fausto-Sterling, 2000, p. 253), in which the individual simultaneously acquires "outside" knowledge about her body and what it means in her culture and incorporates that knowledge "inside," by changing her body.

Thus as we consider the array of reasons that have been advanced to explain observed gender differences and similarities in cognitive performance and aggression, it is important to remember that many factors may conspire to produce such patterns of similarities and differences, and that the either–or dichotomy between nature and nurture is false. One useful way of thinking about this issue is provided by biologist Anne Fausto-Sterling (2000), who invokes the metaphor of Russian nesting dolls to envision the process through which gender is created. Russian nesting dolls are carved wooden figures, identical except for size, that fit one inside the other. Open the first doll, and you will find another just like it within. Open that one, and you will find another, and so on until the last tiny doll is revealed. Fausto-Sterling says,

> I find the Russian nesting doll useful for envisioning the various layers of human sexuality, from the cellular to the social and historical . . . Academics can take the system apart for display

or to study one of the dolls in more detail. But an individual doll is hollow. Only the complete assembly makes sense. Unlike its wooden counterpart, the human nesting doll changes shape with time. Change can happen in any of the layers, but since the entire assembly has to fit together, altering one of the component dolls requires the interlinked system—from the cellular to the institutional—to change. (p. 253)

The Meaning of Difference

Clearly, when researchers go looking for female–male differences, they do find some. That they also find many instances of similarity often goes unremarked. Just how much attention should we pay to the differences that researchers report?

Psychologists who study gender tend to take one of two positions: an emphasis on and exaggeration of differences or a tendency to minimize or ignore differences. The first of these positions is sometimes called an **alpha bias;** the second is labeled a **beta bias** (Hare-Mustin & Maracek, 1990). The alpha bias is the one that has been adopted throughout much of Western psychology's history. As this chapter has noted, researchers have taken pains to prove that women and men differ in abilities and temperament—and thus belong in different spheres. The earliest feminist-inspired research, by contrast, sought to demonstrate that women and men were *not* different, that they were equally capable in every respect. Here, men embodied the implicit standard; the attempt was to show that women were just as good as men. All assertions of gender differences were considered suspect because they implied female inferiority.

In recent years, some feminist researchers have reconsidered the notion of difference. Difference does not have to mean female inferiority, they argue; rather, difference can mean female superiority. For example, a gender difference in moral reasoning might mean that women are more carefully attuned than men are to certain dimensions of morality, or that women are more caring and responsible in relationships than men are (Gilligan, 1982).

A drawback of the alpha bias, both in its prefeminist and feminist versions, is its focus on what women and men are like—implying that certain essential qualities are attached to being female or male. Yet the more we learn about human beings, the more we become aware of how much we are all shaped by our context. The beta bias also tends to ignore context, taking the stance that, "all things being equal," women and men think, feel, and behave similarly. All things are not equal, however, and the beta bias often promotes the examination of women's and men's behavior in situations that have been stripped of social context. Neither of the two positions really supports a careful examination of the ways the environment is different for females and males. Women's and men's thoughts, feelings, and behavior may indeed be different in many respects, and such differences may reflect their different positions in the social hierarchy of power and status rather than their different "natures" (Lott, 1990).

Whether one favors emphasizing or minimizing gender differences, it is wise to remember that the interpretation of such differences is shaped by stereotypes and by a context in which discrimination against women is commonplace. As Favreau (1993) notes, much more has been made of women's lower average scores on certain mathematical and spatial tasks than of certain differences that might appear to disadvantage males. Males' higher average levels of certain types of aggression have not been cited to question men's fitness for careers in diplomacy. The finding that men commit more crimes than women do has not hindered them as a group from being considered for positions as bank managers.

The Question of Differences: The Wrong Question?

At the conclusion of a withering critique of the psychological research on gender differences, two psychologists assert that questions about such differences are not providing a body of useful knowledge:

> [T]he psychological literature on male–female differences is not a record of cumulative knowledge about the "truth" of what men and women are "really" like. Rather it is a repository of accounts of gender organized within particular assumptive frameworks and reflecting various interests. . . . The sex difference question has become the proverbial "wrong question." (Hare-Mustin & Maracek, 1994, p. 535)

One of the reasons these authors want to abandon research on female–male differences is that it encourages categorical thinking when, in fact, the boundaries between categories are indistinct. Categorical thinking becomes more problematic as we increase the number of dimensions we deem relevant. As we pay more attention to the diverse experiences of women from many groups, we may be tempted to divide women into categories and compare them.

But each individual is an intersection of many categories and identities: gender, age, race, sexual orientation, socioeconomic status, nationality, religion, culture. When we make simple comparisons between females and males or between Latinas and African American women, we focus on categories that capture only one part of the experience and social identity of these individuals. Our thinking is often so categorical, though, that we automatically lump together all members of a particular sex, race, or sexual orientation. For example, a gathering of women of only one racial group might include as participants women ranging in age from early 20s to mid-50s, women who are single, married, and divorced; mothers and nonmothers; women whose religious backgrounds include Jewish, Catholic, Baptist, and Mormon; whose occupations include engineer, teacher, dancer, welder, banker, and bartender. Such a gathering may be homogeneous with respect to race, but it encompasses diversity on many other dimensions.

Even such unidimensional categories as gender and race are suspect. We saw in Chapter 1 that gender, which seems on the surface to be so clearly an either–or category, has vague boundaries. Race is even more complex. Many people (perhaps most) are of mixed racial heritage; they do not fall clearly into one racial category. What does it really mean, then, to make such statements as "Black women showed higher self-esteem than either White or Latina women"? Such comparisons may have a limited usefulness (in debunking stereotypes, for example), but they tend to oversimplify complex issues.

Is it better for researchers to choose an emphasis on similarities or an emphasis on differences? Canadian psychologist Meredith Kimball (1995) argues that it is pointless to try to choose between approaches that favor differences and similarities. Rather, she says, we should practice "double visions," refusing to choose either approach as more true than the other. If we deliberately engage the tension between the two approaches when we compare people across genders or other categories that are socially constructed, we will be more in tune with the complexities of the categories and of the process of comparison.

Research on differences has been organized to lead to an either–or answer: Either the sexes are different on a particular dimension, or they are not. Yet, as Favreau (1993) notes, such investigations tend to produce evidence that supports the conclusion of both similarity *and* difference. Groups may differ in average scores and still overlap so substantially in their distributions of scores that they appear very similar. Most members of the two groups may be similar on a particular dimension, whereas a few members of one group or the other stand out as different from both their own and the other gender group. Although we may yearn for a simple, straightforward statement of difference or similarity, the most defensible summary may be not "either–or," but "both."

SUMMARY

Differences between women and men on many dimensions used to be assumed, and the beginnings of scientific research comparing the sexes often focused on showing reasons for male superiority. In psychology, Helen Thompson performed the first laboratory study comparing women's and men's performance on a variety of tasks, finding, to the surprise of many, that there were few differences.

A great deal of psychological research comparing women and men has been carried out since Thompson's pioneering study. However, this research has often been conducted, interpreted, and used in ways that have been harmful to women. From a feminist perspective, there are many criticisms of the ways research has been done. In particular, such criticisms emphasize the researcher–participant relationship and the notion of objectivity. They argue that the traditional notion that the researcher is (and should be) separate from and independent of the person being studied is false. Furthermore, they point out that studying behavior in ways that ignore or strip away the social context in which the behavior normally occurs creates a warped and misleading impression of the extent of and reasons for female–male differences.

Traditionally, psychological research was done in a framework of logical positivism, which assumed that the facts or truth could be discovered through proper applications of research methods. Research also tended to assume that any differences found between women and men were "built-in" or essential. A newer framework, social constructionism, has moderated these viewpoints for many scientists. The social constructionist perspective assumes that there is no completely objective, real truth, but rather that researchers participate in creating reality by the way they study it. Thus, in a sense, the "facts" about gender similarities and differences are not discovered, but constructed by research.

Despite the limitations on research, there are ways to do it that minimize sexist and other biases. Researchers must be careful in their framing of research questions, choice of samples, and methods of measurement to ensure that they are not inadvertently building biases into their investigations. Group comparisons must be done and interpreted with care for the same reasons.

Psychological research on female–male differences has been driven, in the last quarter century, by a landmark study (Maccoby & Jacklin, 1974) in which, after an examination of the studies in many possible areas of difference, two researchers identified only four psychological gender differences as reliably demonstrated: performance in three cognitive areas (verbal, quantitative, and visual–spatial) and aggression. Subsequent research on these four dimensions has tended to show that females perform better than males on tests of some verbal abilities, males perform better than females on some tests of quantitative and visual–spatial abilities, and males behave more aggressively than females. However, these general conclusions must be tempered by findings that social context has a great deal to do with whether and when these differences occur.

Much debate has occurred among psychologists as to the reasons for the patterns of differences and similarities that have been found. For many years, the focus has been on whether or to what extent these patterns were based in biology or in the environment. More recent approaches argue that biology and environment cannot be separated—they always act in concert with each other.

Feminist psychologists do not agree about whether or not it is a good idea to do gender comparison research and about whether it is better to emphasize a search for differences (alpha bias) or a search for similarities (beta bias). However, most research shows evidence for both similarities and differences.

It is clear that, by doing research on gender comparisons, scientists do, in certain ways, construct and then bring attention to certain gender differences. For this reason, some psychologists have argued that we should not be asking questions about whether gender differences exist or how large they are. If we were to focus on different questions, they say, we could find out more about how the process of gender works and take away some of the importance that is placed on gender differences. On the other side of the argument, some researchers argue that gender comparisons can break down stereotypes and that it may provide information that helps to design social interventions to help both women and men. These issues continue to be debated, and gender comparison research continues to be done in psychology.

KEY TERMS

context-stripping	cognitive abilities	generation and maintenance
reflexivity	meta-analysis	of a spatial image
logical positivism	effect size	relational aggression
essentialism	spatial visualization	psychobiosocial model
social constructionism	spatial perception	alpha bias
idiographic	mental rotation	beta bias
nomothetic	spatiotemporal perception	

DISCUSSION QUESTIONS

This chapter argues that research is always shaped by the social context in which it takes place. What are some ways in which the social context that exists now, in your own time and place, may be affecting research on women and gender?

What are some ways that research findings on gender differences in cognitive abilities and aggression are socially constructed?

Is it a good idea to do gender comparative research? Why or why not?

Some researchers argue that cultural ideas about gender become embodied—that we incorporate gender into our bodies and it becomes, not just an abstract set of ideas or expectations, but a set of physical qualities. What are some examples of how this process could take place?

FOR ADDITIONAL READING

Crawford, Mary, & Kimmel, Ellen (1999). Innovations in feminist research. Special issue, *Psychology of Women Quarterly, 23* (1 & 2). This collection of articles offers many examples of feminist-inspired research.

Fausto-Sterling, Anne. (1992). *Myths of gender.* New York: Basic Books. The author, a biologist, examines the myths that surround some of the gender-related differences discussed in this chapter.

Halpern, Diane F. (2000). *Sex differences in cognitive abilities.* Hillsdale, NJ: Erlbaum. A cognitive psychologist who identifies herself as a feminist undertakes a careful examination of the literature on cognitive gender differences.

Hare-Mustin, Rachel T., & Maracek, Jeanne (Eds.). (1994). *Making a difference: Psychology and the construction of gender.* New Haven, CT: Yale University Press. This volume includes a wide-ranging set of articles on the meaning of gender differences and the implications of studying them.

Kimball, M. M. (1995). *Feminist visions of gender similarities and differences.* Binghamton, NY: Haworth. A psychologist delves into the history of research on similarities and differences and shows how the tension between an emphasis on similarities and an emphasis on differences has been productive.

Simmons, Rachel. (2002). *Odd girl out: The hidden culture of aggression in girls.* New York: Harcourt. A journalist's examination of how and why girls can be mean while maintaining the illusion that they would *never* be aggressive.

WEB RESOURCE

Sex Roles: A Journal of Research. Here you can browse the table of contents for this journal, which publishes many studies examining gender differences and gender-related stereotypes and expectations. You can also access a free online sample copy.
www.wkap.nl/journalhome.htm/0360–0025

CHAPTER 3

Growing Up Female:
The Female Body
and Its Meanings

CHAPTER OUTLINE

Actor–comedian Whoopi Goldberg created a skit in which she plays a little girl who is morosely dissatisfied with her dark skin and short, nappy hair. She finds comfort by draping a white blouse over her head—discovering that it magically transforms her into a White girl with long, swinging blond hair.

First performed in the 1980s, the skit pokes fun at the broad issues of vanity and the culturally approved female obsession with appearance and longing to be what one is not. More specifically, it takes aim at the issue of racism in standards of beauty. If she accepts the standard, still promulgated in much of the media, that beautiful means blond and blue-eyed, just what is a young Black girl to do?

In Iran, young women flock to cosmetic surgery, and the fresh bandages that signify a nose job have become a status symbol ("All Things Considered," 2001). Plastic surgeons say they are booked up for weeks in advance for the procedure, which allows Iranian women, who must cover their heads and bodies when in public to "work with what shows." Rhinoplasty is not the only popular procedure, however. The women of Iran also seek out breast reductions and augmentations, tummy tucks, and other types of cosmetic surgery. Why do this if they cannot display their ever more perfect bodies? For their husbands, they say.

Girls and women the world over have been taught to focus on their bodies: their appearance, their fertility, their purity. North American research shows that appearance is more central to women's self-concept than to men's, and examples from many cultures illustrate that women are often urged to transform their bodies drastically in order to meet standards of beauty and perfection. Fertility and sexuality impart important meanings to women's bodies as well. In some cultures, the female body's processes of menstruation, pregnancy, childbirth, and lactation are considered mysterious and powerful. In some, virginity is obsessively guarded.

The idea that women are defined by their bodies, and that the female body is defined by sexual and reproductive functions, has a long history. Rousseau argued in the 18th century that a man could transcend his sexual nature, but a woman remained female "her whole life," dominated by processes such as menstruation, childbearing, nursing, and nurturing (Rousseau, 1762/1979, pp. 357–358). During the second half of the 19th century, the view flourished that the female body was entirely organized for sex and reproduction. At the end of that century, one scientist could write that the sexual instinct was the "essence and the raison d'être of woman's form, the expression of the cause of her existence as a woman" (Balls-Headley, 1894, p. 1).

The female body is associated with vulnerability in many cultures, both because of assumed physical or moral weakness and because of the female capacity to be impregnated. This perceived vulnerability often leads to the sheltering of girls and women—even to their seclusion and veiling in some countries. It also leads to drastic steps to restrict their sexuality, such as female genital mutilation and virginity testing. Yet despite the concern over female vulnerability, the female body has, in many cultures, been relentlessly sexualized until every aspect of a woman's appearance is judged on her ability to attract a man sexually. Women who do not fit the dominant definition of attractiveness, such as old women, disabled women, or those who have undergone mastectomies, are in many cases marginalized and made to feel as if they are not *real* women.

This chapter deals with the processes of sexual differentiation that result in the development of a female, as opposed to a male, body, the consequent biological differences, and the cultural interpretations of those differences. In the latter realm, we shall pay particular attention to the issues of beauty and vulnerability.

Sexual Differentiation:
How Bodies Become Female or Male

Having a body that is classified as female or male has enormous implications in most cultures. In many countries it determines what legal rights a person has, what kinds of occupations a person has access to, what kinds of behaviors are deemed acceptable, even the terms people use when they address the individual. If easy classification into female or male is not possible, social confusion and anxiety result. For example, consider the case of one Levi Suydam of Salisbury, Connecticut, who, in 1843, approached the city fathers to allow him to vote in a local election (Fausto-Sterling, 2000). The authorities were reluctant, because to some Suydam appeared more female than male, and at that time, women did not have the right to vote. A doctor examined him and pronounced him male, and he went on to help his candidate win by a single vote in the bitterly contested election. However, a few days later, the doctor discovered that Suydam had regular menstrual periods and a vaginal opening. History has apparently not recorded whether Suydam lost the right to vote, in light of this discovery. However, the story illustrates both the importance people place on "correct" sexual classification and the fact that not everyone can be easily classified into one of two sexes.

Sex is not a completely either–or matter: An individual's biological femaleness or maleness can be somewhat indistinct and is determined by a combination of factors. Indeed, researchers who study various animal species have found in nature an amazing diversity of ways individual organisms become female or male. For instance, one-third of tropical fish species change sex during their development. All members of the sand tile species are born female, then a few of them change into males in late adulthood as required for reproduction. In a rarer pattern, all clown fish are born male, and they all change into females upon reaching later adulthood (Rabin, 1998).

A dramatic example of the interaction between genes and environment in the determination of sex is provided by alligators. Alligators lay their eggs in a mass of decaying swamp vegetation, and the heat given off by the rotting plants incubates the eggs. Depending on just how much heat is given off, the eggs will hatch as either females or males. If the temperature is below a certain level, all the hatchlings will be female; if it rises higher than that, all will be male (Rabin, 1998).

So, in the case of these fish and reptiles, the embryos begin with the potential to be either male or female, and the sex they become is determined by environmental factors interacting with their biology.

What about humans? Do we too start out as embryos with the potential to be either sex? Not exactly, but the biological process of human sexual differentiation does show some malleability in interaction with the environment. That malleability results in the production of individuals whose anatomy ranges widely around the prototypical images of female and male. It also results in the birth of a significant number of individuals—1.7 percent of all births according to one estimate (Fausto-Sterling, 2000)—who cannot easily be classified as female or male. Such individuals are called **intersexuals** because their biology signals that they are *between* female and male: They possess a mixture of the anatomical features that we associate with males and females. If this estimate is correct, Fausto-Sterling comments, a city of 300,000 has 5,100 such individuals. Compare this, she suggests, to the frequency of albinism, another uncommon trait in humans, but one that most people have encountered. Albinism occurs about once in every 20,000 births—a rate of .005 percent—making it far less frequent than intersexuality. Yet intersexuals are an almost invisible minority in a society that likes to think that people come in only two sexes. *♦ usually can't tell on the outside (genitals)*

Human sexual differentiation is a process. Sex is not determined all at once, but occurs in a series of steps; during each of them genetic potential and environmental influences interact. These steps are usually consistent with the production of an individual who can be classified as biologically female or male, but in certain cases these steps move the individual in a female direction at one stage and a male direction at another. The steps begin at conception, when the individual receives a combination of sex chromosomes from the two parents. The configuration of these chromosomes influences the development of sex glands or gonads. These in turn secrete hormones that direct the sexual differentiation of the internal reproductive tract, the external genitalia, and perhaps some areas of the brain.

Step 1: The Chromosomes

Normal human cells contain 23 pairs of chromosomes. In the joining of an egg and a sperm cell that results in the conception of a new embryo, each parent contributes half the chromosomes—one member of each pair. It is the 23rd pair of chromosomes that concerns us here, for, unlike the other 22, this pair differs for females and males. Called the **sex chromosomes,** the 23rd pair is an XX for females and an XY for males. The Y chromosome that determines maleness must be contributed by the sperm cell; only males carry this chromosome. Thus the genetic aspect of the embryo's sex is determined by the father. The Y chromosome is small and carries little genetic information; however, it does contain the sex-determining region (SRY) on the gene that, when it activates at about the eighth week after conception, starts the development of testes in the fetus's abdominal cavity (Angier, 1999). The X chromosome is larger and carries a great deal of genetic information.

Most human embryos bear one of the two normal configurations of the sex chromosomes: XX or XY. Sometimes, however, errors in cell division produce chromosomal abnormalities—extra or missing sex chromosomes. An individual may develop with a single X chromosome (XO; Turner's syndrome), an extra X or Y chromosome (XXX or XYY), or other patterns, such as XXY (Klinefelter's syndrome). Unless there is at least one Y chromosome the individual's body will tend to develop as female. Every zygote (fertilized egg) tends to develop into a female unless the pattern of development is altered by the presence of a Y chromosome, which stimulates testosterone production, or the addition of testosterone from another source, such as the adrenal cortex or progestin taken by the mother (Sloane, 2002). This has led some biologists to characterize the basic pattern of mammalian development as female and even to label females as the "ancestral sex" and males as the "derived sex" (Angier, 1999). ☺ interesting

Studies show that males are more biologically vulnerable than females, beginning at conception. It is estimated that 140 genetic males are conceived for every 100 genetic females; however, the ratio of male to female live births is only 105 to 100 (Halpern, 2000). It is unclear why this greater male vulnerability exists. However, some scientists have argued that it may result from the necessity to change the basic (female) pattern of development in order to produce a male. An early advocate of this perspective, medical researcher Alfred Jost, declared in 1946 that "Becoming a male is a prolonged, uneasy, and risky adventure; it is a kind of struggle against inherent trends toward femaleness" (quoted in Fausto-Sterling, 2000, p. 204).

Step 2: The Gonads

The anatomical development of XX and XY embryos is similar for the first 6 weeks after conception. A neutral or "indifferent" **gonad** (or sex gland) develops, as well as two sets of internal ducts (one potentially female and one potentially male) that will eventually become internal reproductive organs (Money & Ehrhardt, 1972).

During the seventh to eighth week, the neutral gonad, apparently under the influence of the sex chromosomes, begins to differentiate according to sex. If two X chromosomes are present, development proceeds in a female direction and the gonad develops into an ovary. In fact, in the absence of any interference, the neutral gonad always tends to turns into an ovary. Researchers have not yet discovered a biological "trigger" that sets the process of ovarian development in motion; however, some studies have suggested that the construction of ovaries is more than simply a "default" process (Angier, 1999). If a Y chromosome is present, however, it promotes the formation of a protein called the H-Y antigen, which influences the gonad to differentiate as male—into an embryonic testis.

Step 3: Hormones

A major function of the gonads, once formed, is to secrete the **sex hormones**: the **estrogens, progesterone,** and **androgens.** These chemicals, and the developing body's response to them, control the remaining steps of sexual differentiation.

If the developing embryo is female, the ovary begins to secrete estrogen and progesterone. In this case, the male duct system degenerates and the female duct system becomes specialized into the internal organs of the female reproductive system. Exactly what causes the male duct system to degenerate, other than the absence of testosterone, is still unclear (Sloane, 2002).

If the developing embryo is male, the testis synthesizes **testosterone** (a type of androgen), which influences the male reproductive tract to begin developing. It also produces a hormone called **Müllerian Inhibiting Substance (MIS),** which blocks the development of the female duct system and causes it to degenerate (Yahr, 1988).

Partly because of their role in sexual differentiation, the estrogens and progesterone are called female hormones and the androgens are called male hormones. Nonetheless, all three types of hormones are present in both female and male bodies. All can be produced in the ovaries, testes, or adrenal glands (Becker & Breedlove, 1992).

After prenatal sexual differentiation is finished, the effects of sex hormones are not particularly obvious again until puberty. At puberty, a rise in the level of sex hormones promotes secondary sex characteristics such as breast development for females and beard growth and muscular development for males. Again, both the "female" and "male" hormones are present in both women and men. For example, testosterone is responsible for the growth of body hair (such as hair under the armpits and pubic hair) in both sexes (Angier, 1999).

Step 4: The Internal Reproductive Tract

In female embryos, once the ovaries begin to secrete hormones, the basic pattern of female development continues to unfold. The female duct system develops into Fallopian tubes, a uterus, and a vagina. Meanwhile, the male duct system atrophies. The extent to which estrogen plays a role in this process is still being investigated and debated (Collaer & Hines, 1995). It is clear, however, that if testosterone is present in sufficient amounts, it interferes with this process of female development, causing development to go in a male direction. The female duct system withers away, and the male ducts develop into vas deferens, epididymis, seminal vesicles, urethra, and prostate.

Step 5: The External Genitalia

Until 8 weeks after conception, the external genital appearance of both sexes is identical (Money & Ehrhardt, 1972). At that point, if testosterone is present in high enough concentrations, the genital tubercle develops into a penis and the labioscrotal swelling becomes a scrotum. If the hormone balance favors female rather than male development, differentiation occurs somewhat later. By the 12th week, the genital tubercle in females has turned into a clitoris and the labioscrotal swelling has become the lips of the vagina. By the time this step is completed, the embryo is anatomically female or male or some mixture of the two.

The Language of Sexual Differentiation

The language used to discuss the way an embryo develops female and male characteristics is a good example of how seemingly "hard" scientific evidence can be understood in different ways. In discussing the steps in prenatal sexual differentiation, the language used is sometimes reminiscent of male and female stereotypes. Female development sounds rather passive: At each stage it seems that "if nothing happens to interfere" then the embryo develops in a female direction. On the other hand, male development requires that something active happen. This understanding of sexual development has its origins in the work of Alfred Jost, whose 1940s research on rabbit fetuses demonstrated that, in the absence of a testis, even genetically male rabbits developed a female reproductive system, whereas removing the ovary of a female fetus did not seem to interfere with the development of female reproductive organs (Fausto-Sterling, 2000). He theorized that females became female "because they *lacked* testes, while the testes played the principle role in separating male from female development. . . . The male embryo struggled against the inherent push toward femininity" (p. 203). Thus femaleness began to be characterized as the neutral or default pathway of development, whereas developing maleness took on the aura of an active struggle. This "rhetoric of female absence" (Fausto-Sterling, 2000, p. 203) fit nicely into the prevailing notion that femaleness was associated with the lack of something (a penis, a strong intellect, "soul heat"), whereas maleness was associated with completeness.

In the light of scientific acceptance of the notion that the female body represented simply the unfolding of a basic natural template while development of the male body required aggressive action, researchers ignored the question of just what did control female development. If female development was automatic or the default pathway, it did not require explanation (Fausto-Sterling, 2000). Thus, for decades this particular interpretation caused researchers to focus away from questions about female development, and only in the 1990s did theories about female development begin to appear. Scientists still know very little about what causes ovaries to develop and the role that estrogens play in the developing fetus.

Yet some have regarded the narrative of femaleness as the basic, natural pathway in a more positive light. Natalie Angier (1999) notes that since "female is the physical prototype for an effective living being," woman came first—woman is the legitimate First Sex. Woman was not created from Adam's rib, she scoffs—it was the other way around! Citing the work of biologist David Crews, she puts forth the notion that "the female is the ancestral sex while the male is the derived sex. The female form came first, and eventually gave rise to the male variant" (p. 40). This way of talking about sexual differentiation gives a very different "feel" to the same scientific observations.

Does the Brain Differentiate by Sex?

Some animal research shows that exposure to different levels of sex hormones at critical periods either in utero or postnatally can affect the animal's brain organization and behavior. In rats, for example, exposure to testosterone at a critical period just after birth causes a later sensitivity of the brain to male hormones and an insensitivity to female hormones (Levine, 1966).

Because sex hormones circulate throughout the body, they could conceivably affect distant targets. Furthermore, it is around the time in human fetal development the sex hormones begin to be secreted (7 weeks) that the first brain cells begin to form a rudimentary brain. In humans, some basic sex-related brain differences may be linked to prenatal hormone levels. As we shall see later in this chapter, menstruation is orchestrated by the hypothalamus and the pituitary gland, both of which are structures in the brain. Some female–male differences in the hypothalamus can be observed at the microscopic level (Breathnach, 1990). The differences in these structures may be associated with the easily observable difference that women, but not men, menstruate. There is no indication, however, that differences in these structures have anything to do with intellectual functioning.

In terms of anatomy, female and male brains are not distinguishable. They are the same shape, the same size relative to the rest of the body, and show the same degree of complexity. But researchers continue to search for less obvious differences.

Because of the findings of sex-related differences in cognitive performance discussed in Chapter 2, some researchers (e.g., Geschwind & Behan, 1982; Geschwind & Galaburda, 1987) have speculated that a brain basis for such differences exists. They propose that the intellectual functioning of the human brain may be affected by sex hormone levels at critical periods, producing female or male brains that are differentially prepared to handle certain types of cognitive tasks.

Researchers argue that hormones may "organize" the brain differently for females and males. It has been suggested, for instance, that the presence of testosterone at critical periods prenatally might "masculinize" or "de-feminize" the central nervous system, preparing it so that the individual is predisposed to learn masculine behaviors more easily (Collaer & Hines, 1995). Some researchers have also linked early exposure to high levels of estrogen with differences in cognitive performance and have suggested that estrogen too exerts an organizing effect on the developing brain (Fitch & Denenberg, 1998; McCardle & Wilson, 1990).

One important thing to remember in evaluating these and other approaches to understanding sex differences and similarities in brain organization is that, once formed, the brain is not static. Rather, brains are very plastic, and may be affected by hormones and other factors throughout life. Indeed, the list of environmental factors that can affect brain development is almost endless: for example, home environment, obstetric complications, maternal smoking, myopia, nutrition, and lead exposure all affect the brain (Halpern, 2000). Learning and experience affects the brain as well: "What people learn influences brain structures, such as dendritic branching and cell size; brain architecture, in turn, predisposes individuals to seek additional experiences" (Halpern, 2000, p. 191).

To understand the approach taken by researchers in this area, it is necessary to know some basic facts about brain structure. The human brain is divided into two halves, or hemispheres (right and left), which are connected by a band of neural fibers called the **corpus callosum.** The cerebral cortex, the large, wrinkled outer portion of the brain, is where processing for complex cognitive functions is done. Different functions, such as producing speech, recognizing objects, and recognizing words, seem to be performed at specific locations in the cortex. Thus when a particular part of the brain is injured, the functions associated with that location are often lost.

Research with brain-damaged patients and behavioral studies of normal individuals have demonstrated that each brain hemisphere controls the opposite side of the body. The left hemisphere receives sensory information from the right ear, the right visual field, and the right side of the body and controls the motor responses of the right side of the body. The right hemisphere receives information from and controls the left side of the body. Also, the two hemispheres appear to differ in their relative importance to particular cognitive tasks. For the average, right-handed person, the left hemisphere is more proficient at or specialized for language, and this hemisphere also tends to be most involved in mathematical, analytical, and sequential information processing. The right hemisphere seems to be more specialized for certain perceptual, nonverbal, and spatial information processing and musical abilities (Banich & Heller, 1998; Springer & Deutsch, 1993). This pattern does not hold for left-handed individuals.

Researchers exploring the notion of sex-related differences in the brain have focused on the theory that the differences have something to do with the way various abilities are distributed across or within the two hemispheres. Their work has emphasized three possibilities: sex differences in **brain lateralization,** intrahemispheric sex differences, and sex differences in the size of the corpus callosum, the band of neural fibers that connects the right and left hemispheres (Halpern, 2000).

Theories of sex differences in brain lateralization suggest that female brains tend to be more "bilaterally organized" for some cognitive abilities than male brains. In other words, females are likely to have verbal abilities "spread across" both hemispheres, whereas males are more likely to have verbal abilities located only in the left hemisphere. For females, then, spatial abilities would have to share neural space with verbal abilities in the right hemisphere, perhaps allowing spatial abilities less potential to develop. Not all studies find differences in lateralization between males and females, but studies that do find differences generally find that females show less lateralization than males. Voyer (1996) concluded, on the basis of a meta-analyis of 396 comparisons, that males showed more lateralization than females for both visual and auditory tasks.

Theories of intrahemispheric sex differences propose that *within* the left and right hemispheres, certain functions are more focally organized (localized in a more restricted area) in female brains and more diffusely organized (spread out) in male brains (e.g., Kimura, 1987, 1999). Kimura concludes, on the basis of her own research and that of others, that both language and manual dexterity areas are more focally organized in female than in male brains. If such differences do exist, it is not clear what the implications are for cognitive performance. Do the brain differences help to produce performance differences? Do performance differences help to produce brain differences? Or both?

Regarding the corpus callosum, some researchers have found that its posterior portion is larger in females than males, thus potentially making the two hemispheres more efficiently connected in females (e.g., Allen, Richey, Chai, & Gorski, 1991). Other researchers have found no sex difference (e.g., Byne, Bleier, & Houston, 1988). This has been an area of intense controversy, and it is impossible to draw definitive conclusions from this research. For one thing, there is enormous individual variation in the shape and size of the corpus callosum. As Fausto-Sterling (2000) notes, this variation produces so much "background noise" that it is difficult to detect sex differences: "the corpus callosum is a pretty uncooperative medium for locating differences. That researchers continue to probe the corpus callosum in search of definitive gender differences speaks to how entrenched their expectations about biological differences remain" (p. 145).

Even if this brain difference *were* to be reliably demonstrated, its significance for cognitive functioning would be uncertain. Does a corpus callosum that is larger in one area confer an advantage (or disadvantage) in processing information? Who knows? The size of the corpus callosum is probably responsive to experience. For example, one study shows that musicians who started their training at a young age have larger corpus callosa than those who did not (Schlaug, Jancke, Huang, Staiger, & Steinmetz, 1995), reflecting, perhaps, the impact on the brain of early and extended practice in using both hands to produce music.

At this point, the impact of early hormone levels on the developing human brain remains an area of research and controversy, although many researchers (e.g., Halpern, 2000) are persuaded by the available evidence that some sex differences exist in brain organization and structure that relate to cognition. It certainly appears that if such sex-related brain differences exist, they are part of a complex interplay of moderating variables such as handedness, reasoning ability, age, and maturation rate. It is also clear that there are far more similarities than differences in the ways that female and male brains are organized and that what differences may exist are very subtle. In this area of gender research, as in so many others, it is wise to be wary of simplistic conclusions. Statements such as "Women are more right-brained than men" are patently ridiculous.

The Next Step: Rearing

Alice Dreger (1998) notes that "Whatever our physical make-up, none of us is fully a 'boy' or a 'girl' until that identity is made for us by our family and community and embraced by us. One's physical equipment is the signal, not the determinant, of gender identity" (p. 199). Indeed, the prenatal development of a particular anatomical configuration is only part of the story of the way a person becomes gendered. A developing individual learns through social interactions to place herself or himself in a gender category and accept a particular gender identity. S/he also learns what behaviors are considered acceptable and normal for a person in that category—s/he learns to "do" gender.

The process of rearing a child to be a girl or a boy can begin even before the child is born. One study (Sweeney & Bradbard, 1988) found that parents who saw an ultrasound picture of their fetus still in the womb rated female fetuses as softer, littler, calmer, weaker, more delicate, and more beautiful than male fetuses! And from the day of an infant's birth, North American parents view their female infants as softer and more delicate than their male infants and see their male infants as firmer, stronger, hardier, and more alert (Rubin, Provenzano, & Luria, 1974). We also know that parents treat daughters and sons differently in areas specifically related to gender expectations: giving them different toys, dressing them differently, and assigning them different tasks (Lytton & Romney, 1991). So how is it possible to tell how much "femaleness" and "maleness" are related to these differential patterns of rearing and how much they are related to the biological process we have just described?

Of course, as we have seen already, no precise answer to the "how much" question can ever be given. Yet some intriguing research hints at the complex interweaving of biological and social forces that produce an individual who is female or male. John Money and Anke Ehrhardt (1972) described a case in which a 7-month-old boy was the victim of a surgical accident that destroyed his penis, and his parents decided to rear him as a girl. When the child was 17 months old, his name, clothing, and hairstyle were changed to fit feminine norms, and surgery was performed to feminize the appearance of his genitals. This child had an identical twin brother, providing researchers with a unique opportunity to compare the way two children with exactly the same genetic and prenatal background developed when one was reared as a boy and the other as a girl.

According to Money and Ehrhardt, the child who was reassigned as a girl quickly developed typical feminine interests and behavior, whereas the other child maintained his masculine ones. Moreover, they said, the girl clearly thought of herself as a girl (that is, she formed a female **gender identity**), whereas the boy's self-concept was unambiguously masculine. Thus, they reported, the gender identity of each child was apparently shaped by the sex of assignment and rearing more than by genetic or other physiological determinants.

But was it this simple? Later developments have caused some rethinking of Money and Ehrhardt's conclusions. A follow-up of the sex-reassigned individual, now an adult, revealed that he had reclaimed a masculine gender identity during his teens and that he remembered always feeling uncomfortable and "not right" as a girl—even though he had no idea about the accident and the drastic solution (Colapino, 1997; Diamond & Sigmundson, 1997). In her mid-teens, almost immediately after being told what had happened, the individual adopted a male name and demanded male hormone treatments and surgery to change herself back into a male. He had his breasts surgically removed and a rudimentary penis constructed just prior to his 16th birthday. At age 21, he underwent surgery for the construction of improved male-looking genitalia. At the age of 25, he married and is now living an apparently well-adjusted life as a man.

Some researchers have argued that the outcome of this case shows that gender identity is innate—that our bodies, through hormones and their effects, tell us whether we are (or should be) female or male (Diamond & Sigmundson, 1997). Others, however, point out that there are many other possible reasons for the way this case turned out. For example, when this child was young, tension in the family was very high about whether the sex-reassignment would "take," and consequently many of the child's behaviors that were seen as gender-relevant took on a huge significance. The child was the target of enormous pressure to be feminine and created a great deal of anxiety (and more pressure) when she did not conform. Bernice Hausman (2000) suggests that this child, in digging in her heels and returning to a masculine identity, was claiming the right to determine her own identity, resisting "the coercive attempts at feminization" and the "heavy-handed plot to turn her into a girl" (p. 123). And indeed, this child had endured much in the service of becoming a girl. She had made yearly visits to Johns Hopkins Hospital, for reasons that were never explained to her. At those visits, she had been examined repeatedly by large groups of doctors, told to peruse pictures of nude females that she could be like, and placed into conversations with male-to-female **transsexuals** who tried to convince her of the advantages of being female and of having a vagina surgically constructed. It would not be unreasonable for her to have concluded that people were trying awfully hard to make sure she was female—and to be suspicious of their motives.

Interestingly, the man this child has now become does not define masculinity in terms of biology—even though his case is often used to "prove" that gender identity is biologically based. He says, "From what I've been taught by my father, . . . what makes you a man is you treat your wife well. You put a roof over your family's head. You're a good father. Things like that add up much more to being a man than just *bang bang bang*—sex" (quoted in Colapinto, 1997, p. 97).

A number of other studies have suggested that people form their **core gender identities** (their sense of themselves as being female or male) according to whether, from an early age, they are labeled and treated as girls or boys (Collaer & Hines, 1995). However, the outcome of the famous twin case, as well as scattered findings that girls and women who have been exposed to excessive androgens prenatally may be somewhat less content with female gender identity (see Collaer & Hines for a review), suggest that there is no simple answer to the question of what causes a person to form a particular gender identity. As in other areas of female–male differences, core gender identity must be a product of a continuing interaction between genetic potential and environment.

Supporting this notion is the existence of controversy about whether early gender identity is necessarily fixed. One study examined individuals in a small area of the Dominican Republic who were born with ambiguous-appearing genitalia. The children were genetically male (they had XY sex chromosomes), but they looked more like females and were initially reared as girls. At puberty, however, they developed male secondary sex characteristics and most of them changed their gender identity to male (Imperato-McGinley, Guerrero, Gautier, & Peterson, 1974). The fluidity of the core gender identity in this case was likely related to the fact that the disorder affecting these children was a relatively common one in that region. The children were labeled *machihembra* ("first woman, then man"), creating an expectation for gender identity change that may have been incorporated into their self-concept. Once again, though, the possible contribution of a hormonal influence interwoven with environmental variables cannot be dismissed.

Intersexuality and Behavioral Gender Differences

A great deal of research aimed at disentangling the biological and environmental determinants of **behavioral gender differences** (behavior for which a disparity exists between the average female and the average male, although there may be a large overlap between the two sexes) has been done with intersexed individuals (persons who are born with mixed indicators of biological sex). These individuals bear the marks of either a rare chromosomal configuration (such as XXX or XO rather than the conventional XX or XY) or of a sexual differentiation process in which differentiation occurred in a female direction at some stages and in a male direction in others. Such a "mixed" process of sexual differentiation can result from drugs administered to the pregnant mother, stress she experienced, or a genetically based glandular malfunction, any of which could cause the embryo to be exposed to an unusual dose of hormones at some early stage of prenatal development. Whatever the origin, this prenatal dose of hormones causes the baby to be born with sexual anatomy that is mixed: neither completely female nor completely male. An intersexed baby may be born with ambiguous external genitalia, or with genitalia incongruous with internal reproductive structures.

What happens when a baby cannot be classified easily as female or male on the basis of external genitals? Essentially, the doctors "choose" a sex for the infant on the basis of factors such as chromosomes, genital appearance, and internal reproductive structures. They inform the parents that the baby is "really" a male or female. They then perform "corrective" surgery (often involving a series of operations over several years) to bring the child's appearance into line with her/his "true" sex (Kessler, 1998). The child may be prescribed drugs such as cortisone, and at puberty, the child often must begin taking hormones to produce the appropriate secondary sex characteristics. Thus, the intersexed child, in industrialized U.S. society, is fated to be brought up relying on medical care to fit into the two-sex system. Most of the decisions are made before the child is old enough to know or understand what is going on, and the child is neither given the option of forming an intersexual identity nor of choosing whether to be female or male. Indeed, the child is often not told what the reason is for all the interventions and learns the story only in adulthood.

By studying the behavior and personality of individuals with many types of intersexuality, investigators have hoped to discover the connections between specific aspects of physiological sex, identity, and behavior. However, one thing that should be clear from the above paragraph is that intersexed individuals have a very different experience of growing up than does the average child whose genitalia proclaim clearly at birth that s/he is female or male. The trauma of many medical procedures, the necessity of taking medications as they grow older, and the confusion about what exactly is going on are all bound to have an impact, and thus it is difficult to know just what to make of the research.

The connections researchers have found among physiological aspects of sex and other aspects of gender are still somewhat controversial. Studies of girls who were exposed to higher than normal prenatal levels of androgens (congenital adrenal hyperplasa, or **CAH**) suggest that their behavior may be somewhat "masculinized": showing more energy expenditure and tomboyism, preference for functional over attractive clothing, less interest in and rehearsal for marriage and motherhood roles (Ehrhardt & Baker, 1974; Money & Ehrhardt, 1972) and participation in male-typical activities (Berenbaum, 1999). These behaviors are all well within the realm of normal behavior for girls, however, and many confounding variables, such as parental expectations and drugs given to the girls to treat their condition, make it difficult to know whether it was the prenatal androgenization or postnatal differences in the social environment that caused the differences.

Though none of the studies can rule out all possible confounding variables, some reviewers argue that we can discern a pattern by looking at the findings of a large number of studies. In general, these reviewers report that the most consistent finding for CAH girls is a higher probability of male-typical "rough" play (Collaer & Hines, 1995). These girls also tend to report more aggressive tendencies; there is no evidence, however, that they actually *behave* more aggressively than other girls.

Not all research on the impact of the prenatal hormonal environment has been done with intersexuals. Richard Udry (2000) investigated the notion that levels of prenatal hormones might be linked to gender role behavior of women even in adulthood. He studied 163 27- to 30-year-old adult women whose mothers had provided blood samples during the second semester of pregnancy (thought to be a critical period for the impact of testosterone on the developing brain). He measured how feminine the women's adult behavior was by assessing their interests, the importance they placed on home and family, their job status, and their scores on psychological scales of masculinity and femininity. Udry found a correlation between mother's hormone levels during pregnancy and their daughters' gender-related behavior 30 years later. The lower the level of testosterone available to the fetus, the more typically feminine the daughter scored on the indicators of gender role behavior.

Whatever the early impact of prenatal hormones, the environment plays its hand as the child matures. For example, one study followed into adulthood 12 girls who had been exposed prenatally to masculinizing hormones. The researchers found that none of the girls maintained an active participation in sports, despite a high level of interest and participation during high school (Money & Mathews, 1982). These girls were apparently channeled by their social environment into more "feminine" pursuits as they grew into adulthood.

In some individuals, the issue is not an "overdose" of hormones, but their bodies' ability to respond to hormones. Persons with Androgen Insensitivity Syndrome (**AIS**) have bodies that cannot respond to androgens. They have a nonworking version of the gene on the X chromosome that is responsible for producing an androgen receptor protein, and without such a protein the body cannot sense and react to androgens (Angier, 1999). During prenatal development, a genetic male with AIS develops testes, which secrete androgens; however, the androgens do not have any effect. They do not produce the usual changes in the external genitalia that occur in the development of a male body, and instead the individual develops with female-appearing genitals. At birth, the infant may be classified as female, and the discovery that her internal organs do not match this designation may not occur until many years later, in adolescence.

A person with AIS will be raised as a female and will likely think of herself as female. In adolescence she must take estrogen to promote the development of breasts and to protect her bones. She will not menstruate, and she cannot become pregnant, because she does not have ovaries, a uterus, or fallopian tubes. However, despite all this, and despite their Y chromosome, AIS women look like women—beautiful women (Angier, 1999). They have clear skin and thick hair because testosterone, which their bodies can't respond to, is what causes acne and most cases of thinning hair. They have full breasts, because androgens are what normally keep breast growth in check. They tend to be tall, and they naturally have hairless armpits and very little hair on their legs. In short, these persons with mixed male and female biological characteristics fit the cultural notion of womanly beauty better than most women whose biology in incontestably female. And they *are* women in their self-definition and in the eyes of others.

We may learn important things about gender and gender identity by listening to intersexuals themselves, rather than focusing only on the outcomes of research papers. Some intersexed individuals have organized to protest the system of "managing" intersexuality; their arguments and their stories can be found on the Web site and in the publications of the Intersex Society of North America. This activist group fights to end "shame, secrecy and unwanted genital surgeries for people born with anomaly of the reproductive system" and "to end the idea that intersexuality is shameful or freakish" (Instersex Society of North America, 2001). As we ponder the question of how sex and gender are defined and what makes a person female or male, it is useful to remember that our cultural notion that everyone must fit into one of two clearly demarcated sexes is challenged by the experiences of many individuals.

The Female Body

Even the preceding brief overview of the process of sexual differentiation shows that the main physical differences that develop between females and males (even in the brain) are reproductive and sexual. The female develops with ovaries, a womb, a vagina, and a clitoris, and these characteristics become defining aspects of her femaleness. She menstruates. She can become pregnant. She cannot make anyone else pregnant, but someone else can make her pregnant against her will. She can give birth and can suckle an infant. Enormous meaning is assigned by societies, and by individual women, to these processes. Even though a woman may spend only a small proportion of her life (or none at all) being pregnant, even though the bearing and rearing of children may be only one aspect of the life's work of many women, even though women and men do undergo a huge number of similar experiences, this potential for reproduction is often considered the central fact about being female.

The female capacity to become pregnant plays a crucial role in the way girls are socialized toward vulnerability or power in many cultures. As girls reach puberty they face changes in expectations that reflect their emerging capacity for mature sexuality and for pregnancy. In many societies, the transition from girlhood to womanhood involves a new set of restrictions designed to safeguard females from the attentions of unauthorized males —and to safeguard males from a female sexuality that is viewed as dangerous and tempting. As they reach puberty girls may become the targets of repeated warnings, be forbidden to participate in certain activities, even be physically restricted. In societies that emphasize female vulnerability, the result can be a sense of inferiority, shame, and shaken self-confidence that lasts into adulthood. In societies that emphasize female power, the cautions that surround the development of a woman's body are interpreted as respect for the power and mystery that are entwined with such processes as menstruation, pregnancy, and childbirth. In either case, the onset of menstruation brings important changes into a girl's life—changes that are based on the development of her body, but that go far beyond the physical to the social and cultural.

Menstruation

In Ntozake Shange's novel *Sassafras, Cypress & Indigo* (1982), an African American girl making the transition into womanhood tells the following "marvelous menstruating moment" to her dolls as she busies herself making each of them a velvet menstrual pad:

> When you first realize your blood has come, smile; an honest smile, for you are about to have an intense union with your magic. This is a private time, a special time, for thinking and dreaming. Change your bedsheet to the ones that are your favorite. Sleep with a laurel leaf under your head. Take baths in wild hyssop, white water lilies. Listen for the voices of your visions; they are nearby. Let annoying people, draining worries, fall away as your body lets what she doesn't need go from her. Remember that you are a river; your banks are red honey where the Moon wanders. (pp. 19–20)

It is apparently rare for a girl in White North American culture to encounter **menarche,** the beginning of **menstruation,** with such positive images. Indeed, the popular literature about menstruation in the United States is filled with negative images. A content analysis of popular press articles about menstruation encountered such titles as "Dr. Jekyll and Ms. Hyde," "Coping with Eve's Curse," and "The Taming of the Shrew Inside of You" (Chrisler & Levy, 1990).

For the young women of some cultures, information about menstruation is dispensed gruffly and unwillingly by adults, and the whole process is regarded as something not to be discussed. Nisa, a member of the !Kung people of the Kalahari Desert in southern Africa who was interviewed by anthropologist Marjorie Shostak (1981), recalls that her first glimpse of menstrual blood, when her mother was "seeing the moon" (menstruating), was cause for shock and anger.

> I repeated, "Mommy . . . Mommy . . . there's blood there!" She said, "Where is there blood? Don't you know that some day, when you grow up, your genitals will also do that, and you, too, will menstruate? Why are you staring at me like that?" I said, "What? Me? I won't menstruate. I dont have what's needed to do that. I'll *never* menstruate." She said, "Look at yourself. You've got a vagina, right over there, and some day you *will* menstruate. You don't know what you're talking about." Then I said, "Why don't you wipe the blood away. Mommy, take something, some leaves, and wipe it away." She wouldn't. Then she slapped my face. I started to cry and cried and cried. (p. 72)

Many of the young Chicana women studied by Aída Hurtado (2003) reported that menarche, "'becoming *una señorita'* (a young lady)" (p. 51), was a traumatic experience characterized by a lack of information and physical discomfort. They spoke of being given elaborate instructions by their mothers on how to store (". . . in the closet, always at the bottom, where no one can see it" p. 52) and dispose discreetly of sanitary napkins so that no one would see them. And several told stories of losing their close relationships with their fathers after the fathers learned that they had begun to menstruate.

In other cultures, where menarche represents a clear and rigidly marked public transition, girls anticipate and discuss it. In Saudi Arabia, Muslim tradition dictates that at

In Saudi Arabia, Muslim tradition dictates that beginning at menarche a young woman must begin covering herself from head to toe and wearing a veil when in public.

menarche, a young woman must begin wearing a veil and be separated from all males except her father and brothers. As one Saudi Arabian woman remembers:

> The coming of women's menses is a source of easy conversation in the Muslim world. Suddenly, at that moment, a child is transformed into an adult. . . . In Saudi Arabia, the appearance of the first menses means that it is time to select the first veil and *abaaya*—with the greatest of care. Even the shopkeepers, Muslim men from India or Pakistan, inquire with ease and respect as to the time the girl-child becomes a woman. . . . A child enters the store, but a woman emerges, veiled and, on that day, of a marriageable age. Her life changes in that split second. (Sasson, 1992, pp. 58–59)

For many Native American groups, the onset of menstruation signifies a young girl's emerging womanly power, and a girl's first period is marked by a celebration. Girls in these cultures are taught that menstruation is a sign not of contamination or weakness, but of feminine vitality and power.

> Menstruating (or any other) Crow women do not go near a particularly sacred medicine bundle, and menstruating women are not allowed among warriors getting ready for battle, or those who have been wounded, because women are perceived to be possessed of a singular power, most vital during menstruation, puberty, and pregnancy, that weakens men's powers—physical, spiritual, or magical. The Crow and many other American Indians do not perceive signs of womanness as contamination; rather they view them as so powerful that other "medicines" may be canceled by the very presence of that power. (Allen, 1986, p. 253)

Menstruation is so weighted with symbolism because it is the first outward sign that the female body is prepared for pregnancy. The menstrual flow is the extra layers of uterine wall that have been developed and thickened in preparation for the possible implantation of a fertilized egg and are now being sloughed off. It is the last step in a complex process of hormonal feedback loops that involve the hypothalamus, the pituitary gland, the ovaries, and the uterus.

Gonadotropic releasing hormone (GnRH) from the hypothalamus signals cells in the pituitary gland to secrete follicle-stimulating hormone (FSH). The FSH signals a follicle (a sac that holds eggs) in one of the ovaries to secrete estrogen and bring an egg to maturity. While responding to FSH, both the follicle and the egg secrete estrogen, causing a rise in estrogen levels. The high levels of estrogen influence the cells lining the uterus to develop and differentiate, causing a thickening of the uterine wall. When the egg matures, the follicle ruptures to release it, in a process called **ovulation.** At the same time, the high estrogen levels cause the hypothalamus to produce LH-releaser, which in turn stimulates the pituitary to produce a surge of LH (luteinizing hormone). The LH elicits changes in other developed follicles, which cause an increase in progesterone levels. It also stimulates the ruptured follicle to turn into a glandular mass called the corpus luteum, which secretes both estrogen and progesterone. As progesterone levels rise, they cause the uterine walls to develop and thicken even more. If the egg has been fertilized, it will burrow into the uterine wall and secrete hormones that keep the corpus luteum active—the woman is pregnant.

If no fertilization occurs, the high progesterone levels, through feedback to the pituitary, cause it to reduce the production of LH, which causes the corpus luteum to degenerate after 10 to 14 days. Without the corpus luteum producing estrogen and progesterone, the levels of these hormones drop sharply. This decline causes the cells in the uterine wall to slough off. These cells, and blood from broken blood vessels, flow out through the vagina during the menstrual phase of the cycle. The whole cycle is diagrammed in Figures 3.1 and 3.2.

Menarche usually occurs at about age 12 or 13. However, it is preceded by earlier signs that the girl is moving into puberty: breast development and the appearance of pubic hair. Recently, researchers have noticed a trend toward earlier puberty in girls. In the United States, by the age of 9, about 77 percent of Black girls and one-third of White girls have started developing breasts or pubic hair, and a significant minority of both groups show these signs by age 7 (Earlier puberty, 2001). Scientists have speculated that the cause of the earlier puberty may be environmental pollutants, byproducts of cosmetics and plastics, that may stimulate estrogen production. Another possible cause is body fat, which can also affect hormones.

Why do women menstruate at all? According to one perspective, it seems rather wasteful to go through this complicated cycle of building up and sloughing off the uterine wall every month, just on the remote chance that the body will have the opportunity to become pregnant. One provocative theory was presented by Margie Profet (1993), who suggested that menstruation was the female body's way of ridding itself of pathogens—bacteria or viruses that might cause disease. Such pathogens may be carried into the uterus by sperm after sexual activity, and the monthly flow would allow the body to protect itself. Other researchers have disputed this theory, and so far there is little evidence to support it (Angier, 1999). The interesting thing about this controversy, however, is that it is the first time scientists have given serious attention to the "why" of menstruation. As more women

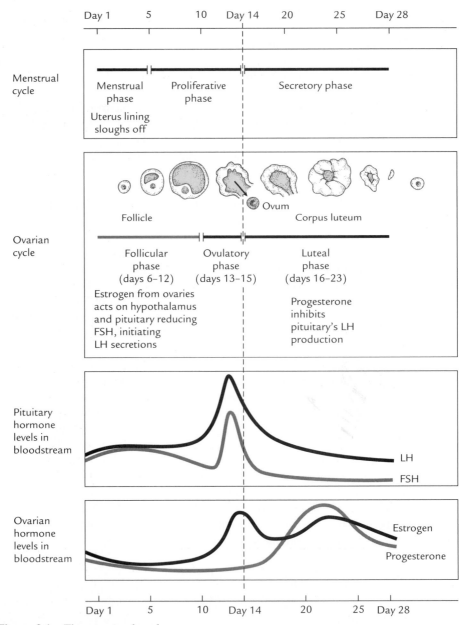

Figure 3.1 The menstrual cycle

become scientists, more attention is being paid to questions about female biology that seem to have been profoundly uninteresting to the men of science.

PMS, Lunar Cycles, and "Menstrual Joy" Considerable research energy has been devoted to examining the menstrual cycle for possible hormone-related variations in mood

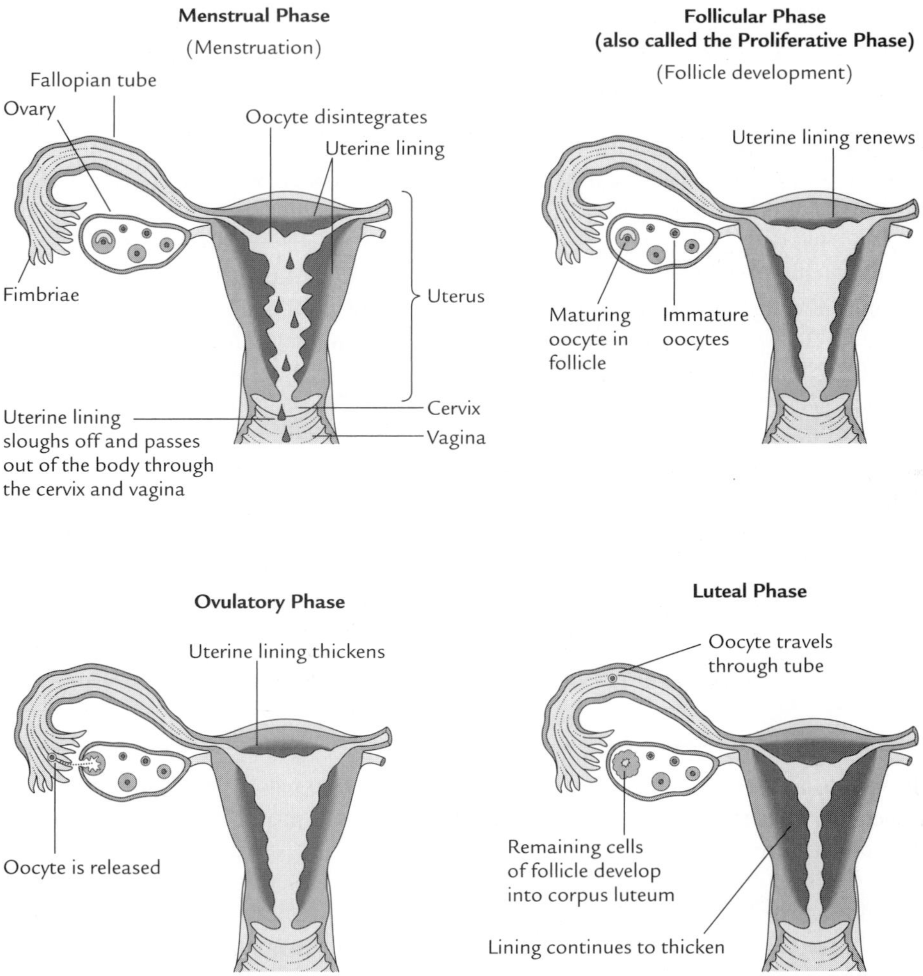

Figure 3.2   Diagrams of female reproductive system during menstrual cycle phases

and behavior. This research is motivated by an awareness that hormone levels do change fairly dramatically across the menstrual cycle, and also by the existence of Western cultural beliefs that certain "times of the month" (notably premenstrual and menstrual) are difficult for women. Indeed, the American Psychiatric Association has reified the concept of the "premenstrual syndrome" (**PMS**) by including it in the latest edition of its *Diagnostic and Statistical Manual of Mental Disorders,* the DSM-IV, as "premenstrual phase dysphoric disorder" (**PMDD**). This was done over the objections of many feminist psychologists, who argue that it turns women's normal physiological processes into sources of pathology.

There is a large and vague list of "symptoms" associated with this disorder, none of which are unique to menstruation (Chrisler, 1996). Moreover, there is evidence that focusing on premenstrual changes as evidence of a specific illness influences women and men to

BOX 3.1 MAKING CHANGE
Organizing to Celebrate Women's Bodies

"Let the good times flow" is the motto of one small group of determined women who are trying to institute Menstrual Monday: a holiday in honor of women's menstrual cycle. By turning something that is often regarded with distaste into a celebration, they hope to change attitudes. Their designated date is the Monday before Mother's Day. However, their main point is not the specific date but "to create a sense of fun around menstruation; to encourage women to take charge of their menstrual/reproductive health care; to create greater visibility of menstruation, in film, print, music, and other media; and to enhance honesty about menstruation in our relationships." To mark Menstrual Monday, they suggest, do something appropriate: Create a potluck meal from the five Menstrual Monday food groups (poppy seed, chocolate, spinach, eggs, and red stuff), have a Power Egg throwing tournament, or hold a Sister Menses costume contest. Take their suggestion and, with a group of friends, find a way to celebrate menstruation together. For help, inspiration and guidance, go to their Web site at **www.moltx .org/index.html** and read some of the "menstrumonials," or order the Menstrual Monday Starter Kit (including a Power Egg, Ovum Fan, Message from the Ovum Office on Womb House stationary, and more). Or make up your own kit.

define the changes as problematic. In one study, persons who read a description of PMDD with the label attached viewed menstrual symptoms as more problematic for women than did persons who read the same description with the label "Episodic Dysphoric Disorder" (Nash & Chrisler, 1997).

Could women's cycling hormone levels be causing significant mood shifts? Once again, it is difficult to separate biological processes from social context and learned expectations. Do we look for a hormone-based reason for women's moods just because we know the hormonal fluctuation occurs? Are women who have grown up learning to expect "premenstrual blues" primed to attribute bad moods to their menstrual cycles rather than to some other cause? There are ample reasons for caution, once we are aware that researchers, and all of us, tend to construct knowledge from questions and observations that embody and reflect current beliefs. We can now read, for example, that medical researchers in the late 19th century were convinced that men as well as women could menstruate; they interpreted periodic nosebleeds, discharges of bloody urine, and other forms of bleeding observed in men as indicators of male "vicarious" menstruation (Moscucci, 1991). Their interpretation stemmed from a general belief that women and men had similar reproductive organs, and that periodic bleeding was necessary to reestablish the body's equilibrium.

Our own beliefs may make us similarly susceptible to misconceptions in conducting and interpreting research on menstrual symptoms. For years, much of the research on these symptoms has been based on retrospective reports; that is, women were asked to remember how they felt during their last premenstrual phase, or how they "usually" felt during this phase. Such a procedure is problematic, both because memory is unreliable and because it may affect women's responses by causing them to focus on their expectations for menstrual symptoms. And research shows clearly that expectations and attitudes are important—both in the ways women experience their own menstrual cycles and in the ways other people perceive menstruating women. For example, young women who learn to view their bodies as objects that are evaluated based on appearance may feel negative about menstruation since it may interfere with their self-presentation as fresh and clean. Tomi-Ann Roberts (2004) studied the relationship between women's preoccupation with their physical appearance as a way of controlling their treatment in the world and their menstrual self-evaluations. She found that women who had internalized a strong "objectified" view with their physical selves (a view that their value is strongly influenced by others' view of their bodies) tended to have more negative attitudes and emotions—including shame and disgust—about menstruation. Other research has shown that people who view women through the lens of hostile sexism are likely to hold negative impressions of menstruating women (Forbes, Adams-Curtis, White, & Holmgren, 2003). These researchers also found that, in general, both women and men rated the menstruating woman as less energized and sexy and as more irritable, sad, and angry than the average woman—and that men also rated her as less clean and fresh, nurturing, and reasonable and as more spacey and annoying!

Some researchers have used prospective reports (daily symptom or mood reports given over a period of several menstrual cycles) from women who are not aware that their menstrual cycle is being studied. Frequently, such reports do not match retrospective reports from the same women (McFarlane & Williams, 1990, 1994). The situation looks even more complex when researchers include men in their samples and when they broaden their focus to include the possibility of other cycles, such as lunar and day-of-week. Jessica McFarlane and Tannis MacBeth Williams (1994) followed 60 women and 10 men for 12 to 18 weeks, obtaining daily mood data. Mood ratings were later matched against information about menstrual cycles, lunar cycles, and days of the week. They found that two-thirds of both the women and the men showed cycles in their moods. Thus it might be viewed as "normal" for a person to have a regular pattern of emotional ups and downs. These mood cycles were very different for each individual, however, and few of them matched such expected patterns as premenstrual blues or weekend "highs." The data showed that more of the women had a negative mood phase at some other point in their menstrual cycle than premenstrually, and that 55 percent had no mood changes correlated with the menstrual cycle. Also interesting was that women's self-labeling as sufferers of PMS bore little relation to the kind of mood cycles their daily data indicated. The findings suggest that both researchers and their female respondents may, for years, have been concentrating too exclusively on the menstrual cycle as a cause of emotional distress. McFarlane and Williams advise that "a biomedical approach that focuses narrowly on a PMS pattern, to the exclusion of other positive and negative menstrual cycle patterns and, importantly, to other equally negative and positive nonmenstrual patterns, is misleading" (p. 368).

The notion that the hormonal changes associated with menstruation are the major influence on women's emotional patterns was assaulted years ago by cross-cultural research. Marjorie Shostak (1981) describes a study in which she conducted daily interviews with eight !Kung women across two menstrual cycles. Simultaneously, she obtained regular blood samples from the women in order to assess their hormone levels. When she later analyzed the data, she found that "[k]nowing what phase of the menstrual cycle a woman was in would enable one to predict little or nothing about her behavior or mood. Much more powerful were such influences as the behavior of husbands, relatives, and friends, or the availability of food and water, or minor illnesses" (p. 354). Moreover, Shostak found that her informants had no expectation of a premenstrual or menstrual syndrome or any other effect of the menstrual cycle on moods.

Recently, some researchers have challenged the idea that menstrual cycle research should focus so narrowly on *negative* emotions. Would the findings change if researchers asked different questions, looking for positive instead of negative changes? As an illustration of the possibilities, one group of researchers developed the "**Menstrual Joy** Questionnaire," which asked respondents about their experience of high spirits, increased sexual desire, vibrant activity, revolutionary zeal, intense concentration, feelings of affection, self-confidence, sense of euphoria, creativity, and feelings of power during their menstrual cycle (Delaney, Lupton, & Toth, 1987). When another group of researchers later administered the questionnaire to female college students, they found that it seemed to "prime" the respondents to include more positive responses in later, broader measures of attitudes toward menstruation (Chrisler, Johnston, Champagne, & Preston, 1994). Clearly, the questions asked by researchers shape what we "know" about menstruation.

Menstrual Synchrony   Although most research has focused on how the physiological changes of the menstrual cycle may affect moods, behavior, and task performance, it is clear that this relationship can also work in reverse: Behavior, stress, and other environmental factors can affect the menstrual cycle. A striking example is the existence of **menstrual synchrony,** which means that women who spend a lot of time together tend to have their periods around the same time. This finding was first reported with respect to women in college dormitories, who over time became increasingly likely to start their menstrual periods on the same day (McClintock, 1971). It has also been observed with mothers and daughters living together, women roommates in private residences (Weller & Weller, 1993), lesbian couples (Weller & Weller, 1992), women in Bedouin families (Weller & Weller, 1997), and Israeli basketball players (Weller & Weller,1995). One study indicated that a majority of women sampled (university students and office and professional workers) reported personal experience of menstrual synchrony (Arden, Dye, & Walker, 1999).

Menstrual synchrony does not always occur, and it is more likely to develop between women who engage in frequent activities together and report stronger emotional bonds. Some research shows that it occurs often among sisters and close friends, even when they do not live together (Weller, Weller, & Roizman, 1999). These researchers suggest that there is an optimal amount of "togetherness" that promotes menstrual synchrony: too much or too little mutual exposure, and the synchrony may not occur.

Why does menstrual synchrony occur? Some researchers suggest that the women are responding to pheromones, chemicals secreted by the axillary sweat glands, which tend to vary with menstrual cycle changes (Russell, Switz, & Thompson, 1980). Indeed, there is

BOX 3.2 LEARNING ACTIVITY
Measurement of Menstrual Changes

Psychologists and medical researchers have often measured menstrual changes by using retrospective reports and "symptom" checklists. But how might researchers affect responses by the very process of measurement? How much does the list of particular menstrual changes included on questionnaires affect participants' views of their own experience? Below are some of the items from two questionnaires that are used to measure menstrual changes. If you are someone who menstruates, answer them for yourself. Does each set of items make you think differently about menstruation? Find two friends who menstruate and ask each one if she would be willing to answer the items from one of the questionnaires. Afterward, ask each person how she feels about menstruation. Does each set of questions produce different feelings about the menstrual cycle?

Set 1 (items from the *Menstrual Joy Questionnaire,* Chrisler et al., 1994; Delaney et al., 1988)

Instructions: Rate each of the following items on a 6-point scale according to the degree you experienced it during your most recent menstrual period. If you did not experience the feeling at all when you were menstruating, rate that item 1. If you experienced a feeling intensely when you were menstruating, rate that item 6.

_____ high spirits	_____ sexual desire	_____ vibrant activity
_____ revolutionary zeal	_____ intense concentration	_____ affection
_____ self-confidence	_____ euphoria (extreme well-being)	
_____ creativity	_____ power	

Set 2 (items from the *Modified Menstrual Distress Questionnaire,* Clare & Wiggins, 1979)

Instructions: Rate each of the following items on a 6-point scale according to the degree you experienced it during your most recent menstrual period. If you did not experience the feeling at all when you were menstruating, rate that item 1. If you experienced a feeling intensely when you were menstruating, rate that item 6.

_____ clumsiness	_____ accidents	_____ decreases in efficiency
_____ avoidance of social activities		_____ crying spells
_____ difficulty sleeping	_____ confusion	_____ tension
_____ headache	_____ dizziness	

evidence that women who become synchronized with their college dormitory roommates are more sensitive to the smell of one particular pheromone (Morofushi, Shinohara, Funabashi, & Kimura, 2000). Pheromones may be only one of several factors promoting synchrony, but so far other factors remain unexplored.

BOX 3.3 LEARNING ACTIVITY
Media Portrayals of Pregnant Women

How do popular magazines portray pregnant women? Or do they portray them at all? Choose several magazines oriented toward female audiences and search for pictures of pregnant women. How often are pregnant women pictured? What are they doing in these pictures? How are they dressed? Do you get an impression that the pregnant body is considered attractive? Strong? Now search some magazines that are not specifically geared toward female audiences. What differences to you find? Did this exercise tell you something about society's attitudes toward pregnant women?

Pregnancy and Childbirth

In North American society, pregnancy is often viewed as a joyful and privileged state. Pregnant women are said to "glow," and are sometimes treated with extra consideration and even deference. On the other hand, pregnant women are in some cases made to feel fat and ugly and are the targets of nasty jokes. Many women are abused by their male partners during pregnancy; intimate partner violence is more common than many other conditions (such as diabetes) for which pregnant women are routinely screened (National Center for Chronic Disease Prevention and Health Promotion, 2001). Young, unmarried women who become pregnant are the objects of strong social disapproval, yet in many cases are denied the choice to end their pregnancies. Perhaps because pregnancy and childbirth are the visible outcomes of sexual activity, and perhaps because they are part of a process that is not experienced by men, the social response to them is filled with contradictions.

Such contradictions abound in many cultures. Traditional Chinese beliefs held that childbirth was an act of extreme spiritual pollution, even though, by having a child, a woman gained status and some power in her husband's family. Some Chinese writings held that women were tortured in hell—"placed in a pond of bloody birth fluids"—for committing the "sin" of childbirth, and that in giving birth, women pollute both Heaven and Earth (Reed, 1992, p. 165).

Nisa, the !Kung woman whose words were recorded by Marjorie Shostak (1981), describes the beginning of her first pregnancy: "I was angry and cried a lot. My heart was full of rage and felt pain, but I didn't know why. Whenever I ate meat, I threw up, and whenever I ate sweet berries, I threw up. But when I ate water root or pounded gwia leaves or do roots, I didn't throw up" (p. 186). The older people in her village told her that her symptoms meant she was pregnant; it was considered commonplace for !Kung women to experience extreme mood fluctuations, as well as nausea, during pregnancy.

A woman's body changes considerably during pregnacy (see Figure 3.3). Women in many parts of the world acknowledge some physical discomfort associated with pregnancy, although there are wide individual variations in the way pregnancy is experienced. A substantial minority of women in North American samples report nausea and vomiting in early pregnancy (Lips, 1982, 1985; Macy, 1986) and feelings of heaviness, general

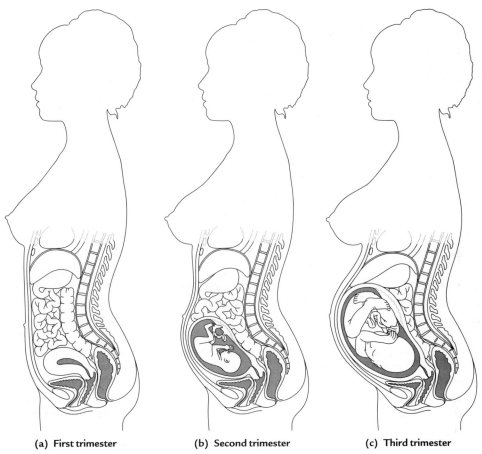

(a) **First trimester**   (b) **Second trimester**   (c) **Third trimester**

Figure 3.3   Changes in a woman's body during pregnancy

aches and pains, and backache in late pregnancy (Lips, 1985). Strong stereotypes link pregnancy to emotional changes such as irritability, mood swings, or glowing contentment. Women's own reports on these emotional dimensions of pregnancy are more mixed, however. Studies in North America suggest higher rates of depression may be associated with pregnancy (Gjerdingen, Froberg, & Kochevar, 1991; Lips, 1985), but other negative emotions such as irritability and anxiety do not seem, in general, to distinguish pregnant women from nonpregnant women. Only a small minority of women reported increased psychological well-being during pregnancy in one study (Condon, 1987). A recent large-scale study in Britain found that pregnant women were as likely as other women to be depressed—a finding that was startling to the press and made headlines because it contradicted the stereotype that pregnancy is a time of special emotional well-being (Study: Depression in pregnancy common, 2001). Studies of expectant mothers in Great Britain, Greece, and the United States suggest that negative emotions during pregnancy are linked with stressful life events and a felt lack of social support (O'Hara, 1986; Thorpe, Dragonas, & Golding, 1992).

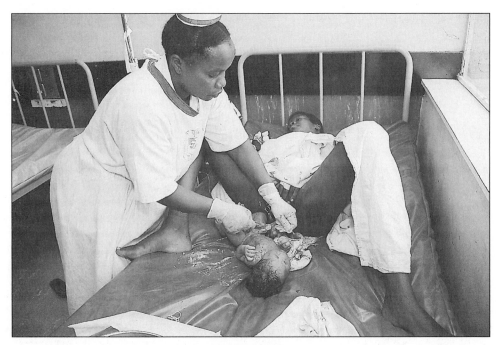

The woman giving birth in this maternity hospital in Nairobi, Kenya, faces a different set of risks than her counterparts in North America. Giving birth is a dramatic event for women, and one that is moderated and shaped by cultural context.

Childbirth is a dramatic event for women, and one that is moderated and shaped by the cultural context. Physically, it involves tremendous effort and a large, rather sudden change in body chemistry and shape. Emotionally, it marks the transition to a new set of family relationships. In North America, where women tend to give birth in hospitals with the physical support of medical personnel and the emotional support of a partner, they may experience little fear of death, but much loss of control, feelings of vulnerability and pain, and anxiety about the baby. The woman may be treated as a passive patient, given little information about the unfolding process, and even bullied into submission to hospital routines.

When a woman gives birth alone, without help, advice, or the knowledge of what to expect, the process can be truly terrifying. This can happen in any culture. Nisa, the !Kung woman, describes her first birth as one that was frightening.

> I didn't really know what a baby did or how much it hurt or how it actually got born. . . . I was in pain and wasn't sure what I was supposed to do. . . . I walked a short distance from the village and sat down beside a tree. I sat there and waited; she wasn't ready to be born. I lay down, but still she didn't come out. I leaned against the tree and began to feel the labor. The pains came over and over, again and again. (Shostak, 1981, p. 193)

Among the !Kung, it was said that "the pain of childbirth is fire and. . . . a child's birth is like an anger so great that it sometimes kills" (Shostak, 1981, p. 195). Yet in this culture, as in many others, women try to be stoical and not to cry out in pain. Nisa recounts that she kept herself quiet as labor began, lest her in-laws laugh at her.

In some cultures, women take control of the birth process, and the woman giving birth is viewed as a traveler on a difficult journey or a warrior going through a challenging rite of passage. In such cultures, women's reproductive biology is not viewed as a limitation they cannot transcend; rather, it is one source of their power. The Arapaho Indians believed that dying in childbirth was spiritually equivalent to dying in battle (Allen, 1986).

Many cultures follow careful rituals to mark the woman's transition to motherhood after childbirth. For example, traditional Chinese custom provides that the new mother "do the month." For the first month after giving birth, the woman must avoid washing, not venture outside, not eat raw or cold food, not be blown by wind or move about, avoid sexual intercourse, and neither read nor cry. Following these rules allows the mother to rest and receive extra attention from her family (Pillsbury, 1978). Such customs allow the mother to recover properly from childbirth, and they give her rewards and structures that ease her into her new role.

Modern North American culture, by contrast, has few rituals that involve the new mother; most of the attention is focused on the well-being of the infant. This lack of ritual may, according to some observers, contribute to the **postpartum depression** that some women experience (Cox, 1988). However, there is little evidence that postpartum depression—depression that occurs after the birth of a baby—is a specific type of depression or that such depression is an especially common response to childbirth. At 8 weeks after childbirth, women are no more likely to be depressed than at other times in their lives; the rate of depression found in one sample of 9,000 British women who were followed through and beyond their pregnancies was 13.5 percent at the 32nd week of pregnancy and 9.1 percent at the 8th week postpartum (Evans, Heron, Francomb, Oke, & Golding, 2001). The most striking thing about these findings, according to some observers, is not that depression is a problem associated with pregnancy or the postpartum period, but rather the unremitting level of depression among young women.

Controlling the Female Body

Perhaps because women's sexual and reproductive biology can be a source of power, determined attempts to control and limit female sexuality and reproduction are made by many cultures. Such control can take many forms, from physically impairing the woman's capacity for sexual pleasure to forcing her to bear unwanted children.

Female Genital Mutilation

About 130 million women worldwide have been "circumcised"—an invasive, painful, and dangerous operation that involves excision of all or part of the clitoris and is often carried out under medically risky conditions. The practice, which is generally referred to as **female genital mutilation (FGM),** is followed in at least 20 African countries, in the Arab countries of Oman, South Yemen, Egypt, and the United Arab Emirates, and among the Muslim populations of Indonesia and Malaysia (Arbesman, Kahler, & Buck, 1993). One survey showed that 97 percent of married Egyptian women between the ages of 15 and 49 had undergone the procedure (Lancaster, 1996). In the African country of Tanzania, FGM affects about 18 percent of the female population, and "mass circumcisions" are carried out in which thousands of girls are genitally mutilated (Tanzania fails to enforce law, 2001). In one such ceremony, after 5,000 girls were subjected to FGM, 20 died from medical complications. The surgery, most often performed on girls between the ages of 4 and 8 years, usually results in pain and heavy bleeding and can lead to such complications as infection, shock, difficulties with menstruation and urination, and painful intercourse.

In some countries such as Ethiopia, Tanzania, Eritrea, and Egypt, girls are subjected not only to clitoridectomy but also to infibulation, the cutting away of the labia and the sealing of the wound to leave only a tiny opening for menstruation and urination. If infection from the procedure does not kill them, these girls may suffer for years from pelvic infections caused by trapped urine or menstrual fluid. Their scarred birth canals create unnecessary dangers and agony each time they give birth; the baby's head may become trapped, leading to a hemorrhage or a ruptured bladder. The practice predates both Christianity and Islam and is not mandated in the scriptures of either religion, but many people practice it as if it were a religious requirement.

Egyptian writer and psychiatrist Nawal el Saadawi (1998), co-founder of the African Women's Association for Research and Development, remembers the night when, at the age of six, she was taken from her bed and carried into the bathroom of her home for the amputation of her clitoris:

> I was frightened and. . . . there were many of them, and . . . something like an iron grasp caught hold of my hand and my arms and my thighs, so that I became unable to resist or even to move. I also remember the icy touch of the bathroom tiles under my naked body . . . a rasping sound which reminded me of the butcher when he used to sharpen his knife. . . . my thighs had been pulled wide apart. . . . Then suddenly the sharp metallic edge seemed to drop between my thighs and there cut off a piece of flesh from my body. . . . I screamed with pain despite the tight hand held over my mouth, for the pain was not just a pain, it was like a searing flame that went through my whole body. After a few moments, I saw a red pool of blood around my hips." (p. 174)

For centuries, women in certain cultures have been taught that these painful and dangerous procedures are important for their health and beauty. Aset Ibrahim, a 28-year-old Eritrean woman interviewed by Geraldine Brooks (1995), commented:

> My mother, my grandmother and my great-grandmother all told me it was right, that without it a woman wouldn't be able to control herself, that she would end up a prostitute. . . . I even learned to believe that it looked nicer that way. We grew up reciting the saying, "A house isn't beautiful without a door." (p. 35)

Why subject a young girl to such a dangerous and painful procedure? Popular belief holds that the operation will ensure "the attenuation of sexual drives, thus protecting the woman against her oversexed nature, saving her from temptation, suspicion, or disgrace, and preserving her chastity" (Abdel Kader, 1987, p. 37). But it is not only (or mainly) the woman who is protected. Defenders of the practice argue that women who have not been subjected to FGM are impolite and oversexed—and thus make bad wives. Women's actions are seen to have tremendous implications for the honor of their male relatives in many Middle Eastern and African countries; adultery or premarital sex committed by a wife or daughter dishonors father, brothers, even the entire family. Thus the curtailing of sexual pleasure through clitoridectomy and infibulation protects male relatives by "protecting" women from temptation.

Political and legal challenges to female genital mutilation have been many, and at least 41 countries have addressed the issue in their laws (Fighting female genital mutilation, 2001). Nine African countries have outlawed female genital mutilation, including Guinea, Egypt, and Tanzania. Women's groups in Africa have been active in lobbying to increase awareness of female genital mutilation and to pass laws against it. In Kenya, a nongovernmental organization called *Maendaleo Ya Wanawake* has developed alternative rite-of-passage ceremonies that emphasize positive rituals and do not include FGM. The United Nations has supported the right of its member countries to offer refugee status to women who flee their countries in fear of mutilation. Thus, whereas the practice of female mutilation is a complex and widespread issue, there are indications that it will gradually decline.

The history of female genital mutilation is not limited to Africa and the Middle East, however. During the 19th century, clitoridectomy was endorsed by physicians in Britain and the United States as treatment for "hysteria, epilepsy, melancholy, lesbianism, and excessive masturbation" and is reportedly still (rarely) prescribed for treatment of "female masturbation and sexuality" (American Medical Association, 1995, p. 1714). The practice was originally popularized by a British gynecologist, Isaac Baker Brown, who theorized that most diseases experienced by women could be attributed to overexcitement of the nervous system and that particularly powerful in this respect was the pudic nerve, leading into the clitoris. He argued that habitual stimulation of this nerve through masturbation put enormous stress on a woman's health, and would cause, in turn, eight stages of progressive disease: hysteria, spinal irritation, hysterical epilepsy, cataleptic fits, epileptic fits, idiocy, mania, and eventually, death (Coventry, 2000). His cure was drastic: "a complete excision of the clitoris with scissors, packing the wound with lint, administering opium via the rectum, and strictly observing the patient. Within a month, the wound usually healed, and according to Baker Brown, intractable women became happy wives; rebellious teenage girls settled back into the bosom of their families; and married women formerly averse to sexual duties became pregnant" (Coventry, 2000, p. 2).

Although physicians may have deluded themselves and the public into thinking that such a procedure was a way to save women from disease, it was clearly a way to control unruly girls and women. Clitoridectomy is no longer justified by medical practitioners as a way to dampen women's sexuality; however, the operation is still frequently performed. Now, however, surgery on the clitoris is performed cosmetically, to make a child "look" like a girl. Removal or reshaping of all or part of the clitoris, called **clitoroplasty,** by modern surgeons, happens about five times a day in the United States (Coventry, 2000). An infant girl who is born with a clitoris that appears "too large," whether or not she is regarded as intersexual, is at risk for such surgery, often on the basis only of a doctor's subjective impression (Fausto-Sterling, 2000). Intersexual rights activists argue that, not only is such surgery a drastic response to genital appearance, but also there is little or no follow-up information to say whether the practice is ultimately helpful or harmful to the patient. And, most troubling, the surgery is done long before the individual is able to make the choice for herself. These procedures unavoidably cut some of the nerves lacing the clitoris—nerves that make the person responsive to sexual stimulation. For the most part, physicians have failed to ask the question: Would most women, given a choice, be willing to sacrifice sexual sensitivity and perhaps orgasmic potential in order to have a "normal-looking" clitoris?

Virginity Testing

In many countries, it is considered crucial that a woman be a virgin—sexually inexperienced—when she is married. It is a sign that her husband truly "owns" her; she has never given herself to anyone else. It also, of course, certifies her husband's paternity if she becomes pregnant. In some villages in Iraq, Saudi Arabia, and Turkey, a bride is returned to her father in disgrace if the sheets from the wedding bed are not bloody. (The rupturing of the hymen, the membrane that partly closes the vagina, during first intercourse results in bleeding.) If the sheets are bloody, they may be presented to the bride's mother-in-law, so that she can display to her friends and relatives that she has acquired an honorable and pure daughter-in-law (Sasson, 1992).

The consequences of nonvirginity can go beyond shame and disgrace. In one incident, five young Turkish women attempted suicide by swallowing rat poison and jumping into a pool of water after the director of their state foster home ordered them to undergo a virginity test when they returned late to their dormitory (Couturier, 1998). The girls survived their suicide attempts, and while they were recovering in a hospital, doctors there were authorized to carry out the tests on them.

The Controversy over Abortion

For centuries, women in many cultures have found ways to prevent and end unwanted pregnancies. The women of ancient Greece looked for signs that they were carrying a male fetus and made decisions accordingly about whether to carry the pregnancy to term. If a mistake was made, infanticide was a final option (Pomeroy, 1983). Women of the Hagen tribe of Papua New Guinea hired women experts in abortion to pummel their abdomens in order to kill the fetus. Women in Chinese peasant societies used herbs and drugs to induce abortion (Tiffany, 1982). !Kung women used chemical agents from plants; they also believed that they could induce an abortion by having sex with a man other than the father (Shostak, 1981).

Women's access to abortion has been restricted in many cultures, forbidden by religious doctrine or hampered by legal and practical strictures. Yet abortion is a common occurrence. In North America, hundreds of thousands of abortions are performed every year, despite the frequent necessity for women seeking abortions to run a gauntlet of protesters. Among American women, about 49 percent of all pregnancies are unintended and almost half of those unintended pregnancies are terminated through abortion. Worldwide, an estimated 46 million abortions are performed every year (Alan Guttmacher Institute, 2003). On the African continent, where abortion is illegal in most countries, tens of thousands of women undergo illegal back-street abortion and at least 20,000 women die every year as a result of these procedures (Illegal abortions claim thousands of lives, 2001).

Studies of the psychological aftermath of abortion suggest that most women feel relief, happiness, and lowered depression and anxiety when an unwanted pregnancy is terminated (Lunneborg, 1992; Martucci, 1998; Turell, Armsworth, & Gaa, 1990). A woman is more likely to experience distress if she has no support from significant others, is very young, has no other children, has a "late" abortion, or is strongly religious (Turell et al., 1990). It is also quite possible for a woman who feels secure and confident in her abortion decision to experience, nevertheless, a sense of loss: "Sadness, even the most gripping sorrow, may accompany abortion, but this does not necessarily mean the decision is regretted" (Hoshiko, 1993, p. 103).

Life circumstances play a large part in the way abortion is experienced and the way decisions about it are made. For example, women who feel that abortion is stigmatizing and that they must keep it a secret from friends and family experience more psychological distress over abortion (Major & Gramzow, 1999). Latina women who live in the border regions of Texas have been found to be more affected in their abortion decisions by factors such as poverty and the availability of abortion providers than their Latina counterparts who do not live along the U.S.-Mexico border (Brown, Jewell, & Rous, 2000). When the abortion experiences of native Israeli women are compared to those of recent immigrants to Israel from Russia, it appears that the immigrant women experience more stress, perhaps because they their lives are more unsettled and they have less social support (Remennick & Segal, 2001). Among one sample of teenage women in Tanzania, abortion, although illegal, was perceived as presenting fewer cultural and practical barriers than obtaining and using contraception (Silberschmidt & Rasch, 2001).

Attitudes toward abortion vary widely. Studies of Canadian and U.S. women activists who are for or against the availability of abortion as a choice for women have shown that the two groups differ greatly on other issues as well. The pro-choice women are more likely to believe in equal rights and responsibilities for women and men and not to accept parenthood as the primary role for women. The women who characterize themselves as antiabortion are more likely to have made family roles central to their lives, are much more likely than the other group to attend church regularly, and are concerned about perceived threats to the family from feminism and homosexuality (Luker, 1984; Rauhala, 1987). A study of abortion attitudes among Mexican Americans, Puerto Ricans, and Cuban Americans, using data from the Latino National Political Survey, indicated that attitudes toward abortion among Latinos are related to feminism, religiosity, and demographic characteristics, just as they are in the non-Latino population (Bolks, Evans, Polinard, & Wrinkle, 2000). The relationship of religiosity and other variables to attitudes toward abortion may differ somewhat among ethnic or cultural groups, however. One study found that African Americans who are church attenders and theological conservatives hold more pro-choice attitudes than do their White counterparts (Gay & Lynxwiler, 1999). A cross-cultural examination of abortion attitudes in Eastern Europe and the United States showed that the link between gender role attitudes and approval of abortion was stronger in Slovenia than in the other countries studied (Wall et al., 1999).

In the United States, although abortion is legal, women who go to abortion clinics often encounter antiabortion picketers and protesters who try to influence them not to go through with their decision. How does it affect a woman who is making what is likely a difficult and painful decision to be confronted in such a way? Most women report that it makes them feel angry rather than guilty (Cozzarelli, Major, Karrasch, & Fuegen, 2000). However, women who are feeling conflicted about abortion are more likely to experience guilt, and these feelings of guilt and conflict predict depression immediately after the abortion.

Not only the women who obtain abortions, but also the people who provide them, are affected by the social context surrounding abortion. For example, clandestine abortion providers in Latin America, working in contexts where abortion is illegal, report that a lack of medical support; the necessity of secrecy; and threats of violence, extortion, and prosecution make their work more difficult (Rodriguez & Strickler, 1999). These health professionals undertake this risky work for a variety of reasons: a sense of calling, a desire to help women, personal experience with abortion, a commitment to political change. They report a sense of great satisfaction with what they do, noting that they are saving women's lives, participating in a supportive network of colleagues, and empowering women by giving them choices in very difficult life situations.

Confining the Female Body: Seclusion and Veiling

When the Algerian runner Hassiba Boulmerka earned a gold medal in the women's 1,500 meters at the 1992 Barcelona Olympics, reactions to her achievement were mixed. Although some Algerians celebrated her achievement, many of her country's most conservative Muslims expressed outrage that she had behaved immodestly, running with naked legs in front of crowds of strangers that included many men (Yesko, 1995).

Many cultures have had traditions that involve the seclusion and hiding of women. Usually, these traditions, which involve concealing a woman's body in swaths of clothing once it becomes defined as sexual, apply to young women who have passed the age of puberty; they may not always extend to old women. In Muslim countries, the most orthodox tradition dictates that women be well covered with a headscarf, face veil, and cloak from head to foot. The donning of these items may be eagerly anticipated by young girls as a sign of being grown up; indeed, for upper-class women in very traditional Muslim countries they may still signal that the woman is beginning her participation in the private, virtually all-female society of the harem. For poor peasant women, there may be no physical veil, simply a strongly enforced code of modesty and seclusion from contact with strangers. In Iran, for example, women from poor rural families have traditionally spent most of their lives behind the high walls of the *andarun*—the women's quarters of traditional homes.

In either case, one result is that women are hidden from view and kept apart from many of the public functions of daily life. The veil has often been seen as a symbol of restriction and invisibility. In a famous precedent-breaking act, Huda Sharawi, returning to Egypt after traveling to the Ninth Meeting of the International Women's Suffrage Association in 1923, publicly removed her veil. As she commented, "The veil, even though so light, is the most serious obstacle in the face of the participation of women in public life" (quoted in Abdel Kader, 1987, p. 95).

In some cases, wearing a veil is an active choice, a woman's symbolic gesture of affirmation and loyalty for her culture and its traditions. By wearing the veil, a woman may be signaling that she does not want to be "Western" just because she is educated or employed. In Egypt in the 1970s, for example, many educated, professional women who had adopted Western dress began to wear veils covering their heads and faces, as specified by Muslim traditions. These women were apparently trying to blend their new "modern" status with an authentic adherence to Islamic moral values; they showed no sign of wanting to leave their professions, abandon their newly won political participation, or return to traditional harem life. Women in Egypt had a difficult time getting this complicated message across, however, even to the men in their own country. Strong pressures developed for the "retraditionalization" of women, a process whereby women would leave their jobs and return to the full-time care of their children. A hostile attitude toward employed women appeared in the Egyptian media, and women's gains in legal rights started to slip away during the 1980s (Abdel Kader, 1987). The women of Egypt have *not* been "retraditionalized," but the women of some other Muslim countries, such as Iran and Afghanistan, have been less fortunate.

Muslim women in many places are actively debating the restrictions that have been placed on women through Islamic traditions and laws. In the United States, one group of women recently founded *Azizah,* a new magazine for contemporary Muslim women. *Azizah* founding editor, Tayyiba Taylor, says of the practice of veiling: "The objectification of a woman can be done in two ways. . . . You can strip her naked and use her to sell excitement at a basketball game . . . [or] you can cover her up completely and then demand her silence and her absence. . . . and then when she enters public space she becomes sexual. . . . The second way has been mastered by the Islamic society . . . so that, instead of seeing a woman's modesty as a passport to public space, it becomes a further barrier" (Weekend Edition, 2001).

Little attention has been paid in Muslim countries to Islamic requirements for *male* modesty. The Prophet Muhammad's tradition specified that women cover all but their hands and feet, and men cover their bodies from the navel to the knees with garments loose fitting enough to hide the bulge of their genitals. But while Hassiba Boulmerka was vilified for her gold-medal–winning run in shorts, male soccer players who play in shorts are national heroes in many Muslim countries.

Displaying the Female Body

Beauty is often defined as a peculiarly feminine attribute, and preoccupation with appearance is one aspect of stereotypical femininity in many cultural groups. Indeed, Susan Brownmiller's best-selling book *Femininity* (1984) is almost totally concerned with the female body: body shape, hair, voice, clothes, and skin. Her work asserts that, in many ways, we equate femininity with beauty—and beauty with youth. This impression is reinforced if we read the writings of the many women who have clearly feared that in accepting "middle-age spread" or gray hair, they would be losing their femininity. Germaine Greer (1992) suggests that femininity is a "condition of perpetual girlishness" (p. 52).

Among North Americans, physical attractiveness seems to be a more central part of the self-concept for women than for men (Lerner, Orlos, & Knapp, 1976). Many women are dissatisfied with their bodies—a phenomenon that has been found in various cultures (Brownmiller, 1984; Fallon & Rozin, 1985; Forbes, Doroszewicz, Card, & Adams-Curtis, 2004; Tiggemann & Pennington, 1990).

The German researcher Frigga Haug and her colleagues (1987) coined the phrase "body-identified identity" to describe their observation that in a culture that values women according to appearance, women construct their identities mainly through their relation-ship to their bodies. More recently, **objectification theory** (Fredrickson & Roberts, 1997) proposes that a culture's emphasis on treating women's bodies as sexual objects has a vari-ety of negative psychological consequences for women. Foremost among these is that girls and women learn to internalize observers' sexualized perspectives on their bodies: They are socialized to continually monitor their appearance and to worry about how others, especially men, will judge them based on their bodies. In support of this theory, research shows that young women who believe they will be interacting with a man report more shame and anxiety about their bodies than do women who expect to be interacting with a woman (Calogero, 2004). Other researchers have found that even young women who self-identify as feminists, and thus have an alternate way to analyze and understand the cultural messages and to resist negative images of themselves, are still affected by this process. These young women report conflicts between their feminist beliefs and their often uncom-fortable feelings about their own appearance (Rubin, Nemeroff, & Russo, 2004).

Standards of beauty vary across time and place, and women are pressed to conform. As Greer (1992) notes in writing about women's aging, it is often not until a woman begins to lose her youthful beauty that she realizes how much she has counted on her appearance to make her visible and give her influence in her world. Indeed, the evidence is that women's beauty is linked to career success: Women who are less attractive are less likely to succeed in the labor force, particularly in the many fields in which women are clearly "on display" (Wolf, 1991).

Body Shape and Weight

In North America, dieting has become an obsession for many women. In this culture, thin-ness is a major aspect of feminine attractiveness. When some Canadian women students were asked what kind of activities or situations would make them feel less feminine, more than 50 percent of them endorsed the item "being overweight" (Lips, 1986). In the United States, women spend 95 percent of the $2 billion that flow annually to commercial weight loss programs; women also account for 90 percent of prescriptions for diet pills (Solovay, 2000).

When some African American women are asked about satisfaction with their bodies, higher body weight and body mass is related to lower body image satisfaction (Falconer & Neville, 2000; S. M. Harris, 1995; Thomas, 1989). Another study also shows that among African American women, greater body mass is associated with dissatisfaction with body areas, the total body, and physical appearance. But other studies of African American women reveal less evidence of body dissatisfaction and concern with body weight than studies of European American women do (Gray, Ford, & Kelly, 1987; S. M. Harris, 1994). Perhaps some of the difference between Black and White women is due to the ways they are portrayed in the media. Among White women, viewing a lot of mainstream television programming is related to poorer body image; among Black women mainstream television viewing is unrelated to body image, but viewing Black-oriented programming is related to a *healthier* body image (Schooler, Ward, Merriwether, & Caruthers, 2004). Why should exposure to same-race models on television have different effects for White and Black women? Perhaps, the study's authors suggest, it is because the casts of Black-oriented shows include a wider range of female body types than predominantly White casts (Tirod-kar & Jain, 2003).

North American women's quest for thinness is related to strong cultural pressures: Obesity triggers more negative evaluations of women than of men. In one study, hundreds of visitors to a summer fair were shown silhouettes of fat and thin women and men. The fat women were rated more negatively than the fat men (Spigelman & Schultz, 1981). Studies of personal ads carried in U.S. newspapers show that men are more likely than women to emphasize the desired partner's physical appearance (Davis, 1990; Smith, Waldorf, & Trembath, 1990) and are much more likely than women (33.6 percent versus 2.2 percent) to specify that they want someone who is thin (Smith et al., 1990). Interestingly, however, when men who had or had not included the designation "thin" in their personal ads were shown a set of female figures and asked to indicate which were acceptable, these two groups of men differed very little in the figures chosen, and both groups accepted a wide range of body sizes (Miller, Smith, & Trembath, 2000).

Media images of women play a strong role in the development of expectations about thinness. Both girls and boys are apparently affected in their views of women and girls by exposure to media images of thin ideal women (Hargreaves & Tiggemann, 2003; Murnen, Smolak, Mills, & Good, 2003). Women report feeling significantly worse about their bodies after being exposed to thin-ideal media images than after viewing images of average or "plus-sized" women (Groesz, Levine, & Murnen, 2002). And women apparently have learned through the media to associate thinness with life success (Evans, 2003).

Perhaps the association of thinness with life success has some truth to it: American women may even pay an economic price for being fat. One 8-year study of more than 10,000 people showed that fat women were more likely than other women to lose socioeconomic status independent of their family's status and income, and independent of their own scores on achievement tests at adolescence (Gortmaker, 1993). The fat women were also less likely to marry, had household incomes that were lower by $6,710, and were 10 percent more likely to be living in poverty. The relationship between obesity and low socioeconomic status may be a two-way one: Discrimination against fat women tends to decrease their income, and poor women may find it more difficult than richer women to get enough exercise and to follow a healthy diet. The discrimination starts early: One researcher found that parents were less likely to financially support heavy daughters in college—and the effect was most pronounced for daughters of the politically conservative parents who were most likely to be paying for their children's education (Crandall, 1995).

The cultural pressures toward female thinness are not unique to North America. Industrialized societies in general seem to impose thinness on women as a standard of beauty (Sobal & Stunkard, 1989). In contrast, developing societies often link fatness with beauty. In Chapter 1 we noted that the Hima people of Uganda, as well as some other African cultures, have traditionally linked fatness with beauty and prepared young women for marriage by fattening them up (Tiffany, 1982). Another researcher noted the criteria for sexual desirability among the Siriono, a Bolivian Indian people: "Besides being young, a desirable sex partner—especially a woman—should also be fat. She should have big hips, good-sized but firm breasts, and a deposit of fat on her sexual organs. . . . Thin women are summarily dismissed as being *ikaNgi* (bony)" (Holmberg, 1946, p. 181, quoted in Anderson, Crawford, Nadeau, & Lindberg, 1992).

BOX 3.4 WOMEN SHAPING PSYCHOLOGY
Maria Root

the time she had completed her master's thesis, she realized that a different area of psychology was the best place for her—she applied and was accepted into the clinical psychology program at the University of Washington. There, under the mentorship of Stanley Sue, whose support was very important to minority students in that program, she completed a dissertation project on the treatment of disordered eating. In the course of this project, she developed her interest in how women's symptoms were affected by their historical and social context. She also began to focus on the ways in which the gendered experience is related to ethnic and racial identity.

After completing her graduate work, she worked in community mental health and private practice for several years. During this time, she continued to develop her thinking about the importance of identity and social context in women's lives, and about minority mental health, with an emphasis on Asian Americans' mental health. She co-edited a book about feminist therapy and the social issues affecting the lives of women of color (Brown & Root, 1990). She also

Maria Primitiva Paz Root was born in the Philippines in 1955, the oldest child of "an international, intercultural, interclass, and interracial relationship" (APA, 1998, p. 398). Raised mainly in the United States, she graduated from the University of California, Riverside, with a double major in psychology and sociology, and went on to enroll in a Ph.D. program in experimental psychology. However, by

Some researchers have also argued that antifat attitudes are rooted in cultural notions of responsibility and blame. Christian Crandall and Rebecca Martinez (1996), comparing the antifat attitudes of students in Mexico and the United States, found that Mexican students were less concerned about their own weight and more accepting of fat people than U.S. students were. This difference appeared to be linked to an ideological difference between the two cultures whereby U.S. respondents, but not Mexicans, held individuals responsible for being fat and blamed them for not controlling their weight. This pattern may be part of a broader difference between the two cultures: The United States is an independence-oriented culture with strong beliefs that individuals control their fate,

---

BOX 3.4 WOMEN SHAPING PSYCHOLOGY (continued)
Maria Root

began to focus increasingly on multiracial or mixed-heritage identity issues—a focus that was grounded in her own experience. As a visiting professor at the University of Hawaii, she began the work that would ultimately lead to the publication of *Racially Mixed People in America* (Root, 1992), an edited collection of articles about mixed-heritage people, by contributors of mixed heritage or from interracial families. As the first work of this kind, this book had an enormous impact. It received a human rights award from the Gustavus Myers Center and it became "required reading for the U.S. Census Bureau as it struggle[d] to determine how to inquire into racial identity classifications for the year 2000 census" (APA, 1998, p. 398).

In 1995, Root joined the faculty of the American Ethnic Studies program at the University of Washington. There, she continued her work on mixed-heritage ethnic identity and on women, producing a flood of publications on these issues. In 1997, she was presented with the American Psychological Association's award for Distinguished Contribution to Psychology in the Public Interest. Currently, she works as a clinical psychologist in Seattle, Washington. Her recent book, *Love's Revolution: Interracial Marriage,* based on interviews with 200 people from a broad range of ethnic and racial backgrounds, has been described as an insightful and comprehensive analysis of interracial marriage.

Read More about Maria Root

American Psychological Association (1998). Awards for distinguished contribution to psychology for the public interest, 1997. *American Psychologist, 53*(4), 398–403.

Read What She Has Written

Brown, L., & Root, M.P.P. (Eds). (1990). *Diversity and complexity in feminist therapy.* New York: Haworth Press.
Root, M. P. P. (Ed.). (1992). *Racially mixed people in America.* Newbury Park, CA: Sage.
Root, M. P. P. (1994). Mixed race women. In L. Comas Diaz & B. Greene (Eds.), *Women of color and mental health: the healing tapestry* (pp. 455–478). New York: Guilford Press.
Root, M. P. P. (2001). *Love's revolution: Interracial marriage.* Philadelphia, PA: Temple University Press.

---

whereas Mexico, a more interdependence-oriented culture, places less emphasis on individual self-determination.

Whatever the cultural preference for a particular female body type, women's identification with their bodies leads to frantic, often painful, attempts to achieve the ideal weight and shape. In the days of the corset, women subjected themselves to the perpetual squeeze of 20 to 80 pounds of pressure and were literally unable to take a deep breath. Today, women diet themselves into illness and even death. The constant monitoring of her body robs a woman of the energy for accomplishment and makes her perpetually self-conscious.

Yet our bodies are, in one sense, the expression of our genetic inheritance. As Clarissa Pinkola Estés (1992) queries in her discussion of women's bodies, how can a woman retain her pride in the body type that was passed on to her by her ancestors if she is caught up in harsh judgments about her body's acceptability?

> If she is taught to hate her own body, how can she love her mother's body that has the same configuration as hers?—her grandmother's body, the bodies of her daughters as well? How can she love the bodies of other women (and men) close to her who have inherited the bodies of their ancestors? To attack a woman thusly destroys her rightful pride of affiliation with her own people . . . (p. 203)

Using herself as an example, Estés illustrates the impact of cultural perceptions on body image satisfaction. As a child she had been told that her large body signified her lack of self-control. As an adult, she visited the home of her ancestral people in Tehuantepec, Mexico, where she found "a tribe with giant women who were strong, flirtatious, and commanding in their size" (p. 201). These women told her that she was not quite fat enough, and exhorted her to try harder. As a woman, they said, she was made in the image of *la tierra,* the earth, round because it holds so much.

Estés also tells the story of her African American friend Opalanga, who was teased as a child for being tall and who was told that the gap between her front teeth signified that she was a liar. Opalanga too had traveled to the home of her ancestors, in her case to Gambia, West Africa. Her ancestral tribe, she discovered, was filled with very tall, slender people like herself. Many of them had a gap between their front teeth as well—a gap they told her was named "opening of God" and was regarded as a sign of wisdom.

Face, Skin, and Hair

A girl making the transition to adolescence and beginning to be self-conscious about feminine beauty focuses anxiously on her skin. At that dangerous age when the face can suddenly erupt into blemishes, she may scan the mirror hourly for signs of imperfections. Later, as she makes the journey into middle age, she may scan it just as anxiously for wrinkles.

The face and the complexion has often been seen as the key to female beauty, and the cosmetics industry makes millions on women's desire for flawless skin. Western European tradition equates fair skin with beauty and includes many glowing references to peaches-and-cream and lily-white complexions, white shoulders, alabaster brows, and pale beauty. Ladies in the royal courts of Europe would powder their faces, diligently avoid the sun, and even eat small quantities of arsenic in order to achieve the requisite pallor (Brownmiller, 1984). In feudal Japan too, aristocratic women used powder to appear lighter-skinned. Fair, blue-eyed, silky-haired blondes are still a mainstay of Hollywood's crafted images of female perfection, and children still read that Snow White was "the fairest of them all."

Women of dark or olive complexions have sometimes been frustrated because they cannot match the standards of beauty promoted by White culture (Collins, 1991). African American college women who are dissatisfied with their skin color are also likely to be dissatisfied with their body image (Falconer & Neville, 2000). In the United States, the writings of African American women illustrate the pain of perpetually facing a standard of beauty that is shaped by White images. Toni Morrison's novel *The Bluest Eye* (1970) shows a young African American girl confronting the realization that "the world agreed a blue-eyed, yellow-haired, pink-skinned doll was what every girl-child treasured." Maya Angelou's autobiographical *I Know Why the Caged Bird Sings* (1969) opens with a young girl's fantasy, which prefigures the Whoopi Goldberg skit mentioned at the beginning of this chapter: "Wouldn't they be surprised when one day I woke out of my black ugly dream, and my real hair, which was long and blond, would take the place of the kinky mass that Momma wouldn't let me straighten?" (p. 2).

Companies such as Johnson Products and SoftSheen, the makers of cosmetics for Black women, have amassed fortunes selling products that are supposed to lighten skin and straighten hair. Cosmetics designed especially for Black women have been big business since the era of Madam C. J. Walker. Walker, the Louisiana-born daughter of former slaves, became the first woman (of any race) to make herself a millionaire when she developed and marketed a secret formula for hair care for Black women in the 1910s. Walker started out mixing soaps and ointments in her home washtub and selling them door to door. Before her death she was employing more than 3,000 workers—mostly Black women. She was adamant, however, that her products were not "hair straighteners" and that she was not in the business of helping Black women to look White (Russell, Wilson, & Hall, 1992). A stamp honoring Madam Walker was issued by the U.S. Postal Service in 1998.

Many dark-skinned women have experienced rejection by others, even by members of their own racial or ethnic group, because of the notion that "fair is beautiful." History tells of color-conscious African American church congregations that would not welcome new members who failed the paper-bag test: Put an arm inside a brown paper bag, and show that the skin on the arm was lighter than the color of the bag. Studies of dating and marriage in the Black community suggest that some Black men still view a light-skinned partner as an asset and consider light-skinned women more attractive than dark-skinned women (Russell et al., 1992).

Not only complexion, but also facial features have been a source of anxiety for women whose faces are different from the ideals of beauty promoted by the media. Women pluck their eyebrows to make them seem thinner, line their eyes to make them seem larger, change their hairstyles to make their faces seem thinner, their cheekbones higher. More drastically, hundreds of thousands of women in developed countries have cosmetic surgery every year to reshape a nose that seems too long, cheeks that seem too fat, a jawline that doesn't seem quite right. About 87 percent of the 244,370 face-lifts performed in the United States in 2000 were performed on women; American women are far more likely than men to have such procedures as nose surgery, chemical peels, and eyelid surgery (American Academy of Cosmetic Surgery, 2001). The women seeking such surgery are often trying to move in the direction of homogeneity with the dominant culture's ideal of beauty. Caucasian women try to get rid of wrinkles and to make their faces more youthful. Asian American women in large numbers have opted for eyelid surgery that makes their eyes seem more round and "Western," and African American women have favored lip and nose reduction operations (Kaw, 1997).

Not surprisingly, a relationship appears to exist between cultural variables, such as racial identity, and women's body attitudes. For example, African American women who hold more positive views of Black identity also hold more favorable views of their appearance (Falconer & Neville, 2000; S. M. Harris, 1995). And Chinese Americans who identify most strongly as Chinese indicate greater satisfaction with their bodies and put more emphasis on behavior and psychological traits when assessing female attractiveness than do their more "Americanized" counterparts (Cheng, 2001). Clearly, women's investment in, and attitudes toward, their appearance are shaped by the values promoted in the culture that surrounds them.

Women in many times and places have been pulled, squeezed, bleached, painted, and starved (or force-fed) into the "right" appearance. We have been judged by our bodies and have judged ourselves by them. The female body can be a source of joy and pride and pleasure, but research tells us that for many women it is the opposite. Women are frequently ashamed of or embarrassed by their shape, their skin, their hair, their menstrual changes, their physical reactions to pregnancy. This sense of shame happens most when women's value is linked only to her attractiveness to men. Perhaps poetry can do a better job than psychology of capturing the sense of self-acceptance that a woman can feel as she comes to terms with her body. A character in Ntozake Shange's play *for colored girls who have considered suicide / when the rainbow is enuf* (1976) sums up this self-acceptance in a few words:

> here is what i have . . .
> poems
> big thighs
> lil tits
> &
> so much love

SUMMARY

Having a female body is heavily weighted with significance, first because it defines an individual as female in the eyes of society. At, and sometimes even before, birth, infants' anatomy is used to classify them as female or male. The series of prenatal steps through which that anatomy develops—chromosomes, gonads, hormones, internal reproductive structures, external genitalia—usually proceeds in a consistent manner and produces an infant that appears obviously female or male. However, in some cases, this biological unfolding takes a female direction at some stages and a male direction at others, producing an individual who is intersexed. In North America and other Western cultures, an intersexed infant is assigned as female or male. Often, surgery is performed to make the child's body fit her/his assigned sex.

Researchers have queried whether the physiological processes that differentiate female and male bodies also differentiate the brain according to sex. In particular, the hypothesis that prenatal hormone levels may affect brain organization differently in females and males has been explored. Currently, there is controversy over the existence of sex differences in brain lateralization and in the shape and size of the corpus callosum. One important thing to remember in evaluating these approaches to understanding sex differences and similarities in brain organization is that brains are very plastic and may be affected by hormones and other factors throughout life.

Although our sex is defined and labeled at birth, we construct our gender identities and roles through a process of self-definition and validation by others. This process is inevitably bound up with our bodies; for example, if we look "feminine" it is easier to form a female gender identity and behave in ways consistent with feminine roles because our appearance causes people to treat us in ways consistent with them. However, sometimes individuals can and do form gender identities that contrast with their bodies. Controversy remains over the extent to which assigning and rearing a child to be one sex can overcome biological and anatomical indications that s/he is the other sex. Many cases exist in which intersexed individuals, raised as male or female, formed gender identities that matched the sex in which they were reared. However, such rearing usually includes altering the individual's body, through surgery and/or hormones, to make it match the sex to which the person is assigned.

The female body is defined in large part through reproductive processes, and women have been largely defined through their bodies in many times and places. Menarche is often seen to mark the beginning of womanhood, and with it come a host of rules and restrictions associated with femininity. The processes of menstruation, pregnancy, and childbirth are fraught with meaning in most cultures. These most female of biological processes are sometimes sources of power for women, but they are often also the sources of negative stereotypes and restrictions.

Much emphasis has been placed on controlling women by controlling their bodies. An example is the practice of female genital mutilation, which is done to keep women's sexuality in check. Virginity testing is also carried out in some cultures to ensure that a woman does not engage in illicit sexual activity. Laws governing abortion often give a woman no choice about continuing a pregnancy.

Women's bodies and the temptations they may provide are also an excuse for confining women. The veiling and seclusion of women in some countries—hiding women's bodies and restricting their ability to go into public places—is rationalized as a way to prevent any illegitimate sexual activities.

On the flip side of such restrictions is the emphasis on displaying the female body. No matter how much or how little of their bodies women are allowed to show, we are taught to be very concerned with appearance. Women are supposed to be beautiful, although the definition of beauty is different in every culture. Women in Western countries often express dissatisfaction with their bodies, and women far outnumber men among people who seek out cosmetic surgery.

KEY TERMS

intersexual	progesterone	corpus callosum
sex chromosomes	androgen	brain lateralization
gonads	testosterone	gender identity
sex hormones	Müllerian Inhibiting	transsexual
estrogen	Substance (MIS)	core gender identity

behavioral gender	ovulation	female genital mutilation
differences	PMS	(FGM)
CAH	PMDD	clitoroplasty
AIS	menstrual joy	objectification theory
menarche	menstrual synchrony	
menstruation	postpartum depression	

DISCUSSION QUESTIONS

What exactly is a woman? What biological and/or social qualities define a person as female?

What do you think the research on intersexuals tells us about femininity and masculinity?

How would you compare the practices of female genital mutilation as practiced in some times and places to control women's sexuality and the practice of clitoroplasty currently used to make an individual look more like a woman?

Why do you think some cultures treat menstruation as something embarrassing? How might it change the culture if menstruation were looked at as something to proclaim ("I'm menstruating today!") instead of hide?

What parallels are there across cultures in the ways that have been or are used to control women by controlling their bodies?

FOR ADDITIONAL READING

Angier, Natalie (1999). *Woman: An intimate geography.* Boston: Houghton Mifflin. Writing in a clear and engaging way about the female body, Angier takes on topics that range from intersexuality to breasts, pregnancy, hormones, hysterectomy, and menopause.

Bornstein, Kate. (1994). *Gender outlaw.* New York: Routledge. Bornstein talks about the restrictions of the either–or gender categories and tells her own story of rejecting the category into which she was born.

Dirie, Waris, with Cathleen Miller (1998). *Desert flower: The extraordinary journey of a desert nomad.* New York: William Morrow. The author, who grew up in Somalia, tells the story of her girlhood and her life since she fled that country. Included is her account of her own clitorodectomy when she was a child. Dirie now has a career as an international supermodel and as a United Nations Special Ambassador for the Elimination of Female Genital Mutilation.

Fausto-Sterling, Anne (2000). *Sexing the body: Gender politics and the construction of sexuality.* New York: Basic Books. A biologist examines the history of our categories of sex and gender, concluding that what we think we know about femaleness, maleness, heterosexuality, and homosexuality has been shaped by cultural attitudes.

Russell, Kathy, Wilson, Midge, and Hall, Ronald. (1992). *The color complex: The politics of skin color among African Americans.* A historical and sociopolitical examination of how standards of appearance have been applied within the African American community and how those standards have been shaped by the wider context.

Ward, Martha C. (1998). *A sounding of women: Autobiographies from unexpected places.* Boston: Allyn and Bacon. A collection of autobiographical sketches of a very diverse set of women. Included is one by an anonymous Native American woman, who gives a remarkable account of her introduction to womanhood at the onset of menstruation, and Egyptian writer Nawal el Saadawi's account of some parts of her life, including her childhood clitoridectomy.

Wolf, Naomi. (1991). *The beauty myth.* New York: Morrow. The author examines how the necessity to be beautiful is used to control American women.

WEB RESOURCES

Intersex Society of North America. This Web page contains basic information, latest news, frequently asked questions, and links to other Web sites on intersexuality, including sites based in Australia, Sweden, Japan, New Zealand, and the United Kingdom. **www.isna.org**

Stop FGM! Online practical information about FGM for women who are or have been affected by it, their physicians, other health care providers, social workers, counselors, teachers, and attorneys. **www.stopfgm.org**

Menstrual Monday. Web headquarters of a group that has established a yearly holiday in honor of menstruation. The site contains recommendations for "Flofilms," "menstrumonials" from people who have successfully celebrated Menstrual Monday, poems, artwork, and political commentary—all with a menstrual theme. **www.moltx.org**

CHAPTER 4

Growing Up Female II: Expectations, Images, and Identities

CHAPTER OUTLINE

A story in the *Washington Post* concerning the National Conference of Black Physics Students begins with the description of a 20-year-old memory by Dr. Cynthia McIntyre, a young physics professor. She recalls an *Ebony* magazine article she read as a youngster: a profile of Shirley Ann Jackson, the first African American woman to earn a doctorate at the Massachusetts Institute of Technology.

"Nuclear Physicist at Fermi Lab," read the headline. "Young Ph.D. holds her own in white male-dominated world."

That image of this woman was frozen in my mind," said McIntyre . . . "I can still describe in great detail the pictures, which I haven't seen in years" (Tousignant, 1995).

Years later, McIntyre followed in Shirley Ann Jackson's footsteps, becoming one of a handful of African American students to earn a doctorate in physics from MIT in 1980. The article she had read as a child helped her to picture herself as a physicist; that image of herself became a magnet that drew her into physics despite the many barriers and the relative lack of role models she encountered. It was critical in helping her to construct a **possible self** as a physicist.

The term *possible self* was coined by Hazel Markus and Paula Nurius (1986) to describe the way an individual pictures personalized images of the self in various future roles, selves she or he might possibly become. According to Markus and Nurius, a person's pool of possible selves is based on what she sees around her: categories made salient by media images, people she encounters and observes, and her social experience. A person who has never met or heard of a nuclear physicist will have difficulty imagining herself in such a role. A girl who sees only male airline pilots, priests, or corporation presidents will not easily construct possible selves that encompass these occupations.

For each of us, our collection of possible selves is an intersection of our notions of "who I am" and "who I could be." Our possible selves reflect our identity and our expectations. They provide concrete guidelines as we make choices and shape our future.

One important function of a possible self is to act as a motivator. If a person has no concrete vision of herself in a particular role, she may have difficulty keeping up the hard work necessary to achieve that role. As one college student said to me just before she dropped out of her engineering program, "I'm doing well, and I like the courses, but *I just can't picture myself as an engineer.*"

How does an individual's interaction with her social surroundings shape her notion of who she is, how she should behave, and who she might become? How does a person's categorization as female or male figure in the development of her or his sense of self and the behavior patterns she or he adopts? Psychologists have proposed a variety of theories to explain this process of social development. The theories focus on the intersection between the development of roles (habitual patterns of behavior) and identities (the sense of self).

Psychological theories about how individuals develop identities and characteristic patterns of behavior usually include some premises about how gender can make a difference in this process. How does an individual develop behavior patterns that are culturally acceptable for her/his gender (that is, fit into the culturally approved **gender role**)? How does a child learn to think of herself as female or himself as male (**gender identity**)? Such theories may emphasize intrapsychic forces (psychoanalytic theories), biological processes (evolutionary theory), direct socialization processes (social learning theories), the individual's role in conceptualizing environmental expectations (cognitive development and self-schema theories), or social structure and roles (social roles theory). We will look at each of these in turn.

Most theories acknowledge the importance of the images of femininity that are presented to girls as they grow up. These images vary across cultures and are presented in a variety of ways: parental and other role models, stories and oral histories, television shows and music videos. Following a brief overview of the theories mentioned above, we shall examine the images and role models for femininity that are presented to girls in various cultures.

As each individual develops a sense of self and a set of behaviors, she or he is blending a variety of identities. A young woman may think of herself in terms of her gender, her ethnicity, her nationality, her religion, her sexual orientation, her talents, her accomplishments, her appearance, her relationships. In the final section of this chapter, we shall focus on the processes of identity formation—the complex matter of blending gender, ethnic, and other identities.

Theories of How Gender Shapes Who We Are

As noted in Chapter 2, a theory seems "reasonable" to the extent that it fits in with the accepted ideas of the time and place. The degree of acceptance conferred on the theories to be discussed here has varied depending on popular notions of women and femininity, trends within psychology, and other aspects of the cultural milieu. One of the most controversial of all theories of gender and personality development has been the psychoanalytic approach developed by Freud in the early 20th century.

Psychoanalytic/Identification Theories

Sigmund Freud, a physician whose career started in Vienna, Austria, in the 1880s, proposed that human beings are not strictly rational in their behavior, or even knowledgeable about their own motives. He argued that much of human behavior is governed by unconscious instinctual motives involving sex and aggression, and that human personality has its origins in early childhood relations between children and their parents. **Psychoanalytic theory,** the approach to personality founded by Freud, had a big impact on psychology's views of women. A major feature of psychoanalytic theory was Freud's belief that from a very early age, little girls inevitably learned to feel inferior to and envious of males. Critics of Freud later argued, however, that his interpretation of what his patients told him was shaped by his own masculine biases and the patriarchal culture in which he lived.

Sigmund Freud Freud (1924/1960) theorized that children moved through three stages of psychosexual development: the oral, anal, and phallic stages, during the first 5 or 6 years of life. At each stage, strong pleasurable feelings (sexual feelings, according to Freud) were associated with particular body zones. Sucking was very pleasurable during the oral stage, elimination during the anal stage, and masturbation during the phallic stage.

The important divergence between females and males supposedly took place during the phallic stage, when children's appropriate feminine or masculine identification was precipitated by the development and resolution of the **Oedipus complex.**

Freud named the Oedipus complex after an ancient Greek myth. In this myth, as presented in a trio of plays by Sophocles written in the 4th century B.C., Oedipus kills King Laius and takes over his kingdom of Thebes. He marries Jocasta, Laius's widow. The two reign as husband and wife, producing two daughters and two sons. Only later does a shocked Oedipus learn that King Laius was in fact his own father, and that Jocasta, Oedipus's wife, is also his mother. Upon making this dreadful discovery, the distraught Oedipus puts out his eyes and Jocasta hangs herself. Blind, Oedipus spends the remainder of his life wandering the land, accompanied by his dutiful daughter (and half-sister) Antigone. Antigone serves as Oedipus's eyes. Because of his dependence on her, she sets aside her own needs and devotes herself to him.

Freud read this myth as a parable of a son's incestuous attraction to his mother. He argued that during the phallic stage (between the ages of 3 and 6), a boy develops an intense attraction and attachment to his mother. He sees his father as a rival for his mother's affections and feels hostile toward him. But he cannot acknowledge these negative feelings toward his father. Instead, he unconsciously projects his hostile feelings onto his father, thus coming to believe that his father sees *him* as a rival.

To the small boy, the father seems a powerful and terrifying rival. The boy becomes fearful of what his father may do to him. His fear crystallizes around the possibility of castration. Why? Because, in this phallic stage, the penis is the source of intense pleasure; losing it is one of the worst things that could happen. Fueling the boy's castration anxiety is his discovery that not everyone has a penis. At this stage, he is likely to notice for the first time that women and girls are apparently missing this important organ. According to Freud, the boy's fear becomes so intense that he is literally forced to resolve the Oedipus complex in order to dispel it. He finds resolution by identifying with his father (accepting his father as a model and incorporating many features of his father's personality into his own) and squelching his desire for his mother. In the end, his feelings toward women are contemptuous or fearful or both; he unconsciously blames women for the trouble "caused" by the mother.

If the little boy is propelled into masculine identification by the fear of losing his penis, what of the little girl? Freud described the penis (actually, the lack of a penis) as central to her development as well. During the phallic stage, she notices that boys have a penis and she does not. The realization that she lacks something so important produces what Freud (1925/1974) called "penis envy." She feels that she has been castrated, and she blames her mother (who, she has noticed, is also lacking a penis), withdrawing her affection from her. She develops a sense of inferiority, contempt for her own sex, and general feelings of jealousy. She rejects masturbation, since her own organ, the clitoris, is so inferior to the penis.

Freud argued at one time that penis envy caused girls to enter a female version of the Oedipus complex, the **Electra complex:** attraction to the father and jealousy of the mother. He claimed, "She gives up her wish for a penis and puts in place of it a wish for a child; and *with this purpose in view* she takes her father as a love object. Her mother becomes the object of her jealousy" (1925/1974, p. 34). She resolves the complex gradually by realizing that she can never possess her father. So she grudgingly reestablishes her feminine identification with her mother and concentrates on becoming an attractive love object for some other man.

If Freud's story of female development, with its focus on the lack of a penis, sounds somewhat labored and improbable to us, we should note, in all fairness, that it eventually came to seem improbable to him as well. Freud later believed that he had overstated the parallels between the sexes in terms of the Oedipus complex; he never developed another model to replace it, however. Thus his story of female psychosexual development has influenced psychoanalytic therapists and theorists for years. One consequence has been a tragic tendency, questioned only in recent years, to assume that women who spoke of being molested by their fathers were describing not real occurrences, but fantasies based on unconscious incestuous wishes.

Karen Horney Horney was an early member of Freud's circle and a well-respected European psychoanalyst when she began to critique Freud's theory of female development. She felt that he had overemphasized the role of the penis in the psychology of both sexes, and she discounted the idea that girls automatically view their bodies as inferior. Furthermore, she noted, male envy of the female womb and breasts was as important and intense among her therapeutic clients, if not more so, than female envy of the male penis (Horney, 1926/1973).

According to Horney, many of men's behaviors could be explained by this envy of the female capacity for pregnancy and the suckling of babies. For instance, men's strong desire to achieve and create could be an overcompensation for their inability to match women's creative process of reproduction. Men's tendency to be contemptuous of women could also be an expression of their unconscious sense of inferiority and envy.

Horney proposed that a girl's psychosexual development centered on her own, rather than the male's, anatomy. A girl's rejection of the female role could be caused, she argued, by an unconscious fear of vaginal injury through penetration—not by resentment over lack

craziness, in my opinion !

of a penis. Thus Horney's critique of Freud repudiated the notion that women's development was driven in a major way by envy of the male body.

In her later work, Horney moved away from the early psychoanalytic focus on the biologically based instinctual drives of sex and aggression. Instead, she emphasized the cultural context in which children developed (Westkott, 1986). This approach provided her with a new way to analyze the situation that Freud had dubbed the Oedipus complex. She theorized that the social environment in which a child was raised could create harm in two ways: **devaluation** (parents' failure to respect the child as a unique and worthwhile person) and **sexualization** (adults' taking a sexual approach to the child, an "emotional hot-house" atmosphere). Horney argued that a child's attachment to one parent and jealousy toward the other was not a sign of Freud's Oedipus complex, but the child's anxious way of coping with devaluation and sexualization practiced by the parents (Horney, 1939).

In a society that valued males over females, girls were more vulnerable than boys to the insecurities caused by devaluation and sexualization, Horney maintained. Girls might well adopt feelings of inferiority if they were clearly valued less than their brothers. If they were treated, as many daughters were, as if their sexuality were the most important aspect of their identity, they were likely to become anxious and dependent. Thus, although Horney constructed her story of female development within the family framework emphasized by psychoanalysis, she became one of the first members of that school to recognize the effect of cultural variables on these family dynamics.

Nancy Chodorow Freudian theory has often been labeled **phallocentric**—centered on the penis. Horney, by contrast, adopted a perspective that was in many ways **gyno-centric**—centered on the female womb. Freud's theory emphasized the critical importance of the father–child relationship; Horney and some of her contemporaries focused more on the mother–child relationship.

Sociologist Nancy Chodorow (1978) elaborated on the latter emphasis to propose a theory of psychosexual development based primarily on the early mother–child bond. She focused on the pre-Oedipal relationship with the mother as a critical time in the process.

Freud had noted that the pre-Oedipal phase of attachment to the mother played a more important role in female than in male development. Chodorow and some other feminist psychoanalytic theorists such as Dorothy Dinnerstein (1976) have directed their attention to this phase. Chodorow has argued that since women do most of the primary parenting of young children, girls, but not boys, experience their closest adult caregiver as someone they can identify with. They develop an emotional closeness with the mother that boys cannot experience.

In Chodorow's view, the consequences of this early difference in the ease of identification and closeness with the caregiver are profound. As adults, she argues, women try unsuccessfully in their intimate relationships with men to reexperience the emotional unity they felt with their mothers. Men, not having experienced this sense of unity as children, do not have the same relational needs. Thus attempts at intimate relationships between women and men often prove emotionally frustrating. depressing

Moreover, because of the early attachment to the mother, boys' formation of a masculine identity is a negative process involving separation and denial. Because of boys' need to separate from the mother, the process of identity formation is more difficult for them

BOX 4.1 WOMEN SHAPING PSYCHOLOGY
Karen Horney (1885–1952)

Born in Germany to an affectionate mother of noble ancestry and a stern, remote Norwegian sea captain father, Karen Danielsen soon discovered that she would have to forge an intellectual life for herself if she wanted to be happy. Her parents preferred her brother, and her father's derogatory comments about her appearance and her intelligence continued to haunt her into adulthood. Deciding that, if she could not be beautiful, she could certainly be smart, Karen decided to study medicine. She applied for advanced schooling to prepare for medical school, but her father initially refused to grant her his permission and to pay the tuition. She finally prevailed upon him to do so only

with the help of her mother, teachers, brother, and aunt and with the promise that, if he acceded to this request, she would never ask him for anything else.

In 1906, she entered medical school at the University of Freiburg, one of the first universities in Germany to admit women, where she became one of only 58 women among 2,350 students. She excelled in her studies, and while in medical school she met her future husband, economics student Oskar Horney. She married Oskar in 1909 and gave birth to three daughters while completing the rest of her medical studies. Working flat out to juggle the demands of motherhood, marriage, her profession, and her unusual role as an ambitious, intellectual (and therefore, in her society, deviant) woman, Karen Horney struggled constantly against exhaustion.

Horney joined the Berlin Psychoanalytic Society and soon became one of its most prominent members. She opened her own private practice and soon gained a reputation as one of the best training analysts in Europe. However, she soon became uneasy with the orthodox psychoanalytic approach to women's psychology. In a 1924 paper, she questioned the Freudian assumption that women felt their bodies were inferior and became one of the first psychoanalysts to explore the role of culture on psychosexual development. Several years later, in a reply to Freud's theory that feminine psychology could be explained by penis envy and the awareness of having been castrated, Horney (1926)

BOX 4.1 WOMEN SHAPING PSYCHOLOGY (continued)
Karen Horney (1885–1952)

wrote a stronger paper: *The Flight from Womanhood,* in which she argued that the Freudian view was a product of male bias and that men's ideas of female inferiority stemmed from their own unconscious fear that they might be "reabsorbed" into the vagina. In this essay, she also wrote about women's sexuality, asserting the pleasurable aspects of clitoral stimulation, and about boys' envy of motherhood.

Horney's rebellion against Freudian views earned her some supporters, as well as many enemies. She continued to expand on her theory of female development, becoming an increasingly controversial figure. In 1932, the same year she moved to Chicago, she published *The Dread of Woman,* in which she argued strongly that the castration anxiety felt by males was due, not to a fear of loss of the penis, but to a dread of and desire not to become a woman. In this paper, she asserted that "it was the man, not the woman who suffered a psychic wound from which he could not recover and who felt anxiety over his physical inferiority. As a means of compensation the male then demeaned the female sex as a whole, deciding that women were not his equal in the sexual, ethical, or intellectual sphere" (Garrison, 1981, p. 684). Freud vigorously disputed her arguments, and his final word on the subject was simply that "a female analyst who has not been sufficiently convinced of her own desire for a penis [will] also fail[s] to assign an adequate importance to that factor in her patients" (quoted in Garrison, 1981, p. 685).

Horney was eventually disqualified as a training analyst by the New York Psychoanalytic Society and lost many of her allies because of her rejection of some aspects of psychoanalysis. However, she gained fame and wealth through her writing and continued to lead an active professional life until her death from cancer in 1952. Her challenge to Freudian orthodoxy was a pivotal factor in shaping psychological debate and theory concerning women.

Read More about Karen Horney

Garrison, Dee (1981). Karen Horney and feminism. *Signs, 6*(4), 672–691.

O'Connell, Agnes N. (1990). Karen Horney (1885–1952). In A. N. O'Connell & N. F. Russo (Eds.), *Women in psychology: A biobibliographic sourcebook* (pp. 184–196). New York: Greenwood Press.

Kimball, Meredith (1995). Female from the start: Karen Horney and maternal feminisms. In M. Kimball, *Feminist visions of gender similarities and differences* (pp. 53–78). Binghamton, NY: The Haworth Press.

Read What She Wrote

Horney, K. (1926). The flight from womanhood: The masculinity complex in women as viewed by men and women. *International Journal of Psychoanalysis, 7,* 324–339.

Horney, K. (1932). The dread of woman. *International Journal of Psychoanalysis, 13,* 348–360.

Horney, K. (1967). *Feminine psychology.* H. Kelman (Ed.), New York: Norton.

than for girls. And <u>males' difficulty with identification ultimately creates problems</u> for <u>females</u>. Boys and men devalue femininity in their flight from it, creating a consensus among themselves that femininity is inferior. As girls mature, they encounter this societal notion of femininity as inferior, and they become ambivalent about identifying with a negatively valued gender category.

Chodorow attributes the differences in female and male relational needs to family arrangements that give primacy to the mother–child bond. She suggests that if parenting were more equally shared between women and men, such differences would be reduced. Close identification with the primary caregiver would no longer be unique to girls, eliminating the necessity for boys to devalue femininity as they struggle to form their own identity through separation. Presumably, this would pave the way for more egalitarian and emotionally satisfying relationships between adult women and men.

The thesis that shared parenting would result in more egalitarian gender roles and relationships is an interesting one. Little evidence exists to support or debunk it, however. It has been argued that without a change in the surrounding social context, changes in parenting arrangements can have little impact (Kaschak, 1992). For example, a daughter being raised by a single father with strong patriarchal attitudes in a culture that devalues women is unlikely to escape the ambivalence about feminine identity. A son being raised under the same conditions might end up with an extra-strong dose of attitudes that women are inferior.

The question of whether family roles or societal values are the primary cause of notions of feminine inferiority is a chicken-and-egg one. Chodorow argues that family parenting arrangements create conditions that result in the entrenchment of certain societal attitudes about women. Ellyn Kaschak argues that family structure and parental attitudes merely reflect the patriarchal attitudes that are prevalent in society; real change must begin at the level of social values. It appears that both arguments are correct, since families exist in a societal context, both influencing and being influenced by that context.

Chodorow (1999) has further explored the issue of context in her more recent theorizing. She notes that children develop their fantasies about gender from a host of culturally available images, not only from parent–child relations. Further, she says, notions of gender vary widely along with culture and include not only expectations that females and males will be different, but also that femaleness and maleness differ in their value and power.

Ellyn Kaschak In an attempt to develop a new psychology of women's experience, Kaschak (1992) reexamined the Oedipal myth to look for fresh insights. She noted that Freud and other psychoanalysts had approached the story from a masculine viewpoint, focusing on the plight and pain of Oedipus and treating the female characters as peripheral. What kind of theory would we get, she asked, if we focused instead on Antigone, the dutiful daughter who gave up all chance of an independent life in order to be blind Oedipus's guide and companion?

Antigone is seen mainly as an extension of Oedipus—as his eyes. Her own needs and emotions are not explored in the story. Kaschak argues that for men in a patriarchal society, the Oedipal analogy is that through early experience the male learns to regard females, beginning with the mother, as extensions of himself, as people who exist to gratify him.

The male soon extends what Kaschak calls his attitude of **infantile grandiosity** from the mother to other women, eventually to wife and daughters.

The Oedipal male experiences himself as subsuming others, as superior to females, as entitled to gratification from women. He is driven by a need for power and by competition with other males—"an eternal adolescent in an adolescent culture" (p. 73). Kaschak posits that this Oedipal complex is rarely resolved in a patriarchal society, which reinforces these tendencies in individual men. When resolution does occur, however, it is characterized by the relinquishment of grandiosity and the sense of entitlement and by the ability to look at women as full persons. In resolving the Oedipal complex, the man "discovers that he is not a king, just a human being in a world of other humans and living creatures, all of equal importance with him" (p. 73).

To understand women in a patriarchal society, Kaschak argues, we can use this story to examine the **Antigone complex.** In a patriarchal family, the daughter's early attachment to the mother is intertwined with learning that men are central and women are secondary. This is what Kaschak labels the "early Antigonal phase." The daughter's loyalty to her mother is mixed with rage against her mother's complicity with this hierarchy. The girl learns to limit her expectations and to deprecate herself. As she grows up, she learns to experience herself as an extension of the men in her life: first her father, then her husband or partner. She becomes compulsively oriented toward relationships and treats her own identity as secondary. She becomes concerned with appearance as a central aspect of her worth.

If a woman manages to resolve the Antigone complex in adulthood, she rediscovers positive relationships with women and develops her own sense of identity. She stops making males central and nurtures her own vision. According to Kaschak, in a patriarchal society many pressures block a woman's resolution of the Antigone complex, and women must work together to avoid being "engulfed in masculine meanings." In retelling the Oedipal story from the feminine point of view, Kaschak herself strikes a blow against such engulfment.

Psychoanalysis and Cultural Difference   Freud used the Oedipus myth as an analogy for family relationships in his own culture—which was unabashedly patriarchal. The other theorists discussed here, Horney, Chodorow, and Kaschak, have also, in different ways, used this approach to understand relationships in a patriarchal culture. It may be considerably less relevant for analyzing relationships in cultures where the father is not so automatically the authority in the family and men are not so automatically seen as "in charge." The psychoanalytic model also assumes that the child develops appropriately gendered behavior as a consequence of identification with a same-sex adult model in the context of a nuclear family. The assumption that most children grow up in such families is untenable, even in Western industrialized countries where the nuclear family is often idealized as normative. For example, it is common in African American families for several generations of women to share in childcare tasks, making the assumption of a single female role model inappropriate (Reid, Haritos, Kelly, & Holland, 1995). As Reid and her colleagues note:

> [P]articularly problematic is [the] assumption that a child has one model and one set of values. In today's world of single parents, lesbian and gay parents, blended families resulting from divorce and remarriage, and multigenerational families, nuclear families are no longer the

norm . . . economic necessities and changing expectations have led most mothers to join the labor force, which means that many children may experience multiple female care givers outside the family. With the possibilities of no male models, multiple females models, and contradictory values, it is unclear how psychoanalytic theory can predict which gender behavior a girl will accept or reject. (p. 96)

Evolutionary Theories

Have women and men evolved to be different? Have certain sex-related behaviors become "built in" to our genes because they have been useful for survival? These are questions posed by theorists who study gender from the point of view of evolution. **Evolutionary theory** argues that in any species, including humans, certain characteristics persist across generations—passed along genetically—because they help the species to survive. The processes involved in passing along particular characteristics were delineated by Charles Darwin (1859; 1871) as **natural selection** and **sexual selection.** In natural selection, a trait that enhances survival and thus increases the chances that an individual will survive and have offspring is favored in the evolution of a species. Organisms that possess certain qualities are more likely than others to survive and to reproduce. Thus these qualities are passed on to future generations. For example, if an acute sense of smell helps an organism detect food and/or danger, individuals with an acute sense of smell are more likely, on average, to live longer and to have more offspring. Over the generations, the pressures of finding food and avoiding danger will make it increasingly likely that individuals with an acute sense of smell survive and reproduce. Eventually, this acute sense of smell may become a common characteristic in the species. Evolutionary theorists would say that such a characteristic had been selected for in the process of evolution, or that the species had adapted to selection pressures by evolving to possess this characteristic.

According to the **big mother hypothesis** put forward by zoologist Katherine Ralls, one characteristic that is naturally selected in some species is large size in females (Hrdy, 1999). In certain species such as many bats, spiders, and fish, females grow larger than males, and larger females produce more young. Large size has many potential reproductive advantages for females: "Depending on the species, big mothers produce bigger babies, deliver larger quantities of rich milk more quickly (as whales do), outcompete smaller females so as to monopolize resources available in their group, or, as spotted hyena females must do, not only defend their place in the chow line but also defend their infants from carnivorous and extremely cannibalistic group mates." (Hrdy, 1999, p. 48). The big mother hypothesis has been used to explain why, as *homo erectus,* the ancestors of modern humans, evolved from earlier australopithecine apes, they showed a dramatic decrease in the size difference between females and males. Among the australopithecines, males were about 50 percent larger than females, but among *homo erectus,* males were only about 20 percent larger than females—the same average size difference that occurs in modern humans. The change from 50 percent to 20 percent occurred because *homo erectus* females grew larger than their predecessors. Why did they grow larger? Evolutionary theorists speculate that selection pressures favoring larger size became more important for females than for males as hominid species descended from the trees and spent more time on the ground. Perhaps males were already at an optimal size for hunting and pursuing

↑ bigger females
↑ today better
adopt?

game, but increasing size for females would confer new advantages. Larger females might have been stronger, better able to defend themselves and their babies, and more able to forage for food effectively. Maybe a larger mother would be better equipped to bear a large baby, and then to carry that baby over long distances (Hrdy, 1999). If these speculations are correct, then large size might have been selected for in females more than for males, resulting in the decreasing size difference between them.

If large size in females is so advantageous, why haven't human females (or the females of many other species) just kept on getting bigger and bigger until they are larger than males? Evolutionary theorists rely on sexual selection as an explanation. Sexual selection involves competition and choice. In any species that reproduces sexually, including our own, successful reproduction involves not one individual, but two. Individuals affect the survival of their own genes (their **reproductive fitness**), not only by their own characteristics, but also by their choice of mate. Darwin (1871) argued that certain traits that made an individual more likely to have access to a mate would be selected for, even if they had no other survival value. Such traits might help an individual to have more offspring in several ways: by conferring the ability to fight off or dominate mating rivals (e.g., large size, sharp teeth), by making the individual more attractive to potential mates (e.g., bright colorful feathers), or by making it possible to destroy another individual's genetic contribution and replace it (e.g., a tendency to kill off infants sired by others). In general, Darwin believed that sexual selection had two aspects: male–male competition for females, and female choice among available males. Through sexual selection, human males may have stayed larger than females because size conferred an advantage in competing with other men for access to women and because women tended to choose larger, stronger men as mates.

Why should males compete and females choose? Why not the other way around? An answer to this question was suggested by Trivers (1972) in the form of **parental investment.** Parental investment is the energy, time, and other resources that a parent uses to promote the survival of an offspring—and that also detracts from the parent's ability to support other offspring. Trivers noted that, biologically, parental investment by mothers and fathers was very unequal for most mammals. The father merely had to ejaculate; the mother had to ovulate, carry the pregnancy to term, and lactate. Thus, each offspring tied up the mother's reproductive capabilities for a long time—and meanwhile the father could go on fertilizing other females. Thus, he argued, females made a much greater investment in each offspring than males did. Because of this greater investment, females would be more selective in their choice of mates. After all, they had only so many chances to get it right. Males, on the other hand, could go along fertilizing females unselectively because they had to invest so little in each potential offspring. And they would tend to compete with other males for access to females—the limiting resource in their quest for reproductive fitness. In doing so, they might seek to restrict access to "their" females by herding or secluding them, by excluding other males from their territories.

The different qualities favored by the female and male patterns of parental investment —sexual selectivity by females and sexual promiscuity, competitiveness, and a tendency to "hoard" females among males—should, according to this theory, be reinforced through sexual selection. Females and males who engaged in these behaviors would be more likely to reproduce successfully, and thus these behavioral tendencies would be more likely to be passed on, becoming "normal" patterns for the species. This argument has sometimes been used to support notions that human males are "naturally" polygamous, whereas human females are "naturally" monogamous, that women have a "natural" tendency to choose mates who control many resources, or that men have a "natural" tendency toward rape. But such notions are far too simple as interpretations of the complex findings of research in evolutionary psychology.

In the first place, female choice in many species is more multidimensional than evolutionary theorists first suspected. Apparently, females do not necessarily limit themselves to choosing a particular mate—the one who outcompetes the other males—and then making themselves available only to that individual. Rather they choose, within the constraints available, the behavior that increases their reproductive fitness. For example, in some primate species, such as chimpanzees, bonobos, and langurs, females solicit and copulate with many partners, many times (Hrdy, 1999). Primatologists speculate that this behavior makes it difficult for any male to be certain of paternity, and thus it may protect the infants. For example, among the langurs of Nepal, some 30 to 60 percent of infant mortality is due to males killing infants. However, according to DNA tests, none of the infants are killed by any male who *could* have sired them—a male who had sex with the infant's mother (Hrdy, 1999). Thus the mother's sexual "promiscuity" protects her infants by manipulating information about the infants' paternity.

The above example shows that the selection pressures identified as aspects of parental investment may not be the whole story. Patricia Gowaty (2001) argues that there are other selection pressures besides female choice of mates and male–male competition that may be important to adaptation. One of these pressures is the necessity to produce offspring that survive, and the pressure to do this may counteract the pressures toward female sexual selectivity. Gowaty also notes that female resistance to male coercion of their reproductive decisions may be adaptive in some circumstances: Females who successfully resist exploitation or coercion may have more reproductive success.

Researchers are also beginning to understand that there is a great deal of variation among females, and that the social and physical environment must be factored in to any understanding of this variation. For example, Jeanne Altman showed that, among the baboons she was studying, high- and low-ranking mothers differed in their probability of giving birth to a son or daughter. Low-ranking mothers bore more sons; high-ranking mothers bore more daughters. This pattern seemed to be an adaptation to a particular social situation: Daughters of low-ranking mothers were less likely to survive than sons because higher-ranking females harassed mothers of daughters but not mothers of sons (Hrdy, 1999).

If the social situation is important for baboons, how much more important might it be for humans, whose social environments are so diverse and whose cognitive response to those environments is so rich and varied? Researchers studying humans find that the patterns expected by evolutionary theory—a male tendency to want more sexual partners and to prefer women who are young and attractive (presumably signs of fertility) and female tendencies to be more selective and to choose mates with plenty of resources—are not universal. Rather, they seem to vary among societies according to the status held by women. Alice Eagly and Wendy Wood (1999) found, for example, that in societies where there was more gender equality, women reported less preference for mates with good earning capacity than they did in societies where there was less gender equality. Clearly, although humans are the product of evolution, we are not inexorably "programmed" to behave in particular ways, regardless of the environment. What we may, in fact, be "programmed" to do is to be flexible and responsive to environmental constraints and possibilities (Gowaty, 2001).

Human females and males may, like our animal relatives, have some biologically based tendencies to behave differently with respect to sexuality and reproduction. However, as individuals we are not pulled or pushed inexorably into particular behaviors by our inherited biological tendencies. And emerging evidence suggests that there is a lot that we do not yet understand about how evolution has shaped sex differences in the human species. For example, it is simply not universally true that women tend to carefully choose one man and then try to hold on to him, whereas men tend to try to have sex with as many women as possible. Among some traditional forager societies in South America (such as the Ache of Paraguay and the Bari of Venezuela), a child is thought to have multiple fathers, and married women often take several lovers during pregnancy (Angier, 1999). All of the lovers are considered fathers to the baby—and have some responsibility to feed and protect it. It is also not always true that men "invest" only in their own biological children. In some hunter–gatherer societies, such as the Hadza people of Tanzania, male hunters bring home food to share with the whole village, showing no particular favoritism toward their own children (Angier, 1999).

Like other theoretical approaches to women's psychology and gender, evolutionary theories offer a partial view, a limited understanding. These theories suggest ways in which behavior is grounded in biology, but other theories illustrate how we transcend our biology and respond to a multitude of social forces.

Social Learning Theories

Social learning theory is a lot less complicated than either psychoanalytic or evolutionary theories. Its focus is not on intrapsychic or innate biological forces but on the individual's internalization of her culture's messages about acceptable behavior (Bandura, 1977). According to this approach, a child's gender identity and role are *learned.* This learning takes place through a combination of modeling, imitation, and reinforcement: A child observes and imitates the behavior of adults and peers and is rewarded, punished, or ignored for such behavior. In this theoretical framework, parents, particularly the same-sex parent, play an important role not *because* they are parents but because they have the characteristics that make them excellent models: They are seen by the child as powerful, nurturant, and similar to the self (Mischel, 1970).

Parents, teachers, peers, media figures, and other socializing agents illustrate gender roles for the child through their behavior. When the child imitates them, she is usually reinforced if her behavior falls within the culturally approved gender role, and ignored or punished if it does not. Gradually, the child's behavior is shaped to conform to her gender role. As early as age 3, children imitate same-sex models more than other-sex models, and this tendency increases with age (Bussey & Bandura, 1984).

In the process of being repeatedly reminded that she is a girl (or he is a boy) and rewarded for behaving appropriately, the child learns to attach a positive value to membership in this gender category. According to this perspective, the formation of socially acceptable gender role behaviors precedes and lays the groundwork for the development of gender identity.

The socialization process, as described in this theory, sounds deceptively linear: Parents and others shape the unresisting child into conformity with the culture. But there are a number of indications that this is not exactly what is going on. At least one meta-analytic study shows that parents do not treat their daughters and sons differently on many dimensions (Lytton & Romney, 1991). One dimension on which some parents clearly *do* treat daughters and sons differently, though, is the encouragement of gender-typed activities (Lytton & Romney, 1991). In this way, parents try to influence their children in the direction of culturally approved gender roles.

Research shows that the child is not passive in this process; rather, she is an active participant in her socialization. Through reciprocal interactions, the child often influences the parents. These reciprocal influences can magnify the effect of initially small differences between children. For example, if a female infant and a male one differ slightly in activity level, parents may find that it works a little better to engage the male in certain kinds of active play than to engage the female in the same activity. Gradually, because of the differences in the children's responses, parents may emphasize active play more and more with the boy, while emphasizing different activities with the girl. Thus the parents are socializing the boy in the direction of greater activity than the girl, but at the same time, the parents' choices are also being shaped, in part, by the children's behaviors. The cycle becomes self-reinforcing; the initial small differences snowball.

The reciprocal influences between the child and the social environment continue as the child matures, creating what some psychologists call **continuities in interactional style** that last into adulthood (Caspi, Bem, & Elder, 1989). Beginning in childhood, an individual selects and creates environments that fit her preferred form of behavior. A sociable child will seek social environments; a shy child will seek environments that are sheltered from high levels of social interaction. These selected environments, in turn, reinforce and sustain the child's preferred behavior. As the child matures, the process becomes cumulative, reinforcing more and more strongly the original behaviors. Appropriately enough, the process is called **cumulative continuity.**

A second type of continuity, **interactional continuity,** refers to the transactions between the child and others in the environment. The child's behavior elicits reactions from others—reactions that promote continuity in the original behavior by confirming the child's expectations. An aggressive child, for example, expects others to be hostile, and so behaves in ways that provoke hostile reactions in others. In a vicious circle, these hostile reactions confirm the child's expectations and make it even more likely that she or he will behave aggressively in the future.

This pattern does not mean that the way a child grows up is predetermined by personality factors first evident in infancy. However, it is easy to see how the processes of continuity might magnify initially small gender differences in interaction style, or how the interaction between the child's expectations and those of others in the environment might reinforce gender-stereotyped behavior.

A further argument against the notion that the child is just passively shaped by the environment is that the child exercises considerable judgment about which models to imitate. Young children seem impervious to feedback from certain sources, with boys responding more to male peers and girls responding more to teachers and female peers (Fagot, 1985). Also, they resist imitating the behavior of models whom they have categorized as inappropriate. Children seem to observe the different frequencies with which females and males perform certain behaviors, using these observations to construct abstract models of acceptable feminine and masculine behavior (Perry & Bussey, 1979). Having constructed such models, the child uses them to decide whom to imitate, choosing same-sex individuals whose behavior generally seems representative of the child's gender category. Thus if a girl thinks her mother is atypical of females or "weird," she will not imitate her. So a child is an active participant in socialization, and makes choices about whom to imitate and when to do so. This notion is incorporated in a reconceptualization of social learning theory as **social cognitive theory** (Bandura, 1986; Bussey & Bandura, 1999). This newer version of the theory suggests that, although children may initially learn gender roles through external rewards and punishments, as they mature they begin to regulate their own actions through internal rewards and punishments. As they grow older, they also begin to incorporate the influence of the social structure outside the family, and this process continues throughout the life course.

It appears that a child is actually socialized not only by a set of individual agents, such as parents, but by a whole culture. The theory of **group socialization** (J. R. Harris, 1995) postulates that children become socialized primarily by identifying with their peer group and taking on that group's norms for attitudes and behavior. According to this theory, cultural knowledge and behavior are transmitted not directly from parents to their children, but from the parents' peer group and other cultural sources to the children's peer group. The peer groups filter cultural transmissions. For example, children quickly learn what behaviors from their home context are acceptable to their peer group. They do not transfer behavior learned at home to the peer group unless it is shared and approved by most of the other children. If children come from what they feel are atypical homes, their behavior tends not to get transferred to the group.

In middle childhood, peer groups are often gender-segregated and may develop quite different group cultures (Maccoby, 1990). Children's attempts to fit into these different cultures may explain the persistence of strong gender roles among children even in cases where parents have tried to rear them in non-gender-stereotyped ways (Serbin, Powlishta, & Gulko, 1993). It also may explain some intriguing cross-cultural differences in the degree to which children learn to differentiate their behavior by sex. J. R. Harris (1995) notes that in societies where the population density is too low for viable separate groups to form, girls and boys play together, and their behavior is much less gender-stereotyped than in populations big enough to support separate groups for boys and girls.

Although the outline of the socialization process may be similar across cultural and ethnic groups, the content of what is learned may vary significantly from group to group. Even within the United States, researchers have noted, for example, that parental expectations for girls' achievement may differ among groups: African American and Latina mothers hold higher expectations for their daughters than European American mothers do for theirs (Stevenson, Chen, & Uttal, 1990). Girls growing up in African American homes have been found to be more likely than girls growing up in European American homes to have adult role models who blend characteristics commonly associated with both femininity and masculinity (Reid et al., 1995). Retrospective reports from adult Latinas, however, indicate that their families treated girls differently from boys in terms of freedom and

Peer groups are important transmitters and arbiters of cultural norms and values.

responsibility, and that parents often worked hard to enforce feminine behavior. Traditional socialization in these families seems to have included a curtailment of girls' activities and an insistence that, even though it was important to take advantage of new opportunities for women, it was also important to learn and practice traditional feminine skills. As one young woman in this study said of her father: "He wanted the best for us, he wants the best education for us and everything and the best opportunities, but women still need to have their traditional roles of being able to cook, being able to clean, being able to look nice. . . ." (Rafaelli & Ontai, 2004, p. 291).

Cognitive Developmental Theories

Proponents of **cognitive developmental theories** (Kohlberg, 1966; Kohlberg & Ullian, 1974) argue that a child's notions about gender are tied to the stages of intellectual development. The key intellectual threshold for the child to cross is **gender constancy**—an understanding that a person's gender is fixed and cannot be changed simply by adopting a different hairstyle, dress, or name. Most children supposedly reach this threshold between the ages of 3 and 5. Before that age, a child may have learned that people can be categorized into female and male but may sometimes make errors in classifying people or may think that arbitrary changes in classification can occur.

According to this approach (Slaby & Frey, 1975), gender identity is formed in three stages: first, an awareness that two sexes exist; second, an understanding that gender does not change over time (stability); and third, an awareness that gender does not change across situations and behaviors (constancy). Most of this research has not, however, addressed differences in the experience and interpretation of gender roles in different cultural, ethnic, and social-class groups.

Clearly, this approach is firmly rooted in Western cultural notions of gender. As discussed in Chapter 1, certain cultures *do* think of gender as changeable or categorize individuals into more than two gender categories. For such societies, the notion of gender constancy might be regarded as inappropriately rigid. Indeed, even some individuals in North American society complain that they do not fit easily into either gender category and argue for more fluidity in the concept (e.g., Bem, 1993; Bornstein, 1994). To fit in with mainstream Western culture, however, a child must learn to think of gender as dichotomous and constant.

The cognitive developmental approach postulates that children use their gender self-categorization as an organizing focus for attaching value to behaviors. Children begin to value behaviors that are appropriate to their own gender; performing such behaviors becomes more self-reinforcing than performing behaviors that are not gender appropriate. In validation of her own gender category, the little girl seeks out and embraces "feminine" behaviors. She identifies with her mother, using her as a guide for establishing correct behavior for her own gender category. She also seeks feminine models among her teachers and her peers, in the stories she reads, and in the television programs she watches. She gathers clues from the way people react to her behavior, from the rewards and punishments she receives. She uses all this information to piece together the puzzle of how she is supposed to behave, given her gender category.

Proponents of the cognitive developmental approach emphasize the child's motivation toward competence and correct behavior. They see the child as an active searcher for information, not as someone who is merely shaped by the environment. Yet the environment is what provides the clues the child uses to formulate a pattern of "correct" behavior, so the content of environmental messages matters enormously.

Beyond Childhood: Social Roles

Cultural messages about gender are not directed solely toward children. They are woven into the fabric of social organization, often so pervasive that we do not even notice them—unless we violate them. A U.S. female college student who sets out to major in chemistry, for example, may encounter feedback from a number of sources that she is on the wrong track. She may, as happened to one of my students, find that she cannot study her chemistry textbook in a public place without having to endure a series of jocular comments from strangers along the lines of "What's a pretty girl like you doing reading something like that?" Her family and friends may respond to her career plans quizzically or with outright disapproval. She may find herself in a small female minority in her chemistry classes. Everything conspires to let her know that she is out of step with the expectations for her gender.

Our human desire to fit in with our social surroundings often exerts both subtle and obvious pressure on us to blend in with and reproduce these surroundings. Thus, for example, the pattern of the division of labor between women and men in a society tends to be self-perpetuating. Alice Eagly (1987), proposing a **social roles theory** of gender-related differences, argued that female–male differences in social behavior often occur because of a two-pronged process. First, women and men are disproportionately assigned to jobs and tasks on the basis of gender stereotypes and expectations prevalent in their culture. For instance, women are more likely than men to work as secretaries and nurses. One reason for this outcome is that people expect women, more than men, to have the qualities necessary for such positions: adaptability, willingness to accept authority, responsibility, a caretaking orientation. The second part of the process, according to Eagly, is that women and men, having been assigned to different roles, tend to learn and emphasize different qualities and skills *because* those qualities are necessary to successful performance of the role. So, in a kind of group version of self-fulfilling prophecy, women and men learn to be and behave more in line with gender-stereotyped expectations, and their behavior confirms and reinforces the stereotypes.

Models and Media Messages around the World

In Costa Rica, a television commercial for cookies raised objections from many women and helped launch a nationwide protest about the portrayal of women in the media. In the commercial, which played for several days on television, an indigenous family comes to a market to buy some cookies. When the husband realizes that he has no money to pay for the cookies, he offers to leave his wife behind as payment!

Many Costa Rican women were outraged, noting that the advertisement defined the Indian wife as an object of exchange, a commodity, a possession of the husband to be disposed of as he saw fit. "If my daughter asks me why the father and son leave the mother behind, I can't give her the answer that this is a payment for a package of cookies. I can't answer my daughter, a citizen of the future, this way," fumed one woman in a letter to the editor of a national newspaper (quoted in Nieto, 1993, p. 5).

Even though most advertisements for household goods are aimed at female consumers in Costa Rica, as in many other countries, the content of these advertisements often belittles or degrades women. One survey showed that 52 percent of Costa Rican women interviewed believed that women were not portrayed favorably in commercials (Nieto, 1993).

The message that men are central and women peripheral, that men are the important people and the experts around whom the world revolves, pervades the popular media in many countries. For example, women are a clear minority among people featured in the world's news media: television, radio, and newspapers. A study across 71 countries showed that women comprised 43 percent of journalists, but only 17 percent of people interviewed or quoted in the news (Mediawatch, 1995), and a study with a similar international scope five years later showed that these number had barely changed (Ngangoue, 2001). Moreover, women who are interviewed are more likely than men who are interviewed to be victims of accidents, disasters, or crimes, and far less likely than men to be politicians, experts, or government spokespersons. European research shows that 47 percent of "ordinary citizens" and 37 percent of victims portrayed on television are women, whereas 72 percent of politicians and 80 percent of "experts" are men (United Nations,

---

BOX 4.2 LEARNING ACTIVITY
Media Portrayals of Women

How much attention do the popular media give to women? For a week, pay attention to the front page of your local newspaper and keep track (in writing) of how many times women, as opposed to men, are pictured there. How many stories on the front page are about women? For a week, take a careful look at several television prime-time shows and record your observations. What percentage of the time are women the main characters? How often are the women portrayed as strong and smart? How much ethnic and racial diversity is there among the female characters? How are poor women portrayed?

At the end of the week, look back over your observations. Are women and men receiving equal attention in these media? To what extent are the media portrayals reinforcing gender stereotypes?

2000). A recent study showed that on the three major U.S. broadcast networks, 87 percent of the sound bites by "experts" were provided by men (Media Report to Women, 2001).

The strong focus on men in the news may reflect male dominance of world news organizations. In the United States, women now hold 26.5 percent of television news director positions and 39.3 percent of all television news jobs. In radio, women are 14.4 percent of news directors (Media Report to Women, 2003). However, the numbers are even lower in many other countries. In Africa, women make up 8 percent of broadcasting managers and 14 percent of managers in the print media; in Latin America, women are 21 percent of broadcasting managers and 16 percent of print media managers (International Women's Media Foundation, 2001). Women, have, however, made progress as presenters of the news. In North America, 55 percent of those who present the news on television and radio are women. Comparable figures are 48 percent for Africa, 53 percent for Asia, and 55 percent for Europe (Ngangoue, 2001).

In prime-time television series and in advertising, women have a much bigger presence than they do in newscasts, but they are shown in stereotypical ways. Male television characters are more likely than female characters to be shown at work and to talk about their work, whereas female characters are more likely to talk about romantic relationships (Media Report to Women, 2001). Female characters are far more likely than males to be young; one study found only 15 percent of prime-time TV characters were women aged 45 and older (Media Report to Women, 2001). Women continue to be underrepresented as primary characters during most commercials shown in prime time—except those for health and beauty products. Moreover, women still tend to be cast in younger, supportive roles relative to men (Ganahl, Prinsen, & Ntezley, 2003). One study showed that in 28 percent of the cases where a female model appeared in a television advertisement, comments about her appearance were included in the script; comments about the appearance of male models occurred in only 7 percent of cases, and on television and in movies women are far more likely than men to be shown "grooming" or "preening" (Children NOW, 1997).

Women's voices make up only 25 percent of those heard in commercials (Media Report to Women, 2001). Women and men are portrayed in stereotypic ways in television commercials in many countries, including Britain, France, and Denmark (Furnham & Skae, 1997), Australia (Mazella, Durkin, Cerini, & Buralli, 1992), Turkey (Uray & Burnaz, 2003), and Kenya (Mwangi, 1996). Canadian television also reflects gender stereotypes, with women infrequently seen as experts and portrayed most often in domestic settings (Dalcourt, 1996; Rak & McMullen, 1987).

The series shown on prime-time network television in the United States have featured a lower percentage of female (35 percent) than male (65 percent) characters for decades (D. M. Davis, 1990). In the prime-time programs, men are more likely than women to be shown as active, and women are more likely than men to be shown in provocative dress. A content analysis of prime-time television characters across the 1970s, 80s, and 90s reveals that women consistently receive less recognition and respect than men on television. Women continue to be underrepresented in relation to their numbers in the population, although the percentage of women portrayed as employed outside the home and as holding prestigious occupations has increased over the past 30 years (Signorielli & Bacue, 1999).

In programming directed at children and adolescents, not only are there fewer female than male characters, but males are more likely than females to be portrayed as having an impact on their environment. In animated cartoons, male characters are given more prominence, appear more often, talk more, and engage in a wider range of behaviors than female characters do (Thompson & Zerbinos, 1995). In commercials shown on Music Television (MTV), male characters outnumbered females more than 2 to 1, and the female characters are more likely to have beautiful bodies, wear skimpy clothes, and be the object of others' gaze (Signorielli, McLeod, & Healy, 1994).

Despite media reinforcement of gender stereotypes, there is also evidence that the media sometimes offers strong positive role models for girls. One content analysis of the top 25 television shows and the top 15 movies favored by girls aged 12 to 17 showed that the female characters in these shows often relied on themselves to solve their problems and achieve their own goals, acted in honest and direct ways, and used intelligence to achieve goals (Children NOW, 1997).

Perhaps because of a growing interest in nontraditional role models for girls, some children's programs featuring female "superheroes" have emerged in recent years. One popular children's TV show, a Japanese animated feature called *Sailor Moon,* is directed at girls between 6 and 11. The show, with a theme song that celebrates "fighting evil by moonlight, winning love by daylight, never shrinking from a real fight," features five Caucasian schoolgirls (in a Japanese city!) who regularly do battle with diabolical villains. Unfortunately, the program manages to promote many gender stereotypes even as it portrays the girls as strong and courageous. They primp before every battle—and are regularly rescued at especially difficult moments by a male figure called Moonlight Knight! The world of cartoons also presents children with the *Powerpuff Girls:* three perfect little girls (Buttercup, Blossom, and Bubbles) whose superpowers are used to fight evil and rescue those in distress. Although portrayed as tough and smart, they are also depicted as almost unbearably cute and diminutive, with large eyes and tiny bodies. Another program, *Xena: Warrior Princess* (now out of production, but shown in reruns), presents a live-action fantasy whose title character fights injustice and defeats cruel despots. Young adults enjoy this series because of its satire, and it has a large following among lesbian viewers. The strong friendship between Xena and her sidekick Gabriele is central to the story. Xena never has to be rescued by a man and, although she does her fighting in revealing clothes, she is scornful of the notion that her appearance is the most important thing about herself. In one episode she tells a male enemy who approaches with lust in his eyes, "It's not my body that makes me who I am—it's my deeds."

On the whole, however, the pervasive message in the public media of many countries is that women are less important and less interesting, and play a smaller role in events of consequence than men do. Women are valued for their beauty or sexuality, for being quiet, helpful, and nice. Men are valued for their expertise, their ability to intervene in danger-ous situations and to act decisively and authoritatively. How do such portrayals affect girls' construction of their pool of possible selves? Research has for years pointed to the conclusion that the more television children watch, the more accepting they are of gender stereotypes (e.g., Frueh & McGhee, 1975; Morgan, 1982; Signorella, Bigler, & Liben, 1993).

The emergence of the Internet and World Wide Web as a source of media content has added some new wrinkles to the portrayal of girls and women. The use of this technology has been dominated by men, who made up two-thirds of Internet users and accounted for 77 percent of total online time as recently as 1997 (Morahan-Martin, 1998). However, these figures are changing rapidly, and one source estimates that women will comprise 60 percent of Internet users by 2005 (Media Report to Women, 2001). Perhaps because cyber-space has tended to be male dominated, the "Internet culture" has sometimes tolerated hostility to women and girls and forms of communication that are more comfortable for males than females. In addition, the Internet has added a new and easy source for porno-graphic images of women and girls; males are significantly more likely than females to say they have accessed sexually explicit materials online (Goodson, McCormick, & Evans, 2001).

However, the Web also provides a place where alternative visions of girls, women, and gender can flourish. For example, actress and artist Lila Lee created a weekly comic strip on the Web to express some of the anger she felt as a Korean American girl growing up in a society that always seemed to regard her as "different." *Angry Little Girls* features, among others, "the angry little Asian girl" Kim (who looks like a nice little Asian girl, but is really a fireball of angry ambition), the "disenchanted princess" Deborah (a beautiful blonde girl who seems to have everything, but who feels empty), the "crazy little latina" Maria (an idealist who gets caught up in things that don't always make sense to others), and the "fresh little soul sistah" Wanda (a smart upbeat girl who "moves on" when she doesn't like something). The comic strip, accessible on the Web, pokes fun at racist and sexist stereotypes while giving the reader some alternative ways of looking at the world (Noguchi, 2001).

The Internet provides for unprecedented access to information and communication among those fortunate enough to connect to it, and women everywhere have used it to advantage in networking, community-building, and carving out areas of control of infor-mation and images about women and gender. The first virtual women's newspaper, *World-woman,* founded in 1999, brings international news that has been selected, written, and edited by women to a global audience. Women's groups all over the world use electronic

BOX 4.3 MAKING CHANGE
Protesting Offensive Media Images of Girls and Women

How often have you seen something in the media that you feel is insulting to women? Or how often have you NOT seen coverage of issues that you believe are important to women and deserving of more attention? Speak out and make your voice heard about such situations. One way to do this is through Web sites that provide links to major media, such as television networks and newspapers. If you live in Canada, go to **www.mediawatch.ca**, where you will find complaint forms that you can fill out and submit online. In the United States, go to the Women's Desk of FAIR, an organization dedicated to fairness in the media: **www.fair.org/womens-desk.html**. You can monitor this page for action alerts and, by keeping track of the issues that appear there, you can participate in the organization's work of analyzing sexism, racism, and homophobia in the media and working to get a broad range of feminist perspectives included in public debate. Or you can become involved in the Girls, Women + Media Project at **www .mediaandwomen.org/ican.html**. Here you can sign up for the "I can" network, which provides you with opportunities to join in letter-writing campaigns against offensive portrayals of girls and women in the media.

To make an effective complaint, you must be specific about the name of the program or advertised product and the time and date that you saw or heard it. When complaining, be clear about your concerns. Don't just say you didn't like something—explain if the material portrayed women in an unfair and inaccurate manner, was discriminatory because . . . , demeaned women by . . . , did not realistically reflect the role of women in society because . . . , and so on.

Remember, the media are shaped by the concerns of the community—and the concerns of the community are often measured by the number of complaints. Also, it certainly would not hurt to pass on compliments to the media when they do a particularly good job of covering women.

communication as a tool for action in fields such as health and human rights. For example, the Asian Women's Resource Exchange (AWORC) promotes resource sharing among women's information centers in Asia and supports Internet literacy and activism by individual women and women's organizations (United Nations, 2000). Yet, it is women in North America who benefit most from this technology. In 1999, more than 201 million people in the world had Internet access—but over half of those people were from two countries: Canada and the United States. By contrast, Africa, with 13 percent of the world's population and a scarcity of telephone lines, personal computers, and Internet hosts, had less than 1 percent of the total Internet users (United Nations, 2000). The World Internet Project (2004) reports that there is still a worldwide gender gap among Internet users, with an average of 8 percent more men than women using the Internet. As seen in Table 4.1, the size of the gap varies dramatically among countries.

TABLE 4.1   Female and Male Internet Users around the World

Country	WOMEN		MEN	
	% Who Use Internet	Average Hours Spent Online per Week	% Who Use Internet	Average Hours Spent Online per Week
Britain	55.0		63.6	
China		10.0		14.3
Germany	41.7	10.7	50.4	12.4
Hungary	15.1	4.1	20.3	6.3
Italy	21.5	7.0	41.7	9.5
Japan	46.2	4.3	54.7	7.3
Korea	53.8	12.1	67.8	15.9
Macao	28.8	8.1	37.8	10.2
Singapore	34.0	15.9	47.2	14.9
Spain	27.2	8.0	46.4	13.3
Sweden	64.4	5.8	67.7	9.4
Taiwan	23.5	9.9	25.1	11.6
United States	69.0	10.1	73.1	13.1

Source: (UCLA World Internet Project, 2004)
http://www.ccp.ucla.edu/downloads/UCLA_World_Internet_Project.doc

What Does It Mean to Be "Feminine"?

If someone is biologically female, does that automatically make her feminine? Most of us would answer no. We are aware of the cultural definitions of femininity and the variations in the extent to which different girls and women adhere to them. We are also aware of differences among women in how strongly they identify with women as a group and how much their identity as women means to them. Clearly there are several issues to be explored when considering what femininity and female identity might mean in women's lives.

Three distinct issues have been explored with respect to gender and individual identity. The first, gender identity, is defined as the individual's private experience of the self as female or male. This aspect of the self-concept is formed early in childhood and is, in most cultures, extremely resistant to change. The second, gender role, refers to the set of behaviors culturally defined as appropriate for one's sex. A woman who acts in accord with cultural prescriptions of feminine behavior is following a feminine gender role. Gender identity and gender role do not necessarily mesh neatly. A woman may have a firm gender identity as female while still rejecting the rules and restrictions for women's behavior in her society. Others may say she is acting in a unfeminine manner, but she may feel no conflict at all between her gender identity and her role behavior. The third issue, **sexual orientation,** refers to an individual's preference for love relationships and sexual partnerships with persons of the same or the other sex. Three broad categories of possible orientations are heterosexual (sexually attracted to and forming love relationships with individuals of the other sex), homosexual (sexually attracted to and forming love relationships with individuals of the same sex), and bisexual (sexually attracted to and forming love relationships with individuals of either sex). Again, there is no necessary set of congruencies between this orientation and the other two issues. A woman may love other women, be firm in her private sense of herself as female, and behave in accordance with many of the social norms for femininity. Or a woman may love men, be firm in her sense of herself as female, and choose to behave in ways that many people would label masculine.

Psychological Androgyny

As presumed experts in human behavior, psychologists have had a long history of pronouncements on what to consider "normal" with respect to gender. Within the prescriptive and therapeutic domain of psychology, tradition held that it was normal for a woman to be feminine—that is, for her not only to think of herself as female (gender identity), but also to act in the ways considered by society to be feminine (gender role) and confine her romantic and sexual attachments to men (sexual orientation). An "unfeminine" woman was, by definition, a maladjusted woman, as was a lesbian woman. Naturally, such pronouncements were often irritating, unnerving, and even frightening for women whose sense of self did not mesh easily with the cultural constructions of femininity.

One crack in this prescriptive edifice was made by psychologist Sandra Bem, who first incorporated the notion of **androgyny** into the psychological discourse about femininity and masculinity. Androgyny, a concept that has been explored in mythology and literature for years (see Heilbrun, 1973, for an overview), literally means a merging of masculine and feminine: the Greek *andro* means man and *gyne* woman. Traditions in many parts of the world, such as Chinese Taoism and Hinduism in India, hold that feminine and masculine must be reconciled in a single individual in the interests of harmony and wholeness. These ideas were echoed to some extent in the psychological theories of Carl Jung (1953) and David Bakan (1966), but for many years did not figure in Western mainstream psychology.

In the realm of psychology, an androgynous person is one who displays both feminine and masculine qualities. Yet for years, psychologists had no language except the language of maladjustment for talking about such a person. Personality tests were designed with femininity and masculinity as opposing poles of a single dimension. A person taking such a test could score as more feminine only by scoring as less masculine, and vice versa. It was considered a sign of psychological problems, and perhaps homosexuality, if a woman scored high on masculinity, or if a man scored high on femininity on these tests (Lewin, 1984).

Sandra Bem (1974) helped the field of psychology break from this tradition by using the notion of androgyny to design a new personality test: the Bem Sex Role Inventory (BSRI). The unique feature of this test is that it treats femininity and masculinity *not* as opposing poles of the same dimension, but as two separate independent dimensions. Thus a person taking the test can end up scoring high on both femininity and masculinity, high on one and low on the other, or low on both. On this test, in contrast to all earlier ones, a woman who admits to some stereotypically masculine qualities would not automatically see her femininity score drop.

On the BSRI, a person who scores high on both femininity and masculinity is labeled androgynous. The label is not code for "maladjusted." In fact, research by Bem and her colleagues has suggested that androgynous individuals are often more flexible and cope better with a variety of situational demands than individuals whose responses to the questionnaire classify them as either feminine or masculine (Bem, 1975; Bem, Martyna, & Watson, 1976).

Androgyny is a useful concept because it allows us to see that a broad range of qualities can coexist in an individual, and that a person need not be *either* stereotypically feminine *or* masculine. Yet it is important to remember that androgyny is meaningless apart from femininity and masculinity, and that all three concepts are culturally defined. Within the field of psychology, femininity and masculinity have been defined only as the two sets of qualities that seem most reliably to distinguish females from males (Constantinople, 1973). These distinctions vary a great deal across time and place. In some cultures, men can weep unashamedly in public; in others, such behavior would signal a lack of masculinity. In some cultures, a sexually aggressive woman is considered unfeminine; in others, she would be seen as the epitome of femininity.

Bem's inventory would produce strange results in a culture that conceptualized femininity and masculinity very differently from the way the California college students on whom she normed the test did. Once again, we come to the notion that femininity and masculinity are culturally constructed. One implication is that tests that purport to measure these concepts cannot be transferred from culture to culture in any meaningful way. Thus, for example, a researcher interested in gender roles in Latin America would not use the BSRI in Spanish translation. Rather, she would use a test that had been developed and normed in Latin America, such as the Latin American Sex Role Inventory (Kaschak & Sharatt, 1983/84).

Gender Schema Theory

In the effort to understand why some individuals adhere strongly to society's gender roles and some do not, researchers now argue that femininity and masculinity are not simply constellations of personality traits (nurturant, gentle, soft versus ambitious, assertive, goal-oriented), but ways of looking at the world. According to this perspective, femininity and masculinity are associated with cognitive structures called **self-schemas** (Markus, Crane, Bernstein, & Siladi, 1982) or **gender schemas** (Bem, 1981). A *schema* is a mental framework or filter that is part of the way a person notices, assesses, and organizes incoming information—analogous in some ways to a mental filing system.

Each of us has many schemas—about the tasks we do, our families, the books we like to read, the people we work with. We each also have a big collection of self-schemas, cognitive structures that guide incoming information about the self. One of those self-schemas may have to do with gender, another with race, another with ethnicity, another with age,

BOX 4.4 LEARNING ACTIVITY
Femininity, Masculinity, and Androgyny

Below are a few of the items from the Bem Sex Role Inventory (BSRI; Bem, 1974). For each item, rate yourself on a 1 to 7 scale in which 1 means you don't have that quality or never engage in that behavior, and 7 means you possess that quality to a high degree or engage in that behavior very frequently.

1. ____ self-reliant	8. ____ yielding	15. ____ independent
2. ____ shy	9. ____ athletic	16. ____ affectionate
3. ____ assertive	10. ____ flatterable	17. ____ ambitious
4. ____ forceful	11. ____ analytical	18. ____ sympathetic
5. ____ understanding	12. ____ self-sufficient	19. ____ dominant
6. ____ soft-spoken	13. ____ warm	20. ____ aggressive
7. ____ gullible	14. ____ childlike	

On the BSRI, these items are scored as feminine: 2, 5, 6, 7, 8, 10, 13, 14, 16, 18. These items are scored as masculine: 1, 3, 4, 9, 11, 12, 15, 17, 19, 20. Did you rate yourself higher on the feminine than on the masculine items? Or higher on the masculine than the feminine items? Or about equally high on both? What do you think your self-ratings reveal about your "femininity" and "masculinity"?

Do you agree that these items accurately represent feminine and masculine qualities? Do the two sets of traits seem equally positive? Why or why not?

another with body weight, and so on. In different people, the strength and importance of these various self-schemas will vary. A person who has a strong gender schema, or self-schema for femininity or masculinity, would tend spontaneously to organize incoming information about herself or himself around the concept of gender, rather than around some other notion, such as age or nationality. An individual who is *gender schematic* (has a strong gender schema) would simply be more ready than someone who is *gender aschematic* (has a weak gender schema) to process information about the self in terms of gender. She or he would, for example, be more likely to remember things relevant to gender than things relevant to nationality and to make faster, easier, and more confident decisions about the applicability to herself or himself of gender-related than nationality-related traits. For instance, a person with a strong self-schema for gender and a relatively weak self-schema for nationality would respond more quickly and easily to the question "Are you very feminine?" than to the question "Are you very American?" In a similar vein, a person with a strong gender schema may be more ready to process information not just about the self but also about other people in terms of their gender than in terms of other categories such as nationality.

Sandra Bem (1985) argues that highly feminine and masculine individuals may differ from others "not in their *ability* to organize information on the basis of gender but in their *threshold* for doing so spontaneously" (p. 197). Being gender schematic does not translate automatically into being highly feminine or highly masculine, however. For example, a woman who does not describe herself as stereotypically feminine may still have a strong tendency to process information in gender-related ways, perhaps because she is oriented toward gender for academic or political reasons (Freedman, 1991). A young woman may define herself as a feminist, and may disdain certain aspects of stereotypically feminine behavior that she finds demeaning, but she may still be gender schematic—spontaneously processing and analyzing incoming information in terms of gender ("Did this professor rebuff my question because I am a woman?" "If I take this engineering course, will I be the only woman in the class?").

Gender schema theory provides one useful perspective on the way individuals create their own identities in interaction with cultural constructions of femininity, masculinity, and androgyny. People with very different repertoires of traits and behaviors might think of themselves as feminine or as masculine, simply by noticing and paying most attention to those qualities in themselves that fit the gender stereotypes and ignoring the others. The theory also suggests that by adjusting their notions of what qualities are relevant to gender, individuals may adapt to changing cultural expectations for women and men without suffering damage to their belief in their own femininity or masculinity. Finally, self-schema theory in general helps us to appreciate the ways that different people tend to emphasize different dimensions of their identities when processing information. Where one person sees issues first and foremost in terms of gender, another may see the same issues primarily in terms of race, and another may focus on nationality or on social class as organizing principles. Such individual differences stem from social experiences that affect the way we view the world, and from the peer and reference groups that are relevant to each of us.

Gender-Based Identity and Other Identities: Shaping the Pool of Possible Selves

I try to be me. What am I? An Orthodox Jamaican–American woman raised in a Jewish neighborhood and married to an Irish-American son of atheists. I've hidden all my life. Like all black women, I'm a great observer of the games folks play in life. Yet, I am not like all black women. I have been told that often enough. (McDonnell, 1994, p. 126)

So what is my identity? . . . What is empowering for me? To say this: I am, first, a third generation (my parents were born in the United States and are the offspring of immigrants), half Sicilian, half Southern Italian North American, a woman of mixed-heritage, and a working-class lesbian. I am neither Anglo nor a woman of color. I am something else and because I don't have the exact language, the perfect word, doesn't mean I am not claiming a truth that is apparent to me. It means I am deeply in search of this truth—even as I know it, utterly, I am also searching. (Leto, 1998, p. 212)

I feel funny saying my family is "working class or blue collar." These are not words my family would use to describe themselves. They didn't define themselves by their work. That wouldn't occur to them. They worked hard. They were good at what they did. They mostly voted Republican. So these labels, although accurate, sound condescending. . . . I feel as if I betray my family every time I use those words. (Herman, 1998, p. 177)

Who am I? Who could I become? Many people struggle repeatedly with these questions. We spend our lives constructing and reconstructing our identities, using the building blocks provided by our interactions with others, our assessment of how we fit into our social networks, and the cultural surround. Gender, as a category that defines each individual to some extent in the eyes of others, must play a role in our identity. But each person's sense of identity as a woman or man must interact in a constant dance with other aspects of identity: race, ethnicity, sexual orientation, social class, nationality, age, religion, political affiliation, occupation, family status.

Social identity theorists (e.g., Tajfel, 1981) suggest that each individual's personal sense of identity is tied to her or his **reference groups.** A reference group is a group with which we identify, to which we look for ideals and perhaps approval. For instance, a person might have the following set of reference groups: female college professors, Canadians, feminists, political liberals, people who enjoy exercise. If she overhears an attack on feminists, she will become irritated because that is by implication an attack on her. Similarly, if she reads a newspaper article about the positive aspects of Canadian society, she will feel, in some obscure way, as if she herself has been complimented. When one of "our" groups is criticized, we become defensive; when one is in the limelight because of a successful achievement, we bask in the glow of that achievement. This happens because our *personal* identities are strongly linked to our *social* identities.

Group socialization theory, discussed above, also focuses on the importance of group affiliations in defining who we are. Peer groups, according to this theory, are the transmitters and arbiters of cultural norms and values. It is each individual's links to important peer groups that shape behavior to fit that group's interpretation of the larger culture. If a preadolescent girl is part of a peer group of girls who are obsessed with playing soccer, she is likely to think of playing soccer as important and to judge herself in a significant way according to how she plays. If a girl comes from a soccer-playing family but finds herself in a peer group in which the idea of a girl playing soccer is simply "weird," she will likely try to shed that aspect of her identity, at least when she is with that particular group.

But what determines which groups a person feels drawn to, feels a part of? Proximity is one factor, of course. We tend to become part of the groups that are around us. Awareness is another factor; we cannot identify with a group we know nothing about. Power and status also come into play; individuals are motivated to identify with groups that seem dominant, successful, and highly valued. Yet much research on identity formation shows that individuals change their reference groups over the years, sometimes through a gradual process of discovery and sometimes in a conversionlike response to events in their lives. In the latter process, a group that was formerly a "them" can suddenly become an "us," or vice versa.

For example, a woman, though certain of her personal gender identity as female, may not identify with women as a group. She may feel that most women are uninteresting and may accept the stereotype that women are less competent, logical, and ambitious than men. She may make comments such as "I don't really get along well with other women; most of my best friends are men." She knows she is a woman, but she sees herself as different from other women. Most other women are "them." She is not accepting women as a reference group—perhaps because she is buying into the attitudes of a culture that says men are better than women; perhaps because she is dazzled by the power and status of the men in her social environment and disappointed in the relative powerlessness and lack of influence among the women.

Then something happens to change the way she looks at her social world. Perhaps she finds herself a target of sexual harassment or sexist comments at work and then discovers that she is only one of many women who have been victimized in this workplace. Perhaps a promotion is given to a less qualified male colleague. She may begin to view what is happening to her personally as part of a pattern of behavior that is directed at women. She suddenly focuses on herself as a part of a group category, women, membership in which has real consequences for how she is treated. She begins to identify more strongly with women as a group. As she does so, she may begin, not only to place a strong priority on her identity as a woman, but also to identify as a feminist. Feminist identity development is theorized to progress in stages from unawareness of sexism and acceptance of traditional gender roles to active commitment (Downing & Roush, 1985).

How do young women go about understanding their experience of gendered selves and coming to terms with gendered identities? Laura Abrams (2003) interviewed young women in two very different communities about how they defined their identities as women. Her respondents in both settings told her that their ideas about what it means to be female were influenced by encounters with male power. For example, many respondents indicated that they encountered persistent disrespect from boys and men, and part of their identity as women involved resistance to such disrespect. The young women from the White middle-class suburban community anchored their resistance in a sense of personal power that was grounded in their gender identity (e.g., "I'm really using my voice . . . I'm proud of the fact that I'm a woman who's making a difference," p. 69). The young women from the urban, working class community of color found a sense of personal power in their identification with their ethnic or cultural heritage—and also in trying to prove that they were "tougher than guys" (p. 69). The two groups of women claimed their identities as women while resisting stereotypes of femininity.

Other important group identities, which certainly intersect with gender and may or may not conflict with gender for the individual's primary allegiance, are also formed in response to life events. Theorists of racial identity (e.g., Cross, 1971; Helms, 1993) suggest that such identities may progress through a series of stages, or, less linearly, through recurrent phases. For example, Cross (1971, 1978) presented a model of Black racial identity in which an individual moves through four stages. In the **preencounter stage,** the individual idealizes White culture and disassociates herself from Black culture, using Whites rather than Blacks as a reference group. In the **encounter stage,** the individual may realize that her being Black will always be salient to others and affect their evaluations of her. In this stage, the person decides that it is futile to identify with the dominant White culture and begins a struggle to find a new identity. The individual may begin to affiliate more with other Blacks and searches for a Black identity that she can adopt. Entry into this stage may be triggered by an instance of discrimination that cannot be ignored or rationalized.

In the **immersion/emersion stage,** the person begins work on constructing a Black identity. She may withdraw as much as possible into a Black world and may "act Black" in very stereotypic ways. Eventually, she may move beyond these stereotypes by finding a supportive Black community in which she can explore positive aspects of Black and African culture, deal with her anger at discrimination, and evaluate which aspects of Black culture are important to her. Finally, in the **internalization stage,** she constructs a positive personal identity that incorporates being Black, blending her notions of her own unique qualities with an acknowledgment that being Black influences who she is.

Somewhat similar theories have been offered to explain the formation of ethnic identity. There may be an initial phase in which ethnicity is largely unexamined or ignored, then a period of questioning and exploring the meaning of one's ethnicity, leading ultimately to a committed ethnic identity (Phinney, 1989, 1990). As in the Black racial identity model, the exploration stage may be triggered by a significant event that awakens the person to an awareness of the implications of her ethnicity (Kim, 1981).

A somewhat different process is postulated for the development of identities relevant to gender and sexual orientation, since this aspect of one's self is not obvious from infancy and must be discovered and, in the case of lesbian, gay, bisexual, or **transgendered** identity, disclosed. One model of this process of **coming out** outlines five stages in the formation of a positive sexual identity (Coleman, 1982). In the *pre–coming out* stage, the person is confused about her sexual orientation, perhaps worried that she may be lesbian or bisexual, but convinced that it would be better to be heterosexual. Sure that people would reject her if they knew her sexual orientation, she tries to "pass" as heterosexual.

In the *coming out* stage, she stops fighting her sexual orientation and begins to disclose to others that she is lesbian or bisexual. In the third stage, labeled *identity acceptance and exploration,* the woman increases her contacts with the lesbian community and develops a support system. In the fourth stage, secure in the support of other women and her own increased self-acceptance, she may develop her *first serious sexual relationship*. In the *integration* stage, she unites her public and private identities. She takes pride in being a lesbian or bisexual woman; it becomes a strong, positive aspect of her identity. The stages are not invariant in their order, or even in their occurrence, but they do describe some of the common experiences of the coming-out process.

A similar process of questioning, discovery, and coming out may be experienced by individuals who are uncomfortable with their assigned or assumed gender identity. Some eventually resolve their dissatisfaction by changing their gender identity: making a transition from male to female or from female to male. In the process, they may begin to question binary gender categories, feeling that they do not fit neatly into either one. Eventually, some may reject conventional feminine or masculine identities and claim an identity as transgendered (e.g., Bornstein, 1994).

Recent research on a national sample of more than 2,000 lesbians of all races, socioeconomic classes, geographic regions of the United States, ages, and abilities suggests that existing models of lesbian development are too limited (Rabin & Slater, 2004). Joan Rabin and Barbara Slater found a lot of diversity among their respondents in the timing of the coming out process. Almost 6 percent of the women reported they had recognized their lesbian identity by age 12, and 35 percent said they had done so by age 18. More than half had recognized their identity by age 21. Women who recognized their lesbian identity early in life were more likely than those who recognized it after age 22 to experience a long time interval between recognizing their lesbian identity and coming out to another person. Preliminary observations from these researchers suggest that a long time interval between coming out to oneself and coming out to another person may be associated with negative emotional consequences. Interestingly, a full 76 percent of this large, diverse sample reported that their experience of coming out to another person was a positive one.

Just how many identities can a person have? And how do they work together? Kay Deaux and Abigail Stewart (2001) suggest that the notion of **intersectionality** is useful in understanding how multiple identities work. Intersectionality means that two "separate" identities (such as gender and race) are not simply additive (i.e., a person doesn't merely add the fact that she is White to the fact that she is female). Rather, "experience in [a] particular race-inflected status is qualitatively different. The experience of 'being a woman' is different for a Black woman and a White woman, because womanhood is defined and socially constructed differently for the two groups. Moreover, the individual woman can never separate her experience[s] into some that are due to her race versus others due to her gender: She is always and everywhere both raced and gendered, and her experience cannot be wholly attributed to only one of these characteristics" (Deaux & Stewart, 2001, pp. 92–93). This perspective suggests that a person's gender identity may be different as it intersects with other identities such as race, class, sexual orientation, age, and even role identities such as "parent."

The experience of intersecting identities may be particularly poignant for women who are living as minority members in a culture that often fails to acknowledge them. As Aída Hurtado (2003) notes, "In the writings of women of Color, the overriding metaphor for women's consciousness is multiplicity. . . . [M]any women of Color have been forced into cultivating multiple social identities. . . . many of my respondents . . . were indeed the bridge between their family members, between different communities of Color, and between different communities of Color and white communities. From an early age they were compelled to juggle multiple social groups while still maintaining, in fact needing, a strong coherent individual self to prevent the relationships around them from colliding" (pp. 100–101).

Experientially, integration of one's various identities can be difficult. A personal and moving description of this kind of struggle to reconcile different identities is provided by Shamara Shantu Riley (1994) in her account of developing her identity as a Black lesbian during her college years. As she says in her introduction,

> Because of my multifaceted identity as a Black lesbian, I have often simultaneously felt like a "sistah" and yet still an "outsider" in the Black, lesbian, and womanist communities. In this contradictory space of sistah-outsiderhood, I am often expected to negate some component of my identity in the name of "unity" or in order to pass someone's litmus test of acceptance. (p. 92)

In a similar vein, Espín (1987) notes that Latina lesbians sometimes feel they must choose to emphasize *either* their ethnic identities *or* their lesbian identities because of the negative labels attached to lesbianism in Latin cultures.

Sometimes, however, with appropriate cultural support, different aspects of identity can be reconciled and strongly integrated. An example of this process is given by Alex Wilson (1996) in her account of her own life journey toward claiming the identity of a **two-spirit person,** a term used by many lesbian, gay, and bisexual Native Americans to describe themselves. She cites a tradition of recognizing the existence and value of two-spirit people in most Native American cultures, people who are thought to be born "in balance," incorporating a blend of feminine and masculine qualities, of female and male spirits. They are considered part of the community, and this tradition helps individuals reclaim their connection to their communities and traditions when they reclaim their identity with this name.

Wilson describes the moment in her childhood when a friend accused her of "dancing like a boy" as a crucial one in questioning her identity:

> Knowing became not knowing, and the sureness of my experience was replaced by a growing certainty that I could not be the girl that was wanted outside of my family. Being "different" was no longer a gift, and my self-consciousness led me to learn ways to pretend and ways to hide myself. (p. 311)

Feeling confused and diminished by homophobia and by the racism of some people in her small community, Wilson says, she began to refuse to identify herself as Cree, and even began to avoid her relatives. Moving to the nearest city, she tried to escape the negative judgments of some of her peers and to explore her lesbian identity in a more anonymous environment. However,

> as an Indigenous woman, I could not find a positive place for myself in the predominantly White, gay scene. I looked there for support in my lesbian identity, and instead found another articulation of racism. Although a large number of gay and lesbian Indigenous people live in the city, the Indigenous community remains segregated from the mainstream, non-Indigenous gay and lesbian community. (p. 312)

She rediscovered her connection to her Indigenous community when she came out to her parents—who told her that they already knew.

> This puzzled me. How could they know and I didn't? I understand now that they respected me enough not to interfere, and enough to be confident that I would come to understand my sexuality when the time was right. Throughout my life, my family had acknowledged and accepted me without interference: my grandfather gave me hunting lessons and my parents brought me the toys that I would enjoy. As I was told by another child that I had danced the "wrong" dance, the elders of my community [had] smiled and clapped, quietly inviting me to continue. (p. 312)

In recognizing her family's and the elders' acceptance of her, Wilson says, she realized that her development had been guided by a traditional Indigenous worldview, and she began to feel integrated into her community as a lesbian and empowered by her identity. She gained strength from discussions with the community elders, who explained to her that "as an Indigenous woman who is also a lesbian, I needed to use the gift of my difference wisely" (p. 313). She realized that all aspects of her identity were interconnected, and that the experience of her sexuality was inseparable from the experience of her culture.

Identity Flexibility and Change

One thing that becomes clear as we think about identities is that they are not static, but seem somewhat flexible in response to life events and situations. Identities are subject to negotiation and change (Deaux & Stewart, 2001). When a young woman is at school, she may be most aware of her identity as a student; when she visits her parents, she may be more focused on her identity as a daughter, for example. And major life events have a way of shifting our identities in ways that have implications for how we experience our gender. For instance, as a woman goes through the process of becoming a mother for the first time, she constructs a new and important identity for herself. This new (and often central) identity as "mother" is not independent of her other identities (such as spouse, employee), but affects them, often making them seem less important (Ethier, 1995). It is likely that the mother identity also intersects with the new mother's experience of being female, thus changing the experience of female identity as well.

One experience that can have fundamental implications for identity is the process of immigration to a new country. As Oliva Espín (1999) notes, "For the person who has migrated, identity issues are further complicated by their polyvalent circumstances. One is aware that both life's losses and failures and life's possibilities and triumphs are magnified and distorted by the lens of the migration experience. Migration for me, as for most immigrants, has provided a dual and contradictory legacy. It has given me safety and success, yet it has also brought losses and silences about them. Mention of them is easily confused with self-pity or even ungratefulness to the new country." (p. 2)

Immigration is a critical issue for women. Eighty percent of the world's refugees and displaced persons are women and their children (Women's Commission for Refugee Women and Children, 2001) and over 47 percent of people who migrate for economic reasons are women (United Nations, 2000). Researchers who have studied immigrants' reports of their experiences note that, in the process of taking on new identities (e.g., "immigrant," "new American," "Mexican American") these individuals often also change the ways they experience their gender. For women, immigration often entails a struggle between old and new identities as their families tug them toward tradition while their new environment beckons them to explore new ways of being. As Italian American writer Maryann Feola (1998) remembers, "Memories of my girlhood daydreams and adventures are mixed with images of those numerous great aunts dressed in black warning me not to forget who I was. My interests, dress, and plans for the future might stem from personal taste: however, they must not break with the traditions that offered security" (p. 284).

Oliva Espín (1999) argues that immigrant communities often emphasize traditional roles for women in an attempt to maintain cultural continuity in the midst of a sense of dislocation. Women in immigrant families, she says, face restrictions on their behavior and are often expected by their families to behave, in terms of gender norms, clothing, and ritual, as if they were still in the old country.

> It is as if the immigrants' psychological sense of safety and their sense of self depended on a sharp contrast between two sets of cultural values conceived as rigidly different and unchangeable. The preservation of old versions of women's roles becomes central to this sharp contrast. For people who experience a deep lack of control over their daily lives, controlling women's sexuality and behavior becomes a symbolic demonstration of orderliness and continuity and gives them the feeling that not all traditions are lost. This is why women themselves frequently join in adhering to traditions that, from the point of view of outsiders, appear to curtail their own freedoms and opportunities for self-fulfillment. (p. 7)

If women do want to adapt to their new culture, such adaptation is easily interpreted as disrespectful of their elders and their home culture's values. Conflicts about dress, dating, and sexuality may be especially intense. Even women who immigrate alone rather than with families may face disapproval from their immigrant communities for their non-conformity to traditional gender roles. Thus women must negotiate their new identities carefully, and they may often feel a great deal of ambivalence.

Clearly, identities are complex and multilayered, responsive to life changes and historical context. As Deaux and Stewart (2001) note, identity development is not a neat, linear process leading to a stable, unchanging outcome. Furthermore, they note, there is not a single "gender identity," but rather "multiple gendered identities" (p. 87). There is no single answer to the question of what it means to be feminine; there are many answers, many ways to be feminine.

The Self as a Cultural Construction

Most of the identity searches and struggles described here have been, despite their links to reference groups and to social acceptance, intensely individual. "I have to discover, become, and stay true to who I am" might be the theme. This independent, individual sense of self is not, apparently, an inevitable fact of human nature. Rather, it, like gender, is a cultural construction, and it receives a great deal of emphasis in some societies but not in others.

Hazel Markus and Shinobu Kitayama (1991) assembled an impressive collection of evidence that "people in different cultures have strikingly different construals of the self, of others, and of the interdependence of the 2" (p. 224). They suggest that one broad distinction between cultures is the sense of the **self as independent** versus the **self as interdependent.** The independent construal of self involves the idea that each person is separate and distinct, with unique attributes, and that the person's developmental task is to become independent from others and to express those unique attributes. The interdependent construal of self involves the idea that human beings are fundamentally interconnected and that the task of each person is to maintain those connections. In Japanese, for instance, the word for self, *jibun,* means "one's share of the shared life space" (Hamaguchi, 1985, cited in Markus & Kitayama, 1991). In this interdependent orientation, "[p]eople are motivated to find a way to fit in with relevant others, to fulfill and create obligation, and in general to become part of various interpersonal relationships" (p. 227). Self-esteem, within this orientation, would be achieved through belonging, fitting in, maintaining harmony with others, and occupying one's proper place.

And how would the notion of identity be described within an interdependent cultural orientation? Perhaps, in part, by describing one's relationship to one's community. For example, Maria Izabel, a Mayan woman from Guatemala, had this response to a question about her definition of herself as Mayan: "[I]f one only says, I am indigenous, and one's activities are otherwise, and one does not make an effort to learn one's language, to get closer to one's people . . . one's definition is very empty . . ." (Lykes, 1994, p. 109).

According to Markus and Kitayama, the independent construal of self is most characteristic of American culture and of many Western European ones; the interdependent construal of self is seen in Asian, African, Latin American, and some southern European cultures. They are quick to note, however, that within a given culture, there may be much variation among subgroups. For instance, in American culture, the tendency toward an independent self may be strongest among White, middle-class men of Western European extraction; it may be less characteristic of women or of men and women from other social classes and racial groups. In fact, some American feminist psychologists have worked to develop the notion of **self-in-relation**, arguing that independence is only one aspect of identity development, and the development of one's connections with others is an equally important aspect (Jordan & Surrey, 1986; Markus & Oyserman, 1988; Miller, 1986). They argue, in fact, that it is likely both females and males construct identities that include both independent and relational aspects, although gender-related expectations may lead them to place differential emphasis on these two components. Perhaps the agonizing that women sometimes do over reconciling their various identities stems from the importance they place on the self-in-relation. Maintaining proper relationships within all of their reference groups is of crucial importance to them.

It is unlikely that members of any cultural or gender group construct selves that are purely independent or purely interdependent. Cathy Louie (2000), who studied European American students and recent Asian American immigrant students, found evidence for a **dual self:** All participants seemed to have *both* independent and interdependent dimensions of the self, with each dimension developed to a different degree in different groups. Asian American students had a more developed interdependent dimension, whereas European American students had a more developed independent dimension.

The field of Western psychology has been all but impervious to the relational aspect of the self and to other alternative conceptions of the self—perhaps because, until fairly recently, the field has been dominated by the White, middle-class men who are most easily characterized by the independent notion of self. This narrowness of vision illustrates the reciprocal influences between culture and psychology as a discipline. Based on their own experience and culturally supported view of the world, psychologists describe the self in a certain way. In describing it, they help define and limit it since the description helps other people to focus only on certain ways of looking at the self: the ways that are "named" by psychologists. Far from being an objective description of an essential reality, any psychology of the self is a social construction that is limited by culture.

SUMMARY

How do we construct and modify our notions of who we are and who we might become? We do not do it as isolated individuals, but as members of a family, a peer group, a culture. We learn to dance in step with our social partners, often not realizing we are doing so.

Theorists have suggested many ways to understand how individuals become "gendered." Psychoanalytic theories focus on inner psychological dynamics that arise from early caretaking relationships and the individual's awareness of her or his body. Evolutionary theories, on the other hand, argue for biological inheritance of characteristics thought to have been differentially useful for females and males in their quest to reproduce. Theories of social learning place their focus squarely on the social environment in which the individual must function, arguing that all of us learn how to be feminine or masculine by watching others, imitating them, and being rewarded for doing so. A more recent version of this approach, social cognitive theory, adds an emphasis on self-regulation through internal rewards and punishments and active choices by the individual about which models are and are not appropriate to imitate. Cognitive developmental theories postulate that the process of forming gender identities and roles is moderated by the child's intellectual maturity, suggesting, for example, that a child cannot achieve gender constancy (the idea that a person's gender is fixed) until s/he reaches a certain level of intellectual development. Finally, social roles theory proposes that gender-related differences throughout the life course occur because of the interaction between societal expectations about what roles women and men will fill and the attempts of women and men to acquire the skills and habits that make them successful in these roles.

Many of the theories about gender invoke the environment as a source of information and pressure about what women and men should be like. An examination of one major aspect of our social environment, the popular media, shows that it provides many messages about gender. In the news media, women are less visible than men as important figures and as experts and more visible as victims. In popular television shows, women and girls are portrayed as more relationship oriented and less work oriented than males, and appearance is emphasized more for females. The new media domain of the Internet offers many negative images of women, but it also provides scope for women to challenge traditional images and stereotypes. Access to this technology, potentially a very useful tool for women, is far greater in developed regions such as North America and Western Europe than in poorer regions, and the technology is still used more by men than women.

In the face of the many different images and pressures to be feminine encountered by girls and women, just what does it mean to be feminine? Much of the old research on femininity and masculinity treated these concepts as opposites. However, Sandra Bem, who developed a measure of psychological androgyny, showed that many people of both sexes report that they possess and display qualities associated with *both* femininity and masculinity. Furthermore, such androgynous persons appear to be well-adjusted, flexible, and responsive to their environments.

Another theory, gender schema theory, proposes that femininity and masculinity are, in some respects, learned cognitive frameworks that individuals use to process information and to decide whether particular behaviors are appropriate for themselves or for others.

Gender is one basic category with which a person must come to terms. Each of us must find a way to integrate it with a set of other social identities, based on race, ethnicity, age, sexual orientation, nationality, and so on, into what we call our "self." The integration is never set, never settled, never finished. Instead, it must be recreated as our lives change. Important to this process are our reference groups and events that we encounter that may propel us to new stages in our identity formation. Such events may include particular occurrences such as discrimination, or life changes such as having a child or immigrating to a new country. And the way we integrate such experiences into our sense of self will depend to some extent on the culture in which we are grounded—whether that culture emphasizes independence or interdependence in the formation of self.

Our gender is a crucial aspect of our identity. As one of the very first categories we accept as part of our self-definition, gender influences how we try to fit in, and with whom. The way an individual's culture constructs and organizes gender can influence that individual's sense of possibilities for the self. We are not passively shaped by such cultural constructions, nor are we ever immune from them. Each woman everywhere creates her sense of meaning and identity in the context of her culture. Thus there are multiple possible feminine identities.

KEY TERMS

possible self
gender role
gender identity
psychoanalytic theory
Oedipus complex
Electra complex
devaluation
sexualization
phallocentric
gynocentric
infantile grandiosity
Antigone complex
evolutionary theory
natural selection
sexual selection
big mother hypothesis

reproductive fitness
parental investment
social learning theory
continuities in interactional
   style
cumulative continuity
interactional continuity
social cognitive theory
group socialization theory
cognitive developmental
   theory
gender constancy
social roles theory
sexual orientation
androgyny
self-schema

gender schema
reference groups
preencounter stage
encounter stage
immersion/emersion stage
internalization stage
transgendered
coming out
intersectionality
two-spirit person
independent self
interdependent self
self-in-relation
dual self

DISCUSSION QUESTIONS

Which theory (or combination of theories) makes the most sense to you as an explanation of how human behavior and personality becomes gendered?

Are there ways in which it appears that theoretical approaches to the psychology of women have been shaped by male-centered views of the world?

What factors help to determine which of our identities (e.g., gender, ethnicity, race, nationality) we feel to be primary?

Do the media help to shape an individual's identity and sense of possibility? What changes would you like to see in the media's treatment of girls and women?

FOR ADDITIONAL READING

Ciatu, Angelina, Dileo, Domenica, and Micallef, Gabrielly (Eds.). (1998). *Curaggia: Writing by women of Italian descent.* Toronto: Women's Press. A collection of intensely personal stories, poems, autobiographical narratives, and pictures explores the ethnic and other identity issues, stereotypes, and life choices of women of Italian heritage.

Hrdy, Sarah Blaffer (1999). *Mother nature: Maternal instincts and how they shape the human species.* New York: Ballantine Books. A respected primatologist and evolutionary theorist brings a feminist lens to evolutionary theory about motherhood.

Hurtado, Aída. (2003). *Voicing Chicana feminisms: Young women speak out on sexuality and identity.* New York: New York University Press. A psychologist distills information about identity, power, sexuality, and family relationships from her extensive interviews with 101 Chicana women between the ages of 20 and 30.

Kaschak, Ellyn. (1992). *Engendered lives: A new psychology of women's experience.* New York: Basic Books. The author takes a critical look at theories of female and male development, particularly psychoanalytic theories, and offers a new feminist theoretical perspective.

Landrine, Hope (Ed.). (1995). *Bringing cultural diversity to feminist psychology.* Washington, DC: American Psychological Association. A collection of articles by researchers and theorists who are exploring the means for psychology to expand beyond its traditional focus on White, middle-class women. It includes chapters on specific issues, such as childhood socialization, health research, and therapy, as well as on particular groups: American Indian, Latina, Asian American, and Black women.

Wilson, Alex. (1996). How we find ourselves: Identity development and two-spirit people. *Harvard Educational Review, 66*(2), 303–317. An account of the development of lesbian identity in the context of Native American culture, in an article that combines theory and an intensely personal story.

WEB RESOURCES

Angry Little Girls. The site presents a bittersweet weekly comic strip that explores and pokes fun at the racist and sexist stereotypes that children often must confront as they grow up and form their identities. The site includes a chat room and an "angry board," where readers share their own experiences. **www.angrylittlegirls.com**

International Women's Media Foundation. The organization was started in 1990 to strengthen the role of women in the news media around the world. The Web site contains research reports about women's roles in the media, provides a forum for the exchange of ideas, and includes links to such international projects as the African Women's Media Center and the Latin America Media Initiative. **www.iwmf.org**

CHAPTER 5

Getting the Message: Self-Confidence, Assertiveness, and Entitlement

CHAPTER OUTLINE

> I told the teacher that I didn't know what I'd be doing when I'm bigger. I told the teacher that I might turn into a caribou, and run away, and never come near the village. I might become a polar bear, and watch our village from some ice out on the harbor. The teacher didn't like the way I was talking! But I didn't like the way the teacher was talking! The teachers who come here usually stay for two or three years. They want us to think just as they do. They tell . . . [us] . . . to dream of airplanes and submarines and snowmobiles and radios . . . (Coles & Coles, 1978, p. 185)

This story of a young Alaskan Inuit girl's outspokenness and self-confident resistance to the imposition of another culture is in sharp contrast with the following observations by Annie Rogers (1993) about her interview with a 13-year-old European American eighth-grade girl:

> I want to learn from Marcia about the lives of girls. She studies me in swift glances, her face closed, as I set up my tape recorder. During this interview I listen to the cadence of Marcia's quick sentences, punctuated by the phrases: "I don't know" and "this doesn't make any sense." We hear these phrases sharply increase in our longitudinal interviews, marking a repression of knowledge as girls enter early adolescence . . . I feel Marcia slipping away from me; her confusion and the dismissal of her knowledge resonates with the voices of girls her age whom I have interviewed over several years. I begin to wonder if girls lose not only clarity, self-confidence, and voice—but also their courage—as they come of age in androcentric cultures. (p. 272)

Rogers defines **courage** as having spirit, liveliness, a quality of boldness, the ability "to speak one's mind by telling all one's heart" (p. 275). Her definition encompasses qualities each of us has observed in some women. Yet the prevailing image of women in many cultures is not of courage or confidence, but of tentativeness and timidity. Rogers and others (e.g., Brown & Gilligan, 1990) conclude from their research on mostly White, middle-class girls in the United States that during the transition to adolescence many girls in this culture begin to pay attention to the cultural message that they are not supposed to be bold, direct, or courageous.

Obviously, the silencing of girls, their acceptance of the message that it is not safe for them, if they value their relationships, to speak their mind and take bold stands, is not inevitable. Niobe Way's (1995) research on a small group of urban poor and working-class adolescent girls suggests that as girls in this group move through adolescence, they may place increasing importance on the ability to speak their minds, to be clear in their expressions of feelings, to refuse to let others treat them with insensitivity. As one young African American woman in her senior year of high school said in her interview:

> [I am] outgoing, outspoken and out everything. Yeah. Out everything. If I [have] something to say I'm just gonna say it. Some case it'd be rude and I know it'd be rude, but, you know, when you're not listening to me, sorry, I'm rude. I'm rude. So I never let anyone intimidate me . . . (p. 116)

Such outspokenness may not, as some participants in this study themselves pointed out, always mean that a girl has high self-esteem. Rather, speaking out may be a style of resistance that developed *because* a girl's self-esteem was under constant bombardment.

As they enter adolescence, then, with its pressures to be feminine, popular, beautiful, liked, some girls retreat into silence or quiet "niceness"; others become increasingly passionate about speaking their minds. How does culture contribute to the ways femininity is constructed by these young women? In this chapter, we examine the evidence concerning girls' self-confidence and self-esteem in childhood and the ways it is challenged at adolescence. We will look at the links between these issues and the kinds of educational and life choices young women make. We will consider the expectations that girls and women hold for their own performance and discuss the ways those expectations may relate to their sense of entitlement to rewards and recognition for their work.

Confidence and a sense of entitlement are linked to power, and girls' and women's use of power is the focus of the second half of the chapter. We shall see that an individual's sense of entitlement can affect the way she attempts to influence others—and that reactions to a woman exercising power are apparently shaped by observers' notions about potential conflicts between femininity and power. Finally, we examine some of the specific ways that cultures restrict girls' and women's sense of entitlement.

Self-Confidence, Courage, and Femininity

Stories told to young girls in many cultures celebrate extraordinary acts of daring or power by women. The Chinese myth of the woman warrior tells of a brave woman whose feats in battle became the envy of male troops. Native American tales describe goddesses who brought powers such as fertility and fire to humans, and great female healers who intimidated their male counterparts. Islamic tradition speaks respectfully of Muhammad's wives and daughters, some of whom rode into battle with him.

It is not necessary to look so far back to find stories of women whose courage carried them past barriers and difficulties: Consider Harriet Tubman, the African American woman who risked her life repeatedly to lead more than 300 slaves to safety in the 1850s; Susan LaFlesche Picotte, the first Native American woman to overcome the obstacles of prejudice to become a doctor; Emily Carr, the Canadian artist who endured fear and discomfort to travel to remote Indian villages in the early 1900s to paint the disappearing totem poles; Alice Paul and her fellow suffragists in the United States (and Emmeline and Sylvia Pankhurst and their sister militants in Britain) who, in the 1910s, were beaten, imprisoned, and force-fed as they struggled to establish women's right to vote; Chinese writer Ding Ling, who traded her favored position for official criticism in 1942 when she suggested publicly that women were being neglected by the Communist revolution and that "if women want equality, they must first strengthen themselves"; winner of the 1991 Nobel Peace Prize

Aung San Suu Kyi, the Burmese woman who faced imprisonment rather than abandon her fight for democracy in her country. Then there are the stories of countless unsung women who have given birth to children under unspeakably difficult conditions, who travel for miles to obtain food or medical attention for their children, whose backbreaking labor makes the difference between starvation and survival for their families.

These and thousands of other examples of courageous women, although inspiring, have not seemed sufficient to offset the notion of girls and women as somewhat timid, self-deprecating, and more likely to seek protection and reassurance than to accomplish difficult, dangerous, challenging feats. In much of North American culture, as in some others, the cultural construction of women as less confident and weaker than men is pervasive enough that all these examples of strong and courageous women can be seen as exceptions to the rule.

Girls' Self-Confidence

Jeanne Block, a psychologist who pursued a pioneering longitudinal study of children's development, concluded from her observations that girls were socialized to develop "roots," whereas boys were taught to develop "wings." Girls were encouraged to stay close, to form bonds; boys were urged to explore, to take risks (Block, 1984). From an early age, then, girls may not be challenged to develop and expand their **self-confidence**—although there is little reason to believe that girls start out with any less tendency toward self-confidence than boys do.

Some studies have indeed shown a tendency for girls more than boys to seek proximity to adults, indicating, perhaps, a higher need for reassurance or some general desire to affiliate rather than to stake out their independence. Is this a sign of girls' shaky self-confidence? Not necessarily. Girls' proximity-seeking is apparently pragmatic and depends on the social context; in particular, it depends on whether or not there are boys in the room.

In a careful study of this phenomenon, Greeno (cited in Maccoby, 1990) brought groups of four kindergarten or first-grade children into a playroom full of toys. An adult woman sat at one end of the room and moved to a seat at the other end when the play session was half over. Observers monitoring the behavior of the four children noted that the gender composition of each quartet made a big difference to patterns of proximity and affiliation. First of all, when a quartet was made up of two girls and two boys, there was extreme gender segregation: Each child behaved as if she or he had only one other potential playmate (the one of the same sex) rather than three. Second, girls behaved quite differently with respect to the adult woman depending on whether they were in an all-girl quartet or a two-girl dyad sharing the room with two boys. In all-girl groups, girls actually played farther from the adult than boys in all-boy groups did, changing their location when the adult moved in order to maintain their distance. On the other hand, when boys were present, girls tended to play significantly closer to the adult than the boys did, and moved *with* the adult when she moved in order to stay relatively close. It appears, then, that the tendency to seek proximity to adults is not a general trait of girls; rather, girls may look on an adult as a potential moderator of boys' rough or boisterous behavior. Girls' discomfort rises when boys are present, and they use the adult as a buffer against potential threats.

Why should girls want an adult around to moderate boys' behavior? Because, beginning at a very early age, girls and boys play and interact differently. These differences are magnified and reinforced by the strong tendency of children from the age of 3 onward to choose same-sex playmates—a tendency that is found in most, but not all, cultures. In a circular, self-reinforcing process, most girls and boys choose same-sex playmates because they are most comfortable with the way children of their own gender interact, and then these segregated playgroups socialize their members into increasingly divergent styles of interaction (Maccoby, 1990). These divergent styles take girls more and more in the direction of building community and sustaining social relationships, whereas they take boys more and more in the direction of emphasizing dominance and competition. Girls develop an interaction style that is collaborative and supportive; they are more likely than boys to express agreement with other speakers, pause to give other girls a chance to speak, soften their directives to playmates, and use strategies to mitigate conflict when it occurs. Boys, in contrast, develop a style that is self-assertive and openly competitive; they are more likely than girls to interrupt other speakers, use commands, threats, and boasts, and refuse to comply with other children's demands. Thus girls are socializing one another to value community and social relationships; boys are socializing one another to value power assertion and successful competition. Given these two very different styles, it is understandable that girls might avoid playing with boys and might feel more comfortable with an adult close by if boys are in the room. Boys, they know from experience, are unlikely to cooperate with them or accede to their requests.

These findings about collaboration among girls do not mean that girls are all "sugar and spice." In fact, girls display their share of conflict and meanness. As noted in Chapter 2, girls display **relational aggression** in their conflicts with other girls: They compete with and retaliate against other girls by withdrawing their friendship, excluding them from social groups, and spreading negative gossip about them (Maccoby, 1998). The success of such methods, however, stems from the importance girls have learned to place on relationships and supportive social interactions.

In cultures that exert no strong pressures for boys and girls to be different, the tendency to choose same-sex playmates—and thus the tendency for girls and boys to be socialized by their peers into very different interaction patterns—is considerably muted. For example, Marjorie Shostak (1981) reported that among the !Kung people of the Kalahari Desert in southern Africa, boys and girls played together and shared most games, and they showed no preference for playing only with children of their own sex. She notes that !Kung girls and boys were equally active and capable of sustaining attention to tasks, and equal in the amount of time spent playing with objects. Both girls and boys were allowed to express the full range of emotions, and neither sex was trained to be submissive, fierce, or competitive.

Even in a culture such as the United States where girls *are* taught to be accommodating and unassertive, in their own space they are often supremely confident. Indeed, one survey of fourth-grade and senior high school girls in all-girl schools found that 92 percent thought that a woman should be elected president of the United States—a result that is startling in a country that has shown such resistance to female political leaders (Mann, 1992). Yet girls are often socialized away from this confidence by parents and teachers who overprotect and underestimate them, or who simply ignore them when boys are around.

For example, many studies in the United States show that teachers, often without realizing it, treat boys and girls differently: They pay more attention to boys than to girls in the

BOX 5.1 WOMEN SHAPING PSYCHOLOGY
Jeanne Humphrey Block (1923–1981)

Jeanne Humphrey Block was fascinated by the way that socialization toward gendered expectations influenced the development of girls and boys. She investigated this process in a now-famous longitudinal study, in collaboration with her husband, Jack Block, in which they tested a group of 130 children at ages 3, 4, 5, 7, 11 and 14. She was also an early practitioner of cross-cultural research in psychology, studying the socialization practices of the Scandinavian countries, England, and the United States. With these studies and her written reflections about their results, Jeanne Block left a lasting mark on psychology.

Jeanne Humphrey grew up in a small town in Oregon and graduated from high school during the Second World War. Although she started college as a home economics major, she was soon disenchanted with both college and home economics and left after one year. She enlisted in the women's unit of the U.S. Coast Guard, was commissioned an ensign in 1944, and served with distinction. During her service, she was scalded over much of her body and nearly died. However, she was able to return to active service after treatment with skin grafts, and she continued to serve until 1946.

After her demobilization, Humphrey enrolled at Reed College and completed a degree in psychology, then went on to Stanford for graduate work in clinical psychology. At Stanford, she found important mentors: Ernest Hilgard and Maud Merrill James. There she also met and married fellow graduate student Jack Block. By the time she completed her doctoral dissertation in 1951, she was pregnant with her first child. Through the next decade, she bore four children and devoted much of her energy to home and family. However, she continued to be involved in psychological work on a part-time basis, beginning some influential research on factors predisposing children to asthma, and writing and publishing articles with her husband. It was not until 1963 that she again found herself in a position to be a full-time psychologist. That year, she was awarded a Special Research Fellowship from the National Institute of Mental Health and moved to Norway (with her family) to take up a one-year appointment at the

BOX 5.1 WOMEN SHAPING PSYCHOLOGY (continued)
Jeanne Humphrey Block (1923–1981)

Norwegian Institute for Social Research. It was during this time that she conducted her cross-cultural research on childhood socialization.

When she returned to the United States, Jeanne Block did not have a full-time position. However, she continued to apply for and receive grants to do research. She also marched in protest against the Vietnam War, volunteered for Eugene McCarthy's presidential campaign, and helped start the Committee for Social Responsibility (now the Physicians for Social Responsibility). It was not until 1968—17 years after completing her doctoral work—that Block was able to embark on a truly focused career in psychology. That year she was awarded a National Institute of Mental Health Research Scientist Development Award and she and her husband began the longitudinal study that became the main focus of the rest of her career. In thoughtful articles about this research, Block subsequently reflected on the ways biological and cultural factors have shaped gender expectations and roles. She noted that, because qualities that are important for self-expression were considered masculine, "Socialization for women . . . becomes associated with control of impulse expression and the renunciation of achievement and autonomy" (Block, 1973, p. 525). In developing their identities, girls were urged to put down roots, she mused, whereas boys were encouraged to spread their wings. She argued that the reason more women did not take on achievement-

oriented and ambitious behaviors was that "it was simply too difficult and too lonely to oppose the cultural tide" (p. 526). She never held a regular faculty position; however, her work had an important influence on our understanding of gender and culture.

Block was at the peak of her research career when she was diagnosed with pancreatic cancer in May of 1981. She died before the year was out, leaving some of her most important work to be published posthumously in the book, *Sex Role Identity and Ego Development* (Block, 1984). Her many contributions are honored through the Radcliffe Institute's Jeanne Humphrey Block Dissertation Awards, which support woman doctoral candidates researching sex and gender differences or some developmental issue of particular concern to American girls or women.

Read More about Jeanne Humphrey Block

Block, Jack (1990). Jeanne Humphrey Block. In A. N. O'Connell & N. F. Russo (Eds.), *Women in psychology: A bio-bibliographic sourcebook* (pp. 40–48). New York: Greenwood Press.

Read What She Wrote

Block, J. H. (1973). Conceptions of sex role: Some cross-cultural and longitudinal perspectives. *American Psychologist, 28,* 512–526.

Block, J. H. (1984). *Sex role identity and ego development*. San Francisco: Jossey-Bass.

Many studies in the United States show that teachers, often without realizing it, pay more attention to boys than to girls in the classroom.

classroom, spend more time outside of class talking with boys than girls, and respond differently to boys' and girls' successes and failures (Dweck, 1999; Okpala, 1996; Sadker & Sadker, 1994). In a *USA Today* write-in survey of a nonrandom sample of 222,653 U.S. teens in grades 6 through 12, one-third of the boys and 42 percent of the girls said that they had some teachers who called on boys more often than girls in class (Pera, 1996/1998). Similar patterns have been found in other countries, such as Costa Rica (Huber & Scaglion, 1995) and Taiwan (She, 2000). The differences are such that they tend to undermine girls' sense of proficiency and competence in comparison to boys. Among European American elementary school students, girls speak up less in class than boys do; this difference is reinforced by teachers who call on boys more frequently than girls. African American girls, on the other hand, begin school with a strong tendency to speak up; however, the teachers, by ignoring them or refusing to encourage their outspokenness, gradually shape them into the same pattern of inconspicuousness as their European American counterparts (Irvine, 1986). One study found that as African American girls advanced through their years of school they received less and less attention from their teachers (Nelson-LeGall, 1990). Eventually these girls may reassert their outspokenness, but they may have to leave the social control of the school in order to do so.

Some critics have argued that, if there is a problem with gender and schooling in North America, it is the boys and not the girls who are having more trouble (Sommers, 2000). After all, girls get higher grades than boys all through school; boys are more likely than girls to drop out of school and less likely than girls to go on to college. And students who responded to the *USA Today* survey reported by a wide margin that teachers were tougher on boys than on girls and that girls received more positive attention than boys in the classroom (Pera, 1996/1998). If girls do better and get more positive feedback in school and boys are "picked on" and more likely to drop out, why should we be concerned about girls? One answer to this question lies in the *kind* of attention that girls and boys receive.

When boys are punished by teachers, it is more likely to be for rowdy behavior; when they are praised, it is more likely to be for correctly solving a problem or some other successful task performance. Girls often receive more praise than boys, but when girls are praised, it is as likely to be for good behavior or for their appearance as for successful task performance. Boys who fail at a task are exhorted to try harder and assured that they can do it if they work hard enough. Girls who fail are often given little feedback or encouragement to keep working at it—thereby receiving the message that the task is a "hopeless" one for them (Dweck & Leggett, 1988; Elliott & Dweck, 1988). The teachers seem to be guided by the idea that boys do not work hard enough, but that girls (always such well-behaved, good little workers) are already doing their best. The impact of the teachers' behavior is a negative one for girls, leading them to feel that their performance is limited mainly by their low ability, and that it is no use putting more effort into succeeding at the task. Girls who start out in school doing very well may be particularly affected by this strategy. If they succeed a lot without trying very hard, they learn that they are "smart" (i.e, they attribute their success to high ability). However, when they encounter a really difficult task—one on which they initially fail—they react with helplessness because they are not used to responding to failure with increased effort or new approaches (Dweck, 1999). Thus, in spite of all the positive attention they have received in the past, these girls may end up with low self-confidence in some academic situations. Evidence is quite consistent that girls, as compared with boys, "are more likely to avoid challenging and competitive situations, lower their expectations more following failure, shift more quickly to a different college major when their grades begin to drop, and perform more poorly than they are capable of on difficult, timed tests (Eccles, Barber, Jozefowicz, Malenchuk, & Vida, 1999).

Summarizing the implications of her research, Dweck (1999) argues that it is essential for teachers to communicate an emphasis on challenge, strategy, and effort when they help girls to make attributions for their performance. If girls are taught that failure is not necessarily the result of low ability, but perhaps of inadequate strategy or effort, then they are likely to be better equipped to keep trying to master difficult educational challenges. Perversely, though, what often happens to bright girls studying subjects that are thought to be "masculine" is that their failures are attributed to low ability while their successes are chalked up to extraordinary efforts. For instance, an analysis of the processes within one South African classroom showed that girls were treated as hard-working, but without a natural flair for mathematics, and the qualities necessary for high achievement in mathematics were ascribed to boys (Macleod, 1995).

Studies suggest that after years of differential treatment in school, many girls begin to feel silenced—to be afraid to speak out about their opinions, nervous about proffering answers in the classroom, intimidated at the prospect of risking failure or disapproval by saying what they think. By the time they reach college classrooms, female students may be more apprehensive than male students about speaking up in class (Jaasma, 1997). But the differences are apparent years before that. Peggy Orenstein (1994) observed that even girls who were expressive and outgoing in informal situations with their friends became quiet and deferential in classroom situations. They feared the humiliation of publicly stating a wrong answer, and they seemed to have learned that they would not get their questions answered by the teacher. Boys, on the other hand, felt entitled to shout out answers—even incorrect answers—and to persist until they were heard by the teacher. As one middle-school boy commented to her, "I think my opinions are important, so I yell them out. . . . The teacher'll tell you not to do it, but they answer your question before the people who raise their hands. Girls will sit there until the bell rings with their hands up and never get their questions answered. . . . Forget that!" (p. 13).

Myra and David Sadker (1985) found a ratio of approximately eight boys to every girl among students who call out answers and demand virtually constant attention from the teacher. And boys are clearly used to receiving teachers' attention. One teacher reported to Orenstein (1994) that she had instituted a careful policy of calling on girls and boys equally by using her attendance roster. After 2 days of this policy, the boys rebelled: They accused her of calling on the girls more frequently than the boys and were reluctant to believe her when she demonstrated that she was indeed calling on girls and boys with equal frequency. As she commented, "[F]or the boys, equality was hard to get used to; they perceived it as a big loss" (p. 27).

Perhaps, then, there are reasons besides differences in interaction styles with peers that cause girls to avoid boys during childhood: Boys demand, and get, more than their share of attention and encouragement from adults. Girls safeguard their self-confidence for a time by staying away from boys; however, at adolescence this strategy is no longer feasible as relationships with boys begin to loom larger in importance.

A Loss of Self-Esteem at Adolescence?

The transition to adolescence provides many challenges, challenges that some theorists argue seem to stress girls' self-confidence more than boys'. Studies of children's **self-esteem** have found that young girls have marginally higher self-esteem than boys, but this effect is reversed at adolescence (Eccles et al., 1999; Feingold, 1994b). Studies of personality in samples of high school students, college students, and adults show a pattern of small but significant gender differences in self-esteem, anxiety, and assertiveness: Males score higher on both self-esteem and assertiveness, and females score higher on anxiety (Feingold, 1994b). The tendency for males to indicate more assertiveness than females has been found to be greater in some countries (e.g., Canada, the United States, Poland) than others (e.g., China, Finland). According to paper-and-pencil measures, males are also more narcissistic than females and have a more inflated sense of their own intelligence and attractiveness (Gabriel, Critelli, & Ee, 1994). Beginning in adolescence, females experience depression at a rate of up to twice that of males (Nolen-Hoeksema, 1987).

One large study of American junior high and high school students found that self-esteem varied by ethnicity as well as gender (Dukes & Martinez, 1994). On "core" or central self-esteem, males of all ethnic groups (Black, Hispanic, White, Native American, and

Asian) scored above the mean for the entire sample. Among females, only Black females scored above the mean; all other female groups scored below the mean. On "public" self-esteem (self-confidence about the ability to perform well in institutional contexts), females of all ethnic groups except Blacks again scored lower than their male counterparts.

These findings fit with the notion that, at least in North America, adolescence is a time of great vulnerability and risk for many girls, a time when the culture's message that girls are supposed to be tentative, compliant, subordinate, and adaptable to the wishes of others begins to sink in (Gilligan, 1990; Pipher, 1994; Rogers, 1993). As many girls move from childhood to adolescence, these psychologists argue, they seem to show a loss of self-confidence, of voice, of trust in the authority of their own experience, of the courage to say what they feel, to "speak one's mind by telling all one's heart." What may be driving this change during adolescence is a process of **gender intensification,** a deepening personal and cultural emphasis on gender roles, particularly for girls, in response to bodily changes and the development of more abstract ways of thinking (Galambos, Almeida, & Petersen, 1990). As adolescent girls experience the intensification of the feminine role, with its emphasis on niceness, maintaining connections to others, and relative helplessness, it may be little wonder if their sense of individual self-confidence and assertiveness is shaken.

A large national survey of preadolescent and adolescent girls and boys in the United States appears to support the notion that for a girl in this country, the passage into adolescence can be marked by a loss of confidence in herself and her abilities and an increasing sense of personal inadequacy. The survey, sponsored by the American Association of University Women, gathered responses from 3,000 girls and boys between the ages of 9 and 15 (AAUW, 1990). Included were questions about their attitudes toward self, school, family, and friends. The researchers found that among the adolescent respondents, girls showed consistently less self-esteem than boys did—a finding that was not evident among the younger, preadolescent respondents. The most dramatic gender gap among the teenagers was in the area of self-perceived competence. Boys were more likely than girls to report that they were "pretty good at a lot of things," whereas girls were much more likely than boys to say that they were not smart enough or not good enough to fulfill their aspirations. Although the study, which did not follow individual girls and boys across time from the age of 9 to 15, did not demonstrate an actual *drop* in self-esteem in adolescence, the much larger gender gap in self-esteem among 15-year-olds than among 9-year-olds is suggestive of such a drop.

A gender gap in confidence was particularly noticeable in the realm of mathematics and science. By the age of 15, even girls who said they enjoyed mathematics and science were much less likely than boys to feel competent in them. The study found that confidence in mathematics seems to both reflect and affect overall self-confidence; the loss of confidence in math, the researchers argue, is not one that can be isolated from confidence in other realms of achievement. The researchers also report that a link between liking math and aspiring to professional careers is stronger for girls than for boys.

Other research has also shown clear evidence of lower self-confidence in mathematics among female than male students—and the gender gap in perceived competence is considerably greater than the gender difference in actual performance. On the other hand, there is also a gender gap in confidence in English, in which girls show higher confidence than boys (Eccles et al., 1999). Apparently, academic self-confidence parallels gender stereotypes.

BOX 5.2 LEARNING ACTIVITY
Grrlstories

Inspired by Mary Pipher's *Reviving Ophelia,* documentary photographer Joanna Pinneo began developing a Web site of photographs, stories, and sound bites dedicated to adolescent girls. The site features photographs and stories of girls such as Shantel, who was 12 when she discovered she was pregnant; Rachael, legally blind, who became a fearless dog sled racer; and LeAnne, who reacted to being teased about her clothes by entering and winning a beauty pageant. These and other girls tell their own stories on this site. In addition, the site provides a place to learn about coming-of-age rituals for girls.

Go to the site: **www.grrlstories.org**

Read the stories of any two of the girls, taking time to look at the pictures and listen to the audio.

Write down your reactions: What did you admire about these girls? What concerns do their stories raise for you? What are the ways you think society could provide more support for girls at this age?

Go to the *Rites of Passage* section of the Web site. Read about the coming of age ceremonies that some African American women have developed for girls. Follow the links in the Educational Activities section to find out more about the Sunrise Ceremony, the Apache coming of age ritual. Write down your reactions: How do you think such ceremonies affect the transition from girlhood to adolescence? Do you wish such a ceremony had been available to you?

Follow the links on the site that lead to other resources for girls. Are you surprised to find such resources available? How useful do you think they are for typical girls? Can you think of ways to make them more useful?

If we consider the findings of a gender gap in self-esteem that emerges at adolescence in light of Eleanor Maccoby's (1990) observations on the different ways groups of girls and boys socialize their members, some possible connections appear. It is at adolescence that, in North American society, the strong segregation of girls and boys begins to break down. Girls and boys begin to become important companions for each other, at least in some domains. When they begin spending time together, they are forced to cope with each other's interaction style. Girls may find themselves unexpectedly squelched by their new male companions when they proffer ideas and opinions. Boys encounter the rather unfamiliar experience of being listened to and agreed with. This aspect of the transition to adolescence is likely to be unsettling and confidence-sapping for girls, but not for boys. Indeed, even the majority of Way's (1995) "outspoken" urban adolescent girls reported that they could not speak their thoughts and feelings in their relationships with boys. They fear losing their relationships with boys if they speak openly, and they are worried that they cannot trust their male peers not to betray and manipulate them.

Others have argued that girls' vulnerability to low self-esteem at adolescence stems partly from their realization that male concerns are central to the classroom—and to the

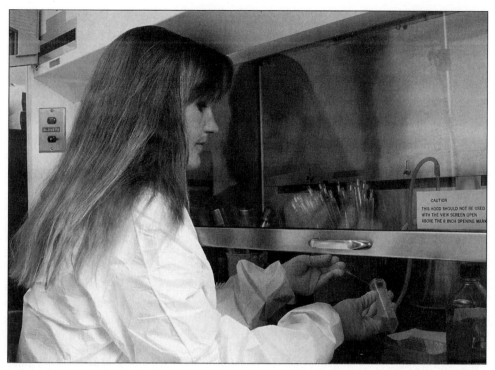

Many theorists and researchers have argued that one of the things that makes science and mathematics feel alien to girls and women is its presentation as something that is devoid of people, human feelings, and emotions.

culture (Orenstein, 1994). Adolescents notice that teachers encourage boys to be more assertive, that girls are valued more for their appearance than for their accomplishments, that men rather than women are at the helm of most important cultural endeavors. Discouraged, girls may give up their dreams or ambitions, beginning to see them as unrealistic.

A third suggestion is that adolescence is a time of many transitions: often a move to a new school, new friends, and the significant bodily changes of puberty. Since girls mature physically earlier than boys do, they are more often facing the changes in their bodies—and all the implications of these changes—at the same time as the changes in school. Boys, because they mature later, are more likely to be able to deal with these changes sequentially, instead of all at once (Eccles et al., 1999). Put this possibility together with the high importance placed on physical beauty for women, and the recipe for threatened self-esteem among adolescent girls is obvious.

Race/Ethnicity and the Gender Gap in Self-Esteem   One of the most intriguing findings of the AAUW survey is the pattern of differences it reveals among racial/ethnic groups. Girls in all groups reported lower self-esteem than boys, but the size and nature of the gender difference varied among European American, Latina, and African American groups.

African American girls were far more likely than girls in the other two groups to feel good about themselves and their families and to feel competent in a variety of areas. However, they were *less* likely than the other girls to feel confident about their schoolwork or their relationships with teachers. Latina girls seem to fare worst of all in general feelings of self-worth. Thirty-eight percent fewer of the Latina 15-year-olds than the Latina 9-year-olds agreed with the statement that "I am happy with the way I am." In comparison, the difference between the 15-year-olds and the 9-year-olds was 33 percent for European American girls and only 7 percent for African American girls. The pattern is similar to the one found by Dukes and Martinez (1994) cited above: African American girls were the only group of girls who did not score lower than their male counterparts on core self-esteem. Also similar are findings of research on sixth and seventh-graders in which African American girls had higher self-esteem than either European American girls or African American boys, similar or higher perceived competence in academic abilities than European American girls, and no evidence of a drop in self-esteem during early adolescence (Eccles et al, 1999). In a seemingly parallel pattern, some researchers have found African American girls to be more resistant than their European American counterparts to pressures to be silent in the classroom (Orenstein, 1994).

What are the forces that promote more self-doubt, more self-silencing among the girls of some racial/ethnic groups than others? Peggy Orenstein (1994) argues that the "hidden curriculum" teaches girls that they will gain teachers' approval and affection by being quiet, compliant, well-behaved, and nice. Carol Gilligan and her colleagues found that adolescent girls invented a "perfect girl" ideal self who was nice and kind, calm and quiet, never mean or bossy (Brown & Gilligan, 1990). As some girls strive to emulate the quiet, well-behaved model, they may silence themselves and become enormously self-critical. This pattern seems to describe what happens to White, middle-class girls, and perhaps to Latina girls, in the United States—but what about African American girls?

One study of 1,100 adolescents in a racially mixed African American majority county in Maryland attempted to discern whether different variables predicted self-esteem among African American and European American girls (Eccles et al., 1999). As the researchers sifted through their data, the first striking pattern they found was that the African American girls reported more positive, confident, views of themselves than European American girls did. The African American girls had higher confidence than the European American girls in their femininity, their "masculine" skills (physical strength and assertiveness), their physical attractiveness, and their popularity. The difference between their educational aspirations and their actual expectations was also higher. The European American girls, by contrast, were higher than their African American counterparts in worrying about their weight and in social self-consciousness. The differences between the African American and European American girls on these variables accounted for all the differences between the groups in self-esteem.

Next, the researchers looked within each group to see what variables predicted individual differences in self-esteem. For both African American and European American girls, the best predictors of self-esteem were confidence in femininity and attractiveness and lack of worry about their weight. The researchers concluded that girls' self-esteem in early adolescence is most closely tied, not to academic self-concept, but to the physical changes and physical image pressures that become especially salient to girls as they reach puberty. African American girls view themselves more positively on these dimensions than European American girls, and thus are more likely to be protected from a precipitous drop in self-esteem.

Intriguing though it is, this research does not answer the question of *why* African American girls seem to be more resistant than European American girls to negative self-concepts. Some clues are offered by Janie Ward's (1996) interview study of African American adolescents and their parents. She found that the parents often saw themselves as "raising resisters" and taught their children that "silence is often the voice of complicity" (p. 90). They talked to their children about their own experiences with racism, and they tried to instill in them a sense of racial pride and self-respect. Perhaps because of the bonds these strategies developed, the daughters often anchored their self-esteem in their closeness to their families and their identification with Black culture. In a similar vein, Jill Taylor and her colleagues (1995) found, in an in-depth study of 26 diverse "at-risk" adolescents, that the Black girls stood out in reporting that their mothers provided ways of looking at femininity that were at odds with the dominant culture, thus helping them construct a feminine self that was not compliant with middle-class standards of femininity.

African American girls often show more willingness to speak up in the classroom and to initiate contact with teachers, and less fear of the "stigma" of giving a wrong answer (Grant, 1985). In fact, these girls may speak up out of a sense of resistance to being silenced, a refusal to be ignored. As one girl commented, in response to a query about why she raised her hand even when she did not know the answer, "I guess I raise my hand because I want to be part of the class . . . I just want to talk and feel part of that, you know?" (Orenstein, 1994, p. 180). However, African American girls often report that even though they speak up, no one listens to them, and they feel invisible and silenced (AAUW, 1990). They are not imagining this; researchers report that teachers more frequently ignore and rebuff African American girls than their European American counterparts. Furthermore, in a pattern that parallels the differing teacher responses to boys and girls, teachers often direct praise to Black girls for nonacademic performance such as good behavior and enforcing rules, whereas they reward White girls for their academic progress (Grant, 1985). They also make different attributions for similar levels of success by different race and gender groups. In one study, when African American girls achieved at the same level as European American boys, teachers told the girls that their success was due to their hard work—but they told the boys that they were not working hard enough to fulfill their potential (Grant, 1984).

Some researchers argue that African American girls, confronted by a sense of devaluation by teachers and other authorities, may try to protect their self-esteem by disconnecting from academic achievement and basing their self-worth on other things (Robinson & Ward, 1991). The use of this strategy might help to explain how African American girls, in contrast to European American and Latina girls, maintain their overall self-esteem at adolescence even though they feel more pessimistic about school than either of the other groups. Outside of school, these girls may search for and find "'alternative contexts' in which their strengths, competencies, and voices could flourish on their own terms" (Fine, 1992, p. 133). The outlets they find instead of school may not necessarily serve them well in the long run; they may devote their energies to jobs with no possibility of advancement, early motherhood, substance abuse, or dangerous behaviors with friends who have similarly disengaged from school. Additionally, as Michelle Fine notes, when these alternatives, seen as more creative by the participants, *replace* formal schooling, they may not lead to the success or happiness that the student leaving school envisions. Yet for some students in this group, physically or emotionally leaving school is the only way they can think of to find a voice.

For Latina adolescents, the search for a secure self-concept and self-expression may be hindered by ideals of femininity that inhibit them from voicing opinions that conflict with their own families and cultures (Taylor et al., 1995). Muños (1995) notes that Latinas must often integrate two cultures and two languages into their sense of self. She relies on a metaphor developed by writer Gloria Anzaldúa (1987) for the Chicana psyche: *la frontera*—the borderland. In Anzaldúa's words, a frontera is "a bordertown, the edge and intersection where two cultures interact and where both are constantly being negotiated" (p. 56). When Muños interviewed Puerto Rican adolescents, she found that many of them were engaged in struggles to blend their familial and cultural traditions with the aspirations encouraged in the dominant culture, to reconcile the visions of femininity in their own cultural communities with the desire to accommodate expectations in the dominant culture they may encounter at school or with friends. These young women are often bilingual as well as bicultural, yet this does not make it any easier for them to find their voice.

Yet Latina girls do not necessarily acquiesce to the notion that they should accept a loss of voice and power at adolescence. Some research shows that these girls develop ways of negotiating around the often contradictory cultural expectations of femininity in an effort to both maintain their own voice and retain the approval of those around them. Jill Denner and Nora Dunbar (2004) interviewed a small group of Mexican American girls aged 12 to 14. They discovered that these girls noted and critiqued the different rules for boys and girls and gender inequalities. They complained that their own and their mothers' mobility and freedom was limited by gendered expectations and they noted that their mothers sometimes seemed to accept these limitations and not speak of these issues. Yet they themselves did *not* accept the idea that they should be silent in the face of sexism or that they should not engage in dialogue about the restrictions on girls and women. As one participant noted, "I have to stick up for myself, because if I don't they're going to . . . you know how girls have been treated unfairly a lot, so when I think about me being a girl I want people to start respecting my sex" (p. 306).

These young Chicana girls often negotiated gender role expectations by speaking out in their relationships—especially with their peers and nonparental adults. Such speaking out was sometimes justified as standing up for others, such as their mothers, peers, or younger children. Thus they could violate the expectation of silent acceptance of authority if they did so in the cause of protecting others or of standing up for what they saw as right. And sometimes they used the traditional feminine role to maintain control over situations, as in the case of the respondent who noted that she "act[ed] like a little girl" to avoid pressure for sex (p. 310).

However it is done, finding a voice is crucial for girls who are marginalized not only by their gender, but also by their race and ethnicity. Although White, middle-class girls may achieve some rewards by being quiet, compliant, and "nice," African American,

Latina, and other minority girls, and poor or working-class girls, may feel an urgent necessity to speak up for what they want and need if they are to have access to any opportunities at all. Niobe Way (1995) suggests,

> Black and Puerto Rican parents, and parents from other ethnic communities living in the inner city (in the United States), socialize their daughters to be outspoken and strong because they realize that if their daughters are passive and quiet, they may simply disappear in a society in which they and their daughters are already pushed to the margins. (p. 124)

The differing outcomes for different ethnic or racial groups in the United States suggest that the low self-esteem many girls experience in adolescence is shaped by the treatment they receive: socialization by family and peers, reactions from teachers, a popular culture that communicates that male concerns take precedence. Do girls in other cultures encounter the same pressures toward a loss of self-esteem and confidence, toward silence, as girls in the United States? And, if so, do they respond in similar ways? To answer such questions, we have little research, but we can find some clues in the personal accounts of women's lives. An Alaskan Inuit woman, remembering her girlhood, paints a picture of strong pressures to limit herself and conform to a feminine ideal—but she identifies those pressures not with her own Inuit culture, but with the ministers and teachers who are messengers of White culture from the south:

> I'm working with my father. He and I have been building a house, and my cousins have asked why I'm doing it with him. I'm a girl, they tell me. They are girls, and they are reminding me that I'm a girl! I thank them! I tell them that it's a good thing they told me I'm a girl, because if they hadn't I wouldn't know. Finally, I asked them where they got their idea of what I should do and what I shouldn't do. They went to school, they remind me. They listened to the teachers. They go to church; they listen to the minister. . . . They think I should sit and smile and wait for one of their brothers to come and ask me for a ride in the snowmobile. They think I should be dreaming of the five or ten children I'll have one day. They think I should be cooking with my mother, not telling her good-bye, and going out to stand beside my father and try to help him. I'm too "restless," a teacher once told them. (Coles & Coles, 1978, p. 190)

Remembering her girlhood, one !Kung woman tells the story of gaining approval by contributing to her village's food supply. In her story, she is praised for her success, not castigated or thought strange for "unfeminine" behavior:

> We started to follow the tracks and walked and walked and after a while, we saw the little kudu lying quietly in the grass, dead asleep. I jumped up and tried to grab it. It cried out . . . it freed itself and ran away. We all ran, chasing after it, and we ran and ran. But I ran so fast that they all dropped behind and then I was alone, chasing it, running as fast as I could. Finally, I was able to grab it. I jumped on it and killed it. Then I picked it up by the legs and carried it back on my shoulders. I was breathing very hard . . . When I came to where the rest of them were, my older cousin said, "My cousin, my little cousin . . . she killed a kudu! . . . We men here . . . how come we didn't kill it, but this young girl with so much 'run' in her killed it?" (Shostak, 1981, pp. 101–102)

Both of the cultures mentioned above traditionally have given wide latitude to girls and boys in behavior, and neither one has depended on institutions such as schools and churches to regiment and train children. However, neither North American culture nor

BOX 5.3 MAKING CHANGE
Providing Mastery-Oriented Feedback to Girls

If you teach or work with young girls, or if you have younger sisters, notice the kind of feedback you give to those girls. Is most of your positive feedback of the "You're so pretty" or "You're so nice" variety? If so, try to place more emphasis on the accomplishments of these girls and give out praise for doing well instead of for following the rules of femininity. When a girl tries something difficult and fails, praise her for taking on a tough challenge and encourage her to try again. And when you praise a girl for succeeding at a task, don't focus only on her ability as a reason for that success (i.e., "You're so smart"). Praise her also for her determination, her strategy, her hard work. This kind of feedback helps girls to become "mastery-oriented" with respect to difficult tasks, and may well make a difference in the kinds of educational and career choices they eventually make.

schools are necessary to produce a diminished sense of confidence in girls as they mature. Parents make an important contribution, often transmitting and reinforcing a cultural message that boys come first. Phyllis Bronstein (1984) studied Mexican families and found that fathers treated daughters and sons in ways likely to produce more confidence and skill development in boys than girls. These fathers listened more to boys than to girls and were more likely to show boys than girls how to do things. They treated girls especially gently, but with a lack of full attention and a readiness to impose opinions on them. Thus they communicated to their children that boys' opinions were more important and boys' skills more susceptible to development.

More research is needed on girls' self-esteem and self-confidence in a variety of cultures. The examples we have seen, however, suggest that gender differences in self-esteem can be produced or not, depending on what children learn about the relative importance of males and females. Teachers, parents, and peers all help to produce the difference when they tolerate domineering behavior in males and squelch it in females, when they yield the floor more often to males than to females, when they reward the loudest children with attention and ignore those who are not disruptive, when they assume that boys are ambitious and intelligent but are surprised when girls show these qualities. The lessons children learn about self-esteem and confidence reflect cultural assumptions about males and females—and they have lifelong implications, as the next section makes clear.

In thinking about the ways that institutions such as schools may affect girls' self-confidence and self-esteem, we would do well to remember that, for many of the world's girls, simply being enrolled in school is considered a victory. In North America, girls and boys have equal access to primary and secondary education, and women are actually in the majority among university students (United Nations, 2000). However, as Table 5.1 shows, in some countries girls lag far behind boys in access to education. During the past two decades, access to basic education has actually declined because of war or economic prob-

TABLE 5.1   Gender and Access to Education around the World

Whereas girls and boys have approximately equal access to education in North American and other economically developed regions of the world, large gender disparities still exist in many countries. The table below shows the ratio of girls to boys (i.e., the number of girls for every 100 boys) enrolled in primary and secondary education in various countries.

Country	Ratio of Girls to Boys Enrolled in Primary and Secondary Education	Country	Ratio of Girls to Boys Enrolled in Primary and Secondary Education
Afghanistan	45.6	India	78.6
Bangladesh	104.7	Iraq	76.3
Bulgaria	97.5	Morocco	85.1
Cambodia	83.9	Nicaragua	105.3
Canada	99.8	Nigeria	80.0
Ethiopia	69.0	United States	100.4
Ghana	88.6	Yemen	55.6

Source: (World Bank, 2002)

lems. In some countries, where primary education was once free for everyone, it now costs families a fee to send their children to school. For poor families, this often means either that none of their children can attend school or that choices must be made about which children to send—and such choices often favor boys. As we turn to a consideration of education and life choices, it is useful to remember that, for girls in some parts of the world, education is sometimes no choice at all.

Confidence, Education, and Life Choices

Sylvia Chavarria, a professor at the University of Costa Rica, recalls her enjoyment of mathematics as a child. She liked mathematics, she says, because it was

> ordered, had one right answer, one correct way of looking at the world. It allowed me to be dichotomous, to have everything in my life either right or wrong, making the world easy to understand, and having one correct view. I did not have to memorize anything, hear anybody's point of view, negotiate anything with or about them. I could remain isolated in my own world. I felt that I had a special type of authority just by understanding mathematics. I think that . . . I too enjoyed excelling in a subject that was considered to be more difficult, that was viewed as male. In some cases, I could even dream that I shared the men's power. (Chavarria, 1993, p. 2)

Later in her career, Chavarria came to question her traditional view of mathematics, along with the notion that it was, by definition, an endeavor that was more suited to males than to females. She read about the history and philosophy of mathematics and found that, far from being infallible, unchangeable, neutral, universal, and value-free, mathematics as we know it reflects the values of particular groups. For example, she learned that the development of mathematics had been guided by very different values among the Hindus and the Greeks. The Hindus, whose algebra emphasized formulas and trial and error, utilized mathematics to help ordinary people solve computational problems. The Greeks, on the other hand, thought of mathematics as an endeavor for the elite and developed a very rule-oriented discipline, with formal axioms and deductive solution strategies. The latter approach has dominated the mathematics curriculum in Western cultures—but it has no legitimate claim as the only *real* mathematics.

Chavarria, along with many others, argues that girls and women often lose their confidence when faced with mathematics because it seems alien to them: It does not reflect their values, their preferred way of approaching problems. Both their discomfort with the classroom presentation of the subject and the obvious appearance of mathematics as a male-dominated field makes them feel that their approaches to mathematical problem solving are illegitimate. This does not, she argues, mean that girls and women do not fit into mathematics, but rather that mathematics has developed in such a way that it does not fit many girls and women—and that there is no reason why mathematics cannot change.

An interesting example of the pattern of belittling females' approaches to problem solving, despite their effectiveness, comes from research on computer programming. A study that followed first-year Harvard University students as they negotiated their first computer programming course showed that students were instructed to adopt a formal approach to programming: "a rule-driven system that can be mastered in a top-down, divide-and-conquer way. . . . This approach decrees that the right way to solve a programming problem is to dissect it into separate parts and design a set of modular solutions that will fit the part into an intended whole" (Turkle & Papert, 1990, p. 136). But for many students (more women than men), this approach feels alien. Their preferred approach is to "play with the elements of the program, to move them around almost as though they were material elements—the words in a sentence, the notes in a musical composition, the elements of a collage" (p. 136).

The dominant culture of computing, however, dictates that the latter approach is "wrong," even though it can be used effectively and creatively in programming. Turkle and Papert (1990) tell the story of Lisa, a student who wants to "manipulate computer language the way she worked with words as she writes a poem" (p. 133). In her desire to learn computing in her own way and to feel comfortable with the computer, Lisa initially resists her teachers' pressures to think in a formal, hierarchical style. Two months into the course, however, she "ends up abandoning the fight, doing things 'their way,' and accepting the inevitable alienation from her work. She calls her efforts to become 'another kind of person with the machine' her 'not-me-strategy' and begins to insist that the computer is 'just a tool'" (p. 134). According to Turkle and Papert, Lisa and others like her are excluded from the computer culture

> not by rules that keep them out, but by ways of thinking that make them reluctant to join in. They are not computer phobic; but they are computer reticent. They want to stay away because the computer has come to symbolize an alien way of thinking. . . . In this way, discrimination in the computer culture takes the form of discrimination against approaches to knowledge . . . (p. 135)

The tendency for science and technology to be presented in a manner that privileges a certain approach to knowledge may partially explain the discomfort and lack of confidence girls and women sometimes experience in these areas. Many theorists and researchers have argued that one of the factors that make science and mathematics feel alien to girls and women (and to some boys and men as well) is their presentation as something that is divorced from any social context (e.g., Harding, 1989; Longino, 1989). Science is often presented in the classroom as an activity that is devoid of people, and of human feelings and emotions. Girls may resist this presentation more than boys do. Two Canadian researchers found that elementary-school girls were more likely than boys to include the personal aspects of their work when writing about their science lab experiences (Pieterson & Geddis, 1993). When diagramming their task of using a single wire and a battery to light a light bulb, for example, one little boy draws a picture of the three objects, along with instructions about how to connect them. A little girl completing the same assignment draws a picture of herself standing at the table connecting the wire. When describing the activity of making a paper airplane, one little girl writes the following, showing how much her feelings and relationships are part of her science lab experience:

> We made air planes. It was a lot of fun. I like Miss P_____ because she is very nice. At first my airplane turned and turned. Then I put paper clips on the nose. I wish that I could come and work with Miss P_____ every day. After I put the paper clips on, it really worked. It was flying all over the portable. Once my airplane hit a girl named Melissa. Then her airplane hit me to get me back . . . (p. 102)

A little boy writes of the same activity:

> We made an airplane. It looked like this: [diagram]. then we made some changes I cut two slits in the back to help it lift I soon found out I needed more weight on the front and sides so I put two slits on the sides. (p. 103)

When girls try to put human context or feelings into their work in science classes, their efforts may be trivialized. Pieterson and Geddis (1993) tell the story of girls in an elementary-school science class who had to construct projects demonstrating the use of electrical circuits. One pair of girls built an elaborate house out of a cardboard box, with window lights that could be switched on and off. They spent a lot of time painting and decorating their house in a Christmas theme. Another pair of girls devised a skit in which handheld generators powered the two main characters: an egg-carton submarine and a margarine-tub jellyfish. The researchers comment:

> In each of these projects, the girls put a great deal of effort into providing a context—decorating and adding details—that went far beyond the simple connecting up of electrical circuits. Another teacher casually observing the class working on their projects commented that some of the projects, Jenny's and Sally's in particular, "seemed more art than science." On the surface, this comment appears valid. We do not expect science projects to include details like paint, candy canes, artificial snow, and wallpaper. The addition of decorations and "frills" left the project suspect in terms of the quality and depth of the science involved. Yet a close examination of the girls' work revealed that their projects contained as many and as sophisticated circuits as the more standard projects devoid of decoration or a story setting. The girls had demonstrated a sophisticated understanding of electrical circuits, but they had gone beyond this to situate this understanding in a context that was meaningful to them. (p. 105)

Some researchers suggest that girls may value "connected" knowing—knowledge that is linked to experience and to concrete concerns—more than boys do (Belenky et al.,

1986). It is a hypothesis that calls for more research, not only in North America but in a wide variety of other cultures. It may be that, at least in countries such as the United States, where girls and boys tend to play separately and socialize one another into either cooperative or competitive interaction styles, girls, more than boys, do learn to value connection more than abstraction. Such a gender difference might not be expected in cultures where the genders are much less separated in childhood because girls would not be the only ones socialized in the direction of connection.

However, examples of girls' reception of the cultural message that men are the ones who can and should do science can be found in a variety of cultures. A study in Malta (Chetcuti, 1993) found that high school girls who were asked to draw a picture of a scientist invariably drew a man and made comments such as "those who are with them . . . the women scientists . . . seem to be more to help the scientists than anything else . . . instead of doing things themselves . . . they pass them things" (p. 213). A Danish study found girls demoralized by the lack of female science teachers (Mallow, 1993). A project in Jordan showed that female university students showed more confidence in their performance in chemistry class when their instructor was female (Tel, 1993). Science appears to be an area where girls are especially vulnerable to the message that they are not as good as males, and where barriers encountered at an early age produce life-changing consequences.

Perhaps part of the reason many girls move away from science is the values that are associated with it. Research by Eccles and her colleagues has demonstrated that the value a person attaches to a task or academic subject is a powerful predictor of whether s/he will pursue success in that task or academic field (Eccles et al., 1999). One study showed, for instance, that among women who had very high confidence in their math and science abilities, the value placed on helping other people was an excellent predictor of occupational plans. The women who placed a very high value on helping others aspired to careers in the health-related fields; for these women, helping others was the value they rated most highly. On the other hand, the women who ranked helping others lowest in value (and who also ranked being able to work with math and computers highest) aspired to Ph.D.-level science careers. A lack of interest in helping others is stereotyped as unfeminine, so girls are often socialized toward values that lead them to prefer particular career choices.

Further pressures from the push to conform to feminine role expectations can be seen in the conflicts that girls report, sometimes as early as elementary school, between their own aspirations and the desire to fit in. L. A. Bell (1989) interviewed an ethnically diverse sample of gifted girls in an urban elementary school. In describing the dilemmas they faced with respect to personal achievement, these girls spoke of a number of issues related to femininity. They worried that they would hurt others' feelings when they won out in competitive achievement situations. They were concerned that they would seem to be bragging if they expressed pride in their accomplishments. They fretted over their physical appearance and the requirements of beauty. They feared that they might be too aggressive in seeking the teachers' attention. In general, they described being pulled between the requirements of femininity and the requirements of ambition and seemed to see the two as contradictory. Clearly, constructions of femininity can start very early to affect life choices.

Whether caused by a lack of confidence, discomfort with particular values, or particular constructions of femininity, a gap between young women's self-perceived abilities in math and science and their plans to pursue accomplishments in these areas seems to widen as they progress through their education. For high school girls, self-perceptions of academic strength in math and science are paralleled by perceptions of future possibilities for themselves in these academic areas. However, by the time students are enrolled in university, this is not the case. Young women in university who perceive themselves as strong in science and mathematics are far less likely than their male counterparts to anticipate future study in these areas; the gender gap is much larger with respect to these students' possible selves than with respect to their current self-views (Lips, 2004). Thus, the stage is set for a continuation of existing gender disparities in careers in the sciences, engineering, and technology.

Culture and the Construction of Entitlement

A newspaper article describes an exercise in career preparation for children, Camp Hyatt Career Day (Grimsley, 1996a). Twenty-four fifth-grade students spend a day in a large hotel in northern Virginia, trying out particular jobs by shadowing the adults who hold them. Two little girls are reportedly thrilled to have been granted positions in the hotel laundry room. One little boy has captured the position of national sales director, while another is working as the banquet manager. The "sales manager" talks about learning a lot about decision making and about not abusing power. One of the "laundry room workers" chirps animatedly about it being a dream job: "I'm the oldest of four children. I always do the laundry, and this is even more exciting because of the big machines." Clearly, the executive positions involve more power and more pay than the laundry room positions, but this is not a source of concern for the little girl who loves the laundry room: "I don't depend on making a lot of money because my husband will have a very good job."

The article provides a disconcerting glimpse of the divergent aspirations and sense of entitlement of girls and boys in the United States. Apparently, many boys grow up with some expectation that they will compete for attention and rewards, give direction to others, and be the center of attention in at least certain situations. Girls seem less likely to adopt such a perspective.

The masculine stereotype includes a strong element of unquestioning self-confidence and a sense of **entitlement.** In many times and places, this stereotype has been a source of humor for women, who have poked fun at men's assumptions of superiority. The 19th-century American essayist Gail Hamilton, in an article "American Inventions," commented:

> It is said that women can not invent, even in matters that concern themselves. . . . Man has to plan the very tools with which woman does her work. Very likely. And after he has planned them, he ought to use them. The very fact that a man invented the flat iron is *prima facie* evidence that he ought to do the ironing. . . . Having invented all, he is but an unprofitable servant, and has not done half that which it is his duty to do. Still, I am glad he has done something. (Hamilton, 1873/1972)

This type of humor has been used to bolster women's own confidence, reminding them that the cultural message of male superiority should be taken with a large grain of salt. But apparently, no challenges to the notion that men are more competent, logical, and skilled in important areas than women are have shaken men's self-confidence. The research shows that men report more self-confidence than women in a variety of situations.

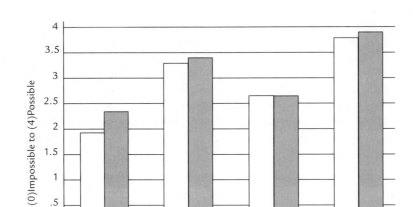

Figure 5.1 University students rated the likelihood that they would achieve various powerful positions in the future. Particularly for the politician and self-defined powerful roles, men were more likely than women to anticipate that they would actually achieve such positions. (Source: Data reported in Lips, 2000)

Studies of North American men often show that they tend to overestimate how well they will perform on tasks, whereas women underestimate future performance. This phenomenon appears first in childhood, as boys give inflated estimates of how well they will do in laboratory tasks and in school grades, while girls tend to err in the direction of pessimism or modesty (e.g., Frome & Eccles, 1995). It continues to appear among college students, among whom men anticipate higher grades in mathematics and science than women do, even when the performance of the two groups has been equivalent in the past (Lips, 1989). In some studies, males and females each overestimate their performance in realms that are gender-stereotypic: males in math and sports, females in reading and social skills (Eccles et al.,1999).

The tendency toward greater male than female self-confidence shows up in students' estimates of the likelihood of achieving powerful careers. In one study, students at a U.S. university were asked to imagine themselves as persons with power—and then to estimate the level of possibility that they would actually achieve such positions. Male and female students provided equally ambitious fantasies in answer to this question, imagining themselves as presidents, millionaire businesspeople, famous media personalities, or high-status professionals. The males, however, thought it significantly more likely than the females did that their fantasy could come true, as seen in Figure 5.1 (Lips, 2000).

Are males overconfident and females overly modest everywhere, or is this phenomenon limited to particular cultures? Research evidence on this point is mixed. Among university students in Spain, no gender differences were found when researchers inquired, in a study parallel to the one described above, about the likelihood that respondents could achieve the powerful roles that they imagined for themselves (Back, Diaz, & Lips, 1996).

Furthermore, researchers in the United States have found that it is not even necessary to change cultures in order to find exceptions to the overconfident male–overly modest female pattern. There are some conditions under which males and females are similar in their self-confidence: when the two groups are equivalent in successful experience on the task, when they can make their estimates of success in private, and when they are given clear feedback (Lenney, 1977).

Women's and men's differing views of their own performance apparently affect their assessments of how much they are entitled to be paid for their work. In general, women tend to pay themselves less than men do when dividing rewards between themselves and others (Major, 1987). Moreover, women's standards of what is fair pay for themselves are lower than those of men. When women and men are instructed to work on a task and then to assign themselves fair pay for their performance, women pay themselves significantly less than men pay themselves—and they also report that less money is fair pay for their own work. This outcome occurs even when women and men give similar evaluations to their own performances. Furthermore, when asked to work as much as they think is fair for a specified amount of money, women work longer, do more work, and do it more correctly and efficiently than men do (Major, McFarlin & Gagnon, 1984). Outside the laboratory as well, women seem to be satisfied with less: Women report as much satisfaction with their jobs as men do, despite the fact that they tend to hold jobs that are lower in status and more poorly paid than men's (American Management Association, 1999). When asked to estimate their future salaries, young women consistently give lower estimates of both entry-level and peak pay than young men do (Heckert et al., 2002). Women, at least under some conditions, seem to feel that they deserve less reward for their work than men do. In fact, Major (1994) notes that many women experience what she calls a "paradoxical contentment": They report being satisfied with their situation and seemingly do not regard as illegitimate any gender inequalities they may notice.

Where does women's lower sense of entitlement come from? The possibilities range from women's socialization toward low self-esteem, to their training to appear becomingly (femininely?) modest and/or unselfish, to an historical–social context that devalues women and rewards them less than men for their work. Certainly, it appears that in judging how much they should pay themselves, or how hard and long they should work for a given amount of money, women compare themselves mainly with other women—not with men (Bylsma & Major, 1994). This finding makes it clear that, perhaps beginning in childhood, women have learned two important messages: First, gender is an important distinction when performance is being evaluated and rewarded; females and males are not to be judged according to the same standards. Second, in most instances, women must work harder and better than men to earn equivalent pay or approval.

Girls and Women Using Power

Entitlement and the Use of Power

Eagly and Johnson's (1990) meta-analytic study of gender and leadership style showed that, on the average, women tend to lead in a more democratic and less autocratic style than men. Eleanor Maccoby (1990; 1998), as noted above, has written about the way girls

BOX 5.4 LEARNING ACTIVITY
The Price of Feeling Unentitled

Suppose you were just out of school, being interviewed for a job you wanted, and the interviewer said "The job is yours if you want it—we'll start you at $30,000"? What would you do? According to the research on entitlement, it is likely that a woman in this situation would accept the offered salary and a man would negotiate for a higher one. Why? Because men have grown up thinking their work is worth more and women have been socialized to think they deserve less (and to be reluctant to ask for it, even if they think they deserve more). But according to Leslie Whitaker and Elizabeth Austin, authors of *The Good Girl's Guide to Negotiating,* a woman's passive acceptance of the first salary offer can end up costing her a small fortune over the course of her career.

Consider this: In the above scenario, imagine that a young woman accepts the initial salary offer of $30,000. A young man, by contrast, counters with a demand for $37,000 and then settles for an offer of $35,000. Both stay on the job for 10 years, working hard and getting pay raises of 5 percent every year. What will be their salary difference at the end of the 10 years? (Hint: To get the salary for each year, multiply the previous year's salary by 1.05. Keep doing this until you get to the 10th year).[1] If the salary difference is this large at the end of 10 years, imagine how large it could be by the time the two people are ready to retire! Interestingly, Whitaker and Austin (2001) note that women are sacrificing not only money, but also esteem when they accept a salary offer without negotiating: Employers are more impressed with an applicant who negotiates a better compensation package.

Write down the reasons why you think women may be reluctant to ask for more reward for their work. If you were in this position, what guidelines would you write down for yourself before talking to your prospective employer about your salary?

1. *Answer*: At the end of 10 years, she will be making $48,869 and he will be making $62,722.

and boys, playing in same-sex groups, develop habits of interaction that can be characterized, respectively, as **enabling** and **constricting.** Girls, she says, develop communication styles that involve a lot of turn-taking, listening, and supportive reactions to other speakers. Boys develop styles that involve power assertion, competition for the floor, interruptions, and open disagreement with other speakers. Sociolinguist Deborah Tannen, in her popular book *You Just Don't Understand* (1990), elaborated upon those distinctions. Tannen summarizes gender differences in communication styles by saying that women's communication reflects a concern with intimacy and connection, whereas men's communication reflects concerns about independence and status. (See Chapter 6 for more on this subject.)

Do these stylistic differences in the exercise of power and influence reflect gender differences in the sense of entitlement? Perhaps to some extent they do. It is easier to be direct and assertive when one feels entitled to make a particular demand; a more tentative, diffident style is likely to accompany a feeling of uncertainty about one's right to push for a particular outcome. As will be discussed further in Chapter 14, influence styles can vary according to the degree of legitimacy a person attaches to her request or demand. A woman, socialized in the direction of cooperation and "enabling" interactions, may not feel entitled to hold the floor for a significant length of time or to demand assertively from others that they follow her wishes. And should she "forget" that she is not entitled to engage in such behaviors, others in her environment will hasten to remind her through their disapproving, or even outraged, reactions.

Reactions to Female Power

One source of uncertainty for girls and young women as they develop their notions of entitlement may be their observations of how women with power are treated. Public reactions to powerful women, as reported in the popular press, are frequently characterized by ambivalence or by downright hostility. For example, high-profile political women in the United States, such as Geraldine Ferraro, Hillary Clinton, and Elizabeth Dole, have often been lightning rods for public criticism and disapproval. Clinton, for instance, was sharply criticized, even by women, for being too ambitious—a criticism that would have sounded bizarre if leveled at a male politician (National Public Radio, 2000). Dole, on the other hand, was caricatured during her run for the U.S. presidency as being too robotlike, even too "ladylike" (Reed, 1999). When Canadian politician Kim Campbell first began receiving press as the likely front-runner for the prime-ministership of Canada in 1993, she too was greeted with ambivalent reactions. For instance, she had allowed her photograph to be taken for a book about professional women as she stood behind a partition, with only her head and the tops of her bare shoulders showing above it. The photograph was a dignified one, but the bare shoulders earned her the disparaging sobriquet "the Madonna of Canadian politics." Apparently there is a narrow range of acceptable behavior for a woman seeking political power.

Not just in politics, but in many areas, women leaders receive negative reactions. Linda Carli (2001) reviews literature showing that women who act in highly assertive, confident or competent ways sometimes find that they have trouble influencing others, particularly males. Moreover, she notes, people respond with dislike, hostility, and rejection to such assertive women, presumably because these women are violating expectations for gender-appropriate behavior. And indeed, gender stereotypes prescribe that toughness, assertiveness, and the competent exertion of power are masculine (Heilman, 2001; Schein, 2001).

Much of the literature on reactions to women leaders shows women giving higher ratings than men to female leaders—a finding that, according to one meta-analysis, seems to reflect mainly a prejudice against female leaders by men and a relative lack of such prejudice in women (Eagly et al., 1992). This parallels findings in the political arena that men show a pro-male bias, whereas women, rather than showing a pro-female bias, are "equal-opportunity voters" (Sigelman, Thomas, Sigelman, & Ribich, 1986). Women in some studies, however, do indicate a pro-female bias: They expect more of powerful women than they do of powerful men (Jabes, 1980; Mikalachki & Mikalachki, 1984). Support for female political candidates sometimes appears to be based in part on the notion that women will be better politicians *because they are women*—they will be more principled, more sensitive to the concerns of their constituents, more dedicated, and harder-working than their male counterparts.

Some of the negative reactions to powerful women obviously stem from the unflattering stereotype of women as incompetent. It also appears that some of the negative reactions stem from *positive* stereotypes of women as warm, caring, kind, gentle people —and as people who are especially likely to be supportive of other women (Eagly & Mladinic, 1994). So what happens when a woman in authority violates those positive stereotypes? The research literature on teacher evaluations provides some sobering indications that powerful women may be held to a higher standard of cordiality and consideration: Women professors who do not fulfill students' expectations that a woman will be "nice" and "nurturing" are punished with negative evaluations. For example, women perceived as tough graders are judged more negatively than women who are perceived as easy graders, but the ratings of male instructors are less likely to be related to their image as "hard" or "easy" graders (Unger, 1979a). In rating hypothetical instructors, students have been found to give lower ratings to a female instructor portrayed as not socializing with her students outside the classroom, whereas socializing had no relationship to ratings of male instructors. The sociable female instructors received about the same ratings as the sociable and the unsociable male instructor; the *un*sociable female instructor was rated less positively than any of the others (Kierstead, D'Agostino, & Dill, 1988). In a similar vein, student ratings of female and male instructors who were portrayed in a slide–tape presentation as smiling or not smiling showed a bias against the woman who did not fall into the "nice" feminine stereotype. The unsmiling man was rated somewhat more favorably than the smiling man, but the smiling woman was rated much more favorably than the unsmiling woman (Kierstead et al., 1988). These findings parallel others showing that women instructors are judged more harshly than men if they do not meet stereotypically feminine standards of behavior with respect to friendliness, student contact, and support. Students do not necessarily give higher ratings to men who give them greater time and attention. Interestingly, students of both sexes hold women faculty to these higher standards.

A meta-analytic study of gender and the evaluation of leaders underlines the tendency to judge women leaders harshly when they depart from expected feminine behavior. Eagly, Makhijani, and Klonsky (1992) found in their overview of studies that women leaders were devalued more than men when they were exhibiting leadership styles characterized as masculine, such as autocratic and directive styles. Women and men were given equivalent ratings, however, when the leadership style portrayed was stereotypically feminine, the democratic and interpersonally oriented styles. As they note, their findings parallel those on conformity and status in small groups explored by Cecilia Ridgeway (1982): Friendly, cooperative, interpersonally oriented behavior enhanced women's status and their influence over other group members, but such behavior by men had little or no impact on men's status and influence. Ridgeway speculated that the stereotypically feminine behavior demonstrated women's group-oriented values and their lack of self-aggrandizing motives. Men did not have to demonstrate these qualities because group members saw them as having an inherent right to lead! Carli (2001) supports this notion, finding that women can reduce resistance to their influence by being careful to display the "feminine" virtues of warmth and collaborative orientation.

How are these attitudes toward powerful women conveyed? In a telling laboratory study, Dore Butler and Florence Geis (1990) trained female and male confederates to try to become the leaders in mixed-gender four-person groups. The males and females used the same scripts, made the same suggestions, using the same words, and followed similar tactics in trying to get the other group members to follow their lead. Butler and Geis found that women trying to take leadership of the groups became the targets of nonverbal disapproval. People—both men and women—frowned at them as they talked, and the more they talked, the more the other group members frowned! When men, using the same script as the women, tried to take leadership of *their* assigned groups, the nonverbal reactions were much more favorable. Their suggestions (the *same* suggestions, remember) were greeted with smiles and nods, not frowns. It appeared that group members were made uncomfortable by the idea of a woman taking charge of a mixed-gender group—although these research participants said, when asked, that they had nothing against female leaders, and they were not aware of their nonverbal discouragement of the female leader.

In the United States, all this disapproval of strong, direct female leaders is not lost on young women. American female university students contemplating leadership positions apparently get the message that leadership can be dangerous to their relationships—that people may not like or trust them if they behave in the ways required by certain powerful roles (Lips, 2000; 2001). They are more likely than men to anticipate that relationship problems will accompany powerful positions.

Eagly and Johnson (1990) suggest that disapproval is directed specifically at women leaders who violate gender expectations by leading in an autocratic and directive manner *because* such a leadership style by a woman is particularly disruptive to expected patterns of gender deference. Is such disapproval expressed in all cultural groups? Presumably it depends on the expectations for women that a particular group holds. Some scholars have argued, for example, that African American women have a tradition of speaking their minds and asserting their opinions, as a consequence of "an Afrocentric expectation that both men and women participate in the public sphere" (Collins, 1991, p. 94), and that African American women and men communicate more nearly as equals than their White counterparts do. Would African American women receive the same disapproval from the men in their own group as European American women would for leading in a directive, authoritarian manner? What would the results of such a study be for the women of the African countries of Ghana or Senegal? India? China? Research does not seem to have addressed these questions yet.

Yet there are disturbing signs of commonality among women in their experiences of self-doubt and limited entitlement. Alice Walker, a renowned African American writer, recounts her dismay and crisis of self-confidence when, in reading about the life and work of an earlier renowned African American writer, Zora Neale Hurston, she found that Hurston had been mercilessly attacked by critics.

[I]f a woman who had given so much of obvious value to all of us (and at such risks: to health, reputation, sanity) could be so casually pilloried and consigned to a sneering oblivion, what chance would someone else—for example, myself—have? . . . Zora was a woman who wrote and spoke her mind—as far as one could tell, practically always. People who knew her and were unaccustomed to this characteristic in a woman, who was, moreover, a. sometimes in error, and b. successful for the most part, in her work, attacked her as meanly as they could. Would I also be attacked if I wrote and spoke my mind? And if I dared open my mouth to speak, must I always be "correct"? And by whose standards? (1984, pp. 86–87)

Indeed, women need a large dose of courage to speak their minds in a cultural context that provides little in the way of structural or moral support. Regrettably for women, such cultural contexts are all too numerous.

SUMMARY

Although there are many examples of courageous, self-confident girls and women, the stereotype of female timidity, uncertainty, and caution remains in place in many cultural contexts. Girls are often overprotected, underestimated, and socialized less toward exploration and adventure than boys are.

Some researchers argue that girls and boys are socialized by their own same-sex peer groups to emphasize different qualities: collaboration and supportive (enabling) interactions for girls and competitive, dominance-oriented (constricting) interactions for boys. Then, when the two groups begin spending more time together during adolescence, young women encounter males who argue instead of listening, whereas young men encounter females who are agreeable, supportive listeners. This change in the social context may present a challenge to young women's self-confidence and self-esteem, and may lead women to feel silenced.

In the United States, many girls, especially European American and Latina girls, seem to internalize a series of cultural messages that they are not entitled to speak their minds, that they must not make mistakes if they are going to be liked, and that the way to acceptance is through quietness and compliance. African American girls are less successfully indoctrinated by these messages, but they are not immune to the notion that girls and women are often valued less than boys and men. In this chapter, we have looked at some of the ways culture helps to shape such differences between the genders, and some of the ways girls resist the threats to their self-esteem and sense of entitlement. Many of the cultural messages may occur in the classroom, where teachers treat girls and boys differently, spending more time and attention on boys and making different kinds of attributions about the failures and successes of their female and male students. Thus, even when girls do well in school, they may feel a lack of solid confidence in their abilities to do intellectually challenging work. When this lack of confidence combines with cultural attitudes that certain academic realms, such as physical science and mathematics, are best suited to males, the result is that many girls and young women avoid these fields.

In adulthood, women may still be haunted by a sense that they are entitled to less than men: They tend to underestimate their future performance in school and in careers; in laboratory studies they assign themselves less pay than men for the same work, and they work harder and longer than men do for the same amount of pay. Furthermore, they protect their self-esteem by comparing their rewards only with those of other women. When women depart from their deferential attitudes and behaviors, at least in some groups, they risk being punished with disapproval and rejection. Powerful women are the targets of unflattering stereotypes and of behavior that undermines their power.

The dynamics of these interactions are not necessarily unique to gender. Indeed, social psychologists who study power and social identity are quick to note that *any* devalued group will show a tendency to protect self-esteem by making comparisons only within the group, and that disapproval and rejection (even from within the group) are quickly visited on those who threaten the status quo. Thus there is nothing particularly mysterious about the observations that researchers have made with respect to female self-esteem, confidence, and entitlement. Girls and young women are adapting to a set of cultural messages that they are valued less than boys and men. To change their feelings and their behavior, it is necessary to change that message.

KEY TERMS

courage	self-esteem	enabling interaction style
self-confidence	gender-intensification	constricting interaction style
relational aggression	entitlement	

DISCUSSION QUESTIONS

After reading this chapter, do you have any new ideas about why women make less money than men? About why there are relatively few women in positions of public leadership?

What role does socialization by peers play in the development of girls' self-confidence? What kinds of changes might make a difference?

Why might girls from different ethnic groups in the United States show different patterns of changes in self-esteem at adolescence?

What future do you predict for yourself, in terms of power and success? How do you think your predictions are influenced by your peers? Your school experiences? Your family? The media?

FOR ADDITIONAL READING

Fine, Michelle (Ed.). (1992). *Disruptive voices: The possibilities of feminist research.* Ann Arbor: University of Michigan Press. In this collection of articles, the voices of a diverse group of female adolescents who are participating in research offer a revealing picture of why it can be so difficult for researchers to discern what girls are really thinking.

Leadbeater, Bonnie J. R., and Way, Niobe. (1996). *Urban girls: Resisting stereotypes, creating identities.* New York: New York University Press. This volume includes articles on the ways inner-city adolescent girls of various ethnicities construct their identities and cope with family and peer relationships, sexuality, health, and career development.

Orenstein, Peggy. (1994). *Schoolgirls: Young women, self-esteem, and the confidence gap.* New York: Doubleday. The author captures the voices of girls in two very different middle schools in the United States.

Pipher, Mary. (1994). *Reviving Ophelia: Saving the selves of adolescent girls.* New York: Putnam. Pipher, a psychologist who has seen many adolescent girls in her practice, explores the forces that can push girls to give up or hide their "authentic selves" as they enter adolescence.

WEB RESOURCES

Girlpower. This is the Web site of a national public education campaign sponsored by the U.S. Department of Health and Human Services to help encourage and motivate 9- to 14-year-old girls to make the most of their lives. It includes sections for girls and adults and a section on research and news about girls. **www.girlpower.gov**

Equity Online. This is the Women's Educational Equity Act Resource Center, containing current information about the efforts of the U.S. government and nonprofit organizations to promote equity. On this site you will find a guide for promoting gender equity in the science classroom, resources to infuse equity in classrooms, and a large section containing biographies of "women of achievement." **www.edc.org/WomensEquity**

United Nations Educational, Scientific and Cultural Organization (UNESCO). Here is a good source for information about the educational participation of girls and women worldwide. It includes information about programs for change adopted by the organization and statistics about education from countries throughout the world. **www.unesco.org**

CHAPTER 6

Connections: Communicating with and Relating to Others

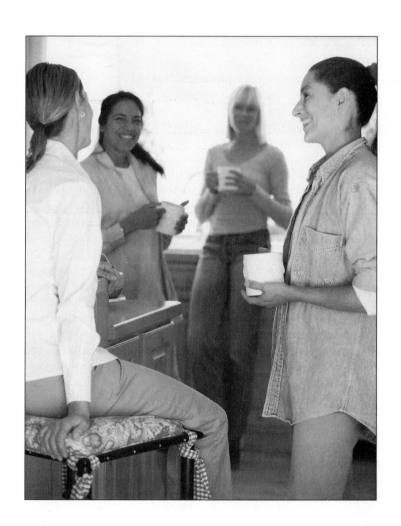

CHAPTER OUTLINE

The Australian scholar Dale Spender (1989), informally investigating the degree to which her male colleagues tended to dominate conversations, tape-recorded a series of conversations between female and male academics at her university. Upon reviewing the tapes, she was annoyed (but not particularly surprised) to learn that the woman's side of the conversations was always shorter than that of the man she was speaking with: Women spoke for between 8 percent and 38 percent of the conversational time. Furthermore, each of the women involved stated, before knowing the results of the investigation, that she had had a *fair* share of the conversation. Clearly, women are so unaccustomed to holding the floor in interactions with men that they feel satisfied with much less than half the speaking time. As Spender noted, "[I]f she tries to talk for half the time[, it] feels unfair, rude, and objectionably overbearing" (p. 10).

Spender herself reported that, try as she might, she had never been able to keep the floor for half the interaction with a male academic colleague because when she employed the strategies necessary to keep the floor, no man stayed to talk with her for the 3 minutes she had set as the minimum interaction time. In her "best score" conversation, she determined to claim her half of the speaking time. Doggedly, she refused to be interrupted, to give up the floor before she was finished speaking, to say less than she wanted to say in order to yield speaking rights to her male colleague. By the end of the conversation, she felt uncomfortable and somewhat guilty—as if she had been rude and ungracious to her colleague and had demanded more than her share of the conversational dominance. He too was uncomfortable—and somewhat irritated, accusing her of being unreasonable and of not listening to him. Is this what it takes, Spender wondered, for a woman to claim her fair share of attention and speaking time when she converses with men? But her discomfort quickly turned to anger when she reviewed the tape of this conversation and found that, her male colleague's aggrieved accusations notwithstanding, she had managed to control only 44 percent of the speaking time! Clearly, what both he and she had learned to think of as "normal" in male–female discussions was weighted heavily in the direction of male talking and female listening.

The notion that gender is socially constructed has been raised frequently in earlier chapters. How we think we should be and behave as women is a set of ideas that is gradually shaped and articulated as we grow from childhood to old age—largely as a function of cultural expectations about femininity, masculinity, and their interrelationship. If we are concerned, as we are in this book, with the question of just *how* gender is constructed and maintained by our interactions with one another, we must focus on the processes of communication.

Communication with others is a major way that cultural expectations are transmitted, acted out, and reinforced. Thus communication both creates and sustains gender. The way we communicate reflects social norms about gender and the ways we, as individuals, have internalized those norms and made them part of our own identities and habits. As researcher Julia Wood (1996a) notes, "When we observe a specific man interrupt a particular woman and see her allow it, we are witnessing a concrete performance of gender. He assumes he should assert and dominate, which is consistent with social prescriptions for masculinity. She displays deference in keeping with social views of women" (p. 11).

Communication also reflects and embodies cultural expectations and distinctions based on race and class and the ways these variables interact with gender. When we assert that femininity involves deference to men, are we universalizing an observation that is actually based mainly on middle-class White women and men in the United States? Perhaps. For example, some researchers have shown that African American women are less deferential than European American women—less likely to smile at and defer to men (Halberstadt & Saitta, 1987). And studies of nonverbal communication in a variety of cultures do not always reveal parallel gender differences (Hall, 1984). It is important, as noted many times in the preceding chapters, to look beyond blanket statements of gender differences to investigate more carefully the differences among women. Such investigations are likely to make it increasingly clear that there is nothing *essentially female* about deference or essentially male about dominance. Rather, each cultural group produces and sustains gender in its own way through the interactions of its members, and the differences vary from context to context.

Furthermore, we must keep in mind that gendered patterns in particular behaviors may not mean the same thing when observed in different groups. For example, we have already noted the research suggesting that African American women show less verbal and nonverbal deference to men than European American women do. Does this mean that African American women have more confidence and/or more power relative to men? That is one possible interpretation; however, as bell hooks (1996) notes,

> in traditional southern-based black life, it was and is expected of girls to be articulate, to hold ourselves with dignity. Our parents and teachers were always urging us to stand up right and speak clearly. These traits were meant to uplift the race. They were not necessarily traits associated with building female self-esteem. An outspoken girl might still feel that she was worthless because her skin was not light enough or her hair the right texture. (p. xiii)

Hooks argues that the propensity to speak up is not necessarily a sign of female empowerment among African Americans, and she laments the tendency of researchers to assume that such behaviors have similar meanings across cultural groups.

We begin this chapter with an examination of the role of gender in the processes of communication, both nonverbal and verbal. Does gender shape the ways we look at, touch, gesture to, and make room for one another? Does it affect the ways we speak to one another: how and how much we talk, what we talk about, and how much we reveal about ourselves in those conversations? How do race and social class figure into these patterns? And how similar are the patterns across cultures?

Communication is the basis of getting acquainted and forming friendships. This chapter focuses next on women's friendships—with one another and with men. And since there are many differences among women, we will examine not only the various ways women of various racial, ethnic, and cultural groups define and act out friendship, but also the challenges and rewards of women's friendships that bridge such boundaries.

Communication

We communicate whenever we ask a question, give direction, exclaim in anger, refuse to meet someone's gaze, move over to let someone sit down, or gesture impatiently at a person who is in our way. Whether or not words are involved in such interactions, messages are sent and received and information about feelings and/or thoughts is conveyed. In **verbal communication,** we use words to get our message across; in **nonverbal communication,** we use a variety of other means: facial expression, tone of voice, gesture, posture, touch, eye contact. In both forms of communication, gender plays a role.

Verbal Communication

Chapter 5 noted that when children play in separate same-gender groups, they tend to socialize one another into gender-specific styles of interacting—different "communication cultures." In other words, they develop some shared assumptions and understandings about how to communicate and how to interpret one another's communications—at least within the context of their own group. These gendered patterns of interaction are likely to persist into adulthood. Among adults, these gender differences are evident in some aspects of verbal communication, such as **conversational dominance,** and less frequently observed in some other aspects, such as language style.

Conversational Dominance   North American researchers have typically found that men try to control conversations; they are concerned with using conversation to establish status and authority, compete for attention and power, and achieve instrumental status and goals (Wood, 1996b). Women tend to use communication to build connections with others, to be inclusive, supportive, cooperative, and responsive to others. Perhaps it is not surprising, then, that men tend to talk more than women do and to try to hold the floor, even when they are not saying anything, by using **filled pauses**—nonwords such as *um* or *ah* (Hall, 1987). In many situations men also tend to interrupt women more often than women interrupt men, and these interruptions often effectively silence women (DeFrancisco, 1991; Tannen, 1990). This gender difference is most obvious in **intrusive interruptions**—interruptions aimed at taking away another speaker's turn to speak. Whereas men often seem to interrupt in order to take control of a conversation by stating an opinion or changing the topic, women more often interrupt to show support and agreement to the speaker (Anderson & Leaper, 1998). Anderson and Leaper also found that men's intrusive interruptions of women were more likely to occur in naturalistic than in laboratory or office settings and in unstructured than in structured activities.

Some kinds of interruptions are perceived to be more serious violations of polite conversation than others. If a woman does interrupt a man, she may become a target of disapproval, evaluated as too assertive and disrespectful (Farley, 2000; LaFrance, 1992), particularly if she is a White woman interrupting a White man. It appears that, although circumstances can moderate this effect, men's dominance of conversations and women's conversational deference mirror the prevailing cultural notion that men should be in charge.

In cultures where the general expectation of male dominance is missing or less pronounced, is the gender imbalance in conversational control so evident? Research is still silent or inconclusive on this question—perhaps because few such cultures exist. However, research comparing the social interactions of African American and European American adolescents in same-race, mixed-gender groups suggests that greater gender equality is evident in conversations among the African Americans (Filardo, 1996). In the European American groups, but *not* in the African American groups, a significantly higher percentage of the females' than of the males' utterances were interrupted and never completed. Similarly, in the European American groups, but not in the African American groups, males made significantly more influence attempts than females did. In fact, when all four groups were compared, European American women showed speech patterns that were more tentative, conciliatory, polite, and less powerful than any of the other three race–gender categories. Furthermore, the data indicates that the gender equality noted in the African American groups is not a consequence of especially facilitative or gender-egalitarian behavior on the part of the African American men. Indeed, African American men had significantly lower levels than their female counterparts of the kinds of speech forms (seeking input, consideration for the other's viewpoint) that invite or encourage participation and influence by others, and they had the highest percentage of speech that expressed commands or a lack of consideration for the viewpoint of others (e.g., "That's stupid," or "*This* way!") of any of the four groups. It appears that the gender equality in social interactions among these African American adolescents was due to the active and assertive behavior of the women, rather than to any accommodating behavior on the part of the men.

Listening and Conversational Maintenance   Keeping a conversation going requires work: effective listening, the communication of attention, and interest. Most people will stop trying to communicate if the person they are talking to displays no sign of wanting to hear more. Girls in North America tend to learn at an early age to pay attention to others and to indicate that attention in a variety of ways: nodding their heads, maintaining eye contact, using facial expressions that say "I'm interested," and issuing an almost continuous stream of what Deborah Tannen (1990) calls "listening noises" such as "I know what you mean" and "Mm-hmm." Boys are less likely to learn such a pattern of ongoing responsiveness; although they may be listening, they do not signal it in such clear ways (Wood, 1996b). In the United States, these patterns are most obvious among European American women. Emily Filardo's (1996) study of social interactions among same-race, mixed-gender groups (mentioned above) showed that simple positive responses expressing nothing more than agreement (e.g., "yeah," "uh-huh") made up more than one-third (36 percent) of European American female adolescents' speech acts, but only between 12 percent and 17 percent of the speech acts of the other race–gender categories. African American women and men did not differ on this measure. However, there were other gender differences in the African American groups that suggested the young women were signaling "I'm listening" more than the young men were: Women more frequently sought input and/or agreement or dialogue from others. This pattern of greater female than male work at conversational maintenance persists among adult women and men; a frequent complaint among women is "He's not listening to me." This complaint can be baffling to a man who really is listening, but who has not been socialized to demonstrate his attention as women have been.

Besides communicating their attention, women also work to keep conversations going by asking questions, responding to what others say, and probing for more information. Such behavior aimed at maintaining conversations is less frequently displayed by men. In fact, researchers have found that men are more likely than women to undermine conversations by interrupting, giving no response or a delayed minimal response (such as a long pause, followed by a barely interested "Mm-hmm"), or failing to pursue a topic that another speaker has raised (DeFrancisco, 1991; Fishman, 1978).

Once again, this gender difference is likely to be related to culture. Girls and boys learn lessons about whether, when, and how to communicate interest and responsiveness, and women, more than men, learn that it is important to communicate positiveness in their interactions with others (LaFrance, 2001). In a culture that values males more highly than females, girls and women are taught to do the "work of relationships" and to communicate their support of male concerns. Boys and men, conversely, are taught to expect such support from females but not to provide it.

"Troubles Talk" Some researchers have argued that women and men tend to differ in the extent to which they provide supportive responses when another person confides a problem: that women are more supportive than men (e.g., Tannen, 1990). Others have found indications that not only gender, but also gender role (i.e., femininity and masculinity) are correlated with supportive communication—with highly feminine individuals tending to be more supportive than highly masculine individuals (Basow & Rubenfeld, 2003). Yet the notion that women and men differ in their tendency to provide supportive responses remains controversial. In one recent study, adult women and men read scenarios describing a friend as upset about a personal problem, and they were instructed to respond to the situation by talking "as if your friend was actually there in the room with you" (MacGeorge, Graves, Feng, Gillihan, & Burleson, 2004, p. 153). The respondents' words were transcribed and analyzed for the presence of various themes, such as sympathy, offering help, and describing the emotion as a shared experience. Overall, these researchers found that men and women were equally responsive to the hypothetical friends' problems: They were equally likely to express sympathy, share similar problems with the distressed friend, and try to discourage worry. There was a small tendency for men to give more advice than women, and for women to provide support by affirming the other person and by offering help.

These researchers also found, in a separate study, that women and men did not differ dramatically in their responses to comforting messages. Although women responded more positively than men did to highly person-centered comforting messages (e.g., "I know you must be feeling down"), and men responded more positively than women to comforting messages that were less centered on the person (e.g., "there's no reason to make such a big deal of it"), both women and men evaluated the very person-centered messages much more positively than the low person-centered messages.

These authors conclude that the overlap between women and men in their supportive communication is far more impressive than the differences between them, and they argue that the notion that women and men communicate so differently as to represent "different cultures" is false. Here, as in many realms of gender and behavior, researchers continue to argue about the extent to which differences or similarities should be emphasized.

Speech Styles   Do women and men talk differently—do they prefer different words or differ in their use of tentative or direct requests, questions, or assertions? Robin Lakoff (1975, 1990) argues that the two genders show very different styles: that women are more likely than men to use qualifiers, to end their statements with tag questions (e.g., "Isn't that right?") in order to elicit signs of attention and agreement, and to be generally more polite and tentative in their speech. Evidence for these assertions is mixed, however. Some researchers report few gender differences in **speech styles** (Cameron, McAlinden, & O'Leary, 1993). Others report that women are more likely than men to use "proper" English (Adams & Ware, 1995), perhaps because women are more worried than men are about the influence they may lose by speaking in a low-status way or because men feel that the use of nonstandard language illustrates their toughness.

One study of the request styles used by female and male Korean and U.S. students found that women in both countries were more polite than men (Holtgraves & Yang, 1992). In the latter case, however, the target of the request was always portrayed as male, making it difficult to know whether the gender difference in politeness was a function of the situation (a same-sex versus other-sex target) or the gender of the person making the requests. Researchers have also found that girls and women use less contentious language than males do. For example, men use more slang and more swearing than women do (Adams & Ware, 1995). Several studies of African American girls have found that although they were very familiar with the forms of "verbal dueling" common in their communities, they used these forms with greater restraint than boys did (e.g., Folb, 1980; Heath, 1983).

Mary Crawford (1995; 2001) notes that it is impossible to interpret gender differences in speech styles and other aspects of communication without an awareness of the cultural context in which the patterns appear. Women are not a single, global category, all following the same rules of speech; rather, they are responsive to the customs, constraints, and opportunities in their own diverse communities. For example, Patricia Nichols (1983) found that speech patterns in African American communities in rural South Carolina tended to reflect occupational opportunities. In these communities, the best jobs for men were in construction and trades—jobs in which the use of standard or "proper" English was unnecessary. The best jobs for women were in sales, nursing, and teaching—jobs that required the use of standard English. Women and men in these communities *did* differ in their use of standard English; that difference, however, seemed to be driven by women's desire to gain and keep good employment rather than by a tendency to be conservative or to safeguard their influence.

Women's variable tendency to be tentative rather than assertive is likely a reaction to the social context and to what they perceive as the "payoff" for being gentle or blunt in

BOX 6.1 LEARNING ACTIVITY
Observing Gendered Patterns of Communication

Next time you are with a group of women and men, sit back and observe the patterns of communication among them. Who does most of the interrupting? Is there a gender difference in the kinds of interruptions (supportive versus taking over the conversation)? How do people communicate that they are listening attentively to a speaker? Do women and men differ in this respect? Do men and women use different kinds of nonverbal communication?

From your observations, do you conclude that communication in this particular group is gendered? In what ways? How well did the patterns you noticed fit with the research findings that are discussed in this chapter? If they do not fit, can you think of reasons why this may be so?

their speech. For example, Linda Carli (1990), studying women and men interacting in mixed-sex or same-sex pairs, found that women were more tentative only when they were interacting with men. Furthermore, women who spoke tentatively were more influential with men, and less influential with women, than women who spoke assertively were. Thus these women seemed to be reading the situation correctly and adjusting their behavior accordingly in order to maximize their effectiveness.

When perceptions of the social context clash, women from different groups may mislabel the emotions associated with blunt speech. For example, bell hooks (1989) writes of the reaction to her first book manuscript, a treatise on Black women and feminism:

> When the white woman editor at South End who was working with the manuscript first talked with me about the book she told me that members of the [publishing] collective felt it was a very angry book and were concerned that it did not have a positive bent. I responded by saying that though I had written in the direct blunt manner that is the customary mode of discourse in my black southern family, I was not angry. Our different perceptions of the implication of my speech, of my tone were important signifiers of the way in which race and class shape our ways of speaking and reading. Many outspoken black people have had an experience in which the passions, intensity, and conviction in our speech is interpreted by white listeners as anger. (p. 153)

Hooks's experience of being misperceived is not unusual in cross-racial communication. As a group, African Americans are more likely than European Americans to be forceful and confrontational in conversations among themselves (Ribeau, Baldwin, & Hecht, 1994). The different styles sometimes cause misunderstanding: Whites may view Blacks as rude or hostile; Blacks may see Whites as cold and overly reserved. African American women sometimes report that European American women seem dishonest and deliberately distant because they speak quietly and unemotionally; they just don't seem to be really *engaged* in the dialogue (Houston, 1994).

Language Topics: What Do We Talk About? When a group of women in conversation is joined by a man, or when a woman sits down at a table where two men are talking, the impact on the conversation is often dramatic. Conversational topics are shifted, either from a desire to avoid sharing "gender-private" information or from a motive to include the new person in the interaction. Does this happen because, as the stereotype suggests, men are always talking about sports and women are always talking about relationships? Partly. Researchers in North America have often found that women and men talk about different things and do not understand what is important to the other gender. Women do tend to enjoy discussing feelings, whereas men are more likely to prefer talk about sports, politics, or other less personal topics (Shields, 1995; Wood, 1996b). The differences are strong enough that when 150 male and female undergraduates read transcripts of conversations between same-sex or cross-sex friends from which all gender identifiers had been removed, they could often tell the sex composition of the conversing pair simply by the topic under discussion (R. Martin, 1997). Such differences may have their roots in childhood when, as some studies have shown, parents focus on discussions of emotions more with their daughters than with their sons (Kuebli & Fivush, 1992) and reinforce daughters and sons differently for expressions of emotions such as sadness and fear (Garside & Klimes-Dougan, 2002). The differences may also spring from social contexts in which women and men, searching for common ground with their same-sex peers, gravitate to topics that they assume will be acceptable, given the cultural expectations for women and men.

Men and boys may learn to emphasize shared activities as the route to closeness; women and girls may learn to value shared self-disclosure (McNelles & Connolly, 1999). A small but reliable gender difference in self-disclosure has been found, showing women revealing more about themselves and their feelings than men do (Dindia & Allen, 1992). Some researchers, however, have shown that when same-gender friends are communicating with each other, men actually disclose more than women do (Leaper, Carson, Baker, Holliday, & Myers, 1995). Women's and men's responses to self-disclosure in such situations were different, however: Men were more silent and women were more verbally supportive in response to friends' self-disclosures.

There are apparently some situations in which men and women self-disclose equally. In particular, when women and men meet for the first time, they seem to disclose the same amount about themselves (Clark et al., 2004). This may be because each is trying to make a good impression on the other person—and it works: In this study both women and men were rated more favorably by their partners the more they self-disclosed. Both women and men believed that self-disclosure would generate positive reactions in their partners, but men seemed to believe this more strongly. So perhaps men in this situation self-disclose to women in hopes of "gaining points" with their new acquaintance by violating the masculine stereotype of being tight-lipped.

Whatever gender difference in disclosure of feelings may exist, there appears to be a general pattern of shared interests between North American women and men. For example, Bischoping (1993) reports that in informal conversations among students recorded in public places on campus, *both* women and men spent the most time talking about work and money, a category that included such topics as studying, jobs, and career goals. Yet men were still more likely than women to talk about sports and entertainment activities, and women talked about men 4 times as much as men talked about women!

In the context of heterosexual relationships, the different communications topics favored by women and men often lead to misunderstanding and hurt feelings. Women

---

BOX 6.2 MAKING CHANGE
Challenging Sexist Language

Many major publishers now have guidelines for avoiding sexist language, so it is unlikely that you will find language that is obviously sexist in your college textbooks. However, such language still lingers in many areas: organizational brochures, advertisements, newsletters, publications by community groups, even college catalogs. Be alert for sexist language in your own writing and that of others. For example, if you find male pronouns or "man" being used to indicate "all people," point out the problem and ask to have it changed. The Web Resources list at the end of this chapter contains a site that provides tips for nonsexist writing.

---

like to talk about the relationship in order to increase its intimacy; men often see no point in talking about it unless something is seriously wrong (Wood, 1996b). When the man avoids discussing the relationship, the woman may believe he does not care about it. Furthermore, women enjoy talking about the details of their daily lives in order to enhance their sense of connection with others (Becker, 1987); men often regard such talk as boring since it is unrelated to achieving a goal or "getting to the point." Here again, women may experience men's lack of interest as a lack of concern about them or about the relationship.

Language as a Way of Making Masculinity the Norm   "Each student should leave his books at the door." "The candidate for the degree must schedule his oral examination before the deadline." "Every taxpayer should know his rights." Do these sentences apply to males only, or would it be safe to assume that they include female students, degree candidates, and taxpayers? Most people would guess that the sentences are meant to apply to both sexes, arguing that English uses the generic *he* to mean "both he and she." Linguistically, the proponents of such a view may be correct, but how does the use of generic masculine pronouns and other masculine terms to refer to people in general shape the way we think about women and men? Many scholars have argued that saying *he* all the time causes us to think about men as the normal ones and women as the unusual or different "other."

Can such simple linguistic conventions really have such a big impact on our thinking? Try these sentences on for size: "No person should let his doctor talk him into having a hysterectomy against his will." "An individual who has been raped should call the police immediately to report his experience." Why do these sentences sound so strange, if the use of the masculine pronoun does not make us think immediately of men in particular? In fact, studies on the use of the generic *he* or the companion generic term *man* show that these terms are more likely to make respondents think of men, rather than of people. For example, when students were asked to provide drawings of the sex-unspecified people in a paragraph that used either the generic *he, he or she,* or *they,* they were more likely to produce images of men when the pronoun used was *he* (Khosroshahi, 1989). And when asked to submit photographs appropriate for chapters of an introductory sociology text, students were more likely to submit male-only photos when the chapter titles used the generic *man* ("Urban Man," "Political Man") than when they did not ("Urban Life," "Political Life") (Schneider & Hacker, 1973).

Of course, not every language has different pronouns for females and males. Chinese, for example, uses the same pronoun to refer to *she* and *he.* Still other languages, such as Spanish and French, apply gender labels to virtually every noun.

Language as a Way to Stereotype, Categorize, and Belittle Women   In English, grown women are frequently referred to as *girls*—a label that suggests immaturity and lack of status. Parallel labeling of men is not done so frequently or so casually: Calling a grown man a *boy* is usually an insult. Apparently it is a more serious matter to trivialize men than women. When the term *boy* was used, with malice and deliberation, in the racially divided communities of the American South, it was meant to humiliate African American men and to remind them that they were not "real" men.

English usage routinely trivializes women. Karen Adams and Norma Ware (1995) note that studies of slang find many more terms for stupid and/or superficial women (*bimbo, ditz, fifi*) than for stupid, superficial men. These studies also find many more words and phrases describing women than men in sexually derogatory ways. Furthermore, the term *lady,* often substituted for *woman* or *female,* frequently conveys a subtle putdown or trivialization. A *lady professor* or a *lady scientist* sounds like someone who dabbles in her profession, in contrast to a *female professor* or a *woman scientist,* who, despite being marked as unusual by the gender label, sounds perfectly serious.

Languages in many parts of the world encode ways of belittling women. In Japan, the terms for widow are *mibojin* (not-yet-dead-person) and *goke* (after-family). A man whose wife has died is not labeled as though his life is over, and is never considered "after-family." The word for womb, *shikyu,* means "child's palace," a not too subtle reminder that it does not belong to the woman herself (Cherry, 1987).

Language as a Way of Resistance for Women   The linguist Suzette Elgin (1984) wrote a science fiction novel called *Native Tongue,* in which the women, oppressed and kept isolated from one another by men, devised their own secret language. The language was meant not simply to communicate with one another, but to describe their lives in ways that were impossible in the dominant language. Her story fits well with the notion, often advanced by feminist scholars, that it would be impossible to analyze or change the way people think about women, men, and gender while constrained by a language that has been shaped by a male-centered culture.

At least one real-life version of a secret women's language exists. For nearly a thousand years, there flourished in the Hunan province of China a "women's script" that could be written and read only by women (Silber, 1992). In this script, called *nüshu,* women could record the truths of their lives for an exclusively female audience. They did not have to worry about what men would think of their writing, since men not only were untrained in women's script, but apparently belittled it and made no effort to learn it. Gathering for an evening of needlework, women would take turns singing from *nüshu* texts they had written or memorized. Women used this script to write to one another, to cement lifelong friendships, and to record their own knowledge to pass on to daughters. The Communist

Even under difficult conditions, women have found ways to form and strengthen ties of friendship with one another. For nearly a thousand years, women in the Hunan province of China used a "women's script," which could be written and read only by women, to communicate with their friends.

revolution in 1949 brought an end to the practice of young women learning *nüshu,* so this female literary tradition has virtually died out. Yet its long existence is a powerful demonstration of the way language can serve as a means of resistance.

A less exotic, but similarly powerful, way that language has been used by women for resistance is through humor. Humor has often been used to denigrate women, and women are often reminded of their "place" by men's pointed sexist jokes. Given that they are so often the targets of jokes, perhaps it is not surprising that women are sometimes stereotyped as having "no sense of humor." Potentially adding to the stereotype is that in order to tell a joke successfully, a person must be allowed to gain and keep the floor in conversation —something that women are often barred from in mixed-sex groups. However, as Mary Crawford (1995) writes, humor does not necessarily have to reflect and uphold the status quo. Rather, because it allows the speaker to employ an indirect form of discourse, humor can be subversive of existing stereotypes and hierarchies.

Crawford notes that women often use humor among themselves to mock existing power structures and stereotypes, to exact some small revenge on oppressive males, and to express shared meanings. For example, she cites a well-circulated U.S. feminist slogan that pokes fun at the notion of male superiority: "To be seen as equal, a woman has to be twice as good as a man. Fortunately, that isn't difficult" (p. 154); and another that mocks the idea that a woman must have a man in order to be complete: "A woman without a man is like a fish without a bicycle" (p. 155). She also notes that when women tell sexual jokes they defy and undermine the "cultural rules controlling women's sexuality" (p. 150) by violating the norm that women are not supposed to talk about sex in any but the most demure and inhibited way. Witness, for example, the shock value of the following story passed on by Rayna Green, who studied the sexual humor of U.S. Southern women: "Once when my grandmother stepped out of the bathtub, and my sister commented that the hair on her 'privates' was getting rather sparse, Granny retorted that 'grass don't grow on a racetrack'" (Green, quoted in Crawford, 1995, p. 150).

Humor also facilitates the discussion of taboo topics by breaking the tension that surrounds them, and it can raise awareness of unexamined assumptions. Thus when Roseanne jokes, "I'll do the vacuuming when they invent a ride-on vacuum cleaner" (quoted in Crawford, 1995, p. 155), she is pointing out and making fun of, among other things, "strong" men's need for ride-on lawnmowers in contrast to "weak" women having to push a vacuum cleaner across the rug.

Crawford notes that a growing body of feminist humor helps women as a group to resist and defy subordination. This humor can be a source of shared empowerment for women in many circumstances. It is one way that communication need not reproduce and reinforce dominant conceptions of gender.

Computer-Mediated Communication   Increasingly, large segments of people communicate through the computer, using e-mail, chat rooms, and bulletin boards. Many educational institutions have begun to offer courses online, relegating student-to-student communication to these electronic modalities. As many of us have begun to rely increasingly on **computer-mediated communication,** some have wondered whether this type of communication would be gendered, or whether the lack of face-to-face (or at least voice-to-voice) interaction would erase distinctions between women and men in their habits of communication. Researchers have been quick to investigate these questions; however, the answers are not yet clear. Some research comparing computer-mediated interactions in female-only versus male-only groups has shown females and males developing different patterns of communication in this medium. Female-only groups have been observed to send more words per message, use more individually oriented language, and be more satisfied with the group process than males (Savicki, Kelley, & Lingenfelter, 1996a; 1996b). In one study, the examination of 2,692 e-mail messages sent by 1,208 individuals in 27 different online groups revealed that participants in female-only groups were more likely than those in other groups to establish online presence through self-disclosure, by using "I" statements, and by directly addressing their messages to other group members. By contrast, participants in male-only groups tended to ignore the social aspects of the group and to engage in monologues instead of dialogues. Perhaps not surprisingly, participants in the latter groups were less satisfied with their experience (Savicki & Kelley, 2000).

In mixed-sex groups, the patterns of gender differences in computer-mediated communication are somewhat suggestive of male conversational dominance. For example, in one study of the communications of postgraduate distance learners, men sent more messages than women and wrote messages that were twice as long as those of women. However, women contributed more interactive messages than men (Barrett & Lally, 1999).

Another study of a small group of graduate students showed that the women produced more messages and expressed more opinions and agreements in face-to-face communication conditions than they did in computer-mediated conditions (Adrianson, 2001), suggesting that women may be more comfortable with traditional face-to-face interactions.

Nonverbal Communication

Communication is often unspoken. It includes the way we look at and touch one another, the way we carry ourselves, our gestures, even the ways we occupy and control the space around us. Here too, gender expectations shape communication and are reinforced and reproduced by the patterns of give-and-take that make up nonverbal interactions. In fact, nonverbal communication may sometimes be the mode through which *real* messages about gender are transmitted. For example, a woman and a man in formally equal positions of power may be engaged in a verbal dialogue that implies equality between them. Yet the man may stare off into space when the woman talks; the woman may smile and nod whenever the man makes a point. The man may sit in a relaxed and expansive posture whereas the woman perches on the edge of her chair. The underlying message about who has the greater power is clear, despite the apparent contradiction from the verbal aspect of the interchange. This message is conveyed through a variety of channels.

Gaze   In middle-class North America, looking at someone while she is speaking communicates attentiveness and the attachment of significance to her words. It is a sign of politeness and respect. Not surprisingly, high-powered people tend to look at their subordinates while speaking to them and tend to look away when listening to them, a phenomenon referred to as **visual dominance** (Dovidio & Ellyson, 1985). This pattern shows up in cross-gender interactions: One study showed that in mixed-sex pairs, expertise was associated with visual dominance for both women and men, but when there was no difference in expertise, men showed greater visual dominance than women did (Dovidio, Ellyson, Keating, Heltman, & Brown, 1988). In the absence of other cues, gender becomes the most relevant one and people behave according to gender-related norms of male dominance and female submission, probably without being aware that they are doing so.

Eye contact can mean different things in different cultures, so gender-related patterns in gaze may vary or require different interpretations across cultures. For example, a high degree of eye contact has been reported as having positive connotations by Arabs, Latin Americans, Indians, and Pakistanis, but as conveying anger or insubordination by Africans and East Asians (Smith & Bond, 1993). Much research remains to be done on the interaction of gender and culture in nonverbal communication.

Touch   In North American cultures, people tend to "touch downward" in a status hierarchy (Henley & Freeman, 1995). People of high status are freer to touch their subordinates (such as putting a hand on a shoulder, holding an arm) than vice versa. Touch seems to communicate or mirror dominance as well as (or instead of) affection or intimacy. In fact, the interpretation of touch may be confusing for this reason. An employer who puts an arm around the shoulder of an employee may intend to communicate liking;

however, the fact remains that the employee (regardless of the affection that may exist between the two individuals) is less free to put an arm around the shoulder of the employer.

Researchers also report that men are more likely to touch women than women are to touch men—an asymmetry that suggests touch can be an expression of male dominance as well as affection or intimacy. Furthermore, men are often in positions of higher status than women, which further complicates the issue. When a male manager touches his female secretary or a male professor touches his female student in a casual way, what is being communicated? Power? Affection? Sexual interest? Perhaps all of these, whether intended or not. But the person who is touched reacts as if it means *something.* Research shows that when a 10-second touch on the wrist by a stranger occurs without any obvious reason, it produces a physiological reaction: increased heart rate and blood pressure (Nilsen & Vrana, 1998). The largest cardiovascular increases are found with women being touched by men, perhaps because a woman who is touched in this way can interpret it in so many ways. In some contexts, a touch may be interpreted as sexual harassment, leading to feelings of threat and anger.

The patterns of touching between women and men seem to vary according to relationship context. One study based on observations of 4,500 dyads interacting in public places in the Boston area showed that in younger couples, males touched females more, but in older couples, females touched males more (Hall & Veccia, 1990). This pattern might mean that male dominance is acted out more strongly in younger couples, or that length of relationship is related to changes in the ways both power and affection are expressed.

The groundwork for patterns of touching that vary by gender and ethnicity may be laid in infancy. Some North American research has suggested that parents tend to touch infant boys less often and more roughly than infant daughters and that daughters are handled more gently and protectively (Wood, 2001). However, when ethnicity and other variables such as maternal depression are taken into consideration, this pattern is not so clear. For example, Stepakoff (2000) found that maternal ethnicity and maternal depression were related to the ways female and male infants were touched by their mothers. Among her findings were that Black, nondepressed mothers touched sons more than 7 times as often as daughters, and that Latina depressed mothers engaged in rough touch more than 20 times as often with boys as with girls. The findings indicate the importance of attending to ethnicity as well as gender in studying communication and suggest that cultural differences in the way we communicate by touch may be maintained and passed on through the mother–infant dyad.

Posture   Starting at a young age, females in North America sit, stand, and walk differently from males. Females adopt a more constricted stance, keeping their legs together and their arms and hands close to their bodies. Males spread out, occupy more space, sitting and standing with their legs apart. This pattern may signal that males feel entitled to more space, that females have absorbed the message that being "ladylike" or "feminine" involves adopting a dignified posture, that females' clothing is more restrictive than males' clothing, or that females begin early on to feel that they are objects of scrutiny to males and so learn to sit and stand in ways that protect their privacy. Probably each of these factors plays a role.

In other cultures, similar gender differences in posture apparently exist, as suggested by studies of photographs and paintings from a variety of countries (Frieze & Ramsey, 1976).

Facial Expression A woman I know was taken aback and irritated one day when, walking down a busy street deep in thought, she was stopped by a strange man who urged her, "Smile! You'll look so much prettier!" Without realizing it, this woman had been breaking a "rule" for women in North America: Women are supposed to smile.

Researchers report that women do, in fact, smile more than men (LaFrance & Hecht, 1999), as revealed, for instance, by studies of photographs in magazines and yearbooks (Halberstadt & Saitta, 1987; Regan, 1982) and of strangers interacting in groups (Frances, 1979). This research is, however, largely based on European American women; African American women smile less than European American women (Wood, 2001). When White women do not smile, they are judged as less attractive, less happy, and colder—judgments that are not made about men who fail to smile (Deutsch, LeBaron, & Fryer, 1987; Stoppard & Gruchy, 1993). White men can get away with being somber and serious without creating negative reactions; their female counterparts cannot.

Perhaps because there is so much pressure on them to smile, many women smile even when they do not feel particularly happy or friendly. They smile to please others or to cover their discomfort (Frances, 1979). Their smiling has a good effect on those they are conversing with: As every lecturer knows, positive nonverbal responses encourage speakers and elicit more confident, competent behavior from those speakers. When interacting with men, women are more often the sources than the recipients of such nonverbal encouragement.

Personal Space Each of us maintains a "comfort zone" of **personal space** around us—a space that others, unless they are intimates, may not breach without causing us uneasiness. There is some evidence that females set smaller personal space zones, approaching others more closely than males do, and that people of both sexes approach females more closely than they do males (Hall, 1984). Culture and gender are both important factors in individuals' preferred use of space. For example, Arabs are often reported to favor closer proximity than Americans, at least when interacting with acquaintances (Smith & Bond, 1993), and many researchers have noted that women in general are often comfortable with closer interpersonal distances than men are. Yet one study of Egyptian and U.S. students found that Egyptian female students wanted males, both friends and strangers, to keep a greater distance than the U.S. women did (Sanders, Hakky, & Brizzolara, 1985). This difference between Egyptian and U.S. women may reflect the strong emphasis in some aspects of Egyptian culture on women maintaining their respectability by keeping separate from men.

Why Should Gender Be Related to Communication Patterns?

Explanations that have been suggested for the relationship between gender and communication patterns include gender differences in social power, childhood socialization, current cultural context, and physical size. As a subordinate group, women may find their well-being depends on understanding and pleasing men. This necessity to understand and to

Culture and gender are both important factors in individuals' preferred use of space.

please may account for some of the observed gender differences in listening, encouraging other speakers, smiling, and deferential posture and gestures. On the other side of the coin, men's tendency to dominate conversations and to occupy more space than women may stem from a sense of entitlement that goes with their higher social power.

Childhood socialization may play a role in orienting individuals to such power differences. Awareness of power differences is probably only one part of the reason for gender-related differences in communication, however. As we have already noted, much childhood socialization is done by same-gender peers. For example, girls seem to learn to be cooperative in their speaking patterns in order to get along well *with other girls,* not with boys. What is responsible for the development of cooperative norms for communication among girls and competitive ones among boys? One contributing factor may be the parental emphasis that girls, not boys, pay attention to emotions. Another may be the pervasiveness of norm-appropriate models presented to girls and boys in the media and other aspects of the culture. And once a set of norms becomes established, social psychologists know that it seems to take on a life of its own, shaping behavior even if there is no particular logic to it. This phenomenon can be readily seen when comparing cultures on dimensions such as gestures, rules of politeness, and so on. The same gesture means different things in different cultures; different rules of politeness govern communication between females and males in different societies. The particular behavior gains its meaning in large part from the significance attached to it by people in the culture.

Finally, a simple explanation for some gender-related differences, particularly in nonverbal communication, may be physical size. Males may take up more space because they are larger, and their size also prompts others to stand further away from them. Their size makes them more easily intimidating to others than women are, perhaps contributing to deferential speech and gestures on the part of women.

There is no single explanation for the relationship between gender and communication patterns. The issues are multifaceted, suggesting a role for power and status differences between males and females, socialization and cultural norms, and the stimulus value of gender. As we turn to a discussion of the friendship bonds that are forged through communication, it becomes apparent that communication shapes relationships and vice versa, perhaps leading to different kinds of friendships for women and men, as well as for women from different cultural groups.

Friendship

The British feminist Mary Wollstonecraft, writing in 1792 on women's rights, declared that friendship was "the most holy bond of society" and "the most sublime of all affections" (quoted in Rose, 1995). A person without friends is considered unfortunate in the extreme, or even flawed in some serious way. In North America, friendships tend to be spontaneous and informal; however, this is not true in every culture. The young Chinese women who practiced the "women's script" discussed above often used it to arrange and promise a permanent, formalized "best friendship" with another woman (Silber, 1992). Among the Bangwa people of Cameroon, parents often arrange a lifelong best friendship for their children in the same way they arrange a marriage (Brain, 1974, cited in Rose, 1995).

Friendships between Women

Despite the generally agreed-upon importance of friendship, women's friendships have often been trivialized and mocked, and women have been portrayed as incapable of true friendship (Rose, 1995). Yet both the historical and psychological research on women's friendships indicates that, far from being trivial and fickle, such friendships tend to be deep, intimate, and enduring. For centuries, women have formed passionate, close friendships, as women's private letters and diaries attest. These relationships have emphasized self-disclosure, emotional closeness, and empathy, and have often been a core part of women's emotional lives (e.g., Faderman, 1981; Smith-Rosenberg, 1975).

A central theme in women's friendships is talking and **self-disclosure.** Even in early childhood, girls talk and share stories with one another, whereas boys are more likely to spend their time together in active play. Girls tend to develop fewer, more intimate, friendships whereas boys are more likely to have large groups of friends with whom they *do,* rather than talk (Johnson, 1996; Rose, 1995). A study of African American girls from preschool to high school showed they spent much more time in talking than in play activity (Goodwin, 1990). Among ninth-grade Hispanic students, girls have been found to be more willing than boys to discuss their feelings with their best friends, with the largest gender difference emerging in the realm of negative emotions: anxiety, apathy, depression, and fear (Kiraly, 2000). In this study, the girls described their friendships as providing more validation, companionship, help and guidance, and intimate exchange and less conflict than the boys did.

Some research suggests that, whereas girls may *have* more intimate friendships, boys are not disinterested in such relationships. Niobe Way's (1996) interviews with a mostly African American and Latino sample of adolescents at an inner-city public high school revealed that the boys longed for close friends with whom they could talk about anything, but they had often given up hope of experiencing this kind of friendship because of betrayals by previous friends. The girls in this sample had also experienced betrayal, but they were more willing to try again for close friendship with someone new, and so were more likely to have close friends.

Adult working-class and middle-class women sometimes report that shared activities with friends are mainly valued as opportunities to get together to talk, and that they bond with other women through talk, support, and sharing feelings (K. Walker, 1994). Research on college students and on upper-class women reveals a similar pattern (Johnson, 1996).

The talking that women do with friends is aimed at building intimacy. Indeed, the most valued function of friendship for women of all ages appears to be intimacy-assistance: discussing private, personal feelings and receiving help (Candy, Troll, & Levy, 1981). The orientation toward intimacy may be particularly intense during adolescence, but the encouragement, support, and affirmation that women receive from female friends is linked for women of all ages and from diverse groups to positive feelings of well-being, high self-esteem, and life satisfaction (Goodenow, 1985; Oliker, 1989).

Most of the research on women's friendships described above has been done within the framework of individualistic, independence-oriented cultures. However, the findings probably do not describe universal patterns in women's friendships. Within more collectivist or interdependence-oriented cultures, the preferred methods of communication and expressions of intimacy may be different (Dion & Dion, 1993). For example, a review of the historical literature on the friendships developed by Asian American immigrant women suggests that

> Verbal self-disclosure and intimacy, so heavily emphasized in the literature on White American women's friendships, have not received the same degree of prominence. Instead, what has consistently been emphasized is the communication and interaction among friends centering on activities, usually undertaken on behalf of families, churches, and communities. Bonds of friendship were forged and expressed through collaboration. Although Asian American immigrant women may have had personal concerns, it did not seem to be in their nature (or socialization) to speak of these. Nonverbal behaviors may have conveyed what remained unspoken and were acknowledged in similar fashion. Reciprocal affection and comfort were expressed

through working together in various activities toward a common goal. (Serafica, Weng, & Kim, 2000).

Women's friendships tend to change over the course of their lives and according to their involvement in heterosexual relationships. Dating or marriage often interferes with women's friendships, and among married couples the man's friends tend to take center stage as the couple's friends (Rose, 1995). Parenting young children may be disruptive of friendships because of the amount of time and energy required; however, women do manage to sustain friendships through these times, often sharing their difficulties and coping strategies. Perhaps not surprisingly, women's friendship networks tend to expand after divorce—following an initial reduction. In one study of European American and Mexican American divorced women, both groups reported that they had more friends after the divorce because their ex-husbands could no longer prevent them from socializing as they chose (Wagner, 1987). Women also tend to expand their network of female friends in later life, probably because many are widows and they depend on other women for support, companionship, and help.

Diversity in Women's Friendships Factors such as culture, social class, race, sexual orientation, and physical ability may be linked to variations in women's friendships. More research is needed to understand how friendships are shaped by the values, resources, opportunities, and restrictions that exist for different groups of women. For example, the Aboriginal women of central Australia have a long tradition of women's camps, or *jilimi*, which serve as refuges for women, places where women's religious rituals are centered and to which women come frequently for conversation and emotional and social support (Bell, 1983). The most permanent members of such camps are widows and married women who do not live with their husbands. The *jilimi* are also more temporary refuges for single girls who are not ready to go to their promised husbands, women traveling without their spouses, women who have temporarily left their spouses because of a dispute, those who are ill or in need of help or support, and those who are in mourning. Sometimes married women come to the camps by day to socialize with other women, returning to their husbands at night. The *jilimi* are taboo to men and provide women with a safe space, a power base, a place where they and their activities are central. These formally designated women's spaces provide opportunities for women to form strong bonds with one another, and such bonds can extend across generations.

By contrast, other cultures in which women often find themselves in spaces that are segregated from men may not provide the same nurturance for female friendships. In the strongly gender-divided world of the Saudi Arabian royal families, for example, girls and young women form friendships that may be based on a shared desire to rebel against men's institutionalized power or on shared commiseration over their anticipated fate of arranged marriages (Sasson, 1992). They may derive comfort but little sense of power from these friendships, which can be broken up at any time by a patriarch's decision to marry off a daughter or divorce a wife and send her away, never to be seen again by the other women in the family or community.

In Europe and North America, social class can affect the form that friendships take. Working-class women may disclose more to their friends than upper-class women do—perhaps because working-class women are less likely to socialize as couples (Rose, 1995).

One British researcher found that White middle-class friendships often spanned a variety of activities and included entertaining friends at home, but the friendships among the White working-class sample tended to be specific to particular activities and settings. The latter group seldom entertained friends at home, which was reserved for the family (Allan, 1977). This difference may reflect not only class values, but also the fact that middle-class women have larger, more comfortable homes for inviting people in (Rose, 1995). Other research, however, suggests that women with limited economic resources are more likely than their more affluent counterparts to integrate friendships into kin relations, counting friends as family rather than segregating them to particular activities (Johnson, 1996). Limited resources may, of course, create an emphasis on more localized friendships—ones that do not require expensive transportation and long-distance phone calls.

For immigrant women, the negotiation of a new culture may provide especially trying conditions for the development of friendships. For example, women who come to the United States from Asia may have to adjust to different cultural norms with respect to social networks. These women often come from cultures in which family networks are most important and in which many supports are available within large extended family networks. Thus, important relationships outside the family have traditionally not been emphasized. In the United States, however, there is a strong cultural emphasis on developing personal networks outside of home and family. Asian American immigrant women, used to having a "built-in" network, and unpracticed in the skills of network building, may face big challenges in forming new social ties in their adopted country, especially if they are not proficient in English (Serafica, Weng, & Kim, 2000).

Racial and ethnic differences in female friendships are also apparent. One small group of White and Black women who were meeting regularly to talk about and try to bridge issues of race reported that they had surprised one another with their discovery, at one meeting, that *all* of the Black women and *none* of the White women had been to one another's homes (K. Allen et al., 1996). This discovery seems to fit with Suzanna Rose's (1995) comment that "a pattern of regarding friends as part of an extended family network appears to distinguish African Americans from white Americans, at least among the poor, working, and middle class" (p. 86). African Americans are more likely than their White counterparts to have an extended network of friends that are counted as family and from whom help and support can be sought.

Black women in professional occupations that are dominated by White men may seek one another's friendship not just for the reasons of help, social support, and companionship already discussed, but also as allies in assessing and coping with issues such as racism at work. As E. Bell (1990) notes, Black women in professional occupations often experience "bicultural" stress, feeling torn between the demands of the White male culture of their job and the Black community. Friendships with other Black women who are feeling similarly torn can help them manage their feelings of conflict and bridge the two cultures.

Sexual orientation may influence women's friendships, but research in this area is just beginning. Research shows few differences between lesbians and heterosexual women in the ways they form friendships. Both groups say that similarities of age, gender, race, and sexual orientation are not important when choosing friends; however, both groups report they have more friends of the same sexual orientation (Bliss, 2000). Also, whereas heterosexual women say they like to make friends through their work, lesbian women are more reluctant to do this, choosing instead to meet new friends through existing friendships. Both lesbians and heterosexual women place high priority on such factors as similar interests, understanding, and support when evaluating friendship with women; however, lesbians emphasize equality and trust within friendship more than heterosexual women do (Rosenbluth, 1990). Among lesbians, friendships with women are highly valued; also, friendship with a lover may be viewed as more important than sexuality and may be maintained after a romantic partnership has ended (Rose, Zand, & Cini, 1994). Also, lesbians often develop close friendship groups, endeavoring to situate their lifestyle and partnership choices in a larger network of social relationships (Johnson, 1996).

Some Paradoxes of Women's Friendships   In her memoir, bell hooks (1996) describes the intimacy that developed among the women in her African American family around the weekly practice of ironing their hair:

> There is a deeper intimacy in the kitchen on Saturday when hair is pressed, when fish is fried, when sodas are passed around, when soul music drifts over the talk. We are women together. This is our ritual and our time. It is a time without men. It is a time when we work to meet each other's needs, to make each other beautiful in whatever way we can. It is a time of laughter and mellow talk. (p. 92)

Years later, as a senior in high school, she decides she never wants to get her hair pressed again; rather, she wants to wear an Afro. At that point, she sees the hair-straightening ritual as a rejection of Black women's beauty, an attempt to look White. In their Saturday morning sessions, she feels, the women supported one another in rejecting their own beauty and conforming to someone else's standards. "The intimacy masks betrayal. Together we change ourselves. The closeness is an embrace before parting, a gesture of farewell to love and one another" (p. 93).

In this example, women friends supported one another, but that support was a mixed blessing because it made them more comfortable with a culture that denigrated them. Do women's friendships in general act to support the status quo? To preserve rather than undermine gender ideologies and gendered social arrangements? Some authors have argued that the answer is yes: At least some of the time, women's support for one another is solidly situated in support for the prevailing gendered power arrangement. Women's friendships tend to keep unsatisfactory or oppressive marriages intact by giving wives an outlet and a source of sympathetic support, by fulfilling needs for intimacy that are unmet within the marriage, and by defusing anger (O'Connor, 1992; Oliker, 1989).

Women's friendships may also unwittingly support women's weaknesses rather than their strengths, and may reinforce stereotypical notions that femininity is synonymous with nurturance and emotionality. Women's friendships allow for a great deal of self-disclosure; however, that self-disclosure is usually focused on weakness and pain, not on strengths and victories. As Suzanna Rose (1995) notes, "in friendships women emphasize their vulnerabilities rather than their skills, their helplessness rather than their power" (p. 98). She also points out that women tend to expect their friendships to be entirely supportive—an expectation that is based on stereotypes. Women may deny parts of themselves and limit their friendships by refusing to acknowledge the existence of more "negative" emotions, such as envy or competitiveness, in their friendships.

Yet women's friendships can also provide a climate in which women can explore new self-definitions and ways to challenge social structures and stereotypes that are detrimental to them. Friends can support one another in resisting the restrictions and limited expectations that women encounter. Louise Bernikow (1980) notes that, across many cultures, "Women friends help each other to remain perpendicular in the face of cultures that attempt to knock them over with the hurricane forces of ideology about what a woman should be or . . . [deny] the validity of their experience, [denigrate] their frame of reference, [reinforce] female masochism, self-doubt, passivity, and suicide" (p. 144).

Women's Friendships across Boundaries of Race or Culture   Diane Bell (1983) describes her quest to form friendships with the Aboriginal women whose community she was studying in Australia. She found she had to answer many questions about her life and her family, and her answers led to the agreement that she had something in common with these women: children, parents, concerns about home and family. Moreover, the fact that her financial support came from a government grant and a university scholarship, rather than from a husband, enhanced her similarity to the Aboriginal women, who received support from the Australian government. Months of dialogue, and her willingness to learn, bridged the cultural gap of mistrust and led to the formation of trust and friendship:

> My economic and emotional independence of the world of men meant that I was "safe" with women's secrets. Aboriginal women often worry that if they confide in a white woman she will repeat the information to her husband. Those who had worked as "house girls" observed that on returning home in the evenings husbands often asked their wives, "What did you do today, dear?" and were told. (p. 26)

Bridging this gap between cultures was no small feat for Bell and her Aboriginal friends. The Aboriginal women regarded the culture associated with "white fella law" as destructive and disparaging to women; they were upset that White-run organizations such as the Institute for Aboriginal Studies had restricted areas in which they housed men's secret sacred material but no comparable restricted areas for women's secrets. They saw little about the White women's lives that they wanted to emulate, and they had only sympathy for the situation of White wives and mothers, whom they saw as virtual prisoners, shut inside all day. Bell was incompetent in many of the skills the Aboriginal women valued—tracking animals, killing and gutting them, distinguishing poisonous plants from edible ones—and she was a novice in understanding the women's system of law. Yet perhaps one of the things that helped the friendship to succeed is that the women on both sides were aware of and openly acknowledged the immensity of the gap between them and approached one another with mutual respect and a willingness to explore and understand differences.

Often women have difficulty forging friendships across gaps of ethnicity, race, and class, gaps that may appear, at first glance, to be much narrower than the one between Diane Bell and her Aboriginal teachers. But perhaps it is the very notion that the gaps are small and unimportant that leads to insensitive behavior and frayed tempers instead of friendship. Midge Wilson and Kathy Russell (1996), writing about friendship between

BOX 6.3 WOMEN SHAPING PSYCHOLOGY
Jean Lau Chin

If someone wanted to begin to understand the role that culture plays in relationships, Jean Lau Chin's work would be a good place to start. Born in New York City, fluent in Cantonese Chinese, and active for many years in professional and community associations that emphasize the importance of diversity, Jean Lau Chin is one psychologist to whom people turn for an understanding of what it takes to be culturally competent.

Now a licensed psychologist with over 30 years of clinical experience, Jean Lau began her training in psychology at Brooklyn College in New York, where she majored in psychology and graduated with honors in 1966. She went on to Columbia University to complete masters (1966) and doctoral degrees (1974) in school psychology, getting married along the way to Gene Chin.

Her clinical and administrative career was underway before she had completed her doctorate. In 1973, she founded her own consulting company, CEO Services, which she continues to run. The organization provides clinical, educational and organizational services, focusing particularly on cultural competence, community-based services, and integrated systems of care. She was co-director of the Douglas A. Thom Clinic between 1973 and 1985, and since then has served as director of several other health organization. She is also a professor in the Department of Family Medicine and Community Health at Tufts University.

Jean Lau Chin's career reflects parallel interests in feminist psychology, Asian American psychology, and empowerment of diverse communities. She conducts training on cultural competence, Asian American women, and diversity. Her extensive writing on these topics has taken the form, not only of books and articles, but also of policy briefs and testimony on expert panels. One place where her interests and expertise in all of these areas is clearly displayed is in her edited book, *Relationships among Asian American Women* (Chin, 2000).

Black women and White women in the United States, note that for many young women, college is the first opportunity for close contact with women of the other race, and that opportunity may take the form of sharing a dormitory room. Although such a situation provides many opportunities for listening, learning, and developing friendships, it also provides opportunities for the woman who is a member of a minority on campus (usually the Black woman) to be made to feel abnormal, on the defensive, and out of place. For instance, the White woman may pepper her Black roommate with questions and comments about the textural differences in their hair, causing the Black woman to feel as if she has to explain herself all the time—even when she is at home in her own room. Wilson and Russell quote one frustrated Black woman:

> White girls are always tripping on Black hair. I used to have to tell my White roommate to butt out. She was so fascinated by my hair and always wondering how I could go two weeks without washing it. I remember one time hearing her on the phone telling her mom how Black people

---

BOX 6.3 WOMEN SHAPING PSYCHOLOGY (continued)
Jean Lau Chin

Chin's work has been recognized through a number of awards and honors, including the *Outstanding Executive Director Award* from the Massachusetts League of Community Health Centers, and the *Women Who Care Award* from Women in Philanthropy. She has been active in the leadership of the American Psychological Association's Committee on Ethnic Minority Affairs and in the APA Division on the Psychology of Women, of which she became president in 2002. Through her work, Jean Lau Chin has helped American psychology broaden its scope, focus on culture as an important issue, and become more aware of the need to empower diverse communities.

Read More about Jean Lau Chin

Who's who in America (2001), vol. 1, p. 904. Chicago: A. N. Marquis.
Profile, Jean Lau Chin. **www.re-inc.com/ProfilesC2.htm**

Read What She Has Written

Chin, J. L. (2000). Paradigms for Asian American women: Power and connection. In J. L. Chin (Ed.), *Relationships among Asian American women,* pp. 223–230. Washington, DC: American Psychological Association.
Chin, J. L. (2000). Mother–daughter relationships: Asian American perspectives. In J. L. Chin (Ed.), *Relationships among Asian American women,* pp. 119–132. Washington, DC: American Psychological Association.
Chin, J. L. (1999). Cultural competence in a multicultural society: A checklist. **www.shpm. com/articles/cultural/cutlure.html**

---

can go two whole weeks without washing their hair. I wasn't on the phone telling my mom how when White people wash their hair it smells like a wet dog. (p. 152)

Among children and adolescents, interethnic friendships are not necessarily perceived as difficult. For example, one Canadian study of teenagers from Anglo-European, East Asian, West Indian, and East Indian ethnic groups found that these teenagers were not ethnically exclusive in their friendship choices, and that gender appeared to be a greater barrier to friendships than ethnicity (A. Smith & Schneider, 2000). However, by late adolescence and adulthood, women from different racial, ethnic, or class groups may have different communication styles, hold different values, and be comfortable in different environments (Houston & Wood, 1996). A first step in building friendship across such differences might be to avoid the assumption that behaviors, choices, or spoken words mean the same thing to members of both groups. For example, going to an expensive restaurant for lunch may mean only pleasure and a chance to talk for an upper-class woman; for her working-class friend, however, it may mean feeling paralyzed with anxiety about how much her lunch is going to cost. Canceling a lunch date with a friend in order to go home to be with a sick aunt may feel like a necessary choice to an African American woman who has been raised with a strong concept of extended family. To her European American friend, whose notion of close family is more restricted, it may seem as if the other woman was merely making an excuse to avoid the lunch.

Marsha Houston and Julia Wood (1996) offer four general suggestions for communicating and forging relationships across group boundaries. First, understand that you may not understand—that your own vantage point and cultural background shape the way you interpret communications. Second, do not impose your own cultural standards on others; shift your response from "That's wrong" to "That's interesting." Third, respect the ways others interpret their experience, and offer, at least, a respectful hearing. Finally, acknowledge but do not totalize differences: Do not pretend not to notice that your new acquaintance is of another race, but also do not relate to her only in terms of race or expect her to "represent" her racial group on every issue.

Women's Friendships with Men

Many pressures militate against cross-sex friendships, foremost among them the suspicion that relationships between heterosexual women and men *always* include sexual attraction. A woman who is married or part of a couple may provoke her partner's jealousy if she invests a lot of energy in a friendship with a man. At least in North American society, there is a tendency, especially by men, to view female–male relationships through a sexual lens, to see sexual attraction as the basis for all such relationships (West, Anderson, & Duck, 1996). Even the phrase "just friends," used only in the female–male context, suggests that such a relationship is second best, a pale imitation of what could be. Consequently, a friendship between a woman and man is often the subject of gossip and/or teasing and a belief that the friends are lying—to others or to themselves—about sexual involvement or attraction.

Reasons for engaging in cross-sex friendships are many. Women report that they receive protection from their male friends, and both sexes say that their friends of the other gender give them useful information about how to attract romantic partners (Bleske & Buss, 2000). People who are involved in such friendships say they enjoy their time together, feel they can talk about anything and be themselves with these friends, have to work less and worry less (than in romantic relationships) to maintain the relationship, and receive important support from these friendships (Reeder, 1997). Heterosexual individuals who have cross-sex friendships often engage in specific strategies, such as not flirting, to keep the relationship platonic. They frequently report that they use these strategies in order to safeguard the relationship (Messman, Canary, & Hause, 2000). This strategy is probably an important one: Flirting is often associated with miscommunication between women and men. For example, men tend to view flirting as reflecting more sexual interest than women do; women are more likely than men to see flirting as fun, or simply as a way of relating (Henningsen, 2004).

Some women form strong friendships with gay men. These friendships can be comfortable and rewarding, and there is no pressure for the relationship to become sexual. But some women (and probably a greater number of men) may feel comfortable defining sex as a part of their cross-sex friendship. One study of college students found that approximately half said they had engaged in sexual activity in an otherwise platonic cross-sex friendship (Afifi & Faulkner, 2000), while another found that sexual attraction was often present in such friendships, particularly on the part of males (Kaplan & Keys, 1997). Men perceive sex with their cross-sex friends as more beneficial than women do (Bleske & Buss, 2000). Steve Duck (1994) argues that whether a relationship is a friendship or a romance is determined not by the presence or absence of sexual activity, but by the meaning of that activity for the relationship. Yet the meaning is quite likely to differ for the two participants and, practically speaking, many women cannot afford the gossip or the threat to their couple relationship that a sexual relationship with a male friend may entail. Furthermore, the possibilities for female–male friendships are limited to certain cultural contexts. In many cultures it is out of the question for an adult woman to have a close friendship of any kind with a man who is not her husband or a relative.

As an increasing number of women move into workplaces that are dominated by men, it is critical for them to be able to form at least casual friendships with their male colleagues. Yet men often exclude women from their social networks on the job. Women and men do form friendships with each other at work, but same-sex ties are stronger than cross-sex ties (Marckiewicz, Devine, & Kausilas, 2000). Women in scientific, professional, and blue-collar occupations all report having difficulty finding male colleagues with whom they can talk, eat lunch, or share ideas—and women in such jobs *must* depend to a certain extent on males for collegiality because female co-workers are in very short supply (Rose, 1995). Moreover, when women are excluded from male colleagues' friendship networks, they miss out on important contacts and information and are denied input into decisions that may affect them. Clearly, friendship has implications beyond the private and personal.

How Friendship Patterns Reflect Social Context

Women in executive positions, according to one interview study, tend to be lonely (Gouldner & Strong, 1987). They do not have the intimate friends and sharing conversations often found among women. Why? Because their social context makes the formation and sustaining of such friendships difficult. These women, because of the inevitable issues of trust and power differences, are reluctant to form friendships in the workplace. They also have little time away from the workplace in which to form and nurture outside friendships. The findings for these women illustrate the impact of context and opportunities on friendship patterns. A more extensive look at such issues reveals that contextual variables may be, in large part, the keys to understanding female–male differences in friendship patterns.

Rose (1995) argues that women's intimate and men's nonintimate styles of friendship are at least partly shaped by the way power and resources are distributed. Since women are expected to cooperate with the notion of male superiority by providing, and not seeking, recognition, and since women have been assigned the difficult, but often thankless, task of maintaining the emotional bonds of the family and society, they may well feel drained and unappreciated. Thus they may be more likely than men to seek nurturance and recognition from their connections with friends. Men are not so likely to need nurturance and recognition from their male friends because they get so much of it from the women in their lives.

In addition, women's friendships are constrained by factors such as time, money, and space. Women have less leisure time than men do because they perform the bulk of domestic and childcare work. Rose (1995) notes, for example, that employed women may have less time than their male counterparts to have lunch with friends, because they use their lunch hours to attend to family matters. Women also earn less than men—a factor that limits the amount of money they can spend on socializing. In addition, women who are financially dependent on men may not feel free to use money for this purpose. Male control of public space also militates against the formation of casual friendship networks by women. Men informally control bars, social clubs, basketball courts, the athletic fields in many parks, and video arcades. Women who visit these spaces with female friends can expect to be stared at, elbowed out of the way, or verbally or physically harassed. Thus men have many more opportunities than women do to form casual friendships based on doing things together. This opportunity factor, as much as any intrapsychic or socialization factors, may explain the different styles of friendship prevalent among women and men.

SUMMARY

Our patterns of communicating and of forming relationships are gendered: They reflect habits and expectations associated with femininity and masculinity in particular cultures and subcultures. Thus, women and men sometimes show different patterns of verbal communication behavior: Men tend to talk and hold the floor more than women, women and men use interruptions differently, and they differ in the way they communicate that they are listening to another.

Language has often been used as a way of reinforcing the centrality of masculinity and the "otherness" of women. Generic male nouns and pronouns create habits of thinking in which females are exceptions. Language that describes women is often belittling. Yet women have used language to resist sexism through developing their own linguistic traditions and through humor.

Nonverbal communication too is gendered. For example, within some populations women smile more than men, and men take up more space than women. Men are more likely to touch women than the reverse; women adopt more constricted "ladylike" postures. Even communication through the electronic medium of the computer reveals some gendered aspects.

Many variables come into play in this gendering of the ways we relate to others. Social power is one: Women's and men's differences in communication may often reflect gender differences in status, dominance, and sense of entitlement. Opportunity structure is another—we have seen, for example, that when opportunities for employment depend on the ability to speak in a certain way, the target group does learn to speak in that way.

Cultural habits, rules, and restrictions also influence the processes of communicating and forming friendships. Among European Americans, women emphasize intimate talk more than men, whereas men are more likely than women to emphasize shared activities in friendship formation. Other groups have been less well researched. However, there is some evidence for a similar pattern among Hispanic Americans. Evidence for African Americans and Asian Americans does not seem to fit the theme of a strong emphasis on emotional talk in women's friendships and a disinterest in such talk in men's friendships; more research is needed to complete our picture of same-sex friendships.

Contact must be allowed before communication can occur, and the setting in which such contact takes place influences the kinds of relationships that can develop. The latter factor has an especially large impact on the formation of friendships between women and men.

Friendships between women have been both limited and fostered by social context variables. Women who are dependent on their husbands for money or transportation may have difficulty giving the desired priority to friendships with other women, and they may find it difficult to arrange to spend time with friends their husbands do not like. But some social arrangements, such as a group of mothers staying at home with small children, or a group of women working together at a job that allows for conversation, or the existence of women's spaces such as the *jilimi* of the Australian Aboriginal women, may promote the prolonged contact between women that leads to friendships. Cross-sex friendships are perceived as valuable by both women and men, but they are perceived somewhat differently.

And such friendships are important. Women need the support of other women to challenge situations in which female subordination is assumed. Women in diverse groups need the friendship and understanding of one another to find common ground and shared solutions to problems. If friendship is indeed "the most sublime of all affections," then perhaps we should be willing to work harder at forming friendships across boundaries of culture, race, class, and other divisions. The work of friendship across such boundaries is difficult but rewarding, as Ellyn Kaschak (1995) notes in her reflections on a series of three-way discussions about racism and anti-Semitism between herself and two other women of different backgrounds:

> Each of us has come to know herself better. We have moved toward each other, learned about some of our differences, as well as about the ways that we share histories of destruction and betrayal. While we are respectful of and interested in each other's experiences, we have begun to be less polite with each other. We feel a little safer together than we did separately. What reason is there for us to trust each other? Yet we begin to. (p. 322)

KEY TERMS

verbal communication	intrusive interruptions	visual dominance
nonverbal communication	speech styles	personal space
conversational dominance	computer-mediated	self-disclosure
filled pauses	communication	

DISCUSSION QUESTIONS

Have you observed a gendered pattern of interruptions in your conversations with friends? If so, does it fit the pattern described in this chapter?

Is it important to use inclusive language (rather than, for instance, the generic *man* to mean humans)?

How do women's and men's close friendships differ? How are they similar? Why might the answers to these questions differ across ethnic and cultural groups?

How easy is it for a woman and a man to be "just friends"? What are some of the sources of difficulty?

How easy is it for women to form and maintain friendships across ethnic, class, racial, or cultural boundaries? What are some of the things that enhance the likelihood of such friendships?

FOR ADDITIONAL READING

Chin, Jean Lau (Ed.). (2000). *Relationships among Asian American women.* Washington, DC: American Psychological Association. The articles in this volume address a variety of issues, such as the ways World War II internment affected relationships of Nisei women, identity development and conflict among Indian immigrant women, and social advocacy among Asian American women.

Crawford, Mary. (1995). *Talking difference: On gender and language.* London: Sage. The author provides an engaging and critical review of the study of gender and language, offering a new understanding of the way language is used to maintain and to disrupt gender inequality.

Raymond, Janice G. (1986). *A passion for friends: Toward a philosophy of female affection.* Boston: Beacon Press. Raymond examines the meaning (and some of the history) of women's friendships.

Tannen, Deborah. (1990). *You just don't understand: Women and men in conversation.* New York: Morrow. This book, full of concrete examples of conversations between women and men, explores some of the reasons miscommunication occurs so frequently in these conversations.

Wilson, Midge, & Russell, Kathy. (1996). *Divided sisters: Bridging the gap between black women and white women.* New York: Anchor Books, Doubleday. Here you will find a lively discussion of the issues that arise when African American and European American women try to build friendships with each other.

WEB RESOURCES

Journal of Nonverbal Behavior. This periodical features articles about all aspects of nonverbal communication. It is a good place to look for information about such communication that may be gendered. **www.wkap.nl/jrnltoc.htm/0191–5886**

Guidelines for Avoiding Sexist Language. This site, provided by the American Psychological Association, provides the rationale for using nonsexist language, as well as concrete suggestions for writing in ways that do not incorporate sexism. **www.apa.udel.edu/apa/publications/texts/nonsexist.html**

Sisterhood Is Global Institute. The capacity to communicate across geographical borders has helped activist women organize in support of their goals. The institute is an international nongovernmental organization that has members in 70 countries, working to support and promote women's rights around the world. The site provides regular "action alerts" and ways to link up with women's organizing efforts. **www.sigi.org**

CHAPTER 7

Family and Intimate Relationships

CHAPTER OUTLINE

> While it was dark, I woke up. I sat up. I thought, "How am I going to jump over him? How can I get out and go to my mother's hut to sleep beside her?" I looked at him sleeping. Then came other thoughts, other thoughts in the middle of the night, "Eh . . . this person has just married me . . ." And I lay down again. But I kept thinking, "Why did people give me this man in marriage? The older persons say he is a good person, yet . . ." [. . .] After Tashay and I had been living together for a long time, we started to like each other with our hearts and began living nicely together. It was really only after we had lived together for a long time that he touched my genitals. (Nisa, a !Kung woman, quoted in Shostak, 1981, pp. 154, 158)

The reflections by Nisa on her marriage as a very young girl suggest a very different beginning to married life than the one that is experienced by women in cultures where marriage is based on an intimate relationship chosen by the couple themselves. Yet Nisa's story reveals that in her culture, as in so many others, the pairing of a woman with a man in marriage is considered a critical step in the formation of new family bonds. Societies take an interest in couple relationships because they have implications for the interpersonal relationships that extend well beyond the couple, and for the direction, strength, and growth of the societies themselves.

In middle-class North America, the couple and the nuclear family are considered the primary relationships. Spousal bonds, the connections between parents and children, the links between siblings—these are the relationships that we often consider most intimate. But there is more than intimacy going on here. Built into these family relationships are many assumptions about gender, power, intimacy, loyalty, privacy, and work. Cultures do vary a great deal in the amount of primacy they give to couple relationships, in the institutionalization of particular kinds of relationships, and in the degree to which the nuclear family is separated from or integrated into the wider social community. With these variations go cultural differences in the expectations women and men have of relationships and of one another. This chapter explores the connection between gender-related expectations and the ways particular kinds of relationships are institutionalized.

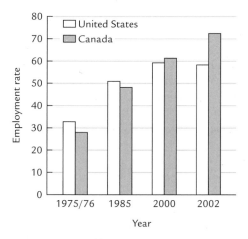

Source: U.S. Bureau of the Census 2001, 2003
and Statistics Canada, 2002

Figure 7.1 Employment rates for mothers with a child three years of age or younger

The Context of Intimate Relationships: Family Structure

In developed countries, several trends have affected families in recent years: a movement of women into the paid labor force, a decline in fertility rates, an aging population, rising divorce rates, and an increase in children born out of wedlock. The combined effects of these changes on the family and the way it works are dramatic.

For example, the employment rate of women with young children has increased dramatically over the past three decades, as shown in Figure 7.1. As Hrdy (1999) has noted, women have always had to combine parenthood with other work, but that work used to be mainly in and around the home. Now, for an increasing number of women, employment means leaving their children with others and going to a workplace that is completely separate from the home. This has changed the requirements of motherhood for many women. The problems associated with balancing family and workplace responsibilities are discussed in the next chapter.

At the same time, the "married, with children" pattern of family life is declining. Birth rates have declined all over the world and are below the "replacement rate" of 2.1 births per woman in all developed countries (United Nations, 2000). Fewer people are getting married: In the United States, the 2000 Census revealed that married couples, with or without children, now make up barely one-half of American households, whereas the number of unmarried partners—gay or straight—rose 72 percent over the past decade (Cohn, 2001a). In Canada, there were only 5.6 marriages for every 1,000 people in 1992, down from 9.2 in 1972 (Statistics Canada, 1995). And women are waiting longer to get married: The average age of women at their first marriage is now 26–27 years in Western Europe, North America, and other developed regions; it is also 27 in Southern Africa, 25 in Eastern Asia, and 28 in the Caribbean (United Nations, 2000). Many women are having children outside of formal marriage: For example, the percentage of births to unmarried women is

32 in the United States, 37 in Canada, 41 in New Zealand, 46 in Denmark, and 64 in Iceland (United Nations, 2000). Women who are married are more likely to divorce now than in previous decades. In Sweden, the most divorce-prone country, there are 51 divorces for every 100 marriages, and the divorce rate for the United States is almost that high. In many other countries, including Belgium, Luxembourg, the Scandinavian countries, and the United Kingdom, there are at least 40 divorces per 100 marriages (United Nations, 2000). Older women make up an increasing share of the population. By 2020, 15 percent of the world's women and 12 percent of the men will be aged 60 or over (United Nations, 2000). By 2041, an estimated 25 percent of Canadian women will be seniors—many of them living on their own (Statistics Canada, 1995). In some developed countries, such as Germany, Japan, and Sweden, at least one-fourth of the women are already 60 years old or older (United Nations, 2000).

What do such trends mean for the shape of the family and for family roles? Certainly, families are smaller, more fluid. Relationships may be more complex when bonds are not formalized—when, for example, children have parents who are not married to each other. There is more pressure for each family member to be a "generalist," instead of a specialist in a certain group of tasks. Women, especially, have the expectation of living alone for a certain number of years, entailing the necessity to be independent—a strange irony in view of the continuing practice of socializing girls to be dependent and compliant.

In the developing world, family size is likely to be inversely related to the power held by women. One study of 79 developing countries showed that fertility rates (the average number of children a woman produces) are strongly linked to illiteracy rates among women, to the percentage of women who are working at home for no pay, and to women's share of paid employment. Women bear more children in countries where their illiteracy rate is high, where a high percentage of them are working at home for no pay, and where they control a low share of paid employment (Dasgupta, 1995). In addition, infant mortality rates in such countries are relatively high; in southern Asia, for example, countries average 70 deaths before the age of 12 months for every 1,000 live female births and 69 deaths for every 1,000 live male births; in sub-Saharan Africa 86 female infants and 98 male infants die out of every 1,000 born—as compared to fewer than 10 deaths for every 1,000 live births for developed countries (United Nations, 2000). Childbirth is risky for women in many developing countries; for example, a woman's lifetime risk of dying from pregnancy-related causes is 1 in 16 for an African woman, but only 1 in 1,400 in Europe (United Nations, 2000). Poverty and inadequate hygiene and health care ensure that life expectancy is short. For this reason, and because various extended-family systems exist in these countries, women are less likely to live alone for any significant period of their lives.

Consideration of women's experience and behavior in families, then, must include acknowledgment of the different issues faced by women in different cultural and economic contexts and of how those issues can change over time.

The Couple Bond

Love

Beginning in adolescence, a great deal of energy is invested in forming couple bonds: intimate, somewhat-to-very exclusive relationships between two people. Such relationships are not only important in meeting needs for intimacy and companionship, they often provide the basis for the formation of families. Indeed, falling in love with the right romantic partner is widely held, in many Western cultures, to be a stage that must be traversed in order to get married and have children.

Psychologists who have studied love argue that people of any age, ethnic group, culture, or gender are capable of passionate **romantic love**—that intense feeling of longing for union with another person that can dominate an individual's emotions. Indeed, cross-cultural work suggests few differences across ethnic and gender groups in the reported intensity of passionate love (Hatfield & Rapson, 1987). These authors also argue that a "Westernization" of attitudes on such topics as gender equality is producing a trend toward love matches in many countries. Such a pattern would fit with changes that have been seen in the United States in attitudes toward love and marriage. Gender differences among U.S. students in responses to the question, "If someone had all the qualities you would want in a mate but you were not in love with that person, would you marry her/him?" used to be quite striking, with many more men than women saying no, they would not marry without love. This gender difference has virtually disappeared—a result, some argue, of the fact that women, no longer necessarily counting on a husband for economic support, can now afford to emphasize love instead of practical considerations when thinking of marriage (Dion & Dion, 2001).

In many other cultures, however, falling in love is still not a necessary part of the process of starting a stable couple union that becomes a family. Traditional practice in India, for example, is for parents to select a spouse for their son or daughter. In such a case, the couple bond may develop after marriage—and it may be quite different from the bond that links couples who first connected romantically on their own. Or an emotional bond may not develop. Indian women have written accounts of the successes (e.g., Murgai, 1993) and failures (e.g., Adhikary, 1993) of such arrangements. In some cultures, a strange blend of romantic love and traditional arranged marriages has developed in recent years. For example, on the island of Lombok in Indonesia, the tradition has been for parents to arrange marriages, and the only way for a bride to marry someone other than her arranged husband was for another suitor to kidnap her and carry her off. These days, when a young couple wants to marry, they plan for such a "kidnapping," often even clearing it with community leaders in advance. After the young man has "stolen" the woman from her parents, he approaches them to negotiate a dowry payment for her. The practice saves the parents (and the daughter) the embarrassment of trying to "sell" their daughter and demonstrates the suitor's independence and bravery. Elders on the island say that 99 percent of couples enact a prenuptial kidnapping (Schuman, 2001).

Women and men may not differ in the intensity of their love relationships, nor do they seem to have different notions about what love means in the abstract. Beverly Fehr (1993) found no gender differences when she asked women and men to rate the prototypical features of love. Cultural expectations surrounding femininity and masculinity may, however, shape women's and men's behavior, experience, and ideals differently with respect to love. Some researchers have found, for example, that men who hold strongly to an ideology that they should be "masculine" do not fit comfortably into intimate affectionate relationships with women. Men's masculinity ideology, as measured by agreement with items such as "A guy will lose respect if he talks about his problems," was related to having had more sexual partners in the previous year, a less intimate relationship with their current sexual partner, and the belief that male–female relationships were fundamentally adversarial (Pleck,

---

BOX 7.1 LEARNING ACTIVITY
Examining Assumptions about Intimate Relationships

One question that has sometimes been asked of research participants is this: "If someone had all the qualities you were looking for in a mate, but you were not in love with her/him would you marry the person?" (Of course, this question assumes that the respondent is open to the idea of marriage in the first place.) For the sake of argument, assume that you are planning to marry, and ask yourself the above question. Why do you think you gave the answer that you did? Ask some of your friends—female and male—and see what they have to say about this question. From your observations and reflections, does gender relate to the way people answer this question? What impact do you think your culture has had on your reaction to this question?

Sonenstein, & Ku, 1993). Obviously, such an attitude fits poorly with many women's expectations of relationships. Researchers have found that over 80 percent of all U.S. women surveyed say that it is more important to have a mate who can communicate about his deepest feelings than to have a husband who can make a good living (Whitehead & Popenoe, 2001).

Although women and men list similar benefits to romantic relationships—companionship, happiness, feeling loved, loving another—their lists of costs and benefits diverge on a number of points. Women list intimacy, self-growth, self-understanding, and self-esteem as significant benefits of a romantic relationship; they list the loss of identity and innocence as important costs. Men, on the other hand, list sexual satisfaction as an important benefit, and the monetary expense of going on dates as a significant cost of involvement in a romantic relationship (Sedikides, Oliver, & Campbell, 1994). And although the "nice guys finish last" stereotype suggests that women do not really mean it when they say they prefer kind, sensitive men, the research says otherwise. College women's ratings of men indicate that both niceness and physical attractiveness are positive factors in men's desirability—and that they view niceness as more important for serious relationships (Urbaniak & Kilmann, 2003).

There is some evidence that, at least in North America, women and men differ in their *styles* of love, with women more likely than men to be pragmatic (practical, compatibility-oriented) and friendship-oriented in their search for a partner, and men more likely to experience love as playfulness, without too much intensity or serious commitment (Hendrick & Hendrick, 1995). These gender differences may transcend sexual orientation. Researchers have found few differences in love attitudes and styles between gay and straight men (Adler, Hendrick, & Hendrick, 1987). They have, however, found some differences between gay men and lesbians; for example, lesbians seem to trust their lovers more than gay men do theirs and remain more satisfied with the relationship over time (Kurdek, 1989).

Every couple must deal with tensions between the partners' needs for closeness and for independence. According to stereotype, women are thought to want more closeness and men more independence—creating an inevitable conflict in mixed-gender couples. Researchers who study couples have actually found few gender differences in the needs for attachment and autonomy: Women and men tend to place equal value on these two needs (Cochran & Peplau, 1985). Where differences are found, they are counterstereotypic: Young women may be more concerned than young men about maintaining their independence in the context of a loving relationship (Peplau & Gordon, 1985).

The partners' needs for autonomy can place strains on a relationship if those needs pull them in different directions. For example, a study of relationship satisfaction in dual-career lesbian couples showed that the more the women experienced role conflict and need for personal autonomy, the less they were satisfied with the relationship (Eldridge & Gilbert, 1990). Differences between the partners' levels of career commitment were also associated with lower levels of relationship satisfaction, whereas shared attachment, intimacy, and power were linked to higher levels of satisfaction.

Both closeness and autonomy can be related to relationship satisfaction, however. In a study of lesbian couples in the Netherlands, Karlein Schreurs and Bram Buunk (1996) found that relationship satisfaction was positively associated with two types of closeness (intimacy and emotional dependency) and with autonomy. The authors speculate that, in this case, autonomy is associated with lesbian–feminist ideology—presumably an ideology that the two partners share and that contributes to their bond.

Studies have found few differences in the ways that lesbians, gay men, heterosexual women, and heterosexual men evaluate the quality of their relationships or in the variables that predict overall relationship satisfaction (McCormick, 1994). For example, poor relationship quality has been attributed in lesbian, gay, and heterosexual couples to arguing about money, intrusion of work into the relationship, spending time apart, and non-monogamy (Blumstein & Schwartz, 1983). In all three types of couples, love for the partner has been linked to the perception that there are many barriers to leaving the relationship and high dyadic attachment (Kurdek & Schmitt, 1986). Reciprocal dependency and equality of power have been found to be particularly important to the perceived relationship quality of lesbian couples; financial equality and similarity of educational level have emerged as especially important for the relationship quality of gay male couples.

Kurdek and Schmitt (1986) found some differences in relationship quality, as well as in the factors that predicted relationship quality, among different types of couples. Cohabiting heterosexual couples had the lowest scores for love for partner and relationship satisfaction relative to married heterosexual, gay, and lesbian couples—who were indistinguishable from one another on these scores. Married partners reported the most barriers to leaving the relationships, and cohabiting heterosexual partners reported the fewest. Gay male partners were more likely than the other groups to believe in "mind reading"—a belief that partners should know each other's thoughts without having to say them out loud. Lesbian couples endorsed shared decision making more strongly than other groups did. Despite the differences, however, the major predictors of relationship quality were the same across the four groups. Dyadic attachment was an important predictor of love for all partner types, and an important predictor of liking for all but cohabiting heterosexual couples. For all groups, relationship satisfaction was linked to seeing few good alternatives to the relationship, high shared decision making, and few beliefs that disagreement is bad for the relationship.

Power, Influence, and Equality in Couple Relationships

Maintaining an intimate relationship involves a continuous series of decisions and compromises that take into account the differing needs and preferences of both partners. Thus it is inevitable that issues of power, influence, and equality figure in the way relationships

WOMEN AND POWER IN INDIA

VANAJA DHRUVARAJAN *was born in India and completed her undergraduate education at the University of Mysore before coming to the United States for graduate work at the University of Chicago. After obtaining her doctorate in sociology in 1981, she took a faculty position at the University of Winnipeg in Canada. She regularly returns to India to continue her research on Indian women. Recently she received a grant to study popular women's magazines and the empowerment of women in India. She responded to questions about the psychology of women and family power relationships.*

Q. What are the most important issues in India with respect to the psychology of women?

A. The psychology of women is a complex issue, particularly in a country like India, which is really a subcontinent. There are tremendous regional, urban–rural, religious, caste, and class differences among women. In addition, as a sociologist, I am acutely aware of the significance of social contexts in determining the psychology of women.

If one were to venture to generalize, I think that the most pressing issue for women in modern India with respect to the psychology of women is how to live up to the traditional ideals of womanhood and achieve personal goals. Changes in expectations for women in urban India have taken place so that they are now encouraged to become empowered economically and psychologically. But these expectations are overlaid on existing traditional expectations that say a wife should be self-effacing and find fulfillment in the service of her family, particularly her husband. A constant preoccupation of women here is how to reconcile these contradictory expectations. The usual strategy adopted is the compartmentalization of roles within the family and the workplace. This is achieved at high personal cost. Some women feel that the lives of their mothers were much simpler and easier to cope with because expectations were clear. On the other hand, they find tremendous self-fulfillment in being able to achieve outside the family

function and in people's satisfaction with their relationships. But just what do we mean by power? Although it is generally understood that power involves the ability to make things happen and to influence others, it can be difficult to analyze in the context of intimate relationships.

For example, a widely accepted theme in social science writings about women in the Philippines is that the woman is "queen of the home"—certainly an image that sounds powerful (Aguilar, 1989). This image arises because Filipino women tend to be the family treasurers, controlling the budget in their households and family businesses, and are believed to be good money managers with sound entrepreneurial sense. Yet these same women are routinely expected to do virtually all household tasks and to defer to their husbands in cases of disagreement. Social scientists have tended to ignore the economic context of these families and "transmute the mundane, tedious, and burdensome duty of housekeeping into that of 'household management' and . . . celebrate as the wife's 'finan-

WOMEN AND POWER IN INDIA (*continued*)

and create a sense of personal space not to mention a degree of financial independence. Most of them would rather live such ambivalent lives than go back to older times. Most do not think that this ambivalence will be resolved in the near future. The reason for such pessimism is that the structural and ideological environment that supports male hegemony shows very few signs of significant change.

Q. In the face of these contradictory expectations, how do women exercise power within the family and elsewhere?

A. Exercise of power and control within the family is considered legitimate as long as it is done discreetly and within the accepted rule of proper behavior for a woman—namely, showing respect to husband and elders, even if it is symbolic at times. Many women in fact exert significant influence in day-to-day family life. Making economic contributions to the family does increase the degree of influence in the family, but, again, to be deserving of respect a woman must follow tenets of proper womanhood.

Exercise of power and control in the workplace is considered legitimate, since empowerment of women has become part of the national agenda. However, such changes have not led to corresponding changes in the arrangements of daily life. My own research indicates that there are rumblings of discontent in some segments of the female population in urban areas. However, the protest is not in any way organized and vocalized in a systematic manner.

To learn more about women in India, read some of Dhruvarajan's work:

Hindu women and the power of ideology. (1989). Granby, MA: Bering and Garvey.

Hinduism, empowerment of women and development in India. In *Women and work in South Asia: Contemporary perspectives* (1996), a special issue of *Labour, Capital and Society,* 29 (1/2), 16–40.

cial prerogative' the painful charge in poverty-stricken families of trying to make ends meet" (Aguilar, 1989, p. 541).

In a similar vein, women in Sri Lankan families may have control over one aspect of a family's decision making but do not necessarily have any control of other areas. Sri Lankan women who are educated and employed have more say in family financial decisions; however, education and employment seem to give them little or no extra influence when it comes to social and organizational matters, such as family friendships or the allocation of household tasks (Malhotra & Mather, 1997).

Research in Western cultures shows that, for most couples, an equal balance of power is considered ideal. Young heterosexuals report that they want equal power in their couple relationships; however, such equality is frequently lacking (Peplau & Campbell, 1989). Lesbian couples also tend to have strongly egalitarian ideals, but a significant minority of lesbian relationships are dominated by one partner (Caldwell & Peplau, 1984; Kurdek,

1989). In both types of couples, an imbalance of power tends to be associated with one partner's being more emotionally invested in the relationship and with disparities in access to resources such as education and employment and to desirable alternatives to the relationship. In heterosexual couples, an imbalance of power usually means that the man dominates the relationship. In order to understand these patterns, it is necessary to pay some attention to social psychological theories about interpersonal power, particularly to notions of **equity,** the **principle of least interest,** and resources as **bases of power.**

Equity and the Principle of Least Interest   One yardstick that couples frequently apply when evaluating their own relationships is fairness. Rules for what is considered fair may vary, but couples in North America often rely on a standard called *equity:* the balance between contributions to and benefits from the relationship. In evaluating how equitable a relationship is, partners ask themselves whether they are getting benefits out of the relationship that are commensurate with their contributions, and whether their own ratio of benefits to contributions is equivalent to their partner's ratio. In other words, each partner asks her/himself: "Am I getting as much out of this relationship as I am putting into it? And am I getting the same level of return on my investment in this relationship as my partner is?" Partners who feel their relationship is equitable tend to feel satisfied; those who feel they are either underbenefited or overbenefited relative to their partners feel dissatisfied with the relationship (Hatfield, Traupmann, Sprecher, Utne, & Hay, 1984).

Just what is a contribution and what is a benefit? A contribution is anything a person brings to the relationship that enhances its attractiveness for the other partner: a pleasing personality, social status, economic security, sexual attractiveness, strong love and appreciation for the partner, the willingness to take on certain tasks in the relationship. Such contributions may be weighted differently by different individuals and in the context of different relationships. Equity theorists argue that it is the participants' *own* weighting of the contributions and benefits, not some outside observer's assessment, that determines whether they experience their relationship as equitable. For example, in one couple it might seem a perfectly fair exchange for one partner to handle all the social arrangements and correspondence with friends and family while the other partner keeps track of the finances and pays the bills, whereas to another couple this arrangement does not feel equitable. In some couples, one partner is willing to take on the financial support of the couple and other practical tasks in exchange for the satisfaction afforded by being with a person who is attractive and sexually interesting, and expresses a great deal of affection; others may find such an arrangement grossly inequitable.

Attitudes about how particular contributions and benefits should be weighted are influenced by self-interest (each individual may view the contributions s/he brings to the relationship as more important and/or effortful than those brought by the other) and by cultural and peer attitudes and expectations. In a social environment that favors traditional gender roles, a marital arrangement in which the wife takes most of the responsibility for household and childcare tasks while the husband takes most of the responsibility for providing financial support would likely seem fair to the participants; in a less traditional environment, the fairness of this arrangement might be challenged. In fact, one study of married couples in which both partners had professional jobs and contributed relatively equally in terms of income revealed that, although wives' and husbands' contributions to housework and childcare tasks were grossly unequal, the wives expressed satisfaction with their husbands' level of contribution (Biernat & Wortman, 1991). Clearly, these wives' perceptions of equity were influenced by societal norms dictating that women are responsible for domestic tasks. Since men's small contributions to the household tasks were in line with cultural expectations, these women denied that the division of labor was unfair. Such perceptions may contribute, in some mixed-gender relationships, to an imbalance of power that favors the man.

When at least one of the partners perceives the relationship as seriously inequitable, it tends to become unstable. The partner who perceives that she is contributing more to the relationship than she is getting out of it feels resentful and may seek a relationship where she will get a better return on her investment—or she may translate her resentment into demands that her current partner take on a larger share of the contributions.

For some partners, the benefits obtained from a particular intimate relationship—the feeling of being loved and needed, economic security, a comfortable place in a given social network—may seem irreplaceable. These partners experience a strong need to maintain the relationship and are heavily invested in it. For others, the benefits associated with their intimate relationship are experienced as somewhat less important, or at least not necessarily tied to the particular relationship they are in. They feel less dependent on that relationship for rewards. When the two partners in a relationship differ in their need for the relationship, the result is an imbalance of power. According to social exchange theorists, the rule that governs such situations is the principle of least interest: The person who is least dependent on the other for rewards—who needs the relationship least—has the most power (Homans, 1974).

Equity and the principle of least interest offer an explanation for the finding, noted above, that in all types of couple relationships an imbalance of power is associated with one partner's being more emotionally invested in the relationship than the other. The person who has the lowest emotional investment, who values the benefits of the relationship least, feels freer to be domineering and is more likely to leave the relationship. Sensing this, the other partner is more likely to make accommodations and compromises to keep the relationship intact.

Resources   When one person tries to influence another to engage in a particular behavior or make a particular decision, the other person has to be given a *reason* to comply—something to back up the first person's demand. Such reasons may vary according to the situation or the relationship. A wife may comply with her husband because she loves him, or because he complied with her wishes last time, or because she fears his anger. One partner in a lesbian relationship may comply with her lover's request because her partner promises a desirable reward or presents an argument that appears irrefutable. A husband may give in to his wife's insistence on a certain issue because he recognizes that she is an expert on that topic. Each of these reasons for complying with another person's wishes illustrates the presence of resources controlled by the influencer.

One of the fundamental ideas in the social psychology of interpersonal power is that power is based on the control of **resources** (French & Raven, 1959; Raven, 1965), and thus on one person's ability to affect what happens to the other person (Thibaut & Kelley, 1959). The more resources relevant to the situation that the would-be influencer controls, the more she can affect what happens to others in that situation, and thus the more power she can exert. For example, in a mixed-gender relationship in which the man brings in most of the income, both members of the couple may feel that he can spend or withhold that income at will. That resource—the control over money—will give him a great deal of power in influencing his partner on such money-related questions as what kind of furniture to buy or how often to eat out, and perhaps on other issues as well. It is important to remember that the translation of power into the ability to influence another is based on both individuals' perceptions of the situation. If another person does not realize how much power you have to affect her life, your attempt to influence her may not work. On the other hand, if she imagines that you have control over resources or outcomes that you really do not have, she may give in to you despite your objective lack of power. Thus if one partner in a couple believes that the other is only weakly attached to the relationship and may decide to leave, that belief gives a great deal of power to the other partner—whether or not her attachment actually *is* weak.

In any society where the distribution of resources is unequal between the sexes, women and men will come to relationships with different probabilities of controlling certain types of resources. For example, in societies where men make more money than women (that is, in most societies), men are likely to bring more power based on financial resources to mixed-gender relationships than women can muster. Interestingly, however, when women *do* have access to financial resources through employment, these resources do not always confer as much power on them as they do on men. One study of White couples in second marriages revealed that some couples in which the man was employed in a low-status occupation did not consider the woman's employment a resource, and hence the woman's employment did not have any positive effect on her marital power (K. D. Pyke, 1994). A case study of Italian immigrants to Canada found that, prior to immigration, the division of household work had been highly sex segregated and couples reported that decisions had been largely made by the men. After immigrating to Canada, most of the wives had become employed outside the home; however, their employment did not seem to have produced any significant changes in decision making or in the way domestic labor was divided. In other words, the income from employment had given these women no added power in their relationships (Haddad & Lam, 1994). Another study of immigrant couples, this time from Korea, showed a similar pattern: The wives had increased their labor force participation dramatically after coming to Canada, with most of them working excessively long hours, but their economic contribution did not seem to have increased their power within the marriage (Min, 1997).

If financial contributions are a concrete resource that women bring to a relationship, why do such contributions not always give women more power in that relationship? Gender ideology is one reason. In societies where men are believed to have a legitimate claim to authority in the family, such authority affords them power in female–male relationships, even when their female partners have financial resources. For example, in the study of Korean couples cited above, one of the reasons the women did not gain in decision-making power within the couple was that husbands and wives often worked together in small businesses and thus were in a situation where it was easy to reproduce the traditional, male-dominant gender role ideology they had brought with them from Korea (Min, 1997).

Other factors figure into the resource equation as well. In societies where males have more access to education than females do, men are more likely than women to hold the power of expertise. Men usually have the advantage of greater size and strength than their female partners, allowing for power based on physical intimidation and violence as well. Further discussion of resources as the bases of power is included in Chapter 14.

The acceptance and use of the power and privilege that go with being male are not necessarily inadvertent or unconscious in intimate and family relationships (although they sometimes are). For example, one study of Hindu gender ideology interviewed adult men in India about joint family living, arranged marriages, restrictions on women outside the home, and interactions between husbands and wives. These men reported that they knew gender inequalities were maintained by their behavior—and that these gender inequalities bolstered their own power. For example, they noted that husband–wife interactions had to be limited so that women would not gain too much control over their husbands, and that women had to be restricted to the home in order to protect the family's (mainly the husband's) honor. One respondent described the situation thus:

> It is the tradition of our place that women here are not left independent. Women here are not free. They are under control. But they can roam around . . . with my desire. If I give my permission, she can go to the cinema—but not alone. She can travel somewhere for pilgrimage—but she goes on the desire of her husband. (Derné, 1994, p. 208)

Another respondent summarized the benefits he received by keeping his wife at home, under his control:

> My wife remains at home doing all kinds of service, adorning the house, the door, and herself. She does household works so completely that when the man comes home and sees the beauty he becomes very happy. [By contrast, if the woman works outside,] there is daily quarrel. The husband comes into the house and knows that his wife has gone outside to earn. The tired husband makes his own tea. He does everything by his own hands. He even has to make his own tea! From this, his mental condition starts deteriorating and every form of corruption is born. (p. 212)

Even in contexts that favor male dominance, however, the balance of power in relationships is based not only on such easily quantified resources as money, expertise, status, and strength, but also on such relationship-specific factors as love, emotional dependence, and personal values about conflict and loyalty. Thus, regardless of societal patterns that promote male dominance in relationships, in some female–male couples the balance of power favors the woman—and within individual couples the balance of power may shift back and forth, according to the situation.

One of the Hindu men interviewed by Steve Derné (1994) betrayed a strong sense of the way emotional ties can affect power within relationships:

> [I]f there is too much relationship and she says to jump in a well, then I will have to jump in a well. But if the relationship remains limited, what she says will not happen and what I want will happen. When the relationship gets too close and the wife says "go to a different house," then the husband goes . . . (p. 215)

Research on mixed-gender and same-gender couples indicates that gender is not always the best predictor of who holds the most power, the types of resources power is based on, or the way power is used (Howard, Blumstein, & Schwartz, 1986; Peplau & Cochran, 1990). Some findings concerning gender are quite consistent; for instance, across both mixed-gender and same-gender relationships, women endorse a stronger preference than men do for equal power in their relationships (Falbo & Peplau, 1980), and, congruently, lesbians are more likely than either heterosexuals or gay men to be in relationships they describe as egalitarian (Caldwell & Peplau, 1984; Kurdek, 1989).

Toni Falbo and Anne Peplau (1980) found that influence strategies in mixed-gender and same-gender intimate relationships varied according to the partners' perceptions of the balance of power in the relationship. In all types of couples, individuals who preferred to have and perceived themselves as having more power than their partner reported the use of more influence strategies that Falbo and Peplau characterized as **bilateral** and **direct.** A bilateral strategy is one that requires a lot of mutual engagement, such as arguing or bargaining, in contrast to a unilateral strategy (such as issuing a nonnegotiable order or walking out on a discussion), which requires no engagement. A direct strategy is one that is open and clear, such as a straightforward request or order, in contrast to an indirect strategy, such as dropping hints or asking leading questions. Bilateral and direct strategies are strong, confident strategies; unilateral, indirect strategies suggest weakness and fear of losing the battle. Presumably, someone who feels powerful in relation to her partner feels uninhibited about being direct in her influence and in opening herself to arguments, which she is confident she can win. A later study suggests that when couples perceive the balance of power in their relationship to be equal, they use fewer power strategies of any kind to influence each other and are more satisfied with their relationships (Aida & Falbo, 1991).

Another study also links the use of weak influence strategies to the feeling that one is less powerful than one's partner. Judith Howard and her colleagues (1986) examined long-term heterosexual mixed-gender and same-gender intimate relationships for the use of the following influence tactics: (1) manipulation (dropping hints, flattering, behaving seductively); (2), supplication (pleading, crying, acting ill or helpless); (3) bullying (threatening, insulting, becoming violent); (4) autocracy (insisting, claiming greater knowledge, asserting authority); (5) disengagement (sulking, leaving the scene); and (6) bargaining (reasoning, offering to compromise). Manipulation and supplication are thought to be weak strategies, used when a would-be influencer feels unsure of her or his ability to affect the other person's behavior. These researchers found that use of these weak strategies was not related to the influencer's gender. However, their use *was* related to the partner's gender. Both females and males with male partners were more likely to use the weak influence strategies than were females and males with female partners. The authors note, "The power associated with being male thus appears to be expressed in behavior that elicits weak strategies from one's partner" (p. 107). The use of weak strategies was also linked to a variety of factors that imply a feeling of less power than one's partner: having less income, seeing oneself as less attractive than one's partner, and depending more heavily on the relationship.

In many relationships and cultural contexts where men view patriarchal authority as legitimate, women resort to indirect and manipulative strategies rather than direct confrontation to influence their male partners. Among the village women of Nepal, for example, resistance to a husband's authority usually brings only vilification and defeat. A favored strategy is to act "appropriately" docile and deferential toward their husbands, winning their affection and boosting their self-esteem in order to gain influence with them (Derné, 1994). Even professional women in such contexts find it useful to hide their competence: "You mustn't 'show off' or try to show up your husband. So you have to be two-faced. At work, I make decisions. At home, I stay in the background" (quoted in Liddle & Joshi, 1986, p. 181).

The most dramatic imbalance of power in an intimate relationship occurs when one partner is physically violent and/or emotionally abusive toward the other. Wives are the most frequent victims of fatal violence in families; in 2001, almost one-third of female murder victims were killed by a husband or boyfriend, but fewer than 3 percent of male murder victims were killed by a wife or girlfriend (U.S. Department of Justice, 2001). Such violence occurs in families all over the world (United Nations, 2000) and is the most destructive expression of power in intimate relationships. Statistics on intimate partner violence are difficult to gather; however, the United Nations (2000) reports that the percentage of women who say they have ever been physically abused by an intimate partner ranges as high as 58 in parts of Turkey and 52 in one sample in Nicaragua, and that many nations, including Egypt, Ethiopia, Chile, Mexico, the United States, Canada, and the United Kingdom, report percentages higher than 20. We will examine this issue, along with other aspects of violence against women, in Chapter 13.

Must Everyone Be Part of a Couple?

In all developed regions of the world, one-person households have increased in recent years, and women make up a majority of these households. Women comprise 61 percent of one-person households in the United States, 58 percent of those in Canada, a full 70 percent in Portugal (United Nations, 2000). Despite the emphasis on finding a person with whom to pair up, there are good reasons for women to explore the positive aspects of single life. For one thing, many women will inevitably live their senior years as singles, given the tendency for men to have shorter lives than women. For another, singlehood affords some women the freedom and independence to pursue careers that are incompatible with traditional couple relationships. Furthermore, a woman who is not afraid to be single will find it easier to extricate herself from a couple relationship that is unhappy or abusive. As one saying goes, "It is better to be alone than to wish you were alone."

Women in most cultures are pressured to marry; however, never-married women express a number of reasons for their choice to avoid traditional heterosexual marriage and to live alone. One study of never-married Chinese American and Japanese American women suggests that many reject marriage because of their observations of their parents' marriage, their status as eldest or only daughter, their educational goals, or the perceived lack of appropriate suitors (Ferguson, 2000). Studies of never-married women reveal that they report active and fulfilling lives (Paradise, 1993) and that, although they may spend considerable time alone, they do not report feeling lonely (Burnley & Kurth, 1992).

Marriage: Legalizing the Couple Bond

In the United States, many young adults plan to marry—and they have very idealistic views of what marriage will be like. In one survey, 94 percent of never-married young adults, male and female, agree that "when you marry, your spouse will be your soul mate, first and foremost," and the majority of respondents were very confident that they will find that special someone when they are ready for marriage (Whitehead & Popenoe, 2001).

Marriage, however, is more than the connection of two soul mates. The formalization of an intimate mixed-gender relationship into a marriage adds a host of legal and economic dimensions to the emotional and interpersonal ones already discussed. Marriage, besides being a public ceremony of commitment between two people, is essentially a contract that those two people make with the state. In the United States and many other countries, that contract makes each spouse the designated "next of kin" of the other and spells out such details as the obligation to sexual exclusivity, inheritance rights, the division of property, and financial support. If a wife and husband make agreements between themselves that violate the state's marriage contract (for example, disavowing sexual exclusivity), these private agreements cannot be legally enforced.

For women, the legalities of marriage have often been associated with disadvantaged status: Historically, in many countries wives have been considered the property of their husbands, have had no access to the couple's resources except through their husbands, and could be divorced more easily by their husbands than vice versa. The custom whereby a new wife takes her husband's surname is rooted in this history. This pattern has changed considerably in some parts of the world, but in many places a married woman is still thought to *belong to* her husband. In parts of India, for example, a married woman moves in with her husband and his family and is expected to do the bidding not only of her spouse but also of her in-laws.

Despite the inconvenience of adding a third party (the state) to the couple relationship, most heterosexual people marry at least once in their life. They may do it in order to provide security for their relationship and for the children they may have, to demonstrate their commitment to each other, or to gain status in their community. However, consensual unions, in which a couple agrees to live together without marriage, are increasingly frequent in many parts of the world (National Marriage Project, 2003; United Nations, 2000). The proportion of women never married varies from 1 percent in some southern and central Asian countries to 22 percent in the Caribbean (where nonformal consensual unions are common). In some countries of sub-Saharan Africa (e.g., Benin, Guinea, Mali, Nigeria), more than 40 percent of women have husbands with at least one other wife—an arrangement that tends to be associated with low education levels for women and less financial support for children (United Nations, 2000). In general, women marry at younger ages than men; some southern Asian and sub-Saharan African countries report that the average age of women at first marriage is below 20 years (United Nations, 2000).

Only 6 percent of young adults surveyed in the United States believe that they are unlikely to stay married to the same person for life (Whitehead & Popenoe, 2001). However, as the statistics reported early in this chapter indicate, a large proportion of marriages do not last. According to the National Marriage Project (2003), in 2002 8.1 percent of males and 10.7 percent of females aged 15 and older in the United States were currently divorced (i.e., divorced and not remarried). The number is higher for women because divorced men are more likely than divorced women to remarry and to do so sooner.

For a married couple, getting out of the marriage contract through divorce is not as simple as deciding to go their separate ways; rather, the state must approve the dissolution of the marriage. This dissolution is easier in some countries than in others; for example, divorce was illegal in Ireland until 1997. In Egypt, a law passed in 2000 made it easier for women to divorce their husbands (Schneider, 2000). This law ended a long tradition in which Egyptian women had to spend years in court and provide irrefutable proof of abuse, adultery, or another serious problem in order to get a divorce, whereas men have traditionally been able to divorce their wives through a simple procedure that involves spending an hour at the local marriage registrar (and does not even require that the wife be informed!).

In the community-based culture of the !Kung, described by Marjorie Shostak (1981), girls or young women may marry several times, on a sort of trial basis, before settling down with a lifelong partner. These early marriages are arranged by parents, but if a girl feels, after some time in the marriage, that she will never have any affection for her husband, she can insist on ending the marriage. In many developed countries there is no formal concept of "trial marriages," yet more than one quarter of the marriages end in divorce (United Nations, 2000). Divorce is especially likely for couples who marry young. For example, in the United States, 59 percent of marriages in which the bride is 18 or younger end in separation or divorce within 15 years; for brides 20 or older, 36 percent of marriages break up in that time (National Center for Health Statistics, 2001).

Finally, in thinking about marriage around the world, it is useful to remember that many girls and young women have no choice at all about whether and whom to marry. The practice of marrying a young girl involuntarily to an older man is common in southern Asia and in parts of Africa. In Bangladesh, 75 percent of girls marry before the age of 18, and in both India and Ethiopia 57 percent do so (Associated Press, 2004). These young brides are robbed of childhood and of the chance for an education. Many die or suffer permanent injuries during pregnancy or childbirth and, because their older, more sexually experienced husbands rarely use condoms, they are at high risk for HIV infection. The practice of child marriage is embedded in cultural traditions and is sometimes assumed to provide girls with security and a safe route to adulthood. Instead, it exposes girls to a host of dangers and makes it impossible for them to make their own life choices.

Gay Marriage?   Ninia Baehr and Genora Dancel, a lesbian couple who say they fell in love at first sight, wanted a wedding on the slopes of a mountain in Maui. When their application for a marriage license was denied, they and two other same-sex couples filed suit against the Hawaii Department of Health. In December 1996, after five years of legal battles, a judge in Hawaii ruled that the state must issue marriage licenses to gay and lesbian couples who wished to marry. Although the ruling was put on hold pending an appeal to the state Supreme Court, it was the closest step that any state had yet taken to legalizing same-sex marriages in the United States. However, the state house of representatives in Hawaii approved a resolution in favor of a state constitutional amendment banning same-sex marriages—a resolution that eventually went to the voters in the 1998 election. By a

BOX 7.2 WOMEN SHAPING PSYCHOLOGY
Ethel Puffer (1872–1950)

The conflicting demands of family and career described in this chapter are not new to women of this generation. Ethel Puffer was one of the first women to earn a doctoral degree in psychology—and one of the first to devote a large segment of her career to a field that we now call women's studies. A hallmark of her career was her struggle to find a way for women to reconcile their career and family lives (Scarborough, 1991).

When Ethel Puffer graduated from Smith College in 1891, there were few opportunities for advanced study for women. Undaunted, she traveled to Germany to pursue her interest in studying esthetics, and eventually became one of the pioneers in the psychology of art. On the way to this achievement, however, she had to face the reluctance of educational institutions to take women students seriously. As a graduate student in Berlin, and later in Freiberg, she found herself the only woman in her classes and she became resigned to being stared at by her fellow students.

Under Hugo Münsterberg's mentorship, she returned to the United States, where she continued her work at Harvard. She was not officially a Harvard student, however, since that institution did not admit women. Rather, she was a registered graduate student at Radcliffe. When she completed her doctoral dissertation and oral defense in 1898, she was granted not an official degree (Harvard did not give those to women) but a signed statement from her examiners attesting that she had performed well on a doctoral level examination and had been found well-qualified. Three years later she requested and got a Ph.D. from Radcliffe, in recognition of this work.

For 10 years after completing her doctoral work, Puffer had an intense and successful career in psychology. She worked as an assistant to Münsterberg at Harvard,

margin of 69 percent to 29 percent, Hawaii voters approved this amendment, effectively giving the State Legislature the power to limit marriage to female–male couples. The state did, however, grant gay and lesbian couples who registered as "reciprocal beneficiaries" certain limited rights associated with marriage, such as hospital visitation, family leave, and property rights (Christensen, 2001).

BOX 7.2 WOMEN SHAPING PSYCHOLOGY (*continued*)
Ethel Puffer (1872–1950)

held academic positions at Simmons and Wellesley Colleges, and in 1905 published a book about her research, *The Psychology of Beauty*. In 1908, however, she decided to marry Benjamin Howes, and this caused a dramatic change in her career. Married women could not hold academic positions at that time, so she was forced to step back from her academic pursuits. She enjoyed marriage and motherhood but felt frustrated by the necessity to confront, as she later wrote, the "persistent vicious alternative, marriage *or* career—full personal life *versus* the way of achievement." (Howes, 1922, p. 731). The choice forced on her was more stark than the one that faces many college-educated women today, but the tension between family and career still feels familiar.

Puffer did not suffer in isolation, however: She tried to find a solution to this dilemma for herself and other women. In 1925, when she was 53, she founded the Institute for the Coordination of Women's Interests at Smith College to study and enhance the status of women. Under her leadership, the Institute studied the ways that women were trying to combine careers and family life and set up demonstration projects to show how this combination could be supported. One very

successful demonstration project was the Smith College day and nursery demonstration schools. Eventually, support for the Institute waned and it closed, but not before Puffer had built a legacy of ideas for the women who followed in her footsteps. Ethel Puffer lost her chance at a full-fledged career in psychology because of the restrictions of her time on married women's employment. However, this loss propelled her to be a pioneer in women's studies. Her life shows us a great deal about the resourcefulness and ingenuity with which women have met discrimination and dealt with the sometimes difficult dilemmas of multiple roles.

Read More about Ethel Puffer

Scarborough, Elizabeth (1991). Continuity for women: Ethel Puffer's struggle. In G. A. Kimble, M. Wertheimer, & C. L. White (Eds.), *Portraits of pioneers in psychology* (pp. 105–119). Washington, DC: American Psychological Association, and Hillsdale, NJ: Lawrence Erlbaum Associates.

Read What She Wrote

Howes, Ethel Puffer (1922). Continuity for women. *Atlantic Monthly, 130,* 731–739.
Puffer, Ethel D. (1905). *The psychology of beauty.* Boston: Houghton Mifflin.

Some gay rights advocates have long argued that legal marriage should be an option for same-sex couples, both in order to secure protections such as inheritance rights; hospital visitation rights; pension rights; joint health, home, and automobile insurance; and family leave to care for a sick partner, and to enhance the public recognition and dignity of same-sex committed relationships. In a "friend of the court" brief filed in the Hawaii case,

Gay rights advocates have long argued that legal marriage should be an option for same-gender couples in order to secure such rights as inheritance, hospital visitation, pension benefits, family leave, and joint insurance, as well as to enhance the public recognition and dignity of same-gender, committed relationships.

a group of psychologists argued that denying marriage to same-sex couples also deprives their children of the material and emotional benefits that go with having two legal parents (Clay, 1997a). These arguments have gained some strength in the United States in recent years. In 2001, Vermont became the first state to legalize same-sex relationships as civil unions; its civil union law extends more than 300 benefits usually associated with marriage to gay and lesbian couples. These benefits include such things as inheritance rights, the authority to make medical decisions for a partner who is incapacitated, and the right to be treated as an economic unit for tax purposes. In addition, the law provides that, if they break down, civil unions may not simply be abandoned: they must be legally dissolved through court proceedings similar to a divorce.

Some barriers to same-sex marriage have fallen recently. In 2003, an appeals court in Ontario, Canada, struck down a ban on same-sex marriage. In 2004, in defiance of a state law banning same-sex marriages, the city of San Francisco issued more than 3,200 marriage licenses to same-sex couples. The legality of the marriages that ensued is expected to be decided by the state's high court. In February 2004, the Massachusetts Supreme Court ruled that no constitutionally adequate reason to deny same-sex couples the right to marry had been demonstrated and gave the state six months to rewrite its marriage laws. A few months later, on May 17th, Massachusetts became the first state to legalize same-sex marriage (Peterson, 2004).

Worldwide, there are signs that the movement toward legal recognition of same-sex unions has increased in recent years. In 2000, the Netherlands became the first country in the world to put gay marriage on the same legal footing as heterosexual marriage (Same-sex Dutch couples gain marriage and adoption rights, 2000). Other countries have moved in this direction. Same-sex marriage is now legal in Canada's three largest provinces: Ontario, Quebec, and British Columbia. France, Portugal, Sweden, Norway, Hungary, and Brazil permit recognized "domestic partnerships" and Germany permits a limited form of gay marriage—sometimes called "marriage lite" by gay activists (Cole, 2001; Goldstein, 2001). However, Australia is moving in the direction of a ban on gay marriage.

In the future, gay marriage may be less controversial in the United States. American teenagers are more likely than their parents to support gay marriage and other legal protections for gay men and lesbians. Two-thirds of 1,000 high school seniors surveyed by Hamilton College researchers, as compared to about one-third of adults responding to Gallup polls, say they support the recognition of gay marriage (Steinberg, 2001). In the present, however, opposition to gay marriage is considerable. Thirty-nine states have passed "defense-of-marriage" laws restricting marriage to male–female couples (Petersen, 2004), and in July 2001 a conservative action group launched a campaign to pass the Federal Marriage Amendment, a proposed 28th amendment to the U.S. Constitution that would define marriage as a bond between a man and a woman and deny the legal aspects of marriage to any other form of couple (Goldstein, 2001).

The 1990 Census in the United States was the first to offer couples the option to categorize themselves as unmarried partners, rather than simply roommates. The 2000 Census shows large increases in the number of same-sex couples listing themselves as partners sharing households, reflecting an increased willingness of such couples to report their living arrangements (Cohn, 2000b). For example, the number of same-sex partners sharing a household reported in Hawaii jumped from 602 in 1990 to 2,389 in 2000 (Christensen, 2001). Members of many such couples report that they feel and act "married." What is missing is not the commitment, but the legal rights that go with marriage. Whereas not every gay and lesbian couple craves the security and legal status of marriage—some argue that gay marriage reflects an unprofitable attempt to imitate heterosexual lifestyles—many believe passionately that the legal protections of marriage should be an option that any couple can consider, and accept or reject.

Families and Parenthood

When middle-class European Americans think of families, they often think in terms of a mother, a father, and two or three children. We have already seen that the majority of family households in the United States do not fit this model. Our notion of family must change to incorporate a variety of different types of households. Could it be possible that the very notion of a family as something that is contained in a household, or as a unit in which children are cared for by one or more parents, is too narrow? Probably. In many African American communities, for example, the family extends beyond the individual household, and children are viewed in some ways as a collective responsibility (Cauce et al., 1996). In the United States, grandparents rather than parents are caring for children in many families. In 1997 there were 3.7 million grandparents maintaining households for their grandchildren; of these, 2.3 million were grandmothers (Casper & Bryson, 1998).

An individual's sense of family may include more than the collection of people with whom s/he shares a household, or even an extended family or community. In Asian cultures, there is a strong tradition of relationship to ancestors who have died. Tradition dictates that a person's behavior will be judged by the ancestors and that they are important sources of advice and support. As Christine Chao (2000) writes,

> How many first-, second-, third-, or fourth-generation Asian Americans have heard . . . admonitions to do better, work harder, study more? These are not just our parents' voices; they are also the voices of the ancestors that underlie a Confucian hierarchy that demands obedience. They are the echoes of what our parents hear, what their parents heard, and what our great, great grandparents hear, and so on down through the ages. (p. 103)

Clearly, cultural, historical, and economic variables come into play when we consider family relationships. In the limited space of this chapter, we cannot examine every aspect of family as it relates to women's psychology, but we will look in detail at some of the ways women shape and are shaped by their families.

Mothers and Children

In the northeastern Brazilian village of Pernambuco, the women, who are usually low-wage day laborers in sugarcane fields, respond to each pregnancy by viewing it not only as the possibility of a new life, but also as the possibility of a new death—another child who will not survive. In this area where it is not uncommon for women to bear more than a dozen children, it is also not uncommon for them to bury most of these infants before their first birthday. These mothers, perhaps cutting their emotional losses, often do not develop a close bond with a new baby until after the first year. They may wait months to give their newborns permanent names. If the infant is very sickly, they may hasten what they view as its inevitable death by withholding food (Preston, 1993).

In pre-Communist China, it was not uncommon for mothers to abandon infants that they did not think could survive. Such a practice, which may appear cruel and inhumane to people who have not confronted the possibility of starvation, was often seen by these mothers as a sacrifice that would allow the survival of remaining family members (Chin, 2000).

People who believe in a "natural" attachment between mother and child are disconcerted by these stories. The scenarios are very different from North American stereotypes about motherhood, which focus on the powerful bond that is thought to form between mother and infant almost immediately. Present-day North American women are expected to adapt relatively effortlessly to being parents and to make a strong emotional investment in each newborn infant—even in the case of a newborn who is ill and unlikely to survive. Indeed, vast medical resources are often devoted to ensuring the survival of premature or very ill babies, and mothers who abandon or kill their newborn infants face serious criminal charges. Evolutionary biologist Sarah Hrdy (1999) argues, however, that there is nothing "unnatural" about mothers cutting their losses when it appears that their infants have no chance of survival. Rather, she says, this way of responding to a difficult and dangerous mothering situation is part of our evolutionary heritage. She recounts many examples of mothers in various animal species who abandon or kill their infants when it appears the infant will not survive—the apparent goal being to ensure that another infant, born later under better conditions, *will* survive. Human mothers too, she says, are sometimes ambivalent about investing in the rearing of children, and this ambivalence is likely to tilt far toward the negative under conditions where resources for child rearing are scarce and little help is available. She points out that literally *millions* of human infants were abandoned at foundling homes in Europe during the 18th century—institutions in which the mortality rate for the foundling babies was often higher than 90 percent. These mothers were abandoning their infants to almost certain death because, in practical terms, they did not think they had the resources to bring them up. The huge numbers of infants involved suggest that such choices did not represent a few "unnatural" mothers, but rather a common response to a situation that was perceived as intolerable.

In some cultures, women are less pleased when they bear a daughter than when they bear a son. For example, a study of women in Punjab, Pakistan, found that they considered daughters a burden and showed a strong preference for sons (Winkvist & Akhtar, 2000). Their preference is not surprising, given that mothers of daughters reported being harassed by their families and by society, whereas mothers of sons reported no such harassment. In China, demographers noticed an epidemic of "missing daughters" when they examined the results of the 1991 census, and they attributed the shortage of girls to sex-selective abortion or infanticide. A preference for sons, enforced by sex-selective infanticide and abortion, has also been well documented for other parts of Asia, some parts of South America, and ancient Italy (Hrdy, 1999). In all cases, the practices appear linked to an ideology that values males over females and cultural practices that reward parents economically for having sons but punish them for having daughters. As one Indian writer noted, "a daughter's birth makes even a philosophical man . . . gloomy [while] a son's birth is like sunrise in the abode of the gods" (Madan, 1965, quoted in Hrdy, 1999, p. 322).

Changing the context helps to shift such attitudes. For example, an action research project being implemented in rural China by Zhu Chuzu and Li Shuzhuo works, apparently successfully, to change families' negative reactions to having daughters (Zia, 2000). The project brings village women together for conversation and training, helping them to find ways to contribute to their families and gain a sense of accomplishment through means other than their traditional roles. It has been the case in these villages that the birth of a son was greeted with the preparation of special foods and the swift arrival of congratulations, but when a daughter was born there was no celebration and the mother might be cursed by her mother-in-law for giving birth to a girl. However, the women are now learning that they can boost their families through various kinds of productivity: cultivating orchards, raising cattle, starting their own businesses—and this brings home the message that a woman (and thus a daughter) can be very valuable to her family. As one woman commented, "Before the program, we never went out; we were too afraid to speak up. Now we feel confident that we can teach others how to have satisfaction within themselves. Now we don't just think about having sons" (Zia, 2000, p. 16). The value of daughters is further reinforced by a new government initiative that encourages men to take their wife's family name at marriage and to join her family, instead of the traditional practice in which the wife joined the husband's family. This allows families with daughters to know that their family's lineage will be carried on, and takes away one more reason for the bias toward sons.

Clearly, the experience of motherhood is shaped by many things: the availability of resources to feed and care for children, the economic consequences of having female and male children, the presence of supportive family networks, the power to decide whether and when to become pregnant, social stereotypes of mothers and infants, medical technology, and control over childbirth. Even the experiences of women within our own culture differ. Certainly, the birth of a child is not guaranteed to provoke the same reaction in every woman; rather, the reaction depends on how much and why she wants and planned for the child, what resources she has to care for it, what kind of supportive relationships she has with the child's father and other family and friends, how being a mother affects her position in the family and community, what kind of medical care is available for her and the baby, and how many other children she has. Motherhood, then, is not an automatic set of feelings and behaviors that is switched on by pregnancy and the birth of a baby. It is an experience that is profoundly shaped by social context and culture.

What is the social context of motherhood in North America? The stereotypes surrounding motherhood suggest that women are supposed to achieve the ultimate fulfillment of their feminine role through motherhood, and mothers are supposed to be warm, nurturing, and selfless, sacrificing their own needs repeatedly to ensure the welfare of their children (Hoffnung, 1995). When women fail to meet the unrealistic demands of this idealized role, society turns on them viciously: Mothers often take the brunt of the blame for failings in their children, and even for failings in society (Caplan, 1989). Young women often believe that as mothers they will be different from their own mothers—less traditional and more self-assertive—yet the power of the stereotypes is very strong (Ex & Janssens, 2000).

One 22-year-old woman, pregnant for the first time, reflects in an interview about how difficult it will be for her to be her "real self" as she embarks on motherhood:

> I think a lot about what kind of role model I will be. That kind of scares me into straightening up my act . . . I guess I'm afraid that I have to have too much fun and I'm not going to be motherly enough . . . I feel like we have to do lots of family things and it's kind of scary . . . Scary that I have to do these kinds of things, that I can't just be myself, you know. And really I can be myself, but will I? (Walzer, 1995, p. 601)

Whether or not a new mother accepts the "motherhood mystique" that mandates favoring the child's needs over her own at every opportunity, the sacrifices involved in motherhood are numerous and real. Most mothers take on the major responsibility for childcare—a set of tasks (feeding, diapering, cleaning up) that is repetitive, messy, and often boring. They lose control of their sleep schedule, often being awakened many times during the night to attend to the baby. They often feel exhausted, incompetent, and frustrated by their inability to accomplish anything beyond the daily care of the infant. Their relationship with their spouse may suffer because of resentment and guilt over changes in the way time is allocated. They may feel trapped in the house. Yet despite these difficulties, most mothers find their relationships with their children rewarding and meaningful—at least some of the time (Hoffnung, 1995). And since much of the drudgery and dispiritedness of motherhood occurs when a woman is at home alone with her children, it is the positive, playful, loving, connected side of motherhood that is most visible in public. Perhaps this is why so many North American women are drawn to motherhood without a full realization of what it entails.

One of the most negative criticisms of a mother in North America is that she is stifling or suffocating her children emotionally by trying to live through them. Stories abound about "stage mothers" and "sports mothers" who push their children too hard and seek to realize their own dreams through their children's successes. Such a result is almost inevitable when mothers are pressured to ignore their own needs and aspirations and devote all their energy to rearing their children. As Michele Hoffnung (1995) notes,

> Because a mother gives up so much to be a mother, because she is educated and achievement oriented, because there is so little family or community support for the contemporary mother, the child has come to mean too much to her. The child cannot grow freely but must succeed for the mother to show that she has done a good job and that her sacrifices have been worth it. Since a woman often puts aside any personal ambition [in favor of] motherhood, the child may be expected to succeed in her stead, to act out her ambitions for her. Or the child may become a substitute for the mother's ambitions, a product she can be proud of . . . (p. 169)

In North America, some mothers who manage to hold on to other aspects of their identity, often by working outside the home, have been found to be more satisfied with their lives and have higher self-esteem than their at-home counterparts (Crosby, 1991; Walker & Best, 1991). Yet the benefits for these women of combining roles are greatest when certain conditions are met: the availability of high-quality childcare, the support of family, the women's perception that their work is important and a legitimate priority. This arrangement can benefit children too: Preschoolers may profit socially and intellectually from childcare outside the home (Clarke-Stewart, 1991).

Motherhood is a complex experience that is only beginning to be studied adequately. It is clear that, at least in some Western cultures, it involves a number of conflicting expectations and contradictory experiences. One pair of psychologists from Israel and the United States (Oberman & Josselson, 1996) have analyzed the experience of motherhood as a "matrix of tensions," arguing that in adjusting to her new identity and to the relationship between herself and her relatively powerless but demanding baby, the mother must maintain a set of tensions—"a balance of conflicting emotions, attitudes, experiences, or states of mind" (p. 356). The tensions they list include

- *Loss of self versus expansion of self.* The child's need of her may threaten a new mother's separate sense of self, yet she has also acquired a new identity as one who nurtures and nourishes.

- *Feeling omnipotent versus feeling liable.* She may feel powerful in her mother role and try to exercise power in controlling the environment for her child. Yet she also faces enormous responsibility and blame for any damage to the child.

- *Life destruction versus life promotion.* Mothers sometimes feel rage at and violent urges toward their children, yet they must reconcile these feelings with love for, and the tending and raising of, those children.

- *Maternal isolation versus maternal community.* Some new mothers may feel isolated and alone with their children. Others become participants in a maternal community that bridges many gaps between women, uniting them "across barriers that divide nonmothers" (p. 353).

*   *Cognitive strategies versus intuitive responses.* Mothers must engage in careful, thoughtful decisions about what is best for their children, yet sometimes they must break their own rules in order to do what they intuitively feel is best for a child in a particular situation.

*   *Maternal desexualization versus maternal sexualization.* A mother must find a way to be a sexual person in the face of social expectations that motherhood and sexuality be completely separated.

These authors seem to have captured some of the conflicts that are built in to the mother role in our culture and certain others. In-depth research may eventually reveal how these and other conflicts are interconnected and how they are affected by a woman's own family history and current social context.

Lesbian Mothers Estimates of the number of lesbian mothers in the United States range from 1 million to 5 million (Patterson, 1992). Comparable estimates for other countries are largely unavailable because lesbian women are invisible in the official statistics of the United Nations and the census reports of countries. It is certain, however, that lesbian-headed families exist all over the world. The children of such families include children who were born into mixed-gender relationships, which later dissolved as one or both parents came out as gay, and children conceived through donor insemination.

Because of the strong bias against homosexuality in many areas, lesbian mothers often must hide their sexual orientation or face a court fight for the right to keep their children. Simply being labeled a lesbian, aside from any particular parental or other behavior, has frequently been used to brand a mother as unfit and to justify taking her children away from her. Research on lesbians' children indicates, however, that they are as likely as children parented by mixed-gender couples to grow up healthy and well adjusted. One reviewer notes that not a single study has found children of lesbian or gay parents to be disadvantaged in any way compared to the children of heterosexual parents (Patterson, 1992). Children of gay and lesbian parents are no more likely than other children to have difficulty with gender identity or gender-role acquisition, and they are no more likely be homosexual in their orientation than children raised by mixed-gender parents (Patterson, 1992; Tasker & Golombok, 1995). Children of same-gender and of mixed-gender parents show no differences in frequency of emotional disturbance, self-concept, locus of control, moral maturity, intelligence, peer relations, social relations with adults, or other measures of cognitive functioning and behavioral adjustment (Flaks, Ficher, Masterpasqua, & Joseph, 1995). In general, the research suggests that children of lesbians fare best when the mother is in good psychological health and living with a lesbian partner, and when the family is in a supportive social environment in which the parents' sexual orientation is accepted by other significant adults. As Charlotte Patterson (1992) notes, "The picture of lesbian mothers' children that emerges from results of existing research is . . . one of general engagement in social life with peers, with fathers, and with mothers' adult friends—both female and male, both homosexual and heterosexual" (p. 1034).

Interestingly, as these children grow up, they may perceive advantages to having a lesbian mother. In one interview study, sons of lesbian mothers said that their mothers had influenced their moral development in important ways, particularly with respect to their awareness of prejudice and discrimination and their acceptance of diversity. They reported that they had gained insights into gender relations and had benefited from acquiring a broader, more inclusive definition of family and from becoming aware that women could be financially and emotionally independent of men (Saffron, 1998).

Single Mothers   In Brazil, women were mobilized to action several years ago when the government agencies handing out emergency food supplies to drought-stricken families refused to give anything to single mothers. Only "heads of households"—men—were eligible to receive the much-needed food (Preston, 1993).

Indeed, in many countries of the world the head of the household is automatically thought to be a man. Yet single mothers head a large proportion of families worldwide, and lone parent families in which the mother is the parent are increasingly common. One-third of all families with children in the United States and 22 percent in Canada are headed by single parents—and 80 percent of those lone parents are women (United Nations, 2000).

Some women choose single motherhood—expressing a wish for a child but not for a partner. Interviews with a small group of American women who were solo mothers by choice revealed that they felt this lifestyle was a legitimate choice for them because of their age, responsibility, emotional maturity, and capacity to support a child economically (Bock, 2000). However, many single mothers do not choose their family circumstances, but are single because of abandonment by their children's father, divorce, separation, or widowhood. Such families are more likely than other family configurations to live in poverty. In most countries, single mothers of children under age 3 are less likely than other mothers of such young children to be employed (United Nations, 2000). In the United States, three-quarters of all unmarried teenage mothers collect welfare within 5 years of giving birth (Boo, 1996). In Canada, two-thirds of divorced single mothers and their children are poor (Gorlick, 1995). In the United States, the Census Bureau reports that there are 3.6 million female-headed families living in poverty—and although only 20 percent of families are headed by single mothers, such families make up half of all families living in poverty (Proctor & Dalaker, 2003).

Single mothers often learn to be very strong: They must often confront daunting obstacles to carve out safe, decent lives for their children. Consider, for example, Elizabeth Jones, a 27-year-old Washington, D.C., woman with three young children, whose story was followed by a reporter as she struggled to leave welfare (Boo, 1996). After a government training program and a brief internship, Jones landed a job as a receptionist at a nonprofit agency. Unable to afford a car, she took six buses and walked two miles to get her children to and from day care and school and herself to and from work. With bills for rent, day care, and food eating up most of her income, Jones had only $207 a month left to cover utilities, emergencies, and clothing for herself and her children. Every "staff development day" at the school meant that she had to pay for a full day of childcare for her children—at $15 per child. She found it all but impossible to save the money necessary to keep her children in winter clothing. Constrained by the time demands of her job, Jones was unable to continue volunteering at her 9-year-old son's school, as she had when she

BOX 7.3 MAKING CHANGE
Challenging Popular Images of "Welfare Mothers"

Media portrayals of and opinion leaders' statements about single mothers who are receiving welfare often imply that such women are lazy and dishonest, that they are getting a "free ride" at the expense of taxpayers. Yet, as the example in this chapter illustrates and as the statistics bear out, single mothers—whether on public assistance or not—are usually anything but lazy and must work very hard to provide a decent life for their children. Arm yourself with some facts about this issue, so that you can challenge such negative stereotyping. Good places to start are the Welfare Rights Organizing Coalition, on the Web at **www.wroc.org/index.htm** and the National Organization for Women's information page on welfare reform at **www.now.org/issues/economic/welfare**. At these sites you will find articles about welfare, welfare reform, and women's experiences of these institutions, links to many other sources of information, and ways to get involved in organizing efforts to achieve economic justice for poor women.

was on public assistance. Her son's problems at school were apparently unnoticed by his teachers; she found it difficult to stay on top of the situation when she could not be at the school during the day. Moving him to a different school would mean adding another stop—and probably another bus trip—to her already complicated daily routine. To make ends meet more easily, Jones searched for a second job that she could work on the weekends, a move that would necessitate finding weekend day care for her children as well. Jones's determination to build a good life for her children was implacable, yet the environment in which she struggled—the inadequate transportation, an inflexible school system, her dangerous neighborhood—would have caused a less courageous woman to give up.

Several years later, Elizabeth Jones had, through determination and hard work, moved her family a little closer to a comfortable existence (Boo, 2001). She had moved from her receptionist job to the police academy and become a police officer on the night shift in Southeast Washington D.C., her own dangerous neighborhood. She also took on a second job as a security officer. The two jobs together brought an income of $39,000, far less than the $52,000 thought to be necessary to provide basic necessities for a family of four in Washington, but enough to make it possible to own a car, to move her family a few blocks away from the public housing project where they used to live, and to have a home computer she and the children could use. But the cost to this single mother in fatigue and lost time with her children has been great. When her 7:30 P.M. to 4:00 A.M. police shift ends, she sleeps for two hours, then gets up to get her three children to three different schools. Then she goes to her second job as a security guard. Finishing there at 5:00 P.M., she picks up her children from their schools, drops them at home, and goes to the police station to begin her shift. She speaks wistfully of missing her children:

> Like, I'm at work chasing after some crazy person and I am thinking, Have my kids taken a bath, did they do their homework, did they turn out the lights—the electricity bill is breaking

me—did they eat dinner, did they go outside like they're not supposed to, did they watch something terrible on TV? (quoted in Boo, 2001, p. 95)

Jones faces the dilemma of all single mothers: working for resources to support her children economically takes her away from them; being a good role model of independence and self-sufficiency takes away her opportunity to be a mother who is available to her children during day-to-day crises. She says it's difficult not to think about what life would be like if she could have real time with her children.

> There'd be time to help them all with homework, answer Dernard's million and two questions, do family things—like make a meal together, me and Drenika, instead of calling her in for a catch-up conversation when I'm taking a shower. . . . We could communicate. We could be a family. (quoted in Boo, 2001, p. 107)

Mother–Daughter Relationships

Mothers present important role models for their daughters. Around the world, research shows that daughters of employed mothers hold less traditional gender role attitudes than daughters of mothers who are not employed (Gibbons, Stiles, & Shkodriani, 1991). The mother–daughter relationship also has implications for daughters' development of feminist attitudes. One study of 24- to 35-year-old American women showed that daughters who identified strongly with feminist mothers held similarly feminist awareness; furthermore, strong, respectful mutually interdependent mother–daughter relationships were linked with high levels of feminist consciousness in both mothers and daughters (Buysse, 2000). On the other hand, this study also showed that some daughters developed high levels of feminist consciousness when they reacted against mothers who were possessive, jealous, and anxious about separation.

Because of the differing contexts in which they exist, there are some differences among cultural groups in the way daughters describe their relationships with their mothers. For example, one comparison of adult daughters from three ethnic groups revealed that Asian Indian American women reported more positive beliefs about and acceptance of hierarchy in these intergenerational relationships than European American women did, with Mexican American women's responses falling between those of the other two groups (Rastogi & Wampler, 1999). The difference may stem in part from the strong Asian tradition of **filial piety,** which counsels respect and obedience toward one's elders (Chin, 2000). The ideal of motherhood in Asian cultures involves a strong element of sacrifice; however, the mother expects to be repaid for this sacrifice by the respect and devotion of her children.

Many African American women report feeling empowered as a result of their mothers. Mothers apparently contribute to this sense of empowerment in several ways: Daughters who described themselves as high in **self-efficacy** were women whose mothers had encouraged them to be family oriented, to use acceptance as a parenting style, to be emotionally expressive, and to form a strong racial identity (Mcwherter, 1999). African American adolescent girls describe their mothers as their biggest source of emotional support, although they do have conflicts with them about independence (Cauce et al., 1996). African American mothers, on the other hand, work hard to protect their daughters from the double-edged dangers of racism and sexism, describing "their children as caught between a rock and a hard place, and their own attempts to exert the right amount of control as akin to threading a needle in the dark" (Cauce et al., 1996, p. 112). Cauce and her colleagues argue that the blend of closeness, conflict, and control that characterizes the interactions between these mothers and daughters is distinctly African American.

A clash of cultures can lead to clashes between generations, and this theme is seen in accounts of mother–daughter relationships among families in which the parents have immigrated from one country to another. As Taylor (1996) describes in her study of Latina and Portuguese daughters in the urban United States, mothers in such families must teach their daughters to become bicultural—to be adept at negotiating the social environments of both the old culture, represented by family and immigrant community, and the new culture, represented by school and the wider social community. Yet these mothers may not be comfortable in the new culture, and their insistence on their daughters' conformity to traditional cultural values may produce conflict that lasts into adulthood. For example, among adult daughters of Chinese American women, conflict with their mothers was related to how **acculturated** (adapted to mainstream U.S. culture) they perceived their mothers to be. Daughters who saw their mothers as less acculturated reported more conflict with them. Interestingly, however, these same daughters reported a more intimate bond with their mothers than did daughters who saw their mothers as more acculturated (Yeung, 2000). A study of Mexican American daughters' perspectives on their mothers suggests a possible resolution to this apparently paradoxical finding: These daughters reported that they rebelled against their mothers in their own struggle to become acculturated, yet when as adults they wanted to reconnect with their mothers, they discovered a new appreciation of their traditional culture (Vera, 1999). For many women who grow up in immigrant families, their relationship to their family's culture of origin may be closely linked with their relationship to their mother.

Because women tend to outlive men, the mother–daughter relationship may confront new and important challenges as the mother becomes elderly. Daughters are likely to become caregivers for their mothers, and this situation presents many potential sources of conflict about mothers' and daughters' expectations. Daughters often confront new responsibilities toward their mothers at a time when they have many other responsibilities. The relationship between the two women must be redefined in certain ways; both mothers and daughters in this situation report an increased awareness of the effects of aging, increased tolerance and acceptance, and putting priority on their relationship (Sheehan & Donorfio, 1999).

Fathers and Children

A study published 10 years ago revealed one remarkable similarity among countries, whether developed or developing, in the role played by fathers in childcare: They did it for, on average, less than 1 hour a day! A 10-country study of the parents of 4-year-olds found that fathers in the United States and Nigeria averaged 0.7 hours a day in solo childcare (that is, looking after the child without anyone else's help). Chinese fathers spent the most time in daily childcare (0.9 hours a day); fathers in Hong Kong spent the least (0.1 hours). Meanwhile, the mothers in these countries spent from 5.2 to 10.7 hours a day in solo childcare; the highest average belongs to women in the United States, the lowest to women in Belgium (Owen, 1995).

This study has not been updated in recent years. However, other research suggests that fathers still spend considerably less time than mothers do with their children. A national study by W. Jean Yeung and her colleagues indicates that, in families where children live with both parents, U.S. children 12 years of age and younger spend an average of 2.5 hours a day with their fathers on weekdays and 6.2 hours a day on weekends (Time U.S. children spend with their fathers, and what they do, 1999). These figures do not represent solo childcare by fathers (i.e., the child's mother may be there at the same time), or even active involvement with children. For about half of the time they are with their children, fathers are directly engaged with them—playing, eating, watching television together, or working together. For the other half of the time, fathers are simply nearby, available to their children if they are needed. In this study, fathers spent an average of 27 minutes on weekdays and 51 minutes on weekend days on the actual work of parenting: feeding, bathing, changing diapers, brushing hair, and so on. Another study of 3- to 12-year-old American children in two-parent families found that they reported spending an average of 22.73 hours per week with their fathers and 30.89 hours per week with their mothers (Children spend more time with parents than they used to, 2001). Once again, these figures represent a combination of times in which the parent was actively involved with the child, or just in the same room.

In Denmark, where fathers are entitled to two weeks of leave from their jobs at full pay after the birth of a child, only 56 percent of new fathers actually use this leave. Many fewer (less than 4 percent) of fathers take the parental leave of up to 12 months, with the equivalent of sickness benefits, to which they are entitled. On the whole, Danish men are absent from work for an average of 2.2 weeks during the first two years of their child's life, whereas women are absent for an average of 45 weeks during pregnancy and maternity leave (European Industrial Relations Observatory, 2001).

And what about fathers who do not live with their children? In the 40 years between 1960 and 2000, the proportion of children living apart from their biological fathers doubled: from 17 percent to 34 percent. Whereas some of these fathers make enormous efforts to stay engaged with their children, one study estimates that about 28 percent of children with nonresident fathers had no contact at all with them over the previous year (National Marriage Project, 2003).

When they do interact with their children, fathers are more likely than mothers to spend time in play activities, and mothers spend proportionally more time in maintenance activities (Tiedje & Darling-Fisher, 1993). Many factors seem to moderate fathers' involvement with their children. Marital satisfaction and a father's love for his wife have been shown to be positively linked with his childcare involvement (Crouter, Perry-Jenkins, Huston, & McHale, 1987). Unemployed fathers may be more involved with their children than employed fathers (Radin & Harold-Goldsmith, 1989). The higher a father's income, the less time he spends with his children during the week; however, the higher the mother's income, the more time the father spends with his children on weekends (Time U.S. children spend with their fathers, and what they do, 1999). One study in the United States showed that noncustodial African American fathers have more daily contact with their children than noncustodial European American, Mexican American, or Puerto Rican fathers do with theirs (Stier & Tienda, 1993). A study of low-income African American fathers demonstrated that the father's self-esteem was the best predictor of his responsiveness to and appropriate playfulness with the child (Fagan, 1996). Self-esteem is also a factor in predicting fathers' *satisfaction* with parenthood, as is age at the baby's birth. Among a group of young fathers, aged 15 to 32, with a mean age of just over 19 years, being older when the baby was born was linked to greater satisfaction with parenting (Thompson & Walker, 2004).

When fathers do spend significant time with their children, the benefits are obvious. In one study of preschool-age children, those whose fathers were responsible for 40 percent to 45 percent of childcare showed higher cognitive competence and greater empathy toward their peers (Lamb, 1987).

In some Turkish families, when men are asked how many children they have, they do not count their daughters (Hortaçsu, Ertem, Kurtoglu, & Uzer, 1990). In Iran, one writer was stunned to hear a frantic father offer her a fortune to find him a woman who would bear him a son: "It's just that I must have a son. My wife, after our daughter, they had to cut her up so she can't have another child. I am nothing in this village without a son" (Brooks, 1995, p. 67). In India, China, the Republic of Korea, and Pakistan, evidence suggests that female fetuses (identified as such by an ultrasound test) are selectively aborted so that parents can try again for a son without having to devote time and energy to bearing and rearing an unwanted daughter (United Nations, 1995). In the United States and Canada, surveys suggest there is a strong preference for a boy as a firstborn child (Hamilton, 1991; Krishnan, 1987).

In patriarchal contexts, where the father is viewed implicitly as the head of the family and boys are valued more than girls, girls may be extremely sensitive to approval and disapproval from their fathers. Perhaps partly for this reason, support and encouragement from fathers are often cited as very important to their daughters' development of self-confidence and strong achievement aspirations. Early research by Tangri and Jenkins (1986) suggested that having a supportive father or boyfriend was an important factor in women's willingness to choose a nontraditional career. The biographies of such female pioneers as Nobel Prize–winning physicist Marie Curie and psychologist Mary Calkins (the first woman to be president of the American Psychological Association) indicate that these women had active support from their fathers in breaking down the barriers to women's acceptance in all-male arenas, and a study of eminent Canadian women indicates that these women saw their fathers as being extremely influential in their lives (Yewchuk & Schlosser, 1995). Yet the typical pattern in the United States is for fathers to be less involved with their daughters than with their sons (Starrels, 1994).

There are important reasons to pay attention to the role that fathers play in the family. In most societies, women's household responsibilities place them at a severe disadvantage in the public world of employment. Workplaces are still largely designed for men who have wives to handle the daily demands of housework and childcare. If any balance is to be achieved between women's and men's work and family roles, conceptions of fathering will have to change. As psychologist Louise Silverstein (1996) has argued,

> Feminine gender role norms now socialize women to perform the couple roles of provider and nurturer. Yet societal institutions do not support them in either role. Redefining fathering to emphasize nurturing, as well as providing, will place men in equivalent dual roles. Men may

then become motivated to revise government and workplace policies to support working parents. (p. 5)

Silverstein's point is underlined by the experience of Lew Platt, former CEO of Hewlett Packard, who, as a rising young manager in the 1980s, suffered the death of his wife and became a single father to two young children. The experience changed his understanding of the obstacles facing employed parents. For example, he remembers being in a meeting that he considered one of the most important meetings of his life—and receiving word that his daughter had been in an accident and was in the hospital. He left the meeting without a backward glance. Later, as CEO of the company, he spearheaded the development of family-friendly policies such as job-sharing (Juggling work and family, 2001).

Women Who Do Not Have Children

In developed countries, a certain number of heterosexual couples, whether by choice or infertility, do not have children. For example, in Canada, over 14 percent of mixed-gender couples have never had children (Statistics Canada, 1995). Attitudes toward childbearing vary across cultures and time periods, of course, but a common and persistent theme is the notion that a woman who does not have children has missed out on the core aspect of being a woman. Historians note that in colonial America, childless women were not necessarily targets of either disapproval or pity, but by the end of the 18th century, marriage and motherhood had been highly romanticized, and childlessness began to be viewed as a personal tragedy. In the early 20th century, White middle-class women were exhorted to have children in order to "save the race" in the context of increasing immigration by poor and non-White people (May, 1995). In the present day, a similar theme, though somewhat muted, is apparent in the willingness of U.S. society to devote resources to helping White middle-class women conceive.

In many cultures, motherhood is the key aspect of women's role, and childlessness is personally, socially, and economically devastating. Childlessness in such cultures is usually the result of infertility, which may run as high as 5 to 7 percent of women in some African countries (United Nations, 2000). In such cultures, women may depend on their children for status in their communities and eventually for economic support. Women who are unable to have children in these cultures may be divorced, abandoned, or physically abused by their partners, and stigmatized or ostracized by their communities. Thus they would be stunned at the idea of *choosing* not to have children. However, under some conditions they may choose to have *fewer* children, and such a choice can be beneficial. All over the world, lower fertility is associated with higher education and opportunity levels for women (United Nations, 2000).

In the United States, couples may be placing less emphasis on having children. In one cross-national comparison among industrialized countries, almost 70 percent of Americans surveyed disagreed with the statement that "the main purpose of marriage is to have children " (Whitehead & Popenoe, 2001). By contrast, only 51 percent of Norwegians and 45 percent of Italians disagreed with that statement. American women who choose to be childfree tend to be well-educated, White, and hold nontraditional beliefs about gender roles. Despite their well-articulated reasons for their choice, they may face some rejection and isolation because they are in the minority at parties and family gatherings and because some stigma of unfemininity is still attached to childlessness (May, 1995). Childfree women report that they are sometimes stigmatized and criticized for their choice not to have children. They are the recipients of unsolicited advice (such as the warning that they are too involved in their work or that they will be lonely in their old age) and of pressure to have children (Mueller & Yoder, 1999). However, childfree women give high ratings of satisfaction with their choice, and do not differ from mothers in their reports of subjective well-being (Mueller & Yoder, 1999). Women who make the choice to be child free reap rewards in the form of time and energy for career, friendship, travel, and creativity. Many such women devote their energy to supporting and building their culture through involvement in politics, education, business, or the media—making contributions that would be virtually impossible for women (but not for men) to combine with childrearing under current social conditions.

SUMMARY

Around the world, the intimate relationships associated with family are shaped by social expectations and structures that relate to gender. The roles and expectations that societies hold out for women help to determine when and with whom women will begin their involvement in intimate relationships—and what they expect from those relationships. In some countries, women are expected to marry very young and start having a long series of babies; in others, there is more tolerance for delay of marriage in order to achieve educational and career goals. But the general expectation that women *will* marry and produce children, and will then be the primary caretakers of these children, transcends cultural differences.

The levels of intimacy, power, and equality expected in close adult relationships are affected by gender in a variety of ways. In mixed-gender relationships, men in many societies hold the power advantage of being viewed as legitimately "in charge," as well as having control of more resources, such as money. Women can sometimes offset this advantage by using power based on attractiveness and affection, but they are generally more likely than men to feel at a power disadvantage in close heterosexual relationships. Women in lesbian relationships are more likely to prefer, and to experience, equality in their relationships. In these relationships too, however, imbalances of power can and do occur.

Marriage has often tended to institutionalize power differences between the sexes, placing women formally under men's control in many cultures. The legal aspects of marriage can supersede a couple's own wishes, conferring advantages in security while taking away flexibility. Despite this double-edged aspect of marriage, many lesbian and gay couples have fought for years for the option to legalize their relationships as marital unions.

Parent–child relationships are gendered too. Women in many cultures find that the mother role is entwined with notions of "proper" femininity; they may feel a great deal of tension between the requirements of that role and the other aspects of their lives or personalities. Mothers must also teach their daughters how to be feminine, and this necessity forms the basis for many mother–daughter conflicts. Such conflicts may be particularly difficult to resolve in immigrant families, where the disagreement is between cultures as well as generations. Fathers have fewer expectations placed on them with respect to childrearing, yet the father–child relationship may be of critical importance for making changes in the family that will support women and girls in broadening their possibilities.

Families are much more diverse than the two-heterosexual-parent model often seen in the media. Social and economic systems are, in certain ways, built around the assumption that families do fit this model, causing some difficulties for those who do not. Single mothers and lesbian mothers face particular challenges in this regard. Women who choose not to have children may be negatively stereotyped for not participating in childbearing and childrearing; however, they report very fulfilling, happy lives.

In this chapter we have seen, once again, that women in many parts of the world confront similar kinds of issues, yet the problems associated with these issues differ in severity and in their exact impact on women. Women, in turn, have different preferences, opportunities, and constraints in how they respond to such problems. A common thread is the resilience that women everywhere show in dealing with the ups and downs of relationships and in caring for family members even under extremely difficult circumstances.

KEY TERMS

romantic love	resources	filial piety
equity	bilateral influence strategy	self-efficacy
principle of least interest	direct influence strategy	acculturation
bases of power		

DISCUSSION QUESTIONS

What do you expect of an intimate couple relationship? How do your expectations mesh with the research findings on what others expect? On what such relationships are like?

How has your own culture and family life contributed to your expectations about intimate relationships, marriage, and family life?

What are the arguments for and against legalizing a heterosexual couple relationship as marriage? Are these arguments the same or different with respect to lesbian couples?

Can you imagine yourself living out your life without having children? Why or why not? What are the sources of encouragement or pressure on women in your own cultural group to have children?

FOR ADDITIONAL READING

Boo, Katherine. (2001, April 9). After welfare. *The New Yorker,* pp. 93–107. This reporter writes a detailed and compelling account of the struggles of single mother Elizabeth Jones and her children to build a life that is independent of welfare assistance.

Brooks, Geraldine. (1995). *Nine parts of desire: The hidden world of Islamic women.* New York: Basic Books. An American journalist who spent 6 years covering the Middle East devoted much of her energy to understanding the daily lives of Muslim women. She presents fascinating vignettes of Muslim women, with a strong focus on female–male relationships and women's family ties.

Lee, Essie E. (2000). *Nurturing success: Successful women of color and their daughters.* Westport, CT: Preager/Greenwood. A series of case studies examines mother–daughter relationships among participants from 13 ethnic groups in the United States.

Rose, Suzanna (Ed.). (2002). *Lesbian love and relationships.* New York: Haworth Press. In a series of chapters, various authors examine such themes as the passionate friendships of early adolescent women, dating experiences of sexual minority women, and the reasons why some lesbian relationships endure and some end.

Shostak, Marjorie. (1981). *Nisa: The life and words of a !Kung woman.* New York: Vintage Books. The author, an anthropologist, gives the reader a unique and detailed glimpse into the life of one woman of the !Kung people of southern Africa, reporting Nisa's own words as she reminisces about her childhood, her early experiences with sexuality, her marriages, motherhood, and her reflections on growing older.

Tan, Amy. (1989). *The Joy Luck Club.* New York: Putnam. This is a novel about mother–daughter relationships in a group of Chinese American women. Read it in combination with psychologist Jean Lau Chin's interesting analysis and commentary on the book in Chin (2000).

Women of South Asian Descent Collective. (1993). *Our feet walk the sky: Women of the South Asian Diaspora.* San Francisco, CA: Aunt Lute Books. This anthology of writing by women of South Asian origin includes poems, stories, and essays about a variety of issues, including arranged marriages, mothers and daughters, identity, sexuality, and stereotypes.

WEB RESOURCES

Human Rights Campaign: Family Net. The latest news and information on legal and other issues for lesbian and gay families. **www.hrc.org/Template.cfm?Section=Family**

National Council of Single Mothers and Their Children (Australia). Their motto is "Single mothers: Half the couple, twice the parent." The site contains the news, information, and a discussion list for single mothers. **www.ncsmc.org.au**

The National Marriage Project. This project, based at Rutgers University, produces a yearly report on "the state of our unions," based on surveys and demographic indicators. Full reports for each of the past several years are available for download at the site. The site also includes some other interesting documents, such as "the top ten myths of divorce." **http://marriage.rutgers.edu**

Women's Work

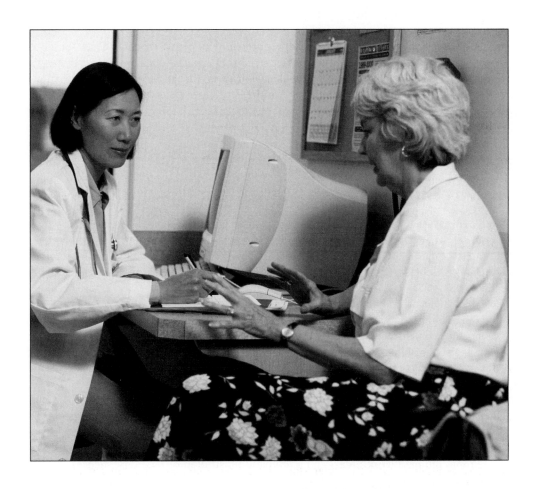

CHAPTER OUTLINE

In October 1996, the women of Afghanistan suddenly found themselves prohibited from going to work. Under an extraordinarily strict interpretation of Islamic law imposed by the rulers of the country, the Taliban militia, women were not allowed to go to school or work and could leave home at all only if covered from head to toe by a flowing garment called a *burqa* (Cooper, 1996).

Many Afghan women were upset and fearful, and most fretted about how their families would get by without their income. Perhaps the largest impact of the new restrictions was not on women themselves, but on the entire economy of the country. At the time, women made up about 70 percent of teachers, half of all civilian government workers, and 40 percent of physicians. Virtually all schools were forced to close down, as was Kabul University, because there were not enough male teachers to handle the load. Hospitals, short-staffed, struggled to treat their usual stream of patients. Relief agencies ceased operations because so many of their staff were female. Without women workers, much of the normal life of the country ground to a halt.

The Afghanistan situation is a good example of the extent to which women have penetrated into the paid workforce—and a dramatic illustration of the consequences of their withdrawal. Women's share of the paid labor force now averages 42 percent or more in all developed regions of the world and is at least 26 percent to 27 percent in the northern African and western Asian countries where it is lowest (United Nations, 2000). In the United States, women's share of the labor force is projected to be 48 percent by 2008 (U.S. Department of Labor, 2000). Around the world, almost 70 percent of working-age women are employed outside the home (Wirth, 2001).

Women's participation in paid employment has economic and behavioral consequences for themselves, their families, and their societies. Furthermore, the presence of women in critical positions can affect the way institutions function. Consider, for example, the practice of obstetrical medicine in Japan, where most physicians are men. Women giving birth are traditionally not given painkilling drugs, even during difficult deliveries. Most women are neither informed about, nor given the choice to take such drugs. If they request them, they are ignored (Jordan, 1997b). If there were more women doctors, some disgruntled patients speculate, there would be more painkillers!

In this chapter, we focus on some of the social and psychological issues surrounding women's economic activity. We begin with an overview of the kinds of work—both paid and unpaid—that women do. Then we turn to an examination of the issues faced by women in the workplace: discrimination, sexual harassment, and expectations with respect to domestic work and childcare.

Women face particular barriers to satisfaction and advancement in the paid workforce. The first of these is gender-based discrimination, first evident in the kinds of encouragement and vocational counseling directed at girls and young women, and later seen in patterns of hiring, salary, and promotion. It can also be seen in decisions about occupational health and safety. We will discuss discrimination and the various remedies, such as education and affirmative action, that have been used to counter it.

A second obstacle for women in the workplace is sexual harassment. The problem is international in scope, from the leers and grabs experienced by female blue-collar workers in the United States, to the *sekuhara* bemoaned by Japanese office workers, to the catcalls of *"Vale! Vale!"* and *"Que chula"* encountered by Mexican women on their way to work. Various approaches to stopping sexual harassment have been proposed and tried; these will be described.

Because domestic work is so strongly associated with women in most cultures, women who engage in paid work also face the stress, in ways that few men do, of trying to balance job and family responsibilities. What impact does it have on women to try to "have it all" (or, perhaps more accurately, "do it all")? What cultural changes and institutional supports would reduce women's stress in this regard? We will consider these questions next.

Finally, what does the future hold for women and work? Some scenarios suggest that women and men will someday be equal partners in the workforce; others predict that women will get tired of "working twice as hard to be thought half as good" as men and will retreat from the workplace. As to the kinds of work that women will do in the future, some foresee a continuing pattern of occupational segregation by gender; others imagine a future in which female construction workers, airline pilots, and corporation presidents will be as common as female nurses and teachers are now. We will examine the trends and projections of women's workforce participation for clues about what to expect in the next century.

Job, Family, and Household Tasks:
All of It Is Work for Women

Jango, a woman in a rural village in western Kenya, described her daily routine to a visiting journalist (Okie, 1993a). According to her account, she rises every day

> at five, prays, wakes her grandchildren, makes tea and sweeps the house. She lets the goats and
> sheep out of their pens. At 7 a.m. she serves tea to the family. Then she works on her farm until

Women in a Brazilian village might laugh at the notion of a "double day," for theirs is often a triple day: working on their husbands' cash crop farm, helping with their parents' land, and maintaining a household.

> 11 a.m., comes home and cooks a hot lunch . . . [then] she collects firewood, walks down the hill to fetch water—a half-hour trip—and grinds millet and cassava by hand for supper. Next, she either goes back to the farm to pick vegetables or makes the two-hour trip to one of the local markets to buy and sell produce. Upon returning, she prepares the evening meal. After supper, the family members talk, tell stories, and go to bed at about 9 p.m. (p. A33)

In rural Brazil, women describe the feeling of being stretched so thin between their work in the fields and their family responsibilities that they fight a continual battle against exhaustion and chronic anxiety. Men are expected to go to bars and dances to relax, but women rarely get such opportunities to escape their responsibilities. Day by day, women and men work in the fields all morning, then men stretch out in hammocks while the women cook lunch for the family. Men eat that lunch sitting down; women eat standing up. These women might laugh at the notion of a "second shift" (Hochschild, 1989), for theirs is often a triple shift: working on their husband's cash crop farm, helping with their parents' land, and maintaining a household (Preston, 1993).

Seen against the backdrop of these women's lives, the question North American researchers often ask about whether it is *good* for women to have a job as well as a family seems almost incredibly naive. Truly, it is only in developed countries that it is possible to separate work and family so neatly and to have the luxury of debating whether or not women *should* work outside the home. Even in countries such as the United States, this question is relevant mainly to European American women whose socioeconomic status is upper middle class or higher; most other women have not had the luxury of choosing to stay home with their families.

It is clear, however, that women everywhere bear the brunt of household labor, regardless of whether and how it is combined with income-producing work. Studies of the division of labor within U.S. households have shown that the movement of wives into the paid labor force has not been accompanied by a complementary shift of husbands into greater participation in household work. Married women who are employed do less housework than their unemployed counterparts, but their husbands do little to take up the slack. In fact, women do more housework than men do in every type of family living situation: married, cohabiting, divorced, living with parents, single (Baxter, 1992; Dempsey, 2000; South & Spitze, 1994; Statistics Canada, 2002). A lopsided division of household labor giving women the greater share of the domestic drudgery is not limited to any one country or culture. It can be found among groups that diverge widely in culture and geographical location: off-reservation Navajo families in the United States (Hossain, 2001), Bengali households in northeastern India (Dutta, 2000), families in modern China (Lu, Maume, & Bellas, 2000), and urban Australian households (Dempsey, 1998). The "double duty" imposed on employed women has costs in terms of stress and exhaustion (Wiersma, 1990). But women also reap psychological rewards from employment: Employed women in the United States report being happier and healthier than homemakers, except when they have small infants to care for (Walker & Best, 1991). The stress can be reduced, and the rewards increased, by high-quality day care and certain kinds of flexibility in the workplace, as discussed later in this chapter.

Women work at home, in the fields, in factories, in hospitals and schools, in business. They may be performing unpaid or barely paid drudgery or challenging intellectual tasks, serving others or supervising them. There is hardly an occupation that does not have some women in it, somewhere in the world. Women's work shows strong patterns of gender segregation, however. Women are more likely than men to be found doing childcare and domestic work in the home, and, in terms of paid employment, about half the world's working women are employed in service-related jobs such as sales, restaurant or hotel jobs, communications, and business and personal services (Neft & Levine, 1997).

The division of labor has economic implications for women: Women, more often than men, are segregated into jobs that do not pay well. It may also have implications for the ways women and men learn to think about themselves, their lives, and their possibilities. As Elsie Clews Parsons, an anthropologist studying the people of the Zuni pueblo in New Mexico in the early 1920s, noted, the household work allocated to women was continuous, whereas the hunting, herding, and farming work assigned to men was seasonal, intermittent, mobile, and easily fitted into the rhythms of religious ceremonial life, the production of art, and the engagement in games. Parsons argued:

> Housework is confining. Hunting, herding, trading lead to a comparatively mobile habit, a habit of mind or spirit which in the Southwest, at least, is adapted to ceremonial pursuit; . . . the differentiation of the sexes at Zuñi proceeds on the whole from the division of labor . . . (Parsons, 1991, p. 104)

Women's Paid Work

Some occupational categories are filled almost completely by women. For example, women make up 98.3 percent of preschool and kindergarten teachers, 96.3 percent of secretaries and 90.2 percent of registered nurses in the United States (U.S. Department of

Labor, 2004). Internationally, the picture is similar; for example, more than 95 percent of secretaries in Finland, France, and Sweden are women, as are more than 89 percent of nurses and midwives and more than 80 percent of domestic helpers and cleaners (International Labor Office, 2004b). Such jobs are often characterized as "traditional" for women; that is, they are jobs people are used to seeing women do and that many would label as "women's jobs." The force of tradition is often used as an argument to keep women segregated in such positions. For instance, in response to the complaint that women in China are often shunted into low-paying jobs such as nursing, elementary and nursery school teaching, and street sweeping, Beijing Labor Bureau official Wang Zhicheng asserted simply, "These jobs have always been done by women, so they are more appropriate for women" (Sun, 1993, p. A24). And as a few Japanese women moved into the formerly male bastion of sumo wrestling, male wrestlers complained that the presence of women will ruin the sport and warn that stepping into the wrestling ring will render women infertile (*60 Minutes,* January 4, 1998).

What jobs are considered traditional for women varies according to time and place, however. Early in the 20th century, most secretaries and bank tellers in North America were men, but now such jobs are so female dominated that they are considered unusual for men. In countries with a strong Islamic tradition, such as Bangladesh, any job that requires a woman to work in the public eye would be nontraditional, since the practice of purdah requires female modesty and seclusion. Hunting and fishing have been traditional work for the Inuit women of the Arctic; this work is considered men's work in many places.

For women in many parts of the developing world, work means some aspect of agriculture. In southern Asia, 66 percent of the female labor force is engaged in agricultural work; in sub-Saharan Africa, the percentage is 65 percent (United Nations, 2000). Even these statistics may be misleading, however, because women's agricultural work may not be counted as "real work" if they do subsistence farming that provides food and shelter for their families rather than generates cash. For example, the 1991 census in India showed that 73 percent of rural women were not "economically active," but a separate survey by the Ministry of Planning indicated that among women who stayed at home and were classified as not economically active, almost two-thirds of rural women collected firewood, maintained kitchen gardens or fruit trees, or raised poultry or cattle—all work activities important to their families' survival (United Nations, 1995).

In much of the world, the notions of "women's work" and "men's work" are in flux. In many countries, women have been making significant incursions into formerly male-dominated (and usually higher-paid) occupations in recent decades. In Canada, for example, the percentage of lawyers who are women rose from just over 21 percent in 1986 to just over 29 percent in 1993, and the percentage of female judges and magistrates rose from 12.5 percent to 20 percent (Statistics Canada, 1995). In 2001, 79 percent of Canadian women workers were employed in teaching, nursing, clerical/administrative and sales/service jobs. However, women made up 54 percent of doctors and dentists, up from 41 percent in 1987. They also made up 50 percent of business and financial professionals (up from 44 percent in 1987) and 20 percent of scientists, engineers, and mathematicians (up from 17 percent in 1987) (International Labor Office, 2004a). According to the International Labour Office, women's percentage share of positions as legislators, senior officials and managers has reached or exceeded 30 percent in a significant number of countries, including the Bahamas, Canada, Costa Rica, Estonia, Hungary, Ireland, Latvia, Lithuania, New Zealand, Poland, Portugal, Puerto Rico, and the Russian Federation (Wirth, 2001). Women now make up more than 50 percent of judges in Eastern European countries, and of 18 judges elected to the International Criminal Court in 2003, seven were women. In Japan, the percent of women working as managers below the section chief level has risen to 11.9 percent, up from 5 percent in 1989, and women now make up 3.2 percent of department heads in companies, up from 1.2 percent in 1989 (International Labor Office, 2004a). In some developing countries, change has been striking: In Colombia the proportion of women managers grew from 14 percent in 1980 to 27 percent in 1990 and 37 percent in 1996; in Chile, the numbers grew from 20 percent in 1980 to 27 percent in 1995 (Wirth, 1997). Since 1995, women's share of managerial positions has jumped significantly: from 26 to 35 percent in El Salvador; from 19 to 27 percent in Ireland; from 31 to 37 percent in New Zealand (Wirth, 2001).

In some countries, however, change has been comparatively slow. For example, in Malaysia women's share of managerial jobs rose only to 10 percent in 1995 from 3 percent in 1986, and the percentage of women in such jobs in Pakistan rose only from 3 percent to 4 percent between 1989 and 1994 (Wirth, 1997). In some countries—Belgium, the Czech Republic, Greece, Republic of Korea, Poland, Romania, Slovenia—there has been a *decline* in women's share of the managerial positions (Wirth, 2001), while in others—Cyprus, Costa Rica, and Bangladesh—there has been a relatively steep decline in women's share of professional jobs (International Labor Office, 2004a).

Not all the historically male-dominated occupations attracting women are white-collar ones. Women have also begun to move, albeit slowly, into blue-collar and trades occupations that have traditionally been dominated by men. In the United States, women make up 2.1 percent of electricians, about 3 percent of construction laborers and firefighters, and 3.3 percent of crane and tower operators (U.S. Department of Labor, 2004a).

Women who move into nontraditional blue-collar occupations often find to their surprise that such jobs are better paid, provide more flexible work schedules, and are more interesting than their previous occupations. For example, a young Costa Rican woman who, after 5 years of working in a garment factory, took on the (for Costa Rica) very nontraditional job of pumping gasoline, commented that she found the work less tedious and easier to coordinate with childcare than her previous job. "It's 'cool' and very different . . . and all the customers treat me nicely," she noted to a reporter intrigued by her unusual job (Palacino, 1994, p. 8). In a similar vein, a 28-year-old U.S. woman who got off welfare by training to be a steamfitter rather than returning to her previous jobs of secretary or beautician noted, "I'm doing something that I never really thought I'd be doing. . . . I had got kind of burned out on doing hair, and I was bored sitting behind a desk all day. . . . This is the best thing I could have done for myself" (Jeter, 1997, pp. B1, B3).

In some countries, however, job opportunities for women are narrowing rather than broadening. For example, as China has moved away from a Communist-based theoretical commitment to women's rights toward a more capitalist-based commitment to profits, female workers have been the first to suffer. In the late 1970s, a higher percentage of women were employed outside the home in China than in most Western capitalist countries, but now women workers there are the last hired and first fired, and 70 percent of jobless young people in the cities are female (Sun, 1993). Similar problems are faced by women in the formerly Communist countries of Eastern Europe, where Communist ideals of egalitarianism have been swept aside and women face discrimination and strong pressures to stay at home rather than seek employment (Lobodzinska, 1996).

Women's Unpaid Work

A Japanese court ruled in favor of a woman who divorced her husband because he demanded that every day she cook him breakfast, press his pants, and clean the house. Even though both spouses worked full time, the husband argued that it was the woman's responsibility to do all the housework, and he had sued her for damages because she had not lived up to the marriage agreement. The judge noted that in the original agreement, the woman had consented to do much of the housework, with the stipulation that the couple would move nearer her place of employment. After the wedding, however, the husband had refused to move—but still demanded that she do all the cooking and cleaning. Japanese women, traditionally expected to do all of the domestic work, were heartened by the woman's victory in court. Perhaps, they speculated, they were seeing the demise of the custom of men lounging around sipping sake and watching television in the evening while women prepare dinner, clean the house, and draw men's baths for them (Jordan, 1997a).

Women's informal and unpaid work is often invisible and uncounted. The prevailing mythology about women and work is that men produce food and women prepare it, that women work mainly to supplement the family income, that women contribute in only a minor way to the world's economy. In fact, statistics show that women produce between 75 percent and 90 percent of the world's food crops, although they rarely hold any ownership of the land they work and are rarely allowed to keep the income that cash crops generate. Researchers have also noted that in the United States, if the economic value of unpaid housework and domestic labor were included in its calculation, economic productivity would be higher by some 25 percent (Ward, 1999). Women do a lot of unrecognized, unpaid work. One often-repeated statistic, which became the informal slogan of the United Nations Decade of Women (1985–1995), is that women do two-thirds of the world's work, receive 10 percent of the world's income, and own 1 percent of the means of production.

Studies of how women and men use their time show that in most of the world, women spend more hours a week working than men do. However, for women a larger proportion of time spent working is devoted to unpaid labor: housework, childcare, and other domestic activities that are not counted when economists try to quantify work (United Nations, 2000). In most countries, women spend about twice the amount of time doing unpaid work as men do—in Japan and the Republic of Korea about 8 times.

In developed regions of the world, two-thirds to three-quarters of the domestic work is performed by women. Women tend to do the cooking, laundry, housecleaning, and ironing; men tend to do household repair and maintenance. In nearly all developed countries, women do between 75 percent and 90 percent of meal preparation and cleanup. They also do most of the childcare, especially when children are young. Even women who are employed full time do most of the domestic work in their households; one Canadian study showed that only 10 percent of wives who were employed full time had spouses who shared responsibility equally for household work (United Nations, 1995). In Canada, surveys show that both women and men spend, on average, about 7.2 hours every day on paid and unpaid work. However, the balance between paid and unpaid work is quite different

Women's informal and unpaid work is often invisible and uncounted.

for the two sexes: women spend about 2.8 hours per day on paid work and 4.4 hours on unpaid work, whereas men spend about 4.5 hours per day on paid work and 2.7 hours on unpaid work (Statistics Canada, 2003).

Women in developing countries do a great deal of unpaid subsistence work, such as carrying water and wood and gardening, as well as unpaid housework. According to the United Nations (1995), women's total work time per week is 53 hours in Bangladesh, 69 in India, and 77 in Nepal, as compared to men's work time in these countries of 46, 56, and 57 hours respectively. In more developed countries, the gap is smaller—about 2 hours— but women consistently work more hours than men (United Nations, 2000).

Women often work outside the home in professional careers only with their husband's permission and moral support—but this does not necessarily translate into sharing household duties. For example, Egyptian engineer Abed Aly, married to an air force officer, noted to a reporter that the main reason she did well in her work was her husband's understanding and help at home. However, when asked if her husband ever washed dishes at home she appeared shocked and cried: "Don't go overboard! . . . He doesn't wash dishes. It never goes that far! But if I come home at 5 o'clock, it's not a problem. He knows I'm working. This is the biggest kind of help" (Murphy, 1993, p. A25).

Equity and Discrimination

In 1974, Shirin Ebadi became the first woman in Iran to be appointed a judge. She was also the last. Five years later, after the revolution, she was forced to step down from the bench because the Iranian constitution guarantees the right to become a judge only to men (Boustany, 1996). In the United States in 2002, the average yearly salary of women managers

---

BOX 8.1 LEARNING ACTIVITY
Learning Activity: Finding Out What You Need to Know to Get Paid Fairly

If you currently hold a job, or if you are getting ready to look for one as you graduate, do some research on salaries to help protect yourself from sex discrimination. Many organizations have published information from salary surveys that will help you find out what the average salaries are for various positions. A good place to access this information is at the Salary Surveys section of the National Committee on Pay Equity Web site: **www.pay-equity.org/info-salary.html**. Here you will find links to several sites that contain salary comparison information.

---

and administrators was just over 68 percent of their male counterparts, and female registered nurses earned 90.9 percent of their male colleagues' income (U.S. Department of Labor, 2004). A survey in Brazil found that female managers often earned only half what male managers earned (Wirth, 1997). In 1995 in Russia, three of every four unemployed persons were women, and women workers earned less than half what men earn. Russian labor minister Gennady Melikyan, when asked about the wage gap between women and men, said: "Why should we employ women when men are out of work? It's better that men work and women take care of children and do housework" (Hockstader, 1995, p. A25). A survey of Canadian female executives revealed that 30 percent of them had left their most recent job because of discrimination or harassment by colleagues or supervisors (Women in Management, 2001). Women are all but shut out of the very top positions in corporate America: In 1999 only 5.1 percent of top executive management positions were held by women, and only 3.3 percent of companies' highest-paid officers and directors were women (Wirth, 2001). Women still make up only 1.6 percent of the CEOs and 5.2 percent of the top earners in *Fortune* 500 companies (National Association of Female Executives, 2004). Many people use the term **glass ceiling** to describe the situation in which qualified women can look upward in an organization and aspire to high-level positions, but invisible institutional barriers prevent them from breaking through.

These reports indicate that discrimination against women in the workplace abounds— and that in the minds of some, it appears justified. What underlies discrimination against women? One obvious factor is men's power and their reluctance to give up resources and control to women. Some men may view women's incursion into male-dominated jobs as a threat to their own future employment or advancement. Yet antifemale discrimination can often come from women as well as men, and even men whose jobs are not threatened and who say they value gender equality may find themselves discriminating against women. Researchers have been exploring these issues for years.

Discrimination in Hiring, Evaluating, and Paying Workers

Undervaluing the Work Done by Women   One of the features of discrimination against women in the world of work is that the quality of women's work tends to be undervalued. Studies that ask respondents to evaluate the quality of a particular piece of work, such as a

TABLE 8.1 Percent of Men's Wages Earned by Women in Various Countries[1]

Country	Women's Percent of Men's Earnings	Country	Women's Percent of Men's Earnings
Japan	65.3	Germany	80.6
Canada	65.8	Greece	83.8
Singapore	75.0	Italy	85.7
United Kingdom	75.7	Spain	86.8
United States	77.9	France	89.2
Austria	78.9	Denmark	89.6
Netherlands	78.9	Belgium	92.7
Ireland	80.2	Portugal	94.1

[1]*Data Sources: (International Labor Office, 2004; Statistics Canada, 2004; U.S. Department of Labor, 2003)*

research article or a painting, have frequently found that the same piece of work is evaluated less favorably when it is attributed to a woman than when it is said to have been done by a man. The tendency to evaluate men's work more favorably than women's is not always found; however, when differences in evaluation are found they tend to favor men. The antifemale bias is most likely to show up in studies outside the lab, in which respondents believe their ratings have real consequences (Top, 1991). Job applications or resumés seem particularly likely to trigger prejudiced evaluations (Harvie, Marshal-McCaskey, & Johnston, 1998; Swim, Borgida, Maruyama, & Myers, 1989). Besides unfavorable evaluations of performance, women also receive other negative assessments of their competence. Their success is often devalued by being explained as "luck," and competent women are sometimes described as "unfeminine" and less likable than competent men (Lott, 1985).

One potential consequence of undervaluing women's work is that women may receive less credit—and pay—for their labors. As seen in Table 8.1, women earn less than men all over the world; Figures 8.1 and 8.2 show that women are paid less than men whether they are in female-dominated or male-dominated jobs. The reasons for the gender pay gap are complex; they include not only the undervaluing of women's work and discrimination against women but also the clustering of women into low-paid jobs and the assumption by women of the largest share of domestic responsibilities. However, all these reasons are linked by gender role expectations.

Making Assumptions about Women's Values There are other threads in the pattern of gender-based discrimination. One concerns stereotypes about the values that women and men hold. Felicia Pratto and her colleagues (1997) proposed that managers' hiring decisions are influenced by their perceptions of job candidates' values. According to this approach, women, perhaps because they are newcomers to the male-dominated power structure, are assumed to hold values that challenge the system, whereas men are assumed to have values that tend to perpetuate it.

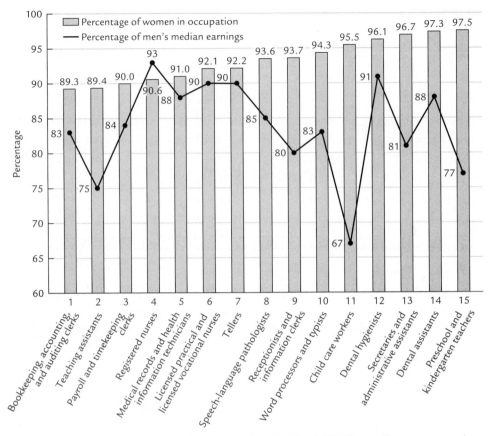

Figure 8.1 Women's percentage of men's earnings in 15 of 499 Census Bureau occupations with the largest majority of full-time, year-round women workers (Data Source: U.S. Bureau of the Census, 2004)

In the theory proposed by Pratto and her colleagues, jobs or roles that promote the interests of the elite, powerful groups in a society are called **hierarchy enhancing,** whereas those that serve the interests of oppressed groups are called **hierarchy attenuating.** Not surprisingly, jobs that enhance the hierarchy are likely to be higher in pay and in status than those that challenge it.

The researchers tested the notion that given the stereotypes about women's and men's values, employers would not simply discriminate against women, but would also be more likely to hire men for hierarchy-enhancing jobs (jobs that maintain and strengthen the status quo) and women for hierarchy-attenuating jobs (jobs that seek to change the system or improve the lot of people who have been marginalized). Indeed, they found that when participants were given the task of placing applicants in positions with different levels of hierarchy-attenuating or hierarchy-enhancing features, they favored women for the hierarchy-attenuating jobs and men for the hierarchy-enhancing ones. This was true even

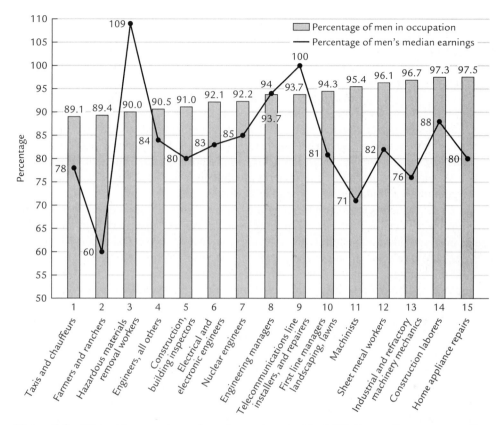

Figure 8.2 Women's percentage of men's earnings in 15 of 499 Census Bureau occupations with a majority of full-time, year-round men workers selected to match the 15 women's percentage majorities (Data Source: U.S. Bureau of the Census, 2004)

when applicants' resumés violated the stereotypes (i.e., women whose career history indicated they were "enhancers" and men whose history indicated they were "attenuators"). Thus stereotypes about women and men that arise from the existing system of power and social dominance are apparently used to perpetuate that system.

Motherhood as a Source of Discrimination Another source of discrimination against women in employment is the idea that women workers cause more trouble and are more expensive to companies than men are because they get pregnant and have childcare responsibilities that may need to be accommodated. Some employers, such as the factories run by large multinational corporations in Southeast Asia, Central America, and other developing regions, simply dismiss women or force them to resign if they have a child. In recent years, some countries have passed new legislation prohibiting employment discrimination on the basis of pregnancy: Such discrimination became illegal in Tanzania, Chile, Cyprus, Sudan, and Zambia (United Nations Population Fund, 2000). However, legislation is only part of the solution. In Mexico, for example, the law prohibits pregnancy-based discrimination, but to avoid paying pregnancy benefits, companies sometimes use pregnancy testing to screen out pregnant job applicants, and women workers discovered to be pregnant are often assigned to the night shift or given extraordinary workloads in order to make them quit (Moore, 1996).

Perhaps the ultimate in refusal to accommodate women's reproductive role can be seen in this account by a woman who worked for a U.S.-based plastics company in the Mexican border town of Tijuana. She was 3 months pregnant and working the night shift when she felt severe pains in her abdomen. Her boss refused her request to leave early, and soon she found herself in the bathroom having a miscarriage. "I left the fetus in the bathroom," she said. "I returned to the floor and even though I was bleeding, they still wouldn't let me go home. I felt like a cow in a market" (Moore, 1996, p. A20).

In China, which has been undergoing a drastic transition in its economy, companies say they are reluctant to hire women because women workers cost more than men. Companies must provide paid maternity leave and may have to set up special rooms for nursing mothers, day care centers, and even special shuttle buses. Some factories have used the rhetoric of "taking care of women" to encourage women to stay home after giving birth (Sun, 1993). Although a 90-day maternity leave is officially required, many work units suggest that a woman stay home for 3 years after having a baby—and a few have urged women to stay home for as long as 15 years.

In the United States, where companies are not legally required to provide paid maternity leave, more than 60 percent of women with young children are in the labor force. Until fairly recently, pregnancy or the potential for pregnancy was used as a justification for discrimination. Until legal rulings in the 1970s forbade such practices, pregnant women were routinely forced to leave their jobs or take unpaid leaves. In addition, women were excluded from certain jobs because they *might* get pregnant. For example, Johnson Controls refused to employ potentially fertile women in its battery-manufacturing operation on the grounds that the lead used in the manufacturing process might harm a fetus carried by a woman worker before she knew she was pregnant. In 1991, the Supreme Court ruled against this practice, saying that potentially pregnant women must not be singled out for discrimination (Freeman, 1995).

Although its laws mandate that it is illegal to discriminate on the basis of pregnancy, the United States remains among a very few countries (the others are Lesotho, Swaziland, Papua New Guinea, and Australia) that do not make any government provision for paid maternity leave for female workers; however, Australia guarantees women a full year of unpaid leave. In contrast, the Family and Medical Leave Act in the United States provides only 12 weeks of unpaid leave and is not applicable to all women workers (Heymann, Earle, Simmons, Breslow, & Kuehnhoff, 2004). The lack of paid maternity leave means that mothers often bear an economic cost for childbearing that is not borne by fathers. Thus, motherhood inevitably becomes a source of discrimination.

The discrimination is intensified by other policies. For example, the provision of paternity leave could allow fathers to shoulder some of the economic (and other) burdens of childbearing. However, only 27 countries provide paid paternity leave, and most of these provide only 3 weeks or less. The United States provides no paid leave for fathers. A few countries provide fairly extensive parental leave benefits: In 11 European countries, paid leave is available to one or both parents until the child is 3 years old. Many countries also support employed mothers of infants by guaranteeing them breastfeeding breaks during working hours. Forty-eight countries guarantee such breaks for 15 months or longer after childbirth; an additional 19 countries guarantee them for at least one year. In the United States, there are no legal provisions for such breaks (Heymann, Earle, Simmons, Breslow, & Kuehnhoff, 2004).

Even when discrimination against mothers is not formal or acknowledged, a social system that assigns the bulk of childcare responsibilities to women produces work–family dynamics in which women's careers are disproportionately affected by family issues. As the Boston Bar Association Task Force on Professional Challenges and Family Needs (1999) recently noted,

> First, in our culture, more women than men have primary responsibility for child care. In many families, there is an agreement that child care should be shared equally, but when this becomes impractical or impossible on a short-term or long-term basis, women tend to be the default child care giver. Second, women who work are judged by their peers and the larger community according to how well they parent and work, but particularly according to how devoted they seem to be to parenting. When children have problems, it is generally women who are expected to alter their professional commitments, and women are more harshly judged than men for not doing so. . . . Fewer women [than men] have the prerogative or the goal of adopting a lifestyle that enables them to devote substantially all their energy to the workplace while receiving behind-the-scenes support for their careers and peace of mind regarding the care of their children. (pp. 14–15)

These societal expectations about the gendering of work–family balance are obvious in the comments from women lawyers gathered by this task force. For example,

> It is difficult to imagine a man being told that he could have one child and be a lawyer, but that having two or more children would be "death to his career." Yet, several women reported being given such "friendly" advice. (p. 15)

Some women reported that they were perceived as less committed to their careers or to their companies because they spent fewer hours in the office than did their colleagues without childcare responsibilities. However, as one woman noted,

> On most days I am taking care of children or commuting or working from the moment I get up until I fall in bed at night. *No one* would choose this if they weren't very committed. (p. 15)

"Women Should Be at Home"   Some of the discrimination against women in employment is rooted in the notion that they do not have the same right as men to be employed: that they belong at home. In the "new" profit-oriented China, men who neglect their household responsibilities for their careers are praised for their dedication, but women who try to do the same face criticism (Sun, 1993). Government bureaucrats and factory managers in countries such as Russia and China, where women are being pushed out of the labor force at an alarming rate, have become fond of asserting to anyone who will listen that women belong at home with their children. A similar message is heard in the formerly socialist republics of central-eastern Europe, where there is "a strong new push toward removing women from gainful employment and toward so-called traditional family values (Lobodzinska, 1996, p. 519).

In countries such as the United States, where such public pronouncements are likely to generate a storm of protest, research shows that there is still a quiet but widespread perception that whereas women should be allowed to work and to advance in their jobs, their employment should always take second place to family concerns. Janice Steil (1995) notes that women and men in the United States still have differing senses of entitlement with respect to their jobs and home responsibilities. For a man, the provider role is assumed to be paramount, carrying the obligation to earn an income and support his family. For a woman, the nurturer role is assumed to be the most important, taking precedence over her job. Such a perception, shared and enforced by many members of the society, entitles the man

> to put his career above his wife's, frees him from a number of responsibilities at home, and entitles him to greater influence. For a woman, the provider role is not socially approved. It is incongruent with her gender role and assumed to interfere with her role as nurturer. Thus, even when she earns more than her husband, she is not entitled to view her career as primary or to significantly decrease her household work. . . . Husbands, employers, and women themselves continue to view childcare as the woman's rather than as the family's responsibility, just as providing is viewed as the man's responsibility. This allows husbands to put their waged work ahead of other family responsibilities. It also allows employers to continue to define equality at work as equality with men under conditions established for men without home responsibility. (Steil, 1995, pp. 157–158)

Despite the disproportionate share of childcare responsibilities, young women now seem to believe that it is important to have both careers *and* families. When Michele Hoffnung (2004) assessed the expectations of 200 college women in 1993, she found that almost all expected to have a career and considered a career important. In addition, however, 78 percent disagreed or strongly disagreed with the statement "I personally could feel completely fulfilled without children." When asked which role would provide the most life satisfaction, 65 percent said family, 20 percent said career, and the other 15 percent chose other roles. Seven years later, when these women were contacted again, most of them had developed reasonably high-level careers and only 15 percent had actually become mothers. Those who had become mothers, however, had significantly fewer advanced degrees and lower career status than nonmothers. Clearly, the reality of trying to combine career and family in a society that provides few supports for this combination is quite difficult.

Discrimination on the Basis of Sexual Orientation   Unlike gender discrimination, discrimination against individuals who are perceived to be lesbian, gay, or bisexual is legal in most workplaces in the United States, although some states, cities, and counties have enacted antidiscrimination ordinances. In the United States military, open acknowledgment of one's homosexuality is grounds for discharge. One review of 21 studies showed that between 16 percent and 46 percent of self-identified lesbian, gay, and bisexual people surveyed reported that they had experienced some form of employment discrimination (Badgett, Donnelly, & Kibbe, 1992). However, heterosexual employees often underestimate the level of discrimination experienced by lesbian and gay employees (Van Den Bergh, 1999). Economic research suggests that lesbian and bisexual women earn about 13 percent to 15 percent less than heterosexual women, partly because they are more likely than heterosexual women to be working in the lowest-paying female-dominated occupations (Badgett, 1995, 1996).

The finding that lesbian and bisexual women earn less than their heterosexual counterparts is striking because there are some reasons to expect exactly the opposite. As Lee Badgett (1995) notes, women who are lesbian or bisexual may have more economic incentives to pursue employment and are more economically penalized for not being employed than heterosexual women are. These women are less likely than heterosexual women to plan to depend on the income earned by their partner. Why? Because if they have a partner at all, it is likely to be another woman, who also faces a discriminatory job market, and they have fewer legal and economic benefits (such as health insurance) of partnership. It might be expected, then, that lesbian and bisexual women, under more pressure to be attached to the labor force, would, as a group, tend to earn *more* than heterosexual women. The finding that they, in fact, seem to earn less suggests the impact of discrimination on the basis of sexual orientation.

Parallel research on the earnings of women of different sexual orientations is not available for other countries. However, countries do vary in their laws regarding discrimination on the basis of sexual orientation. For example, federal law in Canada prohibits discrimination on the basis of sexual orientation, and countries such as Canada and Australia do not bar gay men and lesbians from the armed forces. In fact, the United States is one of the very few member countries of the North Atlantic Treaty Organization (NATO) that ban gay men and lesbians in the military (Baldwin, 1993). Laws against discrimination do not ensure its absence, but such laws *are* a critical first step in changing the attitudes and practices that disadvantage individuals on the basis of their sexual orientation.

Women's Working Conditions   Some people argue that women have less dangerous and difficult jobs than men—after all, most firefighters, police officers, construction workers, and soldiers are men, for example. But jobs dominated by women are also difficult and dangerous. For example, nurses are exposed to infectious diseases and must often lift heavy patients. One investigation revealed that the risk of serious injury for a nursing aide was higher than that for a coal miner or steel mill worker (National Committee on Pay Equity, 2001). In addition to the risk of serious back injuries from lifting and moving patients, nursing aides are also at risk of assaults. Of serious workplace assaults reported in private industry in 1997, 27 percent of the attacks were against nursing aides, compared to 7 percent against security guards.

In much of the world, women are particularly sought after by employers offering certain types of work. Why this discrimination *in favor of* women? Young women are stereotyped as docile and nimble-fingered. Moreover, they work cheaply. Factories and assembly plants making everything from computer parts to shoes in much of the developing world advertise aggressively for "female personnel," and many young single women from poor families flock to answer the call. What they find when they get there is low pay, long hours, and stressful, sometimes dangerous, working conditions. Young women make up the lowest-paid segment of the industrial workforce in developing countries. Most accept the working conditions because they have no choice, and they regard the factory as a stepping-stone to a better life.

Young women are often sought after as workers because they are stereotyped as docile and nimble-fingered and will work for little pay. In developing countries, young women make up the lowest-paid segment of the industrial workforce.

Anthropologist Aihwa Ong (1991), who studied daily life in some Malaysian computer parts factories, found that most of the workers on the floor were young women from rural villages. All the supervisors and executives were men, usually from other countries such as Japan or India. The women were treated somewhat like children: They were subjected to constant supervision, pressured to produce quickly, kept in relative isolation from one another, and could be punished for trips to the locker rooms. Ong noted that the women were called "factory daughters," emphasizing their subservience to male authority.

Accompanying the factories in many developing regions are organized systems of home work, in which women (and often children) produce goods at home and are paid by the piece. In the Philippines, for example, the garment industry is based mainly on women who sew at home in their villages and are paid at a very low rate (Ward, 1999). This system, as well as high-pressure, low-paying factory work, is often justified on the basis that women are a "secondary" labor force, either working only until they can find a husband or to supplement their family income. The stereotype becomes a self-fulfilling prophecy, as women workers burn out from stress and exhaustion and quit after a few years. Some "graduate" into prostitution, as discussed in Chapter 12.

Women workers, although often poorly paid and badly treated, are not simply victims, however. Studies of women factory workers in the Export Processing Zones of Central America show that these young women, 40 percent of whom are single mothers, often do not view themselves as exploited. Rather, they see their jobs as providing income that will buy them not only needed goods but also some independence from the patriarchal authority of their families (Fernández-Pacheco, 2001). And indeed, some women can use poor jobs as routes to empowerment. Louie (2000) tells the story of Ling, a Chinese American immigrant, who went to work in a garment factory sweatshop in New York. She had been living with her in-laws, working in the family's laundry business, and suffering from their rigid control over her for years before finally going to work at the factory.

> In the factory, she related to the other women workers, many of whom had similar experiences. The existing workers taught her how to sew and she in turn helped newcomers. They covered for each others' mistakes, chipped in when one fell behind, and competed with one another for better performance and higher productivity. They took their meals together and commiserated with each other about their hardships. Deep empathy developed among them. . . . Later, Ling, like many other women in the factory, brought her daughter in to work alongside her during after-school hours when she was a preadolescent. Ling . . . [said] that it was better for her daughter to be treated in the factory as a capable girl who is helpful to her mother than being left at home to be treated by her grandmother as someone less valuable than her brothers. (p. 219)

Her work and income at the garment factory, and the relationships with other women there, provided this woman with the foundation for an expanded sense of competence, self-esteem, and empowerment. Whereas the job was in many ways an exploitative one, it helped her to escape from an even more oppressive family situation.

But women should not have to put up with exploitative work situations in order to better their lot in life. Many women have organized to improve their working conditions. In Bangladesh, where women hold the vast majority of jobs in garment factories, working 12 to 14 hours a day under dismal conditions, women organized the Bangladesh Independent Garment Workers Union in 1994. This was the country's first and only union founded and run by women, and it provides a way for women to band together to improve their working conditions without risking the loss of their jobs (Neft & Levine, 1997).

In Search of Gender Equity in the Workplace: Some Remedies

Reducing Gender Stereotypes   Ann Hopkins brought in $25 million in business to the major U.S. accounting firm she worked for, Price Waterhouse. When she applied to be made a partner in the firm, she was turned down, despite the fact that she had generated more revenue than others who received the promotion. The reason? She was told she had an interpersonal skills problem: that she needed to dress and act more "feminine," that she would benefit from a course at "charm school." Would a man who had been so successful at landing new business for his company have been turned down for promotion because he wasn't "charming" enough? Hopkins thought not, and she launched (and ultimately won in 1989) a sex discrimination suit against her employer. In this suit, the American Psychological Association became involved as a friend of the court, and psychologists testified as expert witnesses on the causes and consequences of stereotyping (Fiske, Bersoff, Borgida, Deaux, & Heilman, 1991).

It would be nice to think that the Hopkins case, now well over a decade old, is a relic of times long past, when women were treated unfairly in the workplace. Unfortunately, that is not the case. A steady stream of sex discrimination lawsuits continues, and the details of each one reflect some of the same issues as the Hopkins case. For example,

BOX 8.2 WOMEN SHAPING PSYCHOLOGY
Susan T. Fiske

Susan Fiske came from a long line of independent, feminist women. Her great-grandmother was a leader of the women's suffrage movement in Massachusetts and one of the first women to attend MIT. Her grandmother led parades for women's suffrage at Radcliffe College. Her mother spent much of her life working with citizens' action groups. In her career, she found inspiration from these female forebears as well as from her father, a psychologist deeply committed to his work.

As a child, Fiske attended the University of Chicago Laboratory Schools, where she developed the notion that learning could be fun. She went to Radcliffe College as an undergraduate student and to Harvard as a doctoral student. There she learned an appreciation of social psychology and realized that research in that field was what she wanted to do. Eventually, she became an expert in social cognition—studying attitudes and stereotyping. During the early 1980s, she studied people's reactions to the possibility of nuclear war. At the same time, she began to develop theories and research about the process of stereotyping, amplifying her work on this issue while working as a professor at the University of Massachusetts at Amherst. When she was asked to testify in a sex discrimination case involving a government department, she found that preparing the testimony showed her a lot about what psychology understood and did not understand about sex stereotyping.

Colleen Crangle was fired from her position as a senior research scientist at Stanford University when she filed a complaint about gender bias. Crangle had brought prestige and money to her university department, winning federal grants, writing professional articles and co-authoring a book, and receiving invitations to speak at national and international conferences. Instead of being rewarded for these successes, she was told she could no longer work with other scholars, ordered to add the name of a male peer to her grant applications (although the arrangement would not be reciprocal), and assigned to a programming position for which she had no training. Then she was transferred to another department, where she had no office or computer of her own. What justifications were offered for such treatment? Crangle was criticized for having "strong opinions" and told she ought to be more sensitive to the feelings of her male peer (Saldich, 2000).

BOX 8.2 WOMEN SHAPING PSYCHOLOGY *(continued)*
Susan T. Fiske

That case was settled, but Fiske soon found herself involved in another case—one with a higher profile. This was the *Hopkins* v. *Price Waterhouse* case, in which a female manager had been refused promotion because she did not conform to gender stereotypes. Fiske testified about the impact of stereotyping on Hopkins's evaluation and helped to win the discrimination case for Ann Hopkins. Her testimony was cited favorably at each judicial level, from the trial court to the U.S. Supreme Court. The American Psychological Association filed a friend of the court brief in this case, which became a precedent-setting case in sex discrimination.

In 1991, Susan Fiske received the American Psychological Association's Award for Distinguished Contribution to Psychology in the Public Interest. She has also been awarded the Gordon Allport Intergroup Relations Prize by the Society for the Psychological Study of Social Issues. She served as President of the American Psychological Society in 2002. Fiske continues her work on stereotyping and power, recently applying her theories

to understanding the causes of sexual harassment. She has added greatly to our understanding of the reasons for gender stereotyping and its consequences in the workplace and other settings.

Read More about Susan Fiske

Awards for Distinguished Contribution to Psychology in the Public Interest: Susan T. Fiske. (1992). *American Psychologist, 47*(4), 498–501.

Read What She Has Written

Fiske, S. T., Bersoff, D. N., Borgida, E., Deaux, K., & Heilman, M. E. (1991). Social science on trial: Use of sex stereotyping research in Price Waterhouse v. Hopkins. *American Psychologist, 46,* 1049–1060.

Fiske, S. T. (2001). Stereotyping, prejudice, and discrimination at the seam between the centuries: Evolution, culture, mind, and brain. *European Journal of Social Psychology, 30,* 299–322.

Glick, P., & Fiske, S. T. (2001). An ambivalent alliance: Hostile and benevolent sexism as complementary justifications of gender inequality. *American Psychologist, 56,* 109–118.

When Crangle warned that she would take legal action about this unfair treatment, she was fired within 24 hours. She launched a suit against Stanford University, alleging sex discrimination and retaliation for complaining of discrimination. A jury unanimously supported her claims and awarded her more than half a million dollars in damages. Stanford appealed the decision, but finally settled it in May 2001 (LAF case news: Colleen Crangle case settled, 2001).

Susan Fiske and her colleagues have outlined the kinds of situations that are conducive to stereotyping (Fiske et al., 1991):

- Where the person is the only one or one of a very few of a particular kind of person (a "token") in the work environment (as Ann Hopkins was one of very few women at

---

BOX 8.3 MAKING CHANGE
Fighting Discrimination in the Workplace

Every year, many U.S. women file sex discrimination suits against employers. The outcome of these suits can have implications for many other employed women. Some of the cases are supported by organizations such as the American Association of University Women's Legal Advocacy Fund (LAF), which specializes in cases that involve sex discrimination in higher education. At the Web site for the LAF, **www.aauw.org/laf/cases/index.cfm**, you will find a list of currently supported cases. You can support their efforts by learning more about the cases and adding your voice to the debate—by writing letters, speaking up, and spreading the word about the situations these women are facing. And if *you* are currently experiencing sex discrimination, you can find advice here for navigating the legal system and getting support for your case.

---

her level at Price Waterhouse and Colleen Crangle was one of a minority of women at her level in her department).

- Where members of a previously excluded group are moving into new roles for the first time (Hopkins was trying to enter the almost all-male bastion of partnership. Crangle was trying to take her place among senior university research scientists, a realm where women are few and far between).

- Where the person's social category seems to onlookers not to "fit" the job or role (Hopkins was perceived, as a woman, to lack the aggressive, competitive qualities necessary to be a managing partner—but was negatively judged unfeminine to the extent she *was* perceived to have these qualities. Crangle was perceived as too opinionated and insensitive, but this charge would probably not have been leveled against a man in her position).

- Where evaluation criteria are ambiguous (at Price Waterhouse there were no clear, agreed-upon criteria for promotion, and some people who did not know Hopkins very well made their judgments on the basis of brief impressions and hearsay. Evaluation criteria for university research scientists are fairly ambiguous: A person's colleagues may decide that, even though s/he produced publications and grant funding, her/his work is not important).

- Where organizational norms and policies are tolerant of stereotyping and prejudice (at Price Waterhouse, comments about the inappropriateness of women as partners were made without being challenged at the company's top-level meetings, and there was no policy prohibiting sex discrimination. At Stanford, more than 30 female faculty members have reported discriminatory practices to the U.S. Department of Labor (Saldich, 2000)).

Understanding the circumstances that promote stereotyping and lead to discrimination provides some clues as to how an organization could act to reduce them. Companies can make an effort not to isolate women in particular job categories or levels to avoid problems associated with the stereotyping of "tokens." They can encourage an examination of job-related assumptions by company managers to avoid falling automatically into the notion that "this job requires masculine qualities." They can make evaluation and promotion criteria clear and not base such judgments on impressionistic perceptions. Finally, they can develop formal guidelines about avoiding discrimination—guidelines that top-level management model and enforce.

In some parts of the world, politicians and other leaders can, with relative impunity, publicly make disparaging comments about women's competence, motivation, or fitness for employment. In other countries, prejudice against women in the workplace has, in some ways, gone underground because so many people are aware of the disapproval that greets expressions of gender stereotyping and prejudice. As discussed in Chapter 1, researchers in the United States have identified a constellation of attitudes they label "modern sexism" (Swim, Aikin, Hall, & Hunter, 1995) or "neo-sexism" (Tougas, Brown, Beaton, & Joly, 1995). More subtle than the "old-fashioned" sexism that openly endorses the differential treatment of women and men and the stereotype that women are less competent than men, modern sexism is characterized by a denial that women are still targets of discrimination, antagonism toward women's demands, and lack of support for policies aimed at improving women's status. People who endorse modern sexist beliefs are likely to perceive greater gender equality in the workforce than actually exists, and they tend to believe that the gender segregation of the workforce is due to individualistic factors (such as occupational choice) rather than to discrimination against women.

Modern sexism is difficult to combat, since its adherents do not believe their attitudes are sexist. Information about discrepancies in women's and men's hiring outcomes or salaries is explained as the result of differing qualifications; the shortage of women at the top is attributed to women's choices in favor of family. Perhaps the best strategy in combating the subtle forms of sexism is not argument but example. If administrators make a consistent point of including women in meetings, giving them desirable job assignments, and giving them credit publicly for excellent work, it will improve women's position in the workplace *and* get other workers in the habit of thinking positively of women. Management must take the lead in such efforts if they are to have an impact.

Pay Equity and Affirmative Action   In recent decades, a great deal of effort has been put into concrete programs designed to eliminate gender-based discrimination in the workplace. Terms such as **pay equity** and **affirmative action** have become both rallying cries and points of conflict in the United States, Canada, and some other countries. Yet many people are confused about the meaning of these terms and about the ease with which such programs can be implemented.

Pay equity is the notion that women and men should be paid equally for the same work. In its simplest interpretation, it means that women and men doing the same job at the same level of seniority should be paid the same wage: equal pay for equal work. This principle is enshrined in law in most countries—for example, Argentina, Australia, Bangladesh, Canada, China, Egypt, and the United States all have such laws—but the vigor with which the laws are enforced varies greatly. Some countries have no real sanctions for violating the law and/or no office that is charged with enforcing it.

TABLE 8.2   The Results of One Formula to Determine Comparable Worth

Criteria	Job: Newspaper Librarian (female-dominated)	Job: Truck Loader (male-dominated)
Skill	570	430
Effort	580	590
Responsibility	470	390
Working conditions	450	660
Total	2,070	2,070

Source: (Adapted from Kilpatrick, 1990)

In the United States, equal pay legislation provides that women and men doing the same or "substantially equal" work may not be paid differently, and the Supreme Court has ruled that wage discrimination is illegal even when the jobs performed by women and men are not identical. However, since the Equal Pay Act was signed into law in 1963, the wage gap has closed very slowly. Whereas women made 59 cents for every dollar that men made in 1963, they made just under 78 cents in 2002 (U.S. Department of Labor, 2003). Thus, the gap has been closing at less than half a cent per year.

One reason for the slow closing of the gap may be the gender segregation of occupations. Occupations that are dominated by women tend to be lower paid than occupations that are dominated by men. In some countries, such as Canada, Great Britain, and the United States, the attempt to reimburse women and men equally for their work has led to a refinement of the concept of pay equity to mean not just equal pay for equal work, but equal pay for work of equal value (also referred to as **comparable worth**). This notion is a response to the persistent gender segregation of the workforce, in which women and men tend to be clustered in different jobs (with women in the jobs that pay less). The idea behind the principle of equal pay for work of equal value is that even though women and men may not be working in the same jobs, the work traditionally done by women and that traditionally done by men can be compared in terms of their value. If the jobs are equally valuable, they should be equally reimbursed.

Sound simple? It isn't. Implementation of this idea requires that the value—the composite of skill, effort, responsibility, and working conditions—of jobs normally filled by women and jobs normally filled by men within the same organization be compared. For example, how does the work of a company mail clerk (usually male) compare with that of a secretary (usually female)? How does the work of a grocery store shelving clerk (usually male) compare in value to the work of a cashier (usually female) in the same store? To make such comparisons, organizations may ask supervisors and employees to fill out questionnaires evaluating jobs according to criteria such as amount of education required, deadline pressures, amount of responsibility, and other aspects of working conditions. Then points are assigned to each job category, based on the results of the questionnaire, and job categories with the same number of total points are entitled to the same pay. Table 8.2 illustrates one such scheme.

One publishing company in Ontario, Canada, for example, asked all employees to fill out multiple-choice questionnaires about the nature of their jobs (Kilpatrick, 1990). Each answer had a numerical value (not known to the employees). All the answers were grouped under four categories representing dimensions associated with the job: skill required, effort required, amount of responsibility, and working conditions. Then the total points under each of the four categories were added up. As you can see in Table 8.2, one result of the evaluation was that the female-dominated job of newspaper librarian was rated as equivalent in value to the male-dominated job of truck loader. The librarians, who were making about $3,000 a year less than the truck loaders, received a raise to make the two categories equally paid. Interestingly, according to one management consultant both the librarians and the truck loaders were insulted at being compared with the other category.

There are many other examples of this process. In Los Angeles, a comparison of their jobs found that social workers were comparable to parole officers in terms of skill, effort, responsibility, and working conditions—yet the social workers were being paid less. Similarly, a pay equity study in Portland revealed that the job of typist was equivalent to water meter reader, and their pay was adjusted accordingly (National Committee on Pay Equity, 2001).

Actually, the notion of comparing jobs is not new. Job evaluations have been a much-used management tool for many years. Today, two out of three workers in the United States are employed by companies that use some form of job evaluation. In particular, the federal government has a well-established job evaluation system (National Commission on Pay Equity, 2001).

Why is there a need for such complicated formulas? Partly because the value (and the pay) conventionally assigned to jobs dominated by women or men enshrines, to some extent, the implicit evaluation of women and men that is part of the way we have learned to think about gender. If women are stereotyped as less competent than men, for example, then jobs that are seen as "women's jobs" will be stereotyped as easier, requiring less competence, than those seen as "men's jobs"—and valued lower. In other words, because women and men are perceived and valued differently, work that is gender-labeled "feminine" has a connotation different from that of work that has been labeled "masculine." It is difficult, if not impossible, for people in a society that constructs gender in a certain way to evaluate the worth of an occupation independent of the gender labeling of that occupation.

Affirmative action refers to a set of strategies to increase the proportion of women and minorities hired by organizations, particularly into jobs that they have traditionally been excluded from. The strategies may include special outreach and training programs to counteract the built-in exclusiveness of traditional recruiting methods. In the United States, for example, traditional avenues of recruitment for many blue-collar occupations are high school shop classes, trade schools, and the military. Yet women are very much a minority in such settings, and thus may miss hearing about training and employment opportunities. One aspect of affirmative action is the development of a plan for advertising positions more broadly and actively recruiting candidates from among underrepresented groups. Another aspect involves training for members of such groups to compensate for opportunities that may have been effectively closed to them earlier. For instance, young women in many places have been selectively encouraged to prepare themselves for jobs as secretaries, clerks, or hairdressers and discouraged from learning the skills necessary to be

> ## BOX 8.4 MAKING CHANGE
> **Supporting Pay Equity**
>
> Each year the National Committee on Pay Equity (NCPE) organizes the national obser-
> vance of *Equal Pay Day.* This is a day of speaking out about the gap between women's
> and men's pay. It falls on a Tuesday, to symbolize the point into the new week that a
> woman must work in order to earn the wages paid to a man in the previous week. Find
> out from the NCPE when the day is being celebrated this year, and organize an activity
> —a rally, a speaker, a letter-writing campaign—to join in. Get information at **www.pay
> -equity.org**.

construction workers, plumbers, or steelworkers. Affirmative action plans often give
underrepresented groups special opportunities for training in skills they traditionally have
been systematically discouraged or excluded from learning.

Most affirmative action plans set targets for the proportion of women or minorities
that should be reached in hiring. However, ideally the targets are not quotas, but goals, and
they do not entail hiring unqualified people simply because they are members of a targeted
group. Rather, the programs are designed to bring the level of opportunity for underrepresented groups up to the level that it has historically been for well-represented groups.

The rationale for affirmative action is that it helps balance the scales by improving job
possibilities for groups whose opportunities in education, job training, and employment
have traditionally been limited in comparison to those of White men. In the United States,
affirmative action in employment is based on the Civil Rights Act of 1964, which identified women, people of color, and military veterans as target groups. The Equal Opportunity
Act of 1972 strengthened the enforcement powers of the Equal Employment Opportunities
Commission, which oversees compliance with nondiscrimination laws. The Civil Service
Reform Act of 1978 established a policy that the federal workforce would reflect the
nation's diversity and that steps would be taken to eliminate the underrepresentation of
women and minorities in federal employment. Many individual states also have affirmative
action programs, although in recent years some states (e.g., California, Colorado, Florida)
have weakened or eliminated such programs on the grounds that they constitute "reverse
discrimination" (discrimination against White men). In Australia, the Affirmative Action
Act, passed in 1986, requires all private-sector businesses, trade unions, community organizations, and training programs to establish affirmative action programs for women. In
Canada, the Employment Equity Act, passed in 1986, directs employers to increase the
proportion of women and other underrepresented groups among those they hire. Similar
laws have been passed in France, Germany, Israel, Italy, Sweden, and other countries.

Perceptions of Fairness and Reactions to Affirmative Action

Controversy about affirmative action is pronounced. In the United States, where the chief
beneficiaries of the programs apparently have been White women, polls tend to show that
at least a third of Americans do not support affirmative action policies (Crosby & Franco,

2003). A disgruntled segment of the population argues that affirmative action means discriminating against White men, hiring unqualified women and minorities to fill arbitrary quotas (rarely is speculation heard about quota-driven hiring of unqualified military veterans), and unnecessary interference by the government in the affairs of private companies. Even some members of groups who may benefit from affirmative action experience a sense of unease about it. Few people are pleased with the attribution (by their coworkers or the general public) that it was their membership in an underrepresented group, rather than their qualifications, that got them hired or promoted. And, in fact, that attribution is often made. For instance, in the absence of explicit information about the selection policy, undergraduate students were asked to state the extent to which they thought gender had played a role in the selection of an applicant for a graduate degree program. The students tended to assume that the only woman selected for the program had been selected because of her gender. However, they made no such assumption when presented with an applicant who was the only male selected for the program (Heilman & Blader, 2001). Respondents in another study evaluated an affirmative action hiree as less competent and less likely to have been hired because of qualifications than other hirees, regardless of the person's actual qualifications. Moreover, simply being associated with affirmative action produced negative evaluations in terms of competence and career progress (Resendez, 2002). In fact, this researcher found that evaluators' attitudes toward affirmative action had a stronger impact on the way an individual was evaluated than did the person's actual qualifications.

Women, the largest group to benefit from affirmative action, are often not vocal in their support of it—a silence that gives the floor to opponents of such programs. Researchers puzzled by women's silence have delved into the psychology of the experience of discrimination. They have found that although women are clearly discriminated against in the workplace, many women experience a "paradoxical contentment" (Major, 1994): They report being satisfied with their situation and seemingly do not regard as illegitimate any gender inequalities they may notice. Similarly noted has been a tendency toward "denial of personal discrimination": the perception by individual women that they themselves are being treated fairly, even though they acknowledge the existence of discrimination against women as a group (Crosby, 1984).

To recognize individual discrimination, a person must compare her own situation to those of others. Faye Crosby (1984) argues that women are often not aware of relevant comparison information, such as the salaries of comparably qualified male employees, that would show the existence of discrimination. If a woman is led to make such comparisons, she may experience **personal relative deprivation:** a sense of dissatisfaction stemming from a comparison with others who are being more highly rewarded. She may also experience **collective relative deprivation:** a feeling of dissatisfaction due to perceived inequities between one's own group and a more advantaged group (Runciman, 1966). Clearly, if women are to be aware of the individual and collective discrimination that they face, they must be allowed and encouraged to make appropriate comparisons with men's situations.

If women begin to feel personally or collectively deprived in comparison to men, will they support affirmative action programs? That depends. The women participating in one Canadian study, upset and dissatisfied about inequities in their workplace, declared themselves ready to assert their discontent by denouncing sex discrimination and by participating in a group designed to improve women's position in the workforce, yet they were reluctant to endorse affirmative action (Tougas, Dubé, & Veilleux, 1987). The researchers theorized that even though the women were aware of sex discrimination and of its direct effect on them, they were unwilling to accept a remedy that itself seemed unfair in order to counter this injustice. In a later study, using a sample of French Canadian employed women, the researchers found that strong identification with women as a group was associated with feelings of collective relative deprivation, which in turn were associated with support for affirmative action policies—but only if those policies were not based on preferential treatment for women (Tougas & Veilleux, 1988). In this study, half the women were provided with a description of an affirmative action policy that emphasized preferential treatment of women in order to increase the percentage of women in higher-level job categories. The other half were given a description of an affirmative action program that emphasized the elimination of discriminatory administrative practices and targeted women for special assistance in planning and preparing for career moves. Only the latter program found support among the women studied. The results of this study are congruent with several others. For example, one study of college students found that, of several affirmative action programs for women, passive nondiscrimination was viewed as the fairest response to discrimination (Matheson, Warren, Foster, & Painter, 2000). Another study found that negative attitudes toward affirmative action were linked to the belief that it involved strong actions such as preferential hiring and setting aside jobs (Kravitz et al., 2000).

Why should women feel squeamish about accepting preferential treatment in the face of so many years of discrimination? Perhaps the answer is that long history has had an impact. Women have been socialized to be generally less self-confident about their abilities than men have, so they especially want to feel when hired or promoted that their qualifications and competence, not some system of gender-based preference, is the basis for that decision. Support for this interpretation comes from a laboratory study in which female and male undergraduates were selected as task leaders either on the basis of merit or preferentially on the basis of their gender (Heilman, Simon, & Repper, 1987). Women's, but not men's, self-perceptions and self-evaluations were negatively affected by the gender-based preferential selection method in comparison to the merit-based method. When told they had been selected as leaders because of their gender, women devalued their leadership performance, took less credit for success, characterized themselves as more deficient in general leadership skills, and reported less interest in continuing as leader. It appears that women, who may have more doubts about their competence than men do to begin with, are especially vulnerable to the adverse effects of preferential selection based on non-work-related criteria. Men, on the other hand, do not seem to be plagued by self-doubt about their performance when told they have been selected for a job simply because they are men.

In another study, female undergraduate students showed a number of negative effects of being placed in a task situation in which they were told that another person believed they had been chosen for the job because of preferential selection on the basis of their gender (Heilman & Alcott, 2001). The women's awareness that the other person viewed them as having been selected on the basis of their gender rather than merit produced negative feelings and led the women to conclude that the other person held low expectations of their competence. If the women were uncertain about their own ability to perform the task well, the awareness that they were viewed as beneficiaries of preferential selection also produced timid, performance-limiting task decisions and the tendency to view themselves in an unflattering light. On the other hand, women who were very sure of their own ability to perform well took risks and made ambitious, performance-enhancing task decisions, perhaps trying to make a good impression and counter any negative expectations that might have been held by the other person. Perhaps women resist affirmative action programs based on preferential treatment not because they see them as unfair, but rather because they want the assurance and self-confidence that come with knowing they have been hired or promoted on their merits. They do not want to have to prove themselves over and over again, but to be accepted as competent.

Research shows that when affirmative action programs that have been in place for some time have not produced a significant numerical representation of women in an organization, the women who are there become more discontented about their situation and experience more collective deprivation (Beaton & Tougas, 1997). Furthermore, the stronger women's experience of collective relative deprivation is, the stronger is their support of a variety of affirmative action programs. This finding suggests that women may eventually lose patience with the notion that only certain kinds of affirmative action programs are acceptable remedies for sex discrimination.

Sexual Harassment in the Workplace

Chieko Mitome, an office worker at a Japanese company, was mortified one day when, as she was serving tea to five visitors, her boss introduced her by saying "See this woman who works for me—she has big breasts!" Having already endured months of commentary on her anatomy by male employees, Mitome had reached her limit. She lodged a complaint to a company official about *sekuhara* (**sexual harassment**). Her boss was reprimanded and, as she had requested, she was transferred to another division (Sugawara, 1996).

Monique Evans, now a well-known Brazilian television personality, says her career stagnated for years because she refused to sleep with producers and directors. The anger that she felt, however, was not enough to get her to support legislation against sexual harassment, which she argues is part of Brazilian culture (Buckley, 2001).

For Sandra Rushing, an employee of the Mitsubishi car manufacturing plant in Normal, Illinois, going to work became a terrifying experience when she was transferred to the chassis line at the factory. Male employees would regularly tell coarse jokes about her, and they would surround her, touching her breasts and putting their hands between her legs. One evening, several men waited for her as she came off the night shift and demanded that she have sex with them. Frequent complaints to her supervisor did nothing to stop the harassment, and eventually, in 1994, Rushing became one of the plaintiffs against Mitsubishi in one of the largest sexual harassment suits in the history of the U.S. Equal Employment Opportunity Commission. The suit alleged that 300 to 500 women had been harassed at the plant since its opening in 1988 (Grimsley, Swoboda, & Brown, 1996).

In Israel, most young women serve in the army between the ages of 18 and 20. Such service puts them into subordinate positions with respect to powerful men and makes them vulnerable to harassment. One lawyer who prosecutes such cases notes that, since security is a major issue in Israel, it has been difficult in the past to hold army officers accountable for sexual harassment. However, in recent years, a revolution in social norms has begun, with the value of women's dignity increasing relative to the value of military security. In 2000, she notes, a prominent Defense Ministry spokesman was fired for sexually harassing a female soldier who served in his unit (Shaked, 2001).

Sexual harassment of women in the workplace occurs all over the world, but its incidence is difficult to ascertain. In Israel, where a new law took effect in 1998, 75 women filed complaints in 2000 (Shaked, 2001). In Japan, only about 20 sexual harassment suits had been filed in 1996 (Sugawara, 1996); most women seemed to suffer in silence, and complaints were resolved within the company. Although a government hotline for victims of sexual harassment received several hundred calls a year, many Japanese women had learned to tolerate and even to have mixed reactions to comments about their breasts, unwanted touches, and hugs at work. For many women office workers, employment depends on their fulfillment of the role of *shokuba no hana*—"flowers of the office." Comments about their bodies reassure them that they are still regarded as "flowers"—and that their jobs are, for the time being, secure. However, a 1999 change in labor laws making companies responsible for stopping sexual discrimination and harassment at work has apparently emboldened women. Complaints of sexual harassment rose 35 percent in that one year: The Ministry of Labor received some 9,500 reports of sexual harassment (BBC News, 2000). And recently a Tokyo police superintendent was suspended for having sexually harassed a female colleague on many occasions (Japan Today, 2004).

In the United States, the legal definition of sexual harassment involves two kinds of situations. In the first, labeled **quid pro quo harassment,** an individual is pressured to submit to unwelcome sexual advances or other unwelcome sexual conduct as a condition of employment, promotion, or raises. The second form of sexual harassment involves the creation of a **hostile environment:** making unwelcome sexual advances or engaging in other conduct of a sexual nature that unreasonably interferes with an individual's work performance or creates an intimidating, hostile, or offensive atmosphere. Both women and men can be sexually harassed, but women are the most frequent victims. One review of 18 studies of sexual harassment showed that about 42 percent of American women reported being sexually harassed at work (Gruber, 1990). A 1994 survey of federal workers found that 44 percent of women and 19 percent of men reported experiencing some form of unwanted sexual attention at work—numbers that reflect little change from a survey 15 years earlier (U.S. Merit Systems Protection Board, 1996).

The consequences of sexual harassment can include extreme stress, anxiety, depression, reduced job performance, and job loss. Noncompliance with the quid pro quo harasser or the lodging of a complaint may lead to retaliation: workloads increased, raises and promotions withheld, references jeopardized. One study found that 17.3 percent of the women and 4.8 percent of the men in their samples had quit a job because of sexual harassment (Gutek & Nakamura, 1983).

What behaviors should be classified as sexual harassment is the subject of considerable disagreement among individuals and among cultures. The Japanese businessmen interviewed by one reporter said that they thought most women would take office comments about the size of their breasts as compliments, and they were surprised that such actions were labeled harassment (Sugawara, 1996). In Brazil, where many people pride themselves on their mastery of the art of flirtation and are used to displays of physical affection, some people argue that "making sexual harassment a crime is akin to outlawing samba music" (Buckley, 2001, p. A14). In the United States, men sometimes comment that they are unsure about what behaviors toward their female colleagues at work are acceptable, and some women argue that men "just don't get it." Studies suggest that both observers and victims of sexual harassment are reluctant to conclude that it is taking place, but that they are most likely to notice and label it when the behavior seems out of role or surprising, when it is performed consistently by a particular individual, and when it occurs with more than one target person. In U.S. studies, almost everyone perceives sexual bribery, explicit propositions, unwanted touching, or pressure for sexual activity as harassment. There is more disagreement about such behaviors as sexist comments, suggestive looks, sexual jokes, and coarse language; however, these behaviors too are perceived as sexually harassing by many individuals (Frazier, Cochran, & Olson, 1995; Osman, 2004).

Some have argued that women and men perceive incidents differently as sexually harassing, and this has led to the adoption of a "reasonable woman" (as opposed to a "reasonable person") standard in U.S. courts for determining whether a work environment is hostile enough to warrant legal action. In other words, is the work environment so hostile that a reasonable woman would find it seriously uncomfortable or abusive? To date, however, researchers have found that there is little difference in the way women and men define sexual harassment (Frazier et al., 1995; Gutek & O'Connor, 1995).

Why does sexual harassment occur? John Bargh and Paula Raymond (1995) argue that the men most likely to sexually harass women have a learned association between feelings of power and sexuality. For certain men, they say,

> the idea of power has become habitually associated with the idea of sex, such that when they are in a situation in which they have power over a woman, the concept or motive of sex will become active automatically—without their intention or awareness . . . The concept of sex, once it has been activated or primed outside of awareness by its link to power, would then operate to bias interpretations of both the woman's behavior and the man's perception of her attractiveness. When these men are in a situation in which they have power over women, sexual thoughts and goals come to mind reflexively—immediately and without any conscious thought or intention to think about sex. (pp. 87, 88)

These researchers have shown that, indeed, men who score higher on a measure of likelihood to sexually harass are also more likely than other men to demonstrate an automatic mental association between power and sexuality. Such associations are doubtless fostered by cultural contexts that consistently link power with men and sexuality with women, and that tout access to sexy women as one of the "perks" of male power. This does *not* mean, however, that such men cannot control their thoughts or actions with respect to sexual harassment. Rather, they have learned a bias—one that can be unlearned if they pay attention to their own reactions and practice thinking of women as human beings and colleagues instead of prey.

Researchers Susan Fiske and Peter Glick (1995) suggest that sexual harassment stems from ambivalent attitudes and stereotypes about gender that pervade many workplaces. They note that women often encounter male coworkers whose attitudes combine two brands of sexism: hostile and benevolent. As discussed in Chapter 1, hostile sexism involves dominance-oriented paternalism, the belief that women are inferior, and contemptuous, dominance-oriented heterosexuality; benevolent sexism involves protective paternalism, the belief that women and men are different and complementary, and heterosexual intimacy motives.

Both kinds of sexism can promote harassment, albeit of different kinds. For example, a man who is motivated by benevolent sexist beliefs and heterosexual attraction may persistently shower a woman with sexual attention she does not want—but he may see his behavior not as harassment, but as seeking sexual intimacy. A man who is motivated primarily by hostile sexism may hurl sexual taunts at a female coworker or leave obscene messages in her locker—and he may see his behavior as the justified protection of male turf. Both kinds of sexist attitudes are reinforced by organizational contexts that emphasize a masculine culture in the workplace, a scarcity of information about women, power asymmetries between women and men in the workplace, and the entry of women on a one-at-a-time basis into the workforce. Each of these contextual problems can be addressed by an organization that is serious about eradicating sexual harassment.

In some countries, sexual harassment is a crime, punishable by jail time. In France, a 1991 amendment to the penal code made sexual harassment a criminal offense, calling for up to a year in prison and substantial fines for supervisors convicted of pressuring their subordinates for sexual favors. Similarly, in Israel, Mexico, Sweden, and Britain, sexual harassment is a criminal offense (Neft & Levine, 1997). In other countries, such as the United States, sexual harassment is a violation of civil rights law and can carry stiff financial penalties for employers who violate, or tolerate violation of, compliance guidelines. In Israel, sexual harassment legislation is a tapestry of criminal, civil, and labor law. A woman who has been sexually harassed can seek recourse from both the harasser and the employer—and the most severe penalties are reserved for individuals who try to injure or punish a person because she has lodged a complaint against them (Shaked, 2001). In certain countries, such as Italy, sexual harassment is not illegal, and victims have no access to remedies through the courts.

A Family-Friendly Workplace?
Striving for Work–Family Balance

When Jane Swift took over as acting governor of Massachusetts, she was pregnant with twins. Critics wondered if she would be able to fulfill her duties as governor and manage not to neglect her children. When she said that she would not take maternity leave, they discussed the propriety of her plan to continue running the state from home, and from bed if necessary, while she recovered from childbirth. Although her husband was a stay-at-home father, people had doubts about her ability to balance her family responsibility with a demanding job (C. Goldberg, 2001).

Swift faced, in a very public way, a dilemma that confronts many women more privately: how to balance family and work. An AFL-CIO survey of employed women in two-income families revealed that nearly three-quarters of them did not have access to any childcare benefits from their employers and that more than half could not get paid leave to

Even when women hold heavy responsibilities at work, they are still charged with the main responsibilities for childcare and domestic work.

care for a baby or a family member who was ill. Twenty-nine percent did not receive any paid sick leave for themselves, and 34 percent reported that their employers did not give them any flexibility or control over the hours they worked (Swoboda & Joyce, 2000). The women coped, where possible, by working different hours than their partners, so that at least one parent would be available to the children as much as possible. The survey showed that 46 percent of the women worked a different schedule than their partner. The women often felt that life was a juggling act, in which they had to be compulsively conscious of their calendars and their watches.

Work–family balance is a critical issue for everyone, but especially for women. Women are the ones who are assumed to be primarily responsible for family matters. Before Jane Swift's experience, other governors have had babies while in office, but no one thought it cause for concern. That is because in all those cases, it was the governor's spouse who was giving birth. No one worried about whether the governor could handle the family and political responsibilities—after all, he had a wife.

Childcare: A Thorny Issue

During the highly publicized "nanny trial" in Boston in 1997, in which Louise Woodward, a 19-year-old au pair from England, was accused of murder in the death of the 8-month-old baby in her care, public anger flared not just against the young nanny, but also against the child's mother, a doctor married to a doctor. Why was she not looking after her own child instead of turning him over to an inexperienced stranger? Was her career more important than her son's welfare? How could she be so self-centered? The debate was an uncomfortable reminder to many women in the United States that, in this culture, mothers are still held blameworthy for whatever happens to their children. Here, a woman risks disapproval whenever she turns the care of her children over, even part time, to anyone else. This appears to be particularly true when the woman is financially able to stay at home with her children and yet chooses to be employed. By contrast, women who are on welfare are often exhorted to find employment, regardless of the effect on their families. Irrespective of such blame or pressure, many families place their children in the care of others for part of the week. Fifty-four percent of children 3 years old and under in the United States are cared for in public or private day-care settings (Heymann, Earle, Simmons, Breslow, & Kuehnhoff, 2004).

It is not surprising, in the highly individualistic culture of the United States, that childcare is viewed as a problem to be solved by each family on its own. In America's individual-centered worldview, children are seen as the result of personal choices—and the people who made those choices are supposed to take responsibility for caring for the children. (The reality that children are not always planned or chosen does not fit comfortably into this worldview and is often ignored.) Perhaps what *is* surprising is that in this country that puts so much public emphasis on individual responsibility, only mothers, not fathers, are usually expected to take primary responsibility for their children. No one was angry at the *father* in the nanny case for not staying home with his child.

Many cultures do not share this narrow view of responsibility for childcare. They place a stronger emphasis on the *community's* responsibility for making sure children are raised and nurtured well. Japan, for example, where discrimination against employed women is rampant, paradoxically has a sophisticated, affordable day care system that many employed parents in the United States would envy. Heavily government subsidized, the system, which cares for children a few months to 6 years old, is justified not so much as a way to make life easier for employed mothers, but as an investment in the future of children. In fact, the nursery school environment has become so impressive that many parents feel it is better for their children than home. Some mothers even get fake job certificates in order to make their children eligible for what they consider to be the superior environment of nursery school (Kristof, 1995).

As noted earlier in this chapter, the United States is one of very few countries in the world that do not provide any form of paid maternity leave for employed women when their children are born (United Nations, 2000). In many countries, ranging from the developing nations of Africa such as Algeria, Cameroon, and Morocco to the developed nations of Canada, France, Poland, and Turkey, the cost of paid maternity leave for a certain number of weeks is covered by some form of government-based social insurance. In others, such as Switzerland, Malta, Botswana, Saudi Arabia, Bangladesh, and Singapore, the employer bears the cost. In still other countries, the government and the employer share the cost of paid maternity leave. The provision of paid maternity leave is one of the only formal ways that countries acknowledge that the unpaid work women do in bearing and caring for children is valuable to the society as a whole.

Whether paid maternity leave is available or not, most mothers of young children return to work after a fairly brief absence when their children are born. This raises the issue of how children will be cared for while one or both parents are at work. It is fairly recent that childcare has become something that is part of some workplaces. Some companies and institutions provide on-site day care for the young children of their employees, thus acknowledging that their employees are multidimensional people who have family as well as work responsibilities. In a variety of other ways, some workplaces have moved toward becoming family friendly.

"Best Practices" by U.S. Companies in Aid of a Comfortable Work–Family Balance

Some American companies have been innovators in family-friendly policies, operating on the assumption that their workers will be less stressed and more productive if they are given some help with "the balancing act" (Smith, 2001). For example, IBM offers a 3-year, job-protected family leave, during which company-paid benefits remain intact. Employees may also choose from a variety of flexible work schedules, including one in which they have a 2-hour lunch break to attend to personal business and one in which they may work 20 to 30 hour per week for six months. Greeting-card giant Hallmark offers 6-month unpaid maternity or paternity leave, reimbursement of up to $5,000 for the cost of adopting a child, a referral program for childcare and eldercare, and on-site activities for children during school holidays when their parents are at work. Computer software company SAS provides a free on-site childcare center staffed by specially trained and certified teachers. Fel-Pro, one of the world's largest makers of gaskets, provides a $1,000 savings bond in the child's name on the day an employee's baby is born. Employees' children are eligible for day care at the on-site childcare center, in-home caregiving if they are ill, a summer day camp at the company's own recreation area, tutoring, college counseling, and $3,000 a year toward college tuition. BE&K was the first construction company to offer childcare at a construction site. Boston's Beth Israel Hospital provides on-site day care and an earned-time program, which entitles employees to up to 34 days off per year to attend to family matters.

Companies such as those discussed here are in the minority, however. Most women are on their own when it comes to finding a job–family balance that is workable for them. The result is often a great deal of stress.

Having It All? Stress and the Double Day

In the first decades of the 20th century, higher education was associated with singlehood for women: Half the women in the United States who finished college bore no children, and almost a third did not marry (Wallich, 1996). Elsie Clews Parsons, the prominent anthropologist and folklorist whose fieldwork among Native Americans of the Southwest made her famous in the early part of this century, was one exception. Married and with several young children, she faced the problem of combining her career with a family life. Her solutions were characteristically pragmatic. She developed a work routine when she was at home that ensured her family would take her work seriously. She did her writing in a small cabin on a hill behind the family's house. Every morning she would go up to the cabin to work, coming down only to join her children for lunch. Even though she was "at home," her children soon learned that her working time was not to be interrupted (Zumwalt, 1992).

Parsons had resources that many career women with children would envy: a separate space at home where she could work undisturbed and household help to supervise her children while she was doing so. For many women lacking such resources, the combination of demands from employment and family can be extremely stressful. Yet most young women now in college in many countries want and expect to have a career as well as a family. And the majority of women in the world have virtually no choice but to work both inside and outside the home. What are the implications for women's well-being of combining family and employment roles?

Staying Busy, Staying Healthy?

The combination of family and employment roles adds up to a heavy workload for most women, and studies show that women complain of exhaustion and the stress that results when the two roles one is trying to fill impose conflicting demands (Wiersma, 1990). When it occurs, the sharing of household tasks is associated with lower levels of role strain for women, and many employed women would prefer that their husbands take on more of the domestic chores. One study of Mexican American women in dual-earner couples found that these women perceived themselves as coproviders (Herrera & DelCampo, 1995). They did not subscribe to the myth that they should be "superwomen"—able to work full time and handle all aspects of the housework and childcare.

Stress among employed women comes not only from the burden of unpaid, unrecognized domestic work added to their outside employment, but also from conditions on the job. One study of stress and coping styles among women in professional positions in India showed that the most salient stressors to them were inadequate pay, underutilization of their skills, variability in their workloads, lack of participation in decisions, and conflict between home and job. Women in the United States list similar stressors (Ghadially & Kumar, 1989).

Despite the many sources of stress and strain, combining employment and family roles can be good for women—particularly if they have support from family and friends. Studies done in the United States show that employed women appear to be happier and healthier than homemakers, except when they have infants to care for (Walker & Best, 1991), and that employed women have lower risk of heart disease than either homemakers or women unable to find steady work (Wingard, Kritz-Silverstein, & Barrett-Connor, 1992). Even adult daughters who are employed and also spending many hours per week providing long-term care to chronically ill or disabled parents experience not only stress, but also some positive benefits in terms of health (Martire & Stephens, 2003).

How can all this extra stress sometimes be associated with such positive outcomes for women? One perspective, the expansion hypothesis (Marks, 1977), suggests that people who occupy multiple roles actually expand their resources as a result: They gain an increased sense of mastery, self-esteem, identity, and the social and economic rewards of the different roles. So perhaps women gain self-esteem and satisfaction from their employment roles that translate into greater psychological well-being. Perhaps they make friends and build social networks that can help them resolve problems. Perhaps the higher income gives them access to resources such as better health care or exercise programs. Even in the exploitative sweatshops of Southeast Asia, there is some evidence that young women may glean advantages from their exhausting and stressful jobs. Employment may give them their first freedom from severe family restrictions, help them escape a poor village, offer them some discretionary income, and enable them to live more independently (Ward, 1996).

The Future of Women's Work

Recent decades have seen dramatic increases in women's participation in the paid labor force in many parts of the world. The percentage of women who were economically active in northern Africa, for instance, grew from 8 percent in 1970 to 21 percent in 1990; in the Caribbean regions it grew from 38 percent to 49 percent during that period. And women are doing more paid work. In the United States, between 1978 and 1998, the number of people "moonlighting" (holding down more than one job) increased by 3.4 million—and women accounted for 72 percent of that increase (Costello & Stone, 2001).

The situation for women has also changed with respect to the kinds of paid work they do. Women's share of administrative and managerial jobs in Western Europe went from 12 percent in 1980 to 18 percent in 1990; during the same period this share rose from 15 percent to 23 percent in Latin America. Women's wages have moved closer to men's. In Australia, for example, women in manufacturing jobs earned 57 percent of men's wages in 1970, 79 percent in 1980, and 82 percent in 1990; however, by 2000 the figure had apparently stalled, remaining at 82 percent. In Norway, the comparable percentages were 75, 82, 86, and 86 (United Nations, 1995; World Bank, 2002a).

During the same time period, legislation on a number of fronts has improved women's lot with respect to salary and working conditions. Antidiscrimination laws mandate equal pay for women and men and outlaw sexual harassment in many countries, although there is tremendous variation in the determination with which such laws are enforced.

Women have made inroads even into such traditionally male-dominated fields as the military and professional sports. Most positions in the military have been opened to women in Canada and the United States. The first woman to head an Atlantic Fleet aircraft squadron took up her command in 1992. Women finally attend two military academies that barred them for so long: Virginia Military Institute and the Citadel. There is a viable, thriving women's professional basketball league in the United States. Women have become boxers in the United States and sumo wrestlers in Japan. The 1998 Winter Olympics had the first women's hockey competition—an event that may eventually lead to support for women's professional hockey.

Admittedly, there are places where women have not been able to enter the paid workforce in large numbers. In Saudi Arabia, 25 percent of college-age women, but only 20 percent of college-age men, are enrolled in college. However, women constitute only 16 percent of the labor force (World Bank, 2002a). Nonetheless, an overview of the changes that have occurred with respect to women and work since the 1960s provides, at first glance, an impression of inexorable and inevitable progress. More women are employed, and it has become possible for even mothers of young children to maintain paid employment. Women have gained access to a wider range of jobs and to higher levels of advancement. Day care centers and maternity leave, affirmative action programs that reach out to pull women into nontraditional jobs, and laws against gender-based discrimination and sexual harassment all make employment for women more likely. Surely it is just a matter of time before women reach equality with men in the workplace?

There are reasons to doubt this optimistic assessment, however. Perhaps one of the most dramatic counterexamples to women's progress in the workplace is the experience of women in the changing economies of Eastern Europe. As Eastern European countries moved away from Communism and embraced capitalism, women lost any real assurance of equitable access to job opportunities, promotions, and salary increases. They also lost many of the benefits that used to make labor force participation possible for them: maternity leave, day care for their children, health benefits. In these countries, women's employment has tended to stagnate or decrease in recent years, while it increases in the rest of the world.

The ease with which such an elaborate system of guaranteed workplace equity for women can be undone, apparently scrapped with some relief, by male politicians suggests that progress for women in the workplace is far from inevitable. Indeed, the world scene provides us with other signs that women's progress will be supported and encouraged only up to the point where it becomes inconvenient for men or for the political system in power. The sudden removal of the right to work from the women of Afghanistan, described at the beginning of this chapter, is another example. Yet a third may be the 1995 ruling by the European Court of Justice declaring Germany's affirmative action legislation to be in violation of the European Union's equal opportunity law because under some circumstances (i.e., where women were underrepresented in jobs), it gave women priority to be hired over men.

Laws do not have to be changed for women's progress to be stopped, however. There are many subtle ways of holding women back while appearing to give them equal opportunity. The very necessity for women to do more than their share of unpaid domestic work drains their time and energy in ways that make it difficult for them to give the attention to their jobs that might lead to more rapid advancement—and simultaneously frees men to do just that. Stereotypes of women as being unsuited for the aggressive style of behavior expected in certain top-level jobs cause them to be overlooked for promotion, even when their credentials are exemplary. Token women are used by organizations to "prove" that positions are open to women—while often simultaneously being made the targets of resentment and resistance. The barriers against women have become a little more permeable and a lot less obvious, but many apparently still remain.

Given such barriers, it becomes less surprising to find that although women have entered the labor force in general and jobs that used to be off-limits to women in particular, they are still often clustered at the lower end of the pay and status hierarchy at work (see Table 8.3). For example, a study of female university faculty in the United States—aptly titled *Women Faculty: Frozen in Time*—shows that their share of the highest-level faculty positions has changed little over the years. In 1975, 46 percent of women full-time faculty members had tenure; in 1992, the percentage was still 46 percent. In 1982,

TABLE 8.3   Median Annual Income of U.S. Men and Women by Level of Education in 2000

Education Completed	Women	Men
Less than 9th grade	$15,978	$20,789
High school	24,970	34,303
Associate degree	31,071	41,952
Bachelor's degree	40,415	56,334
Master's degree	50,139	68,322
Professional degree	58,957	99,411
Doctorate	57,081	80,250

Source: (U.S. Department of Education (2003), Table 381. Statistics are for year-round full-time workers aged 25 years and over.)

women who were at the rank of full professor earned 89 percent what male full professors earned; in 1995, women full professors earned 88.5 percent what their male colleagues earned. In 1982, 27 percent of all faculty were women, although women obtained 35 percent of Ph.D.s; in 1994, 31 percent of all faculty were women—although by that time women were earning 47 percent of all Ph.D.s (West, 1995). A more recent study by the American Association of University Professors (2003) shows that women faculty are still "frozen": women at the rank of full professor earn 88.4 percent of what their male colleagues do.

So what is the future of women and work? Clearly it will depend on the social and political context within which they labor. But even in the most favorable contexts that now exist—those countries where gender-based discrimination is forbidden and at least lip service is paid to the idea that women can do anything—women are not even *close* to equality in the workplace. Equality may be in women's future, but not the near future.

SUMMARY

Women work more hours than men all over the world, primarily because women do a greater share than men of unpaid work. Two-thirds to three-quarters of domestic work is done by women. With respect to paid employment, there is considerable occupational segregation; women and men are concentrated in different jobs. Thus, for example, women hold most of the positions as secretaries and nurses. However, the notions of "women's work" and "men's work" are in flux in many places. In many countries, women's share of managerial positions has increased significantly in recent years. Women have shown much smaller increases in their share of some other kinds of nontraditional jobs, however, notably those in trades.

Women often face inequities and discrimination in the workplace. Women earn less than men all over the world and are often overlooked for raises and promotions. A "glass ceiling" seems to block women from the highest positions. Discrimination takes the form of undervaluing work done by women, making unjustified assumptions about women's values, making the workplace difficult for women who are mothers, assuming that women belong in the home and are not as entitled as men to good jobs with good salaries, and defining as "women's work" many low-paid jobs with poor working conditions. Many women also suffer discrimination on the basis of sexual orientation.

Some remedies have been offered to address these issues. Employers are urged to be aware of and put policies in place to resist the tendency toward gender stereotyping. Laws have been passed mandating pay equity, which may include both equal pay for equivalent work, or comparable worth, which is equal pay for work of equal value. Many employers use systems of job evaluation in order to compare jobs, so that those filled mainly by women are not compensated differently than those filled mainly by men. In the United States and many other countries, there are legal mandates for affirmative action, actions taken to combat the underrepresentation of women and minorities in certain jobs and workplaces.

Affirmative action is sometimes viewed with uneasiness. People, even those who benefit from affirmative action, tend to be most in favor of efforts to get rid of discrimination, and least in favor of more active strategies such as preferential hiring. Research suggests that women who know they have been chosen for a position as a result of preferential hiring on the basis of their gender, or who believe that those around them think that is how they got their position, feel uncomfortable and expect others to have low expectations of them. This is particularly likely if the women are unsure of their abilities to begin with. Yet there is also evidence that women become impatient with less active forms of affirmative action if they do not seem to be having any impact after a reasonable time, and they become more supportive of a variety of approaches.

Sexual harassment is a significant problem for women in the workplace. Consequences of being harassed may include stress, anxiety, depression, reduced job performance, and job loss. There is some disagreement about what behavior constitutes sexual harassment. In the United States, most people surveyed perceive sexual bribery, explicit propositions, unwanted touching, or pressure for sexual activity as harassment. There is more disagreement about such behaviors as sexist comments, suggestive looks, sexual jokes, and coarse language; however, these behaviors too are perceived as sexually harassing by many individuals. In other cultures, there may be more disagreement about the latter behaviors. A variety of legal remedies have been enacted to combat harassment. In some countries, such as the United States, it is a civil matter, but some countries treat sexual harassment as a crime punishable by jail time.

Work–family balance is a critical issue for everyone, but especially for women because women are the ones who are assumed to be primarily responsible for family matters. The balance becomes particularly difficult when women have children. In some countries, such as the United States, there is a tendency to treat children as the responsibility of individual parents; other countries, such as Japan, tend to assume that children are in some respects a community responsibility. Most countries in the world have laws that provide employed women with paid maternity leave when they bear children. However, the United States has no such law. Some U.S. companies have, however, developed family-friendly policies that help parents combine their family and job responsibilities. Such policies have an important function in reducing stress, which can be very high among women trying to juggle job and family duties.

Women complain of exhaustion and the stress that results when family and job roles impose conflicting demands. Sharing of household tasks is associated with lower levels of role strain for women, and many employed women would prefer that their husbands take on more of the domestic chores. Combining employment and family roles can actually be good for women—particularly if they have support from family and friends. Studies done in the United States show that employed women are often happier and healthier than homemakers.

The future of women and work is far from assured. Although women have joined the workplace in unprecedented numbers in the last three decades, and although there is an increasing number of legal protections against discrimination and sexual harassment, women have made slow progress in terms of pay equity and making inroads into some kinds of jobs. There are also signs that women's progress can be lost as quickly as it was gained. It is unlikely that women can look forward to equality with men at work as long as inequities persist in the more general treatment of and expectations for women and men.

KEY TERMS

glass ceiling
hierarchy-enhancing values
hierarchy-attenuating values
pay equity
affirmative action

comparable worth
personal relative deprivation
collective relative
  deprivation
sexual harassment

quid pro quo harassment
hostile environment

DISCUSSION QUESTIONS

Women work more hours than men because they do so much of the unpaid work. How could the division of unpaid work be made more equitable between women and men? What factors discourage such changes?

Why do you think there is disagreement about what behaviors constitute sexual harassment?

Why is affirmative action so controversial? Try to imagine an affirmative action program that everyone would accept.

FOR ADDITIONAL READING

Grossman, Hildreth, & Chester, Nia L. (Eds.). (1990). *The experience and meaning of work in women's lives.* Hillsdale, NJ: Erlbaum. This anthology contains accounts of women in a variety of occupations, from psychotherapists to secretaries.

Hess-Biber, Sharlene J., & Carter, Gregg L. (1999). *Working women in America: Split dreams.* This book offers a broad perspective on the diversity of women and their work in the United States, and it places women's work in historical and economic context.

Kung, Lydia. (1994). *Factory women in Taiwan.* New York: Columbia University Press. Kung tells the stories of these women, whose work is so often invisible.

Tucker, Susan. (1988). *Telling memories among Southern women domestics.* Baton Rouge: Louisiana State University Press. An oral history of one group of U.S. women who were household workers.

Zappert, Laraine T. (2001). *Getting it right: How working mothers successfully take up the challenge of life, family, and career.* New York: Simon & Schuster. To gather material for this book, the author, a clinical psychologist and working mother, interviewed 300 Stanford Business School graduates who are now working mothers. While this sample is certainly not representative of all, or even most, working mothers, some of the insights about how to juggle family and employment are practical and useful.

WEB RESOURCES

Sloan Work and Family Research Network. The site contains a newsletter, a searchable database of literature on work–family issues, and dozens of links to other useful sites. **www.bc.edu/bc_org/avp/wfnetwork**

Gender Program of the International Labor Office. This office works on important issues with respect to women and work all over the world. The site provides access to some of the ILO publications and news releases, and links to other sites. **www.ilo.org/bureau/gender**

National Committee on Pay Equity. This committee represents a collaboration among interested individuals and nonprofit, civil rights, and religious groups that are interested in promoting pay equity. The site contains detailed information about the history of equal pay legislation in the United States, current legislation, the status of the gender wage gap, and links to salary survey sites where people can compare their salaries to those of others in the same jobs. **www.pay-equity.org**

CHAPTER 9

*Physical Health, Illness,
and Healing*

CHAPTER OUTLINE

Women's Strength and Fitness

Women and Physical Illness around the World
> **Life Expectancy**
> **Some Major Health Problems for Women**

Factors Related to Women's Health
> **Health- and Illness-Related Behaviors**
> **Poverty and Nutrition**
> **Stress and Social Support**

Women as Patients in Health Care Systems

Women as Healers

In 1993, the first Islamic Women's Games opened in Iran to the spectacle of an 18-year-old Iranian runner, Padideh Bolourizadeh, loping into the arena carrying a torch proudly above her hooded head. As 10,000 onlookers cheered, she ran around the track wearing the world's first combination tracksuit-*hijab:* a suit that covered her from head to toe, allowing not even a wisp of hair to be seen by spectators (Brooks, 1995).

The very occurrence of these games represented an acknowledgment by the Muslim government of Iran that it was important for women to develop their health and fitness through exercise. This acknowledgment did not come without a struggle: Iranian women activists had to quote Muhammad's recommendation that Muslims should have strong bodies and that they should excel in all respects—and then argue that the Prophet had included women as well as men in these recommendations. They had to reclaim time at sports facilities that had been handed over to men after the 1979 revolution by arguing that women, as the heart of the Islamic family, needed sports to become strong and healthy. They had to insist that Western countries would use Muslim women's absence from sports as proof that Islamic countries treated women poorly. Their arguments eventually led to more emphasis on sports in girls' schools, opening certain sports facilities for "women's hours," and banning men from Tehran's Runners' Park 3 days a week so that women could jog without wearing the cumbersome *hijab*. Ultimately, they led to the Islamic Women's Games, in which women's teams from a variety of Muslim countries competed before boisterous all-female crowds.

The Iranian case is only one of many in which the importance of fitness and health for women has had to be argued instead of assumed, and in which women have had to fight for access to health-related resources ranging from sports facilities to proper nutrition to good medical care. All over the world, women face health concerns and suffer health problems different from those of men, not only because of biological differences but because of unequal access to the resources that facilitate good health. These issues of fitness and health have implications well beyond women's physical experiences of feeling well or feeling ill. They are relevant to women's feelings of self-esteem and self-efficacy, the accomplishments they can envision and actualize, their family relationships, and the ways they plan and live their lives.

This chapter focuses on women's physical health and illness, and on women's involvement in the healing process. We begin by examining issues related to women's strength and fitness. Next, we turn to the worldwide data on women's illnesses and life expectancy. This information leads to an examination of research into particular health concerns such as anemia, autoimmune diseases, tropical diseases, reproductive health, heart disease, osteoporosis, cancer, and Alzheimer's disease. Certain specific issues in women's health are examined next: health-related behaviors, stress, and caregiver burdens. Finally, we look at women's status as patients and their roles as healers in various health care systems.

Women's Strength and Fitness

Women are no strangers to heavy physical work. In Nepal, female sherpas carry heavy packs up steep mountain paths in oxygen-thin air, often using straps around their foreheads to secure the weight. Researchers in a University of Nairobi laboratory found that a Kenyan woman who is accustomed to the task can easily carry on her head a load that is equal to two-thirds her body weight (Maloiy, Heglund, Prager, Cavagna, & Taylor, 1986). Women in such traditionally female jobs as waiting on tables and childcare repeatedly lift and carry heavy loads, and they must have the stamina to keep doing it for hours on end. Yet women are often characterized as weak.

In truth, women have plenty of potential to be physically strong, but sometimes cultural forces have not encouraged them to develop their strength. Some cultures have equated feminine attractiveness with frailty, historically carrying the notion to such ridiculous extremes that a sickly pallor was considered beautiful and a tendency to faint was a demonstration of proper feminine delicacy. As noted in Chapter 1, the ancient Chinese tradition of foot-binding literally hobbled women, forcing them to take tiny steps or to be carried in order to conform to the idea of women's fragility. Women in many places still acquiesce to the notion that ease of movement must be sacrificed in the service of feminine beauty, cramming their feet into too-small, pointy-toed, high-heeled shoes that throw them off balance, shorten their tendons, and put them at risk of back injuries and twisted ankles in order to create the illusion that their feet are small and dainty and their legs long and slender.

Although extreme notions of feminine weakness no longer prevail in most places, many forces militate against proper strength and fitness for women. One of those forces has been the pressure for female modesty of dress. We noted at the beginning of this chapter how this pressure has restricted (and continues to restrict) women in some Islamic countries from participation in active sports. Women in many other countries as well have, in the past at least, chafed under similar restrictions. In 1894, the American feminist Amelia Bloomer advocated the garment that bears her name—full, loose trousers gathered at the ankles or knees—to free women from the inconvenience of long skirts while engaged in athletic activities such as bicycling. Up to, and in some cases into, the 20th century, women went horseback riding and ice-skated in long skirts, and swam in bloomers and long stockings. Not only did this take some of the joy and freedom of movement out of the activity, it also made women awkward and vulnerable to tripping and falling (or sinking)!

Women are often characterized as weak, and in many cultures they are discouraged from developing their strength. Women who are accustomed to the task, however, can carry very heavy loads.

Consider, for example, the tradition of the sidesaddle, supposedly invented by Catherine de Medici to improve on the previous method of horseback riding for women, which involved simply sitting precariously sideways on a conventional saddle (Brownmiller, 1984). A woman using a sidesaddle put her left leg in an ordinary stirrup, then swung her right leg over and hooked it onto a pommel on the left side of the saddle. In this way, both legs were kept modestly close together and covered by a skirt. Then the woman had to compensate for the lopsided distribution of her weight and also twist her torso to face forward, causing considerable extra strain on her muscles. Not surprisingly, women riders forced to use this type of saddle tired more quickly than men—thus preserving the myth of feminine frailty.

Women have also been kept from developing their strength by cultural and safety issues that have restricted their opportunities for even leaving the house alone. Women in some Muslim countries are virtually confined to their homes unless accompanied by male relatives. No such law bans women from moving about without men in North America, yet women are often fearful of going out alone, particularly at night, because they feel they are potential targets of assailants. In many places, a woman who simply feels like going for a walk or a jog will find herself unable or unwilling to do so without male company (even though the protection afforded by a male companion may sometimes be more illusory than real). This creates a vicious circle: Women fear to go out alone because they feel unable to protect themselves, and by staying in they lose the opportunity to become stronger.

Some intrepid women, like Amelia Edwards, who was mentioned in Chapter 1, have always found ways to transgress the rules and customs that keep women "safe at home." Isabella Bird, another upper-class Englishwoman, disguised herself as a man to travel through North Africa at the end of the 19th century, and in the second half of the 20th century British adventurer Sarah Hobson used the same strategy to journey to remote parts of Iran. Indeed, wealthy women in the Victorian age often flouted custom in order to travel on their own to remote parts of the world. As English travel writer Mabel Sharman Crawford wrote in 1863, "[I]f the exploring of foreign lands is not the highest end or the most useful occupation of feminine existence, it is at least more improving, as well as more amusing, than the crochet-work or embroidery with which, at home, so many ladies seek to beguile the tedium of their unoccupied days" (quoted in Morris, 1993, p. 44).

The tradition of adventurous women continues, although today's female voyagers are not likely to be escaping enforced crochet-work. For instance, 45-year-old Ann Bancroft and 47-year-old Liv Arneson recently became the first women to cross the Antarctic land mass on skis. This journey required that each of the two women pull a 240-pound sled across more than 2,000 miles of snow and ice. Fighting injury, fatigue, equipment failure, and, of course, subzero temperatures, these two former schoolteachers made the more than 3-month long journey with schoolchildren from five continents following them on the Internet (Glass, 2001).

Closer to home, women have benefited from explicit attempts to make athletic training and facilities available to women. Several decades ago, inequities between women's and men's athletic opportunities in the educational institutions of the United States were overwhelming. For example, in 1975 the women's athletic program at the University of Texas boasted a budget of $58,000 for nine sports; the budget for the men's athletic program in the same year was $2.2 million. Male athletes ate at the elite Longhorn Dining Hall; the hall was closed to female athletes. Ninety-four percent of male varsity athletes were on athletic scholarships; 6 percent of female athletes were (Shipley, 1997). Much greater gender equity exists today as a result of federal legislation known as **Title IX,** the 1972 law that bars sex discrimination in educational programs receiving government financial assistance. In 1972, when Title IX was passed, only 15 percent of college athletes and 7.5 percent of high school athletes were women. In 2001, women made up 43 percent of athletes in college and 41.5 percent in high school (National Coalition of Women and Girls in Education, 2002). As a result of the changes, young women are far more likely now than they were 30 years ago to participate formally in sports—and to aim for college athletic scholarships. Nonetheless, change is slow; women and girls still do not have an equal share of opportunities in competitive sports. For example, although girls and women made up 54 percent of students at four-year colleges, only 23 percent of Division I NCAA colleges came close (within 5 percentage points) to providing female students with opportunities at the same level as their enrollment (National Council of Girls and Women in Education, 2002).

Some of the more stereotypically feminine sports in which girls and women participate place a heavy emphasis on physical appearance; for instance, gymnastics, synchronized swimming, and cheerleading have this emphasis. Girls who participate in these sports get many benefits of exercise and recognition; however, they may also be vulnerable to concerns about their physical appearance (Parsons & Betz, 2001). One of the interesting effects of Title IX is that girls and women are now playing not just these "feminine" sports, but also the "masculine" sports that were formerly off-limits to them. The number of female high school athletes in the United States participating in wrestling increased from 1,629 in 1996 to 2,361 in 1998, while the number of female participants in high school hockey rose from 2,586 to 3,545 (Thomas, 1999). Currently about 4,000 girls wrestle at the high school level, and female wrestling has been included as an Olympic event since 2004 (Burch, 2003). Occasionally, as was the case with Kathy Aldridge of Patrick County High School in Virginia, a homecoming queen accepts her crown while still wearing her muddy football uniform (Female football player for PCHS crowned homecoming queen, 2000). Girls who engage in "masculine" sports find their participation rewarding in many ways. As one female member of her high school's mixed-sex wrestling team commented,

> When I signed up I was terrified. I did it because it was the opposite of what was expected of me —the scrawny girl who barely tipped the scales at 100 pounds in ninth grade. . . . I barely had anything resembling muscle on me when I started and now I am able to flex my arms proudly. . . . I now feel more able to take chances. I no longer rely on the opinions of others to lead my life and make my decisions. I am a wrestler. (Perlmutter, 1999, p. 20)

Girls' participation in mixed-sex sports teams may be helping to change male attitudes toward partnership with females. For instance, one high school wrestler says that her male teammates have been her friends and supporters, and she recounts that when the parents and principal of another school refused to allow their all-male team to compete against the girls on her team, her whole team withdrew from the tournament: "If they were going to be so close-minded, then they didn't deserve to be in our gym. . . . We are all a unified front. We are a team" (quoted in Thomas, 1999, p. 2C). In a similar vein, one girl remembers her first tackle as a football player: "It was freshman year, and it felt really good. My team was really, really proud of me. I can't even describe it, but it was the best moment!" (quoted in Thomas, 1999, p. 2C).

When women do exercise, they quickly become more fit, stronger, and more muscular. Researchers found that in response to the same short-term weight-training program, women and men achieved similar increases in muscle size, and women made greater relative gains in strength (O'Hagen, Sale, MacDougall, & Garner, 1995). And when women train vigorously, as in preparation for athletic competition, they can sometimes turn in performances that rival or surpass those of elite male athletes—particularly if the event in question requires endurance as well as strength. For example, in 1988 Paula Newby-Fraser won the women's division of the Ironman Triathlon with a time that placed her ahead of all but 10 of the hundreds of male contestants, and in 1989 ultramarathoner Ann Trason won the mixed-sex TAC/USA 24-hour race in New York City. In 1995, Trason completed the Leadville 100-mile running race in second place, only 6 minutes behind the first-place man (Maffetone, 2000). In 2000, the women's division of Triathlon USA was won by Melissa Spooner, whose time beat all but 18 of the male professional contestants and even the fastest of the male amateur contestants aged 18 to 24. In endurance swimming as well, women have been very successful. Alison Streeter, known in swimming circles as "Queen of the Channel," holds the record for the fastest swim of the 18-mile North Channel that separates Ireland and Scotland—and has also swum the formidable English Channel more times (40) than anyone else. And Susie Maroney, a marathon swimmer from Australia, broke world distance records when she swam 128 miles from Isla Mujeres to Las Tumbas, Cuba, in 1997.

It is apparent that gender-related expectations have contributed not only to the stereotype that women are weak, but also to the self-fulfilling prophecy inherent in that stereotype. Women in many parts of the world are expected to perform heavy work, yet they are ignored when resources are allocated for facilities and programs related to physical fitness. Women are often expected to prize their modesty above their strength and health, making it difficult and inconvenient to engage in most forms of exercise. In countries where modesty is less of an issue, safety remains a problem for women who want to venture beyond the confines of the gym or the track to get their exercise. For example, female joggers, walkers, and cyclists may be harassed, intimidated, or physically attacked when they traverse public parks or make their route along public streets, even in the daytime. Thus a variety of barriers may keep women from taking the steps necessary to develop their strength.

If building muscles were the only reason for women to exercise, the barriers discussed here would not be so serious. However, regular exercise appears to be critical to women's health in a number of ways: Among young women it builds the bone density necessary to stave off osteoporosis in later years, it is linked to a reduced risk of breast cancer and heart disease, and it promotes increased feelings of self-efficacy (President's Council on Physical Fitness and Sport, 1997). Girls' sports participation is correlated with self-reports of internal locus of control, instrumentality, and personal efficacy (Parsons & Betz, 2001). In older women, exercise can reduce blood pressure and heart rate, thus reducing the risk of heart attack and stroke (Byrne, 2000; Lemmer, et al., 2001). Ironically, it is in the developed countries, where women are likely to live long enough to suffer from such ailments as **osteoporosis,** cancer, and heart disease, that women are most likely to lead relatively sedentary lives that make them vulnerable to these diseases.

Women and Physical Illness around the World

Life Expectancy

Women all over the world live longer than men: almost 14 years longer in Russia, more than 5 years longer in Canada, the United States, and Mexico, and less than 3 years longer in some African countries such as Ethiopia and Somalia (World Health Organization, 2003). Women have a **life expectancy** of 80 years or more in developed countries such as Australia, Japan, Canada, Italy, and Sweden, whereas no country has achieved an 80-year life expectancy for men.

Why do women usually live longer than men? One reason is that more males than females suffer from physical problems that are present from the very beginning of their lives. Males infants are more likely than females to suffer from congenital malformations and from various genetically transmitted diseases. Males are also more likely than females to die from birth-related injuries and in the first year of life (United Nations, 2000). A second reason is that, especially during adolescence and young adulthood, males are more likely than females to die as a result of accidents or violence—a difference that may be linked to cultural expectations tying masculinity to risk taking and aggression. In the United States, the **age-adjusted death rate** from unintentional injuries is about 3 times higher for African American and Latino males than for females in those groups. For European Americans, Asian Pacific islanders and American Indian and Alaskan natives, the injury death rate is twice as high for males as for females (National Center for Health Statistics, 2004). Across the lifespan, the death rate for homicide, suicide, and accidents is higher for males than females: There are 4.15 male deaths by suicide, 3.27 male deaths by homicide, and 2.3 male deaths by accident for every female death by these causes (National Center for Health Statistics, 2004). Third, men are more vulnerable to death from a host of diseases. Even during adolescence, American males are 1.3 times more likely than females to die of natural causes (National Center for Health Statistics, 2000), and for each of the 15 leading causes of death except Alzheimer's disease, the age-adjusted death rate for males is higher than the rate for females (Murphy, 2000). Men's greater likelihood of dying early from disease may be linked in part to their tendency to seek less medical care than women, as discussed later in this chapter. Finally, some have argued that, for reasons that are not altogether clear, women survive better than men under conditions of starvation, exposure, fatigue, and shock (Montagu, 1968). This difference may be partly due to women's greater percentage of body fat (Angier, 1999). Thus, for a complex set of reasons, women tend to outnumber men beginning early in adulthood, and the gap increases with age. Among the elderly, there are many times more women than men.

Life expectancy is linked to such factors as poverty, nutrition, and the availability of good medical care. Where resources are in short supply, both women and men live shorter lives. In many developing countries, women's life expectancy is well under 70 years. In 40 countries in sub-Saharan Africa (e.g., Angola, Mali, Sierra Leone) and Asia (e.g., Afghanistan, Cambodia), life expectancy for women is less than 50 years (World Health Organization, 2003). In Canada, a country where access to medical care is generally good, indigenous women, who are more likely than the average Canadian woman to experience poverty and undernutrition and to live far from good medical care, had a life expectancy 4.8 years shorter than the female average in 1996 (Health Canada, 2002).

The female–male gap in life expectancy is reversed by the different treatment afforded to female and male children in some cultures. In a few countries (e.g., Nepal, Bangladesh, Maldives, Pakistan, Kuwait), men's life expectancy is *higher than* or equal to that of women—an outcome that has been linked to the low cultural value placed on females (World Health Organization, 2003). Boys are given better care (such as nutrition and medical treatment) than girls. As conditions improve in many developing regions, however, women's life expectancy has increased more than men's.

Some Major Health Problems for Women

Historically, medical research on women's health problems has been scant. Women were often left out of studies because researchers were concerned that their cyclic hormonal changes would blur the results of drug tests or that they would become pregnant during the clinical trials. The research that *was* done tended to concentrate on women's reproductive systems, ignoring other health problems such as heart disease and cancer. Furthermore, ethnic minority women have often been left out of medical research. To rectify this situation, the National Institutes of Health in the United States launched the **Women's Health Initiative,** a 15-year set of studies involving 164,500 women ages 50–79 from diverse populations. This study, which the researchers state is the largest and most ambitious study of women's health ever conducted anywhere in the world, began enrolling participants in

1996. It focuses on the prevention of heart disease, breast and colorectal cancer, and osteoporosis in postmenopausal women (Matthews et al., 1997). Since older women are the fastest-growing segment of the population in the United States and in many other developed countries, attention to these diseases, which are the leading causes of death, disability, and frailty for these women, is of critical importance. Data from this study are starting to come in, and researchers are already putting together information showing that behavioral and lifestyle factors are significant in the prevention of these problems.

In developing countries, women have shorter life expectancies. The health problems that plague women in these countries are less likely to be heart disease and cancer (because women may not live long enough to experience these problems) and more likely to involve illnesses that stem from malnutrition, contaminated water, and sexual and reproductive issues. The latter problems are by no means foreign to women in developed countries, however. Sexually transmitted diseases are epidemic in most developed as well as developing countries, for example (United Nations, 2000), and almost 20 percent of pregnant women in the United States suffer from anemia.

Clearly, an overview of women's health problems must cover a wide range. The sections that follow will focus on the major problems, beginning with those that afflict chiefly younger women and ending with those that are most often experienced by older women.

Anemia   Anemia, a deficiency of red blood cells or hemoglobin, often results from inadequate nutrition, particularly a lack of iron in the diet. Although easily treated with oral iron supplements, iron-deficiency anemia is currently the most common micronutrient deficiency in the world (Population Action International, 2003). In all parts of the world, anemia is more common among women than men, and more common among pregnant than nonpregnant women. The symptoms include weakness and fatigue, which cause difficulty in working and learning and a reduced ability to tolerate hemorrhages such as those that may occur during childbirth or abortion.

South Asian women suffer the highest rates of anemia in the world: 58 percent overall and 75 percent during pregnancy (United Nations, 1995). In general, the high rates among developing countries can be attributed to poverty and lack of adequate nutrition. But even in developed countries, an average of 18 percent of pregnant women are anemic. The differences in the rate of anemia that occur among developed countries (e.g., 20 percent in the United States, 8 percent in Denmark) suggest that "anaemia is not an inevitable condition of pregnancy, but a symptom of inadequate support of women's reproductive health" (United Nations, 1995, p. 73).

Autoimmune Diseases   Women are more likely than men to suffer from autoimmune diseases, such as arthritis, lupus, and multiple sclerosis, in which the body literally attacks its own tissues. The higher prevalence among women ranges from a high of 10 to 15 women for every man with systemic lupus to 4 women to every man with rheumatoid arthritis (Lahita, 1996). In the United States, lupus is 3 times more prevalent among Black women than among White women. Black women make up 60 percent of lupus patients, and their survival rate is lower than that of White patients (Blumenthal, 1997).

Most often, autoimmune diseases strike young women sometime after puberty, causing a multitude of symptoms. In multiple sclerosis, for example, the body seems to attack the myelin in the brain and spinal cord, producing areas of scarring and inflammation. The result is a disruption in nerve communication, which can result in weakness, impaired motion, blindness, and other symptoms. This disease attacks mainly women between the ages of 30 and 50 and is most prevalent in Canada, the United States, South America, and Europe. It is virtually unknown near the equator (MS Foundation, 1997).

Reasons for the higher prevalence of such diseases among women are unknown, although researchers suspect a hormonal link. They note that the symptoms sometimes vary with the menstrual cycle and change in severity during pregnancy (Lahita, 1996). The mechanisms through which hormones might affect these diseases are not understood, however.

Tropical Diseases   In some developing countries, tropical diseases such as malaria, schistosomiasis, and leprosy are serious problems. Because of a lack of research, it is not known whether women differ from men in the likelihood of contracting such diseases. However, there are some particular consequences for women in terms of reproductive health. Malaria, for example, may lead to **maternal mortality,** spontaneous abortion, and stillbirth (United Nations, 2000). Studies show that significant gender differences occur in the quality of health care women and men with tropical diseases receive. For example, in Thailand women are less likely than men to attend malaria clinics, perhaps because their families place a low premium on their health. And in India women with leprosy are more likely than men to be asked to leave their homes and to be isolated from their families (United Nations, 1995). Not surprisingly, then, women who develop symptoms of disfiguring diseases such as leprosy may delay seeking care because of the stigma and shame that will result (United Nations, 2000).

Tuberculosis   Tuberculosis, a highly infectious disease of the bronchial system, is now a leading cause of death for young women in many parts of the world (United Nations, 2000). This disease disproportionately affects poorer and younger people. At this time, the majority of deaths are in Asia; however, the highly infectious nature of the disease makes it a potential problem worldwide. Women's lower levels of access to medical care in countries where tuberculosis is prevalent contribute to the problem. In addition, research indicates that women who are in their reproductive years may experience a faster progression from being infected with tuberculosis to developing the disease and that the disease is more likely to be fatal for young women than for young men (Holmes, Hausler, & Nunn, 1998).

Reproductive Health   According to the World Health Organization, more than half a million women die each year because of inadequate reproductive care. The risks vary according to region and economic development. For instance, an African woman faces a lifetime risk of 1 in 16 of dying from a pregnancy-related cause; a European woman's risk is 1 in 1,400 (United Nations, 2000). Maternal mortality is currently decreasing in most of Latin America and Asia, but it is increasing in some countries, notably in Albania, Romania, and some Central Asian countries of the former Soviet Union, where good reproductive care has become a diminishing resource.

What causes most maternal deaths? Hemorrhage, infection, botched abortions, hypertension, and obstructed labor are the most common specific causes. Many of these problems result directly from the low priority given to women's health care (e.g., lack of access to prenatal care or to emergency care to manage complications) and from societal restrictions placed on women (e.g., the lack of access to safe abortions). Worldwide, approximately 19 million unsafe abortions take place each year: Approximately 1 in 10 pregnancies is ended by an unsafe abortion. Each year an estimated 68,000 women die as a consequence of unsafe abortion (World Health Organization, 2004). According to the United Nations (2000), unsafe abortions account for up to one-fourth of all maternal deaths in the Central Asian countries where maternal mortality is rising. In regions such as Latin America, where unsafe abortions are common, deaths from such abortions also represent almost one-fourth of maternal mortality. Obstructed labor, which accounts for about 7 percent of maternal deaths, is often traceable to forms of female genital mutilation in which the vaginal opening has been sewn to make it smaller. Women pay for these societal choices with their lives.

Many women may choose to limit their pregnancies by using contraception. This choice too has disadvantages. Health concerns and side effects (such as menstrual irregularities, pain from uterine contractions, headache) are the most common reasons women discontinue using oral contraceptives. In fact, such concerns are listed much more often than other factors, such as lack of availability, social pressure, husband disapproval, or religious beliefs, by women who stop using contraception (United Nations, 1995). These concerns are often not life-threatening, but they can make life miserable for some women, interfering with their sense of well-being and their ability to function comfortably in their many tasks. Yet such symptoms are often dismissed as unimportant by health care workers.

Sexually Transmitted Infections   Around the world, women have a greater risk than men of becoming infected with **sexually transmitted infections (STIs),** which can lead to cervical cancer. They are also at higher risk of contracting **human immunodeficiency virus (HIV),** the virus that leads to **acquired immune deficiency syndrome (AIDS)** (United Nations, 2000). STIs, which include such infections as gonorrhea, chlamydia, and trichomoniasis, are most prevalent among women in Africa, followed by Asia and Latin America. In developing countries, certain of these infections are particularly prevalent among pregnant women. For example, 44 percent of pregnant women in El Salvador tested positive for chlamydia in 1991, as did 50 percent of pregnant women in Botswana in 1990 (United Nations, 2000). But STIs are a serious problem for women in developed countries as well. In Canada, for example, women account for about 75 percent of all reported cases of chlamydia and women in the 15- to 19-year-old age group contract gonorrhea at a rate of more than 80 cases per 100,000 women (Health Canada, 2000). In women, these diseases often do not display obvious symptoms, and thus they are difficult to detect and treat. Yet the health consequences of these diseases are more serious for women than for men. Possible complications include pelvic inflammatory disease, infertility, pelvic pain, and ectopic (outside the uterus) pregnancy.

HIV is transmitted through blood or semen, often by carriers who have no symptoms themselves. It is passed from person to person through sexual contact, blood transfusions, and the use of contaminated hypodermic needles, and from infected nursing mothers to

---

BOX 9.1 MAKING CHANGE
Organizing to Observe World AIDS Day

Women are the fastest-growing group of people with AIDS. World AIDS Day was conceived and adopted unanimously by 140 countries meeting at the World Summit of Ministers of Health on AIDS in London in January 1988. The observance of World AIDS Day is viewed as an opportunity for governments, national AIDS programs, nongovernmental and local organizations, and individuals everywhere to demonstrate both the importance they attached to the fight against AIDS and their solidarity in this effort. What is your campus doing to observe World AIDS Day, which usually falls on December 1st? To join in this worldwide observance, organize a speaker, a teach-in, or a fundraiser for the United Nations' *Global AIDS and Health Fund.* For more information, log on to **www.unaids.org**.

---

their infants. During heterosexual contact, the virus is up to 17 times more likely to be transmitted from a man to a woman than vice versa (Padian, Shiboski, & Jewell, 1991). Perhaps partly for this reason, women are the fastest-growing category of people living with HIV/AIDS in all parts of the world. They account for about 50 percent of cases worldwide—up from 41 percent in 1997. In Africa, 58 percent of the 22.3 million cases are estimated to be women (World Health Organization, 2003b). In North America, 26.7 percent of HIV-positive adults are women (UNAIDS, 2004).

In the United States, the incidence of AIDS is approximately 9.2 per 100,000 women and is skewed toward poor women and women of color. African American women are 23 times more likely than European American women to be diagnosed with AIDS. Altogether, women of color now constitute 82 percent of U.S. women living with AIDS (National Center for Health Statistics, 2003). The same trend is evident for children: 82.7 percent of children with AIDS in the United States are children of color (Centers for Disease Control, 2002). Most children with AIDS acquire it from their mothers: 93 percent of children with AIDS had a mother with or at risk for HIV infection (Centers for Disease Control, 2002).

Besides the relatively easier transmission of the virus from male to female than vice versa, other factors may help to account for the quickly rising incidence of AIDS among women. Prevention campaigns rarely address measures that women can take on their own to reduce their risk of becoming infected with HIV. Campaigns stress condom use, which is under male control, and monogamy, which depends on the cooperation (and honesty) of both partners. Yet, as Hortensia Amaro (1995) points out, heterosexual encounters often take place "in the context of unequal power and in a context that socializes women to be passive sexually and in other ways" (p. 440). As Chrisler (2001) notes, "If a woman begins to ask a man about his sexual history, it may appear that she is trying to question his authority or fidelity. It takes considerable self-esteem and courage for women to assert themselves in an intimate relationship, and some women will not want to run the risk of

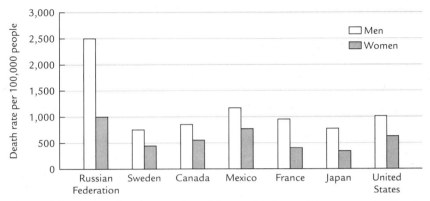

Figure 9.1 In developed countries of the world, heart disease accounts for the most death among both women and men. (Data source: American Heart Association, 2004.)

being rejected by their partners for asking questions" (p. 300). Thus, in many situations, women may feel powerless either to refuse sex or to demand condom use. Amaro (1995) also notes that many AIDS prevention campaigns are not geared to the cultural contexts of different ethnic groups.

A clear example of the link between women's vulnerability to AIDS and gender expectations can be found in Brazil, which has had one of the most aggressive anti-AIDS programs in the world (Faiola, 2001). In that country, the number of new AIDS cases among women increased more than 75 percent between 1994 and 1998, in contrast to an increase of just over 10 percent for men. Most of the Brazilian women contracting AIDS are heterosexual, do not use intravenous drugs, and are married or in long-term relationships. They acquire the infection from their male partners, who are having unsafe sex with others and who refuse to use condoms when they have sexual relations with their wives. Women are expected to put up with a certain amount of "straying" by their partners, but if a woman asks her partner to use a condom it may well be considered an insult. Furthermore, because of the stigma of AIDS as a "gay disease," many infected men refuse to be tested, or they seek treatment without telling their wives. Many women, who think of AIDS as something that does not happen to faithful wives, deny their symptoms until they become overwhelming. As one Brazilian woman says,

> Housewives have become accustomed to denial in this macho country where we pretend that our husbands' love affairs . . . aren't really happening. . . . I laughed when the doctor first told me I had AIDS. . . . AIDS doesn't happen to married women who are faithful to their husbands. But it is happening." (Quoted in Faiola, 2001, p. A34)

Heart Disease Many people think of heart disease as a men's disease. Nothing could be further from the truth. Heart disease accounts for a significantly greater proportion of female than male deaths in most parts of the world; cardiovascular disease accounts for 32 percent of all female deaths and about 27 percent of all male deaths worldwide (World Health Organization, 2003), although, as seen in Figure 9.1, the rate varies among regions. In the United States, cardiovascular disease accounts for almost 30 percent of all deaths in women and is the cause of more mortality in women than in men when all age groups are considered (National Center for Health Statistics, 2003). African American women have a higher death rate from heart disease than other groups of U. S. women do.

Researchers note that the perception of heart disease as a male disease is linked to the earlier onset of heart disease in men than in women. Men in their late 40s are far more likely than women in the same age range to suffer from heart disease, but women tend to catch up at later ages. Cardiovascular disease becomes more prevalent among women after menopause; it is strongly correlated with lowered estrogen levels.

Because of the link between levels of circulating estrogen and vulnerability to cardiovascular disease, researchers pursued the notion that **hormone** (estrogen) **replacement therapy** (**HRT**) after menopause might have a protective effect for women. The results of early observational studies suggested that HRT was associated with an impressive reduction in heart disease. Because these findings were correlational, however, it was impossible to know whether HRT or some associated variable such as access to good medical care was actually producing the protective effect.

The clinical trials of the Women's Health Initiative Study, which followed an ethnically diverse sample of 64,500 postmenopausal women for several years, has provided more definitive information about the impact of HRT on coronary heart disease. In this study, women were randomly assigned to HRT or a placebo, and the groups were compared on the development of heart disease, types of symptoms, and mortality (Matthews et al., 1997). Preliminary results from this study, released in April 2000, were not very positive about the ability of HRT to reduce heart disease risk. In fact, these results showed that the women taking hormones had a small but significantly *higher* risk of heart disease (Meyer, 2000). Another large-scale randomized clinical trial, the HERS study, revealed that, among women with established heart disease, there was no apparent decrease in risk of heart attack and death linked to taking hormones (Meyer, 2000). Research has now shown that estrogen replacement does not protect women from heart disease and that it is linked to an increased risk of stroke and of breast, endometrial, and ovarian cancer (Grodstein, Manson, & Stampfer, 2001; Hulley & Grady, 2004). Thus, many women are now choosing to forgo supplemental estrogen during the menopausal transition.

Cancer   In developing countries, cancers of the cervix, breast, and stomach are the most common among women (United Nations, 2000). About 200,000 women in developing countries die each year from cervical cancer—a cancer that is easily cured if detected early. Yet detection is not easily available to women in developing countries: According to one estimate, only about 5 percent of women in developing countries, as compared to 40 percent of women in developed countries, have been screened for precancerous cervical changes (Reproductive Health Outlook, 2000). Currently, about 80 percent of the new cases of cervical cancer identified each year are in developing countries.

The most prevalent forms of cancer among women in developed countries are lung, breast, and colorectal cancers. Lung cancer, the second leading cause of death for American women, kills as many women as breast cancer and all gynecological cancers combined (Patel, Bach, & Kris, 2004). The lung cancer rate has risen dramatically for women: In the United States, the death rate from lung cancer in women rose an astounding 600 percent between 1930 and 1997, whereas the rate for men has remained relatively stable. Between

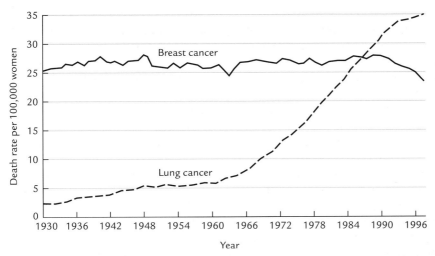

Figure 9.2   Whereas women's death rates from breast cancer have leveled off and even begun to drop, death rates from lung cancer have continued to climb—a trend blamed by the Surgeon General on smoking. (Source: Centers for Disease Control [2001]. http://www.cdc.gov/ tobacco/sgr/sgr_forwomen/ataglance.htm)

1990 and 2003, the yearly number of new cases of lung cancer in U. S. women increased by 60 percent, while the number of new cases in men remained stable. As shown in Figure 9.2, the contrast between the trends in women's death rates for lung cancer and breast cancer are striking: While breast cancer deaths have remained steady and even begun to decrease, lung cancer deaths have increased sharply.

Why the increase in lung cancer cases and deaths among women? Experts link this trend to long-term increases in cigarette smoking among women, who did not begin smoking in large numbers until the 1940s. According to the Surgeon General's report on female smoking, 4 of every 10 Americans who die from smoking are women—a proportion that has more than doubled since 1965 (Rubin, 2001). The Centers for Disease Control estimates that smoking kills 178,000 women in the United States each year (Centers for Disease Control, 2004).

The forecast is similarly bleak for women in developing countries, who are now taking up smoking in increasing numbers. As a result of aggressive marketing campaigns by tobacco companies and the loosening of social restriction, about 20 million women in China have started smoking since the 1990s, and smoking among women in Japan doubled from 9 percent to 18 percent between 1986 and 1991 (Patel et al., 2004).

In developed countries such as the United States, tobacco advertising is increasingly targeted toward African American and Latino communities, in which the gap between the numbers of female and male smokers has traditionally been high. Cigarette smoking among African American 10th graders, which stood at 6.4 percent in 1991, had risen to 9.1 percent in 2002. During the same time period, smoking by White 10th graders decreased from 23.9 to 20.8 percent (National Center for Health Statistics, 2003).

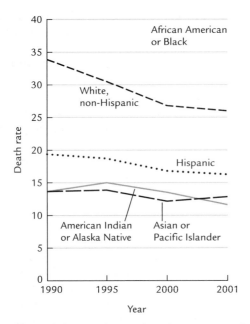

Figure 9.3 Death rates from breast cancer for women of different racial/ethnic groups in the United States. (Data source: Health, United States, 2003.)

In North America, the number of women with breast cancer increased between the 1970s and early 1990s, probably due in part to the fact that women were encouraged to obtain mammograms and so more cases were identified early. Since the mid-1990s, however, the incidence of breast cancer has stabilized and the death rate has fallen. For example, in 2001 breast cancer killed fewer than 26 per 100,000 women in Canada, down from 31 per 100,000 in 1990 (Evenson, 2002). In the United States, the age-adjusted death rate dropped from 33.3 per 100,000 in 1990 to 26 in 2001 (National Center for Health Statistics, 2003). However, there is a widening gap between White and African American women in survival rates. African American women have a 30 percent higher death rate than European American women do (American Cancer Society, 2003). As seen in Figure 9.3, African American women are more likely than any other racial/ethnic group to die from breast cancer. Reasons for the lower survival rate of African American women may include late diagnosis, poverty, undertreatment, and their higher likelihood of developing an aggressive form of cancer (National Women's Health Network 2001).

Osteoporosis   Like heart disease, osteoporosis, a loss of bone density that puts individuals at increasing risk of serious fractures, becomes more prevalent in women after menopause, when the average woman loses 1.5 percent of her bone mass every year—a loss that can eventually result in spinal compression fractures and broken hips from seemingly minor mishaps.

Osteoporosis is associated with lowered estrogen levels in women, whether the reduction happens as a result of menopause or of the seriously calorie-restricted diets sometimes advocated for young girls in athletic training or imposed on women by severe poverty. Artificially raising estrogen levels after menopause, through HRT, may protect women against osteoporosis. In one small but careful experimental study, researchers randomly assigned 94 women who had recently reached menopause to be treated with a combination of estrogen and progesterone or with a placebo (Christiansen, Christiansen, & Transbol, 1981). The women receiving hormones showed an increase in bone density, and the others showed a decrease. Then the women in the two groups were randomly assigned a second time. Those who had started out on HRT but who received a placebo in the second phase lost bone mass. Those who had started out on the placebo but who received hormones in the later phase showed some improvement in bone density, although not as much as the women who received hormones at the beginning. The Women's Health Initiative, described above, has shown that HRT is associated with a reduced risk of hip fracture among postmenopausal women (Hulley & Grady, 2004).

Alzheimer's Disease Because women live longer than men, they are more likely to suffer diseases associated with aging. One of these is Alzheimer's, a progressive, degenerative disease that attacks the brain and impairs memory, thinking, and behavior. Eventually, as the brain deteriorates, the person loses her memory and ability to recognize family and friends, and the functioning of various bodily organs begins to fail. At autopsy, the brains of Alzheimer's victims show fiber tangles within nerve cells and clusters of degenerating nerve endings in areas of the brain that are important for memory and other intellectual functioning. Currently, the disease affects 10 percent of Americans age 65 or older and more than 47 percent of those 85 and older (Alzheimer's Association, 2004). Alzheimer's disease is now the eighth leading cause of death in the United States (National Center for Health Statistics, 2001c). As yet, researchers have not discovered the causes of this disease, nor is there any cure.

Alzheimer's disease and other dementias associated with old age disproportionately affect women in two ways. Not only are they more likely to experience these problems themselves because they live longer, their longevity also makes it more likely that they will have to care for someone with Alzheimer's disease. The caregiver burden for this disease is very stressful, as discussed below.

Factors Related to Women's Health

Health- and Illness-Related Behaviors

Behaviors such as exercise, smoking, dietary choices, visits to health practitioners, and self-monitoring of certain symptoms all have a potential impact on health. Health psychologists often focus on trying to understand and change such behaviors in order to improve people's health. They have found that, in general, women seem to pay more attention to these issues than men do. Women are often more knowledgeable about and interested in health than men are, have more dental and medical checkups, and engage in fewer high-risk behaviors than men do. On the other hand, they are often at higher risk than men are because of poverty, malnutrition, lack of resources for medical care, and high levels of chronic stress.

Diet Women in North America are bombarded with the message that they should watch their diet. The goal of such messages is usually beauty rather than health: Women are reminded repeatedly that they must be thin to be attractive, and such reminders often push young women along the road to the disordered eating patterns of anorexia and bulimia, discussed in Chapter 10. Beauty is not the only, or even the main, reason to be concerned with diet, however. Nutritionists have been arguing for years that health, both in the short and long term, is related to what we eat.

For women, research in industrialized countries points to two dietary issues that may have particular relevance to long-term health consequences: fat intake and levels of calcium and vitamin D. Although more definitive research is needed, dietary fat intake appears to be correlated with risk of heart disease (although most studies have been on men) and with risk of breast cancer (Matthews et al., 1997; One for 2001: Take lifestyle to heart, 2001)). A diet high in calcium and vitamin D is associated with reduced risk of osteoporosis-related fractures (Reducing osteoporosis risk, 2001). Both calcium and vitamin D may correlate with reduced risk of breast cancer, and high dietary calcium is apparently linked with lower incidence of colorectal cancer in women (Matthews et al., 1997). While research into these issues is ongoing, most health experts advise women to limit the amount of fat they eat and to make sure to obtain adequate calcium and vitamin D.

Exercise Between 1985 and 1990, participation in sports and fitness activities declined 12 percent among U. S. adults—and the decline was greater among women than men (Robinson & Godbey, 1993). As seen in Figure 9.4, American women exercise less than men in every age group (National Center for Health Statistics, 2003b). In Canada too, women report less physical activity than men in every age group (Health Canada, 1997). Women over the age of 40 exercise less than younger women (Ransdell & Wells, 1998). At similar levels of socioeconomic status, African American and other minority women report less physical activity than European American women (King & Kiernan, 1997). Yet evidence is mounting that exercise is of critical importance to women's health. Women who exercise more are less likely to suffer from hypertension, heart trouble, diabetes, arthritis, emphysema, recurring migraines, high cholesterol, and emotional problems (Statistics Canada, 1995). Such findings are of critical importance to women, but more research is needed on the effects of exercise for women of particular ethnic groups. For example, in the United States, African American women have the highest death rates from diabetes, and African American and Latina women have the highest rates of obesity (Klonoff et al., 1995). Research on the impact of exercise on these problems for these groups is scant.

Research shows that exercise has the obvious effects of increasing strength and lowering body fat, but it also has less obvious but very important effects: It helps to build the bone density needed to help prevent osteoporosis, produces increased feelings of self-efficacy (President's Council on Physical Fitness, 1998), and is associated with a reduced risk of colorectal and breast cancer (Bernstein, Henderson, Hanisch, Sullivan-Halley, & Ross, 1994).

Smoking It used to be considered "unladylike" to smoke, and that stereotype helped to protect women's health for many years. Now that women have asserted their right to

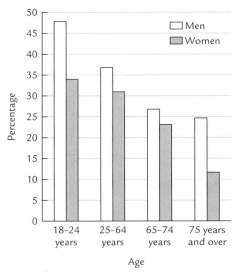

Figure 9.4   Women report that they exercise less than men do in every age group. This chart shows the percent of adults 18 and over who engaged in regular leisure-time physical activity, by sex and age group: United States, January–June 2002 (Source: Data table for figure 7.2. Percent of adults aged 18 and over who engaged in regular leisure-time physical activity, by sex and age group: United States, January–June 2002. U.S. Department of Health and Human Services [2003], Centers for Disease Control and Prevention, National Center for Human Statistics. *http://www.cdc.gov/nchs/about/major/nhis/released200212/figures07_1-7_3.htm*)

smoke, they are paying the same price for that right as men: Tobacco-related deaths among U.S. women under age 70 have been rising dramatically since 1965. Women who smoke are about 12 times more likely to die of lung cancer than women who do not smoke, and 2 to 3 times as likely to die of heart disease (Centers for Disease Control, 2004). Smoking also contributes to osteoporosis; an increased risk of cervical, bladder, esophageal, kidney, oral, and pancreatic cancers; stroke; ulcers; and premature menopause (United Nations, 2000; Weissman, 2001). Smoking-related risks have increased for women as they have begun smoking at younger ages. About 21 percent of American women smoke, but a higher percentage (25.5 percent) of girls who are seniors in high school smoke. A similar picture will likely emerge in developing countries as smoking loses its definition as a masculine habit and young women increase their use of tobacco.

The relatively high incidence of smoking among young women is no accident. Tobacco companies have worked hard to make smoking appear glamorous and sophisticated, and they have deliberately targeted groups that have many nonsmoking members (Weissman, 2001). For example, in Sri Lanka, where smoking among women is very infrequent—only about 1 percent of women smoke—tobacco companies use special advertising and promotional strategies to reach women, such as distributing free cigarettes and holding woman-oriented events (United Nations, 2000). Furthermore, in cultures that stress the necessity for women to be thin, young women may use cigarettes as a way of keeping their weight down (Landrine et al., 1995). One recent study found that, among young women, belief that smoking was an acceptable form of weight control and exposure to magazines depicting ideal women as thin increased the odds that these women would be smokers (Zucker et al., 2001).

Regardless of their reasons for smoking, young women who take up this habit add greatly to their risk of a variety of serious health problems. They also set themselves up for future cosmetic problems: Smoking has been consistently linked with premature wrinkling of the skin (American Lung Association, 2003). Many may begin smoking with the idea that they will give it up "later"; however, since nicotine is addictive, this possibility is slim. About three-fourths of women who smoke say they feel dependent on cigarettes and show signs of nicotine dependence (National Center for Chronic Disease Prevention and Health Promotion, 2001). Whereas tobacco companies may encourage women to think that smoking empowers them ("'See yourself as a King' by smoking Virginia Slims"), the irony is that, rather than being liberating or empowering, for young women smoking means an early "enslavement to a fatally addictive habit" (Weissman, 2001, p. 4).

Seeking Help and Advice   Women visit their physicians more often than men do, and so may be more likely to be diagnosed and treated early for certain illnesses (National Center for Health Statistics, 2003). There are exceptions to this pattern, however. Women delay longer than men in seeking treatment for heart-attack symptoms, possibly because they do not expect to be at risk for heart attacks (Moser & Dracup, 1993). Also, a visit to the doctor does not necessarily mean that a woman will receive satisfactory attention and treatment, particularly if she is poor and/or a member of a minority. For instance, Ntombenhle Torkington (1995) notes that Black immigrant women in Europe are frequently humiliated and refused effective treatment when they seek medical help and that doctors often communicate more interest in restricting their reproductive potential than in treating their illnesses.

In the United States, among women age 40 and over the use of mammograms to screen for breast cancer increased from about 50 percent to over 70 percent between 1990 and 2000. However, screening levels were much lower among poor women and women with lower levels of education (National Center for Health Statistics, 2003). In Canada, about 42 percent of women age 35 and older report that they have had a mammogram in the past two years, and women with higher education and adequate incomes are more likely than other women to obtain mammograms (Health Canada, 1996). In less industrialized countries, many women have no access to such tests.

Poverty and Nutrition

Poor women are more vulnerable to illness and are at higher risk for early mortality and chronic disease than their middle- and upper-income counterparts are—the poorer women are, the worse their health (Adler & Coriell, 1997). This "health gap" persists even in countries that offer universal access to health care (Adler, Boyce, Chesney, Folkman, & Syme, 1993). In virtually every nation of the world, women are more likely than men to be poor (United Nations, 2000). In the United States, the people most likely to be poor are members of minorities, single mothers, and the elderly; one study shows that 15.7 percent of older White women, 46.4 percent of older Black women, and 22.7 percent of older Hispanic women are poor (Lott & Bullock, 2001). The poverty rate among woman-headed households with no husband present is 24.7 percent (U.S Bureau of the Census, 2000b).

Why is poverty associated with increased health risks? Probably because poverty often involves inadequate nutrition, crowded and sometimes unsafe living conditions, lack of easy access to medical care, and perhaps the unavailability of clean water for drinking and washing. It may also be associated with stress. Urban single mothers who are poor may have no help with childcare, for example, or may worry about their children's safety in a neighborhood where criminal activity is high. Poor rural women may live without adequate water, heat, or other necessities. Consider this description of what it means to be poor in the United States:

> You live in substandard, deteriorating housing . . . You are likely to eat a poor-quality diet that negatively affects your health and decreases your energy level. You have inadequate access to private and public resources—to police protection, political power, education, and networks leading to jobs. You shop in smaller stores to which you can walk and that give you credit but sell you older and damaged food at higher prices. You move frequently, because of fires, raised rent, eviction, or a constant search for something better, cheaper, cleaner, or safer. (Lott & Bullock, 2001, p. 199)

What it means to be poor in other parts of the world may be even more grim. The United Nations defines extreme poverty as the lack of sufficient income to satisfy basic food needs, defined on the basis of minimum calorie requirements (United Nations Development Program, 2000). Using this definition, the percentage of people estimated to be extremely poor is alarmingly high in many countries; for example, 30 percent in Botswana, 25 percent in Romania, 27 percent in Pakistan, and 36 percent in Bangladesh. By some estimates, women make up 70 percent of such extremely poor people (PBS online, 2000).

Stress and Social Support

Research has clearly shown that stress increases susceptibility to illness. For example, in one carefully controlled study, researchers inoculated volunteers with one of five different cold viruses or a placebo and measured their level of psychological stress. They found that rates of respiratory infection and clinical colds increased with increases in **psychological stress** across all five cold viruses (Cohen, Tyrell, & Smith, 1991). Stressful life events are linked to somewhat higher risks of some chronic diseases, an increase in recurrent health problems, and a decreased effectiveness of some treatments (Matthews et al., 1997).

There are some reasons to suspect that psychological stress may have a particular impact on women's health. First, some evidence shows that the same stressor may result in more perceived stress for women than for men. When respondents were asked how much stress they would be experiencing now if specific events (e.g., deaths, separations, arguments, threats to self-image, financial changes) had occurred 1 week ago, 1 month ago, and so on up to 3 years ago, women rated all the sets of events as more stressful than men did (Horowitz, Schaefer, & Cooney, 1974). A study that went beyond self-reported perceptions of stress (Kiecolt-Glaser et al., 1996; Researchers link, 1996) showed that routine marital arguments were more stressful for women than for their husbands. In this study of

BOX 9.2 LEARNING ACTIVITY
Is Stress from Sexist Events Affecting Your Health?

Some researchers have argued that women encounter more stressful events than men do, partly because they must deal with regular encounters with sexism. Elizabeth Klonoff and Hope Landrine (1995) developed the Schedule of Sexist Events (SSE) to measure the incidence of sexist treatment reported by women. Klonoff and Landrine found that the women who reported more of these kinds of events in their lives also reported more physical and psychiatric symptoms. The items below are adapted from the SSE scale. How many of these events have happened to you in the last week? In the last year? Ever in your life?

_____ Forced to listen to sexist jokes.

_____ Sexually harassed.

_____ Called sexist names.

_____ Treated with a lack of respect because of being female.

_____ Picked on because of being female.

_____ Hit, shoved, or threatened because of being female.

_____ Lost a raise or promotion because of being female.

90 newlywed couples, the members of each couple were put into a room together with needles in their arms so that blood samples could be taken intermittently without the participants' awareness. A researcher then interviewed the couples, intentionally promoting a discussion that started an argument between them. Blood samples taken during the arguments showed that the women experienced sudden high levels of stress hormones—a steeper increase than the men—as if they were in a situation of great danger. Testing continued through an overnight hospital stay. Just before discharge in the morning, women still had high levels of stress hormones, but hormone levels for the men had returned to normal. Thus the same negative incident, a marital argument, clearly had more negative effects on the women than on the men.

Second, a number of **stressful events** are more likely to happen to women than to men: rape, sexual harassment, spousal abuse, sex discrimination. Two researchers who developed a new scale, the Schedule of Sexist Events (SSE), to measure the incidence of sexist treatment found that 99 percent of the U. S. women they sampled had experienced a sexist event at least once in their lives (Klonoff & Landrine, 1995). The most common events included being forced to listen to sexist jokes, being sexually harassed, being called sexist names, and being treated with a lack of respect because of being female. More than half the women sampled said that they had been picked on, hit, shoved, or threatened because of being a woman, and 40 percent said that being female had cost them a raise or promotion. White women and women of color reported similar kinds of sexist events; however, women of color reported significantly more sexist discrimination than White women did. For the women sampled, scores on the SSE were related to reports of physical and psychiatric symptoms. Knowledge of the SSE scores, added to knowledge of the women's scores on more traditional measures of stressful life events, allowed for significantly better prediction of their symptoms than did knowledge of only the scores on the traditional measures (Landrine, Klonoff, Gibbs, Manning, & Lund, 1995).

One of the variables that is thought to help counteract the effects of stress is **social support:** the perception that others are available to help. Studies have consistently found that social support is associated with longer life and lower disease rates. Many of these studies, however, have not included women—and when women *are* included, the positive impact of social support is not so clear (Matthews et al., 1997). This finding may be due to women's and men's perceptions of different kinds of people and behaviors as supportive, or to measures of social support that exclude variables that are more important to women than to men. A relatively new theory suggests that women, more than men, tend to emphasize caregiving and attachment processes when trying to cope with stress—and that this female–male difference has a biological basis. Women, some researchers argue, respond to stressful situations with a pattern of behavior labeled **tend and befriend:** nurturing their children and affiliating with others to reduce risk (Taylor et al., 2000). So perhaps the ability to provide social support is just as important for women as is the opportunity to receive it.

Caregiver Burden   Because women live longer than men, both the dependent elderly and their caregivers are likely to be female. Research shows that caring for a debilitated relative, such as a spouse or parent with Alzheimer's disease, can be enormously stressful. Caregivers are likely to suffer from depression and malnutrition, for example, because they cannot find the energy and motivation to take proper care of themselves while trying to manage the enormous task of taking care of an invalid. Caring for someone who cannot be left alone often means being housebound, isolated, and lacking in social support. This isolation and lack of social support can have a direct effect on the caregiver's health. Among both older women and older men providing care for a spouse with progressive dementia, those who reported lower social support and high distress showed the greatest and most uniformly negative changes in immune system functioning in a follow-up 13 months later (Kiecolt-Glaser, Dura, Speicher, Trask, & Glaser, 1991).

Janice Kiecolt-Glaser and her colleagues (1995) looked specifically at the impact of the **caregiver burden** on the body's healing response. The researchers administered small, uniform puncture wounds in the arms of two matched groups of women, women who were primary caregivers for a relative with Alzheimer's disease and women who had no such responsibilities. They found that the stress of caregiving apparently slowed the wound-healing process. Women in the caregiver group took an average of 9 days longer to heal than the other women did—a difference that could have important implications for general health and for such specific issues as recovery from surgery. These authors also reported that, in earlier research, caregivers had shown depressed immune system response to flu vaccination, suggesting that these women are more vulnerable to that illness and perhaps to other infections.

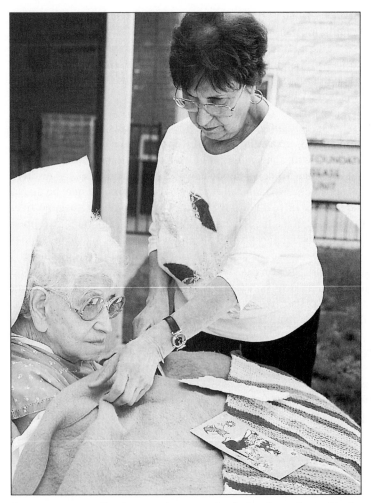

Because women live longer than men, both the dependent elderly and their caregivers are more often than not women.

The psychological and physiological impact of caring for someone with Alzheimer's disease or some other form of dementia is long lasting and does not seem to end immediately with the death of the patient. In a study that compared the immune system responses of current caregivers and former caregivers (whose spouses had died an average of 3 years before), researchers found that the two groups did not differ from each other in their natural killer cell response: the tendency of their natural killer cells to perform their normal function of searching for and destroying infected or malignant cells. However, both groups showed a significantly more suppressed killer cell response than a control group who were not caregivers (Esterling, Kiecolt-Glaser, & Glaser, 1996). It appears that caregivers' immune systems take a long time to recover from the long-term stress of looking after a spouse with Alzheimer's disease.

Women as Patients in Health Care Systems

In developed countries, women go to doctors more than men do and, since they live longer, are also more likely than men to enter long-term-care facilities (Sharpe, 1995). In developing countries, women are often underrepresented among visitors to health clinics (United Nations, 2000). In any country, a woman's interaction with the health care system can be influenced by sexist stereotyping (and by racism and ageism if she is a woman of color and elderly).

Physicians are subject to the gender biases of their culture, and research shows that male doctors tend to feel less warmly toward and to communicate more poorly with female than with male patients (Porzelius, 2000). One study of interactions between female patients and male physicians found that the doctors frequently interrupted their patients and responded to their expressed worries and concerns with jokes and platitudes (K. Davis, 1988). Jokes and platitudes can make a patient feel as if her concerns are trivial. Even empathy and friendliness can be, and often are, as Davis points out, expressed in ways that convey the doctor's power and control over the patient.

The doctor's control lies partly in greater access to information, and although women often work hard to get at this information, one of women's chief complaints in various countries is that doctors do not easily share information with them. Some studies in the United States show that women take a more active role in questioning their doctors than men do, and that they sometimes consequently receive more information, but a study of patient–doctor communication in Mexico showed that in this cultural setting, women did not differ from men in the number of questions they asked—and that men received more information (Waitzkin, Cabrera, Cabrera, Radlow, & Rodriguez, 1996). One study of health care services in Finland showed that a major complaint of women attending hospital maternity clinics was the poor communication they felt they had with their doctors (Kojo-Austin, Malin, & Hemminki, 1993).

If the physician is female, a woman patient may be more satisfied with her health care. Female physicians spend more time with their patients, talk and let their patients talk more, and tend to ask more questions, give more information, and emphasize the doctor–patient partnership more than male doctors do (Bertakis, 1998; Roter, Lipkin, & Korsgaard, 1991). It is not surprising, then, that researchers in the United States and Europe have found greater patient satisfaction with female physicians (Sharpe, 1995).

The asymmetry in the male doctor–female patient interaction may be intensified if the patient is elderly. Studies based on audiotaped encounters show that doctors tend to be more egalitarian, patient, and engaged with younger than with older patients, and they are more likely to be responsive to psychosocial concerns raised by young than by older patients (Sharpe, 1995). The elderly are also treated with condescension by nursing home staff, who frequently use baby talk with them, and by family members, who may discuss them as if they were not present or not capable of understanding. Since women live longer than men, and hence will spend more years as elderly patients, this differential treatment based on age is particularly relevant to them. Women who are lesbian, poor, or members of racial minorities also encounter biases in their interactions with physicians (Porzelius, 2000).

Not just communication between patient and doctor is affected by gender; the type and quality of care are too. Researchers have found that female patients of male physicians are less likely than patients of female physicians to have tests such as Pap smears and mammograms with appropriate frequency (Franks & Clancy, 1993). Physicians are apparently less likely to pursue expensive, high-technology treatment options such as coronary bypass surgery, cardiac catheterization, and kidney transplants for female than for male patients, and they are less likely to take appropriate measures for the detection of lung cancer in women than in men (Sharpe, 1995). In the United States, women who have heart attacks are 50 percent more likely to die than men who have heart attacks, and studies suggest that inferior medical treatment is a major contributing factor (Studies show, 1998). Researchers have also found that women have a higher risk of dying during or soon after coronary bypass surgery than men do—a finding that holds even for female and male patients who have similar risk factors such as age, obesity, and diabetes (Edwards, Carey, Grover, Bero, & Hartz, 1998). Some experts speculate that women's higher risk of dying is related to physiological factors such as their narrower blood vessels; others argue it can be traced to physicians' tendency to refer women for bypass surgery at a later stage of heart disease than they do men.

Why do such gender discrepancies exist? Perhaps men are viewed as more important patients. Or perhaps physicians are less likely to take women's than men's symptom reports seriously, assuming that women are quicker to complain than men are. Whatever the reason, women are apparently in danger of receiving second-class treatment as patients in the health care system—and the danger seems to arise from gender stereotypes.

Health educators and activists have urged women to become more assertive as patients, to ask questions, to reveal their concerns, and to make their opinions known. Clearly, this is an important avenue of change for women. Yet such assertive patients may be perceived simply as "difficult" by health care practitioners accustomed to unquestioning compliance, and their treatment may not improve. For real change to occur, health professionals must be taught to listen, to respect their patients, and to promote patients' involvement in their own care decisions (Sharpe, 1995). Researchers who study health care also have a role to play in making the system more responsive to women. First, as in the Women's Health Initiative study, women must be included in health research, and the illnesses, such as breast cancer and autoimmune disorders, that affect women disproportionately need attention. Second, it is important to include a qualitative aspect to such research (for example, open-ended interviews and focus groups). These methods allow women to raise questions the researcher may have overlooked, and they help the researcher understand the framework within which the quantitative results from surveys or physiological measurements should be interpreted. Perhaps just as important, the qualitative methods help to forge a partnership between the medical research team and the women participating in the research. The women thus help to shape the research agenda

Susan LaFlesche Picotte (1865–1915), an Omaha Indian from a Nebraska reservation, was the first Native American woman to graduate from medical school.

and are viewed as collaborators—a view that may gradually transfer to the physician–patient relationship and help to transform it into one of mutual respect.

Women as Healers

Near the end of the 19th century, Susan LaFlesche Picotte, an Omaha Indian from a Nebraska reservation, became the first Native American woman to graduate from medical school, the Women's Medical College in Philadelphia. She then returned to her home to work with her own people, treating cholera, dysentery, influenza, and tuberculosis. She also became active on the lecture circuit, trying to call attention to the unhealthy and demoralizing conditions on reservations and the consequent prevalence of alcoholism and disease. At the time, hers was one of the few female voices that could speak with the authority of a medical degree—even though that degree came from a women's college, and was therefore viewed by many as second-rate (M. Brown, 1980).

Much has changed in the intervening years. In 1995 the medical schools of Yale, Harvard, Johns Hopkins, and 15 other universities enrolled a first-year class that, for the first time, was predominantly female (Yale 1st-year med class, 1995).

Around the world, women have always been healers, but they have regularly been shut out or kept on the margins of the official health professions and institutions. In the earliest history of medicine, women's practical knowledge of herbs and other treatments for the illnesses they encountered in their families and friends was virtually the *only* medical knowledge. That knowledge was often mined by men, who were in a better position than women to develop it. For example, in 1552 Ambroise Paré, a French military surgeon, was advised by an old woman that raw chopped onions would be helpful in healing burns. He investigated and found it to be true; 4 centuries later, onions were found to have antimicrobial properties. It was the name of the surgeon, not the name of the old woman who gave him the good advice, that passed into history (Farnes, 1990).

The women's medicine that flourished in Europe in the 16th and 17th centuries was herbal medicine, and women herbalists were regularly consulted by people needing relief from a variety of physical complaints. Their perspective was gradually overshadowed and lost, however, by a more aggressive (and ineffective) male-dominated system of medicine, which consisted mainly of bleeding and purging. By the 19th century, women were almost completely excluded from the practice of medicine in Europe and North America. Many women healers had been persecuted and killed as witches, and the nursing profession had been established and achieved respectability as a "suitable" subsidiary role for women in medicine.

Of the few women who managed to penetrate the barriers of official medicine during the late 19th and early 20th centuries, several made stunning contributions to medical knowledge: Florence Sabin did breakthrough work on the lymphatic system and on white blood cells and then went on to attack a number of important public health concerns; Dorothy Reed described the cell characteristic of Hodgkin's disease; Alice Hamilton founded the field of industrial medicine; Maud Slye was a pioneer in cancer research in the early 1900s. Yet women made up only 15 percent of medical school faculty members in the United States until 1980 (Farnes, 1990). A different pattern emerged in Eastern Europe, where, under Communism, advanced education became available to women more quickly, and women actually began to dominate the medical profession. Yet the Communist governments devalued and underpaid physicians, and men left the field for better opportunities, making this victory a hollow one for women.

Of course, women have continued to contribute to healing in ways other than as physicians and medical scientists. In North and South America, significant numbers of medicine women practice in Native American cultures, and *curanderas* help people in various Latin American communities. Their approaches differ significantly from mainstream Western-style medicine. For example, Tu Moonwalker, an Apache medicine woman, describes an emphasis on feelings and the ability to "see" another person as the basis for her healing work: "Half of medicine is psychic . . . You know immediately what's wrong with someone. They won't tell you. Their soul will" (Perrone, Stockel, & Krueger, 1989, p. 52). Moonwalker developed her healing arts partly through training and partly through spiritual quests. Her list of university degrees has not alienated her from her traditional healing practice.

Sabinita Herrerra, a *curandera* who works at a clinic in New Mexico, depends heavily on a knowledge of herbs for her treatments, in the tradition of women's medicine from centuries gone by. Like other *curanderas,* she believes she has been chosen by God to do healing work, and she puts her healing work ahead of obligations to family, church, and friends. The sense of healing as a calling has been with her since she was a small child (Perrone et al., 1989).

By far the majority of women who have worked in the field of modern Western medicine have been nurses and midwives. Midwives have traditionally worked in the margins and nurses in the lower-status echelons of Western medicine, where their skills have rarely been appreciated or rewarded with high salaries. In recent years, however, there have been some signs that nurses and midwives are increasing in status and taking a more prominent place in medical care. Midwives deliver over 70 percent of the babies born in Western European countries (Citizens for Midwifery, 1997). In the United States, certified nurse-midwives, two-thirds of whom hold master's degrees, attended 8 percent of births, usually in hospital settings (Centers for Disease Control, 2002b).

Nurses have come a long way from the 1850s, when Florence Nightingale horrified her wealthy English family by turning down two marriage proposals in favor of pursuing training and experience in the disreputable field of nursing. At that time, nursing was not a profession, and it certainly was no place for a "respectable" woman. Yet Nightingale persevered, reforming inadequate and filthy hospital conditions and the training of nurses, and she eventually became known as the founder of modern nursing. Along the way, she introduced the medical world to the use of statistics, making charts and graphs to force people to see disease, mortality, and the reasons for that mortality in terms of numbers. Her data provided the basis for sanitary reform in medical care (Farnes, 1990). It is a testament to the strength of stereotypes about nursing and about women that her contributions to the science of medicine have been all but forgotten, in favor of the positive but one-dimensional image of her as an angel of mercy, "the Lady with the Lamp."

As Mary Roth Walsh (1977) points out, in the late 1800s doctors who opposed the entry of women into medicine because of women's alleged physical delicacy and weakness were strangely supportive of their entry into nursing. The *Boston Medical Journal,* which in 1867 had railed against the idea of women as physicians because they would be too weak and sensitive to endure the strain of house calls and contact with the rough, vicious public, 30 years later praised nurses for their stamina and strength. The *Journal* noted with approval that nurses regularly braved the slums, tenements, and dark alleys of the city to attend the sick. Clearly, it was acceptable for women to be strong, knowledgeable, and courageous as long as they did work that men did not want to do! Yet the virtues ascribed to nurses were not enough to raise their status from one that was definitely subordinate to that of a physician. As one medical journal noted in 1894, "The doctor's responsibility as to the nursing service is like that of the captain to his ship"; another noted that

BOX 9.3 WOMEN SHAPING PSYCHOLOGY
Hope Landrine

Hope Landrine, a clinical and health psychologist, has spent her career focusing on how issues of race, gender, and class interact with issues of health. Her work has been targeted to address the situation that "even though women of color constitute most of the women in the world and are steadily increasing in the United States, data on such women usually receive a perfunctory treatment that reflects and perpetuates their marginal status in feminist psychology" (Landrine, 1995, p. xxi).

Landrine received her Ph.D. in clinical psychology from the University of Rhode Island in 1983, went on to postdoctoral training in social psychology at Stanford University, and finally acquired additional training in preventive medicine at the University of Southern California. Since that time, she has spent much of her career conducting full-time, grant-supported research in the capacity of Research Scientist at the Public Health Foundation of Los Angeles County. Much of this research is directed at developing interventions to improve the health of African American and Latino children and adults, and of women and girls of all ethnic groups. She has continued this research as an Adjunct Research Professor in the clinical psychology program at San Diego State University.

Under Landrine's editorship, the American Psychological Association published the first book that attempted to address cultural diversity issues in feminist psychology as a whole—focusing on theory and research as well as practice. This groundbreaking book, *Bringing Cultural Diversity to Feminist Psychology,* was recognized with a *Distinguished Publication Award* from the Association for Women in Psychology. The book gathers articles from women of many different groups, and it includes three chapters authored or co-authored by Landrine. In the book, she argues persuasively in favor of taking a

nurses were too often "conceited and too unconscious of the due subordination she owes to the medical profession, of which she is sort of a useful parasite" (quoted in Walsh, 1977, pp. 142, 143).

Subordinate or not, the nursing profession grew rapidly in the United States. In 1890, 30 nursing schools graduated 470 nurses. By 1926, there were more than 2,000 nursing schools, and the number of graduates had risen to 17,500 (Walsh, 1977). Now, nursing

BOX 9.3 WOMEN SHAPING PSYCHOLOGY (*continued*)
Hope Landrine

"contextualist" approach to understanding behavior: conceptualizing a behavior and its context as a single unit. She also argues that the concept of observation is misleading, causing researchers to mistakenly interpret similar behaviors as having similar meanings for people in different ethnic/racial groups. However, her contributions to the broadening of psychology's vision started well before this book appeared, perhaps most notably with a 1985 article that reported what happened when she asked undergraduate students to describe the stereotypes of women who were African American or European American, middle- or lower-class. She found that the stereotypes differed significantly by race and class.

Landrine's work in health psychology has incorporated, among many other things, the impact of stress on health and the impact of sexism on stress. Her research has demonstrated that sexism is an important source of stress for women. Her theoretical and empirical work has challenged feminist psychology to embrace all women.

Read More about Hope Landrine

About the editor. (1995). In H. Landrine (Ed.), *Bringing cultural diversity to feminist psychology.* Washington, DC: American Psychological Association.

Read What She Has Written

Landrine, H. (1985). Race x class stereotypes of women. *Sex Roles, 13* (1–2), 65–75.

Landrine, H. (1995). Introduction: Cultural diversity, contextualism, and feminist psychology. In H. Landrine (Ed.), *Bringing cultural diversity to feminist psychology* (pp. 1–20). Washington, DC: American Psychological Association.

Landrine, H., Klonoff, E. A., & Brown-Collins, A. (1995). Cultural diversity and methodology in feminist psychology: Critique, proposal, empirical example. In H. Landrine (Ed.), *Bringing cultural diversity to feminist psychology* (pp. 55–76). Washington, DC: American Psychological Association.

Klonoff, E. A., Landrine, H., & Campbell, R. (2000). Sexist discrimination may account for well-known gender differences in psychiatric symptoms. *Psychology of Women Quarterly, 24* (1), 93–99.

Landrine, H., & Klonoff, E. A. (2001). Health and health care: How gender makes women sick. *Encyclopedia of women and gender.* San Diego, CA: Academic Press.

accounts for a high percentage of women's jobs in the United States and in other countries. The United States has 2.8 nurses for every practicing doctor; the ratio is 3.8 to 1 in Australia, 4.7 to 1 in Canada (Reddy, 1994). As a profession, it continues to be dominated by women: about 94 percent in the United States and at least 97 percent in such diverse countries as Bulgaria, Japan, and Poland (Thornborrow & Sheldon, 1995; United Nations, 1995). Without nurses, the health care systems of most countries could not function.

SUMMARY

With respect to fitness and health, women have often been caught in a series of double binds. It has been considered unimportant—sometimes even unfeminine—for them to be strong and healthy, yet their presumed frailty has been used as an argument to restrict their activities in everything from sports to the practice of medicine. When women have wanted to engage in activities to build their strength and health, they have often had to fight to gain access to facilities, yet when there has been low-status heavy work to be done, that work has often been assigned to women. Cultural requirements for feminine modesty have often forced women to avoid certain pursuits or to wear such cumbersome clothing that they are literally weighed down; then the observation that they tire more easily is used to confirm the stereotype that women are weak. Indeed, it is a testament to women's motivation and perseverance that so many have managed to cultivate strong, healthy bodies in the face of cultural resistance.

Women live longer than men, and the difference is greater in developed than in developing countries. Their extra years of life are apparently not due to better access to medical treatment or even to an easier life than men, however. In fact, medical researchers have virtually ignored many of the health problems that disproportionately affect women, women in many parts of the world have less access to health care compared to men, and women seem to receive a lower quality of medical care than men do in many respects.

Women's greater longevity is, to some extent, conferred by nature: More males die in infancy or at young ages from hereditary diseases. But women also live longer because they are more cautious: They are less likely to engage in risky behaviors and to die through accidents or violence. In this way, ironically, they may be helped by gender stereotypes that encourage them to be peaceable and fainthearted.

Women are also more concerned about health issues and, in developed countries at least, make more visits to doctors and dentists than men do. They have been, until fairly recently, less likely to smoke—although a change in this pattern has now begun to produce a dramatic increase in the number of women dying of lung cancer. Heart disease, which is also linked to smoking, is the leading cause of death for women.

The rate of HIV/AIDS is growing more rapidly for women than for men worldwide. The virus is transmitted more easily to women than to men during heterosexual contact, and gender-related expectations often make it difficult or impossible for women to insist on safe sex practices.

Many of the health problems that women experience around the world can be linked directly to a lack of access to health care resources. Women in developing countries die of treatable cervical cancer because they have no easy access to Pap smear tests. Maternal mortality in countries such as Romania and Albania is rising as good medical care becomes an increasingly scarce resource. More broadly, women's health problems can be linked to poverty, which characterizes more women than men worldwide, and to stress, such as the burden of caregiving. There is also evidence that female patients are likely to be the recipients of poor communication, and sometimes inattentive treatment, from male physicians.

The submissive, compliant, weak feminine stereotype fits more neatly the role of patient than that of healer—at least the technical, aggressive, interventionist mode of healer that modern medicine has endorsed. Yet women have a long history as healers, in keeping with their image as nurturers. Now, in both the patient and the healer roles, women have begun to resist definition by gender stereotypes. The result of this resistance will likely be improved health and health care for women.

KEY TERMS

Title IX
osteoporosis
life expectancy
age-adjusted death rate
Women's Health Initiative
maternal mortality
sexually transmitted
    infections (STIs)

human immunodeficiency
    virus (HIV)
acquired immune deficiency
    syndrome (AIDS)
hormone replacement
    therapy (HRT)
psychological stress
stressful events

social support
caregiver burden
tend and befriend

DISCUSSION QUESTIONS

Why has the stereotype that women are physically weak persisted for so long? What role do women play in supporting this stereotype?

Why do some diseases that afflict women, such as breast cancer, receive so much attention from the press and the medical research community, whereas others that kill more women (heart disease, lung cancer) are often thought of as men's diseases?

Are gender stereotypes dangerous to women's health? If so, in what ways is this true?

FOR ADDITIONAL READING

Boston Women's Health Book Collective. (1998). *Our bodies, ourselves for the new century: A book by and for women.* Touchstone Books. This is the latest edition of a book that has been the women's health "bible" for American women. It covers virtually every health issue from women's perspectives and is a good source of practical information.

Farnes, Patricia. (1990). Women in medical science. In G. Kass-Simon & P. Farnes (Eds.), *Women of science: Righting the record* (pp. 268–299). Bloomington, IN: Indiana University Press. This fascinating account of the history of women's contributions to medicine allows the reader to discover countless women who have been lost.

Nelson, Mariah Burton. (1994). *The stronger women get, the more men love football.* New York: Avon Books. An athlete presents an insightful feminist analysis of the male-dominated world of American sports.

Perrone, B., Stockel, H. H., & Krueger, V. (1989). *Medicine women, curanderas, and women doctors.* Norman, OK: University of Oklahoma Press. Interviews with several healers from each of the categories listed in the title provide a rare glimpse into the different kinds of healing that women do.

Taylor, Shelley E. (2002). *The tending instinct: How nurturing is essential to who we are and how we live*. New York: Times Books, Henry Holt and Company. A social psychologist describes her theory of how women and men are biologically predisposed to cope with stress differently.

WEB RESOURCES

National Women's Health Network. This is an American national public interest organization dedicated to women's health. Its mission includes both providing reliable health information to women and advocating for policy changes that will support women's health. At the site you will find fact sheets, policy papers, action campaigns in which you can participate, and links to other health advocacy groups. **www.nwhn.org**

Canadian Women's Health Network. This educational and advocacy-oriented site provides news releases, health care alerts and advice, and links to other sites. One resource available in its entirety on the site is *Catching Our Breath: A Journal about Change for Women Who Smoke*. This journal, written for use by individual women at their own pace or by groups of women working together, is aimed at helping women who want to quit or cut down on their smoking, or who simply want to gain a better understanding of the role smoking plays in their lives. **www.cwhn.ca**

British Columbia Centre of Excellence for Women's Health. A wealth of information is available at this site in the form of free downloads. Of particular interest to some will be the report *Documenting Visibility: Selected Bibliography on Lesbian and Bisexual Women's Health,* which provides one of the departure points for establishing a lesbian health research agenda in Canada. **www.bccewh.bc.ca**

UNAIDS. This is the site for the United Nations program on HIV/AIDS. Here you will find information about World AIDS Day, press releases and fact sheets about HIV/AIDS worldwide, and the capacity to search for information by country. **www.unaids.org**

CHAPTER 10

Mental Health, Illness, and Therapy

CHAPTER OUTLINE

At an international meeting, Dr. Philip Gold reported the findings of a study of bone density among depressed and nondepressed women. Everyone expects that depressed women are sadder, more listless, and less optimistic than women whose emotional state is normal, but Gold's study showed that the impact of depression is not limited to emotional effects. The depressed women, who had high levels of stress hormones in their blood, showed a surprising loss of bone density. Although all the women in the study were 40 years old, the bone density of the depressed women resembled that of 70-year-old women (Researchers link, 1996).

This story is one of many that show the close links between body and mind, between physical and mental health. Although physical and mental health are treated in separate chapters in this book, the inclusion of some topics in one chapter rather than the other is, to some extent, arbitrary. For example, eating disorders are classified as mental disorders— but they are undoubtedly physical disorders as well. Cancer is a physical disorder, but research shows that its onset and course can sometimes be affected by psychosocial and emotional factors.

This chapter begins with an examination of the notion of mental health: What does it mean to be mentally healthy? How do gender and culture interact with this definition?

Next, we turn to the question of mental illness. When is a person considered to be mentally ill? Does the gender of the person affect the diagnosis? How might this differ from culture to culture? Then we look at a number of mental illnesses that seem to affect women more than men: depression, the eating disorders, and anxiety disorders. We also examine some other problems as women experience them: post-traumatic stress disorder and the abuse of alcohol and other drugs.

Finally, we examine issues related to the treatment of mental disorders through psychotherapy and drugs. Are women diagnosed or treated differently from men? Can diagnosis be affected by gender stereotypes? How is the process of treatment affected by sexism, racism, or heterosexism? What is feminist therapy, and is it the best approach for emotionally troubled women? Questions surrounding gender and mental health are complex, particularly when they are examined across cultural contexts. One pattern that emerges in the chapter, however, is that an individual's gender *does* have some relationship to whether behaviors are considered normal or symptomatic of mental illness and to the ways mental illnesses are labeled and treated.

Gender and Mental Health

Like physical health, **mental health** is more than just the absence of symptoms. It is often viewed as the ability to function well, to cope with problems, or to be happy or satisfied with one's life. A mentally healthy person is often called "well adjusted."

But what if a person's life situation is too difficult, problematic, and stressful to lend itself to "adjustment"? If a woman is trapped in a violent marriage or a soul-destroying job, is it mentally healthy for her to "adjust"? Or are dissatisfaction and resistance more mentally healthy responses? Clearly, the conception of mental health as adjustment must be tempered by an awareness of both the situation to which the person is being expected to adjust and whether an acceptance of that situation will be beneficial or harmful to her. Yet this very awareness has sometimes been lacking among mental health professionals with respect to women. At various times in history, women who have been overtly dissatisfied or who have refused to play by the rules for the feminine gender have been labeled as deviant and sick; for instance, the early psychoanalysts tended to diagnose as "neurotic" those assertive women who were dissatisfied with their culturally assigned feminine role.

The discussion of mental health and illness in this chapter is inevitably shaped by a Western perspective on these issues. Yet cultures vary widely in how they label, interpret, and respond to mental illness. Although mental illness as a broad set of phenomena may be a universal aspect of human experience, specific diagnostic categories, such as those listed in the American Psychiatric Association's *Diagnostic and Statistical Manual of Mental Disorders,* are not necessarily universal. For example, one study of models of mental illness in sub-Saharan Africa found that spiritual causes were frequent explanations for mental illness and that many patterns that would be labeled mental illness in North America were defined simply as physical problems in African cultures (Patel, 1995). A study of gender and well-being in South Africa underscored the necessity to include spiritual dimensions when assessing mental health in African contexts: Women reported significantly stronger spiritual and religious well-being than men did, and women more often turned to religion as a coping strategy (van Eeden & Wissing, 2000). In a similar vein, a study examining cross-cultural beliefs about depression found significant differences in the meaning that middle-aged native British and Asian-born immigrant women in Britain attached to "symptoms" of depression. The Asian-born women scored higher than the British-born women on a Western measure of depressive symptoms—yet they did not report depression in themselves (Furnham & Malik, 1994). Cultural differences in values, views of the self, habits of attribution for social behavior, and the resources available for treatment may all influence the labeling of particular behaviors or experiences as abnormalities or illnesses.

A Double Standard of Mental Health?

Women and men have traditionally been expected to adjust to different role expectations and behavioral norms. Psychologists from Sigmund Freud onward have had a tendency to use these different role expectations to define what is mentally healthy for women and men. People who conformed to gender expectations—masculine men and feminine women—were considered mentally healthier than those who did not. That has meant, in essence, a **double standard of mental health** for women and men.

The existence of a double standard of mental health among mental health professionals (psychologists, psychiatrists, social workers) was first demonstrated in a classic study in which a sample of these professionals was asked to indicate on a questionnaire what traits they thought should characterize normal, healthy, fully functioning adults (Broverman, Broverman, Clarkson, Rosenkrantz, & Vogel, 1970). The researchers found that the clinicians held different ideals depending on whether the fully functioning adult was described as female or male. The ideal healthy woman was described as more submissive, less independent and adventurous, more easily influenced, less aggressive and competitive, more easily excitable in minor crises, more easily hurt, more emotional, more vain about her appearance, less objective, and less interested in math and science than the ideal healthy man.

Perhaps because this study and others like it have been widely publicized, subsequent studies using the same paper-and-pencil methodology have not often found the same blatant gender bias among mental health practitioners. Investigations of the ways therapists respond to real live clients instead of hypothetical ones suggest that biases based on gender, as well as on race, ethnicity, and class, are still very much alive, however (Comas-Díaz & Greene, 1994a). For example, it appears that some therapists do not recognize the seriousness of the problem faced by a female client who is being abused by her husband and do not want to provide intervention services aimed specifically at stopping the violence. This denial is even more likely when the client is a woman of color (L. E. A. Walker, 1995). As we will explore in more detail in our discussion of diagnosis and treatment, not only is there a double standard of mental health, but both prongs of that standard are based on norms for White, North American, middle-class individuals.

Women and Mental Illness around the World

We have already noted that culture defines what is "normal," and also that the standards of normal behavior and experience are different for women and men. Although mental illness may virtually always indicate real distress, the form in which that distress is expressed is, to a certain extent, dictated by cultural expectations. The distress is real, but the categories of mental illness are social constructions. For instance, in North America it is more acceptable for a woman than a man to be depressed and more acceptable for a man to "drown his sorrows" in alcohol than it is for a woman. Similarly, our cultural expectations mean it will be easier for a therapist to *see* a woman as depressed and a man as alcoholic. This difference in acceptability may well help to produce the gender differences in diagnoses of depression and alcoholism discussed below.

BOX 10.1 LEARNING ACTIVITY
A Double Standard of Mental Health?

Think of a mentally healthy, well-adjusted, fully functioning adult man. On each of the scales below, indicate which pole would probably best describe this man:

Not at all independent _____ Very independent

Very talkative _____ Not at all talkative

Does not hide emotions well _____ Almost always hides emotions

Very tactful _____ Very blunt

Very excitable in a minor crisis _____ Not at all excitable in a minor crisis

Feelings easily hurt _____ Feeling not easily hurt

Very gentle_____ Very rough

Very self-confident _____ Not at all self-confident

Very subjective _____ Very objective

Very submissive_____ Not at all submissive

   Now go back and do the scale again, only this time think of a mentally healthy, well-adjusted, fully functioning adult woman.
   When you have completed the responses the second time, compare your answers for the mentally healthy man and the mentally healthy woman. Were they the same or different? To what extent do you think that being a mentally healthy woman entails different qualities than being a mentally healthy man?
   These items are adapted from the scale originally used to demonstrate that clinicians held a "double standard" of mental health (Broverman, Broverman, Clarkson, Rosenkrantz, & Vogel, 1970). Using the original scale, these researchers found that clinicians expected a normal healthy woman to be more submissive, less independent and adventurous, more easily influenced, less aggressive and competitive, more easily excitable in minor crises, more easily hurt, more emotional, more vain about her appearance, less objective, and less interested in math and science than the ideal healthy man.

   Mental illness, like physical illness, is often a reaction to conditions in the external environment. Yet, historically, mental illness among women has often been attributed to inherent biological or psychological weaknesses. At the beginning of the 20th century, **neurasthenia,** a mental disorder commonly diagnosed in women, was attributed to the weakness of the female reproductive system, as were a number of other disorders. Women were thought to be vulnerable because of internal factors associated with femininity. Accomplished, intellectual women (for example Alice James, Florence Nightingale, and Charlotte Perkins Gilman) often suffered from such "diseases," which probably arose not from female biology, but from the tension and unhappiness of trying to reconcile cultural prescriptions with their own ambitions. Torn between docile femininity and the desire for self-expression or accomplishment, they found that one safe way out of the dilemma was to become ill, and the illness took the form of the diagnosis that was then in vogue for women.

A tendency still exists within the mental health professions to locate the cause of women's emotional problems in internal—hormonal or intrapsychic—factors (see, for instance, the discussion of PMS in Chapter 3). The growth of feminist psychology, however, has led to increased attention to the environmental context in trying to understand and alleviate mental illness. Nevertheless, the language of clinical psychology and psychiatry remains a language of classifications and diagnoses—a language that calls to mind internal, not external, roots of mental illness. The language of diagnostic categories also implies that such categories are discrete and that individuals can easily be classified as "in" or "out" of them, but it is more useful to think of mental illness–related behaviors and symptoms as a continuum. It is also important to remember, while reading about the mental disorders that affect women, that the diagnostic labels represent culturally agreed-upon categories that can change in response to changes in the social environment. Just as the diagnosis of neurasthenia has gone out of fashion now, so in a few decades, the diagnosis of agoraphobia or bulimia may be regarded as a quaint rarity.

Depression

A person who persistently reports feelings of sadness, worthlessness, inadequacy, and helplessness; eating disturbances; social withdrawal; lack of ability to concentrate; tension; lack of energy; anxiety; and insomnia or excessive sleeping is likely to be diagnosed as depressed. **Depression** affects an individual's psychological, physical, and social functioning, making it difficult or impossible to summon up the motivation to pursue daily activities. Depression is one of the most thoroughly studied emotional illnesses; one consistent finding in the research is that women are more likely than men to be depressed.

Studies in the United States have consistently reported that women are 2 to 3 times as likely as men to be depressed, and a similar pattern has been reported in samples from Sweden, Germany, Canada, and New Zealand (Culbertson, 1997). This gender difference first appears in adolescence. Susan Nolen-Hoeksema (1990), who reviewed studies of depression and gender conducted outside the United States, found that a 2-to-1 female–male depression ratio was common in developed but not in developing countries, where gender differences in depression often did not appear.

Researchers do not yet understand why gender differences in depression vary with societal levels of income. However, one possibility is that women in high-income nations are as likely as men to have access to psychiatric care, whereas women in poor countries may have less recourse to or less exposure to such resources than men do. Thus women in some African villages might, for example, be likely to seek help from churches or traditional healers for depressive symptoms, whereas men might be referred to psychiatric institutions (Kisekka, 1990). This would result in men's, but not women's, depression being "counted"—making the depression rate look lower for women than for men.

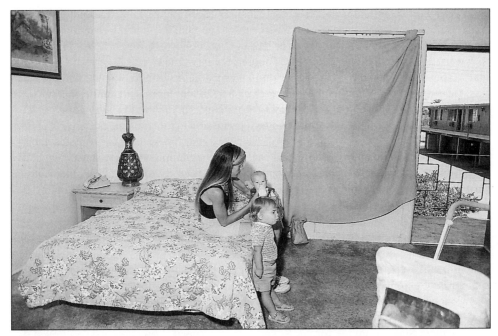

The American Psychological Association's task force on depression in women characterized poverty as a pathway to depression.

Even within countries, the depression–gender relationship may vary according to ethnicity and race. In the United States, female rates of depression have been found to be higher than male rates among European Americans, Native Americans, and various Hispanic American groups and to be lower among African Americans and Asian Americans (e.g., Gratch, Bassett, & Attra, 1995; Russo, Amaro, & Winter, 1987; LaFromboise, Choney, James, & Running Wolf, 1995; Root, 1995). One national mental health survey found that Hispanic Americans were the highest reporters of depression, and African Americans were the lowest; however, the 2-to-1 ratio for depression in women compared to men appeared to hold across groups (Kessler, McGonagle, & Zhao, 1994).

The latter study used a diagnostic instrument that was especially developed for cross-cultural research. Most studies, however, have relied on traditional instruments, and it is difficult to evaluate differences among ethnocultural groups with instruments (such as the scales or symptom categories psychologists have traditionally used to measure depression) that were designed originally for use with European Americans. For example, African American or Asian American women may be more likely than their counterparts in other ethnic groups to express feelings of sadness or hopelessness through physical symptoms or other kinds of behaviors, and thus may not be recognized as depressed. Or women from certain groups may be particularly reluctant to seek help from the mental health system, thus making it likely that their incidence of depression will be underestimated. As yet, there is no definite evidence for significant differences across ethnic groups in the tendency for women to have a higher frequency of depression than men. At least one large study of major depression has reported that in Western industrialized nations, the incidence is about 2 percent for men and 5 percent to 9 percent for women, regardless of race, education, or income group (Agency for Health Care Policy and Research, 1993).

What are the factors associated with depression in women? The American Psychological Association's task force on depression in women in the United States found that married women and mothers with a higher number of children were more likely to be depressed, and that economic status was strongly linked to depressive symptoms. Indeed, they characterized poverty as a "pathway to depression" (McGrath, Keita, Strickland, & Russo, 1990). The authors of this report also noted that the stress from traumas such as physical or sexual abuse was a major contributor to depression in women. Other researchers have reported that among poor inner-city Latina adolescents, acculturation was related to depression: Girls who relied more heavily on the Spanish than the English language were more likely to be depressed, a finding that has been echoed for other immigrant groups (Allen, Denner, Yoshikawa, Seidman, & Aber, 1996). Both poverty and discrimination may contribute to depression by adding sources of stress and undermining potential sources of social support (Belle & Doucet, 2003). Taken together, these predisposing factors suggest stress and lack of social support as important elements in women's risk for depression.

This interpretation is consistent with recent research showing that immigration is positively associated with depressive symptoms in women. For example, among immigrants to the United States from the former Soviet Union, women show more psychological distress than men. The distress seems to be related to the disruption in relationships experienced in the immigration process: In this group of immigrants, having less education, leaving relatives behind, and lacking sponsorship by friends or by a religious organization are factors more strongly associated with distress for women than for men (Aroian, Norris, & Chang, 2003).

Alisha Ali and Brenda Toner (2001) compared Caribbean women and immigrant Caribbean–Canadian women in terms of the life domains from which they derived their primary sense of meaning and their depressive symptoms. They found that the Caribbean women described their primary domains of meaning as relational: They found most of their sense of meaning in family, friendships, and intimate relationships. The Caribbean–Canadian women, on the other hand, were more likely to report that their primary domains of meaning were in the realms of self-nurturance, domains such as career goals and spirituality. Furthermore, the women who had immigrated to Canada reported more depressive symptoms and less meaningfulness for their primary domains than did their counterparts who had remained in the Caribbean. The researchers suggest that the immigrant experience "may be socially isolating and may lead to greater reliance on self-support rather than social support" (p. 179), and they note that immigrating to a new society forces individuals to search for new sources of meaning as they refashion their lives in a new environment. They argue that the higher rate of depressive symptoms among the immigrant women may reflect the lack of social support, the difficulties inherent in searching for meaningfulness in a new country, and the difficulties of living as a woman of color in a predominantly White society after moving from a society in which they were members of dominant racial groups.

But why should women be at higher risk than men for depression? Several explanations for the gender gap have been proposed:

1. The feminine role may predispose women to depression by encouraging them to feel and act helpless and to develop inadequate coping skills.

2. Women may be particularly sensitive to relationship difficulties and thus tend to develop relationship styles that leave them feeling powerless and particularly vulnerable to depression.

3. Women may face more stress than men do and so be more likely really to *be* helpless or powerless.

4. Women may be more vulnerable to depression for biological (hormonal) reasons.

5. Particular feminine qualities that develop in childhood may interact with environmental challenges that occur in adolescence to produce a greater incidence of female depression.

Each explanation may contain some portion of the truth; however, none of them has been supported unequivocally. Let us examine each in turn.

The Feminine-Role Hypothesis   In White, middle-class Western cultures (as well as in certain others), women are stereotyped as having many expressive traits such as emotionality, gentleness, nurturance, and sensitivity, and few instrumental traits such as aggressiveness, competence, ambition, and task orientation. They are expected to focus on their feelings and to suppress "unacceptable" feelings such as anger and competitiveness. Not only have women been socialized to fit these stereotypes, the environment has been structured to reinforce them. A review of the research on childhood socialization shows that girls are literally prepared to be powerless: They learn that the actions of boys are more likely than the actions of girls to have consequences of reward or punishment, that female competence is more likely than male competence to be ignored or greeted with ambivalence, and that work produced by females is less rewarded than similar work produced by males (Lips, 1994). Research on depression has already indicated that the sense of **learned helplessness** that develops when an individual comes to expect her actions will make no difference can lead to depression. It is likely that female socialization is more likely than male socialization to produce learned helplessness, and thus a susceptibility to depression.

There is considerable evidence that gender roles help predispose girls and boys to express psychological distress in different kinds of symptoms: internalizing symptoms such as depression, anxiety, and physical symptoms for girls, and externalizing symptoms such as delinquency, aggression, and conduct disorders for boys (Hoffman, Powlishta, & White, 2004). One aspect of the **feminine-role hypothesis** deals with the stereotypically feminine tendency to focus on moods and emotions, especially when feeling upset or threatened.

Susan Nolen-Hoeksema (1987) noted that men and women show different patterns when responding to their own feelings of depression: Men tend to engage in activities to distract themselves from their feelings, whereas women are more likely to dwell on the depression, its causes, and its implications. These differing reactions fit masculine and feminine gender roles, which discourage men from analyzing feelings and promote self-focus in women. Nolen-Hoeksema argues that the ruminative, inactive response to depression that is associated with the feminine role might amplify and prolong a depressive episode, and an active, distraction-oriented response might dampen and shorten it. Thus the feminine tendency to pay constant attention to one's own mood may be counterproductive in some ways.

Joyce Bromberger and Karen Matthews (1996) investigated the feminine-role hypothesis by looking for a connection between four characteristics associated with the feminine role—limited instrumentality, exaggerated expressiveness, tendency toward self-focus, suppression of angry feelings—and depression among a sample of middle-aged women. They found that when depression was measured 3 years after an initial assessment, the women who were most depressed were those who had earlier scored low on instrumentality, high on the tendency to focus on their emotions, and high on the tendency to suppress their anger. Moreover, those women who tended to reflect a lot on their inner feelings were more negatively affected by stressful events than other women were. No link was found, however, between expressiveness and depression. These findings indicate, the researchers say, that

> there are gender-linked traits that render women vulnerable to psychological distress in midlife . . . [but] . . . it is not the nurturing, socially sensitive, and concerned characteristics that make middle-aged women vulnerable to depressed mood. Rather, it is the more passive, restrained, and ruminative qualities attributed to women that render them susceptible to depressive symptoms, particularly when they experience a chronic problem. (p. 597)

Bromberger and Matthews used a population-based sample for their research, contacting randomly selected women with driver's licenses living within selected ZIP codes in a Pennsylvania county. Thus their sample must have been somewhat ethnically diverse, although they do not report its racial or ethnic composition. An important gap in the feminine-role hypothesis concerning greater female vulnerability to depression involves the tendency to assume that the feminine role is more or less equivalent for all groups of women. This is not necessarily the case, however. As discussed in earlier chapters, there is evidence that African American women are socialized more toward instrumentality than White women are. And we simply do not know whether women of various ethnic and cultural groups are socialized to focus on their feelings or to suppress their anger to the same extent that White, middle-class, North American women traditionally have been.

The Relationship Difficulties Hypothesis The loss of an important relationship is a strong precursor of depression for both women and men. Some theorists have argued that relationships are more central to women than to men and that women are more sensitive than men to disruptions in relationships. Thus women have learned to behave in certain ways to protect their heterosexual relationships—ways that leave them vulnerable to depression. This **relationship difficulties hypothesis** is related to the feminine-role hypothesis because women have learned, as part of the feminine role, that it is their responsibility to maintain their close relationships.

Dana Jack (1991) has proposed a **silencing the self** theory, which posits that women's greater vulnerability to depression springs from their attempts to establish intimate and satisfying connections with male partners within the context of feminine role requirements that do not allow them to assert their own needs in such relationships. She argues that women learn to engage in a set of attachment behaviors called "compliant connectedness" (p. 41), characterized by compulsive caretaking, pleasing the other, and inhibiting self-expression. Cultural prescriptions for feminine relationship behavior, according to Jack, push women to devalue and censor their own experience and feelings in close relationships, suppress their anger, and tolerate a lack of emotional response from their partners. For women, this all adds up to a silencing of the self in close relationships: Women keep quiet in order to make intimate relationships work. Ironically, the more a woman censors herself, the more she loses self-esteem, the less authentic connection she experiences with her partner, and the more vulnerable she is to depression.

To test her theory, Jack (1991) developed a Silencing the Self Scale to measure the extent to which individuals engage in these behaviors. Since then, she and other researchers have been testing her idea that self-silencing is linked to depression in women. Self-silencing was found to be associated with depression in three samples of predominantly European American women: women in shelters for battered women, female college students, and new mothers who used cocaine during pregnancy (Jack & Dill, 1992). When the research is extended to include more ethnically diverse samples, findings have been mixed. A study that compared female African American and European American community college students found that a significant relationship between silencing the self and depression occurred only for the European American women (Carr, Gilroy, & Sherman, 1996). However, Ali and Toner (2001) found a correlation between self-silencing and depression for Caribbean–Canadian women. Another study, which compared the responses of women and men who were African American, Asian, European American, and Hispanic, demonstrated a correlation between self-silencing and depression for both genders in all four ethnic groups (Gratch et al., 1995). Asian Americans showed significantly higher levels of self-silencing than any other ethnic group and, surprisingly in terms of the theory, men showed higher levels of self-silencing than women did. The finding that men reported more self-silencing than women was also obtained by Janice Thompson (1995), whose data came from a Canadian sample of cohabiting men and women. Thompson also found, however, that self-silencing was related to depression for women but not for men, and that women's self-silencing was related to both their own and their partner's relationship satisfaction.

The experiences of immigration and **acculturation** may be related to self-silencing for women. In the study of Caribbean–Canadian immigrant women discussed above, these women were higher in self-silencing than women who remained in the Caribbean (Ali & Toner, 2001). The researchers suggest that since self-silencing reflects pressures to express an outer self that is incompatible with the inner self, "[t]his need may be especially great among immigrant women who may feel that they differ from the accepted norms of their host society." (p. 179). In a similar pattern, research on Asian American women suggests that acculturation is negatively associated with self-silencing: the women who were most strongly Western identified (as opposed to Asian identified) had the lowest self-silencing scores (Wechsler & Rubin, 2000). This study also found, as predicted by the theory, that self-silencing was linked to depression for the women sampled.

Thus some aspects of silencing the self theory have been supported by research, but many questions remain. The finding that men report self-silencing as much as or more than women is difficult to explain. The theory, which grew out of the experiences of primarily European American women, appears to be relevant also to women from other ethnic and cultural groups. More research is needed to determine the scope of its usefulness.

The Stress Hypothesis   Too much stress, particularly uncontrollable stress, can precipitate depression. Perhaps women experience depression more than men do because they lead more stressful lives than men do. Research on this question produces mixed results: On the one hand, there is no conclusive evidence that women experience more **stressful life events** than men do, although, as noted in Chapter 9, women and men may experience the same stressful events differently. On the other hand, women are more likely than men to have low social and economic status and to live under a variety of **chronically stressful conditions**. Around the world, women are more likely than men to be poor, to be heading single-parent families, and to be victims of unpredictable, uncontrollable family violence. They are more likely than men to be trying to perform at least two concurrent full-time jobs: homemaker/mother within the home and paid employee outside the home. They are more likely to be victims of sexist discrimination. All of these conditions promote feelings of a lack of control over one's life—feelings that are usually linked to depression. Thus some of the gender differences in depression may be explainable by differences in exposure to or reactions to stress.

The stressful conditions of violence, poverty, and **gender role strain** may add to women's risk of many kinds of psychological distress, not just depression. As discussed later in this chapter, being a victim of violence is associated with post-traumatic stress disorder. As for poverty, it is well documented that individuals in low income categories are more likely than their high-income counterparts to exhibit not only depression, but also anxiety, substance abuse disorders, and multiple psychological disorders (Roades, 2000). Gender role strain, the feeling that different roles, such as worker, parent, and spouse, are interfering with one another and pulling one in opposing directions, is also a stressor that has been linked to many types of psychological distress (Roades, 2000). One study of women in Hong Kong examined their work and parenting experience and how they thought about their gender roles, in relation to their mental health (Tang & Tang, 2001). These authors found three themes in the ways their sample of Chinese employed women thought of their gender roles: *Traditional Ideal Person* (e.g., "When I assert my own needs I feel selfish"; "I can't feel good about myself unless I feel physically attractive); *Self-sacrifice* (e.g., "I find myself nurturing others but not myself"; "I often give up my own wishes in order to make other people happy"); and *Competence without Complaint* (e.g., "In order to feel confident, I must be able to handle many responsibilities without feeling overwhelmed"; "I feel as though I must push myself to the limit in order not to let other people down"). For these women, the researchers found that low work role quality (i.e., an unsatisfying or unpleasant job) was strongly associated with anxiety, depression, social dysfunction, and physical symptoms. They also found that women who were strong endorsers of the traditional ideal person theme were likely to exhibit psychological distress. And they found that, in some respects, the ways women thought about their gender roles *interacted* with their experience of particular roles to affect their level of distress. For example, among women who reported more worries and concerns than rewards in their mother role, those who subscribed to the traditional ideal person role reported significantly more symptoms than those who did not endorse this ideal. For women in unrewarding jobs, acceptance of the idea that they should be competent without complaint was associated with high levels of depression. And among women who reported high-quality work roles, those who endorsed the self-sacrifice ideal reported more distress than those who did not endorse this ideal—perhaps because they felt guilty about getting so many benefits from their work! These findings illustrate that, in calculating the impact of holding various roles, it is important to know not just what roles a woman is trying to fill, but also her ideas and feelings about how she should fill them.

The Hormone Hypothesis   It has been suggested that women are more susceptible to depression because of hormonal changes associated with their reproductive processes. After all, "everyone knows" that women are at high risk for depression during the premenstrual phase of their monthly cycle, during the early postpartum period, and at menopause because of the wild hormonal fluctuations that occur at those times. In fact, "everyone" is wrong. Menopause has not been convincingly linked to an increase in depression, and research linking depressed mood to the menstrual cycle and to the postpartum period has not demonstrated that the link has a hormonal basis. Cross-cultural research demonstrates, in fact, that the way women experience menstruation, pregnancy, childbirth, and menopause, depends on the cultural meaning assigned to them and the social support provided. One study of the experience of menopause compared rural Mayan Indian women in Mexico with rural Greek women (Beyene, 1989). The only symptom the Mayan women reported was the end of periods, and they looked forward to menopause as a time of health and freedom. The Greek women reported some physical symptoms as well as some irritability and depression, but they considered these to be normal, relatively minor symptoms. Neither group matched the usual North American expectation that menopause is a time when women are vulnerable to serious depression and unsettling physical symptoms.

The Developmental Hypothesis   The **developmental hypothesis** grows out of the observation that it is at adolescence that females begin to display much more depression than males do. This hypothesis suggests that even before adolescence, girls and boys tend to differ on qualities that are risk factors for depression. For instance, girls are more ruminative and self-focused, are less aggressive, and favor an interaction style that is more cooperative and relationship-oriented and less competitive than boys' in many cultures. These early risk factors interact with the challenges posed by adolescence to produce gender differences in depression (Nolen-Hoeksema & Girgus, 1994).

This model does not imply that being cooperative and less aggressive automatically leads girls to become more depressed. Rather, the model suggests that these qualities make girls more vulnerable to a sense of defeat and distress when they encounter the challenges that come with female adolescence: greater restrictions on their activities by parents, greater peer pressure to narrow their activities to fit feminine norms, a dramatic increase in the risk of sexual abuse and harassment. Furthermore, the gender differences in depression that first appear in adolescence lay the groundwork for similar differences in adulthood.

How? Depression in adolescence interferes with performance, thus restricting opportunities for future choices. Depression also creates negative self-perceptions and interpretations of events, influencing decision making about relationships and careers that can affect an individual's life for years into adulthood.

This complex model encompasses many of the factors that seem to contribute to the gender difference in depression, at least in the White, middle-class culture in which it was developed.

Suicide   The most dangerous consequence of depression is suicide, and attempted suicide is common among depressed girls and women. Although women are more likely than men to attempt suicide, men are more likely to complete their suicide attempts. In the United States, more than 4 times as many men as women die by suicide; however, about three times as many women as men report that they have attempted suicide (World Health Organization, 2002). The gender ratio of death by suicide differs around the world. For example, whereas Canada and Australia parallel the U.S. ratio of about 4 male to every 1 female suicide death, the ratio in the Russian Federation and in Mexico is higher than 6 to 1 and the ratio in Singapore and the Philippines is less than 2 to 1 (World Health Organization, 2002).

Other suicide risk factors besides depression seem to include youth, alcohol use, and a perceived lack of family or other support. In the United States, young Native American women, usually between the ages of 15 and 17, make up the largest single group of suicide-related hospitalizations—about one-fifth of young Native American women have attempted suicide (LaFromboise et al., 1995). As seen in Figure 10.1, death rates from suicide differ among the women from different racial/ethnic groups in the United States; the highest rates are among non-Hispanic White women and Native American women (National Center for Health Statistics, 2003). In the general U.S. population, women with professional careers (particularly physicians and chemists) have a higher incidence of suicide than women who are not professionals. This finding may be linked to the combination of high pressure and strong sense of isolation and lack of support that can accompany being in a token or minority position (Comas-Díaz & Greene, 1994b).

There has been some speculation that young women who attempt suicide have exaggerated needs to depend on others and that many suicide attempts could be avoided by helping young women separate from others and establish a healthy sense of psychological autonomy. This speculation stems from the observation that many female adolescents who try to kill themselves are deeply dissatisfied with their relationships. However, a Canadian study that compared adolescent girls who had recently attempted suicide with others who had never made such an attempt found no difference between the two groups on a measure of dependency. What did distinguish the two groups of young women were their perceptions of how adequate and satisfying their relationships were. Those who had attempted suicide were significantly less satisfied than the others with the adequacy and availability of their social networks and their intimate relationships, and they described their interpersonal conflicts as more severe (Bettridge & Favreau, 1995).

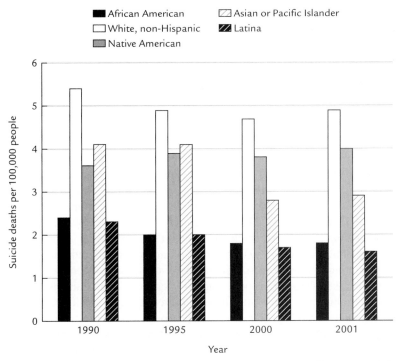

Figure 10.1 Death rates by suicide for U.S. women according to race/ethnicity (Number of deaths per 100,000 individuals). (Data source: National Center for Health Statistics [2003] *http://www.cdc.gov/nchs/data/hus/tables/2003/03hus046.pdf*).

Eating Disorders

Maria, an 18-year-old Argentine high school student, became obsessed with being thin after an ex-boyfriend called her "fatso" in front of her friends. She starved herself for weeks and wrapped nylon stockings and plastic bags around her body to sweat off weight. Soon she appeared gaunt and pale, with sunken cheeks and protruding ribs. She developed black patches under her eyes from malnutrition, stopped menstruating, and could not tolerate the sight of food. Finally, she says, "After three months, people began asking if I had AIDS—I was so glad then. I thought, that means I'm as thin as a model now. Now I'm beautiful" (Faiola, 1997, p. A24).

Maria's case is an example of an eating disorder called **anorexia nervosa:** an obsession with thinness leading to a distorted body image that results in self-starvation. People who suffer from anorexia tend to "feel fat" even when severely underweight, so they starve themselves in order to achieve the thinness they crave. A related eating disorder, **bulimia nervosa,** is characterized by a pattern of binge overeating followed by self-induced purging through dieting, vomiting, or the use of laxatives. This disorder too revolves around an obsession with body weight. Both disorders have, according to media reports, reached epidemic proportions in Argentina, where they are jointly known as "fashion model syndrome." The country's leading supermodel, Raquel Mancini, made headlines when she lapsed into a coma for several days after undergoing liposuction on her already slender body (Faiola, 1997). Eating disorders are most common among young, middle- to upper-class women, although the percentage of male cases in Argentina has increased in recent years from 5 percent to 12 percent.

Studies in the United States also show that women make up the majority of eating disorders cases. Only about 5 to 15 percent of people with anorexia or bulimia are male (National Institute of Mental Health, 2004). The most typical sufferer is a White, middle-class woman under the age of 25. Subgroups of young women for whom thinness is especially important—modeling students, athletes, professional dancers—show a higher than average incidence of these disorders. Data on the incidence of eating disorders among women of various ethnic groups is sketchy. Clinical reports in the 1960s and '70s commented on the conspicuous absence of Black women among anorexic patients, and the literature included few references to women of color (Dolan, 1991). Since then, epidemiological surveys have indicated a lower rate of anorexia and bulimia among women of color than among White women. For example, one study of female African American students found that only 3 percent met diagnostic criteria for bulimia, in contrast to 13 percent in a comparable group of White students (Gray et al., 1987). The strongest predictors of eating disorders are media-promoted body stereotypes and body dissatisfaction—and such dissatisfaction may vary according to the beauty ideals of particular cultural or racial/ethnic groups (Walcott, Pratt, & Patel, 2003). For example, European American girls are more likely than African American girls to report being overweight, being worried about being overweight, and perceiving that their families and friends are concerned about their weight (Thompson, Rafiroiu, & Sargent, 2003). On the other hand, African American girls tend to report being underweight. Body dissatisfaction associated with being either over- or underweight is associated with symptoms of eating disorders (Perez & Joiner, 2003).

It is extremely difficult to know whether African Americans and other women of color are absent from the literature on eating disorders because such disorders are really less prevalent among them or because of biases in the processes of diagnosis and referral. As Bridget Dolan (1991) notes, distress may be shown in different ways in different cultures, and may not always be recognized by White health care providers. And the presumption, based on the clinical literature, that women of color are unlikely to experience eating disorders may create a self-fulfilling prophecy: Clinicians may not recognize or diagnose eating disorders where they do not expect to see them. Supporting this idea are the findings of a laboratory study in which undergraduates were asked to read a passage about an adolescent girl who displayed eating disorder symptoms. Participants all read the same passage, except that for one group the girl was described as Caucasian, for one she was described as Hispanic, and for another she was described as African American. It turned out that participants who believed they were reading about a Caucasian girl were more likely than those who thought they were reading about an Hispanic or African American girl to recognize that she was suffering from an eating disorder (Gordon, Perez, & Joiner, 2002).

When women move from a non-Western to a Western culture, they may be subject to pressures to conform to an ideal of thinness. In one study, female Arab students who were studying at universities in London and in Cairo were compared on the Eating Attitudes Test (EAT). The two groups were quite different in their degree of Westernization: The London group wore typical European clothing; the Cairo group dressed in a traditional Arab manner, some wearing veils. The women in the London group were significantly more likely than those in the Cairo group to score above the clinical cutoff for eating disorders on the EAT, and were more likely to be diagnosed with bulimia (Nasser, 1986). Another researcher found a correlation between becoming acculturated (accepting U.S. values and customs) and being diagnosed with bulimia in young Japanese American, Korean American, and Chinese American women (Yi, 1989).

Culture affects eating behavior by shaping attitudes about what is beautiful. In a study that compared female British Caucasians, Kenyans, and Kenyan immigrants to Britain, Western cultural forces appeared to be associated with attitudes toward body weight. The women were shown the silhouettes of female figures with varying degrees of fatness. Kenyan women responded more positively to the fatter figures and less positively to the thinner figures than the White British women did. However, the Kenyan immigrants to Britain outdid the British women in their approval of the thin figures and disapproval of the fat ones (Furnham & Alibhai, 1983). Apparently, the immigrants were adopting Western attitudes with a vengeance, doing their best to assimilate.

In the United States, an increase in the number of eating disorders over the past 3 decades has coincided with a shift toward thinness as an ideal of feminine beauty and an increased interest in diets and weight reduction. Studies show that young women are very concerned with weight and use extreme and harmful methods to control it. One survey found that nearly one-third of a sample of female U.S. college students reported either self-induced vomiting or laxative use as a weight-loss strategy (Connor-Greene, 1988); another showed that up to 90 percent of U.S. college women had been on diets to lose weight (Dolan, 1994). Such behaviors and symptoms are not limited to middle-class college students; they are also common among rural Hispanic American and Pueblo Indian girls (Snow & Harris, 1989) and inner-city Latinas (Salguero & McCusker, 1996). Moreover, women experience negative social pressures relating to body weight and size from childhood onward. One study of full-figured African American women noted that they remembered being taunted about their size as children and continued to experience overt discrimination based on their size. They were excluded from social events at work, passed over for promotion, and rarely sent to conferences or meetings to represent their organization (Faulkner, 1995). These women's thinner colleagues surely got the message that they would be punished for exceeding cultural standards of size and weight.

Do women experience eating disorders outside a Western or Westernized middle- to upper-class cultural context? Apparently they sometimes do. A few case studies of eating disorders in women in African countries have been reported, and in Japan the disorders, although less frequent than in the United States, are still recognized (Dolan, 1991). Worldwide, the highest number of deaths from eating disorders is reported in the United States and Japan; however, as seen in Figure 10.2, a number of smaller countries have higher per capita mortality from eating disorders.

Eating disorders may be linked to issues of control or disturbed identity; they sometimes appear in women who seem to be trying to reconcile conflicting cultural identities or who feel trapped by or anxious about the requirements of the feminine role in their culture.

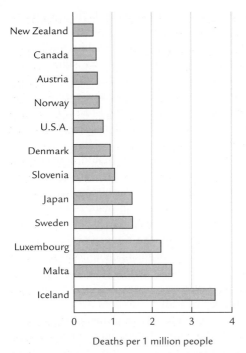

Figure 10.2 Countries with the highest number of death per capita from eating disorders. (Data source: http://www.nationmaster.com [2004])

Episodes of disordered eating are often preceded by negative emotions, such as fear, shame, or helplessness, and they may be one way an individual feels she can deal with such feelings (Lyubomirsky, Casper, & Sousa, 2001). A woman may start trying to control her food intake because that is one thing she feels she *can* control. Unfortunately, what often happens is that her pattern of eating behavior begins to control her instead. She finds, in the case of anorexia, that she can no longer force herself to eat or, in the case of bulimia, that she cannot control her urge to binge and purge. In many cases, she may lose not only control of her eating patterns, but her health and even her life. The physical health consequences of anorexia include bone marrow failure, liver dysfunction, heart arrhythmia, and heart failure. Kidney and endocrine abnormalities, extreme fatigue, and muscle weakness are common among bulimics. Some 5 to 10 percent of anorexics die from starvation or suicide (Chrisler, 2001).

Panic Disorder and Agoraphobia

Panic disorder involves the experience of panic attacks that occur without warning and without any obvious reason. These attacks are bouts of intense physiological arousal that may be characterized by symptoms such as a pounding and/or irregularly beating heart, chest pains, and difficulty breathing (American Psychiatric Association, 1994). Panic disorder is twice as common in women as in men, and it most often begins in late adolescence or early adulthood (National Institute of Mental Health, 1994).

If panic attacks happen repeatedly and seem to be uncontrollable, the sufferer may develop an anxiety disorder such as **agoraphobia** (literally "fear of the marketplace"), a strong fear of venturing out in public (because she is afraid of having a panic attack there). In a small percentage of cases, agoraphobia can occur without a history of panic disorder. In such cases the individual may be fearful of a specific occurrence such as fainting or loss of bladder control while she is out in public rather than a panic attack. In either type of agoraphobia, the phobia may become so strong that the person becomes completely housebound, unable to go to work, to go shopping, or even to go out with friends. A person with severe agoraphobia is literally crippled by fear and finds it impossible to lead a normal life. She follows a strictly circumscribed routine and becomes increasingly dependent on trusted others, such as a spouse.

Women are much more likely than men to be fearful of being alone or of leaving the house alone, and are more likely to be diagnosed as agoraphobic (Watkins & Lee, 1997). In the United States, women account for up to 82 percent of the cases of agoraphobia (Clum & Knowles, 1991). Among Hispanic Americans, European Americans, and African Americans, women are significantly more likely than men to experience panic attacks and to have panic disorder (Katerndahl & Realini, 1993).

Some theorists suggest that these anxiety disorders are caused by a combination of neurobiological factors (such as heartbeat irregularities triggered by stress) with a tendency to misinterpret symptoms (for example, to assume that one is having a heart attack) and a tendency to cope with problems by avoiding them rather than by confronting them. These theories may well explain the immediate mechanism through which a few instances of severe anxiety become transformed into a chronic phobia in an individual, but they do not explain why women should be so overrepresented among sufferers of panic attacks and agoraphobia. To do so, it may be necessary to look at the broader cultural picture of what is expected of women.

In trying to unravel the cause of the female preponderance among agoraphobics, some feminist theorists have suggested that the feminine role makes women particularly vulnerable to the thoughts and behaviors that characterize this disorder. Studies have shown that agoraphobics tend to display, sometimes in rather extreme ways, many aspects of the stereotypical feminine role: unassertiveness, compliant and dependent behavior, difficulty in expressing anger, and passive, avoidant approaches to interpersonal problems (Watkins & Lee, 1997). Feminist theorists have argued that contemporary cultural messages about femininity are ambiguous, conflicting, and often unattainable. Women are supposed to be "assertive and competent in the public world of men, feminine and nurturing in relationships and within the home, and physically 'beautiful' by contemporary normative standards of beauty" (Watkins & Lee, 1997, p. 68). One way a woman can escape from these contradictory demands is to become ill. If the illness she develops is agoraphobia, it both facilitates an extreme version of compliance with society's demand that she be dependent and submissive and simultaneously expresses a request for help. Furthermore, the timidity, helplessness, and dependence that are associated with agoraphobia may be reinforced by the sympathy and attention of those around her. Men who experience similar reactions of

Women who immigrate to a new country face many stressors, including becoming members of a visible minority, the necessity of learning a new language and a new profession, and the reestablishment of old family relationships in a new cultural context.

fear and helplessness are far less likely than women to be reinforced for them; men are supposed to be strong, not fearful.

Post-Traumatic Stress Disorder

> Ba escaped [from Vietnam] with 100 other individuals in a small boat. They encountered pirates on their second day out, who conducted body searches and took all their valuables, food, water, and gasoline, leaving them drifting on the open seas in the hot sun. Ba fell ill, became delirious, and had vivid hallucinations of being raped repeatedly by the pirates. . . . After her recovery, Ba was told by fellow boat members that those hallucinations were actual events . . . (Tien, 1994, p. 481)

After her escape, Ba waited 1½ years to be accepted for immigration to the United States. Her arrival introduced her to a number of new stressors: the cold weather of San Francisco, for which she was not prepared; the experience of being a visible minority woman after growing up in a country where she was a member of the majority; the necessity of learning a new language and a new profession; and the reestablishment of old family relationships in a new cultural context. Some 10 years later, she sought treatment for stress-induced headaches and back spasms that came almost daily. In her initial interview with her therapist, she said that she also suffered from insomnia, nightmares, decreased sexual desire, avoidance of open water, and general anxiety. Her therapist diagnosed her as suffering from **post-traumatic stress disorder (PTSD).**

A person who has experienced one or more severe emotional traumas—such as physical attack, rape, war violence, serious accidents, and physical, sexual, or emotional abuse —may later, and over a considerable period of time, display a set of symptoms characteristic of post-traumatic stress disorder. The symptoms may include depression, insomnia, anxiety, nightmares, feelings of being in danger, and irritability. The diagnosis was originally formulated on the experiences of male combat veterans, but it is common among both men and women.

Women who have been abused by their husbands and have lived in fear for years are likely to exhibit post-traumatic stress disorder, as are women who have been attacked and raped and women who have been the victims of childhood sexual abuse (Koss, Bailey, Yuan, Herrera, & Lichter, 2003). Women who have been targets of aggressive acts of racism, sexism, or heterosexism may experience the chronic anxiety and sense of being in danger that is one facet of PTSD. Refugee women from countries in which war and acts of terror have been common, and who may have been tormented and seen others tortured and killed, often arrive in their new country displaying symptoms of PTSD (Tien, 1994). Trauma can be indirect as well as direct: Women may be traumatized because a loved one has been hurt. Thus, for example, researchers note that in many Native American communities, the women are caught up in a "cycle of endless, unresolved grief and mourning" because of the frequent tragedies (motor vehicle accidents, homicide, suicide) that occur in these communities (LaFromboise et al., 1995, p. 202). The women may respond to these traumas with depression, despair, and anxiety; they are likely to be suffering from PTSD rather than from simple depression. All over the world, women who have been exposed to torture and violence; to the sudden losses that come with epidemics, wars, or natural disasters; or who have been thrown out by their families because of disagreements or disgrace may suffer from PTSD.

Alcohol and Drug Abuse

No matter what country the statistics are from, the pattern is consistent: Women are less likely than men to use and abuse alcohol and illegal drugs (Jernigan, 2001; United Nations, 1995). Although the data from many parts of the world is skimpy, the available studies show male-to-female ratios of alcohol dependence that range from 20 to 1 for patients in Sri Lanka, 6 to 1 for psychiatric outpatients in the Czech Republic, and 4 to 1 for hospital employees in Zimbabwe, to 2 to 1 among survey respondents in Mexico. Women have been identified as 9 percent of registered drug abusers in Greece, 11 percent of drug abuse treatment patients in Brazil, 7 percent of registered opium users in Turkmenistan, and 4 percent of registered heroin users in Sri Lanka. In Canada, among women over the age of 15, 5.1 percent report using marijuana in the past year (as compared to 10.1 percent for men); 0.7 percent report using LSD, speed, or heroin (as compared to 1.5 percent for men); and 0.5 percent report using cocaine (as compared to 0.8 percent for men) (Canadian Centre on Substance Abuse, 2003). In the United States, men are more likely than women to drink and to abuse alcohol and drugs (National Center for Health Statistics, 2003). In some countries, drug treatment facilities are open only to men, because it is

judged more important to devote the limited available resources to them, and many facilities refuse to admit pregnant women (United Nations, 1995).

Within the United States, alcohol use varies among the women of different ethnic and
cultural groups. Latina and African American women are more likely than White women
to report a low incidence of alcohol use (Caetano, 1994), but alcoholism appears to be an
epidemic problem among American Indian women (LaFromboise, Berman, & Sohi,
1994). Acculturation may be associated with increased alcohol use for Latina immigrants
(Caetano, 1994). Research also suggests that lesbians may be less likely than heterosexual
women to abstain from alcohol and more likely to report problem drinking (Hughes &
Wilsnack, 1997).

One risk associated with overuse of alcohol or other drugs by pregnant women is
damage to the developing fetus. Babies born to addicted mothers may be drug-addicted
themselves, and they may suffer a variety of long-term effects on health and ability to
function. In the United States, fetal alcohol syndrome, a combination of irreversible birth
abnormalities resulting from alcohol use by a mother during pregnancy, appears disproportionately among babies born to Native American and African American women, and it
may have profound implications for these groups (Comas-Díaz & Greene, 1994a).

In North America, initial experimentation with drugs and alcohol usually begins in
junior high school or earlier. Studies indicate that Asian, Black, and Hispanic girls consistently report lower rates of alcohol and drug use than White and Native American girls do
(Barnes, Farrell, & Banerjee, 1994). The behaviors that are associated with the use of these
substances include low school achievement, delinquent activities, running away, conflict
with parents, rebelliousness, and nonconformity. Adolescent drug and alcohol users also
tend to show low self-esteem, depression, anxiety, low aspirations, and difficulty in delay-
ing gratification. However, the behavioral and psychological correlates of using drugs and
alcohol may vary across genders and across ethnic and class groups (Gibbs, 1996).

In a study of the use of drugs and alcohol among a multiethnic U.S. sample of urban
girls in the seventh to ninth grades, about 23 percent of the girls reported ever having used
alcohol and marijuana, and 11.6 percent reported having used one or more other drugs
(Gibbs, 1996). White girls were significantly more likely than Black girls to use alcohol
(44 percent versus 14 percent) and other drugs (11.6 percent versus 7.3 percent), but the
two groups reported using marijuana at almost identical rates. A similar pattern appeared
when girls from different income groups were compared: Middle- and higher-income girls
were more likely to use alcohol and other drugs than lower-income girls were, whereas the
incidence of marijuana use did not vary across income groups.

Despite these group differences in the incidence of drug and alcohol use in this sample, the characteristics linked to regular drug use were largely similar for African American
and European American girls. In both groups, girls who used illicit substances were more
likely than nonusers to skip classes, to break school rules, and to have been suspended or
expelled. They were also more likely to be sexually active and to report problems in getting
along with their families. However, there were some suggestions of different precursors to
drug use for the two groups. African American girls attending integrated schools were less
likely than European American girls in the same schools to use alcohol and other drugs;
African American girls involved in extracurricular activities were less likely than involved

European American girls to use alcohol and marijuana. And African American girls who had moved away from friends were more likely to use marijuana than were White girls in similar circumstances. Different factors, then, may increase the vulnerability or resilience of each group; more research is needed to clarify these factors.

Because alcohol and drug abuse have been labeled as male problems, research on women with these problems has lagged far behind that on men. Research in the last 15 years, however, has begun to shed some light on the reasons for alcohol and drug abuse among women. For example, research on twins has now shown that genetics plays a significant role in determining a woman's vulnerability to severe alcoholism. Among 590 pairs of identical female twins (twins sharing the same genetic makeup), a woman was 5 times more likely to experience severe alcoholism if her twin was an alcoholic than if her twin was not. Among 440 sets of fraternal twins (twins who shared the womb, but not their genetic makeup), a woman was only 1.6 times more likely to be an alcoholic if her twin was one. The researchers calculated that genetics accounted for 53 percent to 61 percent of a woman's tendency to become an alcoholic, depending on how alcoholism was defined (Kendler, Heath, Neale, Kessler, & Eaves, 1992). (Such figures may oversimplify the relationship between genes and alcoholism. As noted in Chapter 3, it should be remembered that although genes may provide some potential for susceptibility to a problem such as alcoholism, the expression of this potential depends on a series of interactions between heredity and environment at each stage of the woman's development.)

For many women, having been sexually abused as a child may be a contributor to later alcohol and drug abuse. These women may use alcohol and drugs to help them cope with the long-term emotional aftereffects—feelings of powerlessness, low self-esteem, and isolation—of the abuse (Rohsenow, Corbett, & Devine, 1988). When women entering inpatient treatment for substance abuse are routinely questioned about their childhood history of sexual victimization, they report a much higher incidence of such victimization than that usually reported in community surveys.

In most cultures, women who abuse drugs and alcohol face more of a social stigma than men do. Women are supposed to find "ladylike" ways of coping with distress rather than taking the disinhibiting route of psychoactive drugs. A woman who is drunk is viewed with disgust; a man who is drunk is viewed more tolerantly. Ironically, the very strength of the social rules regarding gender expectations may be one of the factors that push women toward drugs. For example, cocaine can make users feel self-confident, powerful, competent, and in control—feelings that traditional gender roles often deny to women. Indeed, some evidence suggests that among White, middle- to upper-class women in the United States, at least, heroin use may be related to rebellion against the constraints of the feminine role (Friedman & Alicea, 1995).

Jennifer Friedman and Marisa Alicea (1995) interviewed White middle- and upper-class women at two methadone clinics in the United States. These women remembered their initial heroin use as a way of resisting the cultural emphasis on obedience, subservience, selflessness, physical beauty, silence, and devaluation of self-worth they became subjected to as young women. They did not want to be "good girls"; they wanted to be curious, wild, rebellious, and self-confident. They had felt stifled by their parents' expectations of them, as noted by these two study participants:

[My mother] never really pushed me to do anything, except to just eventually get married and have a baby . . . If I would try to get a job that was better, she would say I can't do [it] . . . Anything that I would think that I could do . . . she never wanted me to do it. (p. 436)

I grew up in a very good home . . . I come from a very wealthy family. If I would have stayed home, I could have had anything I wanted. [But] I wanted to do what I wanted to do. I was the black sheep of the family. I was a rebel. Nobody told [me] what to do . . . And finally I kept running away and my parents couldn't keep me home. (p. 437)

Heroin provided a path of rebellion for these women—something unladylike and wild that made them feel good. Unfortunately, what began as an escape from gender roles ultimately trapped these women in even more negative aspects of femininity. Once they became "problems," they were silenced and treated as nonpersons by their male partners and by medical professionals. They were sexually exploited by men. Many resorted to selling sex to support their drug habit—or a boyfriend's drug habit. Many developed low self-esteem and feelings of inadequacy—feelings that persisted as they struggled to escape their heroin habit by becoming clients at the methadone clinic.

Clearly, ethnocultural factors interact with gender in the development of drug or alcohol dependency. For instance, the women in the study just described were rebelling against a specifically Western, White, middle-class set of gender role expectations. Women in other groups may have very different reasons for turning to drugs and alcohol.

Diagnosis and Treatment

If a person is experiencing emotional problems or symptoms that may signal a mental illness, she may seek help from a physician or a mental health practitioner. As is the case with physical symptoms, women are more likely than men to seek professional help for emotional distress. Women may find it easier than men to seek treatment because, in some cultures at least, it is more acceptable for a woman than for a man to talk about emotional issues and to admit a need for help. In White, middle-class, North American society, a woman asking for help with emotional problems is behaving in a way that meets gender role expectations. In fact, some have argued that psychotherapy can be dangerous for such women because it can reinforce the dependency and helplessness that are built into their culture's feminine role (Chesler, 1972). Therapy can put the woman into a dependency relationship with an authority figure, and if the therapist is male it can support the idea that a woman needs a man to solve her problems.

Because the interaction between a therapist and client takes place in the context of cultural expectations and stereotypes, it is bound to be influenced to some extent by these stereotypes. What feelings and behaviors are labeled as problematic, what issues are highlighted or ignored, what solutions are attempted—all can be affected by preconceived ideas held by the therapist (and the client). For example, when a physically abused woman arrives, shaken and upset, at a hospital clinic, she is likely to receive different treatment depending on her race. If she is White, she is more likely to be given psychoactive drugs, such as tranquilizers; if she is a woman of color, she is less likely than her White counterpart to receive even basic pain medication (Walker, 1995).

The Politics of Diagnosis

Putting a label on a cluster of symptoms, providing a diagnosis, inevitably affects the way the person experiencing those symptoms views her problem. It also affects the way others view her and the kinds of solutions that are offered. For example, if a person who has been feeling tired and listless is told she is depressed, she may search for something in her interpersonal life that is causing the depression rather than assuming that she simply needs more rest. Her doctor may prescribe antidepressant drugs rather than examine her eating and exercise habits. The diagnosis of depression assigns a particular meaning to the symptoms and encourages both client and therapist to view those symptoms in a particular light.

In addition to its effect on individuals, the use of diagnostic categories can influence and be influenced by stereotypes of whole groups. Our values and expectations tend to shape both what is considered "normal" for a given group of people and how we notice and label deviations from those norms. In fact, the diagnoses that are most commonly applied to members of specific gender, racial, ethnic, and class groups tend to embody the roles and stereotypes attributed to those groups. Men predominate in disorders that encompass antisocial behavior and aggressiveness; women are most often diagnosed with disorders such as depression and anxiety that involve passivity and helplessness. Hope Landrine (1987) gave stereotyped descriptions of lower-class men, single middle-class women, married middle-class women, and married upper-class men to a sample of clinical psychologists and psychiatrists and asked the clinicians to provide diagnoses for these "cases," explicitly reminding them that the cases might be normal. Landrine found that the stereotype of the lower-class man was labeled antisocial, the stereotype of the married middle-class woman was labeled dependent, the stereotype of the single middle-class woman was labeled histrionic/hysterical, and the stereotype of the married upper-class man was labeled prototypically normal. She found no differences in the ways male versus female clinicians or psychoanalytic versus feminist therapists labeled the cases—suggesting that all were influenced by the prevailing social stereotypes about gender and class.

An example of the politics of diagnosis can be seen in the controversy over the inclusion of **premenstrual dysphoric disorder (PMDD)** in the DSM-IV, the diagnostic manual of the American Psychiatric Association (DeAngelis, 1993). The diagnosis, which had been hotly debated among mental health professionals for years, is intended to be applied to a woman who chronically experiences at least 5 of the following 10 symptoms during the premenstrual phase of her cycle: depressed and hopeless feelings, marked anxiety and tension, tendency toward sudden sadness and crying, persistent anger or irritability, lethargy, decreased interest in life activities, appetite changes, insomnia, a sense of being out of control, and physical symptoms such as swollen breasts, headaches, bloating, and weight gain. The symptoms must markedly interfere with the woman's personal and professional activities for the diagnosis to be applied.

The inclusion of PMDD in the manual met with the unanimous opposition of the psychiatric association's Committee on Women as well as that of many concerned psychologists. Petitions and letters from organizations and individuals representing more than 6 million people opposed the inclusion of this diagnostic category in the manual (Caplan, 2001). Critics of the diagnosis argued that, by calling this set of symptoms a psychiatric (rather than medical) disorder, it was labeling as "mentally pathological" a set of symptoms that are, to some extent, a normal part of the female cycle. Labeling the symptoms as a sign that the woman is somehow "crazy" would, they insisted, magnify the symptoms and actually help women to construe their experience as being "unbalanced." They also pointed out that there is little direct evidence linking the symptoms with the hormonal fluctuations of the menstrual cycle and that the premenstrual phase may simply be a time when some women feel it is more culturally acceptable to vent irritability or anger. Furthermore, they objected to the notion of a single-gender mood disorder, noting that if there are mood disorders triggered by hormonal shifts then men too might experience such disorders. On the other side, advocates of the diagnosis argued that the creation of the PMDD diagnostic category would allow women to have their complaints taken seriously rather than being told that they were overreacting to symptoms that are well tolerated by most women. As Caplan (2001) notes, "some women were so relieved to have their physical discomfort and unpleasant feelings recognized that they rushed to defend the label rather than asking for compassion and help that stopped short of diagnosing them as mentally ill" (p. 1). After years of debate, the PMDD diagnosis was listed in the DSM-IV under depressive disorders, but its criteria were listed in the appendix, indicating that the disorder requires further study.

Mental health policy as it relates to gender and other social categories is not value neutral, but tends to define the behavior of powerful groups as normative and that of other groups as sick. To illustrate this point, Kaye-Lee Pantony and Paula Caplan (1991) mockingly proposed the inclusion of a new diagnostic category, "delusional dominating personality disorder," in the DSM. Among the symptoms of this disorder are the "tendency to use power, silence, withdrawal, and/or avoidance rather than negotiation in the face of interpersonal conflict or difficulty," and a "tendency to feel inordinately threatened by women who fail to disguise their intelligence." The authors posit that this disorder occurs most frequently in males but is occasionally present in females, and tends to be pronounced among "leaders of traditional mental health professions, military personnel, executives of large corporations, and powerful political leaders of many nations" (p. 121).

When diagnoses of mental illness are applied to relatively powerless people, the effect is often to disempower them further, to make them feel and appear flawed and weak. Thus when a woman is diagnosed as depressed, for example, she may feel, and be seen as, inadequate—as if something is wrong inside her—and this perception may contribute to a further cycle of depression and powerlessness. Some therapists have argued, therefore, that diagnoses should take into careful consideration the external circumstances of the individual and place more emphasis on these circumstances as reasons for the symptoms. Many women may show symptoms of depression after terrible events and sudden losses in their lives. For instance, Liang Tien (1994) notes that almost two-thirds of Southeast Asian immigrant women refugees treated in the mental health system in the state of Washington were diagnosed as depressed. Many of these women were severely victimized in their home countries and then entered their new country under extremely stressful social and economic circumstances. Tien argues that a diagnosis of post-traumatic stress disorder would be more appropriate than depression for many of these women, even though the symptoms are much the same. Why? "The diagnosis allows the client to feel less flawed and to interpret her symptoms as understandable reactions to extraordinary life events. It also allows the therapist to explore in depth the traumatic incidents in the client's past, which will eventually lead to the appropriate mourning of the life she lost to war and migration" (p. 496).

In a similar vein, Maria Root (1992) discusses the notion of **insidious trauma:** the continuous stresses of racism, sexism, emotional abuse, class discrimination, and other negative social forces that can erode an individual's well-being over the course of a life-time. Root argues that women of color, living their lives under the shadow of racism, are exposed to greater degrees of insidious trauma than their more privileged White sisters. Such exposure can activate survival behaviors that might be mistaken for symptoms of mental illness by a therapist who did not understand their cause. Similarly, a lesbian, con-scious of homophobia, might display protective hyperalertness, a readiness to identify and deal with dangerous situations. In either instance, a woman who appears more angry and suspicious than expected might receive a psychiatric diagnosis, when her reactions are actually quite reasonable in the context of her own experiences of discrimination.

Laura Brown (1992) suggests a diagnosis that, somewhat like PTSD, takes into con-sideration the impact of the client's sociocultural environment on her emotional reactions to new traumas. **Oppression artifact disorder** is her label for the lack of resilience that might occur in a woman of color who is worn down from dealing with small or large instances of racism on a daily basis. Once again, such a "disorder" would *not* be the result of a flaw inside the person, but rather an understandable reaction to the stresses imposed by the social environment. Brown uses the label as a way of calling attention to the pres-sures that a person of color might sustain in terms of mental health, simply by living in a racist society.

Finally, it is important to consider whether the entire system of psychiatric diagnosis, as represented by the DSM, is helpful to women. Feminist critics of the DSM have noted that it is based on a disease model, in which disorders are considered "real" and are not considered in the context of patients' identities and contexts: their gender, race, and socioeconomic class (Maracek, 2001). Disorders are defined in the DSM as sets of symp-toms unrelated to context or personal meaning. Maracek (2001) argues that "The disease model is inconsistent with the feminist emphasis on the social context, especially the power relationships within that context" (p. 306). Furthermore, she notes that the bound-aries between disorders are artificial and not necessarily congruent with women's experi-ence. She notes, as well, that although the number of categories in the DSM has risen substantially over the years, most individuals who seek help from a mental health profes-sional have problems that do not fit neatly into any DSM category.

Psychotherapy

A person seeking treatment for emotional or mental symptoms will often find herself involved in some form of **psychotherapy.** In all its many variations, psychotherapy involves a client and therapist talking with each other about the issues and/or symptoms that are bothering the client. The ideal is that the therapist will provide the help, support, and guidance the client needs to deal with painful, difficult feelings.

Although psychotherapy can be extremely helpful, it is subject to the same problems as any other interpersonal situation in which one person (in this case, the therapist) has

WOMEN AND MENTAL HEALTH:
A SOUTH AFRICAN PERSPECTIVE

LILY-ROSE MLISA *is a clinical psychologist at the Student Counseling Service at the University of Fort Hare, South Africa. She was the first Black student to complete the program in clinical psychology at the University of Port Elizabeth, and one of only a few Black women registered as clinical psychologists in South Africa. Before becoming a psychologist, she was a nurse and a teacher. Now, in addition to her work at the Counseling Service, she coordinates, on a volunteer basis, a small group of fieldworkers who offer assistance to victims of wife battering and child abuse.*

Q. What do you see as the most important issues with respect to the psychology of women in your country?

A. I think that just psychology per se is something people do not understand. There is a stigma attached to psychological conditions in South Africa. A mental hospital is like a madhouse. People do not know that if you have signs of depression you can go to an outpatient clinic; they don't understand that just talking to a psychologist could help. There is a lot of depression, and doctors will treat depression, even very mild depression, with drugs. Psychologists could help many people without drugs, but professionals often fight each other rather than working as a team.

Also, education in psychology helps with understanding other people's emotions. When I was a nurse, I often had no understanding of what was going on emotionally with a patient or with the relatives. And my training in psychology helped me to understand myself and handle my own emotions too. Women in South Africa need to be educated in this. If women are educated, then the culture is educated, because women have to rear children.

There are more women than men in South Africa, and they have many problems that can be addressed by psychology. For example, almost every woman in South Africa has a post-traumatic stress disorder, resulting from some terrible incident that has never been worked out. Education is a problem too, especially for women in rural areas, where there is a lot of illiteracy.

If more women could be used in psychology as counselors it would help a lot. It has been a male profession in South Africa. Now there is an increase in women, though mostly White women. If there could be an increase among women of other groups it would help. But one problem is that counseling is still taught as a Western-oriented, individualized profession, using U.S.-based literature that is not contextualized for the South African situation. The society, though, is family oriented and people are used to group sharing, not individual counseling.

Q. What about violence?

A. There is a lot of woman-battering, even among professionals. But there may be a big difference between rural and urban women. Rural women often do not see battering

WOMEN AND MENTAL HEALTH:
A SOUTH AFRICAN PERSPECTIVE *(continued)*

as wrong—that's just the way things are. Child sexual abuse is common. Adults pay children for sex; these children are at the mercy of old, rich men.

Also, the mothering role is so tied to protecting the family unit that mothers sometimes do not report incest. They may protect the husband at the expense of the child. The mother is hoping, praying that it will stop, but no one is allowed to talk about it. The child is not believed, or the mother makes herself believe that it is something that will go away. Women should learn the value of reporting this, but it is rarely reported. It is hard to find statistics on this, but our group had 22 cases of child abuse in 1 month.

Rape and sexual abuse are very predominant. They are not reported because women get secondary abuse in the courts. If women could be taught about their bodies—when and how to say no—before they are victims, I think it would help. Sex education is important, and it should be done as early as possible.

Children are suffering. Young women are having lots of children, but they have nothing to care for them. There is high infant mortality and many nutritional problems. Often a child cannot go to school because there is no free education available; these children are socialized as early as 6 or 7 to steal. Even at school there are problems: One day we were called to a primary school where 25 children were "drunk"—they had sniffed benzene. And for adolescents there is an increase in suicidal tendencies. They cannot depend on their elders anymore; they are running away from traditional cultures and depending on their peer groups.

Q.   Are women in South Africa focusing on gender as an issue?

A.   Women are in a very confused state with gender. According to all the cultures in South Africa, men are the heads of families. Women sometimes think that women's emancipation means taking over men. Now men are resisting. Men don't want to attend workshops on gender. But I think we should talk about gender, including males and females.

There is supposed to be a Gender Commission in each institution that reports to the premier's office. But no one knows what the structure should be. How much power should the "head" of this group have? At the end of the day, very little is happening.

Also, we are different women in South Africa and we have been exploited in different ways. We, as women in the "working" class, are often exploiting uneducated rural women, assuming we should think for them. And some of our sisters were perpetrators of our exploitation. When we talk about reconciliation, we ask "how?" There is too much hurt. Whites also have a lot of anger, and they are trying hard to suppress it. White women are trying hard to adjust to the new situation in South Africa, but they are trying not to show how hard it is for them. Barriers of race and culture, with all the stereotyping, will take time to wear down, if ever. But psychology must try to contextualize each women's issue within particular cultures. This is very difficult.

more power than the other (the client). The therapist's values and biases can shape the therapeutic process more easily than the client's values can, and the therapist's values may be inappropriately applied to the client's situation. For example, a woman trying to find the courage to leave or renegotiate an oppressive, unhappy marriage is unlikely to be helped by a therapist who believes that the man is the natural head of the family. Similarly, a therapist's ignorance of the cultural issues affecting a client makes it virtually impossible for the therapeutic process to be helpful to that client. If the therapist in the preceding scenario is unaware that the client comes from a cultural background in which arranged marriages are the norm and that the client's own marriage was arranged, it will be much more difficult for the therapist to understand and be helpful to the client.

Several decades ago, when the psychology of women was an emerging field of study, examinations of the psychotherapeutic process uncovered many examples of sexism. Many instances were reported of therapists being ignorant about sexual and reproductive issues, rigidly fostering traditional gender roles, telling sexist jokes, refusing to take violence against women seriously, and seducing their female clients (American Psychological Association, 1975). Since then, both the American and Canadian psychological associations have published guidelines for therapy with women and materials to help therapists confront and deal with their own gender biases (American Psychological Association, 1978; Canadian Psychological Association, 1980). The goal of these efforts is the promotion of nonsexist or "sex-fair" therapy. **Nonsexist therapy** is based on the idea that gender stereotypes should not guide the therapeutic process—that clients should be treated as individuals first, rather than as women or men. A practitioner of nonsexist therapy would not, for example, use an assumption that "too much" assertiveness in a woman (but not in a man) is a problem or that any woman who does not want to have children is denying her femininity.

Feminist Therapies   **Feminist therapies** go beyond nonsexist therapy in that they not only explicitly disavow traditional gender stereotypic assumptions about behavior, they openly discuss and analyze the stereotypes. There is no single feminist therapy. Rather,

> Feminist therapy is a philosophy of therapy, not a set of specific techniques, nor a theoretical orientation. As such, it is a broad umbrella under which a wide variety of practitioners and practices can flourish. (Maracek, 2001, p. 311)

The many versions of feminist therapy tend to share certain basic principles (Butler, 1985; Maracek, 2001). Feminist therapy acknowledges that women are harmed by living in a society that is often sexist, racist, and oppressive toward women based on their social class, age, or sexual orientation. It emphasizes the sociocultural context as an important factor in the client's experience and behavior. Feminist therapists try to empower their clients, honoring their own perspectives on their lives, helping them to become stronger by setting their own goals and exploring choices that transcend traditional gender stereotypes. When possible, they use all-women group therapy to enable women to support and reinforce one another's strengths, provide role models for one another, and break down their sense of isolation.

The process of feminist therapy can take different forms, but the therapist always tries to demystify the power relationship that exists between therapist and client. In other words, she does not try to be remote and mysterious to her client, but instead is open about her own attitudes and values. At the same time, she is continuously reflecting on and analyzing her own values and practice. In particular, she pays attention to how her own background, including her race, class, and sexual orientation, may be contributing to therapeutic biases or an inability to recognize issues relevant to her clients. Finally, the feminist therapist knows that therapy alone will not solve most clients' problems, and so she encourages clients to explore other ways of making change and finding support in their lives.

Both female and male therapists can adopt the principles of feminist therapy, but many feminists have argued that a female therapist provides a better role model for female clients and that a female therapist–client dyad provides the best context for the development of mutual honesty and respect. The shared life experiences between therapist and client make it easier for the client to feel understood and empowered. Furthermore, the female dyad avoids reproducing the gendered power imbalance that occurs in the culture: male as authority or expert and female as dependent.

Diversity Issues in Psychotherapy   Much mental health treatment in North America reflects an orientation that is most consistent with White, male, and middle-class culture. It rests strongly on notions of individualism, autonomy, free expression of one's thoughts, and the desirability of taking control of one's life. Yet people from various cultural groups might thrive better in therapy that is more oriented toward interdependence with others and accepting of the notion that external forces control various aspects of life (Comas-Díaz & Greene, 1994a). Indeed, the popularity of indigenous healers and of many forms of culturally specific healing practices among particular ethnic groups suggests that mainstream mental health treatments often fall short of meeting the needs of these groups. Some mental health practitioners and organizations now work in concert with traditional healers. For example, the annual Convention of American Indian Psychologists and Psychology Graduate Students focuses on, among other issues, how psychology and Native American spiritual practices can be used together for healing.

Oliva Espín (1994) argues that the best form of therapy for women of color is a feminist ethno-specific approach: a therapeutic context in which the therapist is a woman from the same ethnic/racial background as the client. Such an arrangement is beneficial, she argues, because

1. The therapist has understanding of the client's background, based on firsthand experience.
2. The therapist provides a good role model of what a woman from that particular background can accomplish.
3. The therapeutic relationship does not reproduce the balance of power in which a White, Anglo person is the authority or expert.
4. The therapist is more likely to feel a personal stake in the client's success.

In reality, of course, it is not always possible for an individual to find a therapist who is the same gender, race, and ethnicity. Nor is there any guarantee that finding a good match on these criteria will ensure success in therapy. Male therapists can work successfully with female clients if they understand and are open about the implications of sexism for the client's life and for the therapeutic relationship. Similarly, Espín (1994) notes that a

BOX 10.2 WOMEN SHAPING PSYCHOLOGY
Oliva M. Espín

At Boston University in 1976, Oliva Espín created one of the first courses on cross-cultural counseling and psychotherapy. Her motivation to move psychology in a cross-cultural direction stemmed from her own experiences of migration and acculturation: She knew from these experiences that culture could not be ignored as a factor in psychological health.

Espín was born in Cuba and now lives in the United States, where she is a professor of women's studies at San Diego State University and a core faculty member at the California School of Professional Psychology. In the interim she has lived in several other countries, including Costa Rica, where she earned an undergraduate degree in psychology from the Universidad de Costa Rica, and Canada, where she taught at McGill University. She completed her Ph.D. at the University of Florida, with a dissertation focused on college-educated women in Latin America.

In her distinguished career, Oliva Espín has specialized in the psychology of Lati-

White therapist treating a woman of color must address the negative impact of racism in the therapist–client relationship as well as in the client's life if the therapy is to have a chance of offering the client all that it should. Finally, it is clear that personal as well as social-context variables influence the success of any therapy; if the client and therapist cannot get comfortable with each other the therapy will not succeed, even if the pair is a perfect match in terms of gender, race, and ethnicity.

Some similar issues are present with respect to sexual orientation and therapy. A therapist may show **heterosexist** bias by devaluing same-gender relationships, by emphasizing a search for the cause of a lesbian or gay orientation rather than dealing with current problems, or by expecting the client to be able to be impervious to the widely accepted negative images of lesbian, gay, and bisexual persons. It is difficult for a lesbian client to be helped by a therapist who defines the client's self-identification as a lesbian as the problem, or who does not help the client to analyze her problems in relation to a homophobic cultural context. Because of negative attitudes toward homosexuality, lesbians lead more stressful,

BOX 10.2 WOMEN SHAPING PSYCHOLOGY (*continued*)
Oliva M. Espín

nas, immigrant and refugee women, and women's sexuality across cultures. One of her goals in clinical work is to help Latina women in the United States come to terms with the differing role expectations that accompany the frequent necessity for them to satisfy two different, sometimes conflicting, sets of cultural expectations. She has worked creatively to develop methods of training clinicians to work with people from many ethnic backgrounds and to institutionalize an awareness of the necessity for counselors and educators to understand cultural issues. Her insights and research findings have been regularly shared through her writings, which have spanned topics from the mental health of refugee women to the lives of Latina healers.

Dr. Espín has received the Award for Distinguished Contribution to Public Service from the American Psychological Association and is a two-time recipient of the Women of Color Psychologies Award

from the Association for Women in Psychology. Her work has been a key factor in orienting the psychology of women toward a focus on all women—and many psychologies.

Read More about Oliva Espín

American Psychological Association (1992). Awards for distinguished professional contributions, 1991: Oliva M. Espín. *American Psychologist, 47,* 495–497.

Read What She Has Written

Espín, O. M. (1996). *Latina healers: Lives of power and tradition.* Mountain View, CA: Floricanto, 1996.
Espín, O. M. (1997). *Latina realities: Essays on healing, migration, and sexuality.* Boulder, CO: Westview.
Espín, O. M. (1999). *Women crosssing boundaries: A psychology of immigration and transformations of sexuality.* Philadelphia: Routledge.

and sometimes more isolated, lives than many heterosexual women—a difference that must be acknowledged in the therapeutic process. These issues may feel particularly intractable for lesbian women of color, who may experience conflicting loyalties between their ethnic community and their lesbian community—and who may feel alienated in some ways from both (Greene, 1994). Finding a therapist who shares these experiences would be ideal, but it may not always be possible.

To provide treatment experiences that are meaningful, a therapist must develop **cultural competence** with respect to her clients. To aid in such development, the American Psychological Association has published guidelines for therapists working with ethnically, linguistically, and culturally diverse clients (American Psychological Association, 1993). Maria Braveheart-Jordan and Lemyra DeBruyn (1995) argue that cultural competence

goes beyond "cultural sensitivity," by which we mean having an awareness of the behaviors, norms, and values of the culture of the client with whom one is working. Cultural competence encompasses flexibility in adapting and modifying one's behavior to achieve congruence with a client's behavior. Examples include averting one's own eyes regularly when a client does not utilize eye contact, or using metaphors as a therapeutic intervention when a client uses an indirect communication style. (p. 355)

These writers note, for example, that a Native American woman may not immediately communicate to a therapist the reason she is seeking help. Her reticence may stem from shame about the problem or it may come from a cultural style of indirect communication that deems directly asking for help rude or too aggressive. Similarly, she may avoid eye contact, a behavior that in many Native American cultures is considered a sign of respect, rather than shyness or uneasiness.

Cultural competence involves learning how to ask questions in ways that are most effective and nonthreatening, and also learning to recognize when a "symptom" is actually just an example of culturally normative behavior. For example, Braveheart-Jordan and DeBruyn (1995) tell the story of a Lakota Indian mother, a recovering alcoholic who, after 4 years of sobriety, was trying to regain custody of her daughter. The non-Indian social worker to whom she and her daughter were referred for therapy noted that the mother displayed no physical affection for her child. The social worker concluded that the mother was cold and unfeeling and had not bonded with her daughter. In contrast, a Lakota therapist who saw the mother and daughter later did observe signs of bonding and affection, and she was able to explain to the social services department the traditional value of reserve in Lakota culture that inhibits the expression of affection or *any* strong emotion in front of outsiders.

Cultural competence is not just an issue for traditional therapies. A sensitivity to culture is also important for practitioners of feminist approaches to therapy. For example, as noted above, feminist therapists try to demystify the therapist–client relationship and share power with their clients. However, clients from certain cultures may be used to respecting authority, and they may experience more dismay than relief if the therapist tries to shift power to them (Raja, 1998). In addition, cultural groups differ in the degree to which gender roles are viewed as flexible, in the interdependence between personal and social identities, and the degree to which there is a necessity to maintain "bicultural" loyalties (Worell & Johnson, 2001). Judith Worell and Dawn Johnson (2001) call for a multicultural feminist approach to therapy that incorporates "mature cultural sensitivity and multiple competencies" (p. 323).

The elements of a culturally sensitive and competent approach to therapy are many. However, one group of therapists boiled it down to four key aspects:

1. Being aware of differences between the client and oneself.
2. Knowing about a client's culture.
3. Being able to distinguish between culture and pathology when assessing a client.
4. Understanding how culture affects the process of therapy (Zayas, Torres, Malcolm, & DesRosiers, 1996).

How can a counselor or therapist move in the direction of cultural competence? Karen Fraser Wyche (2001) argues that understanding others begins with self-understanding:

In trying to understand oneself as a cultural being with values, biases, stereotypes, and unique communication patterns, a counselor can begin the process of self-examination. The personal goal is to become a culturally skilled counselor. In this process, one becomes aware of cultural assumptions, biases, stereotypes, and the limitations of one's background. . . . Self-awareness becomes a way to monitor these biases so as to not impose one's own values on clients either verbally or nonverbally. It is not necessary that everyone share the same worldview, but one certainly can learn to monitor biases. It is a process of discovering and understanding our ethnic and cultural identity and the ways in which gender shapes who we are. This exploration must incorporate an analysis of privilege and power in our interactions with others [and] includes examining how differences are conceptualized, being aware of the influences of oppression on clients, and a willingness to work within culturally appropriate treatment frameworks . . . (p. 336)

Drug Therapy

In July 2000, drug company Eli Lilly received approval from the U.S. Food and Drug Administration to market Prozac, an antidepressant, under the new name Sarafem. Sarafem, dispensed as pretty pink and lavender capsules, is aimed squarely at women in their 20s and 30s. Its ostensible use? To treat premenstrual dysphoric disorder (PMDD). As discussed earlier in this chapter, PMDD is a controversial diagnosis—one that many opponents say pathologizes women's ordinary premenstrual symptoms into a mental illness. Women who go to their physicians for help with premenstrual symptoms are now likely to be prescribed Sarafem, and many will not be aware that they are actually taking the antidepressant Prozac. Furthermore, the doctor doing the prescribing will likely be an obstetrician-gynecologist, not someone with special expertise in depression or other mental illnesses (Spartos, 2000).

The metamorphosis of Prozac into Sarafem and the approval of Sarafem to treat PMDD is a gigantic financial plus for the drug company. The patent on Prozac was due to expire, leading to a projected drop in sales from $2.51 billion in 2000 to $625 million in 2003. A new market—the approximately half a million women in North America bothered by severe premenstrual symptoms—boosts profits. Many women who would never have thought of taking Prozac may find themselves taking Sarafem. Meanwhile, other effective nondrug treatments for premenstrual distress, such as calcium supplementation and exercise, receive little attention (Spartos, 2000).

A common clinical response to emotional or mental distress is to prescribe mood-altering drugs such as antidepressants or tranquilizers. In the United States, women are far more likely than men to be treated with drugs for emotional problems; one study showed that 70 percent of such drugs were prescribed for women (Ogur, 1986). A more recent study indicates that women are 48 percent more likely than men to use any "abusable" prescription drug (Simoni-Wastila, 2000). The use of antidepressants is most common among women ages 45 to 64 (Statistics Canada, 1995).

Why are psychoactive drugs prescribed so readily to women? In part, it may simply be the result of women seeking treatment more frequently than men do, and of drug companies taking advantage of this pattern by targeting drugs to women. Presented with similar symptoms, doctors appear more likely to prescribe mood-altering drugs for female than

BOX 10.3 MAKING CHANGE
Monitoring Drug Advertising to Women

An early advertisement for Sarafem featured a woman angrily yanking on a shopping cart that was stuck in its stack, while a female voice-over suggested that she was suffering from PMDD. Many women found this ad insulting, as it appeared to suggest that women "go crazy" every month as their menstrual period approaches. This ad has now been pulled, but if you watch popular magazines and television, you will see others that target women's depression, anxiety, and stress reactions. Try to analyze these ads for gender stereotypes. Are women portrayed as basically unstable, requiring only minor events to push them over the edge? Are they viewed as weak and helpless, unable to cope without the help of a drug? Are any similar ads targeted toward men? Does the information in the ad seem to be misleading? If you see an ad that you believe is insulting to women, write to the company and/or to the television network or magazine publisher to express your disapproval.

for male patients and to continue the prescription over several years (Travis, 1988). And drug companies support this pattern. Drug advertisements in medical journals promote gender stereotypic notions that depression and anxiety in women are due solely to intrapsychic or biological factors, and offer the drugs as an easy solution to female unhappiness (Nikelly, 1995). One frequency analysis of drug advertisements appearing in the *American Journal of Psychiatry* and *American Family Physician* revealed that the ratio of females to males depicted in such ads was 5 to 1, and the elderly were also overrepresented (Hansen & Osborne, 1995). Doctors who feel uncomfortable talking with their female patients about problems, or who have no suggestions for working on the problems, may opt for the simpler route of drug prescription. Paradoxically, however, doctors may be reluctant to accept patients' reports of drug side effects, treating patients' concerns about the drugs as further evidence of their problems. One therapist-in-training reports that she was prescribed Halcion, a hypnotic drug often prescribed for insomnia, over a period of 14 months while her male physician brushed aside her reports of amnesia, confusion, and profound sleep loss. These symptoms were attributed by her doctor to her failure to adjust properly to her recent marriage. Meanwhile, in her work in professional mental health settings, she repeatedly witnessed doctors dismissing their female patients' worries about their medication (Shapiro-Baruch, 1995).

In hospital situations, drugs may be prescribed to keep a patient calm—to keep her from causing trouble. Perhaps it is not surprising, then, that factors such as age and race apparently interact with gender in influencing physicians' readiness to prescribe mood-altering drugs. Older women may be more likely than other women to be given drugs for certain emotional symptoms. For example, women over 65 are more likely than younger women to be taking sleeping pills and tranquilizers (Statistics Canada, 1995).

Unfortunately, the bulk of research on the effects of psychoactive drugs has been done on men, and the appropriate research on women has been begun only in the last two decades. Women were left out of psychopharmacological studies because their menstrual cycles, pregnancy, and lactation would "complicate" their reactions to the drugs, or because the drugs might harm a developing fetus. Yet women are the very ones for whom these medications are most often prescribed! In addition, little research has yet been done examining the ethnoracial differences in reactions to these drugs and how these differences interact with gender. Most of the drugs being prescribed have, until recently, been tested mainly on young, White, male populations. Research now indicates that there are some important gender and ethnoracial differences in clinical responses to specific drugs (Jacobsen, 1994). For example, when taking tricyclic antidepressants, African Americans tend to attain higher blood levels of the drugs than European Americans do when taking the same dose, and may also experience more side effects. In studies using mainly White participants, gender differences in clinical response to drugs have been found for tricyclic antidepressants, mood-stabilizing drugs such as lithium, antipsychotic medications such as Thorazine, and antianxiety drugs such as Valium and Xanax. However, next to nothing conclusive is known about male–female differences within other ethnoracial groups in responsiveness to these medications.

The Social Construction of Women's Mental Disorders

Any person in any culture can experience the distress, disintegration, or sense of disconnectedness that can lead to a diagnosis of mental illness. Yet we have seen that diagnostic categories are fluid and are shaped by expectations arising from gender and culture. We construct classifications of people's "disordered" behavior and experience according to what our culture dictates, and individuals may receive differing diagnoses depending on their gender, race, and social class.

There is some degree of universality to the ways women and men differ in the expression of their distress. For example, women everywhere seem more prone to depression than men do, and women in many places are far more likely than men to suffer from eating disorders. While the field of psychology has had a long historical tendency to search for internal weaknesses or flaws to explain the preponderance of women among sufferers of such problems, biological and intrapsychic explanations have not proven very compelling. In the main, women are not more depressed because of their hormones, nor are they starving themselves because of deep inner conflicts about their femininity. Rather, women are reacting to real and often intolerable pressures from the environment—and they are reacting in ways that cultures have helped them to construct. Cultural messages tell girls and women they are powerless, that they must fear victimization, that they must not express feelings of anger and competitiveness. As young women absorb these messages, many of them become depressed. Some cultures tell young women that the most important achievement they should aspire to is to become thin and beautiful; some young women become obsessed with starving themselves and are diagnosed as anorexic. In these cases, women are taking the cultural prescriptions for femininity to extremes. In a sense, they are getting sick in "approved" ways.

Diagnosis and treatment of mental disorders often perpetuate sexist biases. Diagnoses are social constructions: Mental diseases are created by labels and categories. Yet therapists may apply these diagnoses without regard to the context in which the patient functions or to the patient's own interpretation of her distress.

Feminist therapists help clients analyze their problems as responses to the sociocultural context rather than merely as signs of personal inadequacy or individual pathology. Such interactional work is difficult and challenging, and feminist therapists must constantly examine and reflect on their own biases in order to be useful to their clients. This very process of self-examination and reflection is a model for what is required for the general theory and treatment of mental health and illness. The categories are not static and cannot be understood outside of culture. Feminist scholarship on the psychology of women supports the notion that theories and models of mental illness must be understood as socially constructed and dynamic.

SUMMARY

Mental and physical health are closely intertwined, but mental health emphasizes emotions, patterns of thought, and the ability to cope with one's environment. Standards of mental health are not necessarily universal; what is considered "normal" in one culture may be considered "abnormal" in another. Standards of mental health also vary by gender, class, and ethnicity with cultures. Some researchers have argued that there is a double standard of mental health for women and men.

Mental illness among women has often been attributed to internal weakness: intrapsychic or biological causes. However, the growth of feminist psychology has refocused the emphasis on environmental context in trying to understand and alleviate mental illness.

In most developed countries of the world, women are more likely than men to be diagnosed with depression, a difference that first appears at adolescence. Women are more likely to be depressed if they are poor, have many children, have been traumatized by physical or sexual abuse, or are not very acculturated in the dominant culture in which they live. Several reasons have been proposed for the gender gap in depression. The feminine role may predispose women to depression by encouraging them to feel and act helpless. In an attempt to protect their close relationships in a patriarchal context, women may develop relationship styles that leave them feeling powerless and depressed. Women may face more stress than men do. Women's hormones or hormonal fluctuations may make them vulnerable to depression. And feminine qualities that develop in childhood (such as empathy and nonaggressiveness) may interact with environmental challenges in adolescence (such as sexual harassment) to produce a greater incidence of female depression. No single one of these explanations has been proven to capture the whole truth about gender differences in depression.

Women are also much more likely than men to be diagnosed with eating disorders, and the cultural emphasis on thinness for women is implicated in these patterns. Women are more likely than men to be diagnosed with panic disorder and agoraphobia, a pattern that some feminist theorists attribute to the feminine role's emphasis on vulnerability. Many women are also diagnosed with post-traumatic stress disorder. This disorder, which is a response to trauma, is likely to appear among women who have been raped, physically or emotionally abused, or victimized by hate crimes. It can also appear among women whose loved ones have been traumatized or hurt.

Women are less likely than men to abuse alcohol and drugs; however a significant number of women have substance abuse disorders. There are ethnic group differences in the incidence of drug and alcohol abuse among American women, with White women showing the highest levels. For many women, having been sexually abused as a child may be a contributing factor in later drug and alcohol abuse. Some researchers have also found that, among White middle-class women, the use of heroin may be related to rebellion against the constraints of the feminine role.

The diagnosis and treatment of mental illness take place in the context of cultural expectations and stereotypes and tend to define the behavior of powerful groups as normative. Diagnostic categories reflect these stereotypes. For example, many feminists think the controversial diagnosis of PMDD reflects a stereotype that the menstrual cycle makes women psychologically unstable.

Therapists may implicitly hold different standards of mental health for women versus men, and for people of different sexual orientations, races, and social classes. Also, a therapist may have seriously distorted perceptions and misunderstandings about the life experiences of clients who do not share her racial, ethnic, or social class background, her sexual orientation, or her linguistic and cultural heritage. There is a limited but growing awareness in the mental health professions that it is crucial to try to overcome sexist, racist, heterosexist, and other biases in the therapeutic process.

Feminist therapies have emerged as an explicitly sociopolitical approach to the treatment of mental illness. Practitioners of feminist therapies acknowledge, confront, and explore issues of sexism and other biases with their clients as part of the therapeutic encounter. Many therapists strive for an ideal of feminist culturally competent therapy.

Women are more likely than men to be prescribed psychoactive drugs such as antidepressants and tranquilizers. This may be because women seek treatment for psychological distress more often than men do; however, it also seems to reflect a tendency for doctors to think of women's distress as internally rather than externally caused.

KEY TERMS

mental health	neurasthenia	relationship difficulties
double standard of mental	depression	hypothesis
health	learned helplessness	silencing the self
mental illness	feminine-role hypothesis	acculturation

stressful life events
chronically stressful
    conditions
gender role strain
developmental hypothesis
anorexia nervosa
bulimia nervosa

panic disorder
agoraphobia
post-traumatic stress
    disorder (PTSD)
premenstrual dysphoric
    disorder (PMDD)
insidious trauma

oppression artifact disorder
psychotherapy
nonsexist therapy
feminist therapies
heterosexism
cultural competence

DISCUSSION QUESTIONS

Is there still a double standard of mental health for women and men? Do you think it might be reasonable for clinicians to view different behaviors as "normal" for women and men?

What are some of the reasons why women in different cultures might experience and define mental illness differently?

In what ways might the medical profession and the pharmaceutical corporations benefit from current definitions of mental illness? Do gender stereotypes about mental illness make a difference to such benefits?

FOR ADDITIONAL READING

Comas-Díaz, Lillian & Greene, Beverly (Eds.). (1994). *Women of color: Integrating ethnic and gender identities in psychotherapy.* New York: Guilford Press. This book includes chapters specifically on African American, Native American, Asian American, Latina, Caribbean women, and women of the Indian subcontinent, as well as several "special populations," such as lesbian women of color and Southeast Asian refugee women. There are also contributions devoted to particular types of therapy: psychodynamic, cognitive–behavioral, and feminist. The collection provides a wide-ranging overview of mental health and psychotherapeutic issues relevant to diverse populations of women.

Adleman, Jeanne & Enguídanos, Gloria (Eds.). (1995). *Racism in the lives of women: Testimony, theory, and guides to antiracist practice.* New York: Haworth Press. These readings fall into the three categories listed in the title. They include such diverse offerings as personal reflections on trying to do therapy with clients who do not share one's ethnicity, theory on how women of color can play a central role in constructing psychology, and descriptions of therapists' struggles to develop antiracist practice.

Gottlieb, Lori (2000). *Stick Figure: A diary of my former self.* New York: Simon & Schuster, and Marya Hornbacher. (1999) *Wasted: A memoir of anorexia and bulimia.* New York: Harper Collins. Both of these books are personal memoirs of young women who survived and overcame eating disorders. Their accounts are compelling and very personal.

WEB RESOURCES

Mental Health and Brain Disorders Division of the World Health Organization (WHO). The site contains information about mental health topics for countries all over the world, as well as links to other sites. **www.who.int/mental_health**

Indian Health Service. This site provides access to a wide range of information about mental and physical health issues for American Indian and Alaska Native women. **www.ihs .gov/MedicalPrograms/MCH/WH.asp**

American Psychological Association. Go to this site to find information about depression, stress, and other mental health topics. The site provides access to online brochures about some topics, links to current news items, and a Help Center. **www.apa.org**

CHAPTER 11

Myths and Scripts
for Women Growing Older

CHAPTER OUTLINE

"I just stopped menstruating when I was about fifty. It just disappeared naturally. Everyone says you have physical problems, but I didn't have anything like that. I'd hear you suddenly feel hot and you get headaches and irritable but none of that happened to me. I'd remembered when I was a child that one of the older geisha went to hospital because she had such a bad time with *kōnenki* [the turn or change of life, menopause], and so I was worried. But when it happened I was just relieved that my periods had stopped."

"Do you worry about getting older?"

"Not really. If you have the right attitude there is nothing to worry about."

"So a few wrinkles don't matter?"

"No, of course not. Beauty depends on the way one lives one's life. The accumulation of fifty years of living is not something that's created overnight, and the result is obvious. If a person has a mature *kikoro* [heart, spiritual center], this shows on her face; a middle-aged woman can have beautiful features, the product of experience, whereas young people have beauty that's simply *pitchi pitchi* [bright and lively]." (Kayoko, interviewed by Lock, 1993, p. 185)

Kayoko, a middle-aged Japanese woman who works in a traditional geisha house, was interviewed by Margaret Lock, an anthropologist from the United States, as part of a study on women's experience of aging. Her words may surprise North American readers, most of whom have been taught that aging is something to be feared, especially for women. Clearly, our experiences of and attitudes toward growing older may be products of cultural scripts for aging as much as of physical and mental changes. This issue of cultural scripts for aging is the first we will examine in this chapter: How is women's experience of aging socially constructed by their culture? How does culture teach us to feel about ourselves as we age? How do sexism and ageism interact with each other?

Next, we turn to a specific issue in women's development at midlife: **menopause.** Menopause, the cessation of menstrual periods, is a physical change, but the way it is discussed, experienced, and treated is shaped largely by cultural expectations. These expectations are connected to more general cultural expectations about aging women. In North America, where aging is regarded almost as a disaster for a woman, menopause tends to be viewed as an unpleasant, unhappy transition characterized by symptoms that require medical treatment. In Japan, where older women are not necessarily cut off from admiration and respect, menopause is viewed with less trepidation. We will explore the implications of such differences for women's health and well-being at midlife and beyond.

Finally, we focus on the new roles and challenges women face as they progress beyond young adulthood to midlife and later life. Family roles may change as children grow up and leave home or grandchildren arrive. Work roles may change as women move into different positions, change careers, or begin to plan for retirement. Many older women find themselves single again as intimate relationships break up or their partner dies. New caregiving roles may emerge as midlife women become grandparents or are called upon to look after ailing elderly parents. In sum, the years from mid- to later life are unlikely to be stagnant, or even pleasantly comfortable, ones for women; rather, they are likely to require the learning of new roles, new ways of coping, new ways of relating to others. How do women manage these transitions? What factors have an impact on their ability to adapt and thrive in their new roles? These are the questions we will focus on in the last part of this chapter.

In examining these issues, we will see that cultural myths and scripts shape the experience and meaning of aging. For women, who have a longer life expectancy than men, it is especially important to analyze these cultural messages—one of the most pervasive of which is that a woman's worth declines as she ages.

The Social Construction of Women's Aging

Recently, I overheard a female student comment anxiously to her friend that she would be 20 years old next summer, and that everything would be "downhill" for her after that because she would be "so old." Margaret Gullette, in her book *Declining to Decline* (1997), remembers that at the age of 15, she was already lamenting the fact that she would never again have the "perfect" skin of her younger 12-year-old self. In the film *Lone Star*, one of the female characters comments that, at 30, she is "so old" to still be single that her parents will be overjoyed with whatever man she brings home and says she wants to marry. In some parts of India, the mother of two daughters is considered "old" and is expected to dress in "old" colors. The mother of two sons is not—because the burden of having daughters is thought to age a mother more quickly (Bhardwaj, 2001).

Clearly, the feeling that one is "old" or "declining" is not necessarily tied to any advanced chronological age. How, then, do we form the notions of age, aging, and decline that we attach to our identities as we progress through life? What makes us so certain that aging means decay and why do women latch on to this notion (at least in North America) so early in life? Although the physical processes of aging begin at birth, it is culture that tells us when we are "old" or "aging" and it is culture that tells us what that means. As Gullette (1997) argues, it is culture that ages us; we construct our notions of aging from cultural messages.

Images of Decline: Media Messages about Women's Aging

On late-night television, comedian Jay Leno joked about a report that England's Prince Charles was giving a party for his mistress's 50th birthday. Apparently struck by the incongruity of the terms "mistress" and "50th birthday," he returned to this theme several times during his monologue. Imagine having a 50-year-old mistress! Why would anyone want a mistress who was that old? Imagine telling your buddies that you have a mistress—and that she's *50!* Leno admitted that his own age was 47, but did not seem to entertain the idea that *he* was on the verge of becoming undesirable, or even ridiculous, as a potential sexual partner. Yet he unabashedly mocked the notion that a 50-year-old woman would be worthy of sexual (or perhaps any other form of) attention.

This incident is one of many in the North American media in which women are given the clear message that age inevitably renders them less interesting, less desirable, less valuable. They are bombarded by advertisements that tell them to wash away signs of gray hair, to get rid of wrinkles, to control the signs of aging by taking vitamins, by taking estrogen, by having cosmetic surgery. Many of the newspaper articles and television programs that deal with older women focus on the negative possibilities of aging. Headlines highlight the "plight" of the elderly, the "crisis" in Social Security and Medicare, the "problem" of an aging population (Friedan, 1993). Articles on nursing homes and Alzheimer's disease abound; little coverage is given to people living well in their later years. All these messages conspire to create and reinforce a feeling of dread about aging.

The dread is expressed in negative stereotypes about aging and the elderly. Most people in North America do not like to be called "old," and it is little wonder. The old are stereotyped as lonely, hard of hearing, and rigid, albeit also interesting (Kite, Deaux, & Miele, 1991). And there is a double standard of aging for women and men: The changes in physical appearance that accompany aging are often considered "distinguished" in men but are likely to be labeled "ugly" in women. One study found that ratings of an individual's attractiveness decreased with age when the individual was a woman, but not when the individual was a man (Mathes, Brennan, Haugen, & Rice, 1985). This disparity is reflected in the self-ratings of women and men: Women view aging most negatively in terms of its impact on their appearance, but men view aging as having a neutral or positive impact on their appearance (Halliwell & Dittmar, 2003). The stereotype of the menopausal woman is a negative one that includes the perception that such women often experience bad moods (Marcus-Newhall, Thompson, & Thomas, 2001). Middle-aged and older women have been portrayed in literature, including the works of Chaucer and Shakespeare and onward, within stereotypic frameworks of madness, depression, or frigidity (Maxwell, 1990).

Not only are older women viewed as less attractive than younger women, they are, like older men, frequent victims of discrimination because of their age. A sting organized by the Massachusetts Commission Against Discrimination in 1994 paired women over 45 with 22-year-old women who were similar in education, personal qualities, and work experience. For several weeks the women in each pair applied for the same jobs: entry-level retailing positions that paid a fairly low hourly wage. The 22-year-olds were repeatedly offered full-time, permanent employment with benefits and opportunities for advancement. The women in their 40s, however, were repeatedly rebuffed, and the few jobs they were offered were seasonal and without benefits (Gullette, 1997). A similar sting by the American Association of

BOX 11.1 MAKING CHANGE
Supporting Positive Images of Older Women

Do you find that people around you hold negative, even insulting, images of older women? If you are honest with yourself, do you find that even you sometimes hold these images? It's time to work on constructing positive, strong, inspiring images of older women, images that provide young women with something to look forward to as they age. If you find such images in the popular media, write, e-mail, or call the people responsible to let them know you appreciate what they are doing. If you can't find any positive images (or if you can't even think of any), make it your quest to find some. Good places to look are in organizations dedicated to combating ageism and sexism. Here are two possibilities:

Gray Panthers. **www.graypanthers.org**. Maggie Kuhn, the founder of this intergenerational activist organization, had a much-quoted motto: Speak your mind. Even if your voice shakes, well-aimed slingshots can topple giants. The organization, which has local chapters in many cities, works for peace and health and against ageism and sexism.

Older Women's League (OWL). **www.owl-national.org**. A national grassroots organization that focuses on issues unique to women as they age.

Retired Persons used resumés of women and men whose age was 57 or 32 and found that older applicants encountered age discrimination about 1 of every 4 times they applied for a job (Lewis, 1994). Parallel findings occurred in an Australian study, in which fictitious resumés for accounting assistants, varying only in gender and age (32 or 57) were mailed to over 400 companies. Younger applicants received more positive responses, and older women received negative responses more quickly than older men (Gringart & Helmes, 2001).

Economic researchers find that in the United States a drop in full employment occurs around the age of 50 as people lose once secure jobs and cannot find new ones. The drop is most serious for Black women, then White women, then men. The gender wage gap widens at midlife (U.S. Bureau of the Census, 2004), and at retirement the wage gap translates into an increased risk of poverty for older women. Women retirees receive only half the average pension benefits that men receive (Women's Institute for a Secure Retirement, 2001).

Culture interacts with the way older women are perceived. For example, in many traditional Native American cultures, women elders are deeply respected and their advice is sought on all important matters. However, elderly Native American women in the United States suffer from the more negative and less respectful attitudes of the broader society with respect to women and aging. Interviews with one set of Oklahoma Native American women elders revealed that they were aware of and troubled by these contradictions and that their largely unmet expectations for respect are a source of great pain (Shaver, 1997).

The devaluation of and discrimination against persons based on their age is called **ageism,** and this set of attitudes obviously interacts with sexism and racism. Ageism underlies the surprise in someone's voice when commenting on "how sharp" a 65-year-old administrator is, or "how different from other old people" a healthy, engaged 70-year-old artist is. But perhaps most of all, it underlies the pervasive tendency to ignore older women and render them invisible.

Missing Images: Invisible Older Women

> All one's life as a young woman one is on show, a focus of attention, people notice you. You set yourself up to be noticed and admired. And then, not expecting it, you become middle-aged and anonymous. No one notices you. You achieve a wonderful freedom. It is a positive thing. You can move about unnoticed and invisible. (Doris Lessing, quoted in Warner, 1992, p. 22)

Middle-aged and older women are often ignored, a reaction based on the ageist and sexist notions that the only reason to pay attention to a woman is her sexual attractiveness —and that such attractiveness is limited to youth. Despite the biases that spawn this reaction, its effect is not always purely negative. An older woman may revel in the condition that allows her to go about her business without having to constantly parry unwanted sexual attention.

It is not just individual older women who find themselves becoming "invisible," however. As a group, women of middle age and older are infrequently represented in the media. And that group invisibility has none of the positive, liberating possibilities of the individual invisibility celebrated in Doris Lessing's comment. When Betty Friedan began the research for her book *The Fountain of Age* (1993), she searched women's magazines for images of older women. She found an absence of them. In an issue of *Vogue,* of 290 identifiable faces pictured in advertisements there was 1 woman who looked to be over 60. In the *Ladies' Home Journal,* only 2 of 72 faces in the ads might have been in their 60s. Even the ads for *Ms.* magazine featured not one older woman. Furthermore, when magazines focused on older women in their articles, they tended to run photographs of these women at much younger ages: Imelda Marcos, then in her 60s, was pictured at the age of 45; Jean Harris, then a white-haired older woman, was represented by a picture of her much younger self. It was, Friedan noted, as if the magazines were afraid their buying public would be repulsed by images of age.

A similar pattern of absent older women was found by researchers who compiled data on winners of the Academy Awards between 1927 and 1990. Women over the age of 39 years accounted for only 27 percent of all winners for Best Actress, but men in the same age category had won 67 percent of the Best Actor awards (Markson & Taylor, 1993). Neither is television immune from such patterns. A 1998 study by the BBC showed that older people are underrepresented on television and that among older adults who *are* represented, men outnumber women 72 to 28 percent (Age & Opportunity, 2004).

Images of Power: Stronger, Older Women

> The only defense a person has against change is to learn to step out and face each new wave of life in time with its approach. Whether the waves are surging whitecaps or calm ripples, they must be breasted. (Lyles, 1994, p. 344)

At this time in history there may be more powerful women in the age range of 40 to 65 than ever before. As life-stages chronicler Gail Sheehy quipped, "The boardrooms of America will light up with hot flashes" (quoted in Friedan, 1993, p. 472). Several decades of feminist political action have opened some of the doors to power and influence that had formerly been closed to women, and some women have reached senior positions along with their senior years. In the United States we have recently had the very visible examples in politics of Minority Whip Nancy Pelosi, Attorney General Janet Reno, Secretary of State Madeleine Albright, National Security Advisor Condoleeza Rice, Secretary of Health Donna Shalala, Secretary of Labor Alexis Herman, and Supreme Court justices Ruth Bader Ginsburg and Sandra Day O'Connor; writers, artists, and activists such as Maya Angelou, Betty Friedan, Angela Davis, Toni Morrison, Patricia Ireland, and Ursula Le Guin; and scientists and scholars such as Gertrude Elion, Eleanor Maccoby, and Mary Daly. We have Marguerite Vogt, an 88-year-old molecular biologist still in love with science after three-quarters of a century and still putting in 10 hours a day in her lab at the Salk Institute in San Diego (Angier, 2001). Other nations have provided their own examples of powerful older women: Britain's Margaret Thatcher, Norway's Gro Harlem Brundtland, Palestine's Hanan Ashrawi. Yet it is difficult to escape the notion that these women are exceptions, that they have beaten the odds of age and gender to claim some power and influence through extraordinary talent and determination. What images are there to serve as models for ordinary women, to show that aging is a change and a challenge that must be met, not an insurmountable barrier to achievement and self-worth?

We have the images of older women in a variety of cultures. In many cultures, the reduction of responsibility for childcare that comes with age is associated with an increased involvement in community activities and increased public and spiritual authority.

> The restrictions that encumber young women fall away. Typically, a woman no longer has to defer to a husband, a mother-in-law, or other senior relatives. She can travel, talk back, and be bawdy, outrageous, or independent. In some cases, she can safely take a lover; in other cases, she is relieved never to have sex again. She can drink too much, use forbidden language, or dress in a way that pleases her. The whole complex of obligations or taboos surrounding fertility (menstrual management, birth control, or the possibility of pregnancy) drop away. (Ward, 1996, p. 62)

Among the Aboriginal women of Australia, older women are respected and their advice is sought on matters of importance. They have more of an opportunity to become involved in community decision making and in religious ritual than younger women do and thus to increase in wisdom and status (Bell, 1983). Similarly, among the !Kung of southern Africa, age is associated with increased status, and older people are thought to have stronger spiritual powers. Women wait until their childbearing years are over before seriously exploring their trancing and curing powers; then they can handle taboo and ritual substances that are considered too powerful for those still involved in bearing children (Shostak, 1981). In these cultures, midlife is a new beginning.

We also have the images of real women of accomplishment in our own culture who are not in the limelight but who have lived successful lives: grandmothers and mothers who traversed the various stages of aging with grace and strength; the women who are so busy with the rest of their lives that menopause is simply a small blip on the screen of an active family and/or work agenda and who tell researchers over and over again that it was

Among the Aboriginal peoples of Australia, older women are respected and their advice is sought on matters of gravity and importance.

"nothing" (Martin, 1987); the legislator who leaped to the microphone to respond to a discussion of menopause by saying "About these symptoms, I suppose I'm in the midst of menopause but I just don't pay attention to it. I couldn't tell you at the end of the day if I've had any hot flashes or how many. It's simply one part of your entire life, why not just live it?" (quoted in Friedan, 1993, p. 473). We have the memoirs of women such as Sadie and Bessie Delany (1993), who described 100 years of living full and interesting lives.

Finally, we can find positive fictional images of mid- and later-life women in books and films that treat women over 40 as strong and interesting—and the number is growing. The protagonists of novels by Margaret Atwood, Margaret Drabble, Nadine Gordimer,

BOX 11.2 WOMEN SHAPING PSYCHOLOGY
Una Gault

Australian psychologist Una Gault was as yet untouched by the women's movement when she left her position at the University of New South Wales for a sabbatical at Cambridge University in Britain in 1969.

To questions from her British colleagues, she replied that women's liberation was of less concern in Australia than the really important issue of the Vietnam war. Later, spending the last part of her sabbatical at Northwestern University in Chicago, she recalls that she still did not focus on the activities of the women's movement (Gault, 1993).

When she returned to Australia, however, Gault was soon caught up in the early stages of the feminist movement at her university, where she joined a consciousness-raising group and then became active in a collective that published a women's studies magazine, *Refractory Girl.* Soon she began to try to integrate a feminist approach into her work in psychology, and she became a leader in attempts to institutionalize a recognition of women's importance in psychology in Australia. In 1975 she was the guest editor of a special part-issue of the *Australian Psychologist* devoted to women and psychology. At this time, she was the first woman ever to serve as a guest editor for

---

Doris Lessing, Alison Lurie, Paule Marshall, May Sarton, Jane Rule, and Alice Walker *like* the way they look at 50 or 55 or 60. In Doris Lessing's *If the Old Could,* 55-year-old Jane Somers looks in the mirror and reports

> I saw something else as I stood there, looking from the photograph to me—it was me as I must seem to [a younger woman]. The unreachable accomplishment of it, this woman standing there so firm on the pile of her energetic and successful years. What a challenge, what a burden, the middle-aged, the elderly, are to the young. (quoted in Gullette, 1997, p. 80)

These fictional heroines feel more knowledgeable and confident than they did at 20, and many are freed from the constraints of youth and ready for new possibilities in their

---

BOX 11.2 WOMEN SHAPING PSYCHOLOGY *(continued)*
Una Gault

the journal. She was one of the founders and the first convener of an Interest Group on Women and Psychology, which in 1984 became an official unit under the Australian Psychological Society after several years of sponsoring conference activities. In 1990 she was once again a guest editor of an *Australian Psychologist* special issue (a whole issue this time) focused on women and psychology.

In her research activities as well, Una Gault was influenced by and helped to develop a feminist perspective on psychology. She was one of the authors of a bibliography on women that appeared in the 1975 special issue of the *Australian Psychologist,* and she began research on the use of memory-work to understand the experience of emotions. Memory-work is a collective, social-constructionist research approach to understanding experience. It involves the use of written memories and participants working together as a group to theorize about them. This approach takes into account many of the feminist criticisms of more traditional methods.

Gault is now retired, but maintains her affiliation with Macquarie University and her involvement with the Australian Psychological Society and with the Interest Group on Women and Psychology. As one of the "founding mothers" of feminist psychology in Australia, Una Gault helped to shape psychology into a discipline that is more inclusive and more responsive to women.

Read More about Una Gault

Gault, U. (1993). "Psychology constructs the female": III. A comment. *Feminism & Psychology, 3*(2), 225–229.

Read What She Has Written

Crawford, J., Kippax, S., Onyx, J., Gault, U., & Benton, P. (1992). *Emotion and gender: Constructing meaning from memory.* London: Sage Publications.

Gault, U. (1990). Women and psychology: Introducton. *Australian Psychologist, 25*(3), 236–238.

---

lives. At the end of *Middle Ground,* Margaret Drabble's middle-aged heroine Kate looks forward to the future:

> Anything is possible, it is all undecided. Everything or nothing. It is all in the future. Excitement fills her, excitement, joy, anticipation, apprehension. Something will happen . . . It is unplanned, unpredicted. Nothing binds her, nothing holds her . . . She hears her house living. She rises. (quoted in Gullette, 1997, p. 95)

Such heroines are still relatively rare in the whole realm of literature, but they provide important examples of women resisting the dominant image of aging as stagnation or decline.

Encountering Menopause:
The Cultural Shaping of a Physiological Event

In North America, menopause is regarded by many as the definitive event that marks a woman as "old." Indeed, the discourse about menopause that appears in the popular (and sometime the scientific) press implies that menopause is a kind of "magic marker" (Gullette, 1997): Women on one side are young, those on the other are old. This focus on menopause also makes it appear that women, as the menopausal sex, are the only ones who age!

Furthermore, women are warned early and excessively about the discomforts and dangers associated with menopause: hot flashes, vaginal dryness, depression, irritability, brittle bones, increased risk of heart disease. As Margaret Gullette (1997) notes,

> No other cohort, male or female, at any age, gets told a future health-risk story like this. We do not tell girls of eleven, for example, that the childbirth they will soon be physiologically ready for can involve miscarriage, edema, episiotomy and loss of sexual pleasure, caesarian sections, malformed or diseased children; magazine articles don't tell pregnant women all the things that might go wrong in labor. Although men are now told more often that they can suffer at midlife from sexual decline or impotence, there is, so far, less equivalent discourse striving to make men of forty-plus as anxious about their aging and self-concept. If a man breaks a bone at forty, people say, "Bad luck"; if a woman does, they tut-tut "osteoporosis." (p. 108)

What is menopause and why is so much attention paid to it in North America? It is a physiological change that happens in women's bodies, but culture can magnify or diminish its importance.

The Physical Change

Menopause is the cessation of menstruation. It occurs gradually as, beginning in her 40s, a woman's ovaries slowly stop producing estrogen and progesterone. Menstrual cycles in which no egg is released from the ovaries begin to increase in frequency. The menstrual periods become irregular, often become shorter in duration and less heavy, and eventually stop. When a woman has not had a menstrual period for 1 year, she is said to have reached menopause. The average age of menopause is around 50.

The Experience of Menopause across Cultures

> Most women describe the end of menstruation, like menstruation itself, as a thing of no great importance: "Your body is fine. There is no pain. It's just your moons that stop." When I asked one woman if that made her feel bad, she said, "If I were young, it would. But I'm old." !Kung women do not seem to associate menopause with the physical symptoms reported by women in our own culture. A certain amount of physical discomfort is described for the initial months, but hot flashes and prolonged physical or psychic distress are not reported. (Shostak, 1981, p. 322)

> "The most noticeable thing was that I would suddenly get hot—I'd seen older women have that problem—but then it happened to me, and I thought, Oh, so this is *kōnenki*. It's gone now, it just lasted for about six months or a year. It happened every day, three times or so."

"Did you feel embarrassed?"

"No, I just thought it was because of my age."

"Did you go and talk to anyone about it?"

"No, I didn't go to the doctor."

"Did you take any medicine?"

"No." (Hattori, a Japanese farm woman, interviewed by Lock, 1993, p. 13)

The only physical change that *every* woman experiences and notices in connection with menopause is the cessation of menstruation. There is a wide variation among individual women, and among cultures, in the other changes that are reported to accompany this transition. In North America, the most common symptoms attributed to menopause are hot flashes, vaginal dryness, urinary problems, depression, and mood swings. No clear evidence linking all these symptoms to the drop in hormone levels has been found. Menopause appears to have no significant relationship to the incidence of common psychiatric symptoms such as depression or irritability (Ballinger, 1990). A review of studies of menopause and depression shows no consistent link between the two; in the general population, depression women experience during the menopausal transition may be due to other factors such as life changes. However, a subset of women may be more vulnerable to the effects of hormonal change and may experience depression (Avis, 2003).

In North America, **hot flashes** are the best known of menopausal symptoms; however, their cause is not well understood. During a hot flash, the blood vessels in the woman's skin dilate, her skin conductance increases, she may become flushed—and she feels extremely hot. The experience is transitory, but it may wake a woman from a sound sleep or cause her to be suddenly drenched with perspiration while simply sitting at her desk. A woman may experience hot flashes for a few months, for a few years, or not at all, and researchers have been unable to determine why the experience is so variable. There is no simple relationship between hormone levels and the number and intensity of hot flashes. However, treatment with estrogen can reduce this symptom, suggesting that it is hormone related to some extent. Some women also report relief from herbs such as black cohosh, from dietary changes such as increasing soy intake and decreasing spicy foods and caffeine, and from exercise (Love, 2000), and the reasons for the efficacy of these approaches are not completely understood.

More is going on here than dropping hormone levels, however. Cross-cultural differences in the reporting of hot flashes and other physical and emotional changes associated with menopause suggest that the set of experiences characterizing menopause is culturally constructed. The quote that opens this section indicates that hot flashes were virtually unknown among the !Kung women studied in Africa by Marjorie Shostak (1981). This lack of recognition of or emphasis on hot flashes is not unusual. Comparative research on Japanese and North American women shows that Japanese women are far less likely than their North American counterparts to report hot flashes. Margaret Lock (1993) reports that among her sample of more than 1,300 Japanese women of menopausal age, only 12 percent reported hot flashes, as compared to 35 percent of women surveyed in Massachusetts and 31 percent of women surveyed in the Canadian province of Manitoba.

Indeed, the set of symptoms characterizing menopause differed in several ways among the three samples described by Lock (1993). For the Manitoba and Massachusetts samples, tiredness was one of the most commonly reported symptoms, listed by more than 38 percent of the respondents. Only 6 percent of the Japanese sample reported tiredness.

On the other hand, the Japanese respondents were more likely than the other two groups to report diarrhea or constipation. In general, the Japanese women reported fewer symptoms than the other two groups. The Canadian and U.S. women were similar on many physical symptoms, but the Canadians were less likely than the U.S. women to list emotional symptoms. For example, irritability was listed by 30 percent of the U.S. sample, 17 percent of the Canadian sample, and 11 percent of the Japanese sample; 36 percent of the U.S. respondents said they felt depressed, whereas only 23 percent of the Canadians and 10 percent of the Japanese reported depression. When they describe *kōnenki,* Japanese women characterize the most significant symptoms as headaches and shoulder stiffness; Western women are likely to list hot flashes as the defining symptom of menopause.

Clearly, culture contributes meaning to the physical attributes of menopause, even by labeling such attributes *symptoms.* When Margaret Lock designed her survey for Japanese women, she had difficulty translating the term *hot flash* because there is no specific Japanese term for this experience. In English, however, we have coined the specialized term *hot flash* to refer specifically to the sudden feeling of heat and flushing experienced by menopausal women. Does the availability of this term add significance to something that is not particularly significant? Gullette (1997) notes that "perspiration . . . has been given a special signifier because it's midlife women who are perspiring" (p. 101) and argues that the whole point is to make women embarrassed about being menopausal:

> [B]eing made to use the special term . . . [has] negative effects, making skin-temperature change seem important, even dominant, in the lives of women of a certain age. What is being created is a common emotion: fear of "flushing"—of being *seen* to be a-midlife-woman-in-a-sweat. (p. 101)

A Brief History of Medicine's Approach to Menopause

The medical approach to menopause has proceeded differently in different parts of the world. In Japan, medical literature as early as the 10th century used the phrase "path of blood" to designate the time when the female reproductive system goes into decline, resulting in a collection of "stale blood" in the body (Lock, 1993). This buildup of stale blood was thought to be associated with a number of symptoms such as dizziness, headaches, stiff shoulders, and a dry mouth. This notion has been gradually replaced by the concept of *kōnenki,* first coined at the end of the 19th century, as a medical term for life cycle transition. *Kōnenki* refers not simply to the end of menstruation, but to a diffuse cluster of changes associated with the transition from young womanhood to midlife. It is thought to be related to an imbalance in the autonomic nervous system. According to the Japanese women interviewed by Lock (1993), a woman might be in *kōnenki* for several years—or avoid the symptoms altogether if she is lucky.

Doctors in Japan have traditionally treated the symptoms of *kōnenki* without using medication. Instead, they have recommended that their patients gain control over their autonomic nervous system through the use of meditative exercises. In recent years, however, the use of hormones to treat certain kinds of menopausal symptoms has increased.

European physicians concerned with life stages often used the term **climacteric** to refer to a transition between stages. Beginning early in the 19th century, the term was reserved for the period of life, usually after age 45, when strength and vitality began to decline (Lock, 1993). By the end of the 19th century, *climacteric* was a term associated mainly with women's "change of life."

Many 19th-century physicians ignored menopause, but those who did take an interest in it often discussed it as a relatively sudden transition, dominated by the cessation of reproductive function, the negotiation of which caused the woman to become a very different person. One physician argued

> There is nothing to compare with the almost sudden decay of the organs of reproduction which marks the middle age of woman. Whilst these organs are in vigor, the whole economy of woman is subject to them. Ovulation and menstruation, gestation and lactation by turns absorb and govern almost all the energies of her system. The loss of these functions entails a complete revolution. (Barnes, 1873, quoted in Lock, 1993, p. 309)

Physicians disagreed about whether the changes were dangerous or pathological, but many believed that once a woman had traversed the 1 or 2 years of physical symptoms involved in the change, she would have a healthy, active life. Only at the turn of the century did doctors begin to talk about possible mental changes associated with menopause. Charles Reed, one-time president of the American Medical Association, wrote in 1904 that a woman's enforced change of roles at menopause from a sexual partner to "merely an intellectual companion or a sexless helpmeet" would lead her to contemplate sadly the future of her adult life as "a dreary waste of empty years" (quoted in Lock, 1993, p. 325).

In this era, the change in ovarian and uterine function was attributed to the nervous system; knowledge of hormones was nonexistent. As the endocrine system gradually came to be understood during the early 20th century, doctors focused on the idea that it was the failure of the ovarian secretions that caused the problems associated with menopause. Eventually, some psychiatrists suggested that the sudden drop in estrogen at menopause triggered insanity ("acute involutional psychosis") in women who were vulnerable. Until research in the 1970s showed that no association existed between menopause and major psychiatric disorders, many U.S. physicians espoused the belief that menopausal women were prone to psychosis.

Psychoanalysts weighed in with the notion that women had to unconsciously compensate for the terrible symbolic losses of reproductive capacity and femininity experienced at menopause. As the noted analyst Helene Deutsch wrote in 1945,

> At the moment when expulsion of ova from the ovary ceases, all the organic processes devoted to the service of the species stop. Woman has ended her existence as a bearer of a future life, and has reached her natural end—her partial death—as a servant of the species. (quoted in Lock, 1993, p. 331)

Small wonder women were expected to be depressed at menopause! The only relief, according to Deutsch, was to focus on other forms of creative activity—or on being a grandmother.

During the 1930s and '40s, physicians began to zero in on "estrogen deficiency" as the cause of women's problems at menopause. They began to prescribe supplemental estrogen to women with menopausal symptoms, just as they would prescribe insulin for diabetics or thyroid medication for an underactive thyroid gland. Such prescriptions were not given routinely to any menopausal woman, just to the minority who reported unpleasant symptoms. In the 1960s, however, medical opinion began to coalesce around the notion that most, or even all, menopausal women should receive **hormone replacement therapy (HRT),** not only to ameliorate transient symptoms such as hot flashes, but also to prevent a variety of serious diseases (e.g., heart disease, osteoporosis) against which estrogen may offer protection.

The Debate over Hormone Replacement Therapy

In 1963 Robert and Thelma Wilson published an article in the *Journal of the American Geriatric Association* titled "The Fate of the Nontreated Postmenopausal Woman: A Plea for the Maintenance of Adequate Estrogen from Puberty to the Grave." The article lamented the misery associated with menopause, caused by estrogen deficiency and the resultant "chaos" in the endocrine system. They argued that women's estrogen-starved bodies made them vulnerable to a number of physical and mental disorders: the loss of physical attractiveness, atrophy of the breasts and genitals, arthritis, severe depression or melancholia, and a type of negative emotional state in which "the world appears as through a gray veil, and they live as docile harmless creatures missing most of life's values" (p. 353). Furthermore, the article argued that giving estrogen to these estrogen-deficient women would not only remove the immediate discomforts and disorders of menopause but also would also have a long-term preventive effect on heart disease and osteoporosis.

Robert Wilson went on to promote estrogen replacement to a popular audience in his book *Feminine Forever* (1966), in which he advocated estrogen supplements from menopause until death to stave off the horror and decay associated with female aging. Wilson's research was funded by Wyeth-Ayerst, "the pharmaceutical company with the largest investment in the production and sales of estrogen replacement therapy" (Lock, 1993, p. 348). Although some physicians may have been put off by Wilson's condescending and demeaning descriptions of older women, his call for hormone replacement for all menopausal women did have an impact. His advocacy was the beginning of a trend to put an increasing number of women on hormone replacement at menopause, whether or not they are experiencing symptoms, and to keep them on this medication for the rest of their lives.

Hormone replacement therapy involves either estrogen alone or estrogen in combination with progesterone. The rationale for urging it on women who are symptom-free has been that estrogen was thought to have a protective effect against the high cholesterol that leads to heart disease and against the thinning of bones (osteoporosis) that leads to potentially dangerous fractures in old age. More recently, it was touted as a protection against Alzheimer's disease. These are "killer" diseases. Women are, naturally, afraid of them and want to prevent them. They are also expensive diseases; societies have a strong interest in preventing them for this reason. Thus arguments for hormone replacement found a ready audience in individual women and in policy makers.

Unfortunately, the health impact of HRT is not so positive. Research now suggests that HRT is linked to an increased risk of breast, endometrial, and ovarian cancer (Mayo Clinic, 2001). The claims with respect to prevention of Alzheimer's disease have not been clearly substantiated by research (Otto, 2000; Seshadri, et al., 2001). Claims that HRT lowers the risk of heart disease have been undercut by recent research: The research suggests an increased risk of heart attacks among short-term users who have heart disease, but that risk of heart attack seemed to be reduced among women who kept using HRT for two years (Grodstein, Manson, & Stampfer, 2001). The preponderance of evidence now suggests that hormone replacement therapy entails more risks than benefits for most women. Estrogen plus progestin treatment increases the risk of coronary events, stroke, breast cancer, pulmonary embolism, and dementia. Estrogen alone increases the risk of coronary heart disease and stroke (Hulley & Grady, 2004). Currently, the prevention of osteoporosis is the one area in which the medical community has the most confidence in the effectiveness of HRT (Otto, 2000). The hormonal solution to the serious diseases associated with aging is not as simple as it first appeared.

Why was the research linking estrogen to protection from heart disease not completely conclusive? Few randomized, controlled studies had been done, and while the evidence was fairly consistent, most of came from observation and from comparisons of groups that were not designed to be equivalent. Women who took estrogen at menopause may have been higher in socioeconomic status, healthier to begin with, in more frequent contact with their doctors, and more conscious of other health-related factors such as exercise and diet than women who did not. Without controlled studies, it was impossible to know whether it was the estrogen or these other differences that led to the decreased incidence of heart disease and osteoporosis. On the other side, the extent to which a surveillance bias had overestimated the risks of hormone replacement were hard to estimate. Women taking hormones likely see their doctors more often for tests and physical exams; thus, if they do have cancer, it is more likely to be detected. Moreover, not enough is known about the differences among women of various racial/ethnic groups with respect to reactions to HRT. Some research indicates that, as they approach the age of menopause, African American and European American women have different patterns of certain hormones (Manson, Sammel, Freeman, & Grisso, 2001). These differences may have implications for decisions about health care during menopause.

Given the previous shortage of research, it is surprising that physicians were so ready to prescribe hormones for their menopausal clients. By 1992, Premarin, an estrogen replacement drug, was the fourth most prescribed medication in the United States, and more than 75 percent of U.S. gynecologists prescribed hormone replacement for most of their patients at menopause (Gullette, 1997). In one 4-week period in 2000, roughly 7.4 million prescriptions for HRT products were written by U.S. health care providers (Otto, 2000). As an increasing proportion of women move into midlife, pharmaceutical companies stood to make enormous profits if prescription of such medications was routine, and they protected their interests. Some physicians report that the number of drug company representatives visiting them has increased since the release of studies critical of HRT (Otto, 2000).

Even if estrogen had all the protective effects originally claimed for it, not all women are at risk for osteoporosis and heart disease. Perhaps 1 in 4 women over age 50 suffers from osteoporosis; a good strategy would be for a woman to assess her own personal risk before deciding to take estrogen. As researcher Kathleen MacPherson notes, "To recommend widespread use of hormone replacement therapy . . . to prevent osteoporosis . . . would be the same as recommending that everyone take antihypertensive drugs because so many people develop high blood pressure" (quoted in Friedan, 1993, p. 493).

Noncontroversial recommendations to improve the odds against osteoporosis include adequate dietary intake of calcium and vitamin D, a daily program of weight-bearing exercise including a 30-minute walk, and no smoking (Nagia & Bennett, 1992). For prevention of heart disease, low dietary fat intake and regular exercise are important. Thus women who are concerned about these diseases have alternatives to spending the rest of their lives after menopause on hormone therapy.

An argument in favor of dietary approaches can be made based on the experience of women in Japan and China, where the incidence of osteoporosis is apparently less than half that of women in North America. The mortality from heart disease among Japanese women is only about one-quarter that of North American women (Lock, 1993). In both cases, the difference may be due partly to the very different diets of the two cultures; when Japanese women immigrate to the United States their risk of these diseases seems to increase. Doctors in Japan, then, are considerably less likely than their North American counterparts to push their patients to take estrogen replacement as a preventive measure.

Menopause and the Politics of Aging across Cultures

[W]omen who had broken through the feminine mystique, going beyond the biological role which used to define their lives to a fully human personhood, would experience a completely different aging process—menopause would simply be another milestone of life and growth they would pass through. Now that I have confronted in full force in my own life and among the countless women and experts I have been interviewing the reality of this change, and the forces opposing it, I see that eternal vigilance is needed to ward off both a reversion to the feminine mystique, and a passive acquiescence to the medical model which reinforces the mystique of age even as it seems to defend against it. (Friedan, 1993, p. 496)

If the medical model makes women feel as if they are sick with "estrogen deficiency" when they reach menopause, what are the consequences? Women who, at midlife, are just reaching the senior positions in their careers have their confidence shaken by gloomy predictions about their health. Women who are at crossroads in their lives because their children have grown feel that, instead of being at a new beginning, they are starting a long slide toward decrepitude. Women who are poor or who are struggling against discrimination blame their fatigue and depression on "the change" instead of on the conditions of their working environment. The overall impact is for women to feel disempowered and less hopeful and to accept internal, hormonal explanations for problems they face.

By contrast, menopause can also simply be regarded as a natural development process that signals a life transition in much the same way as puberty does. Puberty may be associated with skin problems and emotional distress, but these problems are not viewed as symptoms of an underlying "clinical disorder" nor are attempts made to prevent puberty by suppressing hormone production. Similarly, according to this model, menopause may be accompanied by hot flashes and the emotional turmoil associated with identity and role issues, but these are dealt with as problems associated with normal and expected transition rather than as indicative of a disease process. The focus is not on "deficiency" and artificially maintaining a particular hormonal state but rather on viewing menopause as an inevitable life stage associated with new challenges and freedoms. (Gannon & Ekstrom, 1993, p. 277)

Whether a woman's culture holds a medical or a life transition view of menopause is likely to affect her attitudes toward this change in her life. When Linda Gannon and Bonnie Ekstrom (1993) asked a large sample of U.S. adults to express their attitudes toward menopause in one of three contexts, they found that the context made a difference. One group gave their attitudes toward three medical problems, including menopause; a second group described attitudes toward three life transitions, including menopause; and a third group responded to three symbols of aging, including menopause. The researchers found that the medical context elicited the most negative and least positive attitudes from respondents. Simply calling menopause a medical issue rather than a life transition influenced people to think more negatively about it.

Thinking more negatively is no trivial matter. Attitudes and expectations can act as self-fulfilling prophecies. Negative attitudes, beliefs, and expectations among pre-menopausal women predict reported distress at the time of menopause (Avis & McKinlay, 1991). For a woman, the feeling that she has entered a period of chronic disease and inevitable decline can cause her to see all her life experiences in this light. It is not a useful light for plotting new beginnings.

New Roles and Relationships

> Midlife represents a crisis. The old breaks up so that the new may emerge. The woman must decide whether she will trust the open future or attempt to hold on to the past. . . . The trust that there are always new levels of growth for the woman even as the past patterns recede and our relationships are forced to change through separation and death is an ability to trust in the movement of life itself. (Washbourn, 1977, pp. 138, 140)

The focus on the losses of middle age has often obscured the equally important gains. At this stage of life, a woman may be freed of earlier responsibilities and concerns and be ready to explore new possibilities. Perhaps the reason the negative emphasis has been so pervasive is that motherhood—the very role that is lost or limited at midlife—has been thought of as the key role for women. If mothering is the most important thing for women, how can she find her post-motherhood life meaningful and happy? This sexist approach, which defined women in terms of their biology, has characterized some of the research on women's adult development, particularly with respect to the "empty nest."

The Empty Nest: Loss or Liberation?

For women who have raised children, the departure of the last child from home may trigger a sense of loss, often called the **empty nest syndrome.** At one time, this stage of life was thought to be a severe crisis for women, often leading to depression and a loss of self-esteem. Certainly, the immediacy of the parenting role diminishes for women at this stage, which may leave some women temporarily floundering, particularly if few other roles are available to them. For other women, however, this change creates longed-for opportunities to develop new roles. Furthermore, researchers have found over the years that women whose children have left home often show higher levels of satisfaction with their lives than do women still caring for children. Researchers in one early study of California empty-nesters reported:

> The majority expressed puzzlement and confusion and even guilt because they were "feeling better than ever," "taking care of myself for once," "much freer and in charge of my own time." . . . [M]ost exulted in the fact that they had some free time in which to explore themselves, takes classes and workshops, and—often for the first time—enter the job market. One woman described herself as a yucca plant "finally blooming after 50 years." (Fiske & Chiriboga, 1990, p. 73)

In contrast, women who find their childcare years extended because of very large families or the necessity of taking on the primary care of grandchildren may feel sad and resentful, as researchers studying one sample of African American grandmothers found (Burton & Bengston, 1985). These women felt that life was passing them by, and that they should have more to look forward to than years and years of being a "nursemaid." Such primary caregiver grandmothers are often depressed (McCallion & Kolomer, 2000). Similar feelings may be experienced by women who are freed of their childcare responsibilities only to acquire a new set of duties as primary caregiver for an aging parent or spouse, as noted in Chapter 9.

Of course, becoming a grandmother is an extremely positive experience for many women, particularly if it is a new role rather than a reprise of the primary caregiving associated with motherhood. Women may feel able to develop more spontaneous, open relationships with their grandchildren than they had with their own children. One study of African American grandmothers aged 85 and older found that they expressed great pride in their longevity and in the numbers of grandchildren, great-grandchildren and great-great-grandchildren in their families (Barer, 2001). A number of these women had special relationships with a particular grandchild. A study of the grandmother role as experienced by lesbian women revealed that they felt it was most important to spend time with their grandchildren. These women too were proud of being grandmothers and had special and rewarding relationships with their grandchildren (Whalen, Bigner, & Clifton, 2000). This possibility for special relationships between grandparents and grandchildren is acknowledged in a variety of cultures. For example, among the !Kung people,

> Alternate generations are recognized as having a special relationship, especially when the child is the grandparent's "namesake." Personal and intimate topics not discussed with parents are taken up freely with grandparents, and grandparents often represent a child's interests at the expense of those of the parent. Also, since older people contribute less to subsistence than do other adults, they have more time to play with their grandchildren. (Shostak, 1981, p. 50)

Despite the big differences between the North American and !Kung cultures, there seems to be a remarkable similarity in the expectations for the grandparent–grandchild relationship.

Career Change and Retirement

Aging often leads to changes in the way people spend their time, and in many parts of the world such changes are regarded as difficult and stressful. For example, in Nigeria a study of women and men in their 60s revealed the perception that the most difficult challenges of aging for women included the departure of children and the prospect of spending less time with children, whereas for men the most difficult things were retirement and increased leisure time (Sijuwade, 1991).

Women who bear and raise children and also hold outside employment have two parallel careers for a large part of their lives. These women experience a series of built-in "career changes" as their families mature, even if their work outside the home remains the same. A woman "retires" from childrearing once her children are able to care for themselves; if raising children has been her main occupation, she must find a new occupation on which to center herself. Perhaps starting over in a new stage of life becomes less stressful if one is used to change.

Still, retirement from paid employment is likely to be experienced by women as a big step, and some studies have suggested that women look forward to retirement with less positive anticipation than men do. This may occur because women may have joined the work force later, after children were in school, or because discrimination and other occupational barriers have slowed their attainment of the jobs they really wanted. At least one U.S. study, however, suggests that the key to understanding gender differences in attitudes toward retirement is economics. This study of a large sample of women and men in their 60s who were not currently married uncovered no differences between never-married women and men in their beliefs that older workers should retire and in their definition of themselves as retirees (Hatch, 1992). In this group of never-married seniors, women actually held a more positive attitude toward life in retirement than men did. The findings were different for the previously married group of respondents, however. Previously married women, who often face a poor financial situation in retirement, were less likely than previously married men to agree that older workers should retire and to define themselves as retirees. The researcher concludes that differences in women's and men's economic circumstances are a major factor causing the differences in their outlook on retirement. And these differences are stark. Women earn less than men over their lifetimes because of the wage gap. The wage gap can translate into an average lifetime loss of over $300,000 for women (Women's Institute for a Secure Retirement, 2001). Nearly half of all women in the United States work in traditionally female, relatively low-paid jobs without pensions. Women live longer than men, so they actually need more money than men do to get them through their retirement, but they usually approach retirement with a lot less money than men do. It is difficult to look forward to a retirement that implies poverty or hardship.

Losing a Life Partner

Aging is often associated with the loss of important relationships, and after middle age a woman often faces the possibility of the death of her long-term partner in life. For married women, the chances of widowhood are high since women tend to outlive men and to be younger than their husbands. For women in lesbian partnerships, the loss of a life partner may be made more devastating by society's lack of recognition of that partner as a spouse. In either case, the loss of a woman's partner forces social and economic changes on her. Increased loneliness is a possibility, as is a decrease in economic resources.

Studies in North America show that women who have lost their partners cope by relying on other sources of interpersonal support: female friends, relatives, and neighbors. In this respect, the cultural expectation that women will nurture relationships may serve them well: Many older women have strong support networks in place because of a lifetime of connecting with others. For older minority women, such contacts tend to be heavily familial; these women often play central roles in their family networks, providing both material and emotional support to their adult children and grandchildren and receiving social support, prestige, and the acknowledgment of their domestic authority in return (Padgett, 1988). For elderly White women, social contacts tend to include both family and nonkin relationships.

Women who feel disconnected often report the most age-related problems. In one study of elderly African Americans, loneliness was found to be the strongest predictor of women's self-reported memory problems (Bazargan & Barbre, 1992). A study of widows in Singapore found that those who coped best were living with immediate family members (Teo & Mehta, 2001).

Yet the changes associated with losing a life partner may trigger new strengths, even among women who had very good relationships, who miss the partner deeply, and who list loneliness as their biggest adjustment problem. One pioneering study of widowhood by Helen Lopata (1973) showed that after the initial grieving for their spouse, women often reported positive changes in themselves. In Lopata's sample of Chicago widows, a majority (63 percent) reported that they had become more independent and competent since losing their husbands, and many also said that they had become "freer and more active" (47 percent) and "more socially engaged" (31 percent). In a similar vein, interviews with widows in Singapore revealed that they found themselves emerging from the shadow of their late husbands, forced to acquire new skills and make new friends (Teo & Mehta, 2001). Australian women's written descriptions of their experience of widowhood often showed they used humor as a coping mechanism and indicated that they had found ways to become tough survivors (Feldman, Byles, & Beaumont, 2000).

Of course, the experience of losing a partner to death is strongly shaped by society's response to this event and by the roles available for older single women in a given culture. For example, in India, a custom (no longer practiced) among certain groups was **suttee** (or **sati**), in which a widow willingly threw herself on her husband's burning funeral pyre as a gesture of virtue and fidelity (Narasimhan, 1990). Although the practice of sati has ended, a widow has virtually no place in many parts of traditional Indian society. She usually cannot return to her birth family because she is considered a liability—another mouth to feed. She does not inherit her husband's estate, so she has no resources to bring to another marriage and thus is not expected to remarry. There is no obvious way for her to support herself. In some parts of India, a widowed woman is considered an "inauspicious" person—thought to bring bad luck—and so would be discouraged from attending even such family events as her own son's wedding (Bhardwaj, 2001).

In other countries, women who outlive their husbands sometimes wonder just how they are supposed to survive. Widows in Australia report worries about their decreased income and anxiety and depression about financial insecurity (Feldman, Byles, & Beaumont, 2000). Elderly widows in Japan are very likely to be poor and can expect relatively little help from social service agencies (Izuhara, 2000). An investigation of the economic impact of widowhood for women in the United States and Germany reveals that women in

The changes associated with losing a life partner may trigger new strengths, even among women who had very good relationships and who miss the partner deeply.

both countries experience drops in their income after the deaths of their husbands. Women in Germany are 2 to 3 times more likely to live in poverty after the deaths of their husbands. Women in the United States are just under twice as likely to be poor after their husbands' deaths as before; however, the poverty rate for older widows in the United States is more than double the rate in Germany. In both countries, the fall into poverty is triggered primarily by a drop in Social Security and pension payments that occur after the husband dies, and secondarily by the loss of the husband's earned income (Hungerford, 2001). Clearly, one reason women may have trouble coping with widowhood is that societies have not taken women's economic needs seriously enough.

BOX 11.3 LEARNING ACTIVITY
Interviewing an Older Woman

Choose an older woman in your family extended family, or community who is willing to spend some time talking and sharing her thoughts with you. Take a pad of paper and pencil with you and think out your questions in advance. Your task is to interview this woman to try to learn more about her life and her reflections about being a woman. Try to find out how she believes being female shaped her life. How was she affected by societal views of women at different stages of her life? How have her experiences as a woman changed over time as she grew from girlhood to young adulthood, to middle age and beyond? How might her experiences reflect those of other women of her social class, religion, race, ethnicity, sexual orientation, physical ability, or national origin? How does she think that the people around her view older women? What are her hopes and fears for the future? What does she think of the lives of younger women today? Add other questions that you think are appropriate. As you go through the interview, it will be helpful to ask her to reflect on *specific experiences* that were important to her or that are good examples of the ideas she is talking about.

The object of this exercise is, first of all, to have a real conversation with an older woman and to get to know her better. Secondly, it should provide you with an opportunity to see how the issues discussed in this chapter with respect to women and aging are relevant to someone's life. Thirdly, it will give you ideas about issues that are new to you and that are not discussed in this chapter.

Rejecting the Message of Decline

The experience of aging is shaped by cultural myths and scripts and by the material constraints that women experience. Women who learn to expect menopause to be traumatic and disabling are more likely than other women to experience it as such. Women who learn that the beauty associated with youth is the most important aspect of their self-esteem are likely to be depressed by the changes in appearance that come with age. Women who face poverty in old age or whose culture provides no roles or social space for older women will approach the process of aging with trepidation.

But cultural scripts can be resisted, and material obstacles can be overcome. Decline does not have to be a necessary part of aging: New strengths can emerge to replace earlier ones. Perhaps nowhere is this clearer than among the select group of hardy older minority women in the United States who survive all the risks associated with day-to-day problems of poverty and discrimination to become examples of "successful aging" (Padgett, 1988). These aging minority women

> are able to draw on strengths—psychological, social, and cultural—which ease the transition to old age. They have spent their lives as strategists, marshaling scarce resources to cope with everyday demands and these coping strategies "pay off" later on in self-reliance. (p. 219)

Societies could make successful aging much more likely for these women and others by providing needed economic support and expanded health care services before age 65 so that more women could reach that age in reasonable economic and physical health. Yet even in the face of social and economic barriers, many women obviously age with grace and strength.

Clearly, aging has, in some societies, been regarded as a catastrophe for women, something to be denied and evaded as much as possible. Yet, as the novelist Ursula Le Guin (1989) notes, the existence of a more dramatic "change of life" for women than for men provides women with an opportunity for a kind of rebirth:

> [I]t seems a pity to have a built-in rite of passage and to dodge it, evade it, and pretend nothing has changed. That is to dodge and evade one's womanhood, to pretend one's like a man. Men, once initiated, never get the second chance. They never change again. That's their loss, not ours. Why borrow poverty? Certainly the effort to remain unchanged, young, when the body gives so impressive a signal of change as the menopause, is gallant; but it is a stupid, self-sacrificial gallantry, better befitting a boy of twenty than a woman of forty-five or fifty. Let the athletes die young and laurel-crowned. Let the soldiers earn the Purple Hearts. Let women die old, white-crowned, with human hearts. (p. 5)

SUMMARY

For women in many modern western societies, aging has become something to dread. Stereotypes of older women are negative: Older women are often portrayed as frail, helpless, irritable, and confused. Sometimes they are not portrayed at all: Older women are often invisible in the popular media. Beauty and youth are often thought of as synonymous for women. Whereas an older man may be viewed as distinguished, an older woman is more likely to be viewed as unattractive. Thus, for women, aging is socially constructed as a time of decline and loss of attributes important to femininity.

Cultures construct these negative images of older women, and thus it is not surprising to learn that, under some circumstances, cultures construct images of older women that are positive and strong. For example, the Aboriginal people of Australia have important, powerful roles for female elders. Even in American culture, a few older women are visible in powerful positions, but these women are often seen as exceptions to the stereotype.

Menopause, the cessation of menstruation, is often thought of as the transition to old age for women—even though most Western women live for two or more decades after reaching menopause. There are many physical and emotional symptoms attributed to menopause, including hot flashes, vaginal dryness, depression, and mood swings. Yet these symptoms vary dramatically among cultures, leading to the conjecture that the symptoms are, at least in part, the result of expectations, stereotypes, and self-fulfilling prophecies. Indeed, some research shows that persons who are asked to describe their attitudes about menopause give more negative responses when it is presented as a "medical problem" than when it is presented as a "life transition."

Nonetheless, menopause has been treated by the medical profession in the West as a disease of estrogen deficiency. During the 1960s, a push began to recommend hormone replacement therapy (HRT) for all menopausal women to keep them "feminine forever." For years, HRT was urged on symptom-free women to protect them from heart disease, osteoporosis, and Alzheimer's disease. However, research debunked the protective effects of HRT.

As they negotiate the transition through middle age, women often confront new roles and relationships. Their children grow up and leave home. They may retire or change careers. They may lose a life partner. The way a woman copes with these transitions is affected by the way her society views and creates opportunities for older women. For example, women may not anticipate retirement with joy because they expect to be poor when their paycheck stops. Or they may have special difficulties with widowhood because their society views widows as useless or "inauspicious."

Women can reject the message of decline that accompanies the move into middle and older age, and they can work together to rewrite the scripts for aging women. Despite stereotypes and age discrimination, many women find ways to be powerful in their later years.

KEY TERMS

menopause	climacteric	empty nest syndrome
ageism	hormone replacement therapy	suttee (sati)
hot flash	(HRT)	

DISCUSSION QUESTIONS

Could the negative stereotypes of older women be changing as the population ages? Have you seen any evidence, for example, that advertisers are promoting images of strong older women?

Do you think menopause is socially constructed? How might the experience of menopause be made more positive for women in North America?

How do financial considerations affect women's experience of aging? What could be done about this?

FOR ADDITIONAL READING

Delany, Sarah, & Delany, A. Elizabeth, with Hearth, Amy Hill. (1993). *Having our say: The Delany sisters' first 100 years.* New York: Kodansha International. Two African American sisters tell the stories of their lives. Insights into their personal struggles and triumphs are combined with a unique window on the history of race and gender relations in the United States.

Friedan, Betty. (1993). *The fountain of age.* New York: Simon & Schuster. The pioneering feminist who named the "feminine mystique" turns her sights on the construction of women's aging in North America.

Gullette, Margaret Morganroth. (1997). *Declining to decline: Cultural combat and the politics of the midlife.* Charlottesville, VA: University Press of Virginia. The author analyzes the ways women in Western countries are often encouraged to feel that life is "all downhill" after middle age.

Lock, Margaret. (1993). *Encounters with aging: Mythologies of menopause in Japan and North America.* Berkeley: University of California Press. An anthropologist discusses the attitudes toward menopause in different cultures and presents the results of her own studies comparing samples of women from Canada, the United States, and Japan.

Shostak, Marjorie (2000). *Return to Nisa.* Cambridge, MA: Harvard University Press. The anthropologist who chronicled the life story of Nisa, a !Kung woman, returned to the Kalahari Desert decades later to reestablish contact with her old friend and informant. Shostak was facing her own death from cancer when she made this trip, and her reflections on culture, aging, anthropology, and friendship between women are remarkable and moving.

WEB RESOURCES

Women's Institute for a Secure Retirement (WISER). This is the site of an independent nonprofit organization devoted to educating women about retirement issues. The site provides access to clear reports about economic and health issues for older women. **www.wiser .heinz.org**

The North American Menopause Society. Run by a scientific nonprofit organization, this site provides the latest scientific research news about menopause. **www.menopause.org**

The National Center on Women & Aging. This research center, based at Brandeis University, provides access to research reports, press releases, a newsletter, and links to other Web resources on women and aging. **www.heller.brandeis.edu/national/ind.html**

Sexualities

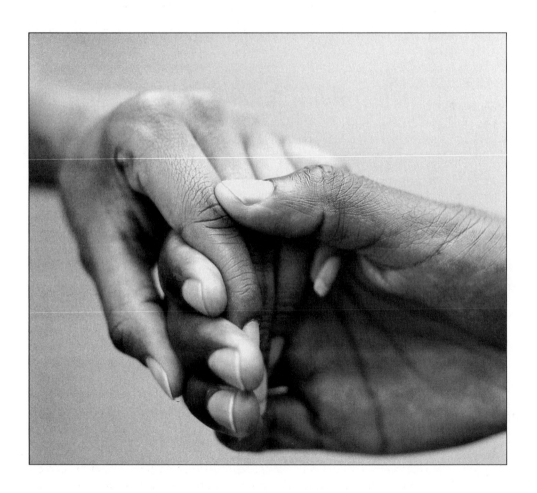

CHAPTER OUTLINE

At the University of Costa Rica in 1995, I listened as a Costa Rican professor lectured to a group of students visiting from the United States. Her topic was the position of women in her country. The students were looking a little bored and restless until the professor hit upon two issues that struck a chord: abortion and prostitution.

She spoke about the fact that abortion was illegal in Costa Rica and noted that most women in her country were, in fact, opposed to abortion. The U.S. students seemed surprised, and they began to listen more closely. A few minutes later, in response to a question, she mentioned that prostitution was legal, and that the government offered various health-related services to prostitutes.

The American students were stunned. "Prostitution is legal?" some cried in consternation. "How can women put up with that?" The Costa Rican professor seemed surprised and taken aback by their reaction. "Why not? It's a job," she replied, and went on to point out that prostitution was, in fact, legal in many countries. She argued that prostitutes were less exploited and better protected from illness and violence when their activities were legal.

One young woman in the front row shook her head in irritation. "I still can't believe it. Abortion is *illegal* and prostitution is *legal*." The discussion heated up and, at the end of the class, the students were still buzzing about the "strangeness" of the country they were visiting. The professor, too, left feeling shaken by the gap between her perceptions and those of the visiting students.

Sexuality is more than simple biology. It is an emotional topic in most cultures, weighed down with moral proscriptions, beliefs about reproduction, and years of traditionally understood meanings. For the middle-class North American students in this particular example, the notion of legal prostitution was not simply an interesting difference between their own culture and that of their host country. Rather, it was something about the host country that seemed terribly wrong. For most of them, it was a first exposure to the idea that prostitution could be legal, and they simply could not imagine, let alone get comfortable with, such a scenario.

Sexuality plays a key role in women's psychology because it plays such an emotional and pivotal role in the cultural dictates concerning women and men. In many cultural groups, women's traditional roles are structured around heterosexual relationships that center on conceiving, bearing, and rearing children. Women are often related to as sexual objects: appreciated for their attractiveness, or subjected to harassment simply because they are women. Rape—an act of violence that is sexual—is one act of violence that is more likely to happen to women than to men, and the fear of rape plays a part in the choices about behavior that many women make. Sexual orientation is a key aspect of a woman's identity—and one that can have strong implications for the ease or difficulty of her life in most societies.

We begin this chapter with a discussion of the ways social scientists have studied women's sexuality. Sex researchers have in many cases been pioneers, daring to investigate emotionally charged issues and hold cherished assumptions up to scrutiny. Every researcher, no matter how incisive, is influenced by personal and cultural biases, however. Thus, like all research, studies of sexuality bear the imprint of the assumptions and understandings characteristic of the time and place in which they occurred. We will see that culture affects what people *know* about female sexual desire, sexual physiology, and sexual response.

Sexual orientation is the next topic addressed. How is a woman defined—by others and by herself—as heterosexual, lesbian, or bisexual? What do we understand about the underlying reasons for sexual orientation? What implications does a lesbian or bisexual identity have in different cultural contexts?

Next we turn to questions about the social contexts of sexual behavior. How do sexual attitudes and behavior differ for women in different contexts? How do sexual attitudes such as the **double standard** affect women's behavior and feelings? How do social contexts influence the sexual experiences of women with disabilities? How does culture shape lesbian sexualities?

Women—members of the sex that gets pregnant—have always been concerned about the consequences of sexual activity. We will look at women's behavior around the world with respect to contraception. Another major potential consequence of sexual activity is sexually transmitted disease. The next section examines how the threat to women from such diseases is magnified by cultural and economic systems that give women little power in sexual negotiation and often make them dependent on male partners for survival.

Cultural attitudes about women, sex, and love help women construct their own attitudes about the meaning of sex and the links between sex and romance. We will examine the role of the double standard in this process. Finally, we will consider the social norms and expectations surrounding prostitution: the exchange of sex for money.

Research on Sexuality:
Where Do Our "Facts" Come From?

In 1914, Marie Stopes, a world-renowned paleobotanist who, when she received her doctorate in 1905, had become the youngest doctor of science in Britain, began making notes for a new and groundbreaking book. The subject was not botany, but human sexuality, and

Stopes was motivated to write it by her own tangled emotions arising from a divorce and the beginnings of a new love relationship. Applying her scientific training to her own life, she began to analyze her own sexual feelings and to chart them daily. Her *Tabulation of Symptoms of Sexual Excitement in Solitude,* prepared as part of her notes for the book, recorded her sensations at different times of the month. Unflinchingly candid in transcribing her personal sexual feelings in notes and charts, she noted, for example, that at certain times she felt "a desire to be held closely round the waist, till corsets become tempting though normally they are abhorrent" (Stopes, 1914, quoted in J. Rose, 1992, p. 85). Stopes also went beyond her own experience, enlisting the cooperation of female friends in the suffrage movement in charting the phenomenology and cycles of sexual desire, and she concluded after much investigation that women experienced peak periods of sexual desire at certain points during the monthly menstrual cycle.

When Stopes finally found a publisher for her controversial book, titled *Married Love,* in 1918, public reaction was mixed. Some readers were repelled by her explicit description of sexual intercourse and her clinical depictions of sexual urges. One distinguished psychiatrist labeled her books "handbooks of prostitution," and a few married women wrote that they were "disgusted with the filth" or upset that she had treated the subject of marital relations so "ruthlessly and inartistically." Yet the majority of letters to her publisher were glowing in their praise for a book that would "clear away the old evil conspiracy of secrecy which has ruined so many women's lives" (quoted in J. Rose, 1992, pp. 14; 114–115).

What made Marie Stopes's book so shocking and unusual was the fact that the researcher and writer was a woman. Previous well-known "sex experts"—Havelock Ellis, Sigmund Freud, Edward Carpenter—had all been men and had focused on "abnormal" sexuality. Stopes had zeroed in on the average married woman's experience of sex. In her book,

> she had dared to stake a claim for female sexuality, for women's sexual needs and sexual rights. Her views challenged the centuries of prejudice and superstition and the accretions of religious teaching which saw women's bodies and women's attractions as desirable but also dirty and corrupting and the lust for women as shameful and sinful. . . . [She] dismissed the idea that "nice" women have no spontaneous sexual impulses . . . (J. Rose, 1992, p. 111)

Because Stopes used research into her own experience and that of her friends as one of the bases of her book, the resulting perspective is somewhat limited, but her contribution was extremely valuable. Subsequent sex researchers have endeavored to be more scientific and objective by studying large numbers of strangers through surveys, interviews, or observation. The trend toward large-scale **sex surveys** was begun by Alfred Kinsey and his colleagues in the 1940s (Kinsey, Pomeroy & Martin, 1948; Kinsey, Pomeroy, Martin, & Gebhard, 1953) and continued by other researchers. The most recent well-known survey in the United States was done by a research group at the University of Chicago, which polled more than 3,000 adults (Michael, Gagnon, Laumann, & Kolata, 1994). Large-scale sex surveys have been conducted in other countries as well. For example, a survey coordinated by Liu Dalin canvassed 23,000 respondents in China over a period of 18 months (Southerland, 1990).

Despite the large numbers of respondents, the perspective provided by these surveys may be as limited, in its own way, as that of the work of Marie Stopes. There are some reasons to be skeptical about the degree to which the survey results reflect the sexual behavior of the general population. Volunteer participants in sex research tend to be more

BOX 12.1 WOMEN SHAPING PSYCHOLOGY
Gail Elizabeth Wyatt

Gail Wyatt grew up in a conservative Southern family that, she says, tried to shelter her from many things. However, they could not shelter her from the images of sexuality portrayed in the media all around her, particularly the images of African American women's sexuality (Grimes, 1999). The prevalent popular images of African American women as either asexual "mammies" or lusty temptresses were unacceptable to her, and she questioned them throughout her years as an undergraduate student at Fisk University in Tennessee. After completing her Ph.D. at the University of California at Los Angeles (UCLA), she focused on sexuality as a research and professional interest and embarked on training as a sex therapist and researcher in the National Institute of Mental Health (NIMH) Research Scientist Career Development Program in 1974. She became the first African American woman to be licensed as a clinical psychologist in the state of California.

Now, having been a sex therapist and researcher for many years, she is a professor of psychiatry and biobehavioral sciences at UCLA and the Associate Director of Behavioral Science Research, Education, and Training for the UCLA AIDS Institute. One focus of her research has been on Black women's sexuality, and she argues that her most important finding does not involve differences among racial groups, but rather diversity among African American women. She notes that there is

experienced and less inhibited in their sex lives than most people, and so may not be a representative sample of the population. Also, particular groups may be deliberately excluded from the research. The original Kinsey report did not include African American respondents, and the University of Chicago survey was limited to respondents over the age of 18. To fill some of the gaps, surveys have been done that focus explicitly on particular groups. For example, Gail Wyatt (1989; 1992) surveyed random samples of 122 European American and 126 African American women in Los Angeles County, and the Indian Health Service surveyed Native American women living on and off the Blackfeet Reservation near Great Falls, Montana (Warren et al., 1990).

BOX 12.1 WOMEN SHAPING PSYCHOLOGY (*continued*)
Gail Elizabeth Wyatt

still much work to be done in the study of Black sexuality in the United States, both in terms of historical data and of the contemporary situation with respect to the impact of stereotypes and other issues. She has also made lasting contributions in other areas, researching and writing about culturally appropriate methods in assessment, treatment, and research with African American families, child sexual abuse, and the effects of abortion. She has testified before the Congressional Committee on Rape and the Los Angeles Commission on Women.

Wyatt herself has done much to fill in the gaps in knowledge about African American women's sexuality. Her research has been presented in a steady stream of articles, and her book, *Stolen Women,* brings a wide range of information on this topic together.

Wyatt has received many awards, including the American Psychological Association (APA) Award for Distinguished Contributions in Research on Public Policy, the Carolyn Sherif Award from the APA division on the psychology of women, and recognition as an outstanding

researcher by the Association of Black Psychologists and the Society for the Study of Ethnicity and Culture of the APA.

Read More about Gail Wyatt

Grimes, T. R. (1999). In search of the truth about history, sexuality and Black women: An interview with Gail E. Wyatt. *Teaching of Psychology, 26*(1), pp. 66–70.
American Psychological Association (1993). Awards for distinguished contribution to research in public policy, 1992: Gail E. Wyatt. *American Psychologist, 48,* pp. 372–375.

Read What She Has Written

Wyatt, G. E. (1992). The sociocultural context of African American and White American women's rape. *The Journal of Social Issues, 48,* pp. 77–91.
Wyatt, G. E. (1997). *Stolen women: Reclaiming our sexuality, taking back our lives.* New York: Wiley.
Wyatt, G. E., Moe, A., & Guthrie, D. (1999). The gynecological, reproductive, and sexual health of HIV-positive women. *Cultural Diversity and Ethnic Minority Psychology, 5*(3), pp. 183–196.

In surveys, the reliance on self-reports of sexual activity has some potential pitfalls. Respondents may distort the picture by tending to exaggerate or minimize their sexual activity, they may be unable to remember accurately events that are long past, and they may have difficulty estimating frequencies and time spent in certain activities. Terms in the survey may mean different things to members of different groups. Moreover, the survey approach provides little information about what the reported activities meant to the participants and, since the participants play no part in shaping the questions in the survey, the survey may omit behaviors and opinions that are critical to the sex lives of the respondents.

William Masters and Virginia Johnson went beyond sex surveys in the 1960s when they undertook research to directly observe human sexual activity and measure the physiological responses associated with sexual arousal and **orgasm.** Using volunteers recruited for their study, Masters and Johnson observed and recorded data from thousands of cycles of sexual arousal and orgasm experienced by 382 women and 312 men. When their book *Human Sexual Response* was published in 1966, it provided hitherto unavailable information about the sequence and patterns of physiological sexual arousal.

The conclusions about human sexual response that Masters and Johnson reached (1966) are presented in the following section. But before studying their findings, it is important to recognize that pioneering as their work was, the picture of human sexuality Masters and Johnson provided is also limited. First of all, it focuses on sexual behavior in the laboratory—outside of any normal social context. The implication is that the physiology of sex is its most basic and important aspect, and this is a very strong assumption built into their research. Second, there were a number of biases in the way participants were selected for the research, making them unrepresentative of many groups (Tiefer, 1995). To be accepted as a research participant, a person had to have a history of achieving orgasm through masturbation and sexual intercourse. Anyone who did not masturbate and who did not regularly have orgasms was excluded from the study. According to Leonore Tiefer, the women who participated were probably less representative of women in general than the male participants were of men in general. The reason? According to a variety of sex surveys, women in the United States are less likely to masturbate and are less consistent in experiencing orgasm—both requirements for inclusion in the study—than men are. The researchers also deliberately sought a sample of participants who were above average in intelligence, education, and socioeconomic status. Furthermore, the volunteers were characterized by a strong interest in effective sexual performance and a willingness to have that performance observed and analyzed, probably making them different from the general population.

Critics have also assailed the omission of sexual desire, attraction, and emotions from the model of human sexual response constructed by Masters and Johnson. Tiefer (1995) argues that the seemingly gender-neutral model actually favors a male approach to sexuality by focusing on the physical aspects of sexuality and leaving out the emotional and intimacy aspects that women in many cultures are trained to value. The Masters and Johnson model, she notes,

> assumes that men and women have and want the same kind of sexuality since physiological research suggests that in some ways, and under selected test conditions, we are built the same. Yet our social realities dictate that we are not all the same sexually—not in our socially shaped wishes, in our sexual self-development, or in our interpersonal sexual meanings. (p. 56)

So what research can we have confidence in when it comes to sexuality? No matter what method researchers employ, they produce a limited picture of human sexuality shaped by their own assumptions and motivations. Must we therefore discount the findings? No, but each piece of research provides only one limited window on sexuality. Any of the methods discussed here produces only a partial picture. No one approach can capture the truth about human sexuality (or most other areas of human being and behavior); it is important to consider all of them.

Sexual Desire and Sexual Response

> [T]he biology presented in these [human sexuality] texts always dwells on the anatomy and physiology of the genital organs, never of the tactile receptors of the cheek or the lips or the physiology of aroma preferences. You'll find the physiology of arousal but not of pleasure, of performance but not of fantasy. (Tiefer, 1995, p. 6)

> According to most sexologists, sex is a biologically driven, mechanical, matter of hydraulics. Heated up by the moment and hormones, body parts swell naturally and genitals connect inevitably. Tab A is inserted into slot B. If she is free of guilt and anxiety, all a woman needs to achieve ecstasy, instantly and easily, is the right partner. (McCormick, 1994, p. 175)

Sex researchers have often reduced sexuality to physiological responses and frequency tables, perhaps because the engorgement of organs with blood is easier to measure than subjective feelings of arousal or pleasure, and questions about "how often" are easier to answer than questions about why a particular sexual activity feels better with one person, or on one occasion, than another.

One reason for the narrow focus has also been a desire to debunk oppressive myths about sexuality, such as the notion that women do not have strong sexual needs or desires or that certain sexual practices will cause problems (e.g., myths that sex during pregnancy or menstruation will be harmful; masturbation will cause insanity). For example, Masters and Johnson (1966) endeavored to show that both women and men responded similarly, in physiological terms, to sexual stimulation. As Tiefer (1995) later argued, they may have worked too hard at forcing female and male sexual response into identical molds. Nonetheless, their research helped to undercut the idea that women did not have strong sexual responses and to discredit the idea that a woman could be labeled "frigid" if she did not experience orgasm or "fixated" if she had the "wrong kind" of orgasm.

Masters and Johnson demonstrated that, at least under certain conditions of sexual stimulation, both women and men followed a pattern of physiological arousal and release in which sexual excitement produced increased blood flow to the genital area (Figure 12.1) and a buildup of muscular tension, heart rate, blood pressure, and pulse, followed by a pleasurable release of that tension through the rhythmic neuromuscular contractions of orgasm. In the process of arousal, the vagina became lubricated with fluid from its walls, making intercourse easier. Masters and Johnson's findings clearly demonstrated that women could become sexually aroused and experience orgasm. They also demonstrated that a necessary, but perhaps not always sufficient, precursor to the experience of orgasm, or even nonpainful intercourse, was sexual arousal brought about by some kind of stimulation.

Another finding from Masters and Johnson's research is that women's orgasms arise mainly from clitoral stimulation, and that there is no physiological difference between orgasms that occur during intercourse and those that occur as a result of manual or oral stimulation of the **clitoris,** a female sex organ located above the urethral opening which is

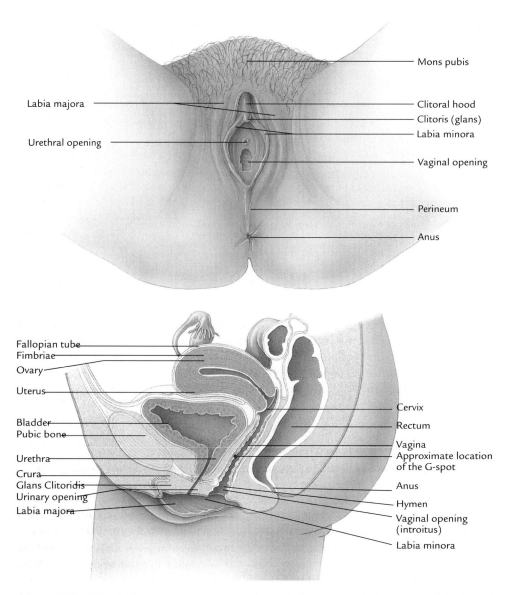

Figure 12.1 Female Sex Organs. *Source:* P. M. Insel and W. T. Roth. (1998), *Core Concepts in Health* (8th ed. 1998 Update) Mountain View, CA: Mayfield, p. 105. Copyright 1998 by Mayfield Publishing Co. Reprinted by permission.

extremely sensitive to sexual sensations. This finding was deemed quite striking at the time, since it undercut the Freudian notion that there were two kinds of orgasm: clitoral and vaginal. Freudian theory held that women who could have orgasms only through clitoral stimulation were displaying a kind of arrested psychological development, and he characterized such orgasms as infantile. A "real woman," according to Freud's theory, would have vaginal orgasms. Yet, as Masters and Johnson found, even orgasms that occur during intercourse seem to be triggered by direct or indirect stimulation of the clitoris, which has as many nerve endings as the penis. In fact, Australian medical researcher Helen O'Connell has shown that the clitoris is not the tiny organ once thought, but extends up to 3½ inches into a woman's body, and is fed by a complicated network of nerves and blood vessels (O'Connell, Hutson, Anderson, & Plenter, 1998). So all orgasms are clitoral orgasms; compared to the clitoris, the vagina is a relatively insensitive organ. Only about 30 percent of women report being able to have orgasms through vaginal penetration alone; most need other, more direct, forms of stimulation of the clitoris (Marrow, 1997).

Of course, Masters and Johnson actually rediscovered information that had been well known by earlier sex researchers but somehow "forgotten" in the context of Freudian theory's popularity. Nineteenth-century medical textbooks made it clear that the clitoris has far more nerve endings than the vagina does, and even in the 17th century it was common knowledge that women's orgasms originated from clitoral stimulation (Laqueur, 1990). The necessity of sexual stimulation for women's enjoyment of intercourse was also known. In her 1918 book, *Married Love,* Marie Stopes provided an apt explanation of why women need to be aroused before they can enjoy sexual intercourse:

> The women's vaginal canal, which has an external opening covered by double lips, is generally of such size as to allow the entry of the erect penis . . . After the preliminaries have mutually roused the pair, the stimulated penis, enlarged and stiffened, is pressed into the woman's vagina . . . [W]hen the woman is what is physiologically called tumescent (that is, when she is ready for union and has been profoundly stirred), local parts are flushed by the internal blood-supply and, to some extent, are turgid like those of the man, while a secretion of mucus lubricates the opening of the vagina . . . It can, therefore, be readily imagined that, when the man tries to enter a woman whom he has *not* wooed to the point of stimulating her natural physical reactions of preparation, he is endeavouring to force his entry through a dry-walled opening too small for it . . . It should be realized that a man does not woo and win a woman once and for all when he marries her: he must woo her before every separate act of coitus . . . (quoted in Rose, 1992, pp. 113–114)

Despite all the physiological research that points to direct or indirect stimulation of the clitoris as the main source of sexual excitement leading to orgasm, the complexities of female sexual response continue to resist such neat definitions. Women (some women, at least) can and do have orgasms without direct clitoral stimulation. Laboratory studies by Beverly Whipple and her colleagues (e.g., Whipple & Komisaruk, 1991; Whipple, Ogden, & Komisaruk, 1992) suggest that stimulation of a part of the anterior vaginal wall, the **G spot** (named for a physician, Grafenburg, who first suggested the possibility that this was an area of sensitivity), provides enough stimulation for orgasm in certain women. Such stimulation of the G spot may actually involve indirect stimulation of the clitoris, as the anterior vaginal wall connects to the urethral sponge that is part of the clitoris. These researchers also report that some women can bring themselves to orgasm through sexual fantasy, without any other stimulation. Perhaps even more remarkably, interviews with a sample of over 300 Sudanese women who underwent clitoridectomy as children indicated that most of them said they had experienced orgasm at some times during their marriages

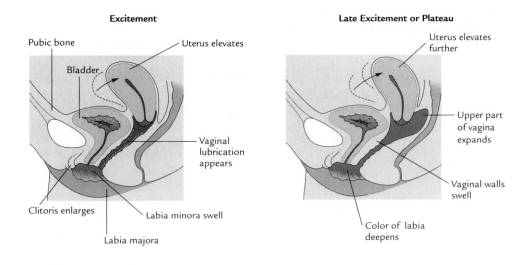

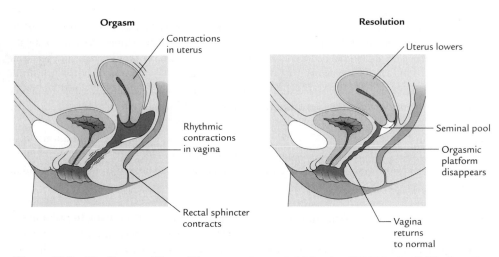

Figure 12.2   The Stages of Sexual Response. *Source:* P. M. Insel and W. T. Roth. (1998), *Core Concepts in Health* (8th ed. 1998 Update) Mountain View, CA: Mayfield, p. 113. Copyright 1998 by Mayfield Publishing Co. Reprinted by permission.

(Lightfoot-Klein, 1989). Finally, certain paraplegic and quadriplegic women report that they can and do experience sexual feelings and even orgasm in the upper parts of their bodies, even though spinal cord injury blocks all genital sensations (Zwerner, 1982). Findings such as these suggest that minds probably have as much or more to do with sexual pleasure than bodies do.

The Medical Model of Sexuality
and the Veneration of the Orgasm

Up until the 1920s, stimulation to orgasm was considered a proper treatment for the symptoms of "hysterical" women. Women suffering from the nervous symptoms associated with hysteria went to their doctors, who performed genital massage until the patients reached orgasm—clinically labeled "hysterical paroxysm" (Maines, 1999). This was a lucrative combination of disease and treatment for doctors, because such patients never died—nor did they recover! Rather, they kept coming back on a regular basis to receive the treatment. However, doctors soon tired of spending the up to one hour that it sometimes took them to massage their female patients to orgasm, and they searched for ways to handle these patients more efficiently and cost-effectively. The vibrator, invented by a British physician in the late 1880s, was enthusiastically adopted by physicians because it reduced the treatment time for hysterical women to about 10 minutes. The women patients, who were strongly discouraged from masturbating, and whose marital sex lives were often unsatisfying, found an approved outlet for their sexual feelings through their "disorder." Female sexuality became, in effect, a troublesome disease that required treatment.

Attitudes toward women's sexuality have changed since then: Women are now expected to find, even demand, sexual satisfaction in their partnered sexual relationships (and a physician who offered genital massage as a treatment would be charged with unethical practice). Partly because of Masters and Johnson, great emphasis has been placed on the female orgasm by sex therapists, sexologists, and North American popular culture in general. Masters and Johnson found that not only could the women in their sample reliably reach orgasm, but often they were multiorgasmic, reaching orgasm several times in the course of one sexual episode. Now, women are coached in how to "achieve" orgasm, and their sexual (and relationship) "adequacy" is often judged according to the reliability with which they reach orgasm during partnered sex (McCormick, 1994). In a medical model of sexuality, the ability to reach orgasm consistently is viewed as a sign of health; any other pattern is viewed as dysfunction.

Do women engage in sex mainly to achieve orgasm? A narrow focus on the physiology of sexual response might suggest such a conclusion, but a look at the bigger picture indicates that the answer is obviously no. A large sex survey in the United States demonstrated that 75 percent of men report *always* reaching orgasm during sexual activity, but only 29 percent of women report this (Michael, Gagnon, Laumann, & Kolata, 1994). One interview study found that 16 percent of sexually active women between 18 and 25 had *never* experienced an orgasm (Marrow, 1997). Moreover, although studies show that women can masturbate to orgasm as easily and quickly as men can, sex surveys have consistently found that women are less likely than men to masturbate—indeed, this is one of the strongest male–female differences in the research literature on sexuality (e.g., Oliver & Hyde, 1993). Clearly, women engage in a lot of partnered sex without reaching orgasm, and many do not want orgasms badly enough to create them on their own. Or perhaps they do not know how to create them on their own. Advocates for women's sexual pleasure argue that women should explore and affirm their own sexuality and empower themselves

BOX 12.2 MAKING CHANGE
"The Vagina Monologues"

Based on interviews with a diverse group of women—from a Long Island antique dealer to a Bosnian refugee—Eve Ensler created a play that explores the humor, power, pain, wisdom, outrage, mystery and excitement associated with vaginas. The powerful series of monologues focuses on topics such as the clitoris, female genital mutilation, "Reclaiming Cunt,"and "If your vagina could talk, what would it say?" Watching the play is a liberatory experience for many women and a revelation for many men. If you have a chance to see it, do so! But even more interesting would be to produce it at your university. Colleges and universities are offered free rights to produce the play under certain conditions and are encouraged to do so during V-day observances on and around Valentine's day each year. To find out about getting the rights to perform the play, or just to find out where you can see it, go the Web site **www.vday.org/main.html**.

sexually by masturbating (McCormick, 1994), and some have even provided supportive instructions for doing so (Dodson, 1974; 1987; Marrow, 1997).

Some explanations for women's less consistent experience of orgasm rest on problems associated with partnered sexuality. For example, women may have partnered sex for a variety of nonpleasure reasons, such as guilt, obligation, fear, the desire to please a partner, and economic need. Also, women may want to reach orgasm during partnered sex but be unable to do so because of the wrong kind of stimulation, fatigue, or distraction. Finally, women, many taught from girlhood to be inhibited about sex, may never have explored their own bodies in a way that allowed them to discover and share with their partners what kinds of stimulation give them sexual pleasure. For the woman who never or rarely experiences orgasm and who wants to do so, one or all of these issues may provide the key. But the notion that orgasm is the sine qua non of female sexuality is in some respects a cultural construction. In North America, largely because of the popularization of Masters and Johnson's findings, we have moved in recent decades from a social environment in which many women did not expect to have orgasms to one in which a woman may be made to feel inadequate and abnormal if she does not have an orgasm (or two or three) with every act of partnered sex.

In a social context where sexuality is socially defined in a male-centered way, "having sex" is interpreted to mean "having heterosexual intercourse." Other sexual activities between women and men are often thought of as foreplay or afterplay—not the real thing. But for women, heterosexual intercourse is not necessarily the best or most important part of sex. If "having sex" were defined in a female-centered way, it might not include intercourse unless pregnancy was the goal of the activity. In fact, one interview study of 350 women of every sexual orientation revealed that their favorite sexual practice was cunnilingus, stimulation of the clitoris or vulva with the lips or tongue, a practice which is much more likely than vaginal penetration to lead to female orgasm. (Marrow, 1997). On the other hand, a sexual experience without orgasm may not be considered a "failure" by every woman (or even by every man) under every condition. Women do not necessarily always find that orgasm, particularly orgasm during intercourse, is central to their sexual satisfaction (Handy, Valentich, Cammaert, & Gripton, 1984/85). Women may link sexual satisfaction to whole-body sensuality, self-disclosure, and mutual sensitivity as much as to genital stimulation and orgasm, at least under some circumstances.

Women experience greater individual variation in the duration and intensity of orgasms than men. Also, for women, orgasm reached through masturbation appears to be more intense than orgasm during intercourse, perhaps because a woman has better control over the stimulation during masturbation. Perhaps for similar reasons, research finds that young lesbian and bisexual women report stronger and more frequent orgasms than heterosexual women (McCormick, 1994).

When women and men report on their experience of orgasm, however, they describe sensations that are very similar. In one study, female and male students gave written descriptions of what an orgasm felt like. A panel of experts (physicians and psychologists) who read the descriptions could not reliably distinguish between those that had been written by women and those that had been written by men (Vance & Wagner, 1976).

Sexual Orientation

In China, a woman can be jailed for participating in a lesbian relationship. In the United States, a woman can legally be fired from her job, lose custody of her children, or be discharged from the military for openly identifying herself as a lesbian. In some West African societies, teenage girls engaged in sexual play with each other as a normal part of growing up—but kept these activities secret from their husbands when they later married. Among Australian Aboriginal peoples, an adolescent girl was allowed to have mutually stimulating sex play with another girl only if she was a cross-cousin (i.e., the mother of one girl and the father of the other girl were brother and sister) (Ward, 1996).

Clearly, the question of whom a woman forms sexual and emotional bonds with has been an emotionally charged one, often surrounded with restrictions, myths, and taboos. Social and behavioral scientists have fallen into the habit of addressing this question under the label of **sexual orientation**—a term that is rather clinical sounding for the complex set of feelings it addresses.

Defining Sexual Orientation

A person's sexual orientation refers in part to her choice of sexual partner or to the group of people to whom she feels sexual attraction. It also refers to her social/affectional attachment to and commitment to women, aspects both separate from and linked to sexual issues. We habitually label people's sexual choices as heterosexual, homosexual, or bisexual, according to whether they are sexually interested in members of the other gender, their own gender, or both genders. But what exactly is "sexual"? As we have already begun to see in this chapter, the answer to that question is not as simple as it seems.

In many cultures it has been and/or is the custom for women to have passionate, romantic friendships with other women, independent of marriage. In the pre-1920s United States, women apparently felt free to exchange passionate love letters, be openly affectionate, sleep together, and pledge permanent commitments. Whether such women were single or had husbands, their relationships were perceived as harmless rather than threatening to society, perhaps because it was generally assumed that the relationships were not sexual or because many of these women also maintained their roles as wives and mothers. According to Naomi McCormick (1994), "Men began to label women's romantic friendships as sexually perverse only after feminists challenged the institution of marriage and competed with men economically" (p. 58).

Were these women lesbians? Were they bisexual? On what factors would the answer to these questions hinge? Some sex researchers would say that the critical factor is whether the women "had sex," meaning "had genital contact." Others would argue that the most important defining issue is the passionate and affectionate love relationship, not genital contact. As McCormick (1994) notes, "Ironically, nobody expects genital proof of heterosexual romance. Heterosexual women frequently see themselves as romantically or sexually involved with men even if genital sex has not occurred" (p. 60). Similarly, many women may define their love relationships with other women more on the basis of emotional bonds and attraction than on whether they have had genital contact. There are and have been many women who consider another woman their "partner," even in the absence of genital sexual activity.

Among women in lesbian communities, there has been some debate about the definition of lesbian orientation. One viewpoint, the idea that being a lesbian has mainly to do with being "woman-identified," was eloquently expressed by the poet Audre Lorde:

> I want to make it clear what I understand by a "lesbian." It is not having genital intercourse with a woman that is the criterion. There are lesbian women who have never had genital or any other form of sexual contact with a woman, while there are also women who have had sex with other women but who are not lesbian. A lesbian is a woman who identifies fundamentally with women and her first field of strength, of vulnerability, of comfort, lies in a network of women. If I call myself a black, feminist lesbian, I am acknowledging by that the roots of my strength, and of my vulnerability, lie in myself as a woman. (quoted in Wekker, 1997, p. 19)

Clearly, this definition reflects the importance not only of an individual close relationship but of a community of women to how many lesbian women identify themselves. Yet there are some women who love women but resist the categories of sexual orientation and focus on their experience of individual relationships. Astrid Roemer, an eminent Black poet from the Netherlands, argued, "I do not call myself 'lesbian' and I do not want to be called 'lesbian' either. . . . If I love a woman, I love that one woman and one swallow does not make a summer" (quoted in Wekker, 1997, p. 18).

Clearly, the question of sexual identity is extremely personal, yet strongly affected by social and political forces. Because heterosexuality is "assumed" in our culture, most women date and have sexual experiences with men, and many marry men. However, many women who have had sexual relationships with men eventually define themselves as lesbian. Similarly, researchers often define an individual as lesbian if she has a same-gender partner, regardless of whether she has enjoyed sexual relationships with men in the past.

Such a definition makes some sense, given that a nonsupportive society places many obstacles in the way of a lesbian identity and may slow down the process of self-discovery of this identity. In a survey of 2,067 lesbians from across the United States, Joan Rabin and Barbara Slater (2004) found that 30 percent of the respondents had been married to men and 78 percent reported having had sex with a man.

One group that is sometimes ignored in discussions of sexual identity are persons who identify themselves as **bisexual,** individuals who can be attracted to persons of either gender. There are unquestionably many people—from 15 percent to 35 percent of the female population in the United States (McCormick, 1994)—who can feel powerfully attracted to members of either sex. Such individuals do not allow the sex of the other person to determine whether they will feel sexual attraction or "fall in love" with that individual.

There seems to be a strong cultural pressure to place people into the either–or categories of heterosexual or homosexual. Yet many theorists have found considerable appeal in a notion of sexual orientation that views hetero- and homosexuality as two poles of a continuum with many possibilities in between. In fact, years ago Michael Storms (1980) proposed a *two*-continuum theory of sexual orientation that encompasses various possible combinations. He argued that sexual orientation is based on two independent dimensions: **homoeroticism** and **heteroeroticism.** A person high only on heteroeroticism (sexual attraction and arousal to members of the other sex) tends to be involved only in mixed-gender relationships; a person high only on homoeroticism (sexual attraction and arousal to members of her or his own sex) tends to be involved only in same-gender relationships, and a person high on both dimensions might be involved in either or both. Of course, the label a person chooses for herself may depend not only on the attractions she experiences, but on the meaning and importance she attaches to them. That meaning and that importance are shaped in important ways by her culture and community. And researchers now believe that, in fact, people's sexual identities often do not fit neatly into categories but can encompass a variety of seemingly contradictory possibilities, change over time and vary across social contexts (Peplau & Garnets, 2000). A woman may define herself as bisexual, yet never experience a strong attraction to a woman, for example. Or she may define herself as heterosexual, yet have homoerotic fantasies while having sex with men. She may go through much of her life having only heterosexual experiences and then fall in love with a woman. Or she may define herself as a lesbian for years and then find herself powerfully attracted to a man.

Because identifying oneself as lesbian or bisexual incurs disapproval, condemnation, and punishment in many societies, female–female relationships have been hidden, making reliable information about them on a global scale hard to find. For example, in China the history of lesbian relationships is difficult to uncover. There are some reports of organized lesbian groups dating back several centuries. One such group, said to have originated in the Guangdong province, was called the Ten Sisters. Couple members of the group, which was founded by a Buddhist nun, went through a formal marriage ceremony in order to be allowed to live together legally as a couple. Members of the Ten Sisters apparently took vows not to marry except among their group. If they were forced into heterosexual marriages because of family pressures, they promised to either commit suicide or eliminate their husbands. Early in the 20th century, groups whose roots went back to this earlier one were reported in Shanghai and Hong Kong (Ruan & Bullough, 1992).

Modern investigations of lesbian orientation in China have also been difficult. In 1926, C. S. Chang, a sociologist at Peking National University, compiled China's first "modern" treatise on sexual behavior, including case histories from anonymous respondents. One female respondent described engaging in sex with other women during her adolescence. However, Chang was forced to resign from the university, and so no one dared to follow up his work. Since homosexuality is still a crime for which an individual can be denounced and jailed in China, it is very well hidden (Ruan & Bullough, 1992).

Is Women's Sexual Orientation Inborn? Discovered? Constructed? All of the Above?

Sexual orientation is no doubt the product of cultural, biological, social, emotional, and experiential factors that are too intertwined to be examined separately. Researchers have been unable to identify any clearly important biological or childhood factors that shape, or even predict, sexual orientation in women (Peplau & Garnets, 2000). Certainly, the research on women's sexual orientation suggests that its determinants are complex—and perhaps different for different women. Some lesbians report, for example, that their sexual orientation is an aspect of themselves that is beyond their control—something that they were born with or that dates back to their earliest memories. Others describe being lesbian as a choice, often made later in life after considerable heterosexual experience (Golden, 1987; McCormick, 1994). When Joan Rabin and Barbara Slater (2004) asked their sample of more than 2,000 U.S. lesbians "Do you feel you had a choice about your orientation?," 58 percent said no, 25 percent said they had a partial choice, and only 11 percent believed that their sexual orientation was a completely free choice. However, when asked what sexual orientation they would choose if they could start their lives over with a choice of being lesbian or straight, more that 78 percent answered that they would choose a lesbian orientation.

Many individuals' stories suggest that sexual identity and orientation can evolve and change across a lifetime; for example, many bisexual women do not have their first sexual experience with a woman until middle age, and many women make the transition from a heterosexual to a lesbian identity in adulthood (Kitzinger & Wilkinson, 1995).

When women are asked to describe their own experience of being lesbian, their stories reflect a variety of patterns. Celia Kitzinger (1987), who examined the personal accounts given by a sample of 41 British women ages 17 to 58, identified five different viewpoints on the meaning and experience of being a lesbian. One viewpoint emphasized *personal fulfillment* and self-acceptance—the idea that being lesbian was right for the individual and that she was doing what she was meant to do. A second group of women emphasized *love* in explaining their lesbian status—they said they were lesbians because they had fallen in love with a particular woman, and that if they should fall in love with a man, they could have a heterosexual relationship. A third group of women described their lesbian orientation as an inborn part of themselves—but as only *one of many important aspects of who they are.* A fourth group expressed the viewpoint that they had *chosen a lesbian identity because of their feminism.* These women identified heterosexuality with the oppression of women by men and chose to label themselves as lesbians and to take only women as lovers as part of their resistance against that oppression. A fifth group of women expressed the viewpoint that being lesbian was a *weakness or flaw*—something they would not have chosen.

It appears that no single factor explains women's sexual orientation. Further, it is clear that many shades of experience exist within lesbian, bisexual, and heterosexual identity. These shades of experience may be constructed from the individual's personality, family relationships, and cultural attitudes toward sexuality.

The Social Context of Sexual Behavior

Not only do patterns of sexual behavior vary across times and places, the meanings of such behaviors vary dramatically as well. As Leonore Tiefer (1995) notes,

> Acts of intercourse, even if they all involve contact between men's and women's genitalia, have no more in common necessarily than haute couture coats and bearskins. And the experience of such acts conducted in wildly different sociocultural settings will have about as much in common as the experience of wearing the Paris coat and the bearskin. (pp. 19–20)

Given this caution, we will not devote a lot of space in this chapter to comparing the frequencies of various sexual behaviors across ethnic or cultural groups. Rather, we will focus on the ways the interaction of gender and sexuality reflects their social and historical context.

Culture and Sexual Scripts

In the former Dutch colony of Suriname, a system of relationships called **mati-ism** has been embedded in the culture of people of African heritage whose ancestors were brought there as slaves. *Mati* means intimate friend, lover, or partner, and the term is used to describe close, emotional relationships between women—who may or may not also have male lovers or husbands (Wekker, 1997). Such relationships are a visible and accepted part of working-class Afro-Surinamese culture, but they have roots in the West African cultures from which people were transported as slaves. In some West African cultures, such as Ashanti and Dahomey, female homosexuality was practiced without negative sanctions and, in fact, anthropologists observed that a woman could formally marry another woman.

In *mati* culture, female couples might engage in practices such as wearing identical dresses, courting each other by wearing and folding their headcloths in certain ways, and composing love songs for each other. There is openness about the relationships, an acceptance of them, and a sense that they fit into the idea of family. In the African American communities of the United States, by contrast, female–female relationships have not been institutionalized so publicly—despite the fact that these communities too have their roots in African cultures in which sexual relationships between women were practiced and accepted. Gloria Wekker (1997) argues that one reason for the difference is that the Afro-Surinamese were allowed, during slavery, to elaborate and maintain their own culture without much interference, whereas slaves in America were forbidden to speak their African languages and were forced into more conformity with the colonists' culture. Clearly, sexuality develops within a social order or context and cannot be considered independent of this context. Culture, in a sense, provides us with a script for being sexual.

Human beings can forge sexual bonds in a variety of ways; the ways they choose are shaped by social, historical, economic, and political factors.

Even within one complex country, the United States, different ethnic, cultural, or social class groups can hold different attitudes about and engage in different practices with respect to sexuality because of contextual factors. Our awareness and understanding of such differences are clouded by widespread stereotypes that often influence the questions that researchers ask and the ways they design and interpret research. For example, there are stereotypes of poor women as sexually uninformed and permissive, of African American women as promiscuous, of Latinas as sexually conservative and inhibited. Research has often confounded social class differences with racial or ethnic differences, making it difficult to draw conclusions about either.

Whatever differences we do observe between groups in sexual attitudes and practices, they are not essential or built-in differences. Rather, as in the case of the differences between the Afro-Surinamese and African American cultures, they seem to be the product of different social and environmental conditions. The ways people experience and give meaning to such conditions can be complex. For example, African American women are the descendants of slaves, many of whom were raped by their White masters, whose babies were routinely taken from them, whose community was barred from holding formal marriage ceremonies. Underlying and upholding such practices was a strong stereotype among the White slave-owning class that Black women were highly sexed and promiscuous rather than restrained and "virtuous"—a convenient fiction that served to justify the sexual coercion of Black female slaves by their White owners. Such a history of sexual stereotyping is bound to have an impact on African American women, who must develop their own sexuality in the shadow of this image. Perhaps in reaction to it, many African American women, especially those in the middle class, seem to be more sexually conservative than their European American counterparts. They often say that they were raised with strong warnings from parents and church against premarital sex, and they report more sexual guilt and less varied heterosexual behavior than comparable European American women (McCormick, 1994; Wyatt, 1982). Warnings from family members and peers about the consequences of sexual behavior, as well as religious beliefs about the morality of various sexual practices, can be important in shaping young African American women's sexual self-concepts, making them feel guilty or motivating them to justify their sexual choices. Their self-concepts can also be affected by experiences in sexual relationships in which they have felt forced or controlled—sometimes leading to a sense that they must take control of their own sexuality (Christian, 2000).

In other cultural groups, sexuality is similarly reflective of historical and cultural factors. Among the indigenous peoples of North America, many (but not all) cultures traditionally gave wide latitude to women's sexuality, tolerating premarital and extramarital sex. In some of these cultures, lesbians and gay men were regarded as "two-spirit" people (as noted in Chapter 4) and were treated with special respect; in others, homosexuality was not tolerated (McCormick, 1994). This wide variation in sexual attitudes and behaviors was squelched by the arrival of the Europeans, who imposed their own more restrictive and less woman-affirming cultural and religious beliefs on the Indian and Inuit peoples. Today, the sexual experiences and values of women from these groups vary greatly, often influenced by such factors as intermarriage, poverty, education, and ethnic identity.

Latina women, whose families originated in the Hispanic countries of Central America, South America, and the Caribbean, are a diverse group with a variety of cultural traditions. Women from these different cultures do tend to share one strong experience, however: the powerful influence of the Catholic church. Women who were raised with the dictates of the church were taught that virginity before marriage is extremely important, that sex without the intention of reproduction is wrong, and that motherhood is the most important and exalted role for women. Women in these communities may be especially vulnerable to unwanted pregnancies because of the church prohibition on contraception, and they may feel that they should not enjoy sex, even with their husbands. Even if they reject this dogma, women are likely to be influenced by it to some extent. Lesbian women and women who are heterosexually active outside of marriage may feel a lot of guilt, and, perhaps more important, may feel they cannot be accepted by their own cultural community (Espín, 1984).

However, for young Latinas, the importance of certain sexual norms may stem as much from cultural and community pride and self-respect as from religious teachings. Interviews with Puerto Rican and Mexican American adolescents suggest that their decisions about sexual behavior may be based on a conviction that maintaining virginity and high self-respect are seen as things that distinguish Latina adolescents from their non-Latina peers (Villarruel, 1998). As one Mexican American girl said,

> I think Mexican girls have more respect for themselves . . . they call them hard to get because they're not as . . . easy . . . a lot of Hispanic girls I know, they don't want to be called easy because it's like nobody will respect you. (quoted in Villarruel, 1998, p. 5)

In many Latino families, parents work very hard at protecting their adolescent daughters by controlling their sexuality. The daughters may chafe at parental restrictions; however, they often cite them as a sign that their parents care for them. And they experience these rules and obligations as quite different from those they see in the families of their Anglo peers. As one young Latina woman commented about her parents' rules:

> To me, I think they're fair. But to other friends that I know that they're not Hispanic, they're so different. . . . They can just go out whenever they want to. And to me it's not the same. You cook, you clean, do your chores . . . take care of your little brother . . . ask for permission if you want to go out. . . . I don't think I would actually want to be like them . . . that would make me feel like my parents didn't care. (quoted in Villarruel, 1998, p. 7)

The Double Standard   One aspect of the social environment that affects sexuality is a set of attitudes often labeled the double standard: two different standards of sexual behavior, one for women and one for men. Generally, it means that women's sexual behavior is more restricted than men's, and that it is easier for a woman than for a man to incur disapproval by engaging in "too much" sex. Acceptance, to various degrees, of a double standard is common in many cultures, although the specific rules may vary from one culture to another. For example, in societies that find extramarital sex unobjectionable, husbands are generally allowed greater sexual freedom than wives. About 54 percent of societies permit men to have extramarital sexual liaisons, whereas only 11 percent allow women the same freedom (Ember & Ember, 1990). Researchers have been unable to find societies that

BOX 12.3 LEARNING ACTIVITY
Test Your Knowledge of Sexual Attitudes

For each of the following items, circle the number you think is closest to the percentage of young American women (aged 20–29) surveyed by the National Marriage Project (2001) who agreed with it:

1. It is common these days for people my age to have sex just for fun, and not expect any commitment beyond the sexual encounter itself.   25%   50%   75%   100%

2. There are people with whom I would have sex even if I had no interest in marrying them.   20%   30%   40%   60%   80%

3. If two people really like each other, it is all right for them to have sex even if they have known each other for only a very short time.   20%   35%   50%   65%   80%

4. I wish men would be more interested in me as a person and less as a sex object.   20%   30%   40%   60%   80%

How accurate were you at guessing the attitudes of these young women? Do you find that your own attitudes tend to fit in with those of the majority of these women? Do you think young men's attitudes would be different? Why or why not?

These researchers did not specify the sexual orientation of their respondents. Do you think the attitudes of lesbian women about the relationship between sex and commitment would be different from those of heterosexual women? Why or why not?

ANSWERS: 1. 75%; 2. 40%; 3. 35%; 4. 60%

allow extramarital sex for wives but not for husbands (Frayser, 1985). Similarly, premarital sex is much more likely to be disapproved for females than for males. One study of 114 cultures revealed that female premarital sex was disallowed in 55 percent of them (although it did occur, despite disapproval); male premarital sex was nearly universal in 60 percent and "typical" in another 18 percent of these societies (Broude & Greene, 1976). Research in the United States shows that girls are still taking the double standard to heart: They tend to believe that "good" girls do not take the initiative in sex and they wait for males to take the initiative (Tolman, 1999).

One example of the double standard is the set of *machismo/marianismo* gender attitudes espoused, in different versions and to varying degrees, by the Spanish-speaking cultures of Latin America. Machismo, an idealized stereotype for men, involves being strong, dominant over women, and sexually virile. Marianismo, the counterpart for women, involves being like the Catholic image of the Virgin Mary: virtuous, sexually pure, subservient, ready to suffer in silence. Within this framework, a man might be allowed, even expected, to have many sexual relationships, whereas a woman would be expected to remain faithful to one man—and even to treat sex with that one man as a duty rather than as a pleasure (Espín, 1984). There is a great deal of variation both within and between different Hispanic cultures in the acceptance and expression of these stereotyped ideals. However, wherever it exists, the machismo/marianismo ideal acts, like other versions of the double standard, to restrict women's behavior and to maintain them in a subordinate relationship to men. Acceptance of the cultural value of marianismo has, for example, been associated among Latina adolescents with postponing both sexual intercourse and contraceptive use (Hovell, Blumberg, Atkins, Hofstetter, & Kreitner, 1994), while machismo has been linked among young Latinos with multiple sexual partners (Beck & Bergman, 1993).

Television portrayals of sexual encounters tend to reinforce the double standard—even in shows that are clearly aimed at young female viewers. One content analysis of prime-time network programs featuring adolescent or college-age characters found that men were portrayed more often than women as initiators of sexual encounters. Furthermore, the emotional consequences of sex were portrayed most often as negative: guilt, rejection, humiliation, and disappointment (Aubrey, 2004). These negative consequences of having sex were more likely to accrue to women than to men and were particularly likely to occur in situations where women had been the initiators of sexual activity. This researcher concludes that "If adolescent girls identify with sexually punished female characters, their own sense of sexual agency and sexual esteem could be reduced, and this, in turn, could disempower them from making healthy sexual decisions" (Aubrey, 2004, p. 513).

What is the basis of the double standard? In many Western cultures it is the assumption that males have a greater desire and need for sexual activity than females do. This supposed difference in males' and females' sexual appetites makes it appropriate for men to be the sexual aggressors and pursuers and for women to be the sexual gatekeepers, maintaining control. In Western cultures, believers in the double standard do not hold a man responsible for pushing an unwilling woman to engage in sexual activity; rather, they maintain, it is the woman's responsibility to set limits. The man, driven by his strong sexual needs, supposedly cannot stop himself; the woman, with her weaker need for sex, can and should.

There are other possible reasons for the persistence of the double standard, though. One is simply that because women are the ones who get pregnant, more restrictive norms for them have arisen to minimize that risk.

The correlates of a society's acceptance of a version of the double standard include valuing virginity more for females than for males, assuming that men will be the initiators of sexual activity, not tolerating single motherhood, and labeling negatively, even shunning, women but not men who are sexually active outside marriage. In our own culture, for example, the connotations of *slut* and *stud* are quite different, although both refer to a person who has many sexual partners.

What are the implications of such attitudes for women's sexual experience? Not surprisingly, they have a dampening effect on women's pleasure and a strengthening effect on women's inhibitions. For example, in the United States, where the acceptance of the double standard is relatively strong, almost 30 percent of women surveyed in one study reported that they did *not* want their first heterosexual intercourse to happen when it did—a response that was especially prevalent among African American women (Michael et al., 1994). Furthermore, for many women, first intercourse is a disappointing, or even painful, experience (Weis, 1985). In Sweden, where attitudes toward sexuality are more permissive and the double standard less entrenched, young women have significantly less negative reactions to first intercourse than their U.S. counterparts do (Schwartz, 1993).

It is obvious how the double standard can influence women's experience of heterosexuality, but what about lesbian sexuality? Here, too, the double standard's message that a "good" woman is not too sexual has an impact. Conditioned by the cultural notion that women are sexually restrained and passive, lesbian and bisexual women, like heterosexual women, may sometimes be inhibited about initiating sex (McCormick, 1994).

In societies where, in contrast to the double standard, female sexuality is accepted as legitimate and women are considered to have significant sexual needs and desires, the discourse about women and sex has a different tone. For example, the following comments by Nisa, the !Kung woman interviewed by Marjorie Shostak (1981), show her matter-of-fact acceptance of women's appetite for sex:

> [W]hen you are a woman, you don't just sit still and do nothing—you have lovers. You don't just sit with the man of your hut, with just one man. One man can give you very little. One man gives you only one kind of food to eat. But when you have lovers, one brings you something and another brings you something else. . . . All women know sexual pleasure. Some women, those who really like sex, if they haven't finished and the man has, will wait until the man has rested, then get up and make love to him. Because she wants to finish too. She'll have sex with the man until she is also satisfied. Otherwise she could get sick. (pp. 271, 287)

Issues in Lesbian Sexualities

Pleasure   Most of the research literature on sexual response and sex therapy ignores lesbian sexuality. The omission is partly due to heterosexism, the notion that heterosexuality is the superior, and the only natural, form of sexual expression. Yet lesbian sexual expression is rewarding for many women. In one sample of 108 heterosexual and 67 lesbian women, the heterosexual women reported that, when they had sex with men, they reached orgasm 52 percent of the time and felt satisfied 63 percent of the time. The lesbians reported that, when they had sex with women, they had orgasms 75 percent of the time and felt satisfied 85 percent of the time (Marrow, 1997). Women do not sacrifice sexual pleasure if they have sex with other women rather than with men.

However, sometimes lesbian women's pleasure may suffer because of a positive-sounding myth: the idea that women know intuitively how to give one another pleasure (McCormick, 1994). Individuals and couples, heterosexual or homosexual, must *learn* what works and what does not, in terms of sexual pleasure for themselves and their partners. For women of any sexual orientation, female socialization toward repression, rather than expression, of their sexual feelings may be a barrier to learning and experiencing good sex. For a couple in which both members are women, the problems stemming from this socialization may be literally doubled. Furthermore, lesbians in most societies live in a homophobic social environment—an environment where discrimination against gay and lesbian individuals is legal and where social and religious sanctions against them are often powerful. In such an environment, it is not surprising that some lesbians internalize anti-gay prejudice and hatred. Such self-hatred is likely to produce feelings of guilt and anxiety about sexual feelings. One result may be inhibited sexual desire and a reluctance to have sex, even with a committed partner. Another may be alcoholism and drug abuse among women who are trying to anesthetize themselves against sexual anxiety (McCormick, 1994).

For lesbians who are self-identified as feminists, another issue may be expectations generated by political analyses of sexuality. Lesbian therapist Margaret Nichols (1987) joked that overzealous concerns about safeguarding equality and repudiating patriarchy can dictate lesbian sexual practices:

> Two women lie side by side (tops or bottoms are strictly forbidden—lesbians must be nonhierarchical); they touch each other gently and sweetly all over their bodies for several hours (lesbians are not genitally/orgasm oriented, a patriarchal mode). If the women have orgasms at all —and orgasms are only marginally acceptable because, after all, we must be process- rather than goal-oriented—both orgasms must occur at exactly the same time in order to foster true equality and egalitarianism. (pp. 97–98)

In real life, of course, lesbian sexuality is as varied as female–male sexuality: sometimes egalitarian, sometimes less so, sometimes satisfying, sometimes frustrating. However, Nichols's satirical commentary reminds us that personal sexual relationships do take place in a political context—one in which, as we have been considering in this chapter, sexuality tends to be male defined and reflective of larger power relationships between males and females. As feminist women of all sexual orientations seek to transform sexuality and unhook it from oppressive assumptions, we are bound to encounter some difficulties. Perhaps a sense of humor is one of the most important ingredients in this transformation.

Danger   Sexual expression is associated with danger in many contexts, particularly in societies that are sexually restrictive. For example, in 1990 a male student was expelled from Beijing University in China for engaging in premarital sexual relations with a young woman (Southerland, 1990). Ironically, although many college students in the United States would be astonished at, and quick to condemn, the expulsion of an unmarried student for engaging in heterosexual sex, some would be just as quick to assert their disapproval and hostility toward a student whose affectional orientation is homosexual.

Lesbian and gay individuals in many contexts face serious prejudice, threats of physical and verbal assault, and discrimination because of their sexual orientation. Research on university campuses in the United States indicates that at least two-thirds of lesbian and gay students report that they have been verbally insulted, one-quarter report that they have been threatened with physical violence, a substantial percentage (42 percent in one study) have been physically abused because of their sexual orientation, and nearly all have overheard derogatory antilesbian/antigay comments on campus (D'Augelli, 1992; Herek, 1993). Most of the harassment comes from fellow students, although some also comes from faculty and staff members. Lesbian students report frightening incidents. For example:

> I was walking through Beinecke Plaza late at night with another lesbian. We were walking without actually touching, but our assailants/abusers assumed we were lesbians (how, it is difficult to know). A group (4–5) of men approached us and shouted terms of abuse—"dyke," "disgusting bitches," etc. Their behavior was threatening and suggested an intended attack. We walked on and for some reason they desisted.

> At a party on Yale property, a lesbian friend and I were physically threatened by some heterosexual men, ordered to kiss in front of them. (quoted in Herek, 1993, p. 19)

The effect of such harassment is to create a climate of fear and to restrict the behavior of lesbian and gay students. Many are secretive about their sexual orientation, reluctant to report incidents of abuse, and careful about public behavior—especially open expression of affection—that may reveal them as lesbian or gay. Contributing to the climate of fear are verbal insults: epithets such as *dyke, queer,* and *faggot,* which convey implicit and explicit threats of violence. Verbal insults are a form of intimidation—a symbolic form of violence and a reminder of the perpetual threat of physical assault. As Linda Garnets and her colleagues note, antigay verbal abuse

> reinforces the target's sense of being an outsider in American society, a member of a disliked and devalued minority, and a socially acceptable target for violence. . . . [It] challenges the victim's routine sense of security and invulnerability, making the world seem more malevolent and less predictable. The psychological effects of verbal abuse may be as severe as those following physical assaults, and possibly more insidious because victims of verbal abuse may find its "psychic scars" more difficult to identify than physical wounds. (Garnets, Herek, & Levy, 1990, p. 373)

Verbal or physical violence directed at individuals because of their presumed sexual orientation falls under the category of hate speech or hate crimes. The targets of such aggression based on bias suffer particularly devastating consequences: One study showed that victims of crimes based on bias experienced significantly higher levels of psychological distress than did victims of similar crimes not based on bias over the same time period (Herek, Cogan, & Gillis, 2002). These authors also note that assaults motivated by bias and hatred have a chilling effect on the entire gay community: "It is not an exaggeration to conclude that bias-motivated attacks function as a form of terrorism, sending a message to all lesbians, gay men, and bisexuals that they are not safe if they are visible" (Herek, Cogan, & Gillis, 2002, p. 336).

Sexualities and Disabilities

In both the scholarly and popular literature about sexuality, women with disabilities are even more invisible than lesbian and bisexual women. People with disabilities are often stigmatized in ways that have nothing to do with their disabilities (e.g., a person in a wheelchair is sometimes treated as if she is deaf or mentally retarded), and that stigmatization often includes the notion that they are asexual, or "sexless." We tend to associate sexuality with young, healthy, *able* bodies. Since women with visible disabilities do not match cultural criteria for female beauty and desirability, the possibility that they might have sexual feelings or be good sex partners is often ignored. In fact, men with disabilities are more likely to marry than women with disabilities, and when disability occurs during a marriage, divorce is more likely when the woman is the one who is disabled (Asch & Fine, 1988).

When therapists or doctors do address the question of sexuality for a disabled woman, they often focus on whether or not she is capable of heterosexual intercourse, not on what feels good to her sexually. For example, after surgery and pelvic radiation for gynecologi-

Because our society associates sexuality with young, healthy, able bodies, the notion that women with disabilities have sexual feelings and can be sexually active is often ignored.

cal cancer, doctors may work to preserve the woman's capacity for sexual intercourse—her sexual availability to a male partner—rather than on helping her to address concerns about pain or bodily changes that may interfere with her enjoyment of intercourse (McCormick, 1994). Little effort is made to help the woman to define alternative forms of sexual expression as preferable, if that is her wish. No one stays young, healthy, and able forever, so we ignore issues surrounding disability at our own peril. Naomi McCormick (1994) argues that maintaining sexual activity in the face of disability or chronic illness often requires finding new ways to be sexual, and that the creativity called for can be a positive factor in sexual expression. For a person contending with a disability, more than anyone else, she asserts,

> the sex act itself needs to be redefined in feminist terms. Sexual intercourse, especially intercourse with the man on top of the woman, may no longer be possible . . . Couples may benefit from experimenting with various forms of oral sex, shared fantasies, and whole body sexual touching. . . . Disability and chronic illness can inspire us to redefine sexuality, rewriting scripts for interacting with loving partners. (p. 212)

Managing the Consequences of Sex

Sexual behavior is about more than lust, or even bonding. Engaging in sex has consequences beyond the emotional ones of satisfaction, joy, guilt, or regret. Heterosexual intercourse can produce the very tangible consequence of pregnancy, and many forms of sexual behavior can result in the transmission of disease between partners. How do women try to control these potential consequences?

Contraception

Since unwanted pregnancy can wreak havoc with a woman's life, and since abortion is often unavailable or dangerous, women everywhere have throughout history sought to prevent pregnancy by a variety of means. Such means involve either timing sexual intercourse so that it does not occur at the most fertile phase of a woman's cycle, taking a drug by mouth that will interfere with conception, or blocking the route of the sperm with some kind of barrier or spermicide. These basic methods have been used since the start of recorded history.

The women of ancient Greece and Rome relied on an oral contraceptive that was derived from a plant called silphion—long since harvested to extinction (Riddle & Estes, 1992). Cherokee folk medicine recommended that women who wanted to become permanently sterile chew and swallow the roots of spotted cowbane for 4 consecutive days. Traditional Arabic literature claimed contraceptive properties for teas made from sweet basil, weeping willow leaves, pulp of pomegranates, and alum, rue, myrrh, and hellebore. Women in India and parts of Appalachia in the United States have been relying on the seeds of the common weed Queen Anne's lace for centuries (Ward, 1996). Traditionally, women have also used barrier methods of birth control: half a squeezed lemon inserted as a cervical cap; sponges steeped in alum or lemon juice; lard or softened beeswax shaped into a cap that could be pressed against the cervix.

Much of the traditional knowledge about contraception has been lost and only recently rediscovered by interested scholars. How could such useful information have vanished so completely? John Riddle and J. Worth Estes (1992) suggest that it was mainly held and transmitted by networks of women—that only women knew what plants to gather and when to gather them, what part of the plant to use, how to extract and prepare the drug, the correct dose and the best time to take it within the menstrual cycle—and with the rise of a male-dominated medical profession, most medical writers (men) failed to learn and record it.

Modern contraceptive practices include a variety of methods: the birth control pill, the condom, the diaphragm, female or male sterilization, and others (see Table 12.1). A newer contraceptive method, a vaginal ring, was recently approved in the United States (FDA approves new birth control option, 2001). This method involves inserting a flexible ring into the vagina, where it releases a continuous dose of estrogen and progestin for three weeks, after which it must be removed and replaced. This method, like many other methods, has come under the jurisdiction of such male-dominated institutions as medicine, religion, and politics. A woman who wants access to such effective methods of contraception as the birth control pill, the vaginal ring, the intrauterine device, the diaphragm, or the cervical cap can obtain them only through a physician. Religions promulgate rules about whether and when it is morally acceptable for a woman to use contraception. Politicians act to give funding to family planning programs or withhold it based on their own views and prejudices about whether family planning practices are right or wrong—and on how the issue is likely to affect their chances of reelection.

TABLE 12.1 A Comparison of Contraceptive Methods

Method	Failure Rate[1] (Typical use)	Failure Rate (Perfect use)	Prescription Required?	Protection against STI[2]
Outercourse	N/A[3]	N/A	No	Some
Withdrawal	27.0	4.0	—	None
The Pill/POPs	8.0	0.3	Yes	None
Male condom	15.0	2.0	No	Good
Diaphragm	16.0	6.0	Yes	Some
Female condom	21.0	5.0	No	Good
Norplant® implant	0.05	0.05	Yes	None
Depo-Provera® (injection)	3.0	0.3	Yes	None
Lunelle® (injection)	N/A	0.05	Yes	None
Intrauterine Device (IUD) ParaGard®				
(copper T 380A)	0.8	0.6	Yes	None
Mirena® (copper T 380A)	0.1	0.1	Yes	None
Cervical Cap (Women who have not given birth)	16.0	9.0	Yes	Some
(Women who have given birth)	32.0	26.0	Yes	Some
Spermicide	29.0	15.0	No	None
NuvaRing® (ring)	N/A	0.3	Yes	None
Ortho Evra® (patch)	N/A	0.3	Yes	None
Sterilization				
Men	0.15	0.1	Yes	None
Women	0.5	0.5	Yes	None
No Method	85.0	85.0	—	None
Emergency contraception				
Contraception pills	*	*	Yes	None
IUD insertion	**	**	Yes	None

*Emergency contraception pills: Treatment initiated within 72 hours after unprotected intercourse reduces the risk of pregnancy by 75–89%.

**Emergency IUD insertion: Treatment initiated within 7 days after unprotected intercourse reduces the risk of pregnancy by more than 99%.

1. Number of pregnancies per 100 women during one year of use.

2. Sexually transmitted infection.

3. Not available because no studies have yet been published.

*Data Source: (**www.plannedparenthood.org** and "Facts about Birth Control" (2004). For more detailed information on these methods, visit the "Your contraceptive choices" section of the Planned Parenthood Web site.)*

Perhaps nowhere is the impact of placing contraception under the control of the medical system more apparent than in the case of the so-called morning-after pill—an emergency method of contraception that a woman can use after she has had unprotected intercourse. The unprotected intercourse may occur because the woman did not plan ahead and so did not use contraception, or it may occur because of contraceptive failure: a broken condom, a diaphragm that slipped out of place, a couple of missed birth control pills. Or a woman may have been raped. There are several types of morning-after pills that, if taken within 72 hours of intercourse, have a high likelihood of preventing pregnancy. For example, Plan B, a product that contains a synthetic progesterone called levonorgestrel, was found by a World Health Organization study to be 85 percent effective in preventing pregnancy (Brody, 2001). The pill suppresses ovulation and also causes changes in the cervical mucous to make it less penetrable by sperm. Thus, it is not an abortion agent: it will not dislodge or destroy a fertilized egg that is implanted in the uterus. It seems to have few side effects and is characterized as very safe, at least for occasional use.

Common sense might seem to dictate that morning-after contraceptives would be readily available so that women could take immediate steps to prevent pregnancy if they have had unprotected intercourse. However, in all states of the United States except Washington, such products are available only by prescription. Recently, the United States Office of Health and Human Services rejected a plan to offer morning-after contraceptives over the counter, dismissing a recommendation from a panel of medical experts that they be made available in this way. Thus, a woman must see a doctor before she can obtain the drug—a situation that means she will likely face a significant delay in taking the pills and thus an increased risk that they will not be effective. If she has unprotected intercourse on Friday night, for instance, she may have difficulty getting the pills until Monday—pushing her close to the 72-hour limit during which the drug works to prevent pregnancy. In Washington, however, as in the Canadian province of British Columbia and in England, France, and Portugal, morning-after products can be obtained directly from a pharmacist without a prescription, and in Norway they are available over the counter (Brody, 2001). The latter places have done women the great service of giving them more control over their own reproduction.

Family planning programs are judged by how many women they can influence in the direction of using birth control. As the Report on the 1994 International Conference on Population and Development noted, individual women's reproductive rights and choices are frequently lost in the process:

> [T]he success of family planning programmes is often evaluated on the basis of contraceptive prevalence rates, usually calculated as the proportion of married women between ages 15 and 44 using contraception. But this measure provides no information about the process by which couples and individuals came to use contraceptives. Nor does it assess whether any coercion took place or determine the extent to which women and men obtained the knowledge to make informed choices or gained access to safe and effective methods to regulate their fertility. Moreover, evaluations using contraceptive prevalence rates often implicitly define "success" as reaching desired levels of contraceptive usage—not knowing whether individuals achieve their reproductive intentions safely. (quoted in United Nations, 1995, p. 78)

Statistics show that the percentage of married women of reproductive age who use modern methods of contraception varies from country to country (see Figure 12.3). In

BOX 12.4 MAKING CHANGE
Equitable Insurance Coverage for Prescription Drugs

Many private health insurance plans specifically exclude birth control pills from their coverage of prescription drugs. This disadvantages women of reproductive age, who must pay for these pills. In an informal survey of 100 major colleges and universities conducted for Planned Parenthood, 53 percent were found to offer student health plans that cover prescription drugs but exclude birth control pills. Does your college health plan follow this practice? If so, you can make a difference by raising awareness on campus and launching a petition drive or letter-writing campaign to get equitable coverage for prescription drugs. New York University changed its student health insurance plan after hundreds of students signed a petition calling for the addition of prescription contraceptives, emergency contraception, and abortion to the plan, and University of Virginia students won contraceptive coverage after sending hundreds of letters to their insurance representative and petitioning the student council.

many developed countries such as New Zealand, Canada, Switzerland, and the United States, about 75 percent or more of such women use contraception. Other developed countries, such as Ireland, Italy, and some Eastern European countries, have lower rates because contraceptives have been unavailable for religious, political, or economic reasons. Rates in developing regions vary widely, from, for example, 8 percent in Ethiopia and 15 percent in Nigeria to 48 percent in India and 58 percent in Costa Rica (United Nations Development Program, 2004). These rates are also dependent on prevailing laws, customs, and religious traditions. When the laws change, the behavior sometimes changes dramatically too. For example, when a law requiring a married woman to have her husband's consent to obtain contraceptives was abolished in Ethiopia, contraceptive use there jumped 26 percent within months (Neft & Levine, 1997).

The statistics just cited are for married women, but many single women are sexually active as well. Moreover, in some countries a single woman who bears a child can have dramatically less support—emotional, social, or financial—for raising that child than a married woman. In some countries of sub-Saharan Africa, the vast majority of women have sexual intercourse before they reach the age of 20. For example, 93 percent of women in Cameroon, 92 percent of women in Niger, and 88 percent of women in Ghana have had sex by the time they reach 20. However, the rate of sexual activity among young women varies widely around the world. Sixty-seven percent of women in Nicaragua, 51 percent of women in Indonesia, and only 30 percent of women in the Philippines have sex before they are 20 years old (United Nations, 2000). In the United States, just over half of all women 15 to 19 years of age have had heterosexual intercourse—and most of these women are single. Only about 30 percent of women in this age range report using any form of contraception; thus, many are at risk for pregnancy (National Center for Health Statistics, 2003).

Among high school students, just over 46 percent of young Hispanic women, 43 percent of non-Hispanic White women, and about 61 percent of African American women

Figure 12.3 Use of contraception around the world. This graph shows the percentage of married women over the age of 15 who use contraception in various countries. (Data source: United Nations Development Program, 2004).

have had intercourse. Just over one-third of high school students surveyed in 2003 were currently sexually active (defined as having had sexual intercourse during the previous 3 months). Among these sexually active students, 63 percent reported that they or their partner had used a condom during their last sexual intercourse and 17 percent said that they or their partner had used birth control pills (Grunbaum et al., 2004).

The 1995 National Survey of Family Growth found that single women in the United States were much more likely now than they were a decade before to use contraception starting with the first time they have intercourse. In the 1990s, 76 percent of single women used contraception in their first intercourse, as compared to 50 percent in the 1980s. Perhaps partly as a result of this change, and also because sexual activity among teenagers has

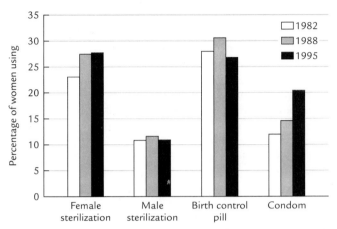

Figure 12.4 Methods of contraception most commonly used by U.S. women aged 15–44. (Data source: National Center for Health Statistics, 2003).

leveled off after increasing steadily for two decades, the pregnancy rate for U.S. teenagers has been falling since the beginning of the 1990s. Whereas in 1957 about 96 births occurred per 1,000 women aged 15 to 19, there are now 45.3 (Alan Guttmacher Institute, 2004). Births to teenagers are more frequent in the United States than in other developed countries. For example, about 45 of every 1,000 women aged 15 to 19 give birth in the United States, whereas 33 of every 1,000 do so in Eastern Europe, 13 of every 1,000 do so in Western Europe, and 4 of every 1,000 do so in Japan (United Nations, 2000). In 2003, 4.9 percent of female high school students had been pregnant (Grunbaum et al., 2004).

Figure 12.4 shows the methods of contraception relied upon in the United States. The most frequent method of preventing pregnancy is female sterilization, used by about 28 percent of women ages 15 to 44 who use contraception. Other methods relied upon frequently are the oral contraceptive pill (27 percent), the male condom (20 percent), and male sterilization (11 percent) (National Center for Health Statistics, 2003). The only dramatic change in contraceptive methods used in recent years has been a rise in the insistence on male condom use by never-married women—from 4 percent in 1982 to 14 percent in 1995 (Centers for Disease Control, 1997). This change may be attributable to educational campaigns stressing condom use as protection against sexually transmitted diseases. For information on the effectiveness of various contraceptive methods, see Table 12.1.

"Safe Sex" and Sexually Transmitted Diseases

As noted in Chapter 9, sexually transmitted infections are a major health issue, and women are at especially high risk. AIDS, the most deadly of them, is the fastest-growing STI among women worldwide. What can women do to protect themselves?

To answer this question, we must examine the context in which women have sex. The standard advice to women for having "safe sex" (sex that does not involve the transmission of disease) is to avoid partners who have been sexually promiscuous or who have been intravenous drug users, avoid the exchange of bodily fluids, and use a condom during heterosexual intercourse. This advice is good, but it assumes that a woman in a sexual encounter with a man has accurate knowledge about him, that she will be able to make a rational choice in a highly emotional situation, and that she has the power to dictate the conditions of sexual activity.

Latex condoms are very effective, although not infallibly so, at preventing the transmission of disease. Men may resist using them, however, and women may, for a variety of reasons, be fearful of insisting. As we have noted repeatedly, women have lower status than men in most societies. This lower social status can translate into lower power in heterosexual relationships, putting women at a disadvantage in negotiating sexual encounters. Hortensia Amaro (1995) describes the findings of one study in which more than 2,500 Latina women and Latino men in the northeastern United States participated. Researchers convened participants into focus groups to discuss HIV risk reduction.

> In nearly 75 percent of 69 women-only focus groups, the issue of power and gender roles emerged as a central barrier to risk reduction. Women talked about this in many ways. For example, they referred to men's stubbornness and unwillingness to use condoms and expressed feelings of powerlessness, low self-esteem, isolation, lack of voice, and inability to affect risk reduction decisions or behaviors with their partners. In contrast, in mixed-gender groups these issues were not discussed as frequently, perhaps suggesting that issues of gender roles and power differentials in relationships are generally difficult for women to discuss openly with men. (p. 441)

Amaro (1995) points out that not only are women often at a power disadvantage in negotiating sexual relationships, many have also been socialized to fear a loss of connection with their partners and thus are reluctant to make their partners uncomfortable. The situation is further complicated for many women by the risk of physical violence and by the fact that male partners often play a critical role in the initiation and progression of drug use among girls and women. She recommends that any model of HIV risk behavior have gender roles as a key component.

Research with young African American and European American women also points to the importance of the balance of power in heterosexual relationship as a determinant of safe sex practices (Soet, Dudley, & Diloria, 1999). Women who saw themselves as dominated by their male partner felt less personally empowered—they had less sense that they could make a difference and less confidence in the outcome of trying to make a difference —with respect to sexual decision making and safe sex. In addition, research with Black and White women in South Africa has shown that unequal gender relations make it very difficult for women to negotiate safer sex practices in their relationships because they fear negative consequences from men when they try to do so (Miles, 1997).

One study of African American women found that their behavior and attitudes with respect to condom use were influenced by a variety of relationship and sexual **scripts:** social norms and expectations that are culturally shared and that guide behavior (Bowleg, Lucas, & Tschann, 2004). For example, a common relationship script is summarized as *men control relationship*s. A number of women in this study mentioned that their male partners expected to control many aspects of the relationship, such as when and with whom they could socialize and their access to money. Another script that came up often was *women sustain relationships:* Women reported that they put up with many things they did not like in order to keep the relationship going. It is easy to see how, when couple relationships are defined by such scripts, women feel little control over whether or not their partner uses a condom during sex.

A dramatic example of the role of gender norms and female powerlessness in the spread of AIDS can be found in the villages of western Kenya. Here, the custom of "wife inheritance" dictates that if a woman is widowed, she and her children will be inherited as a responsibility by her dead husband's brother or by some other male member of the family. The inheritor is supposed to make sure that the widow and her children are fed, clothed, sheltered, educated, and protected. Traditionally, the inheritor is already married and he is not supposed to have sexual relations with the inherited woman. In recent times, however, the latter taboo has broken down, and an inherited woman becomes, often with no choice, a second wife to the man who takes her in (Buckley, 1997). The consequences for the spread of HIV are devastating. If a husband dies of AIDS, after infecting his wife, the brother-in-law who inherits her may then contract the virus from her and transmit it to his first wife. Or if she is not already infected, she may be infected by the brother-in-law, who may have contracted the virus from a prostitute or another lover. Any pregnancies that result run the risk of producing children with HIV. Yet widows, even those who know they have AIDS, see little choice but to go along with the custom. Women who refuse to be inherited are forced from their communities with their children and left to starve by angry in-laws, who sometimes steal their land as well. Kenyan activist groups such as Women Fighting AIDS are directing their efforts to ensuring that women have the resources to survive on their own—something that very few women in the villages are currently in the position to do.

Most of the attention in the fight against AIDS has been directed at gay men and heterosexual men and women; however, lesbian and bisexual women are also at risk. Sex between women does not typically involve the exchange of bodily fluids, making it less risky than heterosexual sex, but some practices, such as oral sex, may involve the risk of virus transmission. A more likely source of risk involves behaviors that are not a part of lesbian sexuality. Research has shown that many self-identified lesbians, even those who have always known they were lesbians, have had sex with men. The factors that are most strongly associated with risk of HIV infection among lesbian and bisexual women are youth, poverty, living in areas where HIV is prevalent, drug use, and sex with men (Clay, 1997b).

Motivations for Sex:
Issues of Desire, Love, Power, and Money

In Western cultures, women are taught that romantic love is the most important element in their lives and that love is the main reason to have sex. The first part of this message is delivered in the fairy tales children learn from books and movies, and the second part is reinforced in romance novels—which account for 25 percent of all sales of paperback books in the United States (E. Brown, 1989)—and in other media such as popular songs and movies. Girls grow up expecting to marry for love, and in many cases, with the belief that "love conquers all." Valuing love as a prime ingredient of committed sexual relationships is not universal, but it seems to be spreading to non-Western countries (Hatfield & Rapson, 1993).

In the version of romantic love most often portrayed in fairy tales and romance novels, the man wins the woman, often rescuing her from a dreary fate. In terms of sex, it is the man who takes the initiative and the woman who succumbs, often after some initial resistance. There is little room in these scenarios for a woman who takes the sexual initiative. Women's sexual desire, if portrayed at all, is shown as the desire to be taken, overwhelmed.

This is the double standard at work. A "good" woman waits to be pursued. Only "bad" women pursue a partner—and these "bad" women are also portrayed frequently in the media, as the scheming, manipulative, power-hungry vixens on soap operas. They are not in it for love, or even lust; they are in it for greed or revenge. The notion that women sometimes actively want sex is not present to any significant degree in any of these portrayals either.

Although women may scoff at these good woman–bad woman distinctions, the culture implacably surrounds us with them and they are pervasively included in norms about sexuality. One result is that women may believe they should not appear too eager for sex. They may sometimes offer **token resistance,** saying no at first even when they intend to agree to sex eventually, as a way of preserving their reputation. One study of unmarried college students in the United States, Russia, and Japan found that 38 percent of the women in the United States, 59 percent in Russia, and 37 percent in Japan had on at least one occasion offered such token resistance (Sprecher, Hatfield, Cortese, Potapova, & Levitskaya, 1994). Interestingly, men too reported offering occasional token resistance to sex, and men in the United States reported it at a higher frequency than women did: 47 percent. The researchers speculate that men's and women's token resistance occurs for different reasons: men's because they more easily define situations as sexual, and women's for the reasons already discussed.

Although these researchers found that women sometimes offered token resistance when they fully intended to have sex, they also found that women often consent to have sex when they do not really want to. Fifty-five percent of the nonvirgin women in the U.S. sample had done this—a much higher percentage than in either Russia (32 percent) or Japan (25 percent). Why was the percentage so much higher in the United States than elsewhere? The researchers suggest that U.S. men may have simply learned to keep the pressure on until the woman gives in, and/or that, because of changing norms, U.S. women do not have the traditional excuses for not having sex and have not developed strategies for asserting their desires when they don't want it.

In this study, most women who had offered token resistance had done it very infrequently—a finding that is supported in other research. Furthermore, women's use of this strategy is linked to their belief that their partner is a believer in the double standard (Muehlenhard & McCoy, 1991). However, there is still some cause for concern. Both token resistance and consent to unwanted sex undercut the perceived importance of women's sexual wishes. It is disturbing that women so often act in opposition to their own desires and that sexual miscommunication is so prevalent. Furthermore, every time a woman acts out an episode of token resistance, it reinforces the stereotype that "women say no when they mean yes"—an assertion that is frequently used by perpetrators of sexual assault and harassment to justify their continued sexual aggressiveness in the face of a woman's resistance or refusal.

The widespread existence of prostitution challenges the myth that sex occurs only or mainly in the context of romantic love.

Obviously, neither love nor desire is the only reason women have sex. However, cultures have a tendency to rank the motivations for sexual activity according to how acceptable the motivation is seen to be. Engaging in sex out of duty or to please a partner is one thing, but what about engaging in sex to make a living? For many believers in the double standard, the ultimate "bad" woman is a prostitute—someone who exchanges nonmarital sexual activity for money. Known as the "oldest profession," **prostitution** has appeared throughout history everywhere in the world, and the women who practice it are often stigmatized as immoral, evil, maladjusted, and/or sick.

But the women who engage in prostitution are not strikingly different from other women. Most see prostitution as a temporary job, until a better opportunity comes along, and most have a steady lover, male or female, apart from their work. Often, prostitution is a part-time job that enables a woman to earn some needed cash. While research does show that girls who enter prostitution as juveniles are considerably more likely than other girls to have been sexually abused, it also shows that women who became prostitutes as young adults are no more troubled or maladjusted than comparable "straight" women (McCormick, 1994).

The main reasons that women enter prostitution are economic. Women can make more as prostitutes than they can in traditionally female work such as clerical and service occupations. Often, it is a question not simply of extra income, but of economic survival. This may be particularly true in the developing world, where young girls and women may literally be sold by families mired in poverty or where homeless abandoned youngsters are forced to hustle to get money for food. Indeed, as discussed in the next chapter, the distinction between prostitution and sex slavery or rape blurs under some conditions, such as when children are involved or when women are forced, through direct coercion or through dire economic distress, to trade sex for money. Two researchers who interviewed juvenile prostitutes in Taiwan found that money was a universal motivation for these young women (Hwang & Bedford, 2004). The women reported that they had become "addicted" to the easy money of prostitution. As one of their interviewees said:

> Once you are in this occupation, you have a kind of mentality—you tell yourself "I'll leave when I make enough money." But when you have earned the money, you have another kind of mentality—you feel the money is so easy, and it does not do harm to you. You'll continue, continue, and continue . . . you cannot leave it. (quoted in Hwang & Bedford., 2004, p. 140)

Poor women everywhere are the most likely to have recourse to prostitution, but this pattern is especially evident in the international trade in sex workers. In some Asian and Pacific Island nations, "sex tourism" is big business. Male tourists from Europe, North America, Australia, and Japan pay in advance for package tours in which a sex partner is included. The women (sometimes girls) receive very little of the money. Most of the profits go to the tour operators and other middlemen, while the women remain poor and dependent on this job as their livelihood. For girls and young women who are forced into prostitution in such situations—perhaps indentured by their families or kidnapped and imprisoned in brothels, there seems to be a gradual transition from resistance to acceptance of their fate (Hwang & Bedford, 2004). The Taiwanese juvenile prostitutes who had worked in such confined situations reported that, at first, they were bitter and angry, and they fought against the customers who were sent to them. Gradually, however, they began to form attachments to some customers, and decided that their lives would be better if they treated their customers well—and that perhaps some customer would help them escape their imprisonment. Eventually, most of the young women abandoned hope of leaving the brothel in the near future, and they fell into depression, drug use, and self-abuse. Finally, however, most of them seemed resigned to prostitution as their fate. As one of them commented: "It was not very tiring, yet not that easy either. Customers came, I lay down, got up, lay down, got up. It's not a big deal . . . The advantage was that I had plenty of food and clothes. As long as I obeyed and did what I was told, I could have whatever I wanted" (quoted in Hwang & Bedford, 2004, p. 143).

Women from developing countries where opportunities are very limited are often recruited as migratory prostitutes who will work very cheaply in more affluent countries. For example, in Japan many women from Latin America, the Philippines, Thailand, Taiwan, and South Korea work as prostitutes at much lower rates than Japanese women. The women are brought in by agents who provide them with a plane ticket, clothing, false passports, and work permits—the costs of which are later deducted from their meager pay (Naoko, 1987). A somewhat similar pattern of exploitation is evident in the "mail-order bride" business, in which Western men "buy" an Asian woman, who is poor enough to be willing to risk everything on a man she has never met. The payment goes, of course, not to the woman but to the company that brokers the arrangement.

When women try to leave prostitution, they are often confronted with a limited set of alternatives: the low-wage traditionally female jobs. For example, when Japanese brothels became illegal after World War II, the prostitutes were given access to social workers, vocational counselors, and job training to help them start new lives. But the training was for positions as maids, factory workers, and sales clerks. Not surprisingly, many eventually returned to prostitution (McCormick, 1994).

Like the students described at the beginning of this chapter, many people may not approve of prostitution or agree with the choices of the women who engage in it. We should be cautious about condemning women who have taken this route to economic survival, however. Identifying prostitutes as the "bad" women in the good–bad dichotomy promoted by the double standard plays too easily into the notions that women's sexuality must be controlled at all costs, and that a woman's worth can be defined and classified according to some hierarchy of sexual virtue. When we use the double standard as the main way of categorizing and judging women, we devalue whole groups of women. Society has often labeled certain women as "loose" as a justification for dismissing or despising them. As Naomi McCormick (1994) notes, "[A] woman doesn't have to be a sex worker to be viewed as a whore. Historically and today, prejudiced men from dominant groups have despised poor women, women of color, immigrant women, and Jewish women as whores" (p. 85).

The widespread existence of prostitution challenges the myth that sex occurs only or mainly in the context of romantic love. Perhaps that is why it arouses such strong emotions in so many people. Yet it is an inescapable conclusion that women do not have sex just for love but for many reasons: money, duty, fear, and, yes, pleasure.

SUMMARY

Women's sexuality has often been defined and explained by male experts such as Sigmund Freud and Havelock Ellis. However, early in the 20th century, one woman, Marie Stopes, provided a female perspective on sexuality in her writings, based on her own experience and research. Subsequent sex researchers, such as Alfred Kinsey, have relied heavily on large-scale sex surveys to determine people's sexual practices and attitudes. Laboratory research on human sexual responses, carried out by Masters and Johnson in the 1960s, led to a model of human sexual response that focused heavily on physiological reactions associated with arousal and orgasm and that portrayed women and men as having rather similar sexual responses. This model has been critiqued by other sexologists for its omission of sexual desire, attraction, and emotion, and the research on which it is based has been criticized for the nonrepresentativeness of the participants. Leonore Tiefer argues that the model is not gender-neutral, but based on a male approach to sexuality.

One purpose that Masters and Johnson's research did serve was to debunk the Freudian idea that "real women" have vaginal orgasms. The vagina is a relatively insensitive organ, and direct or indirect stimulation of the clitoris is the source of female orgasms—even those that occur during heterosexual intercourse. There are, however, a few reports of women able to reach orgasm through fantasy, without any physical stimulation, and of women who are physically incapable of clitoral sensation reaching orgasm. It is difficult to know how to interpret these reports, but they suggest the importance of thoughts and feelings, not just physical stimulation, in sexuality.

Women are much less likely than men to report having orgasms during heterosexual activity. This does not mean that it is harder for women than men to have orgasms; women can masturbate to orgasm as quickly and easily as men. However, women are much less likely than men to masturbate, perhaps because they are inhibited, not interested in solitary sex, or simply have never learned how.

Sexuality is often defined in a male-centered way, with heterosexual intercourse labeled as "having sex," and all other sexual practices relegated to the categories of foreplay or afterplay. Since women's sexual pleasure is less likely to come from vaginal intercourse than from other practices that involve clitoral stimulation, this attitude treats women's sexual pleasure as unimportant.

Sexual orientation, a person's choice of sexual or affectional partners of the same or other sex, has often been discussed as a set of categories into which individuals can be assigned. However, it appears that women's sexual orientation is rather fluid and potentially changeable across the lifespan and that the categories themselves are fuzzy. People may hold contradictory feelings or engage in apparently contradictory behaviors with respect to sexual orientation. There is also disagreement about the meaning of the labels lesbian, bisexual, and heterosexual and about the factors that influence sexual orientation. Researchers have not found clear biological or childhood socialization predictors of women's sexual orientation.

One of the main messages of North American society to girls and women is that, for women, sex should be related to love. Scorn is heaped on women who are promiscuous or who trade sexual activities for money. Although researchers and writers in the field of sexology have helped to change drastically the notion that, for women, sex is not for pleasure but primarily a duty to be endured for the sake of a good marriage and children, strong elements of the double standard remain. Female sexual pleasure is considered to be a good thing in the context of committed mixed-gender relationships, but there is considerable unease about female sexuality when it extends beyond these boundaries. Lesbian sexuality makes much of the culture uncomfortable, and women of any sexual orientation whose sexuality is more overt than discreet incur disapproval. The sexual dimension of life also tends to be acknowledged only for a fairly narrow spectrum of women. Women who are old or disabled or chronically ill, for example, are often considered to have no sexual needs or feelings.

Some cultures interpret sexuality differently. Female sexuality is more restricted than male sexuality in most places, but the disapproval attached to nonmarital sex for women is not universal. Some cultures have interpreted marital sexuality as a practical matter, engaged in for the purpose of maintaining the relationship and producing children, rather than as an outcome of romantic love. In such cultures, women's extramarital relationships with men or other women are sometimes tolerated. In some cultures, lesbian relationships have been institutionalized and accepted.

For women, the practical consequences of sex can include pregnancy and exposure to sexually transmitted diseases. To control these consequences, women need some power in their relationships and in society at large. Women's control over contraception is limited by legal and medical restrictions that reduce their access to various methods of birth control. Their ability to protect themselves from sexually transmitted diseases is often limited by patriarchal social contexts that support male dominance in sexual relationships. Women are often afraid to insist on condom use by their male partners because they fear emotional or physical retribution from them.

While we maintain one meaning of female sexuality (love) at eye level, other meanings (power, economic survival) lurk beneath the surface of the culture. In virtually every culture, many women use their sexuality to survive. Sexual activity is a commodity—sometimes the only commodity women control—that can be exchanged for money, security, and status. A North American high school student may trade it for popularity; a young woman in Bangladesh may trade it for the security of an arranged marriage; a Filipina may trade it for the chance to travel to a new country where she hopes for greater social and economic opportunities; a woman in an African town may trade it for money to feed her family. To romanticize female sexuality too much is to ignore the way it fits into the power structures institutionalized by cultures. When men are the ones with the money, with the status, with the positions of authority, one way—sometimes the only way—for women to gain access to those resources is by using their sexuality. Such exchanges can be dangerous for a woman: She may risk unwanted pregnancy and sexually transmitted disease as well as sexual violence and the contempt of those who feel she is violating standards of proper female behavior. Yet for many women, the risks are seen as necessary and unavoidable.

Sexuality can be thought of as a dangerous aspect of behavior surrounded by rules and restrictions, or as a commodity in the search for power or survival. For many people, it is also thought of as an intense, emotionally and physically pleasurable way of connecting with another person. In a cultural context where equality between women and men is a given, women are more likely to be able to focus on the latter meaning of sexuality.

KEY TERMS

double standard	sexual orientation	mati-ism
sex survey	bisexual	scripts
orgasm	homoeroticism	token resistance
clitoris	heteroeroticism	prostitution
G spot		

DISCUSSION QUESTIONS

What does the phrase "having sex" mean to you? Why do you think you define it the way you do? Did anything in this chapter make you rethink your definition?

How prevalent is the double standard in your social environment? Are women judged differently for sexual activity than men are?

How rigid are the categories of sexual orientation? Can a person identify as a member of one category, such as heterosexual, and yet have feelings or engage in behaviors that do not fit that category? Do you think that people really change their sexual orientation sometimes, or are they simply discovering "who they really are"?

FOR ADDITIONAL READING

Greene, Beverly (Ed.). (1997). *Ethnic and cultural diversity among lesbians and gay men.* Thousand Oaks, CA: Sage Publications. This book explores the lives of gay, lesbian, and bisexual minorities from the perspective of their diverse cultures. The book uses empirical, clinical, and theoretical discussions as well as personal narratives to explore the intersections of sexuality and culture. Chapters include "Native Gay and Lesbian Issues: The Two-spirited, Black South African Lesbians in the Nineties," "Greek American Lesbians: Identity Odysseys of Honorable Good Girls," and "Don't Ask, Don't Tell, Don't Know: The Formation of a Homosexual Identity and Sexual Expression among Asian American Lesbians."

Maines, Rachel P. (1999). *The technology of orgasm: "Hysteria," the vibrator, and women's sexual satisfaction.* Baltimore, MD: The Johns Hopkins University Press. The author explores ways in which a male-defined sexuality allowed female sexual desires and feelings to be defined as symptoms, how the vibrator emerged as "clinical instrument" to treat those symptoms, and how it was later adopted as a way for women to control their own sexual pleasure.

McCormick, Naomi B. (1994). *Sexual salvation: Affirming women's sexual rights and pleasures.* Westport, CT: Praeger. A sex researcher and psychotherapist provides a balanced overview of sexual issues for women, with strong attention to the experience of women from different races, classes, sexual orientations, ages, and abilities. Included are chapters on sexual scripts, intimacy, lesbian and bisexual identities, women sex trade workers, and sexual victimization and pornography.

Rose, June. (1992). *Marie Stopes and the sexual revolution.* London: Faber & Faber. A biography of the woman who, in 1918, wrote the book on sex that she knew would "electrify England." It provides some fascinating history on sexual attitudes and behavior in Britain and Europe.

Tiefer, Leonore. (1995). *Sex is not a natural act and other essays.* Boulder, CO: Westview Press. This collection of essays by a noted scholar in the field of human sexuality takes a witty and piercing look at many assumptions about sexuality. The author stimulates a reappraisal of everything from Masters and Johnson's research to feminist debates on pornography. Guaranteed to make the reader think!

WEB RESOURCES

Sexuality Information and Education Council of the United States (SIECUS). This site is a good starting point for information about many aspects of sexuality. The site includes news releases and reports; pages for teens, parents, and the media; a directory of sexual organizations worldwide; and an international clearinghouse. In the section on global resources, you can find annotated bibliographies on many sexual topics. **www.siecus.org**

Planned Parenthood. This is the gateway to a lot of information about sexuality and reproduction. Here you can find press releases about the latest legislation and research, information about sex education, a special section on emergency contraception, a section that focuses on young people and reproductive freedom, and resources that have been especially developed for teens. **www.plannedparenthood.org**

Prostitution Education Network (PEN). This is the site for a nonprofit organization for sex workers' rights. It allows access to research reports, statistics on prostitution, links to other organizations, and information about advocacy for the decriminalization of prostitution. **www.bayswan.org/penet.html**

CHAPTER 13

Violence against Women:
A Worldwide Problem

CHAPTER OUTLINE

In July 1997, Baskar, a 15-year-old girl from a village near New Delhi, India, married a man selected for her by her conservative Muslim parents. According to tradition, Baskar came to the marriage with a dowry: a refrigerator, furniture, and other household goods. But her family could not afford one of the items demanded by the groom: a motorcycle. On their wedding night the aggrieved groom, apparently feeling cheated because of the missing motorcycle, got drunk and, with three of his friends, took turns beating and raping his new wife. Scared and humiliated, Baskar returned to her parents, who sought justice from the village council. Their ruling, a few days later, was that she should return to her husband and "let bygones be bygones" (Husband, friends raped her, 1997).

In the tiny hamlet of Punsooilri, near Seoul, South Korea, a man who had been married more than 20 years commented to a reporter that he had, of course, beaten his wife regularly during their marriage. "'For me, it's better to release that anger and get it over with,' Mr. Lee said. 'Otherwise, I just get sick inside. . . . Of course, you have to apologize afterward. . . . Otherwise, you can have bad feelings in your relationship with your wife'" (Kristof, 1996). Lee's words reflect the pattern of widespread acceptance of wife beating in South Korea, where one survey revealed that 42 percent of South Korean wives said they had been beaten by their husbands.

In the United States, women working in a large iron-ore mine in Minnesota filed suit against their employer, Eveleth Tacomite, and their union, the United Steel Workers, for failing to stop the sexual harassment that had made their workplace a living hell. The women testified that they had been "groped, grabbed, pressured for sex, threatened with rape, beaten, stalked and subjected to coarse language and graffiti" (Grimsley, 1996b, p. A12). Among the incidents the women recounted: Male workers grabbed women's crotches, stalked them during off-hours, masturbated into their lockers, addressed them with slang terms for parts of the female anatomy instead of names, and threatened them with rape and other kinds of physical violence. The women's complaints had gone unheeded by management and union alike; in 1993 a judge ruled that the women had indeed been subjected to a hostile atmosphere and ordered the mine to pay damages. Meanwhile, however, many of the women had become too fearful to return to work at the mine and had been ostracized by their community because of their accusations (Grimsley, 1996c).

In Istanbul, Turkey, 13-year old Dilber Kina drew the anger of her father because he felt she was dishonoring the family by talking to boys on the street, running away from home, and becoming the subject of neighborhood gossip. Finally, as she tried to run away again, her father grabbed an ax and a kitchen knife, and stabbed and beat her to death. When arrested, the father said "I fulfilled my duty . . . we killed her for going out with boys" (Moore, 2001a, p. A1).

In Gujar Khan, Pakistan, Zahida Perveen's husband came home one day and accused his wife of having an affair with her brother-in-law. She denied the accusation, but in a fit of rage he tied her up and slashed her face with a razor and a knife, cutting out her eyes and slicing off her earlobes and her nose. Months later, as he stood awaiting his trial, the man said, "I did these things, but I was going out of my senses. She was provoking me and ruining my life. What I did was wrong, but I am satisfied. I did it for my honor and my prestige." (Quoted in Constable, 2000, p. A16). Later, when shown photographs of Perveen's badly mutilated face, a group of middle-class men in Islamabad "commented that she 'must have deserved it' and that her husband 'did what a man has to do'" (Constable, 2000, p. A16).

The global problem of violence against women, because it is so widespread and so serious, is a topic that must be addressed in any consideration of the psychology of women. What impact does it have on a woman's psychology for her to know that she may be vulnerable to violence in so many situations? How are her feelings affected by media treatments of violence? By the cultural norms and laws that relate to such violence? How does the fear of violence, or actually being a target of violence, affect her behavior?

These questions are important, but answering them will not be enough to understand the issues surrounding violence against women. For we need to look beyond the psychology of individual women, and of the individual men who perpetrate much of the violence, and try to understand how cultures—not just national cultures, but the "mini-cultures" that evolve and thrive in workplaces and families—cooperate with and reproduce the violence, even while sometimes deploring it. What cultural forces support violence against women? What strategies work to minimize antifemale violence in a society?

All of these questions will be addressed in this chapter as we examine a series of issues in antifemale violence. We begin by looking at physical violence and abuse in close relationships. Such violence is stunning in its frequency and in the damage it does. Also sobering is the amount of violence directed at female children through sex-selective abortion, infanticide, and systematic neglect, issues that we address next. Then, we turn to sexual violence, focusing on rape, the sexual abuse of children, and forced prostitution. We also examine sexual harassment and intimidation. In considering these differing sides of sexual violence, we look also at the role played by the media, both through pornography and through the proliferation of films, music videos, and television programs that graphically depict the victimization of women as entertainment. On another grim note, we examine the torture and abuse of women in custody. On the positive side, the chapter deals next with strategies that have been developed in various countries to combat violence and to protect women. The final section highlights the international focus on freedom from gender-based persecution as a human right—one that should be guaranteed and protected by all nations.

Battering in Close Relationships

Close relationships are, in some respects, the most dangerous ones for women. In the United States, an estimated 30 percent of female homicide victims are killed by an intimate partner (U.S. Department of Justice, 2000). Of the spousal murders committed in the United States in 2002, almost 82 percent involved a wife killed by her husband (Federal Bureau of Investigation, 2002). In some countries, such as Bangladesh, Brazil, Kenya, and Thailand, this figure is higher than 50 percent (Neft & Levine, 1997). Of violent crimes committed against intimate partners in the United States, 85 percent are against women (U.S. Department of Justice, 2000). Whereas intimate partner violence makes up about 20 percent of violent crimes against women in the United States, this type of violence accounts for only 3 percent of violent crimes against men (Rennison & Rand, 2003). Violent acts against women, particularly within families, are ignored, tolerated, or even given tacit approval through law or custom in many parts of the world. Many legal systems offer only limited protection to women and light or nonexistent punishment to the abusers. A woman who is being abused within her own family or close relationship is being threatened and mistreated in an environment that should be her sanctuary, making the abuse doubly hurtful and escape extremely difficult. Physical abuse can begin in dating relationships and can progress to a regular pattern of violence in long-term cohabiting couples.

Dating Violence

In a letter published in Ann Landers's advice column, a young woman described how her boyfriend hit her and called her names when he was angry. She said she loved him and was planning to stay in the relationship no matter what, but she wanted suggestions on how to handle the violence. Landers advised her to get out of the relationship, and so did a flood of letters from women in abusive marriages that Landers later published in her column. The letter writers' message to the young woman was adamant and unanimous: Get out; it will only get worse. Writer after writer described how men who had been physically abusive before marriage became more and more violent afterward, and these women urged the young woman not to get trapped by mistakenly thinking she could change her already dangerous boyfriend.

This public dialogue provided some very dramatic testimony about a widespread problem: At least in the United States, violence has been found to be a part of an estimated 20 percent of dating relationships (Silverman, Raj, Mucci, & Hathaway, 2001), and more than one-third of the women involved in violent dating relationships expect to marry their abusers (Lo & Sporakowski, 1989). Even though they may be physically harmed and emotionally upset, many young women stay in relationships that include violence. One reason may be the causal attributions the women make for their boyfriends' violent behavior. The women often say that the violence occurs when the relationship is somehow threatened

[handwritten margin note: Not good, might see this as the only person who would want them]

TABLE 13.1   Intimate Partner Violence against Women around the World: Some Examples

Industrialized Countries

Canada
- 29% of women in a nationally representative sample reported being physically assaulted by a current or former partner since the age of 16

✗ Japan
- 59% of women surveyed in 1993 reported being physically abused by a partner

United Kingdom
- 25% of a random sample of women from one district had been punched or slapped by a current or former partner in their lifetime

United States
- 28% of a nationally representative sample of women reported at least one episode of physical violence from their partner

Asia and the Pacific

Cambodia
- 16% of women in a nationally representative sample reported being physically abused by a spouse

✗ India
- up to 45% of married men in a survey in one state admitted physically abusing their wives

Korea
- 38% of wives in a random sample of women report being physically abused by their spouse

Africa

Egypt
- 35% of a nationally representative sample of women report being beaten by their husband at some point in their marriage

✗ Kenya
- 42% of women surveyed in one district said they had been beaten by a partner

Uganda
- 41% of the women in a representative sample of women and men in one district reported being beaten or physically harmed by a partner; 41% of men acknowledged beating their partner

South Africa → *interesting, lowest*
- 16% of women surveyed reported being physically abused by a partner in their lifetime

Latin America and the Caribbean

Chile
- 26% of a representative sample of women from Santiago reported at least one episode of violence by a partner and 11% reported at least one episode of severe violence

Mexico
- 30% of women surveyed in Guadalajara reported at least one episode of physical violence by a partner; 13% reported violence within the previous year

✗ Nicaragua
- 52% of a representative sample of women in León reported being physically abused by a partner at least once

Puerto Rico
- 48% of a national sample of women say they have been abused by an intimate partner

Central and Eastern Europe

Estonia
- 29% of women aged 18–24 surveyed said they fear domestic violence; 52% of women aged 65 or older fear such violence

✗ Poland
- 60% of divorced women surveyed reported being hit at least once by their ex-husbands; 25% reported repeated violence

Tajikistan
- 23% of women aged 18–40 reported physical abuse on a survey

Source: (Adapted from United Nations Children's Fund. (2000). Domestic violence against women and girls with additional information from United Nations (2000) The world's women: Trends and statistics.)

through jealousy, dating others, suspicion of sexual infidelity, or a discussion about ending the relationship (Pape & Arias, 1995). Thus they interpret the violence as meaning that the man cares and as a sign of his love or commitment to the relationship. Given this interpretation, they may assume that the violence will cease once they are married and the man is secure in the relationship. Unfortunately, this prediction seldom comes true, and the women who marry their batterers find themselves legally bound to a man whose abuse gets worse every year.

Adolescent girls who report that they have experienced dating violence are more likely than other girls to report a number of other problems. One large study of Massachusetts high school students found that girls who had experienced physical and/or sexual violence in dating relationships were at higher risk for substance abuse, such as cocaine use or binge drinking, and for unhealthy weight control behaviors such as the use of laxatives and vomiting. They were also more likely than their peers to report having their first sexual intercourse before the age of 15 and to engage in such risky sexual behaviors as having a high number of sex partners or having intercourse without using condoms. They were more likely to become pregnant as teenagers and to report that they had considered or attempted suicide. Indeed, young women who had been sexually and physically hurt by dating partners were 6 to 9 times more likely than their peers to say they had recently thought about or attempted suicide (Silverman et al., 2001). Although these data are correlational and thus cannot demonstrate with certainty that violence causes these other behaviors, they suggest that dating violence may be implicated in a host of other problems for adolescent girls.

While staying in an abusive dating relationship is dangerous for young women, so is trying to terminate or avoid it. Many women are stalked and threatened by former boyfriends or lovers and by men who, though they have never actually been in a close relationship with their target, imagine that they have a right to such a relationship.

A particularly horrible form of violence against young women who reject potential suitors emerged in Bangladesh during the 1990s: acid attacks, in which nitric acid is sprayed on the face, causing excruciating pain and severe disfigurement. Hundreds of Bangladeshi girls and women, most between the ages of 11 and 20 years, are the victims of acid attacks every year (Anwar, 1997). In one case that went to court in 1997, Nurun Nahar, a 15-year-old high school student, awoke in the middle of the night to an attack by her rejected suitor and four accomplices. "Suddenly I woke up and found myself in a hell of pain. Everything became dark. My face was burning," she recalled (Anwar, 1997). Nahar, who used to be envied for her beauty, now wraps a sheet of white cloth around her deformed face whenever she leaves her home.

No matter where in the world it occurs, the violence of men against women who they think *owe* them the acceptance of their advances, intimacy, and submission to their will reveals a pervasive sense of masculine entitlement in the arena of heterosexual relationships. On what is such an exaggerated sense of entitlement based? The history and ubiquity of wife abuse provides some answers.

Husbands Abusing Wives

Agnes, a teacher whose husband was also a teacher, said the violence began a few years after she got married, when she caught her husband in bed with a teenage girl. He began to beat her every evening. He forced her to give him her paycheck. He called her his slave. For about two

These young women were the victims of an attack in which nitric acid was sprayed on their faces. Hundreds of Bangladeshi girls and women, most between the ages of 11 and 20 years, are the victims of acid attacks every year. The attacks are carried out by rejected suitors and their friends.

years, the violence eased, but alcoholic rages and financial irresponsibility again became the norm. And the beatings got worse. Nonetheless, Agnes did not tell anyone about the beatings, even those closest to her because, she said, "I was so scared, and I was feeling so embarrassed. I did not want people to know about it." (Buckley, 1996, p. A26)

Where in the world did this happen? In what country are women so vulnerable to violence from their husbands that they bear it for years without leaving and without telling anyone about it? This particular incident happened in the African country of Kenya, but a perusal of the research on wife abuse shows that it could have happened anywhere—that this is a very common story in almost every country of the world. Although it is very difficult to obtain accurate estimates of the frequency of domestic violence, surveys in various countries suggest that the percentage of women reporting that they have ever been physically abused by a male partner may range from a minimum (!) of about 17 percent to 25 percent (e.g., studies in New Zealand, Canada, Belgium, the Netherlands, Norway) to a high of 55 percent to 60 percent or more (e.g., studies in Ecuador, Sri Lanka, Tanzania, and some parts of Mexico and India) (Neft & Levine, 1997). In surveys from 48 different countries, between 10 and 69 percent of women reported that they had been physically assaulted by an intimate male partner (World Health Organization, 2002). A survey in

Tokyo, Japan, revealed that one-third of the women respondents with partners said they had been battered by their husbands or boyfriends (Yamaguchi, 1998). In Chengdu, China, a survey indicated that 13 percent of wives said they had been hit or kicked by their husbands and about 8 percent reported that their husbands had beaten them up (Xu, 1997). One report cites domestic violence rates in Pakistan as high as 90 percent (United Nations Population Fund, 2000).

In many cultures, men have traditionally claimed the right to beat their wives as a matter of authority, superiority, and control over property. According to an old Korean saying, "Dried fish and women both are better after they are beaten" (Kristof, 1996). African social workers report that in some ethnic groups, if a man's wife dies before he has had a chance to beat her he must prove his manhood by beating her corpse (Buckley, 1996). Violence within marriage is linked historically to a legal definition of the family in which the wife is the property of the husband and the husband is the clear authority over her. Under such a legal tradition, which prevailed in ancient Greece and Rome, in Europe in the Middle Ages, and in Britain and North America until at least the last century, and which is still in effect in countries such as Saudi Arabia and Pakistan, a husband is allowed, even encouraged, to exert that authority through beatings. Women are considered unruly, childlike creatures, inferior to men, who bring the beatings on themselves by defying or criticizing their husbands.

It has been, and in some places still is, permissible for a man to "correct" his wife by physical aggression, often with the proviso that she must not be hurt too seriously. Thus a Nigerian husband may not be charged with abuse if his beating does not leave a scar or require a stay of more than 21 days in the hospital; in Mexico, a man whose wife's wounds heal within 15 days is likely to be pardoned or let off lightly (Neft & Levine, 1997). Even in places where the laws have been changed to make spouse abuse a crime, custom often continues to support the behavior.

Research in the United States and Canada (e.g., Frieze, 1986; MacLeod, 1980; L. E. A. Walker, 1979) reveals a pattern of the development of spouse abuse that seems to fit many of the stories told by abused women in other parts of the world as well. Marital violence is usually initiated by the husband, but the wife may sometimes fight back as the pattern continues. The violence tends to increase in severity over time, becoming so dangerous that in one-third or more of the cases the victim must seek medical treatment for her injuries. The woman in many cases becomes isolated from other people and faces a growing sense of powerlessness as she tries and fails to change the situation in some way that will stop the violence. Eventually, she may try to leave the relationship but often returns because she has nowhere to go or feels too frightened and inadequate to make it on her own. If she leaves, the man may track her down, appear contrite, and draw her back to the relationship with promises that the violence will never happen again. But it does happen again—and again. As the violence becomes even more extreme, she may finally leave because she fears for her life or the lives of her children, or she may actually try to kill her husband. If and when she does leave, she risks further violence if her husband hunts her down; risks of extreme violence and murder are highest when the victim tries to escape from the relationship (Pagelow, 1993; United Nations, 2000).

Although both men and women engage in violence toward their partners, men inflict more serious harm (Holtzworth-Munroe & Stuart, 1994). Also, men are more likely than

---

BOX 13.1 MAKING CHANGE
Add Your Voice to the Observance of V-Day

V-Day is a global movement to stop violence against women and girls. Its observance is a catalyst to increase awareness, raise money, and revitalize the spirit of existing antiviolence organizations. V-Day—on or around Valentine's Day in February—is also a day when annual theatrical and artistic events are produced around the world to raise money for antiviolence organizations and to transform consciousness. What is your campus doing for V-Day? To learn more and for ideas about how your campus or organization can participate, go to the Web site **www.vday.org**.

---

women to strike the first blow: Women who report behaving violently toward their spouses are usually responding to abuse by them. However, men who report that they have been physically or psychologically abusive toward their partners are often *not* being treated violently by these women (A. Mason & Blankenship, 1987). About 4 of every 10 female victims of intimate partner violence are injured seriously enough to seek medical treatment (U.S. Department of Justice, 2000).

For many victims of intimate partner violence, the violence is not confined to the home. They may receive threatening telephone calls or be stalked by their partners or ex-partners at work. Researchers estimate that between 35 and 56 percent of employed battered women are harassed at work by their abusers and that one-quarter to one-half of domestic violence victims have lost a job because of the violence (Schafer, 2001). Yet only about 5 percent of employers have any policies in place for helping employees who are victimized in this way, and it is distressingly common for such individuals to be fired because of the trouble the situation causes for the employer.

In North America, some studies show that men who abuse their wives tend to have a marked *need* for power but actually possess little—at least within the marriage. Such research suggests that men may use violence to bolster their sense of power when other sources and strategies of influence are not available (Dutton & Strachan, 1987; A. Mason & Blankenship, 1987). In support of this interpretation is research that shows men who are high in hostility toward women tend to feel personally inadequate: low in their sense of control over their own lives and in their self-esteem (Cowan & Mills, 2004).

One of the reasons wife abuse is often hidden is that in many cultures, the family is considered a private realm. A strong tradition dictates that outsiders not interfere in family conflicts—a tradition that stems at least partly from the notion that husbands own their wives and parents own their children. A very clear example of this attitude occurred in Papua New Guinea some years ago when members of Parliament were asked to consider legal solutions to the widespread problem of domestic violence. According to social anthropologist Christine Bradley (1994), some of the members argued that

> wife-beating is and should remain "strictly a private affair," and that the law should not have the right to intervene in family life. Others asserted that there is nothing wrong with wife-beating

provided the husband has "a good reason," and a minister claimed that paying bride price makes the man the head of the family, so that husbands feel they "own the woman and can belt her any time they like." Another Honorable Member was annoyed that the nation's leaders were being asked to discuss something as trivial as wife-beating: "We are wasting our time instead of discussing the development of the country. We should have something better to discuss than this!"(p. 13)

In many countries, groups that have sought legislation to curb family violence have faced the same kinds of attitudes. And even with strong legislation in place, such attitudes can affect outcomes for battered women. There are still some judges in the United States and Canada who counsel abused women to go back to their husbands, and some police officers who do not view wife beating as a serious crime. However, as the United Nations notes in its resource manual for confronting domestic violence, the right to a private family life does not include the right to abuse family members.

Psychological and Emotional Abuse   The threats, insults, contemptuous verbal and non-verbal treatment, and isolation that comprise psychological abuse are more difficult to measure than physical abuse. However, many women who have survived abusive relationships report that living in fear and being tortured emotionally were more devastating than the physical abuse they endured. And psychological abuse usually accompanies physical abuse by intimate partners. For example, studies in Japan, Zimbabwe and Nicaragua found large overlaps between physical and emotional violence, with only a minority of abused women reporting that they been hurt only physically (United Nations, 2000).

The stress and emotional devastation that results from psychological abuse puts women at risk for suicide. Based on studies in the United States, Fiji, Papua New Guinea, Peru, India, Bangladesh, and Sri Lanka, researchers estimate that women who have been abused are 12 times more likely than other women to attempt suicide (United Nations Children's Fund, 2000).

Wife Murder for Money or "Honor"   The notion of marriage as an economic arrangement is still strong in some parts of India; some parents there literally bribe men to marry their daughters. It is socially shameful and often economically distressing to have a daughter for whom a suitable husband cannot be found, so, as noted at the beginning of this chapter, parents entice potential bridegrooms with promises of dowries of cash and/or household goods. Frequently, in fact, parents go deep into debt to marry off their daughters. Even after the marriage has taken place, however, a husband's family may be unsatisfied with the dowry. They may pressure the new wife to get more goods from her parents, making her life miserable with insults and harassment if she is unwilling or unable to do so (Narasimhan, 1994). The young woman must endure the suffering because she cannot leave the marriage without bringing severe disgrace on her family and herself.

Such situations often end with the death of the new bride. Sometimes, in desperation because the mistreatment has become unbearable, she commits suicide. Too often, however, she is murdered, doused with kerosene by her in-laws and set on fire. The death is reported to authorities as a "kitchen accident"—an explanation that has some surface plausibility because many homes use kerosene stoves for cooking. In 1995, the Indian government reported 7,300 such "dowry deaths" (Neft & Levine, 1997). International organizations estimate that about 5,000 women per year continue to fall victims to dowry-related murders in India (United Nations Children's Emergency Fund, 2002).

A 1961 law prohibiting dowries appears to have had little effect in the face of strong traditions and the difficulty of proving what happened. A more stringent law, passed in 1986, states that in every unnatural death of a woman during the first 7 years of marriage, the husband or in-laws must be presumed responsible by the courts. Yet convictions under this law are rare, and bride burnings continue to increase.

Money is not the only reason that wives can sometimes be murdered with virtual impunity. A strong tradition exists in many societies that a woman who "dishonors" her husband (or sometimes her father) by becoming sexually involved with a man to whom she is not married can legitimately be killed. The remnants of such a tradition can be found in North America, where a husband who kills his wife in a "jealous rage" after discovering her adultery may in some communities be regarded with more sympathy than condemnation. The tradition is more obvious in certain Latin American and Arab countries, where it is reflected in the legal system.

In a famous case in Brazil, a man arrived at a hotel where his wife was staying with another man and asked the bellman to take him to the couple's room. When the wife's lover opened the door at the bellman's request, the husband stabbed him repeatedly in the chest, killing him. The wife ran naked from the room and into the street, where she was pursued by her husband, caught, and stabbed to death.

An all-male jury accepted the argument that the husband in this case had acted in legitimate defense of his wounded honor and acquitted him of the double murder. The decision, after being upheld by an appeals court, was later overturned by Brazil's highest court, the Superior Tribunal of Justice. The Tribunal ordered a new trial, noting that murder could not be considered a legitimate response to adultery and that "what is being defended in this type of crime is not honour but 'self-esteem, vanity and the pride of the lord who sees his wife as property'" (Thomas, 1994, p. 33).

Feminist activists in Brazil, who had for decades been fighting to de-legitimate the "honor defense" and the underlying proprietary attitudes toward women, were buoyed by this decision. In the new trial, however, the husband was once again acquitted of the double killing on the grounds that he had been legitimately defending his honor. Thus, in Brazilian culture, wife murder was still considered an appropriate response to alleged unfaithfulness; a husband could kill his wife with impunity under such circumstances.

Jean Sasson (1992) tells the story of a young woman from a wealthy Saudi Arabian family who violated the cultural restrictions on women by approaching strange men in the marketplace. She engaged in sexual behavior, although not sexual intercourse for fear of the punishment that would befall her if she lost her virginity, with a number of men. She believed herself safe from discovery because she never removed her veil, but eventually she was caught and tried by the Religious Council. They released her to her father for punishment, since they could find no definitive evidence of sexual activity. Her father, however, was enraged and humiliated by her behavior. His chosen punishment? Death. At an appointed time, she was drowned in the family swimming pool with all members of her family looking on. No one was charged with any crime. As her father, he was entitled to punish her in any way he thought appropriate.

"**Honor killings**" to wipe away the shame brought to a husband, father, or brother by a female relative's premarital or extramarital sexual activity are a part of life in certain traditional areas of the Islamic world, including Jordan, Saudi Arabia, Egypt, Bangladesh, Pakistan, and Sudan. In Palestinian villages, according to some estimates, about 40 women a year die at the hands of a male relative—who then becomes a hero for clearing his family name (Brooks, 1995). This type of killing is not necessarily done in a rage, but is sometimes planned and premeditated. The men of the family may gather to vote on the death of the woman and to decide who will carry out the killing. An errant daughter or wife may be lured home with the promise that all is forgiven, then cold-bloodedly murdered. The men may assign the killing to a boy, such as the woman's younger brother, who will receive a lighter prison sentence because of his youth. In any case, shorter prison terms are permitted in some countries, such as Turkey and Jordan, for "honor" crimes than for similar crimes committed for other reasons (Moore, 2001b; United Nations Children's Fund, 2000).

Such killings sometimes take place among families who have emigrated to non-Muslim countries or from more traditional rural areas to cities in which they must reconcile modern lifestyles and freedoms with rural customs that have endured for generations. Researchers estimate that at least 200 girls and women are murdered by their families in Turkey each year as part of this practice, most among families who have moved from villages to rapidly growing modern cities (Moore, 2001a). The United Nations estimates that 5,000 women and girls worldwide were killed by family members for actions that brought "dishonor" to the family, and human rights groups fear that honor killings are increasing in many parts of the world (Moore, 2001b). The killings are likely to be an expression of the feeling that, within the feudal, patriarchal value system that defines these families' tradition, an impoverished family's honor is its only valuable possession. Yet these murders often do not receive official support from the country in which they take place or from the religion, Islam, in whose name they are carried out. For example, in 2000, General Musharraf, the Chief Executive of Pakistan, where hundreds of women are killed each year for "honor," noted that such killings would be treated as murder in his country: "The Government of Pakistan vigorously condemns the practice of so-called 'honour killing.' Such actions do not find any place in our religion or our law" (quoted in United Nations Children's Fund, 2000, p. 6). And Pakistani lawyer, Nayyar Shebana, of a women's advocacy group in Islamabad, notes that it is traditional culture, not religion, that sanctions honor killings: "The concept of honor killing does not exist in Islamic law, but conservative tradition is very strong in our culture. Islam gives rights to women, but society snuffs them out" (quoted in Constable, 2000, p. A16).

Although they are not legally sanctioned, wife murders that arise from jealousy, outraged pride, or wounded egos certainly happen with some frequency in most countries, including the United States and Canada. In both countries, wives are the most frequent victims of fatal violence in families—and such fatal violence is most likely to occur when the woman tries to leave an abusive husband (Pagelow, 1993).

While some stories of male violence against the women in their families are more horrific than others, common themes runs through them: The woman is considered the man's property; the man is believed entitled to wield authority over the woman and to punish her if she defies this authority; the family is viewed as a private institution where the man rules and outsiders should not interfere; the woman is regarded as inferior to the man. These patriarchal cultural attitudes emerge in the courtship violence documented in certain countries, in the wife beatings that occur all over the world, in bride burnings and honor killings. These attitudes are woven into the fabric of many cultures, although their expression is more subtle in some times and places than others and some individuals have been socialized with a stronger dose of them than others in their culture. A decrease in cultural support for violence against wives and daughters would reduce the risks to women around the globe.

Patriarchal attitudes spill over to affect not only violence against women within families, but sanctioned societal violence against all women who violate standards of approved behavior. For example, in many countries prostitutes are at risk of violence because they are considered bad women. If they are beaten or raped, they may have no legal recourse (Koss, Heise, & Russo, 1994), and they may even have to fear the police. In a stark and extreme illustration of this phenomenon, Taliban authorities in Afghanistan gathered hundreds of people in a sports stadium to witness the public hanging of two women convicted of prostitution (Taliban publicly executes 2 Afghan women, 2001). But a woman does not have to be a prostitute to risk death for breaking the rules of "honorable" female behavior. A court in the northern Nigerian state of Sokoto sentenced a woman, Safiya Hussaini Tungar Dudu, to death by stoning for engaging in premarital sex (Nigerian woman sentenced to death for having sex, 2001). Clearly, the attitude that women must conform to restrictive rules defined and enforced by men is a dangerous one for women. However, there are some signs of hope. After an international outcry, Safiya Hussaini's death sentence was overturned by an Islamic appeals court in 2002. In 2003, a second Nigerian women, Amina Lawal, won an appeal against death by stoning for adultery, on the grounds that she had not been caught in the act and had not been given enough opportunity to defend herself (Amina Lawal wins appeal, 2003). Yet the principle that death is an appropriate punishment for a woman who commits adultery remains in place in the northern Nigerian state of Zamfara.

Violence in Lesbian Couples

Not all violence against women in close relationships comes from men. Even in female couples, a pattern of abuse of one partner by the other can develop. Thus it is clear that patriarchal attitudes are not the only factor underlying violence in close relationships.

Until the 1980s, little public information about violence in lesbian relationships was available. Researchers ignored the issue, perhaps because they assumed that violence would not occur between two women, or perhaps because they underestimated the importance of lesbian relationships. Lesbians who were experiencing violence in their relationships rarely talked about it outside the lesbian community, perhaps fearing that such information would give society one more excuse to be homophobic. But researchers have begun to document the occurrence of partner abuse among lesbians, and they now believe the prevalence of domestic violence in lesbian and heterosexual relationships to be similar, with an incidence rate of between 25 percent and 50 percent (Alexander, 2002; Fortunata & Kohn, 2003). Although most of this research has been done with respondents in the United States, there is at least one study documenting the occurrence of violence in same-gender couples in Venezuela (Burke, Jordan, & Owen, 2002). Little documentation about this issue in other parts of the world exists as yet.

Common triggers for verbal and physical abuse in lesbian couples seem to be conflict around issues of commitment to the relationship, jealousy, and autonomy or dependency—a pattern that is similar to that for male–female couples (Lockhart et al., 1994). Some research indicates that, similar to the pattern often observed in male–female couples, violence in lesbian relationships tends to increase in frequency and severity over time (Renzetti, 1992). There is also suggestive evidence that such violence may be associated with the use of alcohol or drugs (Schilit, Lie, & Montagne, 1990) and with the prior experience of abuse as a child (Lockhart et al., 1994). Both of the latter associations require further investigation. On the whole, the research literature tends to suggest that the factors that predict intimate partner violence in lesbian couples are similar in many ways to those that predict intimate partner violence in heterosexual couples and that there is a necessity for providers of physical and mental health services to be alert for the effects of such violence (Burke & Follingstad, 1999).

The growing evidence that intimate partner abuse occurs in same-gender couples with about the same frequency as in mixed-gender couples reminds us that we do not yet understand all the reasons for such violence. An analysis of domestic violence that focuses only on the power and control exerted by a man over a female partner obviously cannot explain the abuse that goes on in lesbian relationships. In fact, at least one theorist has argued that the overreliance on this explanation has contributed to the invisibility and denial of violence in lesbian couples (Ristock, 2002). Janice Ristock argues that another way to look at the violence that occurs in some couple relationships is that power and control can shift back and forth: A member of a couple may be a victim of violence during one period of the relationship and a perpetrator during another period. Domestic violence is complicated, she points out, and those who seek to prevent violence in lesbian relationships must recognize such complications. As theorists examine violence in lesbian relationships, it is likely that they will discover new perspectives on couple violence in general. As is often the case, looking closely at a problem that has been treated as invisible may change researchers' viewpoints on a wider range of issues.

Explaining Partner Abuse

Why is violence so common in intimate relationships? And what determines why certain people become abusive toward their partners and others do not? An understanding of the destructive patterns of partner abuse can be gleaned only by analyzing them at several levels: the sociopolitical/cultural level, the interpersonal dynamics level, and the level of individual personality and temperament (Coleman, 1994).

A *sociopolitical* or *cultural* analysis of partner abuse focuses on the ways cultural beliefs, social structures, and political factors contribute to and support the occurrence of the violence. Using this analysis, it is easy to conclude that the atmosphere of patriarchal societies, which approve and even reward male domination, female subordination, and the exertion of male control over women through violence if necessary, promotes male violence against women—and in particular the violence of husbands against wives. Another sociopolitical factor supportive of antifemale violence would be the rigidity of gender roles and expectations—the narrower the role, the more likely it is that a woman will be motivated to stray from it, thus eliciting anger from her husband. Yet a third sociopolitical factor in domestic violence might be the prevalence of stressors such as poverty, social isolation, or discrimination, causing frustration or self-hatred that erupts in violence against a partner.

At first, it is easier to see how the sociopolitical factors listed above can help explain men's violence against their female partners than to see how they might apply to violence in lesbian partnerships. However, as Valerie Coleman (1994) notes,

> Since we live within a cultural atmosphere of hierarchical structures and patriarchal values, the predominant model for intimate relationships is one of domination and subordination. These values and relationship norms are internalized by women, as well as by men. Consequently, even in a lesbian relationship there is a heightened potential for one partner to seek domination and control over the other. (p. 141)

At the level of *interpersonal dynamics,* the occurrence of partner abuse can be analyzed using *social learning theory* and *social power perspective.* Social learning theory, which says individuals learn behavioral strategies that they feel are effective by watching other people, suggests that the reason people learn to use violence is that they observe it works. In line with this idea, researchers have noted over the years that children who grow up in families where they see others being abused or are abused themselves are more likely to use violence in later relationships (Coleman, 1994). If the use of violence in later relationships works (i.e., if the abuser successfully exerts control over the victim and/or gets what he or she wants), then violence as a strategy is reinforced and will likely increase in frequency.

However, violence does *not* always work as a control mechanism in relationships. In some cases, the target of the violence may strike back or leave or press charges. The person using violence in an intimate relationship usually does so in the belief that it will control the partner, that the partner will put up with it, and that the abuser will suffer no disastrous consequences (such as being arrested, fired from a job, or ostracized by family and friends). What contributes to such a belief in violence as an effective and safe strategy? The abuser must have a sense of possessing greater social power in the relationship than the partner does. Perhaps this sense of power is based on the perception that the partner is emotionally or financially dependent and could not leave. Perhaps it is based on the perception that the partner is socially isolated and has nowhere else to go. Or perhaps it is based on the perception that, culturally, a man is allowed, even expected, to make his wife toe the line by using violence if necessary.

Already it should be obvious that the sociopolitical and interpersonal levels of analysis cannot be cleanly separated. The social and cultural environment, through the promulgation of particular attitudes and values about families, shapes the likelihood that children will be raised in families where they witness or are victims of violence. Similarly, culture shapes attitudes about the legitimacy of male domination and female subordination and about the social acceptability of using violence in many situations. Will the police respond to and take seriously a charge of spousal violence? If not, the abuser has more power. The availability of alternatives in the social environment also affects the likelihood that the victim of violence will leave the relationship. Does she have access to a shelter for victims of abuse? Can she live safely on her own? If not, the abuser has more power. Thus power in interpersonal relationships is, to some extent, shaped by the values and attitudes promoted in the sociopolitical and cultural environment.

Individual personality is also a factor in domestic violence. In both male–female and lesbian couples, abusers are frequently identified as having particular characteristics such as feelings of powerlessness, fear of abandonment, dependency, and low self-esteem. In some cases, these characteristics are rigid and extreme enough that a psychiatrist would label them as borderline or narcissistic personality disorders (Coleman, 1994). Some abusers, particularly males, have many antisocial traits, such as a seeming inability to empathize with others and an absence of guilt or concern about harming others.

An understanding of the personality characteristics associated with partner abuse may encourage the use of therapy to help an abuser break the patterns of domestic violence. However, to the extent that personalities are shaped by the cultural and interpersonal environments in which an individual has been raised, this level of analysis is also interrelated with the previous two. For instance, in most cultures antisocial behavior is more acceptable among men than among women. It must also be remembered that the cultural and interpersonal environment have a strong influence on how individual personality and temperament are expressed in behavior. In a strongly patriarchal culture, a woman who fears abandonment may cling, cry, and plead; a man who fears abandonment may beat his wife so that she is afraid to do anything that makes him feel jealous or insecure.

Sex-Selective Abortion, Infanticide, and Systematic Neglect of Girls

In North America, it is traditional for parents to wish for a son to carry on the family name —and sometimes the family business. There is a lingering tendency to value sons over daughters and to perceive daughters as more burdensome to raise (e.g., parents have to worry about a daughter's becoming pregnant before marriage; the bride's parents are expected to pay for the wedding). This preference represents the remnants of a long, now substantially weakened tradition in which males were valued more highly than females.

The tendency to value males over females is still so strong in some cultures that, as noted in Chapter 7, parents may use abortion, or even infanticide, to ensure that they will not have to raise a daughter. In China, where government policy prohibits parents from having more than one child, many parents try to make sure that their one child will be a boy by aborting female fetuses. One survey in China revealed that 12 percent of all female embryos were aborted or otherwise "unaccounted for" (United Nations Children's Fund, 2000). Similarly, in India, sex-selective abortion is common, and it is estimated that as many as 10,000 infant girls are killed each year by being abandoned, starved, or poisoned (United Nations Children's Fund, 2000). In that country, clinics have been known to advertise their abortion services by declaring it is better to spend 500 rupees today (for a sex determination test and possible abortion) than to spend 500,000 rupees later at the time of the girl's marriage (Narasimhan, 1994). Indeed, the abortion of female fetuses is so common in India that the ratio of women to men in that country is only 93 to 100 (remember that most countries have *more* women than men). In China, the sex ratio at birth is 120 boys to every 100 girls—the highest ratio of male to female births in the world, and the ratio of boys to girls rises as high as 138 in some parts of the country (Riley, 2004).

In many countries, girls are discriminated against in nutrition and access to medical care. When parents have few resources, they spend them preferentially on boys. Thus, girls are more likely to suffer disability or death at a young age. The discrimination that leads to the neglect of girls is the greatest cause of illness and death among girls aged 2 to 5 years in some countries (United Nations Children's Fund, 2000).

Female infanticide, sex-selective abortion, and systematic neglect of female children stem from and perpetuate the devaluation of female lives. For example, traditional values in India have portrayed daughters as economic and social burdens. To get a daughter into a respectable marriage, parents must often impoverish themselves providing a dowry. Only sons are expected to support their parents in old age; daughters must be married off and then they *belong* to their husband's families. When parents die, only sons, not daughters, can perform the religious rites that are considered necessary to benefit their souls. For all these reasons, parents may feel that a daughter is a liability.

The devaluing of females to the point where parents do not feel it is worthwhile to have a daughter has, through the practices described here, led to the phenomenon known as the "missing millions" of women and girls. According to the United Nations Children's Fund (2000), "An estimated 60 million women are simply missing from the population statistics. In other words there are 60 million fewer women alive in the world than should be expected on the basis of general demographic trends. The phenomenon is observed primarily in South Asia, North Africa, the Middle East, and China" (p. 6).

Sexual Violence

A judge in New Zealand provoked a storm of protest when he commented, at the conclusion of a rape trial, that the world would be a much less exciting place if every man in history had stopped his sexual advances the first time a woman said no (Reuters, 1996b). A survey of psychiatrists in the United States revealed that despite research that shows a victim's attire to be an insignificant factor in sex crimes, the vast majority of them believed sexy clothing worn by women was part of the reason rapes occur (Sexy clothing, 1991). It appears that in the minds of some people, rape and other forms of sexual assault are the result of sexual passion rather than aggressive urges—and that there is something titillating about a woman being forced.

Yet **rape, sexual abuse,** and **sexual harassment** are more likely to be crimes of opportunity, planning, and sometimes even ritual and group-participatory aggression than of male sexual urges gone wild.

Rape

At St. Kitzo secondary school in Kenya, 19 girls died of suffocation in 1991 when they crowded into a tiny room to escape a rampaging gang of male students. One teacher regretted the tragedy, but apparently found it inexplicable that the girls had been so terrified. After all, she commented, "the boys did not mean the girls any harm. They only wanted to rape them" (Okie, 1993b, p. A24).

> ## BOX 13.2 MAKING CHANGE
> **Take Back the Night**
>
> Most campuses hold a yearly "Take back the night" march to protest antifemale violence and to empower women. Sometimes it is during October, the month that has been nationally designated as a time to focus on combating violence against women. Sometimes it is in March, Women's History Month. Attending this march and rally is a way to add your voice to the fight to make women's lives safe from violence. Helping with the organization of the event and bringing your friends along are even stronger steps.

One Kenyan father of an 18-year-old girl who was raped by a neighbor on her way home from school found this teacher's comment to be an expression of the tolerance for rape in Kenya and in other African countries. Rape, he noted sadly, "has been taken as a normal thing happening to a woman. . . . people don't take rape seriously" (Okie, 1993b, p. A24).

Indeed, in much of the world rape is not taken particularly seriously and is, in certain cases, condoned and socially approved. Consider the old saying, occasionally revived by insensitive politicians and judges, that "if rape is inevitable, a woman should just lie back and enjoy it." Yet this particular form of violence against women and girls has chilling consequences in terms of social and sexual relationships, as well as in terms of women's physical and emotional health.

The Scope of Rape   In 2002, the rate of forcible rape in the United States reported to the Federal Bureau of Investigation was 64.8 per 100,000 females age 12 or older, a total of 95,136 assaults (Federal Bureau of Investigation, 2002). And there are probably many rapes that are not reported: Almost 8 percent of U.S. women report that their first heterosexual intercourse was not voluntary (National Center for Health Statistics, 2000). These numbers come from crime statistics, acknowledged by most experts to be underestimates of the true frequency of rape because of the underreporting of this crime. In large-scale surveys in the United States, 14 percent to 25 percent of women report being the victims of rape or attempted rape, but only a small minority of those women say they reported the incident to the police (Koss, 1993). A recent study of the prevalence of sexual assault on U.S. Air Force bases concluded that the problem was more serious than officials had thought, and that as many as 95 percent of such assaults might not be reported (Assault study finds problem is widespread in Air Force, 2004). Cross-national studies of college students in Canada, New Zealand, the United Kingdom, the United States, and Korea show that the lifetime rate of being the victim of completed and attempted rape among female college students is above 20 percent across all these countries; researchers have also found that in all countries studied, the majority of rapists are known to their victims and that many of the victims are girls age 15 or younger (Koss, Heise, & Russo, 1994). A recent survey sponsored by the Department of Justice found that during a single academic year, 1.7 percent of U.S. college women were raped and another 1.1 percent were victims of attempted rape. Furthermore, a full 13 percent were stalked (Fisher, Cullen & Turner, 2000).

For many people, the stereotypical notion of rape involves an assault by a stranger in a dark alley. In reality, more than half of all rapes in the United States are committed by friends or acquaintances of the victims, and more than one-quarter are committed by someone with whom the victim has or formerly had an intimate relationship. In 2002, only 28 percent of rapes reported to the FBI in the United States were committed by people who were strangers to the victim (Rennison & Rand, 2003). So powerful is the stereotype of stranger rape that many women who have been raped by acquaintances or intimates do not label the incident "rape," even though they have been traumatized (Fisher, Cullen, & Turner, 2000). Thus researchers frequently find that a woman will answer yes to the question "Have you ever had sex with a man when you did not want to, because he used physical force against you?" but at the same time say no when asked if she has ever been raped (Allison & Wrightsman, 1993).

Under what conditions would a woman who has been pushed or coerced into unwanted sex *not* call such coercion rape? According to researchers, women are less likely to label such an experience rape if they gave in to a whining boyfriend or emotionally needy man, were assaulted by a boyfriend, were impaired by drugs or alcohol and thus not able to resist, or were forced to engage in oral or digital sex. They are most likely to label the experience rape if they knew the assailant less well, were more forcefully assaulted, woke up with a man penetrating them, had strong negative reactions to the experience, or had been sexually assaulted as children (Kahn, 2004; Kahn, Jackson, Kully, Badger, & Halvorsen, 2003).

One reason women may be reluctant to label a coercive sexual experience as rape is that people's ideas about rape and seduction overlap. For example, university students identify as an element of rape the use of manipulative tactics by a man to obtain sex. However, they also identify the use of such tactics as an element of seduction (Littleton & Axsom, 2003). Also, many adolescents and young adults accept social "rules" that specify certain situations under which it is legitimate for a man to initiate sex with a woman even if she does not intend or desire it. In one study, many respondents, particularly males, indicated that it is OK for a man to assume a woman wants to have sex if she "doesn't resist physically," "doesn't say no," "teases," or has an "easy reputation" (Anderson, Simpson-Taylor, & Herrmann, 2004). When Gail Zellman and Jacquelyn Goodchilds (1983) questioned a large sample of Los Angeles teenagers, only 21 percent of them replied that under each of nine specific conditions, it was definitely not all right for "a guy to hold a girl down and force her to have sexual intercourse." Force was viewed as most acceptable when the girl had led the boy on or gotten him sexually excited, or when the couple had been dating for a long time. Both male and female teenagers were reluctant to define forced sex as rape, especially when the couple involved was portrayed as dating steadily, and they tended to assign some of the blame for forced sex to the female.

Even when an experience is acknowledged as rape, it may be viewed as less grave if it was perpetrated by a boyfriend or acquaintance. A study of Turkish university students revealed that date rape was considered less serious than stranger rape (Gölge, Yavuz, Müderrisoglu, & Yavuz, 2003).

One of the difficulties with assessing the prevalence of rape, especially across cultures, is that researchers have not always agreed on a definition of rape. Patricia Rozée (1993) notes that the traditional, and narrowest, definition of rape—nonconsensual, forcible, sexual intercourse with a female—leaves out some of the most violent cases of rape, such as penetration with objects, and also excludes anal or oral intercourse, nonforcible intercourse with underage and incapacitated victims, and also male victims. It also ignores situations in which society may condone the man's behavior even though the woman involved has not given her consent—a situation Rozée terms **normative rape**.

Normative rape situations may include marital rape, ceremonial rape, the rape of servants or slaves by their masters, and the rape of enemy women during wartime. In such cases, force may or may not be used, but the woman has no option to refuse. Historically, for example, this category would include the routine rape of Black female slaves by White masters in the United States, which was not acknowledged as rape at the time because the slaveholder was simply claiming access to his "property." Also included would be the current practices of wedding-night defloration in some societies, in which young girl-brides are forced to submit to intercourse without any prior instruction in sexuality—and without any say in whether and to whom they will be married. Similarly, it would include the use of Korean "comfort women" (sexual slaves) by the Japanese army during World War II and the sexual exploitation of female servants by wealthy masters that has been documented in all corners of the world. It would also include the rapes that have taken place on a massive scale during recent wars in Bosnia, Somalia, Cambodia, and other countries. During the conflict in Rwanda in 1994, rape was systematically used as a weapon; even elderly women, pregnant women, and children were raped. The systematic use of rape has also been documented in Kosovo in 1999 and in East Timor in 1999 (United Nations, 2000).

Patricia Rozée (1993) has argued, and most people who study rape now agree, that the key feature of rape is a lack of choice by the woman to engage in sexual intercourse. A lack of choice "is assumed where there is use of force, threat of force, or coercion; presence of multiple males; physical pain, loss of consciousness, or death; or when the woman is punished or suffers some other negative outcome if she refuses" (p. 502). Under this definition, Rozée found that rape occurs in almost all societies: Normative rape occurred in 97 percent of the cultures she studied. In other words, almost every society has some rules and customs that *allow* men to violate women sexually under certain conditions. Nonnormative rape, "illicit, uncondoned genital contact that is both against the will of the woman and in violation of social norms for expected behavior" (p. 504), occurs in about two-thirds of societies.

A study by Peggy Reeves Sanday (1981) of 156 societies revealed some differences between those in which both normative and nonnormative rape were common and those in which they were rare. Rape most commonly exists in a context of violence, particularly violence against women, Sanday found. Highly rape-prone societies tended to be those in which the use of violence was approved, rape was routinely used to punish or threaten women, violence against women was likely to be tolerated or overlooked, and women had little power relative to men. Sanday's analysis may tell us something about why rape happens so often in the United States: The United Sates is the industrialized country with the highest rate of violence in the world, a country where violence is frequently celebrated in the media (Allison & Wrightsman, 1993).

Attitudes toward Rape and Rape Victims   Obviously, when rape falls into the category of "normative," there is less, if any, disapproval of the rapist and less sympathy and more blame extended to the victim. In many cultural contexts, women who transgress the bounds of "proper" feminine behavior are considered to deserve rape. For example, the notion that a prostitute cannot be raped is common in many societies. In some Latin American countries —Costa Rica, Ecuador, Guatemala—the law has not recognized forced sexual intercourse as rape unless the woman is chaste and honest (Heise, Pitanguy, & Germain, 1993), and in the courts of Pakistan, the testimony of women who are deemed to be of "easy virtue" is heavily discounted. A woman who is categorized as inferior, promiscuous, or insubordinate is often considered to have wanted, or at least deserved, to be raped. Pakistani courts do not even necessarily allow such a woman to testify, and any woman who brings a complaint of rape is likely to be disbelieved and treated with disrespect (United Nations Population Fund, 2000).

important

North American researchers have demonstrated the existence of a widely held set of myths and misconceptions about rape and rape victims (Burt, 1980; Feild, 1978). These myths center on the notions that women can prevent rape if they really want to, that victims precipitate rape by their appearance and behavior, that women secretly want to be raped, and that rapists are motivated by an uncontrollable desire for sex. These ideas have all been discredited. For example, girls and women of every age and appearance—from toddlers to elderly women—are raped, making it clear that a woman does not have to entice a rapist by looking seductive or sexy. And rapists are not sex-starved; most have other outlets for their sexual wants, and many are married (Allison & Wrightsman, 1993). Nonetheless, the myths remain prevalent and tend to encourage the practice of blaming rape victims for their assault.

The acceptance of **rape myths** tends to be linked to other attitudes. People who hold strong gender role stereotypes and strong beliefs that sexual relationships are fundamentally exploitative and manipulative are more likely than other people to believe in rape myths. Acceptance of interpersonal violence—the idea that force and coercion are acceptable ways of persuading others—is a strong predictor of rape myth acceptance (Burt, 1980). Individuals who agree with rape myths are also more likely than others to be prejudiced against other groups and to have personality traits such as rigidity and lack of empathy (Leak, Masciotra, Panza, & Unruh, 1992).

The Impact of Rape   Rape has been called a global health issue for women (Koss et al., 1994). It is well documented that victims of rape suffer psychological, physical, and behavioral consequences. A woman who has been raped may be disturbed by intrusive memories of the event, debilitating anxiety, and a compulsive need to avoid any reminder of the rape. She may blame herself for the rape and suffer from guilt and low self-esteem. Survivors of a single rape often continue to experience negative symptoms for years afterward, and women who have been raped show, years later, higher levels than other women of psychiatric diagnoses such as depression, alcohol and drug dependence, generalized anxiety, obsessive-compulsive disorder, and post-traumatic stress disorder (Koss et al., 1994).

Physical effects of rape begin with injuries caused by the perpetrator during the rape. However, as Mary Koss and her colleagues (1994) note, rape is often a significant risk factor for suicide and murder. In some societies, a woman who has been raped may be blamed for the violation and be considered so permanently stained or dishonored that she is killed by a relative or driven to suicide. In a study of women murdered in Alexandria, Egypt, 47 percent turned out to be rape victims who had been killed by a relative (Graitcer & Youssef, 1993, cited in Koss et al., 1994). Other possible physical consequences of rape are pregnancy and sexually transmitted diseases. Women are much more likely than men to become infected with a sexually transmitted disease during intercourse with an infected partner, and STDs are contracted by 4 percent to 30 percent of rape victims in the United States (Koss et al., 1994). Statistics from rape crisis centers in Mexico, Thailand, and Korea indicate that between 15 percent and 18 percent of rape victims who come to these clinics are pregnant as a result of a rape, and in the United States rape results in pregnancy in about 5 percent of cases (Koss et al., 1994). Faced with the prospect of a forced pregnancy and bearing the rapist's child, women often seek abortions. This quest can lead to serious health problems and even death in countries where abortion is illegal and performed under dangerous conditions.

Even in the absence of pregnancy or sexually transmitted diseases, the aftermath of rape is associated with a range of chronic health problems such as pelvic pain, headaches, gastrointestinal disorders, sexual problems, and premenstrual symptoms. One large study in the United States showed that women with a history of being sexually assaulted were more likely than other women to experience excessive menstrual bleeding, genital burning, painful intercourse, irregular or painful menstrual periods, and lack of sexual pleasure. The reproductive problems (menstrual irregularities) were more likely to occur among women who had been assaulted in a physically violent way by strangers; sexual symptoms (painful intercourse, lack of sexual pleasure) were more likely to be experienced by women who had been the victims of multiple assaults, assaults accomplished by persuasion rather than physical force, or assault by a spouse (Golding, 1996).

Jacqueline M. Golding's (1996) study also revealed some ethnic differences in women's symptoms after sexual assault: Sexual assault was more strongly linked with symptoms for African American and Latina women than for European American women. The author suggests that this difference reflects the exacerbation of the stress of sexual assault by the stress of chronic racism. Being a victim of sexual assault was more strongly linked to menstrual irregularity among African American than European American women —a finding that may be explained by differences in the kinds of assaults women from these two groups reported. The assaults reported by African American women were most likely to involve physical threat. Latina women were more likely than other women to report sexual indifference in the aftermath of rape. Golding speculates that because Latino cultural values place such high importance on women's virginity—and on a woman's duty to guard her virginity—Latina women are especially vulnerable to sexual problems after having been raped.

One of the most insidious possible consequences of sexual assault may be vulnerability to revictimization. A number of retrospective studies have shown that women who are sexually assaulted are more likely than other women to report that they have been sexually assaulted before and that rape victims are more likely than other women to report having been sexually abused as children (e.g., Sorenson, Siegel, Golding, & Stein, 1991; Wyatt, Guthrie, & Notgrass, 1992). Findings in this area are quite consistent; however, such retrospective studies cannot rule out the possibility that victims of sexual assault are simply more likely than other adults to *remember* earlier assaults.

In an effort to rule out this possibility, several researchers have conducted prospective studies, in which women are assessed for their sexual abuse histories and then followed for

In the United States, women who use alcohol while dating and who engage in high levels of consensual sex are more likely to be sexually victimized in college. Researchers suggest that sexually coercive men tend to target women who engage in these behaviors.

a certain period of time to see whether these histories predict later victimization. In one such study, researchers assessed college women's sexual victimization experiences, family adjustment, alcohol use, psychological adjustment, interpersonal functioning, and sexual behavior at the beginning of an academic year, and then reevaluated them 3, 5–6, and 9 months later (Gidycz, Hanson, & Layman, 1995). They found that the more severely a woman had been sexually victimized during one time period covered by the study, the more likely she was to be victimized again during the next time period. They also found some, albeit inconclusive, support for the idea that revictimization is partially mediated by poor adjustment. In other words, a person who has been victimized once may have a shaken sense of self-esteem and may feel powerless and unworthy and thus more vulnerable to the next attempt to victimize her.

In another study, in which 100 women were surveyed as they entered college and then assessed again 32 months later, sexual victimization during college was strongly predicted by precollege sexual victimization in dating relationships (Himelein, 1995). In this study, alcohol use in dating and higher levels of consensual sex were correlated with both precollege and college victimization, suggesting that sexually coercive men may target women who engage in these behaviors.

The impact of sexual assault spreads beyond the victim to her family, friends, and even her therapists. In one revealing study, Laura Schauben and Patricia Frazier (1995) showed that counselors who work with sexual violence survivors can pay a high emotional price themselves. Counselors who had a greater percentage of sexual assault victims in their caseload reported more symptoms of post-traumatic stress disorder and more vicarious trauma (e.g., nightmares, heightened fears, increased feelings of vulnerability) in themselves. Some also reported changes in their beliefs about the world, such as becoming less trusting of men and losing a sense of innocence about people's basic goodness. Some said it was difficult to listen to the details of particularly horrific abuse—and also difficult to forget it after hearing it. On the positive side, however, these counselors reported that they appreciated watching their clients grow and change, even in the face of terrible trauma and pain, and turn from "victims" into "survivors." Even while their work with sexual violence survivors shook their faith in human goodness in some ways, it also gave them confidence in the human spirit's capacity for strength and resilience even in the face of violence.

In any consideration of the impact of rape, it is important to note that such impact is shaped by the sociocultural context in which the survivor lives. As we have already seen, rape is often considered a stain on a woman's reputation, and in some cultures that stain is seen as so serious and so permanent that the woman is considered to have become worthless. Obviously, such cultural values will influence the meaning that a woman attaches to being raped, and thus her emotional response.

Researchers who study stress note that a person's response to a potentially stressful event is determined not by the event itself, but by her cognitive appraisal of her experience, how she interprets it and how it fits into her personal view of the world (Lazarus, 1991). A woman's cognitive appraisal of a rape would be influenced by her own personal history and temperament as well as by her sociocultural context. Variables such as family history, personality, whether and to what extent she has been previously traumatized, the coping styles she has learned, her ethnicity, class, and sexual orientation, and the norms and values of her community with respect to gender, sexuality, and violence are all likely to help shape her emotional response to being raped.

Although that point may seem obvious, little systematic research has been done about the ways women from different groups experience and cope with rape. When different groups are compared, few disparities are found; however, this may be because the measuring instruments, usually designed for White, middle-class, North American college students, do not include items that would show differences. For example, Lily McNair and Helen Neville (1996) indicate that more African American than European American women and men use "prayer" as a general coping mechanism, but questionnaires measuring coping responses to rape do not include references to religious practices.

Gail Wyatt (1992) notes that one difference between African American and European American women is that the latter are more likely to disclose the incident to significant others and to report it to agencies such as rape crisis centers and police. Suggesting sociocultural reasons for this difference, McNair and Neville (1996) point out the long history of mistrust between African American communities and various official agencies. Furthermore, they argue, stereotypical perceptions of African American women work against the desire to disclose and seek help for the rape. The perception that Black women are supposed to be strong, domineering, and matriarchal may keep some women from admitting the vulnerability that seeking help implies. Another persistent stereotype portrays Black women as promiscuous, a stereotype rooted in the era of slavery when White masters justified their routine sexual exploitation of Black female slaves by claiming that the women were lascivious and wanted sex. So successfully was this stereotype promoted that the credibility of Black women rape victims was always suspect, and it was not until the late 1960s that a White man was convicted for raping a Black woman in any Southern state (D. G. White, 1985). In view of this history, Black women may be reluctant to report a rape for fear that they themselves will be blamed for the assault.

Stereotypes and a long history of injustice surrounding Black men may also be a factor in a woman's reluctance to disclose a rape if the assailant is an African American. African American men have historically been unfairly accused of and punished for rape with a high frequency in the United States, and African American women may feel they should protect these men from perceived and actual biases in the justice system (McNair & Neville, 1996).

We have been focusing on the impact of rape on individuals, but it would be a mistake to leave this subject without considering its impact in societal terms as well. Mary Koss and her colleagues (1994) pointed out that the economic costs to a society of women's victimization are extremely high. In the United States, women who have been physically and sexually assaulted in the past visit their physicians twice as often as women who have not been victimized, making the cost of their medical care 2.5 times higher than that of non-victimized women. On a global scale, gender-based victimization accounts for an astounding percentage of the healthy years of life lost to women because of incapacitation or premature death. Koss and her co-authors note that the World Bank has calculated that gender-based victimization (rape and domestic violence) accounts for almost 20 percent of healthy years of life lost to women ages 15 to 44 in developed countries, 16 percent in developing countries where maternal mortality and poverty-related diseases are under relative control, and 5 percent in developing countries overall. This global health burden is comparable to that imposed by other diseases or risk factors such as AIDS, tuberculosis, sepsis during childbirth, cancer, and heart disease.

Sexual Abuse of Children

Examined within a global context, the line between adult rape or sexual assault and child sexual abuse is blurry. For example, a 14-year-old girl may be considered a child in one culture, a grown woman in another. Nonetheless, it is clear from international data that the sexual abuse of young children is prevalent worldwide (Finkelhor, 1994); 40 to 60 percent of sexual assaults within families are perpetrated against girls 15 years old or younger, regardless of what part of the world is being examined (United Nations Children's Fund, 2000). One report indicates that children in Nicaragua listed sexual abuse as the most important health priority facing them in their country (Rompiendo el Silencio, 1992). In the United States, more than 22 percent of women who report that their age at first intercourse was less than 15 years say that their first intercourse was not voluntary (National Center for Health Statistics, 2000). In a random sample of 13- to 14-year-old girls in Jamaica, 17 percent reported that they had experienced attempted or completed rape, half of these before age 12 (United Nations, 2000). A survey of ninth-grade students in Geneva, Switzerland, found that 20 percent of the girls had experienced at least one incident of sexual abuse (United Nations, 2000). Mary Koss and her colleagues (1994) note a trend in many parts of the world for men to seek out younger and younger sexual partners, apparently because they believe younger girls will be free of HIV. In Africa, it has become common to see girls as young as 8 or 9 years old with HIV infections due to rapes by their fathers, uncles, or neighbors. Believing that sex with a virgin is not only safer but can bring mystical powers—or even a cure for AIDS—men in Africa seek out younger and younger girls. The United Nations has found that sexual abuse in the home is a significant reason why many young girls run away. But for many, running away means being exposed to the commercial sex trade on the streets. With as many as 1 in 4 adult men infected with HIV in some parts of Africa, the danger to young victims of sexual abuse is immense (Murphy, 1998).

Many of the effects of childhood sexual abuse are similar to, but even more intense and harmful than, the effects of being sexually assaulted as an adult. Girls are even more likely than adult women to become infected with STDs as a result of rape because at younger ages the reproductive tract is more vulnerable to them. Studies from Nigeria and Uganda have found that up to 16 percent of female patients seeking treatment for STDs were under 5 years of age and as many as 22 percent are under the age of 10 (Koss et al., 1994).

Being sexually abused as a child can have a profound impact on later emotional well-being. Adults who were sexually abused as children are considerably more likely than other adults to have psychiatric problems (Burnham et al., 1988). This early abuse also has strong implications for revictimization: As adults, victims of child abuse are more than twice as likely as their nonabused counterparts to be raped (Wyatt et al., 1992). Studies show that childhood sexual abuse is associated with an increased probability of later use of drugs and alcohol and of entering prostitution (Koss et al., 1994).

Female genital mutilation, discussed in Chapter 3, can be considered a form of child sexual abuse. The operation, in which the clitoris is cut away, is usually performed on girls younger than 8 and frequently results in pain, infection, and later complications associated with sexual intercourse and childbirth. Even more seriously, it is associated with high mortality. Some 80 million women are estimated to have been "circumcised" in this way, most from African countries, Oman, South Yemen, the United Arab Emirates, Indonesia, and Malaysia (Arbesman, Kahler, & Buck, 1993). The operation is intended to make girls acceptable later as brides by guaranteeing their chastity. The effect is to underline the notion that women are property and must be kept "in good condition."

Forced Prostitution and Sex Slavery

During the 1930s and 1940s, Japan forced or coerced some 200,000 girls and women into serving as sex slaves, euphemistically named "comfort women," for Japanese soldiers fighting in Asia during the Second World War. These women, mostly from Korea, but also from other Asian countries, were taken to "comfort stations" near the front, where they were repeatedly raped, sometimes by as many as 30 to 40 men a day (Miller, 2001). In 2001, these women failed in an attempt to win compensation from the Japanese government for their suffering, although that government has expressed deep remorse and apology for the actions of the Japanese military.

It would be nice to think that forcing women and girls into prostitution and sex slavery is a thing of the past. But consider this recent account from a Nepali woman of 19, who was rescued from a brothel in Bombay when she was 15:

> I never saw the sun rise or set because the windows were always locked. Every night they sent me 10 or 15 customers. Sometimes they raped me or burned me with cigarettes. Afterward they gave us tips and we hid them in our clothes to buy food. (quoted in Constable, 2001, p. A14).

BOX 13.3 WOMEN SHAPING PSYCHOLOGY
Lenore E. Walker

Lenore Walker, a pioneer in psychological research and theory on battered women, began her career teaching emotionally disturbed children in New York City schools in 1962. She received her master's degree from City College of the City University of New York, then worked as a staff psychologist in the racially segregated community schools of New York, where, among other projects, she trained parents to help children with their reading skills. Meanwhile, she was raising a family and laying the groundwork for her doctoral research. She received her Ed.D. in psychology from Rutgers University in 1972, having developed a strong commitment to feminist psychology along the way.

With her doctorate in hand, Walker took on the leadership of an educational outreach program in the community mental health center affiliated with Rutgers Medical School. Here, she became increasingly aware that the children she saw were victims of abuse and that many of their mothers were also being abused at home. She carried her awareness and concern about this issue with her when she moved to Denver in 1975, where she taught at Colorado Women's College and developed a private practice. In her practice, she began to concentrate on psychotherapy with women. She also began to collect data on battered women.

In the mid-1970s, there was little solid information on violence against women in the home, and there was no national policy about how to deal with it. Walker and her staff collected and analyzed interviews from over 400 battered women to identify patterns in these cases, and the findings were quickly in great demand. She wrote and published a now-classic book, *The Battered Woman,* in which she detailed the cycle of violence in abusive relationships. She became a highly regarded consultant to task forces, women's shelters, and other

According to human rights agencies, more than 5,000 Nepali girls aged 10 to 20 are smuggled out of the country every year to work as prostitutes in India. Nepali families, often desperately poor and viewing daughters as a burden, contract their daughters to unscrupulous employers who promise to find them jobs abroad. The "jobs" turn out to be

BOX 13.3 WOMEN SHAPING PSYCHOLOGY (*continued*)
Lenore E. Walker

groups working to develop effective interventions for battering. She was soon in demand as an expert witness in court cases, detailing the "battered woman syndrome" now often used as a defense for battered women who kill an abuser in self-defense. She created controversy when she testified as an expert witness for the defense in the trial of O. J. Simpson (see article listed below). She has been a policy advisor to congressional committees and to agencies around the world.

Since her original book, Walker has gone on to write 10 books on the subject of violence and women and has founded the Domestic Violence Institute, a private firm that provides training, conducts research, and consults on social policy issues. She was one of the founders of the *Feminist Therapy Institute* and was also a co-founder of *Women in Psychology for Legislative Action,* a group that supports women candidates who lend their voices to important psychological issues. She has been honored by being inducted into the Hunter College Alumni Hall of Fame and by being named the recipient of the American Psychological Association's *Award for Distinguished Professional Contributions to Applied Psychology as a Professional Practice* in 1987. More recently, she has received the Heiser Award from the APA Division of Psychologists in Private Practice and the 2001 Distinguished Psychologist Award from the APA Division of Psychotherapy. Dr. Walker's efforts to raise awareness and understanding of family violence have helped stimulate scholarship on these issues and to create public policy based on this scholarship, with the result that abused women and children are better protected than they were two decades ago.

Read More about Lenore Walker

Awards for distinguished professional contributions: 1987. Lenore Walker. *American Psychologist, 43*(4), 243–244.

Read What She Has Written

Stahly, G. S., & Walker, L. E. A. (1998). What are nice feminists like you doing on the O. J. defense team? Personal ruminations on the "trial of the century." *Journal of Social Issues, 53* (3), 425–9.

Walker, L. E. A. (1979). *The battered woman.* New York: Harper & Row.

Walker, L. E. A. (1984). *The battered woman syndrome.* New York: Springer.

Walker, L. E. A. (1989). Psychology and violence against women. *American Psychologist, 44*(4), 695–702.

Walker, L. E. A. (1989). *Terrifying love: Why battered women kill and how society responds.* New York: Harper & Row.

in brothels, not carpet factories, and the daughters find themselves trapped and enslaved (Constable, 2001).

In southeast Asia, more that 225,000 people, mostly women and children, are taken across borders and sold, usually into prostitution, each year. At one brothel in Vietnam, the

---

BOX 13.4 LEARNING ACTIVITY
Resources for Women Experiencing Violence

What resources are available on your campus and in your community for women who are experiencing violence? Explore your own environment and identify these resources. Does your school have a sexual harassment policy? Obtain a copy of that policy. Is there a person or group on your campus whose responsibility it is to deal with cases of sexual assault? Find out who that is and what they do in response to a complaint. Does your community have a battered women's shelter? A victim assistant or advocate program for rape victims? An emergency hot line for women who need help and advice about escaping violence? Educate yourself about these resources. Even if you do not need to use them yourself, it will put you in a better position to help a friend who does.

---

madam explained to a reporter how the system works: "Once the girls are brought to me by an agent, I must pay from $350 to $400 for a virgin girl, or from $150 to $170 for a girl who is no longer a virgin. When a customer requests a virgin, we arrange for a hotel where he can take the girl for one week. For this I charge him $300 to $400" (quoted in Flamm, 2003).

Around the world, **trafficking** in girls and women is a serious problem: An estimated 4 million girls and women are bought and sold worldwide, either into marriage, prostitution, or slavery (United Nations Population Fund, 2000). For example, tens of thousands of poor children are sent from the countries of West Africa to the Middle East each year, where many end up as prostitutes (United Nations, Children's Fund, 2000). In poor rural areas of Thailand, families insist that it is their daughters' duty to sacrifice themselves for their families, to pay off family debt (United Nations, Children's Fund, 2000). One study estimates that 45,000 to 50,000 women and children are trafficked to the United States each year; these persons end up as prostitutes or forced laborers in sweatshops or agricultural or domestic settings (United Nations, 2000). Clearly the impact on women of these trafficking practices is severe in terms of health issues such as AIDS and other sexually transmitted infections, pregnancies, injuries from violence, depression, and anxiety. Even women who are not themselves trafficked may reap costs in terms of insecurity, cynicism, and low self-worth.

Sexual Harassment and Intimidation

Many women in Western countries know the experience of walking down a street to the accompaniment of whistles, catcalls, exaggerated kissing noises, or loud sexual overtures. Such behaviors qualify as sexual aggression: They seem designed to make women feel uncomfortable and vulnerable and reinforce the notion that men are sexual predators. Depending on the circumstances, a woman's reaction to this kind of harassment based on her gender may range from amusement to irritation to fear.

Street harassment is not a condition of female existence in every culture. Such behavior from men on the street toward women is not tolerated in certain Muslim societies. However, women pay a price for this protection in restricted movement and restrictive clothing. A woman who does not observe the dress code may find herself the target of intense harassment, as foreign women visiting such countries have frequently discovered (Brooks, 1995). And in certain very restrictive societies, such as existed in Afghanistan under the rule of the Taliban, women may be harassed on the street, not by catcalls from lustful men, but by zealous male vigilantes, who hit them with sticks or flog them with whips or car antennas if their veils accidentally slip from their faces or if they show a glimpse of ankle as they walk (Schulz & Schulz, 1999).

Sexual harassment—unwanted and unwelcome sexual overtures or allusions to sexuality—has been most extensively investigated as a workplace issue and is discussed at length in Chapter 8. But sexual harassment can happen on the street, in public places such as stores and hotel lobbies, on public transportation, in schools, and in churches.

In a survey by *Seventeen* magazine that netted responses from 4,200 young North American women, 39 percent said they experienced sexual harassment *every day* in school. The effect was that many students were reluctant to go to school or to draw attention to themselves by speaking up in class (Mann, 1993). A more recent survey of 8th- to 11th-grade students, sponsored by the American Association of University Women, found that 1 in 3 students fears being sexually harassed in school and that harassment changes students' lives. After they have been harassed, students tend to avoid the person who harassed them, talk less in class, change their seats, and not want to go to school (American Association of University Women, 2001). Research in China shows that college students experience harassment from both peers and professors (Tang et al., 1995). In a study in Tanzania involving interviews with 300 women, schoolgirls, and young female college students, 90 percent said they had been sexually harassed at school, in the streets, or even by cousins, uncles, or brothers-in-law in the home. Street harassment, most reported, consisted of abusive language (Tanzania Media Women's Association, 1994).

In Zimbabwe, a government report concluded that sexual harassment by both peers and teachers is one of the reasons so many girls drop out of school (N. Wyatt, 2000). And in Thailand, the Bangkok Mass Transit Authority began operating "Lady Buses" to protect women from pickpockets and sexual harassment that was occurring on public buses (N. Wyatt, 2000). Sexual harassment, particularly verbal harassment, is common in Swedish schools, where behaviors that would be outlawed in an adult workplace are often condoned (Witkowska, Eliasson, & Menckel, 2000).

Perpetrators of sexual harassment have, in recent years, found a new medium in the easy availability of the Internet, e-mail, and text messaging. Especially among adolescents and young adults, the high use of such media has the unfortunate side effect that hostile or abusive messages can spread quickly and do enormous damage. For example, high school students create online lists of the "hottest" or "ugliest" girls in the school, and in at least one school a list surfaced on the Internet listing the names, phone numbers, and alleged sexual exploits of dozens of girls (Harmon, 2004). Embarrassing photographs can be taken with picture cell phones and circulated on the Internet, digital videos meant for one person can be circulated to thousands in a flash, and nasty text messages can reach their target even when a girl is in a normally "safe" place. This type of abuse is new enough that few effective strategies have been developed to counteract it.

The result of sexual harassment is the intimidation of girls and women and their absorption of the message that they should restrict their activities. This is the same message delivered by other forms of gender-based and sexual aggression: Women should not act independently, and they must seek male protection to avoid male violence.

Pornography and Sexual Violence   **Pornography,** particularly the variety in which explicit violence is mixed with sexually arousing material, is a major purveyor of rape myths and may also be a disinhibiting factor for men who are sexually aggressive. At best, pornography portrays women as objects rather than human beings; at worst, viewers learn to associate the brutalization of women with sexual pleasure. Pornography tends to sexualize the power difference between women and men. Not all **erotica** takes this objectifying, dehumanizing perspective; some erotic materials are explicitly sexual and sensual without being insulting or denigrating to women or men.

In many sexually violent pornographic movies, a woman who is raped, humiliated, or brutalized is shown to resist initially, but eventually to become sexually aroused by the way she is treated. Thus a major rape myth—women secretly want to be raped—is played out on the screen and reinforced for the viewer. Research shows that exposure to sexually violent pornography can increase men's acceptance of rape myths and of interpersonal violence against women (Demaré, Briere, & Lips, 1988; Malamuth & Check, 1981), and that repeated exposure to violent pornography also results in decreased sensitivity to female victims of violence in nonsexual contexts (Linz, Donnerstein, & Penrod, 1984). Laboratory studies in which men are exposed to violent or nonviolent pornography and then given the opportunity to behave aggressively against another person by delivering electric shocks show that exposure to violent pornography increases the men's aggression against women, but not against other men (Donnerstein, 1980; Malamuth, 1984). Exposure to violent pornography is strongly related to men's arousability to rape scenes, acceptance of rape myths, and self-reported likelihood of committing rape (Briere, Corne, Runta, & Malamuth, 1984). Among college males, self-reported use of sexually violent, but not nonviolent, pornography plays a significant role in predicting self-reported likelihood of using sexual force or rape against women and of self-reported use of actual sexual coercion or force (Demaré et al., 1988; Demaré, Lips, & Briere, 1993).

What about the impact of violent pornography on women? At least one study suggests that women who view pornography that supports rape myths—in which a woman is portrayed as becoming sexually aroused when being raped—become sexually aroused themselves. This sexual arousal apparently contributes to judgments that the victim's behavior is typical (i.e., that a woman would typically enjoy being raped) and that they themselves are likely to react in the same way (Norris, Davis, George, Martell, & Heiman, 2004). On the basis on their findings, the authors of the study argue that women who find themselves exposed to and aroused by violent pornography that shows women as willing victims may come to believe that such a sexual encounter is normal and acceptable and that they should submit to sexual victimization.

Certainly, the very fact that the sexual brutalization of women is viewed as entertainment by a certain number of men suggests that violent pornography, at the very least, helps create a climate in which sexual aggression against women is taken with minimal seriousness. Nonviolent pornography may be less cause for concern. However, some researchers, such as Diana Russell (1988), have argued that even nonviolent pornography may have detrimental effects because it can undermine men's inhibitions by objectifying women and by producing overestimates among men of uncommon sexual practices. At the very least, the visible presence of pornography forcefully reminds women that they are considered sexual objects and can make them feel uncomfortable and intimidated about going into the places where it is displayed. In fact, the deliberate display of pornography is frequently used as a way of harassing women in the workplace and making them feel unwelcome, as discussed in Chapter 8.

Intimidation through the Media: Stalkers and Serial Killers on Parade   In *Kiss the Girls,* one of a seemingly endless series of grisly Hollywood films centering on a psychopathic stalker/serial victimizer of women, the mysterious abductor of young women signs his notes to the police "Casanova" (the great 18th-century lover—a misuse of the term *love* if ever there was one) and is characterized by one police officer (with some apparent grudging admiration) as "a real student of the game . . . and he *likes* to play."

The abduction, abuse, rape, and murder of women is not a game, but it *is* routinely treated as entertainment by filmmakers, television producers, and publishers, even outside the realm of pornography. What impact does constant bombardment by such images have on women? Researchers have long known that the portrayal of violence makes people fearful, leads them to exaggerate the probability that they will be victims of violence themselves, and may even teach them to think of themselves as victims if the victims portrayed are like themselves (Morgan, 1983). Thus, some have argued, women who repeatedly view portrayals of other women being victimized are likely to feel vulnerable, intimidated, unable to control their environment, and powerless in the face of threat. This is especially likely in view of the pattern that women are also socialized in many other ways to accept an inferior status in patriarchal societies.

Sometimes, women's victimization in media portrayals is linked to their violation of cultural norms of appropriate female behavior. One genre of films in India, for example, portrays "bad" women, who have returned from a stay abroad wearing blue jeans instead of the traditional sari, as inevitably getting into trouble, whereas the "good" women, who follow Indian social customs in dress and demeanor, reap rewards.

Two researchers in South Africa, Penny Reid and Gillian Finchilescu (1995), conducted a direct test of the notion that viewing violence against women disempowers women. First, they developed a Disempowerment Scale, with items such as "I often feel intimidated in day to day situations" and "I never feel safe from the occurrence of negative events." Then they had female undergraduate students view 10-minute video clips from popular movies that featured instances of violence against either female or male victims. The clip that portrayed female victims included a scene in which a young Vietnamese woman was being abducted from her village by soldiers who obviously intended to rape her, a scene in which a woman was stalked by a man in an underground parking garage, and a scene in which a woman was physically assaulted by her husband. The clip focusing on male victims featured three sequences in which a man alone is attacked, beaten up, and in one case killed by a group of other men. Women who watched the clips showing violence against women showed heightened scores on the Disempowerment Scale afterward, in comparison to women who watched the male-victim clips. In other words, watching the victimization of women made women feel vulnerable in a way that watching the victimization of men did not. Furthermore, viewers of the female-victim films reported more anxiety and tension and a more heightened sense of the prevalence of violence than viewers of the male-victim films did. It appears that the many media portrayals of female victims of violence serve as effective means of social control, reminding women to feel vulnerable and to be fearful of independent actions such as traveling unaccompanied, walking alone, or breaking the rules of dress and demeanor in their societies. While clear research documenting this conclusion is scant, anecdotal evidence suggests that women who are exposed to these portrayals seem to have little difficulty getting the message.

Torture and Ill-Treatment of Women in Custody

Konca Kuris was an Islamic feminist in Turkey who argued that women should be allowed to pray alongside men in the mosques (mosques generally have separate areas for women and men). Her outspokenness cost her her life: She was abducted by a group of militant men—self-appointed guardians of "pure" Islam—who tortured and abused her for weeks before suffocating her and hiding her body. At her funeral, male relatives refused to allow her daughter to pray beside her coffin, which stood in the men's section of the mosque during the service (Associated Press, 2000).

In many parts of the world, a woman does not have to be in the custody of a band of renegades to be tortured—she can be in the hands of the police. Nazli Top, walking home from work in 1992, was stopped at a security checkpoint, then taken to a police station and held for 10 days. During this time, she was beaten, prodded with electric shocks until she went numb, then raped with a truncheon. At the time, she was 32 years old and three months pregnant. Nine years later, when she told her story at Turkey's first public conference on the abuse of women in police custody, she and other conference speakers faced criminal charges for their actions. The charge? Insulting and raising suspicions about the security forces (Moore, 2001b). The torture of women in custody has been documented in countries as diverse as Argentina, Bangladesh, China, Egypt, Israel, Saudi Arabia, Spain, and the United States (Amnesty International, 2001). For example, in China, women migrant workers have been detained and accused of prostitution, then mistreated to elicit lists of their "clients." In the Democratic Republic of Congo, women detainees are frequently tortured and raped. In Turkey, torture methods used on women prisoners reportedly include electric shocks and beatings directed at the breasts or genitals, as well as sexual abuse, including rape. The Women's Commission for Refugee Women and Children issued a report detailing widespread sexual, physical, verbal, and emotional abuse by guards of female detainees in the U.S. Immigration and Naturalization Service's Krome detention facility in Miami (Women sexually assaulted under INS detention to be deported, 2001).

Women who are subjected to violence while they are in custody are in a particularly difficult and dangerous position. They run the risk of being treated even more harshly if they complain or try to report the abuse. They are unlikely to be believed, and their reports may well not even be investigated. And in some cases they may simply be unable to get word out to anyone of what is happening to them. Violence against women in custody, as in situations of intimate partner abuse or other situations in which women are under the control and authority of abusers, is often invisible to the general public and carried out with impunity.

Protecting Women from Violence: Some Strategies

In Brazil, feminist organizations persuaded the mayor of São Paulo to establish a women's police station in 1985. Staffed entirely by women, the station was dedicated to crimes of violence against women, excluding homicide. By later that year, eight such women's police stations (called Delegacias de Defesa Da Mulher) had opened in the state of São Paulo, and by 1990 there were 74 in various parts of Brazil (D. Q. Thomas, 1994). There are now more than 300 women's police stations in Brazil, and some other countries in Latin America, Africa, and South Asia have adopted similar approaches (Vera Institute of Justice, 2004). The presence of these stations has increased the visibility of and police responsiveness to domestic violence. Women are more willing to report being battered and are given more support and help when they do. Some problems remain, however. Many cases are not prosecuted, apparently because of a lack of political will on the part of state prosecutors and other officials. Female police officers find that there is a stigma attached to working at a delagacia, and such work does not help them to get promoted. And many more such stations would be needed to provide full coverage of the country.

Brazil's response to domestic violence was a pioneering one that has now been echoed in the creation of "women's desks," staffed by officers especially trained to investigate domestic violence, at police stations in Bolivia, Nicaragua, Pakistan, Peru, the Philippines, and Spain. A similar principle of a dedicated focus on gender violence has been applied to the court system in some countries. In India, special women's courts have been created specifically to handle cases of violence against women, from sexual harassment to murder. These courts are staffed with female judges and prosecutors, and they have worked to streamline the judicial process in gender violence cases (Neft & Levine, 1997). Bangladesh has also established special courts to handle wife abuse and other forms of antifemale violence.

In 1993, South Africa initiated special "rape courts" to deal with sexual assault, with the goal of handling rape cases in ways that would be efficient and effective and would eliminate additional trauma to the victim. There were 29 such courts in 2003, and they have been successful enough that the government plans to more than double their number (Itano, 2003). South Africa has one of the world's highest rates of sexual assault, and some 70 percent of the victims of these assaults are children. Yet, until the advent of the rape courts, very few rape cases resulted in convictions. Now, with energetic female prosecutors freed from other types of cases and trained female intermediaries who work with traumatized victims to help them prepare to testify, these courts achieve conviction rates of 75 to 90 percent in the cases they bring to trial. In addition, the average length of time to trial has been cut in half.

Around the world, women have organized to stop violence against women and to develop ways of protecting the victims of gender violence. The strategies have included legislative reform, education and legal counseling for women, the provision of shelters, self-defense classes, and various strategies to support the healing and empowerment of survivors of violence. Countries as diverse as Argentina, Costa Rica, Canada, Germany, Ireland, Israel, Japan, Sri Lanka, Sweden, the United Kingdom, and the United States have established networks of residential shelters for battered women. Italy has a government hotline to offer legal and medical advice and help to abused women. In Japan, there is a movement to establish "women only" subway cars so female passengers can ride without being harassed. In Canada, December 6 is designated a National Day of Remembrance and Action on Violence against Women. In a few countries, such as France and Germany, victims of sexual assault are entitled to financial compensation from the government.

On the legislative front, many countries have enacted tougher laws against sexual assault and domestic violence in recent years. In many parts of Canada and the United States, for example, there are mandatory arrest policies for spousal abuse cases in which the police are called. Many countries, including Canada, France, Israel, Australia, Sweden, the United Kingdom, the United States, and South Africa, have laws making marital rape a crime. In Israel, a 1990 amendment to the penal code made all sexual crimes more serious if they were committed within the family. The United States, in 1994, passed the Violence against Women Act, which declared domestic violence a federal crime and recognized violent crimes against women as violations of their civil rights. Perhaps the strongest set of protective laws is that of Sweden. The Restraining Orders Act enables the courts to prohibit an abusive spouse from any contact with the victim, and women in severe danger of being assaulted may be entitled to a bodyguard, a trained police dog, or an electronic alarm to call the police (Neft & Levine, 1997).

Yet there are many countries where little has been done to counter gender-based violence. For example, in 1996 the first and only battered women's shelter in the huge city of Shanghai, China, was forced to close because of bureaucratic red tape: As a "rescue center" it did not fit into any accepted category. Although the center had been open for only a month when it was shut down, it had already sheltered 21 women and taken calls from another 250 (Reuters, 1996a). China still does not have state-funded shelters for battered women, and the problem of domestic violence has reportedly increased in recent years as the country has been wracked by social change (Liu, 2004). In Egypt, the very first shelter for battered women opened only recently (Walker, 2004). In Pakistan, activists have decried conditions in the few state-run shelters for women in which, once a woman enters, she becomes a virtual prisoner and cannot leave without a court order (Integrated Regional Information Network, 2004). Marital rape is still not considered a crime in some countries. For example, in Malaysia, where the country's human rights commission had asked parliament for legislation making marital rape a crime, one of the country's chief clerics, Mufti Harussani Zakaria, came out strongly against such a law. A man has the right to be intimate with his wife, and the wife must obey, he told newspapers. "If the wife refuses, then . . . the husband is not required to provide financial assistance to her" (quoted in Kent, 2004). Even in some countries where marital rape is a crime, public officials may not support the legislation. For example, one attorney in the Philippines recently wrote that "Personally, I do not agree that the State can punish an aggressive (or excited) husband for forcing his wife to have sexual intercourse with him. This is so because a husband has the right to physical access to his wife by virtue of the consent, which she gave at the time of the celebration of the marriage" (Luna, 2004).

The United Nations asked governments to report on their progress in implementing actions to counteract antifemale violence in 1999. These reports indicated that a number of countries had launched public awareness and advocacy campaigns and introduced new legislation aimed at protecting victims and punishing perpetrators of domestic violence. Yet in most countries, "[s]ufficient resources have not been allocated for measures that address violence, and conflicting values and beliefs about women and their place in the family, the community and society undermine the development and implementation of such measures" (United Nations, 2000, p. 159).

Freedom from Persecution on the Basis of Gender:
A Human Right

In 1993, Canada led the world in explicitly recognizing gender-based persecution as a legitimate reason for seeking asylum as a refugee. Acknowledging that women in many countries have no protection from violent husbands or fathers or from certain kinds of violence that are meted out specifically to women, Canada's Immigration and Refugee Board issued new guidelines opening the door to women who are at risk in their home countries simply because they are women. Around the world, women face a variety of threats, from violent retribution for advocating changes in the status of women or violating behavioral norms for women, to officially sanctioned rape and domestic violence. Nurjehan Mawani, chair of Canada's Immigration Board, commented that "in cases where the state makes no effort to protect a severely battered woman, or stop or punish a violent partner, and where no protection can be obtained with her own country . . . she is, in essence, fleeing for her life" (Trueheart, 1993).

One of the examples that brought this issue to the fore in Canada was the case of a young woman from Trinidad, who pleaded that her husband there had threatened to cut her to pieces if she went back. Another was a woman from Saudi Arabia, who argued that her outspoken resistance to the subordinate status of women in her country and her refusal to wear a veil put her life at risk in her own country. Both women were given asylum. More recently, the first such case was successful in the United States. A 19-year old Mexican woman, who argued that she could not return home because her abusive father's violence against her put her life at risk, was granted refugee status as a victim of domestic violence (First battered women granted asylum in the US, 2001).

The kinds of gender-based situations that might cause women to be unsafe in their own countries have been, or are being, played out in many places. In Bangladesh, author Tasmila Nasrin faced criminal charges and the threat that she would be killed after using her novels and newspaper columns to advocate women's right to choose their sexual partners and to have children outside of marriage. Her argument that Muslim women should have the right to take four husbands simultaneously—just as Muslim men have the right to take four wives—enraged Muslim fundamentalists, and she had to go into hiding (J. F. Burns, 1994). Under the Taliban regime that took over Afghanistan in 1996, women were forbidden to go to work or school and were barred from leaving their homes unless wearing a garment that covered their entire body and concealed their eyes behind a mesh cloth. Women who disobeyed were assaulted and beaten by zealous militiamen (Cooper, 1996).

In 1979, by approving the Convention on the Elimination of All Forms of Discrimination Against Women (CEDAW), the United Nations recognized that violations of women's rights are violations of human rights. In other words, it is not acceptable to mistreat women simply because cultural or national tradition dictates "That is how women are treated." Women cannot be beaten, assaulted, or raped just because custom allows it. The Convention includes, among other things, the assurance that women and men will be equal before the law and have equal rights and responsibilities in marriage. CEDAW has now been ratified by 177 countries—about two-thirds of the countries in the United Nations (United Nations, 2001). By ratifying the Convention, a country makes a commitment to pass legislation and promote policies congruent with the treaty's conditions and to submit periodic progress reports on the status of women and the implementation of the treaty. Canada ratified this treaty in 1981; the most recent country to ratify it is Swaziland, in March 2004. The United States signed the treaty in 1981; however, it has never ratified it. Thus, the United States has *not* agreed to actively implement the treaty, only to do nothing in contravention of the treaty's terms. The other countries that have signed but declined to ratify this treaty are Afghanistan and Sao Tome and Principe.

Unfortunately, many women and men (and apparently many political leaders) have never heard of CEDAW. There is a lot of educational and enforcement work left to do around the world before the protections afforded by this Convention can be realized.

SUMMARY

Violence against women and girls is a pervasive, worldwide problem. Women are often the targets of physical and emotional abuse in courtship or dating relationships and by intimate partners. The abuse of women by their husbands is very common, ranging from 17 percent to 90 percent in various cultural settings. Women are murdered by their husbands because of dowry disputes in some countries, and wives and daughters are also murdered by male relatives to preserve "family honor" in some parts of the world. Violence also occurs in lesbian couples.

Females are at risk of violence from the beginning of their lives in certain places. Sex-selective abortion, infanticide, and the systematic neglect of female children has resulted in literally millions of "missing women" in population statistics.

Sexual violence against women is a serious problem all over the world, but statistics are hard to interpret because rape is often unreported. Rape is often committed against women by acquaintances and intimates. It is also, under the protection of social norms, committed against women who are under certain forms of social control, such as slave women and enemy women in wartime. Some have termed the latter behavior as normative rape.

Rape victims are often thought to have "asked" to be raped by their dress or demeanor. Often their accounts are not believed, and they are treated disrespectfully by justice officials. Such behavior and attitudes stem from rape myths, which center on the idea that a woman can prevent rape if she really wants to. Yet rape has serious physical, emotional and social consequences for women. For example, women may suffer sexually transmitted infections, unwanted pregnancies, pelvic pain, and depression. Women who have been raped are also more vulnerable than their peers to revictimization. Many of the same negative consequences accrue, with even more intensity, to children who are sexually abused. And child sexual abuse is very frequent in much of the world. The trauma associated with rape and child sexual abuse is magnified under conditions of forced prostitution and sexual slavery.

Sexual harassment and intimidation remind women that they are vulnerable to violence, keeping them on edge and insecure. Institutions such as schools that do not protect women from such harassment provide implicit support for antifemale violence. Explicit support is provided by sexually violent pornography, which links the subjugation and abuse of women with sexual pleasure for men. Mainstream media images of violence against women as entertainment underscore the idea that women are vulnerable, contributing to a sense of disempowerment.

Although it takes somewhat different forms in different societies, antifemale violence around the world is characterized by common themes. One is a sense of male superiority and entitlement. Another is the notion that what goes on in families is private. A third is that violence is a tolerable behavior and an appropriate response to problems.

The attitude that men are superior to women and should be in charge in the home and elsewhere is implicitly and explicitly used to justify male aggression against women. The notion of male superiority engenders a sense of entitlement among some men: They believe that wives, daughters, female relatives, and female co-workers owe them submission, obedience, pleasure. This attitude, in its most extreme form, suggests that girls and women are literally the property of men and can be used and abused at will. Thus under some circumstances battering one's wife or raping an uncooperative woman is explicitly allowed. This attitude can be so pervasive in some sociocultural contexts that women too are infected by it, internalizing a sense of their own relative worthlessness and helplessness and even cooperating in the perpetuation of customs that enshrine antifemale violence.

Most antifemale violence occurs within families. The latitude for violence given to a man by the notion that he is the head of the family is compounded by the equally ubiquitous idea that the family is a private place, not necessarily subject to outside interference. In this commonly held view, family members are supposed to settle their own problems without recourse to outsiders. Thus the victims of violence may be ashamed to seek help or simply have no resources for help that could protect them from a husband, father, or other family member. The notion of family privacy also helps keep hidden the violence that occurs in lesbian relationships.

Violence against girls and women is most common among individuals who accept interpersonal violence as a way of solving problems and in societies in which violence is tolerated or even celebrated. The combination, in an individual or a society, of patriarchal beliefs and a readiness to use violence as a method of achieving goals is a dangerous one for women. It appears that girls and women cannot be protected from violence in sociocultural contexts where there is no political will to reduce violence in general or to acknowledge women and men as equal.

Such political will has been demonstrated in some countries, where legislation has enshrined various protections for women and where awareness and advocacy campaigns are designed to discourage antifemale violence. On the global front, the work of the United Nations to gain support for CEDAW has helped provide a basis for viewing women's rights as human rights and for reducing violence against women around the world. However, much work is yet needed in terms of education and enforcement.

KEY TERMS

honor killing
rape
sexual abuse

sexual harassment
normative rape
rape myths

trafficking
pornography
erotica

DISCUSSION QUESTIONS

How vulnerable are you to violence in your own life? How much of that vulnerability is connected to your gender?

How does violence against women in North America compare in scope and seriousness to violence against women in other parts of the world? Can you see any underlying causes of antifemale violence that are similar in North America and other countries?

What are the potential psychological effects on women of antifemale violence, even when they are not directly victimized themselves?

FOR ADDITIONAL READING

Davies, Miranda (Ed.). (1994). *Women and violence: Realities and responses worldwide.* London: Zed Books. This collection includes contributions from many countries describing and analyzing causes of and solutions to antifemale violence. Articles address such diverse topics as domestic violence in Northern Ireland, women's police stations in Brazil, sexual harassment in France, mass rape in Bosnia, and Aboriginal women organizing against violence in Canada.

Koss, Mary P., Goodman, Lisa A., & Browne, Angela. (1995). *No safe haven: Violence against women at home, at work, and in the community.* Washington, DC: American Psychological Association. A trio of experts presents a wide-ranging view of the many faces of violence against women.

Ristock, Janice L. (2002). *No more secrets: Violence in lesbian relationships.* New York: Routledge. In her examination of violence in lesbian couples, Ristock questions many of the assumptions about couple violence and asks the reader to pay attention to the fluidity of power in relationships and to the specific contexts of violence.

Weiss, Elaine, & Magill, Michael. (2000). *Surviving domestic violence: Voices of women who broke free.* Agreka Books. The book contains the careful interviews of women who have survived domestic violence, along with thoughtful reflections on their comments. This is an encouraging and supportive book for anyone who feels or has felt trapped in an abusive relationship.

WEB RESOURCES

Centre for Research on Violence against Women and Children. This alliance of five research centers is based at the University of Western Ontario in Canada. Its goal is to promote the development of community-centered action research on violence against women and children. The site includes a library, resources, publications, and links to other sites. **www.uwo.ca/violence**

Global Anti-Violence Resource Guide. This site provides resources related to the global movement to end violence against women. **www.feminist.com/antiviolence/global.html**

Global Campaign to Eliminate Violence Against Women, UNIFEM. This United Nations–sponsored site provides information about awareness campaigns to combat anti-female violence in various regions of the world. **www.unifem.undp.org/campaign/violence**

Violence against Women Office, U.S. Department of Justice. This government site contains information about what communities can do about violence, federal laws and regulations, research and publications, and help and information for women who need assistance (including lists of state hotlines, coalitions, and advocacy groups by state). **www.ojp.usdoj.gov/vawo**

CHAPTER 14

Leadership, Power, and Social Change

CHAPTER OUTLINE

During the 1920s, Liu Qingyang was a fiery, articulate spokeswoman for the revolutionary Communist movement in China. Once a respected teacher at a women's teachers' college, she had become a leader of protests, studied in Europe, joined the Communist Party, and returned to China to assume the editorship of an important women's newspaper. Famous for her independence and for her rousing speeches, Liu modeled herself after a woman warrior.

The revolutionary rhetoric of the early Chinese Communists placed great emphasis on gender equality and the liberation of women from the cruel feudal practices of footbinding and the total subservience of wives, but most male party members squirmed in discomfort at the prospect of a woman as "strident" as Liu. One high-placed leader, Peng Shuzhi, found her "pure hell" to be with, and objected to her presence as a representative of China at an international congress in Moscow. She was, he argued, lacking in culture and politically uncouth. Even Liu's lover, a man who was a strong public proponent of women's emancipation, apparently felt no qualms about insisting on his own dominance within their private relationship—and later insisted that he had written most of her speeches.

Apparently untroubled by the paradoxes involved, most men in the early Chinese Communist movement maintained some traditional expectations of gender roles, even while they argued for women's equality. They wanted women freed from the strictures of arranged marriages and felt it important that women have access to jobs so they could be economically independent. For a long time, however, they saw no necessity to invite women to be official members of the party or to share decision-making power with them in any way (Gilmartin, 1993). They wanted women to be "liberated" in the personal and

485

TABLE 14.1   Gender Empowerment around the World

In 2004, the United Nations Development Program ranked 78 countries on a Gender Empowerment Measure, based on a formula that took into consideration all the factors listed in this table. These are the ratings they produced for some countries:

Country	Gender Empowerment Measure (GEM) Rank	Seats in Parliament Held by Women (% of total)	Female Legislators Senior Officials, and Managers (% of total)	Female Professional and Technical Workers (% of total)	Ratio of Estimated Female to Male Earned Income
Norway	1	36.4	28	49	0.74
Canada	10	23.6	34	54	0.63
New Zealand	11	28.3	38	52	0.69
Austria	13	30.6	29	48	0.36
United States	14	14.0	46	55	0.62
Mexico	34	21.2	25	40	0.38
Japan	38	9.9	10	46	0.46
Venezuela	61	9.7	27	61	0.41
Republic of Korea	68	5.9	5	34	0.46
Pakistan	64	20.8	9	26	0.33
Saudi Arabia	77	0.0	1	31	0.21

Source: (United Nations Development Program, 2004)

sexual sense, but paid no attention to the idea of increasing women's formal political power.

The double messages directed at Liu Qingyang were not unusual in the China of the 1920s. They were not unusual even in the China of the 1990s, where, despite several decades of rhetorical emphasis on gender equality, women were severely underrepresented in powerful political and economic positions (Bauer, Wang, Riley, & Zhao, 1992). In fact, women aspiring to public positions of power and leadership in any culture still face some conflicting messages. Women may be encouraged to be assertive and to take control of their own (personal) lives, but they may be met with surprise and hostility if they try to assume public power as individuals. They may encounter even more resistance if they try to make collective change and insist on justice for women.

Why are power and leadership so often fraught with conflict for women? Part of the issue is the image of power, often at odds with the image of and expectations for femininity. We begin this chapter with an overview of how these warring images can affect the ways powerful women are perceived. A second, connected aspect of the issue may be skills and styles, examined in a subsequent section of the chapter. A third, intertwined aspect involves the practical barriers—from limited funds, to exclusion from important networks, to lack of good childcare—that effectively keep women out of leadership positions. This chapter examines these structural issues before turning to two final question: What happens when women *are* accepted as leaders? And how are women using their collective power to effect social change?

Images and Stereotypes of Powerful Women

Power and Femininity Don't Mix

In 1964, when U.S. Senator Margaret Chase Smith of Maine announced her intention to seek the Republican presidential nomination, the reaction, even from other women in the political arena, was discouraging at best. The headline in the *Arizona Daily Star* that day read "State's female lawmakers shudder at thought of woman president," and the article quoted one female state representative as saying "I certainly hope in my lifetime I never have to see a woman president" ("Margaret Chase Smith," 1995). → ridiculous

When Mina Hassan Mohamed was appointed director of the Keysaney hospital in the Somalian city of Mogadishu, her biggest challenge was winning the respect of subordinates unaccustomed to seeing women in positions of authority. During her first week as director, she was slapped across the face by a man bringing his injured child for treatment; hospital security guards, instead of intervening, merely stood and watched. She received death threats from staff members outraged by the idea of a woman enforcing the rules, insisting on discipline and promptness. Why all the hostility? "They see you as a woman, and they think a woman cannot say something to a man . . . a woman cannot talk [to them] like this. But I say I am just doing my job," said Mohamed, one of the very few Somali women with a medical degree (Richburg, 1993).

Delegates to the annual conference of the Southern Baptist Convention in Orlando, Florida, voted to define a woman's place in the church as a helper, not a preacher or a pastor. One female delegate commented, "I believe in the authority given to man to be pastor. . . . Women *should* be teaching, but men have the responsibility and authority over the flock, for their souls" (quoted in Dodd & Brecher, 2001, p. 3B).

Societies have often set very explicit norms that men should be the public leaders and women should not try to usurp such roles. Even when the explicit norms are more egalitarian, the implicit ones are contradictory at best. As noted in Chapter 5, in many situations a woman in a position of power is measured against two contradictory sets of stereotypical expectations: the tough, assertive, ambitious, take-charge standard associated with leadership and the warm, expressive, accommodating, "nice" standard associated with femininity. Such contradictory standards are difficult for a powerful woman to meet, and she often finds herself treading a narrow path of acceptable behavior. Too much deviation in the direction of "masculine" assertiveness, and she is accused of not being a real woman; too much deviation in the direction of "feminine" niceness, and she is considered too soft to be a good leader.

The contradictions between power and femininity are rooted in gender stereotypes. Gender stereotypes prescribe that toughness, assertiveness, and the competent exertion of power are masculine (Heilman, 2001; Schein, 2001). Some researchers have argued, in fact, that power is the key organizing element of such stereotypes—that our notions of masculinity cluster around potency, dominance, and control, whereas our notions of femininity cluster around submissiveness, frailty, and pliability. Support for these ideas comes from studies in which respondents associate powerholders with stereotypically masculine qualities and link feminine characteristics to people who hold less power. For example, Zbigniew Smoreda (1995) asked men and women in Paris to read a description of a male–female couple and then to imagine them and to describe them on a series of questionnaires. He varied the status attributed to each member of the couple by varying their work roles: In one scenario the man was described as a professional in computing and the woman was described as a housewife. In the other scenario, the woman was described as a professional in computing, and the man was described as a part-time clerk. Respondents attributed more decision-making power to the member of the couple who had higher status, whether that was the woman or the man. Furthermore, for both genders, perceived power was strongly associated with the attribution of stereotypically masculine instrumental traits. A person who was seen as having power was also seen as masculine. This tendency was accentuated when the woman was the person perceived as having greater power. Apparently, the surprise of seeing a female-dominated relationship caused respondents to exaggerate the masculine qualities of the woman involved. The message is apparent: A woman cannot be both powerful and feminine.

The struggle that observers often experience in reconciling femininity and power is amply demonstrated in the U.S. popular culture's reaction to women in positions of visible power. For example, former Attorney General Janet Reno was the target of sharp criticism and merciless satire while she was one of the most powerful women in U.S. politics. The attacks were not the same as those directed at male politicians; they were directed at her femininity and her sexuality. Reno's critics, political opponents, and those who feast on gossip and jokes about celebrities used her apparent unconcern with fashion, her tendency to avoid makeup, and unmarried status to attack or make fun of her. *Saturday Night Live* skits portrayed her as a man in drag. An anonymous videotape shipped to the *Washington Post* was labeled "Janet Reno—Evil Lesbian." On World Wide Web sites her short, practical haircut was superimposed above the faces of Demi Moore, Courtney Love, and Jenny McCarthy, and rude sexual jokes were made at her expense. Indeed, one reporter's search of the Web yielded more references to Janet Reno than to any other Cabinet minister except former Defense Secretary William Cohen—whose entries tended to be standard press releases (Mundy, 1998). People focused on her appearance and commented on her hair, her glasses, and her dresses in a way that simply does not occur with male political figures. It is as if by focusing on her sexuality or appearance, they could bring the "feminine" role to the forefront, discounting the leadership one.

An examination of the reactions to former cabinet secretary and Republican presidential candidate Elizabeth Dole reveals another side of the gender-based criticism of powerful women. Dole was criticized and satirized, not for her lack of femininity, as Reno was, but for being, in some respects too feminine: too nice, too well-behaved, too prone to follow the rules. When she was a member of the Cabinet, she earned the derisive nickname "Sugar Lips" because she achieved some political victories by charming congressmen with what some people thought of as fake sweetness. During the presidential campaign, one columnist called her "Little Miss Perfect," and reporters noted her "penchant for perfection" and "tightly wound efficiency." The Doonesbury comic strip lampooned her as being so robotlike that she had to be "rebooted" (Reed, 1999).

So perhaps powerful women can expect criticism if they deviate in either direction from a narrow set of behaviors: if they emphasize their authority and power and pay little attention to being "feminine," or if they emphasize their femininity too much. Young women in countries such as the United States, Spain, and Argentina are apparently aware of the tension between the requirements of femininity and power. When asked to describe what they would be like if they held powerful positions such as political leadership or corporate presidencies, many female college students in these countries stressed that they would be compassionate even though powerful, kind to employees even though demanding, nice even though tough (Lips, 2000; Lips, de Verthelyi, & Gonzalez, 1996). Some worried that other people would not like them in these roles—a worry that, given the media reactions to female politicians, seems well founded. A sampling of their comments (Lips et al., 1996):

> I would wear business suits every day. My hair would always be up in a bun to symbolize that I am not someone who is a sex symbol just because I am a woman in power. (U.S.)
>
> I would feel alone—no friendships with other employees. (U.S.)
>
> I would be kind and really respect my coworkers . . . hardworking, intelligent, kind, patient and feminine. (U.S.)
>
> Sophisticated . . . but not intimidating. (Argentina)
>
> Nervous, feelings of a lot of responsibility; feelings of insecurity. (Spain)
>
> I can't imagine it—myself with power. (Argentina)
>
> The stress would affect my personal life. (U.S.)
>
> I imagine myself as an authoritarian person: organized, strict, but compassionate at times. (Spain)

Negative stereotypes of powerful women are apparently more commonly held by men than women. In one Australian study, nearly half the male respondents asked to list descriptors for unspecified powerful women made reference to what the researchers called the "iron maiden" stereotype, labeling powerful women as "man-hater," "unfeminine," "asexual," "cold," and "hard" (Onyx, Leonard, & Vivekananda, 1995). Similarly, when respondents in both the United States and Spain were asked for men's thoughts about powerful women, they listed negative attributes: "more obsessed [than men] in reaching power," "pedantic and authoritarian," "[they] try to have power like men do, but without doing it like real women" (Diaz Zuniga, Sattler, & Lips, 1997).

Women who hold powerful positions often find themselves in a double bind. When Linda Carli (2001) reviewed research on women and social influence, the pattern she found was that women who act in highly assertive, confident, or competent ways sometimes find that their ability to influence others, particularly males, is reduced. Moreover, she found, people responded with dislike, hostility and rejection to such assertive women, presumably because these women were violating prescriptive norms for gender-appropriate behavior. The research showed that women can reduce resistance to their influence by being careful to display the "feminine" virtues of warmth and collaborative orientation. Being perceived as warm and likeable makes women more influential and, indeed, appears essential for women trying to wield influence.

So there is ample evidence that women are perceived stereotypically, but do these stereotypes really hinder women's advancement to top positions? Some researchers have noted that the impact of gender stereotypes on the evaluation of candidates for jobs or promotions is small, accounting for about 0.1 percent of the variance in such evaluations (Swim et al., 1989). However, it would be a rare woman indeed whose evaluation was impacted by gender stereotypes only once in her career. When evaluations occur over and over again during a career, as is the case when individuals apply for jobs, ask for raises, or are considered for promotion, the cumulative impact of this "small" effect is magnified (Agars, 2004). For example, imagine that the initial applicant pool for positions in an organization is 500 men and 500 women—all of whom have good qualifications for the position. If hiring choices are not affected by stereotypes, then the organization will hire women for 50 percent of the positions. If stereotypes have their "small" effect, then women will be hired for only 48.2 percent of the positions. However, next year, when the organization decides which of these employees to promote, they are starting with a smaller pool of women and the stereotype will increase the imbalance: Of those promoted to the next level only 46.4 percent will be women. By the time the organization has made a series of four advancement-related decisions, the percentage of women will have shrunk to 41.9 percent (Agars, 2004).

Stereotypes are more likely to impede the progress of female leaders in certain contexts. Foremost among them are situations where people are not used to female leaders: male-dominated occupations or roles, roles that call for a directive "masculine" style, and settings where most of the participants are male. Under such conditions, women leaders are likely to be evaluated more harshly than men, according to a meta-analysis of studies of reactions to women leaders in the workplace (Eagly, Makhijani, & Klonsky, 1992). Women attempting to wield power under some circumstances face such conditions in an extreme way. For example, one study shows that female faculty members at the Citadel, a military academy in Charleston, South Carolina, that admitted only male students until recently, can face a lot of silent resistance to their authority. Cadets sometimes refuse to salute them, and some stare at their bodies or wink at them while they are teaching (Siskind & Kearns, 1997). There is a tendency for the male students to think of and relate to female professors in sexual terms—although they may not think of this tendency as sexist. For example, one cadet commented in an interview,

> I have never heard any cadets make any innuendos or discriminate or put the professor down because she was a woman. Any professor who is a female and who is attractive to the cadets will be talked about in class and not to the professor's hearing. . . . Cadets will say, "Man, I love this class because she is so good looking" and stuff. (quoted in Siskind & Kearns, 1997, p. 505)

In this setting, female professors seem to be given less leeway than male professors to criticize the institution or to articulate opinions students disagree with. They are also subject to a variety of putdowns, such as being labeled "girls," being called Ms. or Mrs., instead of addressed by their academic or military rank as male faculty are, and being called "Sir" in class. In settings where women are expected to predominate, however, females are more likely to be chosen as leaders and are not so likely to face discrimination.

A study by Michelle Hebl (1995) demonstrated that participants working in four-person mixed-sex groups were far more likely to choose men than women as leaders when the activity they were engaged in was a competitive one. When the activity was cooperative, however, women were as likely as men to be chosen as leaders. Apparently, women can readily be perceived as leaders when the activity in question is congruent with stereotypes about feminine behavior—although even in this case, they achieved only parity with men, not dominance of the leadership positions.

Stereotypes about what women are good at do have some positive implications for the evaluation of women leaders in certain settings. In some North American business organizations, new models of leadership emphasize the ability to relate to and inspire employees—qualities that fit the feminine stereotype. In one large study of **transformational leadership,** the capacity to effect change by inspiring employees to be dedicated and creative in their jobs, a research team asked employees in community organizations, manufacturing jobs, and schools to evaluate the leadership qualities of their supervisors (Bass, Avolio, & Atwater, 1996). Women leaders were rated higher than men in three of the components of transformational leadership: recognizing employees' needs and inspiring them to work to their highest potential, serving as moral role models for employees, and challenging outdated assumptions. Women and men scored equally on the fourth component, establishing an optimistic vision of the future. A recent meta-analysis of 45 studies underscores this conclusion, showing that women tend to be more transformational leaders than men (Eagly, Johannesen-Schmidt, & Engen, 2003). Clearly, women make effective leaders.

Yet, if women managers are rated so highly as transformational leaders by their subordinates and if they are so good at the mentoring and empowering of subordinates that constitutes effective leadership, why have they not taken over the leadership of more companies, more organizations, more schools? Perhaps because change is not what a lot of companies and other institutions want. The resistance to female leaders may be as likely to come from above as below, driven by power needs as well as stereotyping. Indeed, many women leave middle-level leadership positions in large organizations to form their own companies, perhaps because they know they will not be allowed to make the changes they envision.

Invisibility

At the beginning of his course on the U.S. civil rights movement, Northwestern University sociologist Charles Payne asks his students to name all the women they can think of who were a part of the civil rights struggle. The names Rosa Parks and Coretta Scott King come up, but then the students are silent. But as Payne points out, "In the early '60s in much of the South, women were leading the struggle. And yet that's been totally wiped out of our collective memory" (S. Russell, 1995, p. 15).

Payne goes on to teach his students about how African American women organized much of the civil rights movement, educating their communities and preparing people to become involved. He teaches them, for instance, about Septima Clark, who started the Citizenship Schools that secretly prepared Black citizens to pass the tests required for voter registration, and about Ella Baker, whose long career included work as a field secretary for

BOX 14.1 WOMEN SHAPING PSYCHOLOGY
Mirta González Suárez

Mirta González Suárez has spent much of her career bridging the gap between the university and the community, supporting the political activism of women in her own

country and elsewhere. She is a firm believer that "the political struggle for women's rights is central to the relation between the academy and the community." (González Suárez, 1994, p. 184). Working together with grass-roots activist groups in the women's rights movement, she found that this collaboration "provided the means of spreading the impact of academic activities at the same time it changed the usual research process from one defined by the researchers to a more participatory model that starts with the communities' interests." (p. 184).

González Suárez, a social psychologist, is currently a professor of psychology at the University of Costa Rica. She received her Ph.D. at the Universidad Autónoma in Madrid in 1977 after completing a dissertation on the topic of education and gender roles. Since that time, she has been active in starting the university's interdisciplinary gender studies pro-

the NAACP and as a major organizer of both the Southern Christian Leadership Conference and the Student Nonviolent Coordinating Committee. These powerful women are often overlooked as driving forces in the civil rights movement. Why? Perhaps Ella Baker's own words provide the best explanation:

> I had known . . . that there would never be any role for me in a [formal] leadership capacity with the SCLC. Why? First, I'm a woman. Also, I'm not a minister . . . The basic attitudes of men and especially ministers as to . . . the role women [play] in their church setups is that of taking orders, not providing leadership. (quoted in S. Russell, 1995, p. 17)

A number of studies show that women's leadership is difficult for many people to see. For example, Paul Hanges and his colleagues bring people to their lab to watch a series of videotapes of a four-person group (two women and two men) working together to solve a group decision-making task. In one condition, participants see a man taking the initial leadership of the group, and then watch his role gradually diminish while that of a woman becomes stronger. By the last tape, the woman has emerged as the clear leader of the

BOX 14.1 WOMEN SHAPING PSYCHOLOGY (continued)
Mirta González Suárez

gram (Programa Interdisciplinario de Estudios de Genero) and in networking with academic and nonacademic feminists in many Latin American countries. In 1993, she chaired the organizing committee for the Fifth International Interdisciplinary Congress on Women, which took place in San José, Costa Rica. In that role she became, of necessity, a person who facilitated links among women of many countries. She is the author of many articles and several books in Spanish, including *Women's Studies: Knowledge and Change* (1988) and *Sexism in Education* (1990). Of all her publications, she is most proud of one called *Learning to be a Woman,* a magazine developed for grassroots women's organizations.

Read What Mirta González Suárez Has Written

González Suárez, Mirta. (1988). Barriers to female achievement: Gender stereotypes in

Costa Rican textbooks. *Women's Studies International Forum, 11*(6), 599–609.

González Suárez, Mirta. (1994). With patience and without blood: The political struggles of Costa Rican women. In B. J. Nelson & N. Chowdhury (Eds.), *Women and politics worldwide* (pp. 174–188). New Haven, CT: Yale University Press.

González Suárez, Mirta. (1995). *Felicidades, falacias y fantasías: feminismo en Costa Rica?: Testimonios, reflexiones, ensayos.* San Jose, CR: Editorial Mujeres.

González Suárez, Mirta (1997). Análisis de relaciones interpersonales: Propuesta para una psicologia respetuosa de los derechos humanos (An analysis of interpersonal relations: Toward a psychology respectful of human rights). *Revista Costarricense de Psicologia, 14*(27), 9–28

González Suárez, Mirta (2002). Feminismo, academia y cambio social (Feminism, academy, and social change). *Revista Educación* (Universidad de Costa Rica), *26*(2), 269–283.

group. In another condition, the order is reversed: The woman starts out as group leader and then gradually loses her position of leadership to a man. As the research participants watch these tapes, they are instructed to move the computer cursor to the name of the person they think is leading the group, and this information is recorded. Findings suggest that participants are more ready to see men than women as leaders. Those who saw the series that began with a female leader noticed the male leader as soon as he started to emerge; those who saw the male leader first did not notice the emergence of the female leader until she demonstrated unequivocally that she had become the group leader (described in DeAngelis, 1997).

Perhaps we should not be so surprised at the invisibility of female leadership. Studies show that even when judging everyday verbal interactions, people in the United States find it easier to see men than women as causing the outcomes of the interaction. In one study, respondents were given brief verbal descriptions of interpersonal events, which varied in terms of the gender of the actors and recipients, and asked to say who had caused the actions (LaFrance, Brownell, & Hahn, 1997). The researchers found that the gender of the participants in the interaction significantly affected respondents' views of who initiated the behaviors. Women acting or feeling in mixed-gender pairs were viewed by these respondents as having caused or initiated their own actions or feelings less than men. Once again, it appears that women's agency is not noticed or taken seriously.

Motivation, Skills, and Styles in the Use of Power

Granted that gender stereotypes mitigate against women's being chosen or seen as leaders, might some of the gender disparities in power be traced, nonetheless, to differences in motivation to hold power over others? To differences in the effective assertion of authority or wielding of influence? Researchers have been examining such questions for years.

Do Women Want to Lead?

Women are just as likely as men are to be motivated by a **need for power** (Winter, 1988). Because of the different social expectations placed on them, however, women and men may show their needs for power differently. In many contexts, women, who are not expected to behave in the authoritative, assertive ways we sometimes associate with powerful positions, must find alternative ways to express their power motivation.

Many leadership positions in organizations are defined around a set of qualities that, in Western cultures, are stereotypically masculine. Traditional business and political organizations, for example, have hierarchical structures, and the requirements for managerial roles in such structures include an orientation toward competition, giving directions to others, acting assertively, and standing out from the group. Management in such organizations involves having a lot of explicit power over others, as well as receiving significantly more rewards and having access to more resources than subordinates. Researchers have found in the past that such managerial roles, probably because they require stereotypically masculine behaviors, are viewed, especially by men, as a better "fit" for men than for women (Heilman, 2001; Heilman, Block, Martell, & Simon, 1989).

Women who adopt the autocratic or directive style of leadership that is traditional for hierarchical organizations are more likely than men to be targets of disapproval (Eagly, et al., 1992). Perhaps because they expect to be penalized for taking on a role that is stylistically masculine, women do show somewhat lower scores than men on a paper-and-pencil measure of motivation to manage (Eagly, Karau, Miner, & Johnson, 1994). The tendency for men to score higher than women on this measure is more pronounced in samples of African Americans than in their European American counterparts and less pronounced among older than younger respondents. Congruent with the idea that gender role requirements are the basis for women's lower scores is the finding that, of the seven subscales of this test, only the five that measure masculine-stereotyped qualities produce higher scores by men. These five subscales measure a desire to compete with peers in games and sports, a desire to compete with peers in work-related activities, a desire to behave actively and assertively, a desire to tell others what to do, and a desire to assume a distinctive, highly visible position. The remaining two subscales, which measure a desire to maintain positive relationships with superiors in the chain of command and a desire to handle the day-to-day administrative tasks of the managerial role, are more congruent with feminine role expectations. On these two subscales of the motivation-to-manage scale, women scored higher than men (Eagly et al., 1994).

If women show a small but significant tendency to be less motivated than men to meet most of the requirements for managerial roles in hierarchical organizations, does this mean they are less effective managers than men? Not at all, many theorists argue. Leadership is being redefined in many organizations. Many new models of management reject the strictly hierarchical, rigidly bureaucratic role expectations for managers, replacing them with roles that emphasize participatory decision making and democratic relationships with subordinates (e.g., Rosener, 1995). As the role requirements for leadership change, so too may women's motivation to hold such positions. It is too soon to tell, but women may be more motivated than men to meet the requirements of these new managerial roles.

Claiming Leadership: Women and Men in Groups

When women and men work together in groups, men are more likely than women to emerge as leaders. Why and how does this happen? Part of the explanation may be that, as discussed in Chapter 6, women and men have, by adulthood, been through years of socialization toward different communication styles: women toward sharing ideas, turn-taking in speech, and listening; men toward asserting ideas, interrupting, and holding the floor. Research suggests, however, that there is more going on in mixed-gender groups than different patterns of socialization. Women's and men's leadership behavior in these groups is apparently influenced by the status that they and others perceive them to have and by the actual amount of power that goes with their position in the group.

According to **expectation states theory,** gender is a **diffuse status characteristic:** a characteristic that carries a general set of expectations for performance. Males are automatically evaluated more highly than females, the theory says, and so whenever women and men are working together in informal task groups, both women and men will expect men to perform better at the task. Because both the men and the women in the group have higher expectations for men, men will be given more opportunities to contribute to the task, actually will contribute more, will receive more positive evaluations of their contributions, and will exert more influence on group decisions than women will. Research has supported these predictions: In informal mixed-gender task groups where participants know little about one another and are not assigned to leadership positions, men tend to talk more, give more directions and explicit suggestions, and emerge as leaders much more often than women do (Lockheed & Hall, 1976; Wood & Karten, 1986).

But what happens when the conditions are changed—when, for example, someone in the group is known to have previous experience with the task or is assigned a formal leadership position? Providing women with task-specific expectations of competence by giving them experience with the task can markedly improve their level of contributions to the group and their chances of emerging as leaders. However, women have to be made to appear *more* competent than men in the group in order to attain the same level of influence (Lockheed, 1985).

Assigning women to formal, legitimate positions of authority in the group also increases their level of influential behavior. When Cathryn Johnson (1993) randomly assigned males or females to be "managers" of a four-person task group, supposedly on the basis of their past work experience, she found that the female and male managers did not differ from each other in the amount of time they talked in their groups or in their rate of compliments or agreements toward their subordinates. Both female and male managers differed from their subordinates of both sexes on these behaviors—as would be expected in any situation where one person is designated as the supervisor. So it appears that explicitly giving women legitimate formal authority can allow them to act like, and to be perceived as, leaders. The generalized lower status and expectations associated with women have some effect even under these conditions, however. Johnson found that both male and female subordinates complimented male managers more than female managers. She also found that whereas managers were more directive toward subordinates of the other sex, this tendency was far more pronounced for male than for female managers.

Clearly, the tendency to expect men to take charge and women to subordinate themselves to male authority can be counteracted to a large extent by putting women in formal leadership positions. But the generalized expectations about women's lower competence mitigate against their being chosen for leadership positions, and if a woman *is* promoted into a leadership position, her advancement may be attributed to affirmative action or favoritism rather than to competence. In such a case, her position will not grant her automatic legitimacy and status as a leader. Because a challenge to men's authority is a challenge to a system that many consider to be not only normative but natural, women leaders are bound to be regarded by some, not as legitimate, but as disruptive, troublesome, and annoying. In fact, research shows that it can be extraordinarily difficult for a woman to gain legitimacy as a leader in certain situations. Janice Yoder and her colleagues (1998) devised a laboratory experiment in which women were placed in leadership positions with all-male groups on a masculine-stereotyped task. This procedure was meant to simulate the position in which women find themselves when they acquire leadership positions in male-dominated organizations. In all three experimental conditions, group members were told that the woman had been randomly appointed by the experimenters to lead the group. In two of the three conditions, the women leaders received special pretask training to give them expertise on the group task. However, in one of these two conditions, the women were told *not* to reveal that they had been trained, whereas in the other condition a male experimenter informed the group that the woman who would be leading them had come in early for special training and that she had information that could be useful to the group as they made their decisions. Thus, the experiment compared the group outcomes for an appointed-only leader, an appointed and trained leader, and an appointed, trained, and "legitimated as credible" leader. Results showed that *only* the women who had been appointed and trained and were legitimated as credible by the male experimenter were effective in influencing the performance of their all-male groups. Women who had been simply appointed leaders tended to be relegated to secretarial roles in their groups. Women who had been appointed and trained but not introduced by the experimenter as experts were continually frustrated in their attempts to share their expertise with their groups: "these women's added expertise gave them the background to influence the group without the power base from which to do it effectively. They interrupted in vain to try to make relevant points; they pleaded for acknowledgment using tag questions, yet they went unheeded" (p. 219). The women who had been trained but had not had legitimacy bestowed on them externally were apparently seen by the male group members as ineffectual and contributing little to the group. The researchers argue, based on these findings, that no matter how competent they are, women in male-dominated organizations often cannot overcome the stereotype that women are not expected to be leaders unless they are empowered by an external endorsement from the organization.

This research provides some understanding of what Rosabeth Kanter (1977) illustrated long ago: that merely holding a managerial position does not automatically imply that one also holds all the authority and access to resources that should go with that position. Kanter has argued that women in leadership positions similar to those of men often do not have the same level of status and clout in the organization and so cannot influence their subordinates in the same ways. Thus they behave in less powerful ways with their subordinates than men do.

Styles of Power and Influence

There are different ways to wield influence. A person can be an autocratic, directive leader who issues orders and spends little time gathering the opinions of subordinates. Or a leader can work to build participation, consensus, and a sense of shared responsibility within a group. Stereotypes would predict that women would tend to exert leadership in a democratic, participative style, and men would favor the more autocratic, directive approach. In this case, the stereotypes seem to be at least partly right. A meta-analytic review of studies showed a small but reliable tendency for the sexes to differ in just this way in their leadership style (Eagly & Johnson, 1990). Why the difference? Perhaps because, as we have just discussed, women are penalized or devalued for using the "masculine" approach. Or perhaps because women and men have each learned to adopt the style that gets them the most compliance. Perhaps different approaches are favored by women and men because they control different resources.

The Bases of Power   One lesson that many of us learned as children is that our influence on others depends on how much and what kind of power we have, and that, in turn, is a function of how many and what kind of resources we control. Pleading, threatening, sulking, arguing—all are ineffective when we have nothing to back them up. As noted in Chapter 5, holding power with respect to another person implies having control over the resources necessary to affect the other person's outcomes.

John French and Bertram Raven (French & Raven,1959; Raven, 1965) outlined six **bases of social power:** types of resources used to buttress influence attempts over others. They argued that the basis of one person's power over another was incorporated into the relationship in the form of some combination of these resources. According to French and Raven, in a hypothetical social interaction between two individuals, Maria and Ira, Maria's power with respect to Ira is based on the following:

- **Reward power:** What kinds of rewards does Maria control that Ira wants?
- **Coercive power:** What kinds of punishment does Maria control that Ira fears?
- **Legitimate power:** Does Ira believe that Maria has a right to influence him in this situation?

- **Referent power:** Does Ira admire, feel affection for, or wish to emulate Maria?

- **Expert power:** Does Maria have presumed knowledge or expertise in this situation that is greater than Ira's?

- **Information power:** Does Maria have information that she can use to persuade Ira?

This list does not exhaust all possible bases of power (Raven, Schwarzwald, & Koslowsky, 1998). However, it is extensive enough to suggest that some bases of power may be more likely to be in the hands of women and others in the hands of men. For example, if men have more money, they may have more reward power; if they have more physical strength, they may have more of the coercive power that rests on physical threat. If men have higher status and are more likely to be perceived as experts, they may have more expert power. If women find it easier to attract people into relationships and make them care for them, then they may have more referent power.

All of these possibilities are too simple, however. Rewards include not just money, but also love and approval. Punishment includes not only the ability to beat someone up, but also the ability to ruin his reputation. Expertise is linked to particular topics. Although women and men may differ in the specific *types* of reward, coercion, legitimacy, and expertise they control, it is probably inaccurate to say that women or men, in general, have more access to any of these bases of power.

The most complex basis of power is legitimacy: the perceived right of one person to influence another. Legitimacy can come from recognized authority or status; for example, a teacher may be seen as having a right to influence her students *because* she is the teacher. It may also come from an accepted obligation, such as a promise. If I have previously promised you my help, you later have a right to request that help. It can also come from role requirements; for instance, a man may influence his wife by reminding her of the requirements for being a "good wife."

This last aspect of legitimate power suggests how it is that women and men in different cultures and in different times can differ so strongly in what they consider reasonable to demand of one another. In some parts of the Arab world, both men and women agree it is legitimate for a husband to demand that his wife not go out in public unaccompanied because this is part of the accepted role of a virtuous wife. In certain other cultures, such a demand would be considered illegitimate and could be enforced only by threats. In any culture, when the shared sense of legitimacy about the requirements of gender roles (or any other major roles) begins to shift, so does the power. For example, in North America it used to be accepted that male supervisors in the workplace had the right to make sexual advances to their female subordinates, whether or not those advances were welcome. Women who objected rarely got a sympathetic hearing, and sometimes lost their jobs. The climate has now changed and, although many men still make such advances, women are seen to have a legitimate right to object, to complain, and even to file charges of sexual harassment.

The resources that people control help to determine how they go about trying to influence others. In general, people in the independent cultures of the West are most likely to use influence styles that are direct, open, and assertive when they feel they are operating from a strong base of power. Thus, for example, a teacher will directly tell her students that she wants them to read particular material: She is the legitimate authority, and she can reward students for compliance or punish them with poor grades if they do not meet her requirements. In other contexts, the same woman may hold fewer resources in terms of legitimacy, reward, and coercion and be less direct in her influence attempts. Thus she may hint to a friend that she would like help with a chore rather than come right out and request such help—particularly if she feels she is already obligated to that friend for previous favors.

Both women and men in the United States say they choose **direct influence strategies** over **indirect** ones when possible (White & Roufail, 1989), and there are indications that the use of direct strategies creates a more positive impression. Influence strategies that are indirect (sneaky or manipulative) and unilateral (rather than discussion oriented) tend to be used when the influencer feels relatively powerless in relation to the person she is trying to influence (Falbo & Peplau, 1980). Could the association between relative powerlessness and indirect strategies be related to the stereotype that women are manipulative?

When gender differences in power and self-confidence are controlled for in a research setting, there are minimal gender differences in the tendency to use direct or indirect influence styles (Steil & Weltman, 1992). In many real-world situations, however, such gender differences in power and self-confidence are not controlled for, and "feminine" behavior is confounded with "powerless" behavior. For example, Maria Strykowska (1995) notes that women in Poland who are in managerial roles are expected to be less direct in their exertion of authority than their male counterparts are, relying on friendly persuasion and coaxing rather than direct assertion and threat. The expectation may be based on women's perceived lack of legitimacy in such roles or on their lack of coercive or reward power within the organization.

Does the link between directness and strong bases of power hold for more interdependent cultures, where directness is sometimes frowned upon and confrontation is considered unseemly? Janice Steil and Jennifer Hillman (1993) examined this question by comparing the responses of college students in the United States, Korea, and Japan to questions about their preferred and most frequently used influence strategies. They reasoned that given the stronger concern with politeness in the Eastern cultures than in the West, directness might be less valued as an influence strategy in Korea and Japan than in the United States. They further hypothesized that the apparently larger status difference between women and men in Korea and Japan than in the United States would produce a stronger association between gender and the directness of influence styles. Their findings, however, showed little support for these hypotheses. Students in all three samples valued direct influence strategies (convince, state importance, reason) more than indirect ones (acquiesce, evade, use an advocate) and associated them with greater power. Among the direct strategies, however, Americans were more likely to try to *convince* others, whereas Japanese students were more likely to simply *state the importance* of what they wanted. Among the indirect strategies, Japanese and Korean students were more likely to *acquiesce* than American students. These differences may reflect the greater concern for politeness among Japanese and Korean students.

Students in all three groups reported having greater power when trying to influence female rather than male targets, although they did not report significant differences in the strategies used with females and males. Also, women and men did not indicate different preferences for strategies of influence. The authors conclude that perceptions of personal power and concerns for politeness, rather than gender, are related to the choice of influence

BOX 14.2 LEARNING ACTIVITY
What Influence Strategies Do You Use?

Imagine you are with a good friend, getting ready to spend an evening together. Imagine further that you have one idea about how to spend the evening, and s/he has an idea that is totally opposite to yours and uninteresting to you. If you were going to try to persuade your friend to go along with *your* idea, what would you do? Rank order the following possibilities in terms of the likelihood that you would use them:

Provide information about all the benefits of doing what you want to do.

Argue clearly for your choice on the basis that it is what you really want to do.

Point out that you did what s/he wanted last weekend, so it's your turn.

Promise to do something for her/him in exchange if you get your way on this issue.

Threaten to cancel your evening together if you can't do what you want.

Act quiet and unenthusiastic in response to her/his suggestion.

Cry, sulk, or pout.

Do what s/he wants, but ruin the evening by refusing to enjoy yourself.

What do your rankings tell you about the influence strategies you tend to use in such situations? About the bases of power you rely on in this kind of relationship? Would it make a difference whether your good friend in this example was female or male? Does this example tell you anything about the way interpersonal power is affected by gender?

strategies. This finding is in line with others based only on U.S. samples (e.g., Cowan, Drinkard, & MacGavin, 1984).

"It's Not in Her Head": Barriers to Power for Women

We have seen that many social and emotional barriers to power exist for women: Women are labeled "masculine" when they hold power, their influence is discounted, and they meet with disapproval when they act in directive ways. Some of these social psychological forces are so subtle and intangible that women may wonder at times if they are imagining the barriers; others are blatant and undeniable to the woman experiencing them, but seemingly invisible to everyone else. One aspect of the barriers is quantifiable: the rewards and visibility talented women leaders gain.

Two Glass Ceilings

What is a "**glass ceiling**"? A barrier that keeps people from rising past a certain point—but a barrier that is virtually invisible until the person crashes into it. Because increasing numbers of women are entering fields that often lead to leadership positions—law, business, politics, education, science—many assume that getting to top positions is a matter of time, energy, and talent. Yet the proportion of women who have made it into high leadership positions remains stunningly small.

The final report of the U.S. government's Glass Ceiling Commission in 1995 noted that the nation's boardrooms remain overwhelmingly White and male: 95 percent of the senior-level managers in the *Fortune* 1000 industries and *Fortune* 500 companies were men and 97 percent were White (Swoboda, 1995). How much have things changed since then? Not very much. Women hold only eight of the CEO positions in *Fortune* 500 Companies—although, as a group, those eight companies significantly outperformed the broader market (D. Jones, 2003); African American women represent only 1.1 percent of corporate officers in such companies (106 out of 10,092 positions) (Catalyst, 2004).

Even women who do crash through the glass ceiling into top executive positions apparently do not reach a place where gender equity is the norm. A study of executives in one multinational corporation showed that the women who had reached this level faced a *second* glass ceiling (Lyness & Thompson, 1997). These women made the same pay and received the same bonuses as their male counterparts, but they managed fewer people, were given fewer stock options, and obtained fewer overseas assignments than the men did. They had the same title as the men; however, as we noted in the discussion of power in groups, being in the same position does not necessarily imply having the same status and clout in the organization. When surveyed, the women reported less satisfaction than the men did with their future career opportunities. Clearly, they had gotten the message that they had moved up as far as they could in their company—whereas the men were more likely to see new opportunities ahead. The differences in the ways the two groups were rewarded were subtle, but they apparently signaled to men that they were valued for the long term and to women that they were not.

A Hostile Environment

The social-structural environment of many institutions is not particularly welcoming for women in management positions, nor is it easy for women to adapt. Maria Strykowska (1995) notes that in Poland, promising women may miss out on promotions because they are not viewed as holding "an attitude considered vital for a managerial post, that is, attachment to the enterprise, readiness to work overtime, and geographical mobility" (p. 9). Many women cannot dedicate themselves entirely to work, as this set of norms requires, because in Poland, as in other countries, women are charged with the main responsibilities of childcare and domestic work. Strykowska notes that when a woman does show the kind of dedication and ambition required of a manager, she is assumed to be asexual, unfeminine, and neglectful of her duties at home.

Women in Poland who aspire to senior management positions face other obstacles as well. One is the very fact that most senior managers are male, and these male managers tend to choose other men for promotion. Women, often outside the information network maintained by existing high-level managers, frequently do not even find out about a vacant position until it has been filled. Another issue is the age thought to be appropriate for entry into senior management. Appointment to higher management ranks usually occurs at about age 40, on the assumption that a manager this age has both accumulated a lot of valuable experience and looks forward to many years of efficient performance before retirement. This pattern of promotion is not an easy fit for women, who may have had to devote much of their energy to their families throughout their 30s. Many women may not be ready for promotion at 40, but when they are ready a few years later, they are considered too old.

The situation in Poland is mirrored in other countries, including the United States. In particular, women seem to face many more difficulties with advancement in organizations that are male dominated, where there are very few women in senior, authoritative positions. Robin Ely (1995) studied women lawyers in firms that were either strongly male dominated or gender integrated. Women in the two types of firms differed in the ways they described themselves, other women, and men, and in the qualities they believed were important for advancement and success in their firms. Women in male-dominated firms tended to believe that masculine qualities were essential for success, and some tried hard to fit the masculine mold. For example, some commented that the women who were going to become partners in the firm were those whose femininity was not obvious or who modeled themselves on men. They did not think that stereotypically feminine attributes were valued in their organizations. One commented,

> I think if I'm going to be a trial attorney I can't really rely on or develop those attributes that are considered sort of feminine. I'm not saying that you should forget about being a woman, but on the other hand, I think what society has defined as being masculine or feminine, it's more the masculine, it seems, that you have to go toward. . . . I think [the male partners] would prefer whatever that professionalism is to be defined probably in masculine terms . . . I think they have a skewed view of what being feminine is. And those attributes just don't mesh well in an established place. (p. 614)

Some of the women in the male-dominated firms tried to model themselves on a masculine standard of aggression and competitiveness, yet they also noted that the men hated women who acted "too much" like men. They still felt the need to rely at times on feminine roles when trying to influence their male colleagues. As one woman said,

> I think that the men in most law firms don't know how to deal with strong professional women because they haven't had the experience yet. And so you have to figure out a way to communicate with these people on their own level. . . . You could be openly sexual but that would bring with it a very much more substantial problem. . . . So it's easier for me to take on the role of [my boss's] daughter or his wife or his mother, or some role that he's familiar with. (p. 620)

Other women in these firms resisted the idea that they should conform to masculine norms, and they expressed anger and frustration—as well as the intention to leave their jobs. Still others blamed themselves for their inability to fit in, saying that they just did not have the qualities, such as the ability to tolerate conflict and pressure, that were necessary for success in that organization. Clearly, women in the male-dominated firms were very conscious of gender stereotypes and tended to see conforming to masculine-stereotyped behavior (without, however, losing their femininity) as vital for success.

For women in gender-integrated firms, the picture Ely (1995) found was quite different. These women were not so likely to categorize feminine behavior in negative terms and tended to see both traditionally feminine and traditionally masculine qualities as important

---

BOX 14.3 MAKING CHANGE
Supporting Women in Leadership Positions

One of the things that is clear from the research discussed in this chapter is that women in leadership positions are judged very harshly when they deviate from a fairly narrow range of behavior. Men in leadership positions are often given more leeway than their female counterparts. Are there women in leadership positions at your school or your place of employment? Do you find yourself and others being extra critical of them? Listen to the way you and others talk about these women. Think carefully about whether or not you are judging them fairly. Consider how gender expectations may come into your judgments. Do you expect women to be "nicer" than men, and then dislike them if they are not? If a woman is firm in her opinions and decisions, do you respond more negatively than if a man were similarly firm? By trying to hold women and men leaders to similar standards, instead of holding women to a higher one, you advance justice for women.

---

for their success. They did not have such a strong notion that they must change in order to fit in; rather, they viewed the profession as changing to adapt to women:

> I think that women are bringing to the practice the sense that you don't have to be so aggressive —you can be cooperative and still do things for your client. You don't have to fight every inch of the way. Being cooperative may actually help your client in the long run because you won't spend as much time fighting over things that aren't worth fighting over, and so you won't spend the client's money. So I think women are changing the profession. (p. 615)

Clearly, working in an organizational environment that included significant numbers of women in top positions helped women lawyers to feel less embattled and made gender roles less stereotypical and less problematic. Even these women, however, sometimes felt that they had to work especially carefully at connecting with the male lawyers who "want you to be feminine as well" (p. 618). They struggled to find ways of relating to their male co-workers that did not fit either the male "golfing buddy" or the female "flirt" roles. Perhaps because the profession of law as a whole is still male dominated at the top levels, women must work harder than men to fit in. The latter argument finds support from legal scholar Lani Guinier and her colleagues (1994), who analyzed what they deemed the hostile environment of law school. In an article titled "Becoming Gentlemen: Women's Experiences at One Ivy League Law School," they noted that women and men enter law school with similar qualifications, yet significantly fewer women than men end up in the top 10 percent of their class. This means that fewer women than men end up in the very top tier of the job market when they graduate, making them less likely to snag the high-status positions that lead to rapid advancement in the profession. Guinier and her coauthors argue that law school culture is designed to encourage a sort of ritualized combat among students —something that comes more easily to men than to women. Women in law school must become "social males," taking on stereotypically masculine qualities such as aggression and willingness to fight and submerging their former selves in order to succeed. Women who do not adopt this style, the authors assert, lose self-esteem, making it even harder for them to perform well.

The environment can also be hostile to women who wish to enter the arena of political leadership. For example, the Roma women of Eastern Europe have found cultural barriers arrayed against them. Carol Silverman (2000) details some of the difficulties faced by women in that particular cultural context, some of which are shared by women everywhere:

> Firstly, women do not feel welcome in the overwhelmingly male context of political meetings in part because they occur in male spaces such as cafes, restaurants, and meeting halls. . . . Secondly, . . . the assembly is almost totally male, so to offer female Romani candidates seems absurd to many. Women are taught in subtle ways that national politics is a male domain—there is a lack of female role models. Thirdly, women find most party platforms . . . lacking in women's concerns, which they define as more practical and focused on economic discrimination and family issues such as child care. (p. 2)

It appears that even though women often blame themselves for their lack of advancement into top leadership positions, a range of subtle and not-so-subtle social-structural barriers are keeping them out. Dismantling these barriers clearly involves a circular, self-reflexive process: More women must be in positions of power before it will become easier for women to achieve positions of power. For the first women to climb over the barriers in any institution, the process is likely to be slow, difficult, and painful.

The Difficult Process of Change

In many places, gender relations are undergoing a slow process of transformation as women gradually gain more access to positions of power. The barriers to be negotiated are often daunting, yet women have evolved a variety of strategies to get around, over, or under them. Consider, for example, South Korea, where women are inching their way into positions of political leadership. Gender relations in Korean society have been based for centuries on the Chinese cosmology of yin and yang: the idea that the feminine passive principle and the masculine active principle are complementary and must be combined in harmony. This philosophy is present along with the traditional Confucian belief in male superiority. Based on these ideas, Korean tradition with respect to gender dictates an ordered hierarchy in which women and men each have their place. Historically, no public roles of high prestige for women existed, and a woman's main duty was obedience: first to her father, later to her husband, and still later to her son (Soh, 1993). Women assuming leadership positions in the public world of politics are violating that order, yet a small number of them have consistently done so. In 1988, the female membership of the Korean National Assembly was 2 percent—the same percentage as the female membership of the U.S. Senate in that year. In the 2004 elections, women won 30 of the 299 legislative seats —just over 13 percent. Many Koreans were surprised at the results and found their gender stereotypes challenged. As one woman commented:

> I expected women to hold quieter, smaller campaigns, due to their relative physical weakness. But I was prejudiced. The women candidates that I saw led campaigns as actively as any man. It was also good to see their husbands helping them. Women are no longer passive followers

Women assuming leadership positions in the public world of politics in Korea are transgressing the traditional social order, yet a small number of them have consistently done so.

of their husbands. I want my own daughters to grow up to be as active as them. (Korea Update, 2004)

Chung-Hee Soh (1993) interviewed 26 of the 42 women who had become legislators in Korea before 1988. She discovered that these women used a variety of coping strategies to manage the conflicting roles of woman and legislator—exercising considerable *nunch'i* (tact and intuitiveness in delicate situations) to maintain proper womanly behavior while still being effectively involved in the processes of political influence and decision making. Korean society is strongly gender segregated. Schools and universities tend to be single gender, and social life is largely segregated as well. Thus it is difficult for women legislators to be included in informal social gatherings with their male colleagues and hence to share in the information and influence that are exchanged at such gatherings. Some of the women organized informal lunch meetings with top officials so that they would get a chance to talk with them. Others enlisted the help of husbands, sons, and other male relatives to accompany them to male-dominated gatherings and to interact with the men on their behalf. Some hired men to be their secretaries and assistants, since male staff members could more easily gather information from the offices of male politicians.

A few of the women legislators were emboldened to join their male colleagues in informal group activities. One took up golf—a very unusual pursuit for a Korean woman.

Another woman sometimes went drinking with the male politicians, who later criticized her behind her back for her immodest and "unwomanly" behavior. One woman reported that she sometimes dined out with her male colleagues, but only if she had ascertained that *all* of them wanted her to join them.

> When she dines out with her male colleagues, even at their invitation, . . . she is expected to behave with *nunch'i* and leave them sometime after dinner, so that the men could entertain themselves freely without the inhibiting presence of their female colleagues. If she does not do so, she will be criticized for being "a woman without *nunch'i*." One informant said that some men would half-jokingly suggest the departure time for their married female colleague by reminding her of her duty to look after her husband, "the big baby," at home. (Soh, 1993, p. 84)

The women were also careful about how they dressed. Elected women tended to wear the *hanbok*—the traditional dress with long skirts—or trousers to cover their legs and present an image of either conservative femininity or sexual equality.

The women handled some of the contradictions between traditional and egalitarian gender role ideologies by compartmentalizing social situations into public and private, formal and informal. For example, a woman legislator having lunch in a public place with male members of her committee would likely share a table with them; however, if she invited the committee to her home she would serve the men first, in the traditional manner, then join the women in another room. These women legislators are apparently managing change as a fluid but discontinuous process—one that will occur slowly and in a careful dance with tradition.

Women in Power

Women as a group have begun to claim an increasing amount of political power, though it is still small in relation to men's. This increase in power is evident in two ways: the election of women to political leadership positions, and the success of women's efforts at grassroots organizing. Researchers have studied what happens to women holding political power and the kinds of changes they produce in the processes of power.

Women as Political Leaders

Wilma Mankiller, chief of the Cherokee Nation for 10 years, stared down the stereotypes about women in political leadership positions. After serving as chief under difficult conditions from 1985 to 1991, this first woman chief was reelected for her final 4-year term with 83 percent of the vote. One of the most visible Native American leaders in the United States, Mankiller oversaw the addition of three health centers, nine children's programs, and a job training center for the United States' second-largest group of Native Americans. During her 10 years as chief, membership in the Nation more than doubled, the budget grew from $44 million to $144 million, and the number of employees nearly doubled to 1,300 (Ferguson, 1995). By the time she stepped down, most of the doubts that people had entertained about having a woman as chief had simply evaporated. Most women who aspire to political leadership, however, do not get the opportunity to prove themselves in this way.

Even decades—or centuries—ago, women occasionally headed countries as heredi- tary monarchs: for instance, Queen Elizabeth I and Queen Victoria of England and Cather- ine the Great of Russia. The first woman *elected* to lead a nation appears to have been Sirimavo Bandaranaike, who became prime minister of what is now Sri Lanka (then called Ceylon) in 1960. From 1960 until 1997, only 31 women around the world were elected or appointed as heads of state (Neft & Levine, 1997). If you have not heard of many of them, it is because, for some, their terms of office were extraordinarily short. For example, Kim Campbell, Sylvie Kinigi, Edith Cresson, and Ertha Pascall-Trouillot were, respectively, prime ministers of Canada, Bolivia, France, and Haiti for less than a year. As of 2000, 39 countries had elected or appointed a female head of state (president or prime minister) at least once, with the most recent being Finnish president Tarja Halonen (United Nations, 2000). There seems to be only one country in which women have held a majority of the top political positions: New Zealand. In New Zealand, a woman, Helen Clark, is the prime minister. A woman, Jenny Shipley, was until recently the leader of the opposition. Another woman, Dame Sian Elias, is the chief justice and yet another, Margaret Wilson, the attor- ney general. Furthermore, the chief executive officer of the nation's largest company, Tele- com, is a woman: Theresa Gattung. And the most recent appointment, to the position of governor general, is yet another woman, Dame Silvia Cartwright (Peters, 2000).

Women have been an increasing presence in national legislatures worldwide, but there is no nation where women hold half of such posts (United Nations Development Program, 2004). As shown in Figure 14.1, the countries with the highest percentage of women in national legislatures are Sweden (45.4 percent) and Rwanda (45 percent). Canada (23.6 percent) and the United States (14 percent) have far lower percentages of women legisla- tors. Some countries are lower still. For example, Japan and Brazil have fewer than 10 per- cent; Turkey and Sri Lanka have fewer than 5 percent, Papua New Guinea and Yemen have fewer than 1 percent, and Saudi Arabia and Kuwait have no women in their national governing bodies (United Nations Development Program, 2004).

Because politics has everywhere been dominated by men, women who achieve posi- tions of political leadership tend to experience a sense of **double marginality:** a sense of alienation from other women because of their unusual job and alienation from male col- leagues because they are unlike them (Apfelbaum, 1993). Consequences include loneli- ness and lack of a sense of entitlement. Sometimes these women try to bridge the gap between their role expectations as women and as politicians by finding a way to merge the two images. For example, female political leaders in Chile and Peru achieve legitimacy by presenting themselves as *supermadres* (supermothers) who use their power to nurture their constituents. Argentina's legendary leader Eva Peron summed up this position well: "In this great house of the Motherland, I am just like any other woman in any other of the innumerable houses of my people. Just like all of them, I rise early thinking about my hus- band and my children. I so truly feel myself the mother of my people" (quoted in Patter- son, ´2000). In a similar vein, Dr. Masooda Jalal, the only woman candidate in Afghanistan's first presidential election, promised to be "the mother for this country" (news24.com, 2004).

Erica Apfelbaum (1993) argues that the particular form women's experience of lead- ership takes is shaped by their culture and their times. Apfelbaum conducted in-depth interviews with 50 women leaders in France and Norway. Sixty percent held cabinet or

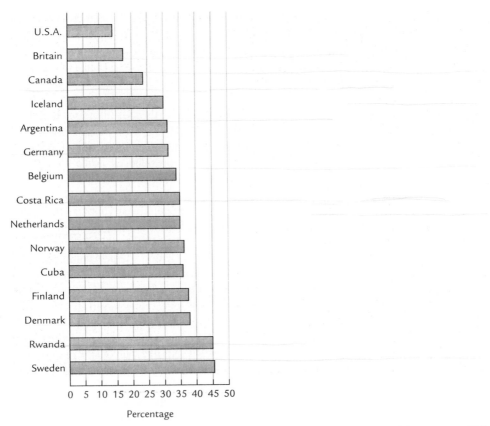

Figure 14.1   Percent of seats in national legislatures and parliaments held by women. This chart shows the countries in which women hold thirty percent or more of the seats in national legislatures and parliaments, and compares them to the lower percentage of such seats held by women in Canada, Great Britain, and the United States. (Data source: United Nations Development Program, 2004)

subcabinet posts, 12 percent headed municipal government agencies of the national capital, and the others were heads of trade unions or directors of major institutions. She discovered that in these two Western European countries, powerful women reported very different experiences. In France, the women leaders spoke of their lives as difficult, burdensome, and filled with conflict and suffering. In Norway, by contrast, the women spoke of their roles positively and with jubilation.

What could account for the differences in tone between powerful women in these two countries? Part of it can be explained by the differing history of the two countries. Power for women is a much older and more established idea in Norway than in France. Norwegian women obtained the vote in 1913, had women representatives in local assemblies beginning in 1967, and have consistently had the support of major political parties in their push to gain equality. It is a country where a woman has been prime minister in three dif-

Mahsood Jalal, the first woman candidate for president of Afghanistan.

ferent governments and where 39 percent of cabinet posts are held by women. In France, women did not win the right to vote until 1944, and they still hold only a small proportion of legislative seats and just 13 percent of cabinet posts. The few token women in high positions are used as examples to "prove" that women are represented at all levels and to discourage further claims.

Clearly, the presence of women who have broken ground as pioneers and role models changes the social landscape for the women who come later, providing them with a legacy of increased confidence and legitimacy. In France, Apfelbaum noted, the women leaders who had obtained their positions in the 1980s were more optimistic and less lonely than those of the previous decade. In Norway, where women had a longer history of role models to draw on, the women "expressed a deeply anchored sense of legitimacy that was totally alien to French women of the first generation and just evolving for the second" (p. 419).

Cultural attitudes about power may also help explain the differing experiences of Norwegian and French women in leadership positions. In Norway, political life apparently revolves around the idea of turnover—the idea that power is transitory and that a leader easily passes the torch to a successor. The power built into a leadership position is not a core part of the leader's identity. Thus men may not feel very threatened by the notion of sharing leadership with women. In France, the political power structure is strongly identified with men, and there is no comparable notion of easy turnover (Apfelbaum, 1993).

Perhaps as a result of the sociohistorical differences between their two countries, Norwegian and French women leaders differed dramatically in two other ways: their allegiance to feminist movements and the ease with which they combined their high-profile positions with marriage. Norwegian women leaders of all political persuasions consistently paid tribute to feminist movements as "the foundation from which emerged the means to fight for the integration of women in the public arena" (Apfelbaum, 1993, p. 421). The French women did not mention feminist movements—except to deny any connection with them. Congruent with these differing emphases on feminism, Norwegian women were much more likely than French women to actively promote their female colleagues, to respond actively and combatively to sexual harassment and everyday sexism, and to place high value on the friendship and support provided by informal networks of women.

The casual observer might think that these combative, feminist-oriented Norwegian women would be less likely than their French counterparts to be able to maintain their close relationships with men. Nothing could be further from the truth, Apfelbaum (1993) found. Whereas 18 of the 20 Norwegian women were married when interviewed, only 5 of the 30 French women were. Most of the Norwegian women claimed to have had few problems balancing marriage with their high-powered career, except for the logistical ones involving time management. The French women were less sanguine about their private lives:

> Almost without exception, they spontaneously raised the issue of their private life as a problematic one and spoke at length about the burdens, the tensions and the difficulty of keeping a harmonious balance in their interpersonal relations with their companions. In this domain, they seemed vulnerable and insecure: The danger of losing a companion was omnipresent, and deep down they knew that being single was the price they might have to pay. French men still seem unable to cope with the social comparison involved once their wives become too visible. (p. 423)

Apfelbaum notes that the French tradition of male–female intimate relationships is strongly based on romance, seduction, chivalry, and game playing—all of which involve notions of conquest and dominance and inequality. Perhaps, she speculates, such cultural traditions mitigate against the easy acceptance in France of relationships in which the woman is visibly more powerful than the man.

The contrast between the leadership experience for women in Norway and France suggests that holding power is likely to involve major social and personal sacrifices for women unless it is done within a cultural context where female leadership is not unusual and female political participation is strong. It also suggests, however, that such a context may be more difficult to achieve in some cultures than in others. Given the discrepancies in the leadership experiences of women from two Western democracies, it is likely that differences in the experiences of women whose cultures diverge even more widely are considerable.

Women, Resistance, and Collective Action: Wielding and Building Power from Below

In many contexts, women are barred from achieving high leadership positions. This does not mean, however, that they have no access to power. Even in the least auspicious circumstances, women find ways to resist patriarchal authority.

Individual Resistance   Sometimes, resistance is carried out on an individual, perhaps nonconscious basis, as in cases where women who are forced to work under impossible conditions develop strange symptoms. Women working in factories in Malaysia, for example, may use spirit possession as a thinly veiled protest against their inhuman treatment. Spirit possession results in attention-getting symptoms and several days' leave from the factory in order to have the spirit exorcised. It is one of few ways these women find to fight back against a system that refuses to take their needs into account (Ong, 1987). Similarly, Erin Moore (1993) noted that young women in one Indian village develop spirit possessions that allow them to behave in antisocial ways (such as falling unconscious in the middle of a task or a meal) that would not otherwise be tolerated by their husbands and in-laws. To be cured, they must take some time off to visit the maulavi, a Muslim healer. It may be, as Moore notes,

> the Nara women's distinctive form of work stoppage. The visit usually requires an overnight stay, meaning that the woman and often her husband or brother are pampered at the home of a relative; . . . she enjoys a needed break from the routine of daily work and a mother-in-law. In addition, the maulavi's cures often require that the patient drink a quarter kilo of warm, sweetened milk and take a warm bath daily. These would be mandated luxuries for a woman in Nara. (pp. 538–539)

Even when they see no mechanism for resisting male authority, women take opportunities to express their disapproval. For example, women in the Taliban-controlled areas of Afghanistan, arguably the most restrictive regime for women in the modern world, responded with a clear voice when surveyed about their experiences by a human rights organization. More than 90 percent of them endorsed equal access for women to work and education opportunities, participation of women in government, and legal protections for the rights of women. More than 80 percent said that women should be able to move about freely and that Islamic teachings do not justify restrictions on women's human rights. Seventy-five percent agreed that women should be able to associate with people of their own choosing. The women almost unanimously (94–98 percent) reported that the policies of the Taliban authorities had made their lives much worse, and they attributed their own declining mental and physical health to these policies (Physicians for Human Rights, 2001).

Collective Action   Often women's resistance is not individual but communal, which is a more effective approach for lasting change. Women around the world have achieved a great deal by developing their own grassroots organizations. The right to vote, now taken for granted by women in many countries, was not simply given to women, but won in each nation only after years of organized struggle by determined women's organizations. The very right to meet in order to organize politically has been precarious for women in many places. In 1994, a political meeting of 100 women in Kenya was disrupted by police, who said it was illegal. When the women refused to leave, the police beat them with batons and fists. In response to such incidents, some women in some African countries began meeting in small groups of three or four, organizing their resistance without drawing police attention (Buckley, 1995).

Women in countries where governments fail to protect their rights or their economic survival have often organized to provide such protections for themselves. In Senegal, rural women organize themselves into groups called *mbootaay,* with an older respected woman as leader. The organization provides familylike support for its members, coming forward with assistance when for example, a woman has a baby or there is a death in her family. Each woman also contributes a small amount of money each month, which provides a source of funds for loans to needy members. The mbootaay have become a force within local politics, mobilizing their members to vote for certain candidates (Patterson, 2000).

In India, self-employed women formed the Self-Employed Workers' Organization (SEWA), which became an international model for women's banking and self-organized financial services. The organization was created through the determination of many poor women who were struggling to support their families on the meager incomes generated by a variety of part-time pursuits (e.g., collecting wood, collecting materials to be recycled, bartering services for food). Their first project was to set up a women's bank, which made small loans to women who needed supplies in order to do their work. Thus a woman might receive a loan to buy a used sewing machine so she could earn money by sewing, or to buy produce that she could sell on the street at a small profit. This organization now supports women in a variety of ways besides the bank. It has helped set up cooperatives for artisans, small farmers, childcare providers and vegetable suppliers. It supports workers' unions for women who labor in agriculture and carpentry. It has been the driving force in the development of community health services and maternity protection plans. And it empowers women directly through group rallies, lobbying, and launching court cases (Ward, 1996). Similar success has been achieved by a union of 240 women entrepreneurs and traders in the West African country of Mauritania. Eighty percent of Mauritania's small businesses are controlled by women; however, many of the women are illiterate and thus become victims of injustice because they do not know their rights. The women's union, tired of being exploited by male businessmen, raised the money to build a shopping center run entirely by women. This Women's Market, planned and funded through the efforts of these women, now stands as a place where women-run businesses can operate with independence (Fullerton, 1998). And in Nicaragua, the Nueva Vida (New Life) women's cooperative to manufacture conventional and organic cotton clothing is the first to be run entirely by female workers—all of whom are partners in the business (Stockman, 2003). This *maquila* (assembly plant) provides an alternative to the sweatshops where many women have to work; in contrast to many other factories it does not mistreat or exploit workers.

Women have organized to claim their power not just in the marketplace and in governments, but in other institutions as well. For example, at the Mount Saint Benedictine Monastery in Pennsylvania, more than 120 Roman Catholic nuns resisted a papal edict that forbade one of their number from attending the first Women's Ordination Worldwide Conference in 2001. They argued that their tradition allowed them to make decisions as a community and that they saw obedience as relational—the product of discussion rather than of a top-down structure in which orders are simply given and carried out without comment. The sisters came together for a process of "discernment" and then sent their prioress to Rome to discuss the issues. In the end, they decided they could not comply with the papal order, and they supported the nun, Sister Joan Chittister, in her attendance at the conference. By their collective action, these women asserted their right to be "a prayerful and questioning presence" in the church rather than being silenced (Murphy, 2001).

Perhaps the best-known example of women's grassroots organizing is the Mothers of the Plaza de Mayo in Argentina. These women were responding to the disappearance of their daughters and sons under the military dictatorship that came to power in Argentina in 1976. Worried relatives could find out no information, and word soon began to circulate that, with the complicity of the government and other institutions, thousands of people who objected to the new regime were being kidnapped, tortured, and killed. Frantically, mothers whose children had disappeared sought information from government and military officials, only to be met with evasion or silence. Finally, a group of these mothers decided to band together to voice their concern and their protest. In 1977, they began to meet every week in the Plaza de Mayo, a large public square in Buenos Aires. Wearing white headscarves to identify themselves, the women walked together in the square, by their presence bearing witness to the terrible events that were taking place in Argentina. They were mocked as *las locas* (the madwomen) and harassed by soldiers. After a few months, 14 of the women disappeared themselves and were never again seen or heard from. Still the mothers kept coming to the square, determined to expose the lies of the Argentine government about what had happened to their children. By 1982, thousands of people had joined them, and in the next year, the military regime fell. This group of women found their power in acting together. Their organization still works to trace missing relatives and to convict the people who killed them. It has also spawned similar organizations in other Latin American countries. A tremendous political force was generated by this determined group of women who said they were "only mothers"—but who refused to accept the political powerlessness traditionally associated with that label (Fisher, 1989).

A New Frontier: Radical Young Feminists. How do young women encounter and become participants in the grassroots power of feminism? Often through music, writing, art, and loosely organized groups of young women who have banded together to challenge traditional notions of gender roles. For example, in the early 1990s, several all-women bands appeared and challenged the macho and often misogynistic attitudes that were common in the world of alternative rock and punk music. In this context, the music world had begun to see commentary about "angry girrrls," and Jean Smith of the band Mecca Normal commented that "We need to start a girl RIOT" (Emplive.com, 2001). The term *riot grrl*, which came to mean a form of punk rock music with a militant feminist stance, was coined at the all-woman opening night of the International Pop Underground convention in Olympia, Washington in 1991 (Wikipedia, 2001). Eventually, the term broadened to include a whole host of activities that centered on an empowerment theme of "doing it yourself" and challenging established wisdom and institutions. Riot grrl meetings soon became important gatherings, where young women talked about music, bands, violence against women, feelings, and other issues, while developing connections with other women.

The energy and questioning spirit spawned by the riot grrl movement has been fueled by feminist punk rock bands such as Bikini Kill and Le Tigre, whose lyrics celebrate women's choices with regard to sex, relationships, and the power to reject abuse and exploitation. Also contributing to the movement has been an explosion of zines: self-published, independent, often electronic magazines that are published and distributed by individuals or small groups of writers and activists. These zines provide an outlet where "critically and politically thinking feminist girls and women, and lesbian, queer and transgender youth from around the globe [can] express their voices without being censored or

BOX 14.4 WOMEN SHAPING PSYCHOLOGY
Collective Voices for Change within the Discipline

As women in psychology discovered, during the 1960s and 1970s, that their voices often went unheard, that psychological theories often either ignored women or dismissed them as inferior to men, that female psychologists were not usually welcome in leadership positions, they began organizing to change the institutions that defined psychology. Without these early and continuing collective efforts, there would be no such thing as a psychology of women course, no psychological journals dedicated to the psychology of women and gender, and few mentors for students wishing to pursue thesis research on aspects of women's experiences. While the situation for women in psychology is far from perfect, the changes wrought in the field by women's collective organizing efforts cannot be ignored.

In Canada, these organizing efforts first reached the awareness of most psychologists when a group of women submitted a symposium, titled *On women, by women,* to the program committee for the 1972 national convention of the Canadian Psychological Association (CPA). The symposium was rejected because it did not "fit in" anywhere on the program (Greenglass, 1973). However, the symposium was held at the convention anyway—an "underground" symposium that defied the notion that the psychology of women was not important. The event proved to be a flashpoint for participants, and it led to the formation of the Interest Group on Women in Psychology. This group later evolved into the CPA Section on Women in Psychology (SWAP) and continues to be one of the largest sections in the association.

In Australia, women psychologists responded to International Women's Year by forming a Women and Psychology Group to present a "hearing" on feminist perspectives on psychology (Dalgliesh, 1975). The organizers were disappointed to find a staggering lack of interest by male psychologists: Of more than 100 men invited, only 15 attended. This perhaps presaged what happened when women petitioned the Australian Psychological Society (APS) for a Women and Psychology Professional Board, which would have been a major professional division of the society. This proposal was rejected on the grounds that it cut across the interests of existing boards. Eventually, in 1984, after several years in which the proponents of a psychology of women group organized conference activities and lobbied, the society approved the formation of an Interest Group on Women and Psychology. The aims of the group were (and are) to encourage research about women, women's studies in psychology, and professional work with women in any field, and as noted by the first convener of that group, "it is a matter of regret that they are not accommodated easily within the aims of existing Divisions" (Gault, 1985, p. 28).

During the late 1970s, women in the New Zealand Psychological Society tried to form a women-only division. The society rejected their proposal on the grounds that it violated human rights policies of nondiscrimination. When the women appealed to the

BOX 14.4 WOMEN SHAPING PSYCHOLOGY (*continued*)
Collective Voices for Change within the Discipline

Human Rights Commission, they were told that they could hold programs for women only, but could not legally have a women-only division. This result slowed the momentum of the group and, although an informal association of women psychologists continued for some time, no formal organization for women in psychology was formed in New Zealand.

And what about the United States? Decades ago, in 1958, the International Council of Women Psychologists opened its membership to men, deleted the word *women* from its name, and applied to become a division of the American Psychological Association (APA). They were turned down because they were perceived as a "women's group" (Walsh, 1985). In 1969, organizing efforts at the APA national convention led to the formation of the Association for Women in Psychology (AWP), a feminist group that still operates outside the organizational structure of APA. It was not until 1973, under lobbying pressure from AWP members, that a formal APA Division of the Psychology of Women (Division 35) was formed, with Elizabeth Douvan as its first president. The spokespersons for Division 35 were careful to claim legitimacy for the group as a scholarly rather than political group, although, as Douvan said, the pursuit of knowledge was intrinsically political: "The existence and growth of the Division will obviously have the effect of legitimizing the study of women. And this is political in the last analysis" (quoted in Mednick, 1978). As a result of joint efforts by AWP and Division 35, APA established a Women's Programs Office in its national headquarters. Thus, there is now a strong presence for women's concerns in APA. Women do not yet have an equal voice in American psychology; however, our progress over the past three decades has been significant.

Read More about Women Organizing for Change in Psychology

Dalgleish, L. (1975). Women and Psychology "Hearing" group report. *Australian Psychologist, 10*(3), 339–344.

Gault, U. (1985, November). Interest Group on Women and Psychology. *Bulletin of the Australian Psychological Society,* p. 28.

Greenglass, E. (1973). Woman: A new psychological view. *The Ontario Psychologist,* 5(2), 7–15.

Mednick, M. T. S. (1978). Now we are four: What should we be when we grow up? *Psychology of Women Quarterly, 3,* 123–138.

Pyke, S. W., & Stark-Adamec, C. (1981). Canadian feminism and psychology: The first decade. *Canadian Psychology, 22*(1), 38–54.

Walsh, M. R. (1985). Academic professional women organizing for change: The struggle in psychology. *Journal of Social Issues, 41*(4), 17–27.

Wilkinson, S. (1990). Women's organisations in psychology: Institutional constraints on disciplinary change. *Australian Psychologist, 25*(3), 256–269.

ridiculed" (grrrlzines.net, 2003). The electronic zines, which include an array of provocative titles such as *Ladybomb, Grrrl Rebel, Driving Blind, Satan Wears a Bra*, and *Persephone Is Pissed*, provide a global forum for young women's outrage, critical thinking, new ideas, and creativity. Comments from some of the participants in this movement illustrate the thoughtfulness and passion that undergirds this newest women's movement:

> When I started the first incarnation of *Pretty Ugly (Kill the Real Grrls)* I hoped to refocus people's attention to feminism as a valid and essential movement, the zine was also a great medium to explore feminist issues and concerns on a personal level. As the zine transformed into the *Pretty Ugly* project, a major goal of ours became to inspire young people, especially women, to write and perhaps make their own zine. (Kelly, *Pretty Ugly*, Australia, quoted on grrrlzines.net, 2003)

> What I love about zines is that I get a lot of new perspective on things. It's inspiring to read what a girl on the other side of the world thinks about feminism or what a girl 2 kilometers from here thinks about rape or whatever. It gives me strength. (Stina B., *(her) riot distro*, Sweden, quoted on grrrlzines.net, 2003)

The young feminist movement has also been strengthened by small radical groups of activists that carry out protests in a wide variety of contexts. One such group that has been active for many years is the Guerilla Girls, a group of anonymous women who take the names of dead women artists and appear in public wearing gorilla masks. Their weapon of choice is humor, which they use to challenge stereotypes and to "re-invent the f-word—feminism" (Guerillagirls.com, 2004). A more recently formed group is the Radical Cheerleaders, whose theme is "protest + performance" and "activism with pom poms and middle fingers extended" (Radical Cheerleaders, 2004). Squads of radical cheerleaders turn up at various events to perform their protest cheers; they take their inspiration from "cheers" that were written, performed, and distributed by the founders of the group, but each squad is independent. The cheers can deal with any issue, but often focus on cultural demands for women to be thin and beautiful. Part of one cheer goes like this:

> Now I'm feeling Healthy And ready to RIOT
> against those demands that i need to DIET!
> I WILL TAKE UP SPACE AND LOVE MY SIZE
> CUZ FAT AND FABULOUS IS ON THE RISE! (Radical Cheerleaders, 2004)

As these examples illustrate, young women all over the world are questioning traditional roles and challenging established women—literally claiming their power.

Women Claiming Power

Farahnaz Nazir, an Afghan woman fleeing the war and the Taliban regime, spoke eloquently about the importance of women's rights in her country: "Afghanistan is like a bird with a broken wing. One wing is the man, and that one works. The other wing is woman, and that one is broken. With one wing broken, the bird cannot fly. A society, without the strength of its women, cannot function" (quoted in Raimondo, 2001).

Nazir's words have relevance to every one of the world's nations: There is no place on earth where women's rights, women's empowerment, are not important to the well-being of the country. It was in support of this belief that, in 1995, delegates from all over the world traveled to Beijing to attend the Fourth World Conference on Women. In the *Beijing Declaration,* adopted at that historic conference, most of the world's governments agreed that they were "determined to advance the goals of equality, development and peace for all women everywhere in the interest of all humanity" and they agreed on a *Platform for Action* that "seeks to promote and protect the full enjoyment of all human rights and the fundamental freedoms of all women throughout their life cycle" (United Nations 2000, p. xiii). It is within this international context that women in many countries have acted collectively to claim power, to promote gender justice, and to improve women's lives. The legitimacy provided by the Beijing documents has been a source of power for women, helping them pressure governments in the direction of better access to education for girls, better political representation for women, improved health care, pay equity, and a variety of other goals. Yet there are many barriers arrayed against these goals, and progress is often slower than women would wish.

The structure of power and authority in many cultures is organized in ways that discourage women from claiming it. Men, in general, hold many more of the powerful positions in government, business, education, and the professions than women do. Women's voices are often silenced in decision making. Such a large imbalance in the distribution of legitimate authority begs justification. After all, some may argue, if women were as good at leadership as men are, would not more of them have risen to the top?

As many social psychologists, beginning with Gordon Allport in 1954, have noted, human beings have a tendency to justify the subordination of one group by attributing characteristics of inferiority to that group. We like to believe that there are good reasons for the way things are—and we do not like to believe in the existence of injustice. Thus many people—women and men—find it easy to accept the notions that most women are not interested in power or are not "cut out for" leadership. Many cultures hold stereotypes of femininity that characterize women as caring, pliable, and nonconfrontational, not tough enough for real leadership, decision making, or power. When women violate these expectations, they are viewed as unfeminine misfits. A woman who takes such reactions to heart can have her self-esteem shaken to the core. Social sanctions go a long way toward keeping women from engaging in powerful behaviors, organizing for social change, or pursuing powerful positions.

Even when women grit their teeth and act in defiance of the stereotypes, they encounter many more obstacles to gaining and using power: discrimination; exclusion from various activities and settings where decisions are made; lack of good, affordable childcare; the double responsibilities of family and work; even laws, restrictions, intimidation, and physical force that steal their courage and prevent them from claiming and using their individual or collective power. Women's strength, however, is not easily undermined. As Afghan women's rights supporter Farahnaz Nazir defiantly asserts, "They can cover us. They can make us cover ourselves, but they cannot close our minds. They cannot close our minds." (Raimondo, 2001, p, A21).

When women understand the social forces that are arrayed against their movement into power and leadership, they can transcend the forces of prejudice, custom, and law that work against them, particularly if they support one another. As Byllye Avery, founding mother of the National Black Women's Health Project, argues, women have to look beyond the seemingly impenetrable structure of male authority in various institutions, envision and talk about ways those structures could change, and "breathe fire, breathe life into ourselves" (1997, p. 536). For power, after all, is the ability to imagine and create change—and change is long overdue for women everywhere.

SUMMARY

Women are often discouraged from exerting formal power or seeking positions of public leadership. Indeed, in many cultural contexts, there is a contradiction between images of femininity and power that is rooted in gender stereotypes. Women are not supposed to have the qualities needed to hold and use power or to be leaders, organizers, or authoritative figures—and if they do have such qualities they are presumed not to be very feminine. Women are aware of the contradictory expectations for power and femininity, and they sometimes adjust their behavior accordingly. On the other hand, some stereotypically feminine qualities *are* considered congruent with transformational leadership, a style of leadership that inspires people to work together and to actualize a vision of change. Perhaps because of the difficulties involved in meshing power and femininity, female leadership is often unacknowledged and invisible.

Some people have wondered whether women really want to lead or hold power. Research reveals that women's need for power is as high as men's, but it may be expressed differently because women who exert power in directive or authoritative ways meet with disapproval. Women do score lower than men on scales of a motivation-to-manage measure that taps into aspect of the managerial role that are considered "masculine." However, on motivation for leadership tasks that are more congruent with feminine role expectations, such as the desire to maintain positive relationships with superiors in the chain of command and a desire to handle the day-to-day administrative tasks of the managerial role, women score higher than men.

In small task-oriented groups, women's and men's leadership behavior is influenced by the status that they and others perceive them to have and by the actual amount of power that goes with their position in the group. According to expectation states theory, women are automatically ascribed lower status than men in such groups, and this must be counteracted by other factors such as experience if they are to achieve power in the group. Some research suggests that no matter how competent they are, women in male-dominated groups or organizations often cannot overcome the stereotype that women are not expected to be leaders unless they are empowered by an external endorsement from the organization.

There is some evidence that women and men use different styles of leadership under some conditions: Women tend to be more democratic and subtle, men more authoritative and direct. Part of the explanation for this difference may be that in some contexts, women and men differ in their bases of social power. For example, there are many cultural contexts in which male authority is viewed as more legitimate than female authority.

Women's work or social environment is often hostile to powerful women. Women pioneers in positions such as political leadership have had to find ways to deal with this hostility without letting it become their main focus. At this writing, women are increasingly visible in political leadership positions, but they are still in a very small minority. Women in such positions may experience a sense of double marginality: a sense of alienation from other women because of their unusual role and alienation from male colleagues because they are unlike them. As research on French and Norwegian women shows, the cultural context is very important in determining the way women experience leadership roles.

Women do not have to be in positions of formal leadership to effect change. Individual women work out strategies to resist patriarchal authority, even under the most difficult conditions. And women everywhere have found ways to empower themselves through collective action for women's rights. The barriers to power for women are many—but so are women's strengths.

KEY TERMS

transformational leadership
need for power
expectation states theory
diffuse status characteristic
bases of social power

reward power
coercive power
legitimate power
referent power
expert power

information power
direct influence strategies
indirect influence strategies
glass ceiling
double marginality

DISCUSSION QUESTIONS

In your experience, do women and men use power differently? After reading this chapter, what explanations would you give for what you have observed?

What kinds of social/cultural contexts would be friendly to female leadership? Have you ever had experience in such contexts?

Do you think that women in different parts of the world think about power in similar ways? Why or why not?

FOR ADDITIONAL READING

Fisher, Jo. (1989). *Mothers of the disappeared.* London: Zed Books. Through interviews and careful piecing together of details, the author tells the story of the Mothers of the Plaza de Mayo in Argentina. It is a dramatic story and a case study in the way power can come from grassroots organizing.

Mendelson, Sue J. M., Shelton, Christine M., and Bourque, Susan C. (Eds). (2001). *Women on power: Leadership redefined.* Boston: Northeastern University Press. This collection includes discussions of women and power from many perspectives and both contemporary and historical case studies. For example, there are articles on the Boston Women's Health Book Collective, women's environmental activism, and motherhood as a catalyst to social activism.

Nelson, Barbara J., & Chowdhury, Najma (Eds.). (1994). *Women and politics worldwide.* Cambridge, MA: Yale University Press. This collection analyzes women's political participation in countries around the world through individual articles. Articles about each country are authored by a woman from that country.

Ortiz, Teresa. (2001). *Never again a world without us: Voices of Mayan women in Chiapas, Mexico.* Washington, DC: EPICA. The author interviewed indigenous women in Chiapas and provides the narratives of women who are trying to be agents of justice and social change in their country.

Rosener, Judith B. (1995). *America's competitive secret: Utilizing women as a management strategy.* New York: Oxford University Press. Rosener explores the "gender paradox" in the realm of management: When qualities associated with women (e.g., cooperativeness, orientation to relationships) are considered negative or of no value, gender is seen as relevant to hiring or promotion; when such qualities are considered positive or valuable, gender is seen as irrelevant.

WEB RESOURCES

Feminist International Radio Endeavour (FIRE). Based in Costa Rica, this is the site of the "first women's Internet radio," and it provides a unique perspective on world events. Here you can hear, in English or Spanish, a variety of current and past broadcasts, search for information on particular topics, and chat with people who are interested in women's rights. **www.fire.or.cr/indexeng/htm**

Grrrl Zine Network. This site includes an overview and some history of the grrrl zine network, along with commentary from zine creators, reviews, and resource lists. **http://grrrlzines.net**

Guerilla Girls. The official site of the activist group, this page includes articles about the Guerilla Girls, copies of their posters, and a schedule of some of their appearances. **http://www.guerrillagirls.com**

Radical Cheerleaders. Here you will find a description of the group, a collection of "girl-positive" cheers, calendar of events, and a way to locate a squad near you. **http://radcheers.tripod.com/RC**

Womenwatch: The UN Gateway on the Advancement and Empowerment of Women. This is an excellent starting place to find out about women's status in various countries. The site contains links to databases and documents, breaking news, women's issues on U.N. Radio, and online forums. **www.un.org/womenwatch**

GLOSSARY

acculturation the process of identifying with and conforming to a new culture

affirmative action a set of strategies to increase the proportion of women and minorities hired by organizations or admitted into universities, particularly into fields from which they have traditionally been excluded

age-adjusted death rate an average measure of mortality risk based on a standard population. By using this standard population to calculate death rates, the age composition among different population groups is held constant, allowing meaningful comparisons

ageism devaluation of and discrimination against persons based on their age

agoraphobia a persistent, irrational fear of being in public places from which escape might be difficult or help unavailable in case of sudden incapacitation

AIDS (acquired immunodeficiency syndrome) a condition caused by the human immunodeficiency virus (HIV), characterized by the destruction of the immune system and consequent vulnerability to life-threatening diseases

AIS (androgen insensitivity syndrome) a syndrome in which the body cannot respond to androgens because the gene on the X chromosome that is responsible for producing an androgen receptor protein does not work

alpha bias a tendency toward exaggerating differences between women and men

androgen a type of male sex hormone

androgyny a blend of feminine and masculine characteristics. An androgynous person is one who combines stereotypically feminine and masculine qualities

anorexia nervosa a mental disorder that involves self-starvation in an effort to maintain an unrealistically low body weight. It is characterized by an intense fear of becoming obese and by a disturbed body image—a tendency to "feel fat" even when severely underweight.

Antigone complex according to Ellyn Kaschak, in a patriarchal family, the intertwining of the daughter's early attachment to the mother with learning that men are central and women are secondary

bases of social power things that can be used to "back up" attempts to exert power

behavioral gender differences behavior for which a disparity exists between the average female and the average male, although there may be a large overlap between the two sexes

benevolent sexism a type of sexism that includes protective paternalism, idealization of women, and desire for intimate relations. Measured by the Ambivalent Sexism Inventory

beta bias an inclination to ignore or minimize differences between women and men

big mother hypothesis the idea that one characteristic that is naturally selected in some species is large size in females

bilateral influence strategy strategy that requires a lot of mutual engagement, such as arguing or bargaining

bisexual someone attracted to persons of either gender

brain lateralization (also called cerebral lateralization or hemispheric lateralization) the degree to which particular functions are localized in one side of the brain

bulimia nervosa a mental disorder that is characterized by an obsession with food and with body weight and involves a pattern of binge overeating followed by self-induced purging through a variety of means, including dieting, vomiting, or laxatives

CAH (congenital adrenal hyperplasia) genetically transmitted syndrome in which the adrenal glands of the fetus malfunction, resulting in a release of excess androgens from the prenatal period onward

caregiver burden the stress associated with caring for someone who cannot be left alone, such as an invalid or Alzheimer's disease patient

chronically stressful conditions ongoing conditions (such as poverty, role strain, sexual harassment at work) that put a strain on a person and require coping

climacteric by the end of the 19th century, a term associated mainly with women's "change of life"

clitoris a female sex organ located above the urethral opening that is extremely sensitive to sexual sensations

clitoroplasty surgical removal or reshaping of all or part of the clitoris

coercive power power based on the ability to threaten harm or punishment to another person

cognitive abilities abilities relevant to thinking, learning, and remembering

cognitive developmental theory proposes that gender, like other concepts, cannot be learned until a child reaches a particular stage of intellectual development

collective relative deprivation a feeling of dissatisfaction due to perceived inequities between one's own and a more advantaged group

coming out acknowledging and disclosing that one's sexual identity is lesbian, gay, or bisexual

comparable worth the principle that persons should earn equal pay for work of equal value, even when their jobs are not identical

constricting interaction style style in which participants in an interaction are more likely to interrupt one another, command and threaten, boast, refuse to comply, and give information.

context-stripping studying and discussing the behavior, thought, or feelings of a person or group as if they were separate from the context in which they are normally embedded

continuities in interactional style reciprocal influences between the child and the social environment that, as a child matures, influence her/his personality in a consistent direction

conversational dominance control over the conversation, in terms of speaking time

core gender identity the individual's private experience of the self as female or male

corpus callosum a mass of nerve fibers that connects the two hemispheres of the cerebral cortex

courage defined by Annie Rogers as having spirit, liveliness, a quality of boldness, the ability "to speak one's mind by telling all one's heart"

cultural competence having the knowledge and flexibility to adapt and modifying one's behavior to achieve congruence with a client's (or student's or friend's) behavior

cumulative continuity the process through which an individual, beginning in childhood, selects and creates environments that fit her or his preferred forms of behavior—and these selected environments, in turn, reinforce and sustain that behavior

depression a mental illness signaled by feelings of extreme sadness and hopelessness and by a loss of interest in most activities

devaluation according to Karen Horney, one of two major environmental dangers to a child's development: parents' lack of respect for the child as a unique and worthwhile individual

diffuse status characteristic a characteristic (such as gender, age, race) that carries a general set of expectations for performance

direct influence strategy one that is open and clear, such as a straightforward request or order

double marginality the feeling a woman in a powerful position can have of being alienated from both her reference groups: from women because she has an unusual role for a woman, and from the other powerful people in her environment because they are all men

double standard the use of two different standards of acceptable sexual behavior, one for women and one for men

double standard of mental health the notion that there are different expectations for mentally healthy women and mentally healthy men

dual self having both independent and interdependent dimensions of the self

effect size the average size of the difference in a particular variable that is associated with a categorical factor (such as gender or age) or with a manipulation (such as the administration of a particular drug)

Electra complex according to Freud, this system of feelings is experienced by girls in the phallic stage. The girl realizes she cannot have a penis, replaces her wish for a penis with a wish for a child, and focuses on her father as a love object and on her mother as a rival.

empty nest syndrome a sense of loss triggered in women by the departure of the last child from home. At one time, this stage of life was thought to be a severe crisis for women, often leading to depression and a loss of self-esteem.

enabling interaction style style in which the interactants seem more interested in sustaining social relationships. They are likely to say they agree with another speaker, acknowledge points made by other speakers, and pause to allow another to speak.

encounter stage in Cross's model of Black racial identity, the stage at which the individual realizes that her race will always be salient to others and affect their evaluations of her

entitlement the sense that one has a right to expect certain treatment, such as respect, a certain level of pay, and the like

equity a good balance between contributions to and benefits from a relationship

erotica sexually explicit material, designed to promote sexual arousal

essentialism a view that gender (along with other characteristics, such as sexual orientation) is something that lies within the individual—a quality that belongs to that person

estrogen a type of female sex hormone

evolutionary theory theory that argues that human nature (including human sex differences) has evolved in certain ways because of pressures to adapt and survive as a species

expectation states theory theory that persons' behavior and effectiveness in interactions with others is influenced by the status that they and others perceive them to have

expert power power based on one person's presumed greater expertise (e.g., a doctor can use expert power with respect to her patients)

female genital mutilation (FGM) an invasive, painful and dangerous operation, ritually performed on young girls in many parts of the world, that involves excision of all or part of the clitoris and is often carried out under medically risky conditions

feminine-role hypothesis the idea that the feminine role may predispose women to depression by encouraging them to feel and act helpless and to develop inadequate coping skills

feminist person characterized by an acceptance of a broad set of attitudes that share certain premises: the notion that inequalities between women and men should be challenged, that women's experiences and concerns are important, and that women's ideas, behaviors, and feelings are worthy of study in their own right

feminist psychology an approach to psychology characterized by a focus on understanding women's own experience, rather than on fitting women into traditional, often male-centered, views of human behavior and social relations

feminist therapies therapies based on a philosophy that not only explicitly disavows traditional gender stereotypic assumptions about behavior, but also encourages open discussion and analysis of the stereotypes

filial piety Asian tradition that counsels respect and obedience toward one's elders

filled pauses nonwords such as *um* or *ah,* used to try to hold the floor, even when a person is not saying anything

G spot an area on the anterior wall of the vagina that is especially sensitive to sexual stimulation in some women

gender the nonphysiological aspects of being female or male—the cultural expectations for femininity and masculinity

gender constancy an understanding that a person's gender is fixed and cannot be altered by a change in hairstyle, dress, or name. According to cognitive developmental theory, this understanding is achieved by a child sometime between the ages of 3 and 5.

gender identity (sometimes called core gender identity) the individual's private experience of the self as female or male

gender intensification a deepening personal and cultural emphasis on gender roles during adolescence, particularly for girls, in response to bodily changes and the development of more abstract ways of thinking

gender role the set of behaviors socially defined as appropriate for one's sex

gender role strain difficulty in conforming to different aspects of expected gender roles (e.g., spouse, parent, worker) because such roles are often contradictory and inconsistent, so it is difficult not to violate them.

gender schema network of cognitive associations (schema) for gender used by individuals to organize incoming information about themselves and others

gender stereotypes socially shared beliefs that certain qualities can be assigned to individuals, based on their gender

generation and maintenance of a spatial image the ability to generate a visual image and then hold that image in memory while answering questions about the way it looks

glass ceiling an invisible barrier that keeps women from advancing into high-level positions in organizations

gonads sex glands: ovaries (female) and testes (male)

group socialization theory postulates that children become socialized primarily by identifying with their peer group and taking on that group's norms for attitudes and behavior

gynocentric literally, centered on the female womb. This term is also used to mean female centered.

heteroeroticism sexual attraction to and arousal by members of the other sex

heterosexism the tendency to view heterosexuality as the norm and to ignore or render invisible the alternatives of homosexuality and bisexuality

hierarchy-enhancing values values that promote the interests of the elite, powerful groups in a society

hierarchy-attenuating values values that challenge existing hierarchies in society and align with the interests of oppressed groups

HIV (human immunodeficiency virus)   the virus that causes AIDS

homoeroticism   sexual attraction and arousal to members of a person's own sex

homosexual   a person who prefers sexual and/or affectional partners of the same sex

honor killing   killing a wife or daughter who has behaved "inappropriately" in order to protect the family's or the man's honor

hormone replacement therapy (HRT)   the prescription of supplemental estrogen, sometimes accompanied by progesterone, to menopausal women

hostile environment harassment   form of sexual harassment that involves making unwelcome sexual advances or engaging in other conduct of a sexual nature that unreasonably interferes with an individual's work performance or creates an intimidating, hostile, or offensive atmosphere

hostile sexism   a type of sexism that includes dominance-oriented paternalism, derogatory beliefs about women, and heterosexual hostility. Measured by the Ambivalent Sexism Inventory

hot flash   symptom associated with menopause in some cultures, in which the blood vessels in the woman's skin dilate, her skin conductance increases, she may become flushed, and she feels extremely hot

idiographic   research method focused on careful, in-depth case studies of individuals' experiences

immersion/emersion   in Cross's theory of racial identity development, the stage during which the person begins work on constructing a Black identity, sometimes by withdrawing as much as possible into a Black world and trying to "act Black"

independent self   a sense of self based on the notion that each person is separate and distinct, with unique attributes, and that the person's developmental task is to become independent from others and to express those unique attributes

indirect influence strategies   methods of trying to exert influence through manipulation or subtlety, rather than through obvious means such as giving orders or making requests

infantile grandiosity   young boy's idea that females, beginning with the mother, are extensions of himself, people who exist to gratify him

information power   power based on having more information about the issue at hand than others do

insidious trauma   the continuous stresses of racism, sexism, emotional abuse, class discrimination, and other negative social forces that can erode an individual's well-being over the course of a lifetime

interactional continuity   the two-way transactions between the person and the social environment in which the person's behavior elicits reactions from others, and those reactions promote continuity in the original behavior through reinforcement, confirmation of expectations, and confirmation of the person's self-concept

interdependent self   a sense of self based on the idea that human beings are fundamentally interconnected and that the task of each person is to maintain those connections

internalization stage   in Cross's model of racial identity, stage in which the person constructs a positive personal identity that incorporates being Black, blending notions of her/his own unique qualities with an acknowledgment that being Black influences who s/he is.

intersexual   person who possesses a mixture of the anatomical features that we associate with males and females

intrusive interruptions   interruptions aimed at taking away another speaker's turn to speak

learned helplessness   the learned conviction that one's actions do not make a difference

legitimate power   power based on the influencer's perceived right to make a certain demand or request

life expectancy   the average number of years that a person in a particular category (e.g., African American women) can be expected to live

logical positivism   approach to knowledge that assumes that reality is independent of the knower and can be discerned "objectively" under the proper conditions

maternal mortality   deaths caused by complications during pregnancy, delivery, or the 42-day period immediately following the end of the pregnancy

mati-ism   in working-class Afro-Surinamese culture, a system of close, emotional relationships between women

menarche   a girl's first menstrual period

menopause   the cessation of a woman's menstrual periods. A woman is said to have reached menopause when she has had not menstrual periods for one year

menstruation   final phase of the menstrual cycle that involves shedding the inner uterine lining, the endometrium, which flows out through the cervix and the vagina

menstrual joy positive feelings such as high spirits, increased sexual desire, and self-confidence associated with parts of the menstrual cycle

menstrual synchrony the phenomenon in which women who spend a lot of time together tend to have their menstrual periods around the same time

mental health the ability to function well, to cope with problems, or to be happy or satisfied with one's life

mental illness disordered behavior or thinking indicating ongoing distress and the inability to cope

mental rotation a type of spatial ability that involves being able to quickly visualize objects from different perspectives. Performance in this category is measured by showing the person a picture or object and asking questions about it that require the visualization of that picture or object from another angle

modern sexism a constellation of attitudes characterized by a denial that women are still targets of discrimination, antagonism toward women's demands, and a lack of support for policies designed to improve women's status

Müllerian Inhibiting Substance (MIS) hormone that, during embryonic development, blocks the development of the female duct system and causes it to degenerate

natural selection process in which a trait that enhances survival and thus increases the chances that an individual will survive and have offspring is favored in the evolution of a species. Organisms that possess such traits are more likely than others to survive and to reproduce.

need for power the motive to influence others and to have an impact on one's social world

neurasthenia a mental illness often diagnosed in women at the beginning of the 20th century but now rarely used, characterized by mind and body fatigue, depression, anxiety, headaches, and gastrointestinal disturbances

nomothetic research approach that combines the responses of similar individuals in order to make summary statements about groups and/or compare one group with another

nonsexist therapy therapy based on the idea that gender stereotypes should not guide the therapeutic process—that clients should be treated as individuals first, rather than as women or men

nonverbal communication unspoken comunication that includes the way we look at and touch one another, the way we carry ourselves, our gestures, and the ways we occupy and control the space around us

normative rape rape that is supported by social norms (and so may not be labeled rape), such as the rape of female slaves, the rape of enemy women in war, ceremonial defloration of women, marital rape

objectification theory theory that the cultural emphasis on women's bodies as sexual objects causes women to internalize observers' perspectives on their bodies and to chronically monitor their appearance out of concern for the way others may judge them

Oedipus complex a system of feelings named by Freud for the mythical Greek character who unwittingly killed his own father and married his own mother. Freud said boys at this stage develop an intense attachment for the mother and begin to see the father as a rival.

oppression artifact disorder the lack of resilience that might occur in a woman of color who is worn down from dealing with small or large instances of racism on a daily basis

orgasm phase of human sexual response in which arousal reaches a critical point, triggering a series of involuntary rhythmic contractions of the pelvic organs

osteoporosis a loss of bone density that puts individuals at increasing risk of serious fractures

ovulation second phase of the menstrual cycle, in which the follicle ruptures to release the mature egg

PMS (premenstrual syndrome) period of high tension, depression, irritability, and assorted physical symptoms that is said to occur during the days immediately preceding the onset of menstruation

panic disorder involves the experience of panic attacks that occur without warning and without any obvious reason. These attacks are bouts of intense physiological arousal that may be characterized by symptoms such as a pounding and/or irregularly beating heart, chest pains, and difficulty breathing.

pay equity paying women and men equally when they do similar work

personal space a "comfort zone" of space around a person, that others, unless they are intimates, may not breach without causing uneasiness

personal relative deprivation a sense of dissatisfaction stemming from a comparison with other individuals who are being more highly rewarded

phallocentric literally, centered on the male penis. This term is also used to mean male centered.

pornography sexually explicit material, designed to elicit sexual arousal, that sexualizes the subjugation/or and abuse of women

possible self personalized images of the self in various future roles: selves a person believes s/he might possibly become

post-traumatic stress disorder (PTSD) A person who has experienced one or more severe emotional traumas—such as physical attack, rape, war violence, serious accidents, and physical, sexual, or emotional abuse—may later, and over a considerable period of time, display a set of symptoms such as depression, insomnia, anxiety, nightmares, feelings of being in danger, and irritability

preencounter stage in Cross's model of racial identity, stage in which the individual idealizes White culture and disassociates herself from Black culture, using Whites rather than Blacks as a reference group

prejudice the negative evaluation of persons or their activities because they belong to a particular group

premenstrual dysphoric disorder (PMDD) a formal (and controversial) diagnosis included in an appendix of the Diagnostic and Statistical Manual of the American Psychiatric Association, which lists a set of psychological symptoms that may occur during the week prior to menstruation

principle of least interest the principle that, in a relationship, the person who is least dependent on the other for rewards—who needs the relationship least—has the most power

progesterone a type of female sex hormone

prostitution the exchange of sexual activity for money or other goods

psychoanalytic theory theory first developed by Sigmund Freud that emphasized the importance of unconscious motivations in personality development

psychobiosocial model model of human behavior rooted in the idea that some variables are *both* biological and social, and so cannot be readily classified as either biological or environmental

psychological stress feelings of threat, upset, worry, discomfort, and general distress associated with events such as spousal arguments, fear of job loss, and other problems

psychotherapy involves a client and therapist talking with each other about the issues and/or symptoms that are bothering the client, with the therapist trying to provide the help, support, and guidance the client needs to deal with painful, difficult feelings

quid pro quo harassment form of sexual harassment in which an individual is pressured to submit to unwelcome sexual advances or other unwelcome sexual conduct as a condition of employment, or when employment decisions that affect the individual, such as promotion or raises, are based on her or his submission to or rejection of such conduct

rape forcing sexual relations on someone against that person's choice

rape myths misconceptions about rape that center around the idea that a woman can prevent rape if she really wants to (e.g., "all women secretly want to be raped")

reference groups a group with which we identify, to which we look for ideals and perhaps approval

referent power power based on the target person's affection, admiration, wish to be accepted by, or wish to emulate the influencer

reflexivity an approach to research in which researchers try to be aware of and to reflect on the ways their identities (for example as individuals in Western society, members of particular ethnic or religious groups, females or males) influence their work and, in turn, how their work influences these aspects of the self

relational aggression harming others by deliberately manipulating and damaging their relationships with their peers

relationship difficulties hypothesis the idea that, because relationships are more central to women than to men, women have learned to behave in certain ways to protect their heterosexual relationships—ways that leave them vulnerable to depression

reproductive fitness survival of an organism's genes

resources items a person controls (such as the capacity to reward someone, or expertise) that give her/him a basis for influencing another person

reward power power based on the influencer's ability to promise positive outcomes to the other person

romantic love intense feeling of longing for union with another person

scripts culturally shared social norms that guide expectations for relationships

self-confidence belief that one can successfully perform certain tasks

self-efficacy a sense of competence, empowerment, and the ability to accomplish goals

self-esteem favorability of one's self-view

self-disclosure telling others about oneself and one's thoughts and feelings

self-in-relation the sense of oneself as a relational being, someone who is developing and growing in the ability to connect with and relate to others

self schema mental framework or filter that is part of the way a person notices, assesses, and organizes incoming information about the self —analogous in some ways to a mental filing system

sex chromosomes the 23rd pair of chromosomes in humans, which differs for women and men. If the individual is female, the sex chromosomes are represented as XX; if male, the pair is designated as XY.

sex differences refers to biologically based differences between males and females

sex discrimination differential treatment on the basis of sex

sex hormones chemicals secreted by the ovaries, testes, and adrenal glands, which control sexual development and are implicated in processes such as puberty, pregnancy, and menopause

sex survey collecting self-reports of sexual activity from sizeable samples of individuals

sexism the brand of prejudice that is based on a person's sexual category. Judgments about a person based on whether s/he is female or male

sexual abuse mistreatment that has a sexual aspect. May include rape, sexual torture, or sexual advances toward a child

sexual harassment unwanted sexual attention and behavior

sexual orientation a person's choice of sexual partner, or the group of people to whom s/he feels sexual attraction, as well as the person's pattern of social/affectional attachments.

sexual selection involves competition for and choice of mates. Individuals affect the survival of their own genes, not only by their own characteristics, but also by their choice of mate.

sexualization in Karen Horney's theory, adults' taking a sexual approach to the child, an "emotional hothouse" atmosphere

sexually transmitted infections (STIs) infections that are transmitted from person to person through sexual contact (e.g., AIDS, gonorrhea, chlamydia)

silencing the self theory that posits that women's greater vulnerability to depression springs from their attempts to establish intimate and satisfying connections with male partners within the context of feminine role requirements that do not allow them to assert their own needs in such relationships

social cognitive theory a modification of social learning theory that suggests that although children may initially learn gender roles through external rewards and punishments, as they mature they begin to regulate their own actions through internal rewards and punishments

social construction a concept (such as gender) that is defined by social agreement and whose reality is created and maintained through social interactions

social constructionism approach to knowledge that assumes researchers do not discover independently existing facts through objective observation; rather, they construct knowledge that is influenced by the social context of their inquiry

social identity suggests that each individual's personal sense of identity is tied to her or his reference groups

social learning theory suggests that the child develops both gender identity and gender role through a learning process that involves modeling, imitation, and reinforcement

social roles theory theory that argues that differential role occupancy by women and men is mediated by the formation of gender roles in which persons of each sex are expected to have qualities that equip them for the tasks typically carried out by that group

social support the perception that others are available to help when a person is having difficulties

spatial perception a type of spatial performance that involves determining spatial relationships with respect to one's own body orientation, in spite of distracting information

spatial visualization a type of spatial performance that involves complicated, multi-step mental manipulations of spatial information. To measure it, subjects may be asked to "disembed" a simple figure from a complex background or to imagine how a piece of paper would look when folded a certain way

spatiotemporal perception a type of spatial ability that involves making judgments about moving visual displays, such as predicting when a moving object will reach a particular spot

speech styles differences in ways of speaking, including preference for different words, differences in the use of tentative or direct requests, questions, and assertions

stereotype threat the awareness that one may be judged by or may self-fulfill negative stereotypes about one's group

stressful life events particular, discrete events (such as the loss of a job, an automobile accident, the death of a family member) that cause strain and distress and require coping

suttee (also called sati) a practice (now rarely observed) in some parts of traditional India, in which a widow willingly throws herself on her husband's burning funeral pyre so that she can die with him as a gesture of virtue and fidelity

tend and befriend a pattern of behavior postulated by some theorists to describe women's response to stress, in which they nurture their children and affiliate with others to reduce risk

testosterone a type of androgen, a male sex hormone

third gender an institutionalized alternative role that allows an individual to opt out of the two gender categories, female or male

Title IX 1972 U.S. federal law that bars sex discrimination in educational programs receiving government financial assistance

token resistance saying no at first even when the person intends to agree to sex eventually

trafficking (in women and children) the recruitment, buying, selling, and transportation of women and children through the use of violence or fraud for the purpose of placing them in forced labor, often prostitution

transformational leadership a style of leadership that inspires people to work together and to actualize a vision of change

transgendered a person who is uncomfortable with the conventional categories female and male and who may live all or part of the time in the identity of the other sex

transsexuals people whose gender identity does not match their biological sex, and who have had or want to have surgery to change their bodies to match those of the other sex

transvestite (also called cross-dresser) person who enjoys dressing in the clothing of the other sex

two-spirit person a term used by many lesbian, gay, and bisexual Native Americans to describe themselves. A two-spirit person is thought to be born "in balance," incorporating a blend of feminine and masculine qualities, of female and male spirits

verbal communication communication using words

visual dominance tendency to look at subordinates while speaking to them and to look away when listening to them

Women's Health Initiative a large-scale 15-year set of studies, sponsored by the National Institutes of Health in the United States, that focuses on identifying factors related to prevention of heart disease, breast and colorectal cancer, and osteoporosis in postmenopausal women

REFERENCES

Abdel Kader, S. (1987). *Egyptian women in a changing society, 1899–1987.* Boulder, CO: Lynne Rienner.

Abrams, L. S. (2003). Contextual variations in young women's gender identity negotiations. *Psychology of Women Quarterly, 27*(1), 64–74.

Adams, K. L., & Ware, N. C. (1995). Sexism and the English language: The linguistic implications of being a woman. In J. Freeman (Ed.), *Women: A feminist perspective* (5th ed., pp. 331–346). Mountain View, CA: Mayfield.

Adhikary, Q. (1993). The marriage of Minnoo Mashi. In Women of South Asian Descent Collective (Eds.), *Our feet walk the sky: Women of the South Asian Diaspora* (pp. 175–190). San Francisco: Aunt Lute Books.

Adler, N. E., Boyce, T., Chesney, M. A., Folkman, S., & Syme, S. L. (1993). Socioeconomic inequalities in health: No easy solution. *Journal of the American Medical Association, 269,* 3140–3145.

Adler, N. E., & Coriell, M. (1997). Socioeconomic status and women's health. In S. J. Gallant, G. P. Keita, & R. Royak-Schaler (Eds.), *Health care for women: Psychological, social and behavioral influences* (pp. 11–23). Washington, DC: American Psychological Association.

Adler, N. L., Hendrick, S. S., & Hendrick, C. (1987). Male sexual preference and attitudes toward love and sexuality. *Journal of Sex Education and Therapy, 12*(2), 27–30.

Adrianson, L. (2001). Gender and computer-mediated communication: Group processes in problem solving. *Computers in Human Behavior, 17*(1), 71–94.

Afifi, W. A., & Faulkner, S. L. (2000). On being "just friends": The frequency and impact of sexual activity on cross-sex friendships. *Journal of Social and Personal Relationships, 17*(2), 205–222.

Agars, M. D. (2004). Reconsidering the impact of gender stereotypes on the advancement of women in organizations. *Psychology of Women Quarterly, 28*(2), 103–111.

Age & Opportunity (2004). Working with the media. [online] **http://www.olderinireland .ie/equality/workingwithmedia.htm**

Agency for Health Care Policy and Research. (1993). *Depression in primary care: Vol 1. Detection and diagnosis.* Bethesda, MD: U.S. Department of Health and Human Services.

Aguilar, D. D. (1989). The social construction of the Filipino woman. *International Journal of Intercultural Relations, 13,* 527–551.

Aida, Y., & Falbo, T. (1991). Relationships between marital satisfaction, resources, and power strategies. *Sex Roles, 24*(1/2), 43–56.

Alan Guttmacher Institute (2003, January). Fact Sheet: Induced Abortion. [online] **http:// www.guttmacher.org/pubs/fb_induced _abortion.pdf.**

Alan Guttmacher Institute (2004, February 19). U.S. Teenage pregnancy statistics with comparative statistics for women aged 20–24. [online] **http://www.guttmacher.org/pubs/ teen_stats.html**

Alexander, C. J. (2002). Violence in gay and lesbian relationships. *Journal of Gay & Lesbian Social Services: Issues in Practice, Policy & Research, 14*(1), 95–98.

Ali, A., & Toner, B. B. (2001). Symptoms of depression among Caribbean women and Caribbean-Canadian women: An investigation of self-silencing and domains of meaning. *Psychology of Women Quarterly, 25*(3), 175–180.

All things considered (2001, July 11). Iran—rhinoplasty. Report by Jennifer Ludden, National Public Radio.

Allan, G. (1977). Class variations in friendship patterns. *British Journal of Sociology, 28,* 389–393.

Allen, K., Bounds, E., Carlisle, B., Cina, C., Pendergrass, B., Plaut, L., Scott, D., Watford, B., & Williams-Green, J. (1996, September). Color conversations. Plenary session and performance for the Racialization, Gender and the Academy Conference, Virginia Women's Studies Association and Fourth Annual Feminist Research and Pedagogy Conference, Roanoke, VA.

Allen, L., Denner, J., Yoshikawa, H., Seidman, E., & Aber, J. L. (1996). Acculturation and depression among Latina urban girls. In B. J. R. Leadbeater & N. Way (Eds.), *Urban girls: Resisting stereotypes, creating identities* (pp. 337–352). New York: New York University Press.

Allen, L. S., Richey, M. F., Chai, Y. M., & Gorski, R. A. (1991). Sex differences in the corpus callosum of the living human being. *Journal of Neuroscience, 11*(4), 933–942.

Allen, P. G. (1986). *The sacred hoop: Recovering the feminine in American Indian traditions.* Boston: Beacon Press.

Allison, J. A., & Wrightsman, L. S. (1993). *Rape: The misunderstood crime.* Newbury Park, CA: Sage.

Allport, G. (1954). *The nature of prejudice.* Reading, MA: Addison-Wesley.

Alzheimer's Association (2004). Statistics about Alzheimer's disease. [online] **http://www.alz .org/AboutAD/statistics.asp**

Amaro, H. (1995). Love, sex, and power: Considering women's realities in HIV prevention. *American Psychologist, 50*(6), 437–447.

American Association of University Professors (2003). *Don't blame faculty for high tuition: The annual report on the economic status of the profession, 2003–04.* [online] **http://www .aaup.org/surveys/zrep.htm**

American Association of University Women. (1990). *Shortchanging girls, shortchanging America: A call to action.* Washington, DC: Author.

American Association of University Women (2001). *Hostile hallways: Bullying, teasing, and sexual harassment in school.* Washington, DC: Author.

American Academy of Cosmetic Surgery (2001). Statistics. [online] **www.cosmeticsurgery.org**

American Cancer Society (2003, October 3). Breast cancer deaths on the decline. [online] **http://www.cancer.org/docroot/NWS/ content/NWS_1_1x_Breast_Cancer _Deaths_on_the_Decline.asp**

American College of Nurse-Midwives. (1997). World Wide Web site, **www.acnm.org**

American Heart Association. (2004). *Statistical Fact Sheet-Populations: International Cardiovascular Disease Statistics* [online] **http:// www.americanheart.org/downloadable/ heart/1077185395308FS06INT4(ebook).pdf**

American Lung Association (2003). *Women and smoking fact sheet.* [online] **http://www .lungusa.org/site/pp.asp?c=dvLUK9O0E &b=33572**

American Medical Association Council on Scientific Affairs. (1995). Female genital mutilation. *Journal of the American Medical Association, 274*(21), 1714–1716.

American Management Association and Business and Professional Women's Foundation

(1999). 1999 AMA/BPW survey. Compensation and benefits: A focus on gender. [online] **www.amanet.org**

American Psychiatric Association. (1994). *Diagnostic and statistical manual of mental disorders* (4th ed.). Washington, DC: Author.

American Psychological Association. (1975). Report of the Task Force on Sex Bias and Sex-Role Stereotyping in Psychotherapeutic Practice. *American Psychologist, 30,* 1169–1175.

American Psychological Association. (1978). Guidelines for therapy with women. *American Psychologist, 33*(12), 1122–1123.

American Psychological Association. (1993). Guidelines for providers of psychological services to ethnic, linguistic and culturally diverse populations. *American Psychologist, 48,* 45–48.

Amina Lawal wins appeal against stoning (2003, September 25). *Feminist Wire.* [online] **http:// www.msmagazine.com/news/uswirestory .asp?id=8064**

Amnesty International (2001). *Broken bodies, shattered minds: Torture and ill-treatment of women.* Oxford, UK: Author.

Anderson, J. L., Crawford, C. B., Nadeau, J., & Lindberg, T. (1992). Was the Duchess of Windsor right? A cross-cultural review of the socioecology of ideals of female body shape. *Ethology and Sociobiology, 13,* 197–227.

Anderson, K. J., & Leaper, C. (1998). Meta-analyses of gender effects on conversational interruption: Who, what, when, where, and how. *Sex Roles, 39*(3–4), 225–252.

Anderson, V. N., Simpson-Taylor, D., & Herrmann, D. J. (2004). Gender, age, and rape-supportive rules. *Sex Roles, 50*(1/2), 77–90.

Angelou, M. (1969). *I know why the caged bird sings.* New York: Bantam.

Angier, N. (1999). *Woman: An intimate geography.* Boston: Houghton Mifflin.

Angier, N. (2001, April 10). A lifetime later, still in love with the lab. *New York Times,* p. D1.

Another chapter in the heart and estrogen story. (2001, April). *Harvard Women's Health Watch, 8*(8), 1–2.

Anwar, S. (1997, May 20). Jilted Bangladeshis take brutal revenge. *Ottawa Citizen,* p. A12.

Anzaldúa, G. (1987). *Borderlands/La Frontera.* San Francisco: Aunt Lute.

Apfelbaum, E. (1993). Norwegian and French women in high leadership positions: The importance of cultural contexts upon gendered relations. *Psychology of Women Quarterly, 17*(4), 409–429.

Arbesman, M., Kahler, L., & Buck, G. (1993). Assessment of the impact of female circumcision on the gynecological, genitourinary and obstetrical health problems of women from Somalia: Literature review and case series. *Women & Health, 20* (3), 27–42.

Archer, J. (2000). Sex differences in aggression between heterosexual partners: A meta-analytic review. *Psychological Bulletin, 126* (5), 651–680.

Archer, J., & Ray, N. (1989). Dating violence in the United Kingdom: A preliminary study. *Aggressive Behavior, 15,* 337–343.

Arden, M. A., Dye, L., & Walker, A. (1999). Menstrual synchrony: Awareness and subjective experiences. *Journal of Reproductive and Infant Psychology, 17*(3), 255–265.

Aroian, K. J., Norris, A. E., & Chiang, L. (2003). Gender differences in psychological distress among immigrants from the former Soviet Union. *Sex Roles, 48*(1/2), 39–52.

Asch, A., & Fine, M. (1988). Introduction: Beyond pedestals. In M. Fine & A. Asch (Eds.), *Women with disabilities: Essays in psychology, culture, and politics* (pp. 1–37). Philadelphia: Temple University Press.

Assault study finds problem is widespread in Air Force (2004, September 1). *New York Times,* p. A16.

Associated Press (2004, June 5). Effort aims to curb child marriages. *Roanoke Times,* p. 4A.

Associated Press (2000, January 31). Islamic feminist brutally slain. *Roanoke Times,* p. A5.

Atkinson, J. W. (1958). *Motives in fantasy, action, and society.* Princeton, NJ: Van Nostrand.

Aubrey, J. S. (2004). Sex and punishment: An examination of sexual consequences and the sexual double standard in teen programming. *Sex Roles, 50*(7/8), 505–514.

Avery, B. Y. (1997). Breathing life into ourselves: The evolution of the National Black Women's Health Project. In E. Disch (Ed.), *Reconstructing gender: A multicultural anthology* (pp. 534–539). Mountain View, CA: Mayfield.

Avis, N. E. (2003). Depression during the menopausal transition. *Psychology of Women Quarterly, 27,* 91–100.

Avis, N. E., & McKinlay, S. M. (1991). A longitudinal analysis of women's attitudes toward the menopause: Results from the Massachusetts Women's Health Study. *Maturitas, 13,* 65–69.

Back, S., Diaz, C., & Lips, H. M. (1996, March). *Possible powerful selves in Spanish university students.* Paper presented at the annual meeting of the Southeastern Psychological Association, Norfolk, VA.

Badgett, M. V. L. (1995). The wage effects of sexual orientation discrimination. *Industrial and Labor Relations Review, 48*(4), 726–729.

Badgett, M. V. L. (1996). Disclosure and discrimination in the workplace. *Journal of Gay and Lesbian Social Services, 4*(4), 29–52.

Badgett, M. V. L., Donnelly, C., & Kibbe, J. (1992). *Pervasive patterns of discrimination against lesbians and gay men: Evidence from surveys across the United States. National Gay and Lesbian Task Force Policy Institute.*

Bakan, D. (1966). *The duality of human existence.* Chicago: Rand McNally.

Baldwin, J. (1993, January 28). In nations where gays serve, many soldiers keep sexuality quiet. *Philadelphia Inquirer,* p. A6.

Ballinger, S. E. (1990). Psychiatric aspects of the menopause. *British Journal of Psychiatry, 156,* 773–787.

Balls-Headley, W. (1894). *The evolution of the diseases of women.* London: Smith, Elder.

Bandura, A. (1977). *Social learning theory.* Englewood Cliffs, NJ: Prentice-Hall.

Bandura, A. (1986). *Social foundations of thought and action: A social cognitive theory.* Englewood Cliffs, NJ: Prentice-Hall.

Banich, M. T., & Heller, W. (1998). Evolving perspectives on lateralization of function. *Current Directions in Psychological Science, 7,* 1–2.

Barclay, R. I., & Barclay, M. L. (1976). Aspects of the normal psychology of pregnancy: The midtrimester. *American Journal of Obstetrics and Gynecology, 125,* 207.

Barer, B. M. (2001). "Grands and greats" of very old Black grandmothers. *Journal of Aging Studies, 15*(1), 1–11.

Bargh, J. A., & Raymond, P. (1995). The naive misuse of power: Nonconscious sources of sexual harassment. *Journal of Social Issues, 51*(1), 85–96.

Barnes, G. M., Farrell, M. P., & Banerjee, S. (1994). Family influences on alcohol abuse and other problem behaviors among Black and White adolescents in a general population sample. *Journal of Research on Adolescence, 4*(2), 183–201.

Barrett, E., & Lally, V. (1999). Gender differences in an on-line learning environment. *Journal of Computer Assisted Learning, 15*(1), 48–60.

Basow, S. A., & Rubenfeld, K. (2003). "Troubles talk": Effects of gender and gender-typing. *Sex Roles, 48*(3/4), 183–187.

Bass, B., Avolio, B., & Atwater, L. (1996). The transformational and transactional leadership of men and women. *Applied Psychology: An International Review, 45*(1), 5–34.

Bauer, J., Wang, F., Riley, N. E., & Zhao, X. (1992). Gender inequality in urban China: Education and employment. *Modern China, 18*(3), 333–370.

Baxter, J. (1992). Power attitudes and time: The domestic division of labour. *Journal of Comparative Family Studies, 13*(2), 165–170.

Bazargan, M., & Barbre, A. R. (1992). Self-reported memory problems among the Black elderly. *Educational Gerontology, 18* (1), 71–82.

BBC News (2000, May 2). Harassment claims soar in Japan. [online] **http://news.bbc.co.uk/1/hi/world/asia-pacific/733609.stm**

Beaton, A. M., & Tougas, F. (1997). The representation of women in management: The more the merrier? *Personality and Social Psychology Bulletin, 23*(7), 773–782.

Beck, K., & Bergman, C. (1993). Investigating Hispanic adolescent involvement with alcohol: A focus group approach. *Health Education Research, 8,* 151–158.

Becker, C. (1987). Friendship between women: A phenomenological study of best friends. *Journal of Phenomenological Psychology, 18,* 59–72.

Becker, J., & Breedlove, S. M. (1992). Introduction to behavioral endocrinology. In J. B. Becker, S. M. Breedlove, & D. Crews (Eds.), *Behavioral endocrinology* (pp. 3–37). Cambridge, MA: MIT Press.

Belenky, M. F., Clinchy, B. M., Goldberger, N. R, & Tarule, J. M. (1986). *Women's ways of knowing: Development of self, voice, and mind.* New York: Basic Books.

Bell, D. (1983). *Daughters of the dreaming.* Melbourne, Australia: McPhee Gribble.

Bell, E. (1990). The bicultural life experience of career-oriented Black women. *Journal of Organizational Behavior, 11,* 459–477.

Bell, L. A. (1989). Something's wrong here and it's not me: Challenging the dilemmas that block girls' success. *Journal for the Education of the Gifted, 12,* 118–130.

Belle, D., & Doucet, J. (2003). Poverty, inequality, and discrimination as sources of depression among U.S. women. *Psychology of Women Quarterly, 27,* 101–113.

Bem, S. L. (1974). The measurement of psychological androgyny. *Journal of Consulting and Clinical Psychology, 42,* 155–162.

Bem, S. L. (1975). Sex-role adaptability: One consequence of psychological androgyny. *Journal of Personality and Social Psychology, 31,* 634–643.

Bem, S. L. (1981). Gender schema theory: A cognitive account of sex typing. *Psychological Review, 88,* 354–364.

Bem, S. L. (1985). Androgyny and gender schema theory: A conceptual and empirical integration. In T. B. Sonderegger (Ed.), *Nebraska Symposium on Motivation: Psychology of Gender* (pp. 179–226). Lincoln, NE: University of Nebraska Press.

Bem. S. L. (1993). *The lenses of gender.* New Haven, CT: Yale University Press.

Bem, S. L., Martyna, W., & Watson, C. (1976). Sex-typing and androgyny: Further explorations of the expressive domain. *Journal of Personality and Social Psychology, 34,* 1016–1023.

Benbow, C. P. (1988). Sex differences in mathematical reasoning ability in intellectually talented preadolescents: Their nature, effects, and possible causes. *Behavioral and Brain Sciences, 11*(2), 169–232.

Benbow, C. P., Lubinski, D., Shea, D. L., & Eftekhari-Sanjani, H. (2000). Sex differences in mathematical reasoning ability at age 13: Their status 20 year later. *Psychological Science, 11*(6), 474–480.

Benbow, C. P., & Stanley, J. C. (1980). Sex differences in mathematical ability: Fact or artifact? *Science, 210,* 1262–1264.

Benbow, C. P., & Stanley, J. C. (1982). Consequences in high school and college of sex differences in mathematical reasoning ability: A longitudinal perspective. *American Educational Research Journal, 19,* 598–622.

Benbow, C. P., & Stanley, J. C. (1983). Sex differences in mathematical ability: More facts. *Science, 222,* 1029–1031.

Berenbaum, S. A. (1999). Effects of early androgens on sex-typed activities and interests in adolescents with congenital adrenal hyperplasia. *Hormones and Behavior, 35,* 102–110.

Bernikow, L. (1980). *Among women.* New York: Crown.

Bernstein, L., Henderson, B. E., Hanisch, R., Sullivan-Halley, J., & Ross, R. K. (1994). Physical exercise and breast cancer in young women. *Clinical Journal of Sports Medicine, 5*(2), 144.

Berry, J. W. (1966). Temne and Eskimo perceptual skills. *International Journal of Psychology, 1,* 207–229.

Bertakis, K. D. (1998). Physician gender and physician–patient interaction. In E. A. Blechman, & K. D. Brownell (Eds.), *Behavioral medicine and women: A comprehensive hand-*

book (pp. 140–141). New York: Guilford Press.

Bettridge, B. J., & Favreau, O. E. (1995). The dependency needs and perceived availability and adequacy of relationships in female adolescent suicide attempters. *Psychology of Women Quarterly, 19*(4), 517–531.

Beyene, Y. (1989). *From menarche to menopause: Reproductive lives of peasant women in two cultures.* Albany: State University of New York Press.

Bhardwaj, S. (2001, August). *Elderly women and widowed women—Legal, economic, physical, social and psychological problems.* Workshop presentation at the triennial conference of the International Federation of University Women, Ottawa, Canada.

Biernat, M., & Wortman, C. B. (1991). Sharing of home responsibilities between professionally employed women and their husbands. *Journal of Personality and Social Psychology, 60,* 844–860.

Bischoping, K. (1993). Gender differences in conversation topics, 1922–1990. *Sex Roles, 28,* 1–18.

Bjorkqvist, K. (1994). Sex differences in physical, verbal, and indirect aggression: A review of recent research. *Sex Roles, 30*(3/4), 177–188.

Bleske, A. L., & Buss, D. M. (2000). Can men and women be just friends? *Personal Relationships, 7*(2), 131–151.

Bliss, G. K. (2000). Self-disclosure and friendship patterns: Gender and sexual orientation differences in same-sex and opposite-sex friendships. *Dissertation Abstracts International, 61*(5-A), 1749.

Block, J. H. (1984). Psychological development of female children and adolescents. In J. H. Block, *Sex role identity and ego development* (pp. 126–142). San Francisco: Jossey-Bass.

Blumenthal, S. J. (1997). Women's health issues, Part 1. Women's Connection Online. **www.womenconnect.com**

Blumstein, P., & Schwartz, P. (1983). *American couples.* New York: Morrow.

Bock, J. D. (2000). Doing the right thing? Single mothers by choice and the struggle for legitimacy. *Gender & Society, 14*(1), 62–89.

Bohan, J. S. (1992). *Re-placing women in psychology.* Dubuque, IA: Kendall/Hunt.

Bolks, S. M., Evans, D., Polinard, J. L., & Wrinkle, R. D. (2000). Core beliefs and abortion attitudes: A look at Latinos. *Social Science Quarterly, 81*(1), 253–260.

Boo, K. (1996, December 15). Two women, two responses to change. *Washington Post,* pp. A1, A28–A29.

Boo, K. (2001, April 9). After welfare. *The New Yorker,* pp. 93–107.

Bookwala, J., Frieze, I. H., Smith, C., & Ryan, K. (1992). Predictors of dating violence: A multivariate analysis. *Violence and Victims, 7,* 297–311.

Bornstein, K. (1994). *Gender outlaw.* New York: Routledge.

Boston Bar Association Task Force on Professional Challenges and Family Needs (1999). *Facing the Grail: Confronting the costs of work–family imbalance.* [online] **www.bostonbar.org/workfamilychallenges.htm**

Bouchard, T. J. Jr., Lykken, D. T., McGue, M., Segal, N. L., & Tellegen, A. (1990). Sources of human psychological differences: The Minnesota study of twins reared apart. *Science, 250,* 223–228.

Boustany, N. (1996, November 22). Tehran's first female judge is also its last. *Washington Post,* p. A42.

Bowen, C-C, Swim, J. K., & Jacobs, R. R. (2000). Evaluating gender biases on actual job performance of real people: A meta-analysis. *Journal of Applied Social Psychology, 30*(10), 2194–2215.

Bowleg, L., Lucas, K. L., & Tschann, J. M. (2004). "The ball was always in his court": An exploratory analysis of relationships scripts, sexual scripts, and condom use among African American women. *Psychology of Women Quarterly, 28*(1), 70–82.

Boyce, L. A., & Herd, A. M. (2003). The relationship between gender role stereotypes and requisite military leadership characteristics. *Sex Roles, 49*(7–8), 365–378.

Bradley, C. (1994). Why male violence against women is a development issue: Reflections from Papua New Guinea. In M. Davies (Ed.), *Women and violence: Realities and responses worldwide* (pp. 10–26). London: Zed Books.

Braveheart-Jordan, M., & DeBruyn, L. (1995). So she may walk in balance: Integrating the impact of historical trauma in the treatment of Native American Indian women. In J. Adleman & G. Enguídanos (Eds.), *Racism in the lives of women* (pp. 345–368). New York: Harrington Park Press.

Breathnach, C. S. (1990). The secondary sexual characteristics of the brain. *Irish Journal of Psychological Medicine, 7*(1), 59–63.

Briere, J., Corne, S., Runta, M., & Malamuth, N. (1984, August). *The rape arousal inventory:*

Predicting actual and potential sexual aggression in a university population. Paper presented at the meeting of the American Psychological Association, Toronto.

Brody, J. E. (2001, April 10). Pregnancy prevention, the morning after. *New York Times,* p. D8.

Bromberger, J. T., & Matthews, K. A. (1996). A "feminine" model of vulnerability to depressive symptoms: A longitudinal investigation of middle-aged women. *Journal of Personality and Social Psychology, 70*(3), 591–598.

Bronstein, P. (1984). Differences in mothers' and fathers' behaviors toward children: A cross-cultural comparison. *Developmental Psychology, 20*(6), 995–1003.

Brooks, G. (1995). *Nine parts of desire: The hidden world of Islamic women.* New York: Doubleday Anchor.

Broude, G. J., & Greene, S. J. (1976). Cross-cultural codes on twenty sexual attitudes and practices. *Ethnology, 15,* 409–429.

Broverman, I. K., Broverman, D. M., Clarkson, F. E., Rosenkrantz, P. S., & Vogel, S. R. (1970). Sex role stereotypes and clinical judgments of mental health. *Journal of Consulting and Clinical Psychology, 34*(1), 1–7.

Brown, E. A. (1989, June 9). Happily ever after. *Christian Science Monitor,* p. 13.

Brown, J. M. (1998). Aspects of discriminatory treatment of women police officers serving in forces in England and Wales. *British Journal of Criminology, 38*(2), 265–282.

Brown, L. M., & Gilligan, C. (1990). *Meeting at the crossroads: Women's psychology and girls' development.* Cambridge, MA: Harvard University Press.

Brown, L. S. (1992). A feminist critique of personality disorders. In L. S. Brown & M. Ballou (Eds.), *Personality and psychopathology* (pp. 206–228). New York: Guilford.

Brown, M. M. (1980). *Homeward the arrow's flight.* Nashville, TN: Abingdon.

Brown, R. W., Jewell, R. T., & Rous, J. J. (2000). Abortion decisions among Hispanic women along the Texas–Mexico border. *Social Science Quarterly, 81*(1), 237–252.

Brownmiller, S. (1984). *Femininity.* New York: Simon & Schuster.

Buckley, S. (1995, February 28). Africa's women make power moves. *Washington Post,* p. A1.

Buckley, S. (1996, May 2). Spousal abuse in Africa viewed as a right and a rite. *Washington Post,* pp. A1, A26.

Buckley, S. (1997, November 8). Wife inheritance spurs AIDS rise in Kenya. *Washington Post,* pp. A1, A18.

Buckley, S. (2001, April 16). Flirtatious Brazil weighs harassment bill. *Washington Post,* p. A14.

Burbank, V. K. (1987). Female aggression in cross-cultural perspective. *Behavior Science Research, 21,* 70–100.

Burch, M. (2003, May 26). Women's wrestling is a forgotten solution. [online] **http://www.wrestlegirl.com/gnews870.htm**

Burgess, L. C. (Ed.) (1994). *An uncommon soldier: The Civil War letters of Sarah Rosetta Wakeman alias Pvt. Lyons Wakeman.* Pasadena, MD: Minerva Center.

Burke, L. K., & Follingstad, D. R. (1999). Violence in lesbian and gay relationships: Theory, prevalence, and correlational factors. *Clinical Psychology Review, 19*(5), 487–512.

Burke, T. W., Jordan, M. L., & Owne, S. S. (2002). Cross-national comparison of gay and lesbian domestic violence. *Journal of Contemporary Criminal Justice, 18*(3), 231–257.

Burnham, M. A., Stein, J. A., Golding, J. M., Siegel, J. M., Sorenson, S. B., Forsythe, A. B., & Telles, C. A. (1988). Sexual assault and mental disorders in a community population. *Journal of Consulting and Clinical Psychology, 56,* 843–850.

Burnley, C. S., & Kurth, S. B. (1992). Never married women: Alone and lonely? *Humboldt Journal of Social Relations, 18*(2), 57–83.

Burns, J. F. (1994, July 16). Furor over feminist writer leaves Bangladesh on edge. *New York Times,* pp. 1, 2.

Burns, R. B. (1977). Male and female perceptions of their own and the other sex. *British Journal of Social and Clinical Psychology, 16,* 213–220.

Burt, M. R. (1980). Cultural myths and supports for rape. *Journal of Personality and Social Psychology, 38,* 217–230.

Burton, L., & Bengston, V. (1985). Black grandmothers: Issues of timing and continuity of roles. In V. Bengston & J. Robertson (Eds.), *Grandparenthood* (pp. 61–77). Beverly Hills, CA: Sage.

Bussey, K., & Bandura, A. (1984). Influence of gender constancy and social power on sex-linked modeling. *Journal of Personality and Social Psychology, 47,* 1292–1302.

Bussey, K., & Bandura, A. (1999). Social cognitive theory of gender development and differentiation. *Psychological Review, 106,* 676–713.

Butler, D., & Geis, F. (1990). Nonverbal affect responses to male and female leaders: Implications for leadership evaluations. *Journal of*

Personality and Social Psychology, 58(1), 48–59.

Butler, M. (1985). Guidelines for feminist therapy. In L. B. Rosewater & L. Walker (Eds.), *Handbook of feminist therapy* (pp. 32–38). New York: Springer.

Buysse, T. M. (2000). The mother–daughter relationship and the development of daughters' feminist consciousness. *Dissertation Abstracts International, 60*(12-B), 6419.

Bylsma, W. H., & Major, B. (1994). Social comparisons and contentment: Exploring the psychological costs of the gender wage gap. *Psychology of Women Quarterly, 18*(2), 241–249.

Byne, W., Bleier, R., & Houston, L. (1988). Variations in human corpus callosum do not predict gender: A study using magnetic resonance imaging. *Behavioral Neuroscience, 102*(2), 222–227.

Byrne, H. K. (2000). The effects of resistance training on resting blood pressure in women. *Journal of Strength and Conditioning Research, 14*(4), 411–418.

Caetano, R. (1994). Drinking and alcohol-related problems among minority women. *Alcohol Health and Research World, 18,* 233–241.

Cahill, L. (2003). Sex- and hemisphere-related influences on the neurobiology of emotionally influenced memory. *Progress in Neuro-Psychopharmacology & Biological Psychiatry, 27*(8), 1235–1241.

Caldwell, M. A., & Peplau, L. A. (1984). The balance of power in lesbian relationships. *Sex Roles, 10,* 587–599.

Callender, C., & Kochems, L. M. (1983). The North American berdache. *Current Anthropology, 24,* 443–456.

Calogero, R. M. (2004). A test of objectification theory: The effect of the male gaze on appearance concerns in college women. *Psychology of Women Quarterly, 28*(1), 16–21.

Cameron, D., McAlinden, F., & O'Leary, K. (1993). Lakoff in context: The social and linguistic functions of tag questions. In S. Jackson (Ed.), *Women's studies: Essential readings* (pp. 421–426). New York: New York University Press.

Canadian Centre on Substance Abuse (2003). Canadian Community Epidemiology Network on Drug Use (CCENDU) 2002 National Report. [online] **http://www.ccsa.ca/ccendu/pdf/report_national_2002_e.pdf**

Canadian Psychological Association. (1980). *Guidelines for therapy and counselling with women.* Ottawa, Ontario: Author.

Candy, S. G., Troll, L. E., & Levy, S. G. (1981). A developmental exploration of friendship functions in women. *Psychology of Women Quarterly, 5,* 456–472.

Caplan, P. J. (1989). *Don't blame Mother.* New York: Harper & Row.

Caplan, P. J. (2001, May/June). "Premenstrual mental illness": The truth about Sarafem. *The Network News,* National Women's Health Network (pp. 1, 5, 7).

Caplan, P. J., & Caplan, J. B. (1999). *Thinking critically about research on sex and gender.* New York: Longman.

Carli, L. L. (1990). Gender, language, and influence. *Journal of Personality and Social Psychology, 59*(5), 941–951.

Carli, L. L. (2001). Gender and social influence. *Journal of Social Issues, 57*(4), 725–741.

Carr, J. G., Gilroy, F. D., & Sherman, M. F. (1996). Silencing the self and depression among women: The moderating role of race. *Psychology of Women Quarterly, 20*(3), 375–392.

Casey, M. B., & Brabeck, M. M. (1989). Exception to a male advantage on a spatial task: Family handedness and college major as factors identifying women who excel. *Neuropsychologica, 27,* 689–696.

Casper, L. M., & Bryson, K. R. (1998). *Coresident grandparents and their grandchildren.* Washington, DC: U.S. Bureau of the Census (Working paper # 26, Population Division).

Caspi, A., Bem, D., & Elder, G. H., Jr. (1989). Continuities and consequences of interactional styles across the life course. *Journal of Personality, 57*(2), 375–406.

Catalyst (2004, February 18). News Release: *Catalyst report outlines unique challenges faced by African-American women in business.* [online] **http://www.catalystwomen.org/press_room/press_releases/2004afric_woc.pdf**

Cattell, J. M. (1909). The school and the family. *Popular Science Monthly, 74,* 84–95.

Cauce, A. M., Hiraga, Y., Graves, D., Gonzales, N., Ryan-Finn, K., & Grove, K. (1996). African American mothers and their adolescent daughters: Closeness, conflict and control. In B. J. Leadbeater & N. Way (Eds.), *Urban girls: Resisting stereotypes, creating identities* (pp. 100–116). New York: New York University Press.

Ceballo, R. (1994). A word and a kindness: The journey of a Black social worker. In C. E. Franz & A. J. Stewart (Eds.), *Creating lives: Identities, resilience, & resistance* (pp. 83–96). Boulder, CO: Westview Press.

Center for American Women and Politics (2003). Gender gap in the 2000 elections. [online] **http://www.cawp.rutgers.edu/Facts/Elections/gg2000.html**

Centers for Disease Control (2001). Women and smoking. A report of the Surgeon General—2001. [online] **http://www.cdc.gov/tobacco/sgr/sgr_forwomen/ataglance.htm**

Centers for Disease Control (2002). *HIV/AIDS surveillance report. Cases of HIV infection and AIDS in the United States, 2002.* (Vol. 14). [online] **http://www.cdc.gov/hiv/stats/hasr1402/2002SurveillanceReport.pdf**

Centers for Disease Control (2002b, December 18). Births: Final data for 2001. *National Vital Statistics Report, 51*(2). [online] **http://www.cdc.gov/nchs/data/nvsr/nvsr51/nvsr51_02.pdf**

Centers for Disease Control, Tobacco Information and Prevention Source (2004, February). Tobacco-related mortality fact sheet. [online] **http://www.cdc.gov/tobacco/factsheets/Tobacco_Related_Mortality_factsheet.htm**

Centers for Disease Control and Prevention. (1997, May). Press Release: Teen sex down, new study shows. [online] **www.cdc.gov/od/oc/media/pressrel/teensex.htm**

Chang, J. (1991). *Wild swans: Three daughters of China.* New York: Simon & Schuster.

Chao, C. M. (2000). Ancestors and ancestor altars: Connecting relationships. In J. L. Chin (Ed) *Relationships among Asian American women* (pp. 101–117). Washington, DC: American Psychological Association.

Chavarria, S. (1993, February). *Mathematics, being a social construction, is biased.* Paper presented at the Fifth International Interdisciplinary Congress on Women, San José, Costa Rica.

Cheng, C-Y. (2001). Acculturation and cultural value orientations of immigrant Chinese Americans: Effects on body image, aesthetics for appearance, and involvement in dress. *Dissertation Abstracts International, 61* (7-A), 2782.

Cherry, K. (1987). *Womansword: What Japanese words say about women.* New York: Kodansha International.

Chesler, P. (1972). *Women and madness.* New York: Doubleday.

Chetcuti, D. A. (1993). Adolescent girls' views on science: A Maltese study. *Contributions to the Seventh International Gender and Science and Technology Conference* (Vol. 1), pp. 208–216.

Children NOW (1997). Reflections of girls in the media: A two-part study on gender and media. [online] **www.childrennow.org/media/mc97/ReflectSummary.html**

Children spend more time with parents than they used to (2001, May 9). News release: The University of Michigan news and information services. [online] **http://www.umich.edu/~newsinfo/Releases/2001/May01/r050901a.html**

Chin, J. L. (2000). Mother–daughter relationships: Asian American perspectives. In J. L. Chin (Ed.), *Relationships among Asian American women* (pp.119–132). Washington DC: American Psychological Association.

Chodorow, N. (1978). *The reproduction of mothering: Psychoanalysis and the reproduction of gender.* Berkeley: University of California Press.

Chodorow, N. (1999). *The power of feelings.* New Haven, CT: Yale University Press.

Chrisler, J. C. (1996). PMS as a culture-bound syndrome. In J. Chrisler, C. Golden, & P. D. Rozee (Eds.), *Lectures in the psychology of women* (pp. 107–121). New York: McGraw-Hill.

Chrisler, J. C. (2001). Gendered bodies and physical health. In R. K. Unger (Ed.), *Handbook of the psychology of women and gender* (pp. 289–302). New York: John Wiley & Sons.

Chrisler, J. C., Johnston, I. K., Champagne, N. M., & Preston, K. E. (1994). Menstrual joy: The construct and its consequences. *Psychology of Women Quarterly, 18*(3), 375–388.

Chrisler, J. C., & Levy, K. B. (1990). The media construct a menstrual monster: A content analysis of PMS articles in the popular press. *Women & Health, 16,* 89–104.

Christian, M. (2000, August). *Development of the sexual self-concept in African American women.* Paper presented at the annual convention of the American Psychological Association, Washington, DC.

Christiansen, C., Christiansen, M. S., & Transbol, I. (1981). Bone mass in postmenopausal women after withdrawal of oestrogen/gestagen replacement therapy. *Lancet, 1*(8218), 459–461.

Christensen, J. (2001, July 25). Same-sex households mark presence in Hawaii. Associated Press Newswires. Available online from Dow Jones Interactive, **http://ptg.djnr.com**

Citizens for Midwifery. (1997). [online] **www.cfmidwifery.org/facts1.html**

Clare, A. W., & Wiggins, R. D. (1979). The construction of a modified version of the Menstrual Distress Questionnaire for use in general practice populations. In L. Carenza & L. Zichella (Eds.), *Emotions and reproduction* (pp. 191–197). London: Academic Press.

Clark, R. A., Dockum, M., Hazeu, H., Huang, M., Luo, N., Ramsey, J., & Spyrou, A. (2004). Initial encounters of young men and women: Impressions and disclosure estimates. *Sex Roles, 50*(9/10), 699–709.

Clarke-Stewart, K. A. (1991). A home is not a school: The effects of child care on children's development. *Journal of Social Issues, 47*(2), 105–124.

Clay, R. A. (1997a, February). Psychology informs debate on same-gender marriages. *APA Monitor, 28*(2), 40.

Clay, R. A. (1997b, February). HIV risk among lesbians is higher than most realize. *APA Monitor, 28*(2), 40.

Clum, G. A., & Knowles, S. (1991). Why do some people with panic disorders become avoidant?: A review. *Clinical Psychology Review, 11,* 295–313.

Cochran, S. D., & Peplau, L. A. (1985). Value orientations in heterosexual relationships. *Psychology of Women Quarterly, 9,* 477–488.

Cohen, S., Tyrell, D. A., & Smith, A. P. (1991). Psychological stress in humans and susceptibility to the common cold. *New England Journal of Medicine, 325,* 606–612.

Cohn, D. (2001a, May 15). Married-with-children still fading. *Washington Post,* p. A1, A9.

Cohn, D. (2001b, June 20). Census shows big increase in gay households. *Washington Post,* pp. A1, A10.

Colapinto, J. (1997, December 11). The true story of John/Joan. *Rolling Stone,* pp. 55–73, 92, 94–97.

Cole, D. (2001, July 31). Germany establishes limited form of gay marriage. Agence France-Presse. Available online from Dow Jones Interactive, **http://ptg.djnr.com**

Coleman, E. (1982). Developmental stages of the coming out process. In W. Paul (Ed.), *Homosexuality: Social, psychological, and biological issues* (pp. 149–158). Beverly Hills, CA: Sage.

Coleman, V. E. (1994). Lesbian battering: The relationship between personality and the perpetuation of violence. *Violence and Victims, 9*(2), 139–152.

Coles, R., & Coles, J. H. (1978). *Women of crisis: Lives of struggle and hope.* New York: Dell.

Collaer, M. L., & Hines, M. (1995). Human behavioral sex differences: A role for gonadal hormones during early development? *Psychological Bulletin, 118*(1), 55–107.

College Entrance Examination Board (1997). *National Report on college-bound-seniors, various years.* New York: Author.

Collins, P. H. (1991). *Black feminist thought.* New York: Routledge.

Comas-Díaz, L., & Greene, B. (1994a). Overview: Gender and ethnicity in the healing process. In L. Comas-Díaz & B. Greene (Eds.), *Women of color: Integrating ethnic and gender identities in psychotherapy* (pp. 185–193). New York: Guilford.

Comas-Díaz, L., & Greene, B. (1994b). Women of color with professional status. In L. Comas-Díaz & B. Greene (Eds.), *Women of color: Integrating ethnic and gender identities in psychotherapy* (pp. 347–388). New York: Guilford.

Condon, H. S. (1999, October 1). Feminist image campaign: Beyond the old stereotypes. *National NOW Times,* p. 1.

Condon, J. T. (1987). Psychological and physical symptoms during pregnancy: A comparison of male and female expectant parents. *Journal of Reproductive and Infant Psychology, 5*(4), 207–219.

Connor-Greene, P. A. (1988). Gender differences in body weight perception and weight-loss strategies of college students. *Women and Health, 14*(2), 27–42.

Constable, P. (2000, May 8). In Pakistan, women pay the price of 'honor.' *Washington Post,* pp. A1, A16.

Constable, P. (2001, April 24). For Nepali girls, a way station to dignity. *Washington Post,* p. A14.

Constantinople, A. (1973). Masculinity-femininity: An exception to a famous dictum? *Psychological Bulletin, 80*(3), 389–407.

Conway, M., Pizzamiglio, M. T., & Mount, L. (1996). Status, communality, and agency: Implications for stereotypes of gender and other groups. *Journal of Personality and Social Psychology, 71*(1), 25–38.

Cooper, K. J. (1996, October 7). Afghani women under virtual house arrest. *Washington Post,* pp. A1, A16.

Coren, S., & Halpern, D. F. (1991). Left-handedness: A marker for decreased survival fitness. *Psychological Bulletin, 109,* 90–106.

Costello, C. B., & Stone, A. J. (Eds.) (2001). *The American Woman 2000–2001: Getting to the top.* Washington, D.C.: Women's Research and Education Institute.

Couturier, K. (1998, January 27). Suicide attempts fuel virginity-test debate. *Washington Post,* p. A18.

Coventry, M. (2000, October). Making the cut. *Ms.* [online] **www.msmagazine.com/oct00/makingthecut.html**

Cowan, G., Drinkard, J., & MacGavin, L. (1984). The effects of target, age, and gender on use of power strategies. *Journal of Personality and Social Psychology, 47*(6), 1391–1398.

Cowan, G., & Mills, R. D. (2004). Personal inadequacy and intimacy predictors of men's hostility toward women. *Sex Roles, 51*(1/2), 67–78.

Cox, J. L. (1988). Childbirth as a life event: Sociocultural aspects of postnatal depression. *Acta Psychiatrica Scandinavica, 78,* 75–83.

Cozzarelli, C., Major, B., Karrasch, A., & Fuegen, K. (2000). Women's experiences of and reactions to antiabortion picketing. *Basic and Applied Social Psychology, 22*(4), 265–275.

Crandall, C. S. (1995). Do parents discriminate against their heavyweight daughters? *Personality and Social Psychology Bulletin, 21,* 724–735.

Crandall, C. S., & Martinez, R. (1996). Culture, ideology, and antifat attitudes. *Personality and Social Psychology Bulletin, 22*(11), 1165–1176.

Crawford, M. C. (1995). *Talking difference: On gender and language.* London: Sage.

Crawford, M. C. (2001). Gender and language. In R. K. Unger (Ed.), *Handbook of the psychology of women and gender* (pp. 228–244). New York: John Wiley & Sons.

Crawford. M. C., & Kimmel, E. B. (1999). Promoting methodological diversity in feminist research. *Psychology of Women Quarterly* (Special Issue: Innovations in feminist research), *23,* 1–6.

Crick, N. R., & Grotpeter, J. K. (1995). Relational aggression, gender, and social-psychological adjustment. *Child Development, 66*(3), 710–722.

Crosby, F. J. (1984). The denial of personal discrimination. *American Behavioral Scientist, 27*(3), 371–386.

Crosby, F. J. (1991). *Juggling: The unexpected advantage of balancing career and home for women and their families.* New York: Free Press.

Crosby, F. J., & Franco, J. L. (2003). Connections between the ivory tower and the multicolored world: Linking abstract theories of social justice to the rough and tumble of affirmative action. *Personality and Social Psychology Review, 7*(4), 362–373.

Cross, W. E. Jr. (1971). The Negro-to-Black conversion experience: Toward a psychology of Black liberation. *Black World, 20*(9), 13–27.

Cross, W. E. Jr. (1978). Models of psychological nigrescence: A literature review. *Journal of Black Psychology, 5*(1), 13–31.

Crouter, A. C., Perry-Jenkins, M., Huston, T. L., & McHale, S. M. (1987). Processes underlying father involvement in dual-earner and single-earner families. *Developmental Psychology, 23,* 431–440.

Culbertson, F. M. (1997). Depression and gender: An international review. *American Psychologist, 52*(1), 25–31.

Dalcourt, P. (1996). Les stereotypes sexuels dans la publicité Québecoise televisée: Le maintien d'une tradition. *Revue Québecoise de Psychologie, 17*(2), 29–42.

Darwin, C. (1859). *On the origin of species.* London. Reprinted 1967: New York: Atheneum.

Darwin, C. (1871). *The descent of man, and selection in relation to sex.* Reprinted 1981: Princeton: Princeton University Press.

Dasgupta, P. S. (1995, February). Population, poverty and the local environment. *Scientific American,* pp. 40–45.

D'Augelli, A. R. (1992). Lesbian and gay male undergraduates' experiences of harassment and fear on campus. *Journal of Interpersonal Violence, 7*(3), 383–395.

Davis, D. M. (1990). Portrayals of women in prime-time network television: Some demographic characteristics. *Sex Roles, 23*(5/6), 325–332.

Davis, K. (1988). Paternalism under the microscope. In A. D. Todd and S. Fisher (Eds.), *Gender and discourse: The power of talk* (pp. 19–54). Norwood, NJ: Ablex.

Davis, S. (1990). Men as success objects and women as sex objects: A study of personal advertisements. *Sex Roles, 23*(1/2), 43–50.

DeAngelis, T. (1993, September). Controversial diagnosis is voted into latest *DSM. APA Monitor, 24*(9), 32–33.

DeAngelis, T. (1997, August). Stereotypes still stymie female managers. *APA Monitor, 28*(8), 41.

Deaux, K., & Lewis, L. (1984). Structure of gender stereotypes: Interrelationships among components and gender label. *Journal of Personality and Social Psychology, 46*(5), 991–1004.

Deaux, K., & Stewart, A. J. (2001). Framing gendered identities. In R. K. Unger (Ed.), *Handbook of the psychology of women and gender* (pp. 84–97). New York: Wiley.

DeFrancisco, V. (1991). The sounds of silence: How men silence women in marital relations. *Discourse and Society, 2,* 413–423.

Delaney, J., Lupton, M. J., & Toth, E. (1988). *The curse: A cultural history of menstruation.* Urbana: University of Illinois Press.

Delany, S., & Delany, A. E., with Hearth, A. H. (1993). *Having our say: The Delany sisters' first 100 years.* New York: Kodansha International.

Demaré, D., Briere, J., & Lips, H. M. (1988). Violent pornography and self-reported likelihood of sexual aggression. *Journal of Research in Personality, 22,* 140–153.

Demaré, D., Lips, H. M., & Briere, J. (1993). Violent pornography, anti-woman attitudes, and sexual aggression: A structural equation model. *Journal of Research in Personality, 27,* 285–300.

Dempsey, K. C. (1998). Increasing the workload of the overloaded housewife. *Journal of Family Studies, 4*(1), 3–20.

Dempsey, K. C. (2000). Men and women's power relationships and the persisting inequitable division of housework. *Journal of Family Studies, 6*(1), 7–24.

Denner, J., & Dunbar, N. (2004). Negotiating femininity: Power and strategies of Mexican American girls. *Sex Roles, 50*(5/6), 30 1–314.

Derné, S. (1994). Hindu men talk about controlling women: Cultural ideas as a tool of the powerful. *Sociological Perspectives, 37*(2), 203–227.

Deutsch, F. M., LeBaron, D., & Fryer, M. M. (1987). What is in a smile? *Psychology of Women Quarterly, 11,* 341–352.

Diamond, M., & Sigmundson, H. K. (1997). Sex reassignment at birth. Long-term review and clinical implications. *Archives of Pediatric Medicine, 151*(3), 298–304.

Diaz Zuniga, C. C., Sattler, S. E. B., & Lips, H. M. (1997, March). *Multicultural perceptions of powerful women and powerful men.* Paper presented at the annual meeting of the Southeastern Psychological Association, Atlanta.

Dindia, K., & Allen, M. (1992). Sex differences in self-disclosure: A meta-analysis. *Psychological Bulletin, 112,* 106–124.

Dinnerstein, D. (1976). *The mermaid and the minotaur: Sexual arrangements and human malaise.* New York: Harper Colophon.

Dion, K. K., & Dion, K. L. (1993). Individualistic and collectivistic perspective on gender and the cultural context of love and intimacy. *Journal of Social Issues, 49,* 53–69.

Dion, K. K., & Dion, K. L. (2001). Gender and relationships. In R. K. Unger (Ed.), *Handbook of the psychology of women and gender* (pp. 256–271). New York: John Wiley & Sons.

Dodd, D. A., & Brecher, E. J. (2000). Church says men to lead. *Miami Herald,* p. 3B.

Dodson, B. (1974). *Liberating masturbation: A meditation on self-love.* New York: Published and distributed by Betty Dodson, Box 1933, New York, NY 10001.

Dodson, B. (1987). *Sex for one: The joy of self-loving.* New York: Harmony Books.

Dolan, B. (1991). Cross-cultural aspects of anorexia nervosa and bulimia: A review. *International Journal of Eating Disorders, 10*(1), 67–78.

Dolan, B. (1994). Why women? Gender issues and eating disorders: an introduction. In B. Dolan & I. Gitzinger (Eds.), *Why women?* (pp. 1–11). London: The Athlone Press.

Donnerstein, E. (1980). Aggressive-erotica and violence against women. *Journal of Personality and Social Psychology, 3,* 269–277.

Dovidio, J. F., & Ellyson, S. L. (1985). Patterns of visual dominance behavior in humans. In S. L. Ellyson & J. F. Dovidio (Eds.), *Power, dominance, and nonverbal behavior* (pp. 129–149). New York: Springer-Verlag.

Dovidio, J. F., Ellyson, S. L., Keating, C. F., Heltman, K., & Brown, C. E. (1988). The relationship of social power to visual displays of dominance between men and women. *Journal of Personality and Social Psychology, 54,* 233–242.

Downing, N. E., & Rousch, K. L. (1985). From passive-acceptance to active commitment: A model of feminist identity development for women. *The Counseling Psychologist, 13*(4), 695–709.

Dreger, A. D. (1998). *Hermaphrodites and the medical invention of sex.* Cambridge, MA: Harvard University Press.

Duck, S. W. (1994). *Meaningful relationships: Talking, sense, and relating.* Thousand Oaks, CA: Sage.

Dukes, R. L., & Martinez, R. (1994). The impact of ethgender on self-esteem among adolescents. *Adolescence, 29*(113), 105–115.

Dutton, D. G., & Strachan, C. E. (1987). Motivational needs for power and spouse-specific assertiveness in assaultive and nonassaultive men. *Violence and Victims, 2*(3), 145–156.

Dutta, M. (2000). Women's employment and its effects on Bengali households of Shillong, India. *Journal of Comparative Family Studies, 31*(2), 217–229.

Dweck, C. S. (1999). *Self-theories: Their role in motivation, personality, and development.* Philadelphia, PA: Psychology Press.

Dweck, C. S., & Leggett, E. L. (1988). A social-cognitive approach to motivation and personality. *Psychological Review, 95,* 256–273.

Eagly, A. H. (1987). *Sex differences in social behavior: A social-role interpretation.* Hillsdale, NJ: Erlbaum.

Eagly, A. H. (1994). On comparing women and men. *Feminism and Psychology, 4,* 513–522.

Eagly, A. H., Johannesen-Schmidt, M. C. (2003). Transformational, transactional, and laissez-faire leadership styles: A meta-analysis comparing women and men. *Psychological Bulletin, 129*(4), 569–591.

Eagly, A. H., & Johnson, B. T. (1990). Gender and leadership style: A meta-analysis. *Psychological Bulletin, 108,* 233–256.

Eagly, A. H., Karau, S. J., Miner, J. B., & Johnson, B. T. (1994). Gender and motivation to manage in hierarchic organizations: A meta-analysis. *Leadership Quarterly, 5*(2), 135–159.

Eagly, A. H., Makhijani, M. G., & Klonsky, B. K. (1992). Gender and the evaluation of leaders: A meta-analysis. *Psychological Bulletin, 111*(1), 3–22.

Eagly, A. H., & Mladinic, A. (1994). Are people prejudiced against women? Some answers from research on attitudes, gender stereotypes and judgments of competence. In W. Stroebe & M. Hewstone (Eds.), *European review of social psychology* (Vol. 5, pp. 1–35). New York: Wiley.

Eagly, A. H., & Steffen, V. J. (1986). Gender and aggressive behavior: A meta-analytic review of the social psychological literature. *Psychological Bulletin, 100,* 309–330.

Eagly, A. H., & Wood, W. (1999). The origins of sex differences in human behavior: Evolved dispositions versus social roles. *American Psychologist, 54*(6), 408–423.

Earlier puberty for girls worries parents, doctors (2001, February 13). *Roanoke Times,* p. A1.

Eccles, J. S., Barber, B., Jozefowicz, D., Malenchuk, O., & Vida, M. (1999). Self-evaluations of competence, task values, and self-esteem. In N. G. Johnson, M. C. Roberts, & J. Worrell (Eds.), *Beyond appearance: A new look at adolescent girls* (pp. 53–83). Washington, DC: American Psychological Association.

Edwards, A. (1987). *Untrodden peaks and unfrequented valleys.* Boston: Beacon Press. (Original work published 1873.)

Edwards, F. E., Carey, J. S., Grover, F. L., Bero, J. W., & Hartz, R. S. (1998). Impact of gender on coronary bypass operative mortality. *Annals of Thoracic Surgery, 66,* 125–131.

Edwards, J. R., & Williams, J. E. (1980). Sex-trait stereotypes among young children and young adults: Canadian findings and cross-national comparisons. *Canadian Journal of Behavioural Science, 12,* 210–220.

Ehrhardt, A. A., & Baker, S. W. (1974). Fetal androgens, human central nervous system differentiation, and behavior sex differences. In R. M. Richart & R. L. Vande Wiele (Eds.), *Sex differences in behavior* (pp. 33–52). New York: Wiley.

Ekehammar, B., Akrami, N., & Araya, T. (2000). Development and validation of Swedish classical and modern sexism scales. *Scandinavian Journal of Psychology, 41*(4), 307–314.

Eldridge, N. S., & Gilbert, L. A. (1990). Correlates of relationship satisfaction in lesbian couples. *Psychology of Women Quarterly, 14,* 43–62.

Ellet, E. F. (1848). *The American revolution.* New York: Baker & Scribner.

Elgin, S. H. (1984). *Native tongue.* New York: DAW.

Elliott, E. S., & Dweck, C. S. (1988). Goals: An approach to motivation and achievement. *Journal of Personality and Social Psychology, 54,* 5–12.

Ely, R. J. (1995). The power in demography: Women's social constructions of gender identity at work. *Academy of Management Journal, 38*(3), 589–634.

Ember, C. R., & Ember, M. (1990). *Anthropology* (6th ed., instructor's edition). Englewood Cliffs, NJ: Prentice-Hall.

Emplive.com (2001). Evolution of grrrl style. [online] **http://www.emplive.com/explore/riot_grrrl/evolution.asp**

Entwisle, D. R., & Baker, D. P. (1983). Gender and young children's expectations for performance in arithmetic. *Developmental Psychology, 19*(2), 200–209.

Epstein, C. (1973). The positive effects of multiple negatives: Explaining the success of Black professional women. In J. Huber (Ed.), *Changing women in a changing society* (pp. 150–173). Chicago: University of Chicago Press.

Espín, O. M. (1984). Cultural and historical influences on sexuality in Hispanic/Latina women: Implications for psychotherapy. In C. Vance (Ed.), *Pleasure and danger: Exploring female sexuality* (pp. 149–163). London: Routledge & Kegan Paul.

Espín, O. M. (1987). Issues of identity in the psychology of Latina lesbians. In Boston Lesbian Psychologies Collective (Eds.), *Lesbian psychologies* (pp. 35–55). Urbana: University of Illinois Press.

Espín, O. M. (1994). Feminist approaches. In L. Comas-Díaz & B. Greene (Eds.), *Women of color: Integrating ethnic and gender identities in psychotherapy* (pp. 265–286). New York: Guilford.

Espín, O. M. (1995). On knowing you are the unknown: Women of color constructing psychology. In J. Adelman & G. Enguidanos

(Eds.), *Racism in the lives of women* (pp. 127–136). New York: Haworth. Reprinted in O. M. Espín (1997). *Latina realities: Essays on healing, migration, and sexuality* (pp. 71–78). Boulder, CO: Westivew Press.

Espín, O. M. (1999). *Women crossing boundaries. A psychology of immigration and transformations of sexuality.* New York: Routledge.

Esterling, B. A., Kiecolt-Glaser, J. K., & Glaser, R. (1996). Psychosocial modulation of cytokine-induced natural killer cell activity in older adults. *Psychosomatic Medicine, 58*(3), 264–272.

Estés, C. P. (1992). *Women who run with the wolves.* New York: Ballantine.

Ethier, K. A. (1995). *Becoming a mother: Identity acquisition during the transition to parenthood.* Unpublished doctoral dissertation, City University of New York.

European Industrial Relations Observatory (2001). *Fathers fail to use full parental leave entitlement.* [online]. **wysiwyg://14/http://www.eiro.eurof...ie/2001/02/Feature dk0102114f.html**

Evans, J., Heron, J., Francomb, H., Oke, S., & Golding, J. (2001, August 4). Cohort study of depressed mood during pregnancy and after childbirth. *British Medical Journal, 323,* 257–260.

Evans, M., Schweingruber, H., & Stevenson, H. W. (2002). Gender differences in interest and knowledge acquisition: The United States, Taiwan, and Japan. *Sex Roles, 47*(3/4), 153–167.

Evans, P. C. (2003). "If only I were thin like her, maybe I could be happy like her": The self-implications of associating a thin female ideal with life success. *Psychology of Women Quarterly, 27,* 209–214.

Evenson, B. (2002, December 17). Awareness turns to terror: Breast cancer: Public relations campaigns belie high survival rate. *National Post* (Canada), p. AL3.

FDA approves new birth control option. (2001, October 4). Feminist Daily Newswire. [online] **www.feminist.org/news/newsbyte/printnews.asp/id=5842**

Faderman, L. (1981). *Surpassing the love of men: Romantic friendship between women from the Renaissance to the present.* New York: Morrow.

Fagan, J. (1996). A preliminary study of low-income African American fathers' play interactions with their preschool-age children. *Journal of Black Psychology, 22*(1), 7–19.

Fagot, B. I. (1985). Beyond the reinforcement principle: Another step toward understanding sex role development. *Developmental Psychology, 21*(6), 1097–1104.

Faiola, A. (1997, July 3). "Epidemic" of eating disorders plaguing Argentina. *Washington Post,* pp. A1, A24.

Faiola, A. (2001, September 30). Brazilian women ravaged by AIDS. *Washington Post,* p. A34.

Falbo, T., & Peplau, L. A. (1980). Power strategies in intimate relationships. *Journal of Personality and Social Psychology, 38,* 618–628.

Falconer, J. W., & Neville, H. A. (2000). African American college women's body image: An examination of body mass, African self-consciousness, and skin color satisfaction. *Psychology of Women Quarterly, 24*(3), 236–243.

Fallon, A. E., & Rozin, P. (1985). Sex differences in perceptions of desirable body shape. *Journal of Abnormal Psychology, 94*(1), 102–105.

Farley, S. D. (2000). Attaining status at the expense of likability: Pilfering power through interruptive behavior. *Dissertation Abstracts International, 61*(3-B), 1694.

Farnes, P. (1990). Women in medical science. In G. Kass-Simon & P. Farnes (Eds.), *Women of science: Righting the record* (pp. 268–299). Bloomington: Indiana University Press.

Faulkner, J. (1995). The full-figured Black woman: Issues of racism and sizeism. In J. Adelman & G. Enguídanos (Eds.), *Racism in the lives of women: Testimony, theory, and guides to antiracist practice* (pp. 271–280). New York: Haworth.

Fausto-Sterling, A. (2000). *Sexing the body: Gender politics and the construction of sexuality.* New York: Basic Books.

Favreau, O. E. (1991, March). *Do the Ns justify the means? Is the median the message?* Paper presented at the annual meeting of the Association for Women in Psychology, Hartford, CT.

Favreau, O. E. (1993). *Sex difference and sex similarity: Does null hypothesis testing create a false dichotomy?* Unpublished manuscript, Université de Montréal.

Federal Bureau of Investigation. (2001, October 22). Press release: Crime in the United States, 2000. [online] **www.fbi.gov**

Federal Bureau of Investigation (2002). Uniform Crime Reports. Crime in the United States, 2002. [online] **http://www.fbi.gov/ucr/02cius.htm**

Fehr, B. (1993). How do I love thee? Let me consult my prototype. In S. Duck (Ed.), *Individuals in relationships* (pp. 87–120). Newbury Park, CA: Sage.

Feild, H. S. (1978). Attitudes toward rape: A comparative analysis of police, rapists, crisis counselors, and citizens. *Journal of Personality and Social Psychology, 36,* 156–179.

Feingold, A. (1988). Cognitive gender differences are disappearing. *American Psychologist, 43*(2), 95–103.

Feingold, A. (1994a). Gender differences in variability in intellectual abilities: A cross-cultural perspective. *Sex Roles, 30*(1/2), 81–92.

Feingold, A. (1994b). Gender differences in personality: A meta-analysis. *Psychological Bulletin, 116*(3), 429–456.

Feingold, A. (1995). The additive effects of differences in central tendency and variability are important in comparisons between groups. *American Psychologist, 50*(1), 5–13.

Feldman, S., Byles, J. E., & Beaumont, R. (2000). "Is anybody listening?" The experiences of widowhood for older Australian women. *Journal of Women and Aging, 12*(3–4), 155–176.

Female football player for PCHS crowned homecoming queen. (2000, September 28). [online] **www.theenterprise.net/story1.html**

Feola, M. S. (1998). An ethnic passage: An Italian-American woman in academia. In N. A. Ciatu, D. Dileo, & G. Micallef (Eds.), *Curaggia: Writing by women of Italian descent* (pp. 282–286). Toronto: Women's Press.

Ferguson, D. (1995, June 17). Wilma Mankiller leaves strong Cherokee Nation. *Dallas Morning News,* p. 30A.

Ferguson, S. J. (2000). Challenging traditional marriage: Never married Chinese American and Japanese American women. *Gender & Society, 14*(1), 136–159.

Fernández-Pacgeco, J. (2001), Female workers in the Central American Export Processing Zones. Geneva: International Labour Office. [online] **www.ilo.org/public/english/bureau/gender/new/index.htm**

Fighting female genital mutilation in Africa (2001). [online] **www.afrol.com/Categories/Women/backgr_fighting_fgm.htm**

Filardo, E. K. (1996). Gender patterns in African American and White adolescents' social interactions in same-race, mixed-gender groups. *Journal of Personality and Social Psychology, 71*(1), 71–81.

Fine, M. (1991, March). *Women with disabilities.* Paper presented at the national conference of the Association for Women in Psychology, Hartford, CT.

Fine, M. (1992). Silencing and nurturing voice in an improbable context: Urban adolescents in public school. In M. Fine (Ed.), *Disruptive voices: The possibilities of feminist research* (pp. 115–138). Ann Arbor: University of Michigan Press.

Finkelhor, D. (1994). The international epidemiology of child sexual abuse. *Child Abuse and Neglect, 18,* 409–417.

First battered woman granted asylum in the US. (2001, June 8). *Feminist Daily Newswire.* [online] **www.feminist.orf/news/newsbyte/printnews.asp?id=5576**

Fischbein, S. (1990). Biosocial influences on sex differences for ability and achievement test results as well as marks at school. *Intelligence, 14*(1), 127–139.

Fisher, B. S., Cullen, F. T., & Turner, M. G. (2000). *The sexual victimization of college women.* Washington, DC: National Institute of Justice.

Fisher, J. (1989). *Mothers of the disappeared.* London: Zed Books.

Fishman, P. (1978). Interaction: The work women do. *Social Problems, 25,* 397–406.

Fiske, M., & Chiriboga, D. (1990). *Change and continuity in adult life.* San Francisco: Jossey Bass.

Fiske, S. T., Bersoff, D. N., Borgida, E., Deaux, K., & Heilman, M. E. (1991). Social science on trial: Use of sex stereotyping research in *Price Waterhouse* v. *Hopkins. American Psychologist, 46,* 1049–1060.

Fiske, S. T., & Glick, P. (1995). Ambivalence and stereotypes cause sexual harassment: A theory with implications for organizational change. *Journal of Social Issues, 51*(1), 97–115.

Fitch, R. H., & Denenberg, V. H. (1998). A role for ovarian hormones in sexual differentiation of the brain. *Behavioral and Brain Sciences, 21,* 311–352.

Flaks, D. K., Ficher, I., Masterpasqua, F., & Joseph, G. (1995). Lesbians choosing motherhood: A comparative study of lesbian and heterosexual parents and their children. *Developmental Psychology, 31*(1), 105–114.

Flamm, M. (2003). Exploited, not educated: Trafficking of women and children in Southeast Asia. UN Chronicle, *XL*(2): [online] **http://www.un.org/Pubs/chronicle/2003/issue2/0203cont.htm**

Fleming, J. (1983a). Black women in Black and White college environments: The making of a matriarch. *Journal of Social Issues, 39*(3), 41–54.

Folb, E. (1980). *Runnin' down some lines: The language and culture of Black teenagers.* Cambridge, MA: Harvard University Press.

Forbes, G. B., Adams-Curtis, L. E., White, K. B., & Holmgren, K. M. (2003). The role of hostile and benevolent sexism in women's and men's perceptions of the menstruating woman. *Psychology of Women Quarterly, 27*(1), 58–63.

Forbes, G. B., Doroszewicz, K., Card, K., & Adams-Curtis, L. (2004). Association of the thin body ideal, ambivalent sexism, and self-esteem with body acceptance and the preferred body size of college women in Poland and the United States. *Sex Roles, 50*(5/6), 331–345.

Fortunata, B., & Kohn, C. S. (2003). Demographic, psychosocial, and personality characteristics of lesbian batterers. *Violence and Victims, 18*(5), 557–558.

Frances, S. J. (1979). Sex differences in nonverbal behavior. *Sex Roles, 5,* 519–535.

Franks, P., & Clancy, C. M. (1993). Physician gender bias in clinical decisionmaking: Screening for cancer in primary care. *Medical Care, 31,* 213–218.

Frayser, S. (1985). *Varieties of sexual experience: An anthropological perspective on human sexuality.* New Haven, CT: Human Relations Area Files Press.

Frazier, P. A., Cochran, C. C., & Olson, A. M. (1995). Social science research on lay definitions of sexual harassment. *Journal of Social Issues, 51*(1), 21–38.

Fredrickson, B. L., & Roberts, T.-A., (1997). Objectification theory: Toward understanding women's lived experiences and mental health risks. *Psychology of Women Quarterly, 21,*173–206.

Freedman, S. A. (1991). *Triggering the gender schema.* Unpublished master's thesis, Radford University.

Freeman, J. (1995). The revolution for women in law and public policy. In J. Freeman (Ed.), *Women: A feminist perspective* (5th ed., pp. 365–404). Mountain View, CA: Mayfield.

French, J. R. P. Jr., & Raven, B. H. (1959). The bases of social power. In D. Cartwright (Ed.), *Studies in social power* (pp. 150–167). Ann Arbor: University of Michigan Press.

Freud, S. (1960). *A general introduction to psychoanalysis.* (J. Riviere, Trans.). New York: Washington Square Press. (Original work published 1924.)

Freud, S. (1974). Some psychical consequences of the anatomical distinction between the sexes. In J. Strachey (Ed. and Trans.), *The standard edition of the complete works of Sigmund Freud* (Vol. 19, pp. 241–260). London:

Hogarth Press and the Institute of Psycho-Analysis. (Original work published 1925)

Friedan, B. (1993). *The fountain of age.* New York: Simon & Schuster.

Friedl, E. (1993). Legendary heroines. Ideal womanhood and ideology in Iran. In M. Womack & J. Marti (Eds.), *The other fifty percent: Multicultural perspectives on gender relations* (pp. 261–266). Prospect Heights, IL: Waveland Press.

Friedman, J., & Alicea, M. (1995). Women and heroin: The path of resistance and its consequences. *Gender & Society, 9*(4), 423–449.

Friedman, L. (1989). Mathematics and the gender gap: A meta-analysis of recent studies on sex differences in mathematical tasks. *Review of Educational Research, 59*(2), 185–213.

Frieze, I. H. (1986, August). *The female victim: Rape, wife-battering, and incest.* American Psychological Association Master Lecture, presented at the annual meeting of the American Psychological Association, Washington, DC.

Frieze, I. H., & Ramsey, S. J. (1976). Nonverbal maintenance of sex roles. *Journal of Social Issues, 32,* 133–142.

Frodi, A., Macaulay, J., & Thome, P. R. (1977). Are women less aggressive than men? A review of the experimental literature. *Psychological Bulletin, 84,* 634–660.

Frome, P., & Eccles, J. S. (1995, April). *Underestimation of academic ability in the middle school years.* Poster presented at the meeting of the Society for Research in Child Development, Indianapolis, IN.

Frueh, T., & McGhee, P. (1975). Traditional sex role development and amount of time spent watching television. *Developmental Psychology, 11,* 109.

Fullerton, E. (1998, August 3). Women blaze trail in business in Muslim Mauritania. *Washington Post,* p. A17.

Fulton, R., & Anderson, S. W. (1992). The Amerindian "Man-Woman": Gender, liminality, and cultural continuity. *Current Anthropology, 33*(5), 603–610.

Furnham, A., & Alibhai, N. (1983). Cross-cultural differences in the perception of female body shapes. *Psychological Medicine, 13,* 829–837.

Furnham, A., & Malik, R. (1994). Cross-cultural beliefs about "depression." *International Journal of Social Psychiatry, 40*(2), 106–123.

Furnham, A., & Skae, E. (1997). Changes in the stereotypical portrayal of men and women in British television advertisements. *European Psychologist, 2*(1), 44–51.

Furumoto, L., & Scarborough, E. (1986). Placing women in the history of psychology: The first American women psychologists. *American Psychologist, 41,* 35–42.

Gabriel, M. T., Critelli, J. W., & Ee, J. S. (1994). Narcissistic illusions in self-evaluations of intelligence and attractiveness. *Journal of Personality, 62*(1), 143–155.

Galambos, N. L., Almeida, D. M., & Petersen, A. C. (1990). Masculinity, femininity, and sex role attitudes in early adolescence: Exploring gender intensification. *Child Development, 61,* 1905–1914.

Ganahl, D. J., Prinsen, T. J., & Netzley, S. B. (2003). A content analysis of prime time commercials: A contextual framework of gender representation. *Sex Roles, 49*(9/10), 545–551.

Gannon, L., & Ekstrom, B. (1993). Attitudes toward menopause: The influence of sociocultural paradigms. *Psychology of Women Quarterly, 17*(3), 275–288.

Garber, M. (1992). *Vested interests: Cross-dressing and cultural anxiety.* New York: Routledge.

Garnets, L., Herek, G. M., & Levy, B. (1990). Violence and victimization of lesbians and gay men: Mental health consequences. *Journal of Interpersonal Violence, 5*(3), 366–383.

Garside, R. B., & Klimes-Dougan, B. (2002). Socialization of discrete negative emotions: Gender differences and links with psychological distress. *Sex Roles, 47*(3/4), 115–128.

Gay, D., & Lynxwiler, J. (1999). The impact of religiosity on race variations in abortion attitudes. *Sociological Spectrum, 19*(3), 49–66.

Geschwind, N., & Behan, P. (1982). Left-handedness: Association with immune disease, migraine, and developmental learning disorder. *Proceedings of the National Academy of Sciences, 79,* 5097–5100.

Geschwind, N., & Galaburda, A. M. (1987). *Cerebral lateralization: Biological mechanisms, associations, and pathology.* Cambridge, MA: MIT Press.

Ghadially, R., & Kumar, P. (1989). Stress, strain and coping styles of female professionals. *Indian Journal of Applied Psychology, 26*(1), 1–8.

Gibbons, J. L., Hamby, B. A., & Dennis, W. D. (1997). Researching gender-role ideologies internationally and cross-culturally. *Psychology of Women Quarterly, 21*(1), 151–170.

Gibbons, J. L., Lynn, M., Stiles, D. A., Jerez de Berducido, E., et al. (1993). Guatemalan, Filipino, and U.S. adolescents' images of women as office workers and homemakers. *Psychology of Women Quarterly, 17*(4), 373–388.

Gibbons, J. L., Stiles, D. A., & Shkodriani, G. M. (1991). Adolescents' attitudes toward family and gender roles: An international comparison. *Sex Roles, 25*(11–12), 625–643.

Gibbs, J. T. (1996). Health-compromising behaviors in urban early adolescent females: Ethnic and socioeconomic variations. In B. J. R. Leadbeater & N. Way (Eds.), *Urban girls: Resisting stereotypes, creating identities* (pp. 309–327). New York: New York University Press.

Gidycz, C. A., Hanson, K., & Layman, M. J. (1995). A prospective analysis of the relationships among sexual assault experiences. *Psychology of Women Quarterly, 19*(1), 5–29.

Gilligan, C. (1982). *In a different voice: Psychological theory and women's development.* Cambridge, MA: Harvard University Press.

Gilligan, C. (1990). Joining the resistance: Psychology, politics, girls and women. *Michigan Quarterly Review, 29,* 501–536.

Gilligan, C., & Attanucci, J. (1994). Two moral orientations: Gender differences and similarities. In B. Puka (Ed.) *Caring voices and women's moral frames: Gilligan's view. Moral development: A compendium (Vol. 6).* (pp. 123–137).

Gilmartin, C. (1993). Gender in the formation of a Communist body politic. *Modern China, 19*(3), 299–329.

Ginorio, A. B., & Martínez, L. J. (1998). Where are the Latinas? Ethno-race and gender in psychology courses. *Psychology of Women Quarterly, 22,* 53–68.

Gjerdingen, D. K., Froberg, D. G., & Kochevar, L. (1991). Changes in women's mental and physical health from pregnancy through six months postpartum. *Journal of Family Practice, 32*(2), 161–166.

Glass, D. (2001, February 13). First two women cross Antarctica. *Ithaca Journal,* p. B1.

Glick, P., & Fiske, S. T. (1996). The Ambivalent Sexism Inventory: Differentiating hostile and benevolent sexism. *Journal of Personality and Social Psychology, 70,* 491–512.

Glick, P., & Fiske, S. T. (2001). An ambivalent alliance: Hostile and benevolent sexism as complementary justifications for gender inequality. *American Psychologist, 56*(2), 109–118.

Gold, A. G. (1993). Power as violence: Hindu images of female fury. In M. Womack & J. Marti (Eds.), *The other fifty percent: Multicultural perspectives on gender relations* (pp.

247–260). Prospect Heights, IL: Waveland Press.

Goldberg, C. (2001, February 15). 2 new jobs for Massachusetts official: Acting governor and mother of twins. *New York Times*, p. A16.

Golden, C. (1987). Diversity and variability in women's sexual identities. In Boston Lesbian Psychologies Collective (Eds.), *Lesbian psychologies* (pp. 18–34). Urbana: University of Illinois Press.

Golding, J. M. (1996). Sexual assault history and women's reproductive and sexual health. *Psychology of Women Quarterly, 21*(1), 101–122.

Goldstein, R. (2001, July 31). The gay marriage bomb. *The Village Voice*, p. 42.

Gölge, Z. B., Yavuz, M. F., Műderrisoglu, S.,& Yavuz, M. S. (2003). Turkish university students' attitudes toward rape. *Sex Roles, 49*(11/12), 653–662.

Goodenow, C. (1985, August). *Women's friendships and their association with psychological well-being.* Paper presented at the annual meeting of the American Psychological Association, Washington, DC.

Goodson, P., McCormick, D., & Evans, A. (2001). Searching for sexually explicit materials on the Internet: An exploratory study of college students' behavior and attitudes. *Archives of Sexual Behavior, 30*(2), 101–118.

Goodwin, M. H. (1990). *He-said-she-said: Talk as social organization among Black children.* Bloomington: Indiana University Press.

Gordon, K. H. (2002). The impact of racial stereotypes on eating disorder recognition. *International Journal of Eating Disorders, 32*(2), 219–224.

Gorlick, C. A. (1995). Divorce: Options available, constraints forced, pathways taken. In N. Mandell & A. Duffy (Eds.), *Canadian families: Diversity, conflict and change* (pp. 211–234). Toronto: Harcourt Brace Canada.

Gortmaker, S. L. (1993, September 30). Social and economic consequences of overweight in adolescence and young adulthood. *New England Journal of Medicine, 329*(14), 1008–1012.

Gouldner, H., & Strong, M. S. (1987). *Speaking of friendship: Middle-class women and their friends.* New York: Greenwood.

Gowaty, P. A. (2001). Women, psychology, and evolution. In R. K. Unger (Ed.), *Handbook of the psychology of women and gender* (pp. 53–65). New York: John Wiley & Sons.

Graham, S. (1992). "Most of the subjects were white and middle class": Trends in published research on African Americans in selected APA journals, 1970–1989. *American Psychologist, 47*(5), 629–639.

Grant, L. (1984, April). Black females' place in desegregated classrooms. *Sociology of Education,* 98–110.

Grant, L. (1985). Race–gender status, classroom interaction and children's socialization in elementary school. In L. C. Wilkinson & C. B. Marrett (Eds.), *Gender influences in classroom interaction* (pp. 57–77). Orlando, FL: Academic Press.

Gratch, L. V., Bassett, M. E., & Attra, S. L. (1995). The relationship of gender and ethnicity to self-silencing and depression among college students. *Psychology of Women Quarterly, 19*(4), 509–516.

Gray, J. J., Ford, K., & Kelly, L. M. (1987). The prevalence of bulimia in a Black college population. *International Journal of Eating Disorders, 6,* 733–740.

Greene, B. (1994). Lesbian women of color: Triple jeopardy. In L. Comas-Díaz & B. Greene (Eds.), *Women of color: Integrating ethnic and gender issues in psychotherapy* (pp. 389–427). New York: Guilford.

Greene, B., & Sanchez-Hucles, J. (1997). Diversity: Advancing an inclusive feminist psychology. In J. Worell & N. G. Johnson (Eds.), *Shaping the future of feminist psychology: Education, research, and practice* (pp. 173–202). Washington, DC: American Psychological Association.

Greer, G. (1992). *The change: Women, aging and the menopause.* New York: Knopf.

Grimsley, K. D. (1996a, March 6). Hyatts serve up a children's special: Trying out a career. *Washington Post,* p. D1.

Grimsley, K. D. (1996b, October 27). Into the abyss of harassment at Eveleth Mine. *Washington Post,* pp. A1, A12.

Grimsley, K. D. (1996c, October 28). In court, women miners felt harassed again. *Washington Post,* pp. A1, A12.

Grimsley, K. D., Swoboda, F., & Brown, W. (1996, April 29). Fear on the line at Mitsubishi. *Washington Post,* pp. A1, A8–A9.

Gringart, E., & Helmes, E. (2001). Age discrimination in hiring practices against older adults in Western Australia: the case of accounting assistants. *Australian Journal on Ageing, 20*(1), 23–28.

Grodstein, F., Manson, J. E., & Stampfer, M. J. (2001, July). Postmenopausal hormone use and secondary prevention of coronary events in the Nurses' Health Study. *Annals of Internal Medicine, 135,* 1–8.

Groesz, L. M., Levine, M. P., & Murnen, S. K. (2002). The effect of experimental presentation of thin media images on body satisfaction: A meta-analytic review. *International Journal of Eating Disorders, 31*(1), 1–16.

Grrrlzines.net (2003). What is this all about? [online] **http://grrrlzines.net/about.htm#zines**

Gruber, J. E. (1990). Methodological problems and policy implications in sexual harassment research. *Population Research and Policy Review, 9*, 235–254.

Grunbaum, J., Kann, L., Kinchen, S., Ross, J., Hawkins, J., Lowry, R., Harris, W. A., McManus, T., Chyen, D., & Collins, J. (2004, May 21). Youth risk behavior surveillance—United States, 2003. In *Surveillance Summaries, MMWR* (No. SS-2), 2–100.

Guerillagirls.com (2004). [online] **http://www .guerillagirls.com**

Guinier, L., Fine, M., & Balin, J., with Bartow, A., & Stachel, D. L. (1994, November). Becoming gentlemen: Women's experience at one Ivy League law school. *University of Pennsylvania Law Review, 143*(1), 1–110.

Gullette, M. M. (1997). *Declining to decline: Cultural combat and the politics of the midlife.* Charlottesville: University Press of Virginia.

Gunew, S. (1991). Margins: Acting like a (foreign) woman. In *Women/ Australia/Theory: A special issue of Hecate, 17*(1), 31–35.

Gutek, B. A., & Nakamura, C. (1983). Gender roles and sexuality in the world of work. In E. R. Allgeier & N. B. McCormick (Eds.), *Changing boundaries: Gender roles and sexual behavior* (pp. 182–201). Mountain View, CA: Mayfield.

Gutek, B. A., & O'Connor, M. (1995). The empirical basis for the reasonable woman standard. *Journal of Social Issues, 51*(1), 151–166.

Haaken, J. (1988). Field dependence research: A historical analysis of a psychological construct. *Signs, 13*(2), 311–330.

Haddad, T., & Lam, L. (1994). The impact of migration on the sexual division of family work: A case study of Italian immigrant couples. *Journal of Comparative Family Studies, 25*(2), 167–182.

Halberstadt, A., & Saitta, M. (1987). Gender, nonverbal behavior, and perceived dominance: A test of the theory. *Journal of Personality and Social Psychology, 53*, 257–272.

Hall, J. A. (1984). *Nonverbal sex differences: Communication accuracy and expressive style.* Baltimore: Johns Hopkins University Press.

Hall, J. A. (1987). On explaining gender differences: The case of nonverbal communication. In P. Shaver & C. Hendrick (Eds.), *Sex and gender* (pp. 177–200). Newbury Park, CA: Sage.

Hall, J. A., & Veccia, E. M. (1990). More "touching" observations: New insights on men, women, and interpersonal touch. *Journal of Personality and Social Psychology, 59*, 1155–1162.

Halliwell, E., & Dittmar, H. (2003). A qualitative investigation of women's and men's body image concerns and their attitudes toward aging. *Sex Roles, 49*(11/12), 675–684.

Halpern, D. F. (1995). Cognitive gender differences: Why diversity is a critical research issue. In H. Landrine, (Ed.), *Bringing cultural diversity to feminist psychology. Theory, research and practice* (pp. 77–92). Washington, DC: American Psychological Association.

Halpern, D. F. (2000). *Sex differences in cognitive abilities* (3rd ed.). Hillsdale, NJ: Erlbaum.

Halpern, D. F. (1994). Stereotypes, science, censorship, and the study of sex differences. *Feminism & Psychology, 4*(4), 523–530.

Halpern, D. F., & LaMay, M. L. (2000). The smarter sex: A critical review of sex differences in intelligence. *Educational Psychology Review, 12*(2), 229–246.

Hamilton, G. (1972). American inventions. In *Twelve miles from a lemon.* Freeport, NY: Books for Libraries Press. (Original edition published 1873.)

Hamilton, M. C. (1991, March). *Preference for sons or daughters and the sex role characteristics of the potential parents.* Paper presented at the meeting of the Association for Women in Psychology, Hartford, CT.

Hampson, E. (1990a). Estrogen-related variations in human spatial and articulatory-motor skills. *Psychoneuroendocrinology, 15*, 97–111.

Hampson, E. (1990b). Variations in sex-related cognitive abilities across the menstrual cycle. *Brain and Cognition, 14*, 26–43.

Hampson, E., & Kimura, D. (1988). Reciprocal effects of hormonal fluctuations on human motor and perceptual-spatial skills. *Behavioral Neuroscience, 102*, 456–495.

Handy, L. C., Valentich, M., Cammaert, L. P., & Gripton, J. (1984/ 85). Feminist issues in sex therapy. *Journal of Social Work & Human Sexuality, 3*(2/3), 69–80.

Hansen, F. J., & Osborne, D. (1995). Portrayal of women and elderly patients in psychotropic drug advertisements. *Women & Therapy, 16*(1), 129–141.

Harding, S. (1989). Is there a feminist method? In N. Tuana (Ed.), *Feminism and science* (pp. 17–32). Bloomington: Indiana University Press.

Hare-Mustin, R. T., & Maracek, J. (1990). Gender and the meaning of difference. In R. T. Hare-Mustin & J. Maracek (Eds.), *Making a difference: Psychology and the construction of gender* (pp. 22–64). New Haven, CT: Yale University Press.

Hare-Mustin, R. T., & Maracek, J. (1994). Asking the right questions: Feminist psychology and sex differences. *Feminism & Psychology, 4*(4), 531–537.

Hargreaves, D. A., & Tiggemann, M. (2003). Female "thin ideal" media images and boys' attitudes toward girls. *Sex Roles, 49*(9/10), 53 9–544.

Harmon, A. (2004, August 26). Internet gives teenage bullies weapons to wound from afar. *New York Times* [online] **http://www.nytimes.com/2004/08/26/education/26bully.html**

Harris, J. R. (1995). Where is the child's environment? A group socialization theory of development. *Psychological Bulletin, 102*(30), 458–489.

Harris, M. G. (1994). Cholas, Mexican-American girls, and gangs. *Sex Roles, 30*(3/4), 289–301.

Harris, S. M. (1994). Racial differences in predictors of women's body image attitudes. *Women & Health, 2,* 89–104.

Harris, S. M. (1995). Family, self, and sociocultural contributions to body-image attitudes of African-American women. *Psychology of Women Quarterly, 19*(1), 129–146.

Harvie, K., Marshal-McCaskey, J., & Johnston, L. (1998). Gender-based biases in occupational hiring decisions. *Journal of Applied Social Psychology, 28*(18), 1698–1711.

Hatch, L. R. (1992). Gender differences in orientation toward retirement from paid labor. *Gender & Society, 6*(1), 66–85.

Hatfield, E., & Rapson, R. L. (1987). Passionate love: New directions in research. In W. H. Jones & D. Perlman (Eds.), *Advances in personal relationships* (Vol. 1, pp. 109–139). Greenwich, CT: JAI.

Hatfield, E., & Rapson, R. L. (1993). Historical and cross-cultural perspectives on passionate love and sexual desire. *Annual Review of Sex Research, 4,* 67–97.

Hatfield, E., Traupmann, J., Sprecher, S., Utne, M., & Hay, J. (1984). Equity and intimate relationships: Recent research. In W. Ickes (Ed.), *Compatible and incompatible relationships* (pp. 1–27). New York: Springer-Verlag.

Haug, F. (Ed.). (1987). *Female sexualization* (E. Carter, Trans.). London: Verso.

Hausman, B. L. (2000). Do boys have to be boys? Gender, narrativity, and the John/Joan case. *NWSA Journal, 12*(3), 114–138.

Health Canada (1996). *Statistical report on the health of Canadians.* [online] **http://www.hc-sc.gc.ca/hppb/phdd/pdf/report/stats/eng15–29.pdf**

Health Canada (1997). *Highlights on the physical activity of Canadians, National Population Health Survey, 1996/97.* [online] **http://www.hc-sc.gc.ca/pphb-dgspsp/ccdpc-cpcmc/cancer/publications/pdf/nphstabe.pdf**

Health Canada (2000, October). 1998/1999 *Canadian sexually transmitted diseases (STD) surveillance report, Volume 26S6.* [online] **http://www.hc-sc.gc.ca/pphb-dgspsp/publicat/ccdr-rmtc/00vol26/26s6/**

Health Canada (2002). *The health of Aboriginal women.* [online] **http://www.hc-sc.gc.ca/english/women/facts_issues/facts_aborig.htm**

Heath, S. B. (1983). *Ways with words: Language, life, and work in communities and classrooms.* New York: Cambridge University Press.

Hebl, M. (1995). Gender bias in leader selection. *Teaching of Psychology, 22*(3), 186–188.

Heckert, T. M., Droste, H. E., Adams, P. J., Griffin, C. M., Roberts, L. L., Mueller, M. A., & Wallis, H. A. (2002). Gender differences in anticipated salary: Role of salary estimates for others, job characteristics, career paths, and job inputs. *Sex Roles, 47*(3/4), 139–151.

Hedges, L. V., & Nowell, A. (1995). Sex differences in mental test scores, variability, and numbers of high-scoring individuals. *Science, 269,* 41–45.

Heilbrun, C. (1973). *Toward a recognition of androgyny.* New York: Harper & Row.

Heilman, M. E. (2001). Description and prescription: How gender stereotypes prevent women's ascent up the organizational ladder. *Journal of Social Issues, 57*(4), 657–674.

Heilman, M. E., & Alcott, V. B. (2001). What I think you think of me: Women's reactions to being viewed as beneficiaries of preferential selection. *Journal of Applied Psychology, 86*(4), 574–582.

Heilman, M. E., & Blader, S. L. (2001). Assuming preferential selection when the admissions policy is unknown: The effects of gender rarity. *Journal of Applied Psychology, 86*(2), 188–193.

Heilman, M. E., Block, C. J., Martell, R. F., & Simon, M. C. (1989). Has anything changed? Current characterizations of men, women, and managers. *Journal of Applied Psychology, 74,* 935–942.

Heilman, M. E., Simon, M. C., & Repper, D. P. (1987). Intentionally favored, unintentionally harmed? Impact of sex-based preferential selection on self-perception and self-evaluations. *Journal of Applied Psychology, 72*(1), 62–68.

Heise, L., Pitanguy, J., & Germain, A. (1993). *Violence against women: The hidden health burden.* Washington, DC: World Bank.

Helms, J. E. (Ed.). (1993). *Black and White racial identity: Theory, research, and practice.* Westport, CT: Praeger.

Henderson-King, D., & Zhermer, N. (2003). Feminist consciousness among Russians and Americans. *Sex Roles, 48*(3/4), 143–155.

Hendrick, S. S., & Hendrick, C. (1995). Gender differences and similarities in sex and love. *Personal Relationships, 2,* 55–65.

Henley, N., & Freeman, J. (1995). The sexual politics of interpersonal behavior. In J. Freeman (Ed.), *Women: A feminist perspective* (5th ed., pp. 79–91). Mountain View, CA: Mayfield.

Henningsen, D. D. (2004). Flirting with meaning: An examination of miscommunication in flirting interactions. *Sex Roles, 50*(7/8), 481–490.

Herek, G. M. (1993). Documenting prejudice against lesbians and gay men on campus: The Yale sexual orientation survey. *Journal of Homosexuality, 25*(4), 15–28.

Herek, G. M., Cogan, J. C., & Gillis, J. R. (2002). Victim experiences in hate crimes based on sexual orientation. *Journal of Social Issues, 58*(2), 319–339.

Herman, J. C. (1998). The discourse of un' propria paparone. In N. A. Ciatu, D. Dileo, & G. Micallef (Eds.), *Curaggia: Writing by women of Italian descent* (pp. 176–179). Toronto: Women's Press.

Herrera, R. S., & DelCampo, R. L. (1995). Beyond the superwoman syndrome: Work satisfactions and family functioning among working-class, Mexican-American women. *Hispanic Journal of Behavioral Sciences, 17*(1), 49–60.

Herstory: The Canadian women's calendar. (1995). Regina, Saskatchewan: Coteau Books.

Herzenberg, C. L., Meschel, S. V., & Altena, J. A. (1991). Women scientists and physicians of antiquity and the Middle Ages. *Journal of Chemical Education, 68*(2), 101–105.

Heymann, J., Earle, A., Simmons, S., Breslow, S. M., & Kuehnhoff, A. (2004). *The work, family and equity index: Where does the United States stand globally?* The Project on Global Working Families, Harvard School of Public Health. [online] **www.globalworkingfamilies.org**

Himelein, M. J. (1995). Risk factors for sexual victimization in dating: A longitudinal study of college women. *Psychology of Women Quarterly, 19*(1), 31–48.

Hines, M. (1990). Gonadal hormones and human cognitive development. In J. Balthazart (Ed.), *Hormones, brain and behavior in vertebrates. Vol. 1. Sexual differentiation, neuroanatomical aspects, neurotransmitters and neuropeptides* (pp. 51–63). Basel: Karger.

Hochschild, A. (1989). The second shift: Working parents and the revolution at home. New York: Viking.

Hockstader, L. (1995, September 1). For women, new Russia is far from liberating. *Washington Post,* pp. A25, A31.

Hoffmann, M. L., Powlishta, K. K., & White, K. J. (2004). An examination of gender differences in adolescent adjustment: The effect of competence on gender role differences in symptoms of psychopathology. *Sex Roles, 50*(11/12), 795–810.

Hoffnung, M. (1995). Motherhood: Contemporary conflict for women. In J. Freeman (Ed.), *Women: A feminist perspective* (5th ed., pp. 162–181). Mountain View, CA: Mayfield.

Hoffnung, M. (2004). Wanting it all: Career, marriage, and motherhood during college-educated women's 20s. *Sex Roles, 50*(9/10), 711–724.

Holmes, C. B., Hausler, H., & Nunn, P. (1998). A review of sex differences in the epidemiology of tuberculosis. *International Journal of Tuberculosis and Lung Disease, 2*(2), 96–104.

Holtgraves, T., & Yang, J-N. (1992). Interpersonal underpinnings of request strategies: General principles and differences due to culture and gender. *Journal of Personality and Social Psychology, 62*(2), 246–256.

Holtzworth-Munroe, A., & Stuart, G. L. (1994). Typologies of male batterers: Three subtypes and the differences among them. *Psychological Bulletin, 116*(3), 476–497.

Homans, C. G. (1974). *Social behavior: The elementary forms.* New York: Harcourt Brace Jovanovich.

hooks, b. (1989). *Talking back: Thinking feminist, thinking Black.* Boston: South End Press.

hooks, b. (1996). *Bone Black: Memories of girlhood.* New York: Henry Holt.

Horney, K. (1939). *The neurotic personality of our time.* New York: Norton.

Horney, K. (1973). The flight from womanhood. In J. B. Miller (Ed.), *Psychoanalysis and women* (pp. 5–20). Baltimore: Penguin Books. (Original work published 1926.)

Horowitz, M. J., Schaefer, C., & Cooney, P. (1974). Life event scaling for recency of experience. In E. K. E. Gunderson & R. H. Rahe (Eds.), *Life stress and illness* (pp. 125–133). Springfield, IL: Charles C Thomas.

Hortaçsu, N., Ertem, L., Kurtoğlu, H., & Uzer, B. (1990). Family background and individual measures as predictors of Turkish primary school children's academic achievement. *Journal of Psychology, 124*(5), 535–544.

Hoshiko, S. (1993). *Our choices: Women's personal decisions about abortion.* New York: Harrington Park Press.

Hossain, Z. (2001). Division of household labor and family functioning in off-reservation Navajo Indian families. *Family Relations, 50*(3), 255–261.

Houston, M. (1994). When Black women talk with White women: Why dialogues are difficult. In A. Gonzalez, M. Houston, & V. Chen (Eds.), *Our voices: Essays in culture, ethnicity, and communication* (pp. 133–139). Los Angeles: Roxbury.

Houston, M., & Wood, J. T. (1996). Difficult dialogues, expanded horizons: Communicating across race and class. In J. T. Wood (Ed.), *Gendered relationships* (pp. 39–56). Mountain View, CA: Mayfield.

Hovell, M., Blumberg, E., Atkins, C., Hofstetter, C., & Kreitner, S. (1994). Family influences on Latino and Anglo adolescents' sexual behavior. *Journal of Marriage and the Family, 56*, 973–986.

Howard, J. S., Blumstein, P., & Schwartz, P. (1986). Sex, power, and influence tactics in intimate relationships. *Journal of Personality and Social Psychology, 51*(1), 102–109.

Hrdy, S. B. (1999). *Mother nature: Maternal instincts and how they shape the human species.* New York: Ballantine Books.

Huang, J. (1993). An investigation of gender differences in cognitive abilities among Chinese high school students. *Personality and Individual Differences, 15*(6), 717–719.

Hubbard, R. (1988). Some thoughts about the masculinity of the natural sciences. In M. M. Gergen (Ed.), *Feminist thought and the structure of knowledge* (pp. 1–15). New York: New York University Press.

Huber, B. R., & Scaglion, R. (1995). Gender differences in computer education: A Costa Rican case study. *Journal of Educational Computing Research, 13*(3), 271–304.

Hughes, T. L., & Wilsnack, S. C. (1997). Use of alcohol among lesbians: Research and clinical implications. *American Journal of Orthopsychiatry, 67,* 20–36.

Hulley, S. B., & Grady, D. (2004). The WHI estrogen-along trial—Do things look any better? *Journal of the American Medical Association, 291,* 1769–1771.

Human Rights Watch (1999). Broken people: Caste violence against India's "Untouchables." New York: Author. [online] **http://www.hrw.org/reports/1999/India**

Hungerford, T. L. (2001). Economic consequences of widowhood on elderly women in the United States and Germany. *Gerontologist, 41*(1), 103–110.

Huntsinger, C. S., & Jose, P. E. (1995). Chinese American and Caucasian American family interaction patterns in spatial rotation puzzle solutions. *Merrill-Palmer Quarterly, 41*(4), 471–496.

Hurtado, A. (2003). *Voicing Chicana feminisms: Young women speak out on sexuality and identity.* New York: New York University Press.

Husband, friends raped her when dowry lacked a motorcycle, bride says. (1997, August 2). *Washington Post,* p. C6.

Hwang, S., & Bedford, O. (2004). Juveniles' motivation for remaining in prostitution. *Psychology of Women Quarterly, 28*(2), 136–146.

Hyde, J. S. (1981). How large are cognitive gender differences? A meta-analysis using ω^2 and d. *American Psychologist, 36,* 892–901.

Hyde, J. S. (1984). How large are gender differences in aggression? A developmental meta-analysis. *Developmental Psychology, 20,* 722–736.

Hyde, J. S. (1994). Should psychologists study gender differences? Yes, with some guidelines. *Feminism & Psychology, 4*(4), 507–512.

Hyde, J. S., Fennema, E., & Lamon, S. J. (1990). Gender differences in mathematics performance: A meta-analysis. *Psychological Bulletin, 107,* 139–155.

Hyde, J. S., & Kling, K. C. (2001). Women, motivation, and achievement. *Psychology of Women Quarterly, 25*(4), 364–378.

Hyde, J. S., & Linn, M. C. (1986). *The psychology of gender: Advances through meta-analysis.* Baltimore: Johns Hopkins University Press.

Hyde, J. S., & Linn, M. C. (1988). Gender differences in verbal ability: A meta-analysis. *Psychological Bulletin, 104*(1), 53–69.

Illegal abortions claim thousands of lives (2001, August 1). Feminist Daily Newswire. New York: Feminist Majority Foundation Online. **www.feminist.org/news/newsbyte**

Imperato-McGinley, J., Guerrero, L., Gautier, T., & Peterson, R. E. (1974). Steroid 5-alpha-reductase deficiency in man: An inherited form of male pseudohermaphroditism. *Science, 186,* 1213–1215.

Instituto de la Mujer. (1993). *Mujeres Latinoamericanas en cifras: Costa Rica.* Madrid: Ministerio de Asuntos Sociales de España Y Facultdad Latinoamerican de Ciensias Sociales.

Integrated Regional Information Network, UN Office for the Coordination of Humanitarian Affairs (2004, August 16). *Pakistan: Activists call for reform of state-run shelters for women.* [online] **http://www.irinnews.org/report.asp?ReportID=42685 &SelectRegion=Central_Asia &SelectCountry=PAKISTAN**

Intel Science Talent Search awards scholarships totaling $530,000 (2001, March 12). Press release, Intel Corporation. [online] **www.intel .com/pressroom/archive/releases**

International Institute for Democracy and Electoral Assistance (2004). Gender and political participation. [online] **http://www.idea.int/ gender/turnout.htm**

International Labor Office (2004a). Breaking through the glass ceiling: Women in management. Update 2004. Geneva, Switzerland: Author. [online] **http://www.ilo.org/dyn/ gender/docs/RES/292/F267981337/ Breaking%20Glass%20PDF%20English .pdf**

International Labor Office (2004b). SECGREGA database. [online] **http://laborsta.org**

International Women's Media Foundation (2001). Leading in a different language: Will women change the news media? [online] **www.iwmf .org/resources**

Intersex Society of North American (2001). [online] **www.isna.org**

Irvine, J. J. (1986). Teacher–student interactions: Effects of student race, sex, and grade level. *Journal of Educational Psychology, 78*(1), 14–21.

Itano, N. (2003, January 29). S. Africa finds "rape courts" work. *Christian Science Monitor.* [online] **http://www.csmonitor.com/2003/0129/ p01s0 4–woaf.html**

Izuhara, M. (2000). Changing family tradition: Housing choices and constraints for older people in Japan. *Housing Studies, 15*(1), 89–110.

Jaasma, M. A. (1997). Classroom communication apprehension: Does being male or female make a difference? *Communication Reports, 10*(2), 219–228.

Jabes, J. (1980). Causal attributions and sex-role stereotypes in the perceptions of women managers. *Canadian Journal of Behavioural Science, 12*(1), 52–63.

Jack, D. C. (1991). *Silencing the self: Women and depression.* Cambridge, MA: Harvard University Press.

Jack, D. C., & Dill, D. (1992). The Silencing the Self Scale: Schemas of intimacy associated with depression in women. *Psychology of Women Quarterly, 16,* 97–106.

Jacobsen, F. M. (1994). Psychopharmacology. In L. Comas-Díaz & B. Greene (Eds.), *Women of color: Integrating ethnic and gender identities in psychotherapy* (pp. 319–338). New York: Guilford.

Japan Today (2004, July 1). Police superintendent suspended over sexual harassment. [online] **http://www.japantoday.com/e/ ?content=news&cat=2&id=304045**

Japanese court won't allow women to use maiden name. (1993, November 20). *Tampa Tribune,* p. 4.

Jernigan, D. H. (2001). *Global status report: Alcohol and young people.* Geneva: World Health Organization. [online] **http:// whqlibdoc.who.int/hq/2001/WHO_MSD _MSB_01.1.pdf**

Jeter, J. (1997, June 27). Off the dole and fitting into new roles. *Washington Post,* pp. B1, B3.

Johnson, C. (1993). Gender and formal authority. *Social Psychology Quarterly, 56*(3), 193–210.

Johnson, F. L. (1996). Friendships among women: Closeness in dialogue. In J. T. Wood (Ed.), *Gendered relationships* (pp. 79–94). Mountain View, CA: Mayfield.

Jones, D. (2003, December 30). 2003: Year of the woman among the "Fortune" 500? *USA Today.* [online] **http://www.usatoday.com/ money/companies/management/200 3–1 2 –3 0–womenceos_x.htm**

Jones, E. E., & Davis, K. E. (1965). From acts to dispositions: The attribution process in person perception. In L. Berkowitz (Ed.), *Advances in experimental social psychology* (Vol. 2), New York: Academic Press, p. 81.

Jones, L. V. (1984). White–Black achievement differences: The narrowing gap. *American Psychologist, 39,* 1207–1213.

Jordan, M. (1997a, August 2). Japanese court rules for wife in housework suit. *Washington Post,* pp. A1, A14.

Jordan, M. (1997b, November 24). Letter from Japan: In search of an anesthetic experience. *Washington Post,* pp. B1, B5.

Jordan, V., & Surrey, J. L. (1986). The self-in-relation: Empathy and the mother–daughter relationship. In T. Bernay & D. W. Cantor (Eds.), *The psychology of today's women* (pp. 81–104). Cambridge, MA: Harvard University Press.

Juggling work and family (2001). A Public Broadcasting Service program and multimedia project. [online]. **www.pbs.org/ workfamily/aboutProgram_story.html**

Jung, C. G. (1953). Two essays on analytical psychology. In *Collected works* (Vol. 7). New York: Pantheon.

Kahn, A. S. (2004). 2003 Carolyn Sherif Award Address: What college women do and do not experience as rape. *Psychology of Women Quarterly, 28*(1), 9–15.

Kahn, A. S., Jackson, J., Kully, C., Badger, K., & Halvorsen, J. (2003). Calling it rape: Differences in experiences of women who do or do not label their sexual assault as rape. *Psychology of Women Quarterly, 27*(3), 213–242.

Kahn, A. S., & Jean, P. J. (1983). Integration and elimination or separation and redefinition: The future of the psychology of women. *Signs, 8,* 659–671.

Kanter, R. M. (1977). *Men and women of the corporation.* New York: Basic Books.

Kaplan, D. L., & Keys, C. B. (1997). Sex and relationship variables as predictors of sexual attraction in cross-sex platonic friendships between young heterosexual adults. *Journal of Social and Personal Relationships, 14*(2), 191–206.

Kaschak, E. (1992). *Engendered lives: A new psychology of women's experience.* New York: Basic Books.

Kaschak, E. (1995). Three perspectives on racism and anti-Semitism in feminist organizations: 3. In the beginning—again. In J. Adelman & G. Enguídanos (Eds.), *Racism in the lives of women: Testimony, theory, and guides to antiracist practice* (pp. 315–323). New York: Harrington Park Press.

Kaschak, E., & Sharatt, S. (1983/84). A Latin American sex role inventory. *Cross-Cultural Psychology Bulletin, 18,* 3–6.

Katerndahl, D. A., & Realini, J. P. (1993). Lifetime prevalence of panic states. *American Journal of Psychiatry, 150*(2), 246–269.

Kaw, E. (1997). "Opening" faces: The politics of cosmetic surgery and Asian American women. In M. Crawford & R. Unger (Eds.), *In our own words* (pp. 55–73). New York: McGraw-Hill.

Kendler, K. S., Heath, A. C., Neale, M. C., Kessler, R. C., & Eaves, L. J. (1992). A population-based twin study of alcoholism in women. *Journal of the American Medical Association, 268*(4), 1877–1882.

Kent, J. (2004, August 23). Malaysian rape law provokes storm. BBC News. [online] **http:// news.bbc.co.uk/go/pr/fr/-/hi/asia-pacific/ 3592740.stm**

Kessler, R. C., McGonagle, K. A., & Zhao, S. (1994). Lifetime and 12-month prevalence of *DSM-III-R* psychiatric disorders in the United States: Results from the National Comorbidity Survey. *Archives of General Psychiatry, 51,* 8–19.

Kessler, S. J. (1998). *Lessons from the intersexed.* Rutgers, NJ: Rutgers University Press.

Khosroshahi, F. (1989). Penguins don't care, but women do: A social identity analysis of a Whorfian problem. *Language in Society, 18,* 505.

Kiecolt-Glaser, J. K., Dura, J. R., Speicher, C. E., Trask, O. J., & Glaser, R. (1991). Spousal caregivers of dementia victims: Longitudinal changes in immunity and health. *Psychosomatic Medicine, 53,* 345–362.

Kiecolt-Glaser, J. K., Marucha, P. T., Malarkey, W. B., Mercado, A. M., & Glaser, R. (1995). Slowing of wound healing by psychological stress. *Lancet, 346*(4), 1194–1196.

Kiecolt-Glaser, J. K., Newton, T., Cacioppo, J. T., MacCallum, R. C., Glaser, R., & Malarkey, W. B. (1996). Marital conflict and endocrine function: Are men really more physiologically affected than women? *Journal of Consulting and Clinical Psychology, 64*(2), 324–332.

Kierstead, D., D'Agostino, P., & Dill, H. (1988). Sex role stereotyping of college professors: Bias in students' ratings of instructors. *Journal of Educational Psychology, 80*(3), 342–344.

Kilpatrick, L. (1990, March 9). In Ontario, "Equal pay for equal work" becomes a reality, but not very easily. *The Wall Street Journal,* p. B1.

Kim, J. (1981). *The process of Asian-American identity development: A study of Japanese-American women's perceptions of their struggle to achieve positive identities.* Unpublished doctoral dissertation, University of Michigan.

Kimball, M. (1989). A new perspective on women's math achievement. *Psychological Bulletin, 105,* 198–214.

Kimball, M. M. (1995). *Feminist visions of gender similarities and differences.* Binghamton, NY: Haworth.

Kimura, D. (1987). Are men's and women's brains really different? *Canadian Psychology, 28*(2), 133–147.

Kimura, D. (1999). *Sex and cognition.* Cambridge, MA: The MIT Press.

King, A. C., & Kiernan, M. (1997). Physical activity and women's health: Issues and directions. In J. S. Gallant, G. P. Keita, & R. Royak-Schaler (Eds.), *Health care for women: Psychological, social and behavioral influences* (pp. 133–146). Washington DC: American Psychological Association.

Kinsey, A. C., Pomeroy, W. B., & Martin, C. E. (1948). *Sexual behavior in the human male.* Philadelphia: Saunders.

Kinsey, A. C., Pomeroy, W. B., Martin, C. E., & Gebhard, P. H. (1953). *Sexual behavior in the human female.* Philadelphia: Saunders.

Kiraly, Z. (2000). The relationship between emotional self-disclosure of male and female adolescents' friendship. *Dissertation Abstracts International, 60*(7-B), 3619.

Kirk, G., & Okazawa-Rey, M. (1998). *Women's lives: Multicultural perspectives.* Mountain View, CA: Mayfield.

Kisekka, M. N. (1990). Gender and mental health in Africa. In E. D. Cole (Ed.), *Women's mental health in Africa* (pp. 1–13). New York: Haworth Press.

Kite, M. E., Deaux, K., & Miele, M. (1991). Stereotypes of young and old: Does age outweigh gender? *Psychology and Aging, 6,* 19–27.

Kitzinger, C. (1987). *The social construction of lesbianism.* Beverly Hills, CA: Sage.

Kitzinger, C., & Wilkinson, S. (1995). Transition from heterosexuality to lesbianism: The discursive product of lesbian identities. *Developmental Psychology, 31*(1), 95–104.

Klonoff, E. A., & Landrine, H. (1995). The Schedule of Sexist Events: A measure of lifetime and recent sexist discrimination in women's lives. *Psychology of Women Quarterly, 19*(4), 439–472.

Klonoff, E. A., Landrine, H., & Scott, J. (1995). Double jeopardy: Ethnicity and gender in health research. In H. Landrine (Ed.), *Bringing cultural diversity to feminist psychology* (pp. 335–360). Washington, DC: American Psychological Association.

Koblitz, A. H. (1988). Science, women, and the Russian intelligentsia: The generation of the 1860s. *Isis, 79,* 208–226.

Kobrin, J. L., Camara, W. J., & Milewski, G. B. (2002). *The utility of the SAT I and SAT II for admissions decisions in California and the Nation.* Research Report No. 200 2–6. New York, NY: College Entrance Examination Board.

Kohlberg, L. (1966). A cognitive-developmental analysis of children's sex-role concepts and attitudes. In E. E. Maccoby (Ed.), *The development of sex differences* (pp. 82–173). Stanford, CA: Stanford University Press.

Kohlberg, L., & Ullian, D. Z. (1974). Stages in the development of psychosexual concepts and attitudes. In R. C. Friedman, R. M. Richart, & R. L. Vande Wiele (Eds.), *Sex differences in behavior* (pp. 209–222). New York: Wiley.

Kojo-Austin, H., Malin, M., & Hemminki, E. (1993). Women's satisfaction with maternity health care services in Finland. *Social Science and Medicine, 37*(5), 633–638.

Koppel, T. (1993, April 16). No girls need apply. *Science, 260,* p. 422.

Korea Update (2004, April 20). Women have greater say in Parliament. [online] **http://www.koreaemb.org/archive/2004/4_2/foreign/foreign3.asp**

Koss, M. P. (1993). Detecting the scope of rape: A review of prevalence research methods. *Journal of Interpersonal Violence, 8,* 98–122.

Koss, M. P., Bailey, J. A., Yuan, N. P., Herrera, V. M., & Lichter, E. L. (2003). Depression and PTSD in survivors of male violence: Research and training initiatives to facilitate recovery. *Psychology of Women Quarterly, 27,* 130–142.

Koss, M. P., Heise, L., & Russo, N. F. (1994). The global health burden of rape. *Psychology of Women Quarterly, 18*(4), 509–537.

Kova, D., & Majerova, M. (1974). Figure reproduction from the aspect of development and interfunctional relationships. *Studia Psychologica, 16,* 149–152.

Kravitz, D. A., Klineberg, S. L., Avery, D. R., Nguyen, A. K., Lund, C., & Fu, E. J. (2000). Attitudes toward affirmative action: correlations with demographic variables and with beliefs about targets, actions, and economic effects. *Journal of Applied Social Psychology, 30*(6), 1109–1136.

Krishnan, V. (1987). Preferences for sex of children: A multivariate analysis. *Journal of Biosocial Science, 9,* 367–376.

Kristof, N. D. (1995, February 1). Japan invests in a growth stock: Good day care. *New York Times,* p. A4.

Kristof, N. D. (1996, December 5). Do Korean men still beat their wives? Definitely. *New York Times,* p. A4.

Kuebli, J., & Fivush, R. (1992). Gender differences in parent–child conversations about past emotions. *Sex Roles, 27,* 683–698.

Kurdek, L. A. (1989). Relationship quality of gay and lesbian cohabiting couples: A 1-year follow-up study. *Journal of Social and Personal Relationships, 6,* 39–59.

Kurdek, L. A., & Schmitt, J. P. (1986). Relationship quality of partners in heterosexual married, heterosexual cohabiting, and gay and lesbian relationships. *Journal of Personality and Social Psychology, 51*(4), 711–720.

Kutova, N. (2000, October). *The Ukranian experience of gender studies development.* Paper presented at the conference on The Future of Women's Studies: Foundations, Interrogrations, Politics, Tucson, AZ.

LAF case news: Colleen Crangle case settled! (2001, May). [online] **www.northnet.org/nysaaus/laf.htm**

LaFrance, M. (1992). Gender and interruptions: Individual infraction or violation of the social order. *Psychology of Women Quarterly, 16,* 497–512.

LaFrance, M. (2001). Gender and social interaction. In R. K. Unger (Ed.), *Handbook of the psychology of women and gender* (pp. 245–255). New York: John Wiley & Sons.

LaFrance, M., Brownell, H., & Hahn, E. (1997). Interpersonal verbs, gender, and implicit causality. *Social Psychology Quarterly, 60*(2), 138–152.

LaFrance, M., & Hecht, M. (1999). Smiling and gender: A meta-analysis. In A. Fischer (Ed.), *Gender and emotion* (pp. 118–142). New York: Cambridge University Press.

LaFromboise, T. D., Berman, J. S., & Sohi, B. K. (1994). American Indian women. In L. Comas-Díaz & B. Greene (Eds.), *Women of color: Integrating ethnic and gender identities in psychotherapy* (pp. 30–71). New York: Guilford.

LaFromboise, T. D., Choney, S. B., James, A., & Running Wolf, P. R. (1995). American Indian women and psychology. In H. Landrine (Ed.), *Bringing cultural diversity to feminist psychology* (pp. 197–239). Washington, DC: American Psychological Association.

Lahita, R. G. (1996). The connective tissue diseases and the overall influence of gender. *International Journal of Fertility and Menopausal Studies, 41*(2), 156–165.

Lakoff, R. (1975). *Language and woman's place.* New York: Harper & Row.

Lakoff, R. (1990). *Talking power: The politics of language in our lives.* New York: Basic Books.

Lamb, M. (1987). The emergent American father. In M. Lamb (Ed.), *The father's role: Cross-cultural perspectives* (pp. 3–25). Hillsdale, NJ: Erlbaum.

Lancaster, J. (1996, November 24). Egyptians stand by female circumcision. *Washington Post,* pp. A33, A37.

Landrine, H. (1987). On the politics of madness: A preliminary analysis of the relationship between social roles and psychopathology. *Psychology Monographs, 113,* 341–406.

Landrine, H., Klonoff, E. A., & Brown-Collins, A. (1995). Cultural diverstiy and methodology in feminist psychology: Critique, proposal, empirical example. In H. Landrine (Ed). *Bringing cultural diversity to feminist psychology: Theory, research and practice.* (pp. 55–75). Washington, DC: American Psychological Association.

Landrine, H., Klonoff, E. A., Gibbs, J., Manning, V., & Lund, M. (1995). Physical and psychiatric correlates of gender discrimination: An application of the Schedule of Sexist Events. *Psychology of Women Quarterly, 19*(4), 473–492.

Laqueur, T. (1990). *Making sex: Body and gender from the Greeks to Freud.* Cambridge, MA: Harvard University Press.

Lazarus, R. S. (1991). Cognition and motivation in emotion. *American Psychologist, 46,* 352–367.

Leak, G. K., Masciotra, T., Panza, S., & Unruh, K. (1992, August). *Personality, attitudinal, and familial correlates of rape myth acceptance.* Paper presented at the annual meeting of the American Psychological Association, Washington, DC.

Leaper, C., Carson, M., Baker, C., Holliday, H., & Myers, S. (1995). Self-disclosure and listener verbal support in same-gender and cross-gender friends' conversations. *Sex Roles, 33*(5–6), 387–404.

Le Guin, U. (1989). *Dancing at the edge of the world.* New York: Harper & Row.

Lemmer, J. T., Ivey, F. M., Ryan, A. S., Martel, G. F., Hurlburt, D. E., Metter, J. E., Fozard, J. L., Fleg, J. L., & Hurley, B. F. (2001). Effect of strength training on resting metabolic rate and physical activity: Age and gender comparisons. *Medicine & Science in Sports & Exercise, 33*(4), 532–541.

Lenney, E. (1977). Women's self-confidence in achievement settings. *Psychological Bulletin, 84,* 1–13.

Lerner, R. M., Orlos, J. B., & Knapp, J. R. (1976). Physical attractiveness, physical effectiveness and self-concept in late adolescents. *Journal of Youth and Adolescence, 11,* 313–326.

Leto, D. N. (1998). Excerpts from a letter. In N. A. Ciatu, D. Dileo, & G. Micallef (Eds.),

Curaggia: Writing by women of Italian descent (pp. 211–215). Toronto: Women's Press.

Levine, S. (1966). Sex differences in the brain. *Scientific American, 214* (4), 84–90.

Lewin, M. (1984). "Rather worse than folly"? Psychology measures femininity and masculinity, 1: From Terman and Miles to the Guilfords. In M. Lewin (Ed.), *In the shadow of the past: Psychology portrays the sexes* (pp. 155–178). New York: Columbia University Press.

Lewis, R. (1994, February). Tests find age bias in hiring. *AARP Bulletin,* p. 1.

Liddle, J., & Joshi, R. (1986). *Daughters of independence: Gender, caste and class in India.* London: Zed Books.

Lightfoot-Klein, H. (1989). The sexual experience and marital adjustment of genitally circumcised and infibulated females in the Sudan. *Journal of Sex Research, 26,* 375–392.

Linn, M. C., & Petersen, A. C. (1985). Emergence and characterization of gender differences in spatial ability: A meta-analysis. *Child Development, 56,* 1479–1498.

Linz, D., Donnerstein, E., & Penrod, S. (1984). The effects of multiple exposure to filmed violence against women. *Journal of Communications, 34*(3), 130–147.

Lips, H. M. (1982). Somatic and emotional aspects of the normal pregnancy experience: The first five months. *American Journal of Obstetrics and Gynecology, 142*(5), 524–529.

Lips, H. M. (1985). A longitudinal study of the reporting of emotional and somatic symptoms during and after pregnancy. *Social Science and Medicine, 21*(6), 631–640.

Lips, H. M. (1986). *Self-schema theory and gender-related behaviors: Research on some correlates of university women's participation in mathematics, science and athletic activities.* ERIC Document ED 263517, ERIC Clearinghouse on Counseling and Personnel Services.

Lips, H. M. (1989). *The role of gender, self- and task perceptions in mathematics and science participation among college students.* ERIC Document ED 297 945, ERIC Clearinghouse for Science, Mathematics and Environmental Education.

Lips, H. M. (1992). Gender and science-related attitudes as predictors of college students' academic choices. *Journal of Vocational Behavior, 40,* 62–81.

Lips, H. M. (1993, March). *Women, power, and sisterhood.* Invited address to the Association for Women in Psychology, Atlanta.

Lips, H. M. (1994). Female powerlessness: A case of "cultural preparedness"? In L. Ratdke

& H. Stam (Eds.), *Power/gender: Social relations in theory and practice* (pp. 89–107). London: Sage.

Lips, H. M. (2000). College students' visions of power and possibility as mediated by gender. *Psychology of Women Quarterly, 24*(1), 37–41.

Lips, H. M. (2001). Envisioning positions of leadership: The expectations of university students in Virginia and Puerto Rico. *Journal of Social Issues, 57*(4), 799–813.

Lips, H. M. (2004). The gender gap in possible selves: Divergence of academic self-views among high school and university students. *Sex Roles, 50*(5/6), 357–372.

Lips, H. M., & Asquith, K. (1995). University students' possible selves as scientists. *GATES: An International Journal Promoting Greater Access to Technology, Engineering and Science, 2*(1), 1–7.

Lips, H. M., de Verthelyi, R. F., & Gonzalez, M. (1996, August). *Gender and students' possible powerful selves: A cross-cultural study.* Paper presented at the International Congress of Psychology, Montreal, Canada.

Liss, M., O'Connor, C., Morosky, E., & Crawford, M. (2001). What makes a feminist? Predictors and correlates of feminist social identity in college women. *Psychology of Women Quarterly, 25,* 124–133.

Littleton, H. L., & Axsom, D. (2003). Rape and seduction scripts of university students: Implications for rape attributions and unacknowledged rape. *Sex Roles, 49*(9/10), 465–476.

Liu, J. (2004, August 4). Wife beating grows in China as economy roars ahead. *San Diego Union-Tribune.* [online] **http://crossword .uniontrib.com/news/features/2004080 4 –050 0–china-women.html**

Lo, W. A., & Sporakowski, M. J. (1989). The continuation of violent dating relationships among college students. *Journal of College Student Development, 30,* 432–439.

Lobodzinska, B. (1996). Women's employment or return to "family values" in Central-Eastern Europe. *Journal of Comparative Family Studies, 27*(3), 519–544.

Lock, M. (1993). *Encounters with aging: Mythologies of menopause in Japan and North America.* Berkeley: University of California Press.

Lockhart, L. L., White, B. W., Causby, V., & Isaac, A. (1994). Letting out the secret: Violence in lesbian relationships. *Journal of Interpersonal Violence, 9*(4), 469–492.

Lockheed, M. E. (1985). Sex and social influence: A meta-analysis guided by theory. In

J. Berger & M. Zelditch Jr. (Eds.), *Status, rewards, and influence: How expectations organize behavior* (pp. 406–429). San Francisco: Jossey-Bass.

Lockheed, M. E., & Hall, K. P. (1976). Conceptualizing sex as a status characteristic: Applications to leadership training strategies. *Journal of Social Issues, 32,* 11–24.

Longino, H. E. (1989). Can there be a feminist science? In N. Tuana (Ed.), *Feminism and science* (pp. 45–57). Bloomington: Indiana University Press.

Lopata, H. (1973). Self-identity in marriage and widowhood. *Sociological Quarterly, 14*(3), 407–418.

Loring-Meier, S., & Halpern, D. F. (1999). Sex differences in visual-spatial working memory: Components of cognitive processing. *Psychonomic Bulletin and Review, 6,* 464–471.

Lott, B. (1985). The devaluation of women's competence. *Journal of Social Issues, 41*(4), 43–60.

Lott, B. (1990). Dual natures or learned behavior: The challenge to feminist psychology. In R. T. Hare-Mustin & J. Maracek (Eds.), *Making a difference: Psychology and the construction of gender* (pp. 65–101). New Haven, CT: Yale University Press.

Lott, B., & Bullock, H. E. (2001). Who are the poor? *Journal of Social Issues, 57*(2), 189–206.

Louie, S. C. (2000). Interpersonal relationships: Independence versus interdependence. In J. L. Chin (Ed.). *Relationships among Asian American women* (pp. 211–222). Washington, DC: American Psychological Association.

Love, Susan M. (2000) (with K. Lindsey). *Dr. Susan Love's breast book.* Cambridge, MA: Perseus Publishing.

Lu, Z. Z., Maume, D. J., & Bellas, M. L. (2000). Chinese husbands' participation in household labor. *Journal of Comparative Family Studies, 31*(2), 191–215.

Luker, K. (1984). *Abortion and the politics of motherhood.* Berkeley: University of California Press.

Lummis, M., & Stevenson, H. W. (1990). Gender differences in beliefs and achievement: A cross-cultural study. *Developmental Psychology, 26*(2), 254–263.

Luna, M. (2004, August 24). Marital rape. *Sun Star Network.* [online] **http://www.sunstar .com.ph/static/zam/2004/08/24/oped/atty .manuelito.luna.constitutional.matters.html**

Lunneborg, P. (1992). *Abortion: A positive choice.* New York: Bergin and Garvey.

Lykes, M. B. (1994). Speaking against the silence: One Maya woman's exile and return. In C. E. Franz & A. J. Stewart (Eds.), *Women creating lives: Identities, resilience, and resistance* (pp. 97–114). Boulder, CO: Westview Press.

Lyles, L. F. (1994). Going through my changes. In P. Bell-Scott (Ed.), *Life notes: Personal writings by contemporary Black women* (pp. 341–344). New York: Norton.

Lyness, K., & Thompson, D. (1997). Above the glass ceiling? A comparison of matched samples of female and male executives. *Journal of Applied Psychology, 82*(3), 359–375.

Lytton, H., & Romney, D. M. (1991). Parents' differential socialization of boys and girls: A meta-analysis. *Psychological Bulletin, 109,* 267–296.

Lyubomirsky, S., Casper, R. C., & Sousa, L. (2001). What triggers abnormal eating in bulimic and nonbulimic women? The role of dissociative experiences, negative affect, and psychopathology. *Psychology of Women Quarterly, 25*(3), 223–232.

Maccoby, E. E. (1990). Gender and relationships: A developmental account. *American Psychologist, 45,* 513–520.

Maccoby, E. E. (1998). *The two sexes: Growing up apart, coming together.* Cambridge, MA: Harvard University Press.

Maccoby, E. E., & Jacklin, C. N. (1974). *The psychology of sex differences.* Stanford, CA: Stanford University Press.

MacGeorge, E. L., Graves, A. R., Gillihan, S. J., & Burleson, B. R. (2004). The myth of gender cultures: Similarities outweigh differences in men's and women's provision of and responses to supportive communication. *Sex Roles, 50*(3/4), 143–176.

Maclean, I. (1980). *The Renaissance notion of woman.* Cambridge: Cambridge University Press.

Macleod, C. (1995). Gender differences in mathematics: A discourse analysis. *South African Journal of Psychology, 25*(3), 191–202.

MacLeod, L. (1980). *Wife battering in Canada: The vicious circle.* Hull, Quebec: Canadian Government Publishing Centre.

Macy, C. (1986). Psychological factors in nausea and vomiting in pregnancy: A review. *Journal of Reproductive and Infant Psychology, 4* (1/2), 23–55.

Maffetone, P. (2000). Are women naturally superior as endurance athletes? Racing the Planet. [online] **http://www.racingtheplanet.com/ medicaltent/women_superior.asp**

Mageo, J. M. (1992). Male transvestism and cultural change in Samoa. *American Ethnologist, 2*(3), 443–459.

Maines, R. P. (1999). *The technology of orgasm: "Hysteria," the vibrator, and women's sexual satisfaction.* Baltimore, MD: The Johns Hopkins University Press.

Major, B. (1987). Women and entitlement. *Women and Therapy, 6*(3), 3–19.

Major, B. (1994). From social inequality to personal entitlement: The role of social comparisons, legitimacy appraisals, and group membership. In M. P. Zanna (Ed.), *Advances in experimental social psychology* (Vol. 6, pp. 293–335). San Diego: Academic Press.

Major, B., & Gramzow, R. H. (1999). Abortion as stigma: Cogntive and emotional implications of concealment. *Journal of Personality and Social Psychology, 77*(4), 735–745.

Major, B., McFarlin, D. B., & Gagnon, D. (1984). Overworked and underpaid: On the nature of gender differences in entitlement. *Journal of Personality and Social Psychology, 47*(6), 1399–1412.

Major, B., Spencer, S., Schmader, T., Wolfe, C., & Crocker, J. (1998). Coping with negative stereotypes about intellectual performance: The role of psychological disengagement. *Personality and Social Psychology Bulletin, 24*(1), 34–50.

Malamuth, N. M. (1984). Aggression against women: Cultural and individual causes. In N. Malamuth & E. Donnerstein (Eds.), *Pornography and sexual aggression* (pp. 19–52). New York: Academic Press.

Malamuth, N. M., & Check, J. V. P. (1981). The effects of mass media exposure on acceptance of violence against women: A field experiment. *Journal of Research in Personality, 15,* 436–446.

Malhotra, A., & Mather, M. (1997). Do schooling and work empower women in developing countries? Gender and domestic decisions in Sri Lanka. *Sociological Forum, 12*(4), 599–630.

Mallow, J. V. (1993). The science learning climate: Danish female and male students' descriptions. In *Contributions to the Seventh International Gender and Science and Technology Conference* (Vol. 1, pp. 78–87). Waterloo, Ontario: University of Waterloo.

Maloiy, G. M. O., Heglund, N. C., Prager, L. M., Cavagna, G. A., & Taylor, C. R. (1986, February). Energetic costs of carrying loads: Have African women discovered an economic way? *Nature, 319*(6055), 668–669.

Mann, J. (1992, June 23). A transformation among schoolgirls. *Washington Post,* p. C20.

Mann, J. (1993, June 23). What's harassment? Ask a girl. *Washington Post,* p. D26.

Mann, V. A., Sasanuma, S., Sakuma, N., & Masaki, S. (1990). Sex differences in cognitive abilities: A cross-cultural perspective. *Neuropsychologia, 28*(10), 1063–1077.

Manson, J. M., Sammel, M. D., Freeman, E. W., & Grisso, J. A. (2001, February). Racial differences in sex hormone levels in women approaching the transition to menopause. *Fertility and Sterility, 75,* 297–304.

Maracek, J. (2001). Disorderly contructs: Feminist frameworks for clinical psychology. In R. K. Unger (Ed.), *Handbook of the psychology of women and gender* (pp. 303–316). New York: John Wiley & Sons.

Marcus-Newhall, A., Thompson. S., & Thomas, C. (2001). Examining a gender stereotype: Menopausal women. *Journal of Applied Social Psychology, 31*(4), 698–719.

"Margaret Chase Smith." (1995, June 1). Editorial, *Arizona Daily Star,* p. 10A.

Markiewicz, D., Devine, I., & Kausilas, D. (2000). Friendships among women and men at work: Job satisfaction and resource implications. *Journal of Managerial Psychology, 15*(1–2), 161–184.

Marks, S. R. (1977). Multiple roles and role strain: Some notes on human energy, time and commitment. *American Sociological Review, 42,* 921–936.

Markson, E. W., & Taylor, C. A. (1993). Real versus reel world: Older women and the Academy Awards. *Women & Therapy, 14* (1–2), 157–172.

Markus, H., Crane, M., Bernstein, S., & Siladi, M. (1982). Self-schemas and gender. *Journal of Personality and Social Psychology, 42,* 38–50.

Markus, H., & Kitayama, S. (1991). Culture and the self: Implications for cognition, emotion, and motivation. *Psychological Review, 98*(2), 224–253.

Markus, H., & Nurius, P. (1986). Possible selves. *American Psychologist, 14*(9), 954–969.

Markus, H., & Oyserman, D. (1988). Gender and thought: The role of the self-concept. In M. Crawford & M. Hamilton (Eds.), *Gender and thought* (pp. 100–127). New York: Springer-Verlag.

Marrow, J. (1997). *Changing positions: Women speak out on sex and desire.* Avon, MA Adams Media.

Martin, D. J., & Hoover, H. D. (1987). Sex differences in educational achievement: A longitudinal study. Special issue: Sex differences in early adolescents. *Journal of Early Adolescence, 7,* 65–83.

Martin, E. (1987). *The woman in the body: A cultural analysis of reproduction.* Boston: Beacon Press.

Martin, R. (1997). "Girls don't talk about garages!": Perceptions of conversation in same- and cross-sex friendships. *Personal Relationships, 4*(2), 115–130.

Martire, L. M., & Stephens, M. A. P. (2003). Juggling parent care and employment responsibilities: The dilemmas of adult daughter caregivers in the workforce. *Sex Roles, 48*(3/4), 167–173.

Martucci, J. (1998). Meta-analysis: Psychosocial predictors of psychological sequelae of induced abortion. *Dissertation Abstracts International, 59*(4-B), 1860.

Mason, A., & Blankenship, V. (1987). Power and affiliation motivation, stress, and abuse in intimate relationships. *Journal of Personality and Social Psychology, 52*(1), 203–210.

Mason, J. (1991). Hertha Ayrton (1854–1923) and the admission of women to the Royal Society of London. *Notes and Records of the Royal Society of London, 45*(2), 201–220.

Masters, W. H., & Johnson, V. (1966). *Human sexual response.* Boston: Little, Brown.

Mathes, E. W., Brennan, S. M., Haugen, P. M., & Rice, H. B. (1985). Ratings of physical attractiveness as a function of age. *Journal of Social Psychology, 125*(2), 157–168.

Matheson, K. J., Warren, K. L., Foster, M. D., & Painter, C. (2000). Reactions to affirmative action: Seeking the bases for resistance. *Journal of Applied Social Psychology, 30*(5), 1013–1038.

Matthews, K. A., Shumaker, S. A., Bowen, D. J., Langer, R. D., Hunt, J. R., Kaplan, R. M., Klesges, R. C., & Ritenbaugh, C. (1997). Women's Health Initiative: Why now? What is it? What's new? *American Psychologist, 52*(2), 101–116.

Mau, W-C., & Lynn, R. (2000). Gender differences in homework and test scores in mathematics, reading and science at tenth and twelfth grade. *Psychology, Evolution, & Gender, 2*(2), 119–125.

Maxwell, M. (1990). Portraits of menopausal women in selected works of English and American literature. In R. Formanek (Ed.), *The meanings of menopause: Historical, medical and clinical perspectives* (pp. 225–279). Hillsdale, NJ: Analytic Press.

May, E. T. (1995). *Barren in the promised land: Childless Americans and the pursuit of happiness.* New York: Basic Books.

Mayo Clinic (2001, October 9). Headline watch: New evidence of ERT risks. [online] **www.mayoclinic.com/home?id=NE00254**

Mazella, C., Durkin, K., Cerini, E., & Buralli, P. (1992). Sex role stereotyping in Australian television advertisements. *Sex Roles, 26,* 243–259.

McCallion, P., & Kolomer, S. R. (2000). Depressive symptoms among African American caregiving grandmothers: the factor structure of the CES-D. *Journal of Mental Health and Aging, 6*(4), 325–338.

McCardle, P., & Wilson, B. E. (1990). Hormonal influence on language development in physically advanced children. *Brain and Language, 38,* 410–423.

McCaughey, M. (1997). *Real knockouts: The physical feminism of women's self-defense.* New York: New York University Press.

McClelland, D. C. (1961). *The achieving society.* Princeton, NJ: Van Nostrand.

McClintock, M. K. (1971). Menstrual synchrony and suppression. *Nature, 229,* 244–245.

McCormick, N. B. (1994). *Sexual salvation: Affirming women's sexual rights and pleasures.* Westport, CT: Praeger.

McDonnell, C. S. (1994). Oreo blues. In P. Bell-Scott (Ed.), *Life notes: Personal writings by contemporary Black women* (pp. 126–141). New York: Norton.

McFarlane, J., & Williams, T. M. (1990). The enigma of premenstrual syndrome. *Canadian Psychology, 31,* 95–108.

McFarlane, J., & Williams, T. M. (1994). Placing premenstrual syndrome in perspective. *Psychology of Women Quarterly, 18,* 339–373.

McGrath, E., Keita, G. P., Strickland, B., & Russo, N. F. (1990). *Women and depression: Risk factors and treatment issues.* Washington, DC: American Psychological Association.

McGrayne, S. B. (1993). *Nobel Prize women in science.* New York: Birch Lane Press.

McHugh, M. C., Koeske, R. D., & Frieze, I. H. (1986). Issues to consider in conducting non-sexist psychological research: A guide for researchers. *American Psychologist, 41,* 879–890.

McNair, L. D., & Neville, H. A. (1996). African American women survivors of sexual assault:

The intersection of race and class. *Women and Therapy, 18*(3–4), 107–118.

McNelles, L. R., & Connolly, J. A. (1999). Intimacy between adolescent friends: Age and gender differences in intimate affect and intimate behaviors. *Journal of Research on Adolescence, 9*(2), 143–159.

Mcwherter, P. L. (1999). Contributions of African-American mothers to their daughters' empowerment. *Dissertation Abstracts International, 59*(11-B), 6073.

Media Report to Women (2001). Industry statistics. [online] **www.mediareporttowomen .com/statistics.htm**

Media Report to Women (2003). Employment levels of women, minorities, in broadcasting mixed, RTNDA study shows. *Media Report to Women, 31*(3), 1, 3.

Mediawatch (1995). Global media monitoring project. [online] **www.mediawatch.ca**

Meece, J. L., Eccles-Parson, J., Kaczala, C. M., Goff, S. B., & Futterman, R. (1982). Sex differences in math achievement: Toward a model of academic choice. *Psychological Bulletin, 91,* 324–348.

Meyer, V. (2000, September/October). Hormones and heart disease: Medical bias disregards best evidence. *The Network News,* National Women's Health Network, pp. 1, 4.

Messman, S. J., Canary, D. J., & Hause, K. S. (2000). Motives to remain platonic, equity and the use of maintenance strategies in opposite-sex friendships. *Journal of Social and Personal Relationships, 17*(1), 67–94.

Michael, R. T., Gagnon, J. H., Laumann, E. O., & Kolata, G. (1994). *Sex in America.* Boston: Little, Brown.

Mikalachki, D., & Mikalachki, A. (1984). MBA women: The new pioneers. *Business Quarterly, 49*(1), 110–115.

Miles, L. (1997). Women, AIDS, and power in heterosexual sex: A discourse analysis. In M. Gergen, & S. N. Davis, (Eds.), *Toward a new psychology of gender* (pp. 479–501). Florence, KY: Taylor & Francis/Routledge.

Miller, B. (2001, October 5). Sex slave suit against Japan is dismissed. *Washington Post,* p. A3.

Miller, C. L. (1987). Qualitative differences among gender-stereotyped toys: Implications for cognitive and social development in girls and boys. *Sex Roles, 16*(9/10), 473–487.

Miller, E. J., Smith, J. E., & Trembath, D. L. (2000). The "skinny" on body size requests in personal ads. *Sex Roles, 43*(1–2), 129–141.

Miller, J. B. (1986). *Toward a new psychology of women* (2nd ed.). Boston: Beacon Press.

Min, P. G. (1997). Korean immigrant wives' labor force participation, marital power, and status. In E. Higginbotham, & M. Romero, (Eds.), *Women and work: Exploring race, ethnicity, and class. Women and work: A research and policy series,* Vol. 6 (pp. 176–191). Thousand Oaks, CA: Sage Publications.

Mischel, W. (1970). Sex-typing and socialization. In P. H. Mussen (Ed.), *Carmichael's manual of child psychology* (Vol. 2, p. 3–72). New York: Wiley.

Moffat, S. D., & Hampson, E. (1996). A curvilinear relationship between testosterone and spatial cognition in humans: Possible influence of hand preference. *Psychoneuroendocrinology, 21,* 323–337.

Money, J., & Ehrhardt, A. A. (1972). *Man and woman, boy and girl.* Baltimore: Johns Hopkins University Press.

Money, J., & Mathews, D. (1982). Prenatal exposure to virilizing progestins: An adult follow-up study on 12 young women. *Archives of Sexual Behavior, 11,* 73–83.

Montagu, A. (1968). *The natural superiority of women.* New York: Collier Books.

Moore, M. (2001a, June 8). Iran's women say yes to Khatami. *The Washington Post,* p. A22.

Moore, M. (2001b, August 8). In Turkey, 'honor killing' follows families to cities. *Washington Post,* pp. A1, A14.

Moore, E. P. (1993). Gender, power, and legal pluralism: Rajasthan, India. *American Ethnologist, 20*(3), 522–542.

Moore, M. (1996, August 21). Rights of pregnant workers at issue on Mexican border. *Washington Post,* p. A20.

Morahan-Martin, J. (1998). The gender gap in Internet use: Why men use the Internet more than women—A literature review. *Cyberpsychology & Behavior, 1*(1), 3–10.

Morgan, M. (1982). Television and adolescents' sex role stereotypes: A longitudinal study. *Journal of Personality and Social Psychology, 43,* 947–955.

Morgan, M. (1983). Symbolic victimization and real world fear. *Human Communication Research, 9,* 146–157.

Morofushi, M., Shinohara, K., Funabashi, T., & Kimura, F. (2000). Positive relationship between menstrual synchrony and the ability to smell 5alpha-androst-16-en-3alpha-ol. *Chemical Senses, 25*(4), 407–411.

Morris, M. (Ed.). (1993). *Maiden voyages: Writings of women travellers.* New York: Vintage Books.

Morrison, T. (1970). *The bluest eye.* New York: Holt, Rinehart & Winston.

Morrow, S. L. (2000). Feminist reconstructions of psychology. In M. Biaggio & M. Hersen (Eds.), *Issues in the psychology of women* (pp. 15–32). New York: Kluwer Academic/Plenum.

Moscucci, O. (1991). Hermaphroditism and sex difference: The construction of gender in Victorian England. In M. Benjamin (Ed.), *Science and sensibility: Gender and scientific enquiry 1780–1945.* Oxford, UK: Basil Blackwell.

Moser, D., & Dracup, P. K. (1993). Gender differences in treatment-seeking delay in acute myocardial infarction. *Progress in Cardiovascular Nursing, 8*(1), 6–12.

MS Foundation (1997). [online] **www.msfacts.org**

Muehlenhard, C. L., & McCoy, M. L. (1991). Double standard/double bind: The sexual double standard and women's communication about sex. *Psychology of Women Quarterly, 15,* 447–461.

Mueller, K. A., & Yoder, J. D. (1999). Stigmatization of non-normative family size status. *Sex Roles, 4*(11–12), 901–919.

Mundy, L. (1998, January 25). Did you hear the one about Janet Reno? Jokes, gender, politics and the attorney general. *Washington Post Magazine,* pp. 6–11, 21–25.

Muños, V. (1995). *"Where something catches": Work; love, and identity in youth.* Albany: State University of New York Press.

Munsterberg, H. (1901). *American traits: From the point of view of a German.* Cambridge, MA: Riverside Press.

Murgai, A. (1993). A marriage proposal. In Women of South Asian Descent Collective (Eds.), *Our feet walk the sky: Women of the South Asian Diaspora* (pp. 330–338). San Francisco: Aunt Lute Books.

Murnen, S. K., Smolak, L., Mills, J. A., & Good, L. (2003). Thin, sexy women and strong, muscular men: Grade-school children's responses to objectified images of women and men. *Sex Roles, 49*(9/10), 427–438.

Murphy, C. (1993, February 17). Lowering the veil: Muslim women struggle for careers in a society ruled by men and religion. *Washington Post,* pp. A1, A24–25.

Murphy, C. (2001, July 14). Nuns stand up to Vatican on obedience issue. *Washington Post,* p. B9.

Murphy, D. E. (1998, August 16). In Africa, child rapes speeding AIDS' sweep. *San Francisco Examiner,* p. A–26.

Murphy, S. L. (2000, July 24). Deaths: Final data for 1998. *National Vital Statistics Reports, 48*(11), whole issue.

Mutsuko, Y. (2001). Compulsory selection of a family name for a married couple. *Japanese Women Now* [online] **http://wom-jp.org/e/JWOMEN/name.html**

Mwangi, M. W. (1996). Gender roles portrayed in Kenyan television commercials. *Sex Roles, 34*(3/4), 205–214.

Nadelhaft, J. (1982, October). The Englishwoman's sexual civil war: Feminist attitudes towards men, women, and marriage 1650–1740. *Journal of the History of Ideas,* 555–579.

Nagia, S. A., & Bennett, S. J. (1992). Postmenopausal women: Factors in osteoporosis preventive behaviors. *Journal of Gerontological Nursing, 18*(2), 23–32.

Nanda, S. (1990). *Neither man nor woman: The Hijras of India.* Belmont, CA: Wadsworth.

Naoko, I. (1987). The traffic in Japayuki-san. *Japan Quarterly, 34,* 84–88.

Narasimhan, S. (1990). *Sati: Widow burning in India.* New York: Anchor.

Narasimhan, S. (1994). India: From Sati to sex-determination tests. In M. Davies (Ed.), *Women and violence: Realities and responses worldwide* (pp. 43–52). London: Zed Books.

Nash, H. C., & Chrisler, J. C. (1997). Is a little (psychiatric) knowledge a dangerous thing? The impact of premenstrual dysphoric disorder on perceptions of premenstrual women. *Psychology of Women Quarterly, 21,* 315–322.

Nasrin, T. (1993, December 5). Death sentence in Bangladesh. *St. Petersburg Times,* p. 3D.

Nasser, M. (1986). Comparative study of the prevalence of abnormal eating attitudes among Arab female students of both London and Cairo universities. *Psychological Medicine, 16,* 621–625.

National Association of Female Executives (2004). Fact sheet: Top 30 companies for executive women. [online] **http://nafe.com/pr_top30_04Fact.shtml**

National Center for Chronic Disease Prevention and Health Promotion (2001). Intimate partner violence during pregnancy. [online] **www.cdc.gov/nccdphp/drh/violence**

National Center for Chronic Disease Prevention and Health Promotion (2001b). Pattern of tobacco use among women and girls—fact sheet (from the Surgeon General's Report 2001). [online] **www.cdc.gov**

National Center for Health Statistics. (1996, June 24). Teenage births drop for third straight year. News release, NCHS Press Office. [online] **www.cdc.gov/nchswww/releases/96news**

National Center for Health Statistics (2000). *Health, United States, 2000.* Hyattville, MD: Author.

National Center for Health Statistics (2001, May 24). 43 percent of first marriages break up within 15 years. News release [online] **www.cdc.gov/nchs/releases/01news/firstmarr.htm**

National Center for Health Statistics (2001b). *Health, United States, 2001.* Hyattville, MD: Author. (released Sept. 25, 2001).

National Center for Health Statistics (2001c, September 25). New CDC report on U.S. mortality patterns. News release [online] **www.cdc.gov/nchs/releases/01facts/99mortality.htm**

National Center for Health Statistics (2003). *Health, United States, 2003.* [online] **http://www.cdc.gov/nchs/hus.htm**

National Center for Health Statistics (2003b). Data table on percent of adults aged 18 and over who engaged in regular leisure-time physical activity. [online] **http://www.cdc.gov/nchs/about/major/nhis/released200212/figures07_ 1–7_3.htm**

National Center for Health Statistics (2004, June 2). Deaths: Injuries, 2001. *National Vital Statistics Report, 52*(21). [online] **http://www.cdc.gov/nchs/data/nvsr/nvsr52/nvsr52_21acc.pdf**

National Center for HIV, STD and TB Prevention (2001). *Basic statistics.* [online] **www.cdc.gov/hiv/stats**

National Coalition of Women and Girls in Education (2002). Title IX at 30: Report card on gender equity. [online] **http://www.ncwge.org/title9at3 0– 6–11.pdf**

National Committee on Pay Equity (2001, February). Information about pay equity. [online] **http://www.feminist.com/fairpay/peinfo.htm**

National Institute of Mental Health (1994). Anxiety disorders. [online] **http://www.nimh.nih.gov/publicat/anxiety.cfm**

National Institute of Mental Health (1999). Suicide facts. [online] **www.nimh.nih.gov/research/suifact.htm**

National Institute of Mental Health (2004). Eating disorders: Facts about eating disorders and the search for solutions. [online] **http://www.nimh.nih.gov/publicat/eatingdisorders.cfm**

National Institutes of Health. (1997, April 23). Risks of cigarette smoking for women on the rise. Press release, National Cancer Institute Press Office. [online] **www.os.dhhs.gov/cgi-bin/wai**

National Marriage Project (2003). *The state of our unions, 2003.* Piscataway, NJ: Rutgers University. [online] **http://marriage.rutgers.edu/Publications/SOOU/SOOU2003.pdf**

National Public Radio (2000, March 31, Hour 1). Morning Edition. [Transcript]. Livingston, NJ: Burrelle's Transcripts.

National Women's Health Network (2001). Fact sheet: Breast cancer and African American women. [online] **www.womenshealthnetwork.org/advocacy/wocbreastca/african.htm**

Neft, N., & Levine, A. D. (1997). *Where women stand: An international report on the status of women in 140 countries.* New York: Random House.

Nelson-LeGall, S. (1990). Academic achievement orientation and help-seeking behavior in early adolescent girls. *Journal of Early Adolescence, 10,* 176–190.

News24.com (2004, August 12). Running for president. [online] **http://www.news24.com/News24/World/News/0,2–10–1462_1571915,00.html**

Ngangoue, N. R. (2001, June 15). Men make most headlines—Women stay newspaper victims. *Worldwoman.* [online] **www.worldwoman.nte**

Nichols, M. (1987). Lesbian sexuality: Issues and developing theory. In Boston Lesbian Psychologies Collective (Eds.), *Lesbian psychologies: Explorations and challenges* (pp. 97–125). Urbana: University of Illinois Press.

Nichols, P. C. (1983). Linguistic options and choices for Black women in the rural South. In B. Thorne, C. Kramarae, & N. Henley (Eds.), *Language, gender and society* (pp. 54–68). Rowley, MA: Newbury House.

Nieto, S. C. (1993, September/October). Mujeres ganan batalla contra publicidad sexista. *Mujeres, 40,* 5–6.

Nigerian woman sentenced to death for having sex (2001, October 17). Feminist Daily Newswire. [online] **www.feminist.org/news/newsbyte/printnews.asp?id=5882**

Nikelly, A. G. (1995). Drug advertisements and the medicalizaion of unipolar depression in women. *Health Care for Women International, 16* (3), 22 9–242.

Nilsen, W. J., & Vrana, S. R. (1998). Some touching situations: The relationship between gender and contextual variables in cardiovascular responses to human touch. *Annals of Behavioral Medicine, 20*(4), 270–276.

Noguchi, I. (2001, August 27). 'Asian Girl': Comic strip of a different stripe. *Washington Post,* pp. C1, C7.

Nolen-Hoeksema, S. (1987). Sex differences in unipolar depression: Evidence and theory. *Psychological Bulletin, 101*(2), 259–282.

Nolen-Hoeksema, S. (1990). *Sex differences in depression.* Stanford, CA: Stanford University Press.

Nolen-Hoeksema, S., & Girgus, J. S. (1994). The emergence of gender differences in depression during adolescence. *Psychological Bulletin, 115*(3), 424–443.

Nordquist, R. (2004, March). *Sojourner Truth's Ain't I a Woman: Print the Myth.* Paper presented at the annual meeting of the Southeastern Women's Studies Association, Savannah, GA.

Norris, J., Davis, K. C., George, W. H., Martell, J., & Heiman, J. R. (2004). Victims's response and alcohol-related factors as determinants of women's responses to violent pornography. *Psychology of Women Quarterly, 28*(1), 59–69.

O'Connell, H. E., Hutson, J. M., Anderson, C. R., & Plenter, R. J. (1998). Anatomical relationship between urethra and clitoris. *Journal of Urology, 159*(6), 1892–1897.

Oberman, Y., & Josselson, R. (1996). Matrix of tensions: A model of mothering. *Psychology of Women Quarterly, 20*(3), 341–359.

O'Connor, P. (1992). *Friendships between women: A review.* New York: Guilford.

Ogur, B. (1986). Long day's journey into night: Women and prescription drug abuse. *Women and Health, 11,* 99–115.

O'Hagen, F. T., Sale, D. G., MacDougall, J. D., & Garner, S. H. (1995). Response to resistance training in young women and men. *International Journal of Sports Medicine, 16,* 314–321.

O'Hara, M. W. (1986). Social support, life events, and depression during pregnancy and the puerperium. *Archives of General Psychiatry, 43,* 569–573.

Okie, S. (1993a, February 15). Where choosing a good mate is the "will of God." *Washington Post,* p. A33.

Okie, S. (1993b, February 17). The boys "only wanted to rape them." *Washington Post,* p. A24.

Okpala, C. O. (1996). Gender-related differences in classroom interaction. *Journal of Instructional Psychology, 23*(4), 275–285.

Oliker, S. J. (1989). *Best friends and marriage: Exchange among women.* Berkeley: University of California Press.

Oliver, M. B., & Hyde, J. S. (1993). Gender differences in sexuality: A meta-analysis. *Psychological Bulletin, 114,* 29–51.

One for 2001: Take lifestyle to heart (2001, January). *Harvard Women's Health Watch, 8*(5), 1–2.

Ong, A. (1987). *Spirits of resistance and capitalist discipline.* Albany: State University of New York Press.

Ong, A. (1991). The gender and labor politics of postmodernity. *Annual Reviews of Anthropology, 20,* 279–309.

Onishi, N. (2001, February 12). On the scale of beauty, weight weighs heavily. *New York Times,* p. 4.

Onyx, J., Leonard, R., & Vivekananda, K. (1995). Social perception of power: A gender analysis. *Perceptual and Motor Skills, 80,* 291–296.

Orenstein, P. (1994). *Schoolgirls: Young women, self-esteem, and the confidence gap.* New York: Doubleday.

Osman, S. (2004). Victim resistance: Theory and data on understanding perceptions of sexual harassment. *Sex Roles, 50*(3/4), 267–276.

Otto, M. A. (2000, April 18). Hormone therapy market remains strong despite critical studies. *Washington Post,* Health Section, p. 6.

Owen, K. (1995, February 20). U.S. dads lag in child-care duties, global study finds. *Los Angeles Times,* p. 5.

Oyewumi, O. (1997). *The invention of women: Making African sense of Western gender discourses.* Minneapolis: University of Minnesota Press.

Oyewumi, O. (1998). De-confounding gender: Feminist theorizing and Western culture: A comment on Hawkesworth's "Confounding gender." *Signs, 23*(4), 1049–1062.

Padgett, D. (1988). Aging minority women: Issues in research and health policy. *Women & Health, 14*(3/4), 213–225.

Padian, N. S., Shiboski, S. C., & Jewell, N. P. (1991). Female-to-male transmission of human immunodeficiency virus. *Journal of the American Medical Association, 266*(12), 1664–1667.

Pagelow, M. D. (1993). Justice for victims of spouse abuse in divorce and child custody cases. *Violence and Victims, 8*(1), 69–83.

Palacino, A. (1994, March 13). Empleo no tradicional. *La Nacion,* p. 8.

Pantony, K., & Caplan, P. J. (1991). Delusional dominating personality disorder: A modest proposal for identifying some consequences of rigid masculine socialization. *Canadian Psychology, 32*(2), 120–135.

Pape, K. T., & Arias, I. (1995). Control, coping and victimization in dating relationships. *Violence and Victims, 10*(1), 43–54.

Paradise, S. A. (1993). Older never married women: A cross-cultural investigation. *Women & Therapy, 14*(1–2), 129–139.

Parsons, E. C. (1991). *Pueblo mothers and children: Essays by Elsie Clews Parsons, 1915–1924* (B. A. Babcock, Ed.). Santa Fe, NM: Ancient City Press.

Parsons, E. M., & Betz, N. E. (2001). The relationship of participation in sports and physical activity to body objectification, instrumentality, and locus of control among young women. *Psychology of Women Quarterly, 25*(3), 209–222.

Parsons, T. D., Larson, P., Kratz, K., Thiebaux, M., Bluestein, B., Buckwalter, J. G., & Rizzo, A.A. (2004). Sex differences in mental rotation and spatial rotation in virtual environment. *Neuropsychologia, 42*(4), 555–562.

Partnow, E. (Ed.). (1977). *The quotable woman.* Los Angeles: Pinnacle Books.

Pascoe, P. (1990). Gender systems in conflict: The marriages of mission-educated Chinese American women, 1874–1939. In E. C. DuBois & V. L. Ruiz (Eds.), *Unequal sisters: A multicultural reader in U.S. women's history* (pp. 123–140). New York: Routledge.

Patel, J. D., Bach, P. B., & Kris, M. G. (2004). Lung cancer in U.S. women: A contemporary epidemic. *Journal of the American Medical Assocation, 291,* 1763–1768.

Patel, V. (1995). Explanatory models of mental illness in sub-Saharan Africa. *Social Science and Medicine, 40*(9), 1291–1298.

Patterson, A. S. (2000, September). Women in global politics: Progress or stagnation? *USA Today, 129* (issue 2664), p. 14.

Patterson, C. J. (1992). Children of lesbian and gay parents. *Child Development, 63,* 1025–1042.

PBS Online (2000). Facts about global poverty and microcredit. [online] **www.pbs.org/toourcredit/facts_one.htm**

Peiffer, J. (1991). La littérature scientifique pour les femmes au siècle des Lumières. In M. Hurtig, M. Kail, & H. Roche (Eds.), *Sexe et genre: De la hiérarchie entre les sexes* (pp. 137–146). Paris: Centre National de la Recherche Scientifique.

Peplau, L. A., & Campbell, S. D. (1989). The balance of power in dating and marriage. In J. Freeman (Ed.), *Women: A feminist perspective* (4th ed., pp. 121–137). Mountain View, CA: Mayfield.

Peplau, L. A., & Cochran, S. D. (1990). A relationship perspective on homosexuality. In D. P. McWhirter, S. A. Sanders, & J. M. Reinisch (Eds.), *Homosexuality/heterosexuality: Concepts of sexual orientation* (pp. 321–349). New York: Oxford University Press.

Peplau, L. A., & Garnets, L. D. (2000). A new paradigm for understanding women's sexuality and sexual orientation. *Journal of Social Issues, 56*(2), 329–350.

Peplau, L. A., & Gordon, S. L. (1985). Women and men in love: Gender differences in close heterosexual relationships. In V. E. O'Leary, R. K. Unger, & B. S. Wallston (Eds.), *Women, gender, and social psychology* (pp. 257–291). Hillsdale, NJ: Erlbaum.

Pera, G. (1996). The great divide: Teens and the gender gap. *USA Weekend.* Reprinted in R. Bredin (Ed.) (1998), *Perspectives: Women's Studies* (pp. 73–77).Boulder, CO: Coursewise Publishing, Inc.

Perez, M., & Joiner, T. E., Jr. (2003). Body image dissatisfaction and disordered eating in black and white women. *International Journal of Eating Disorders, 33*(3), 342–350.

Perlmutter, R. (1999, December 21). Wrestler proud of accomplishments. *USA Today,* p. 2C.

Perrone, B., Stockel, H. H., & Krueger, V. (1989). *Medicine women,* curanderas, *and women doctors.* Norman: University of Oklahoma Press.

Perry, D. G., & Bussey, K. (1979). The social learning theory of sex differences: Imitation is alive and well. *Journal of Personality and Social Psychology, 37,* 1699–1712.

Peters, G. (2000, August 24). Clean sweep for women. *The Evening Post* (Wellington, NZ), p. 1.

Peterson, K. (2004, June 17). 50–state rundown on gay marriage laws. Stateline.org. [online] **http://www.stateline.org/stateline/?pa=story&sa=showStoryInfo&id=353058**

Phinney, J. S. (1989). Stages of ethnic identity in minority group adolescents. *Journal of Early Adolescence, 9,* 34–49.

Phinney, J. S. (1990). Ethnic identity in adolescents and adults: Review of research. *Psychological Bulletin, 108*(3), 499–514.

Physicians for Human Rights (2001, May 17). Women's health and human rights in Afghanistan: A population-based assessment. [online] **www.phrusa.org/campaigns/afghanistan/afghanreport**

Pieterson, C., & Geddis, A. N. (1993). Elementary school girls confront an androcentric science. In *Contributions to the Seventh International Gender and Science and Technology Conference* (Vol. 1, pp. 98–106). Waterloo, Ontario: University of Waterloo.

Pillsbury, B. L. K. (1978). "Doing the month": Confinement and convalescence of Chinese women after childbirth. *Social Science and Medicine, 12,* 11–22.

Pipher, M. (1994). *Reviving Ophelia: Saving the selves of adolescent girls.* New York: Putnam.

Pleck, J. H., Sonenstein, F. L., & Ku, L. C. (1993). Masculinity ideology: Its impact on adolescent men's heterosexual relationships. *Journal of Social Issues, 49*(3), 11–29.

Pomeroy, S. B. (1983). Infanticide in Hellenistic Greece. In A. Cameron & A. Kuhrt (Eds.), *Images of women in antiquity* (pp. 207–222). Detroit, MI: Wayne State University Press.

Population Action International (2003). Fact Sheet: How family planning and reproductive health services affect the lives of women, men, and children. [online] **http://www .populationaction.org/resources/ publications/worldofdifference/rr2_facts _english.htm**

Porzelius, L. K. (2000). Physical health issues for women. In M. Miaggio & M. Hersen (Eds.), *Issues in the psychology of women* (pp. 229–250). New York: Kluwer Academic/ Plenum Publishers.

Pratto, F., Sidanius, J., & Siers, B. (1997). The gender gap in occupational role attainment: A social dominance approach. *Journal of Personality and Social Psychology, 72*(1), 37–53.

President's council on Physical Fitness and Sport. (1997, May). *Physical activity and sport in the lives of girls: Physical and mental health dimensions from an interdisciplinary approach.* Washington, DC: Author.

Preston, J. (1993, February 15). For rural women, a millstone of poverty. *Washington Post,* pp. A1, A32–A33.

Pringle, P. (2003, July 27). College Board Scores with Critics of SAT Analogies. *Los Angeles Times.* **http://www.latimes.com/news/ education/la-me-sat27jul27002421,1 ,2926050.story?coll=la-news-learning**

Proctor, B. D., & Dalaker, J. (2003). *Poverty in the United States 2002.* U.S. Census Bureau, Current Population Reports P60–222. Washington, DC: U.S. Government Printing Office.

Profet, M. (1993). Menstruation as a defense against pathogens transported by sperm. *Quarterly Review of Biology, 68,* 335–386.

Pyke, K. D. (1994). Women's employment as a gift or burden? Marital power across marriage, divorce, and remarriage. *Gender & Society, 8*(1), 73–91.

Rabin, J. (1998, March). *Using developmental-interactionist and feminist perspectives in teaching ethology and comparative psychology.* Paper presented at the annual meeting of the Association for Women in Psychology, Baltimore.

Rabin, J. S., & Slater, B. R. (2004, March). *Feminist psychology, science and practice: The lesbian development study.* Paper presented at the annual conference of the Association for Women in Psychology, Philadelphia.

Rabinowitz, V. C., & Martin, D. (2001). Choices and consequences: Methodological issues in the study of gender. In R. K. Unger (Ed.), *Handbook of the psychology of women and gender* (pp. 29–52). New York: John Wiley & Sons, Inc.

Radical Cheerleaders (2004). [online] **http:// radcheers.tripod.com/RC/**

Radin, N., & Harold-Goldsmith, R. (1989). The involvement of selected unemployed and employed men with their children. *Child Development, 60,* 454–459.

Raffaelli, M., & Ontai, L. L. (2004). Gender socialization in Latino/a families: Results from two retrospective studies. *Sex Roles, 50*(5/6), 287–299.

Raimondo, L. (2001, October 19). 'Small steps' for Afghan women's rights. *Washington Post,* p. A21.

Raja, S. (1998). Culturally sensitive therapy for women of color. *Women and Therapy, 21,* 67–84.

Rak, D. S., & McMullen, L. M. (1987). Sex role stereotyping in television commercials: A verbal response mode and content analysis. *Canadian Journal of Behavioural Science, 19,* 25–39.

Randhawa, B. S., & Gupta, A. (2000). Cross-national gender differences in mathematics achievement, attitude, and self-efficacy within a common intrinsic structure. *Canadian Journal of School Psychology, 15*(2), 51–66.

Ransdell, L. B., & Wells, C. L (1998). Physical activity in urban white, African American and Mexican-American women. *Medicine and Science in Sports and Exercise, 30,* 1608–1615.

Rastogi, M., & Wampler, K. S. (1999). Adult daughters' perceptions of the mother–daughter relationship: A cross-cultural comparison. *Family Relations, 48*(3), 327–336.

Rauhala, A. (1987, April 2). Religion is key for anti-abortionists, study finds. *Toronto Globe and Mail,* pp. A1, A5.

Raven, B. H. (1965). Social influence and power. In I. D. Steiner & M. Fishbein (Eds.), *Current studies in social psychology* (pp. 371–381). New York: Holt, Rinehart & Winston.

Raven, B. H., Schwarzwald, J., & Koslowsky, M. (1998). Conceptualizing and measuring a power/interaction model of interpersonal influence. *Journal of Applied Social Psychology, 28*(4), 307–332.

Reddy, M. A. (Ed.). (1994). *Statistical abstract of the world.* New York: Gale.

Reducing osteoporosis risk (2001, March). *Harvard Women's Health Watch, 8*(7), 3–4.

Reed, B. E. (1992). The gender symbolism of Kuan-yin Bodhisattva. In J. I. Cabezón (Ed.), *Buddhism, sexuality, and gender* (pp. 159–180). Albany: State University of New York Press.

Reed, J. (1999, July 12). Running against Hurricane 'W,' Scrambling for dollars: Elizabeth Dole was raised to be in control. Now she's trying to keep smiling in a storm. *Newsweek, 134*(2), 28.

Reeder, H. M. (1997). What Harry and Sally didn't tell you: The subjective experience of heterosexual cross-sex friendship. *Dissertation Abstracts International, 57*(7-A), 2742.

Regan, J. M. (1982). Gender displays in portrait photographs. *Sex Roles, 8,* 33–43.

Reid, P., & Finchilescu, G. (1995). The disempowering effects of media violence against women on college women. *Psychology of Women Quarterly, 19*(3), 397–411.

Reid, P. T. (1988). Racism and sexism: Comparisons and conflicts. In P. A. Katz & D. A. Taylor (Eds.), *Eliminating racism* (pp. 203–221). New York: Plenum.

Reid, P. T. (1993). Poor women in psychological research: Shut up and shut out. *Psychology of Women Quarterly, 17,* 133–150.

Reid, P. T., Haritos, C., Kelly, E., & Holland, N. E. (1995). Socialization of girls: Issues of ethnicity in gender development. In H. Landrine (Ed.), *Bringing cultural diversity to feminist psychology* (pp. 93–111). Washington, DC: American Psychological Association.

Reid, P. T., & Robinson, W. L. (1985). Professional Black men and women: Attainment of terminal degrees. *Psychological Reports, 56,* 547–555.

Remennick, L. I., & Segal, R. (2001). Sociocultural context and women's experiences of abortion: Israeli women and Russion immigrants compared. *Culture, Health & Sexuality, 3*(1), 49–66.

Rennison, C. M., & Rand, M. R. (2003, August). Criminal victimization, 2002. Bureau of Justice Statistics, National Crime Victimization Survey. [online] **http://www.rainn.org/ncvs_2002.pdf**

Renzetti, C. (1992). *Violent betrayal: Partner abuse in lesbian relationships.* Newbury Park, CA: Sage.

Reproductive Health Outlook (2000). Cervical cancer prevention. [online] **http://www.rho.org/html/cxca.htm**

Resendez, M. G. (2002). The stigmatizing effects of affirmative action: An examination of moderating variables. *Journal of Applied Social Psychology, 32*(1), 185–206.

Researchers link stress hormones with disease. (1996, November 16). *Roanoke Times,* p. A4.

Reskin, B. F. (1998). Bringing the men back in: Sex differentiation and the devaluation of women's work. In Myers, K. A., Anderson, C,. D., & Risman, B. J. (Eds), *Feminist foundations: Toward transforming sociology.* Gender and society readers, Vol. 3 (pp. 278–298). Thousand Oaks, CA: Sage.

Reuters News Services. (1996a, April 19). Beijing, China.

Reuters News Services. (1996b, July 4). Wellington, New Zealand.

Ribeau, S. A., Baldwin, J. R., & Hecht, M. L. (1994). An African-American communication perspective. In L. Samovar & R. Porter (Eds.), *Intercultural communication: A reader* (7th ed., pp. 140–147). Belmont, CA: Wadsworth.

Richburg, K. B. (1993, February 18). "I would like to be President—really": Somali women defy repressive customs to help repair their damaged country. *Washington Post,* p. A35.

Riddle, J. M., & Estes, J. W. (1992, May–June). Oral contraceptives in ancient and medieval times. *American Scientist, 80*(3), 226–233.

Ridgeway, C. L. (1982). Status in groups: The importance of motivation. *American Sociological Review, 47,* 76–88.

Riley, N. E. (2004, June). China's population: New trends and challenges. Populations Bulletin, 59(2), entire issue. [online] **http://www.prb.org/pdf04/59.2ChinasPopNewTrends.pdf**

Riley, S. S. (1994). Sistah outsider. In P. Bell-Scott (Ed.), *Life notes: Personal writings by contemporary Black women* (pp. 92–108). New York: Norton.

Ristock, J. L. (2002). *No more secrets: Violence in lesbian relationships.* New York: Routledge.

Roades, L. A. (2000). Mental health issues for women. In M. Biaggio & M. Hersen (Eds.), *Issues in the psychology of women* (pp. 251–272). New York: Kluwer Academic/Plenum Publishers.

Roberts, D. (1994, August). Men didn't have to prove they could fly, but women did. *Smithsonian, 25*(5), 72–81.

Roberts, T.-A. (2004). Female trouble: The menstrual self-evaluation scale and women's self-objectification. *Psychology of Women Quarterly, 28*(1), 22–26.

Robinson, J. P., & Godbey, G. (1993). Sports, fitness, and the gender gap. *Leisure Sciences, 15,* 291–307.

Robinson, T., & Ward, J. V. (1991). "A belief in self far greater than anyone's disbelief": Cultivating resistance among African American female adolescents. In C. Gilligan, A. G. Rogers, & L. Tolman (Eds.), *Women, girls and psychotherapy: Reframing resistance* (pp. 87–103). New York: Haworth Press.

Rodriguez, K., & Strickler, J. (1999). Clandestine abortion in Latin America: Provider perspectives. *Women & Health, 28*(3), 59–76.

Rogers, A. G. (1993). Voice, play, and a practice of ordinary courage in girls' and women's lives. *Harvard Educational Review, 63*(3), 265–295.

Rogoff, B., & Chavajay, P. (1995). What's become of research on the cultural basis of cognitive development? *American Psychologist, 50*(10), 859–877.

Rohsenow, D. J., Corbett, R., & Devine, D. (1988). Molested as children: A hidden contribution to substance abuse. *Journal of Substance Abuse Treatment, 5,* 13–18.

Roma Rights (2000). Roundtable: Romani activists on women's rights. Number 1. [online] **http://www.errc.org/rr_nr1_2000**

Rompiendo el Silencio. (1992, October–November). *La Boletina,* p. 9. Managua, Nicaragua: Puntos de Encuentro.

Root, M. P. P. (1992). The impact of trauma on personality: The second reconstruction. In L. S. Brown & M. Ballou (Eds.), *Personality and psychopathology* (pp. 229–265). New York: Guilford.

Root, M. P. P. (1995). The psychology of Asian American women. In H. Landrine (Ed.), *Bringing cultural diversity to feminist psychology* (pp. 265–301). Washington, DC: American Psychological Association.

Rose, J. (1992). *Marie Stopes and the sexual revolution.* London: Faber & Faber.

Rose, S. (1995). Women's friendships. In J. C. Chrisler & A. Huston Hemstreet (Eds.), *Variations on a theme: Diversity and the psychology of women* (pp. 79–105). Albany: State University of New York Press.

Rose, S., Zand, D., & Cini, M. (1994). Lesbian courtship rituals. In E. D. Rothblum & K. A. Brehony (Eds.), *The Boston marriage today: Romantic but asexual relationships between contemporary lesbians* (pp. 70–85). Amherst: University of Massachusetts Press.

Rosenberg, R. (1982). *Beyond separate spheres: Intellectual roots of modern feminism.* New Haven, CT: Yale University Press.

Rosenbluth, S. (1990, August). *Intimacy: Women's experience of same-sex and cross-sex couples.* Paper presented at the meeting of the American Psychological Association, Boston.

Rosener, Judith B. (1995). *America's competitive secret: Utilizing women as a management strategy.* New York: Oxford University Press.

Rossi, J. D. (1983). Ratios exaggerate gender differences in mathematical ability. *American Psychologist, 38,* 348.

Roter, D., Lipkin, M., & Korsgaard, A. (1991). Sex differences in patients' and physicians' communication during primary care medical visits. *Medical Care, 29,* 1083–1093.

Rousseau, J-J. (1979). *Émile: Or, on Education,* Book 5 (A. Bloom, Trans.). New York: Basic Books. (Original work published 1762.)

Rozée, P. D. (1993). Forbidden or forgiven? Rape in cross-cultural perspective. *Psychology of Women Quarterly, 17*(4), 499–514.

Ruan, F. F., & Bullough, V. L. (1992). Lesbianism in China. *Archives of Sexual Behavior, 21*(3), 217–226.

Rubin, J., Provenzano, F., & Luria, Z. (1974). The eye of the beholder: Parents' views on sex of newborns. American *Journal of Orthopsychiatry, 44,* 512–519.

Rubin, L. R., Nemeroff, C. J., & Russo, N. F. (2004). Exploring feminist women's body consciousness. *Psychology of Women Quarterly, 28*(1), 27–37.

Rubin, R. (2001, March 28). Female smoking deaths double. *USA Today,* p. 1A.

Rudman, L. A. (1998). Self-promotion as a risk factor for women. The costs and benefits of counter-stereotypical impression management. *Journal of Personality and Social Psychology, 74,* 629–645.

Rudman, L. A., & Glick, P. (2001). Prescriptive gender stereotypes and backlash toward agentic women. *Journal of Social Issues, 57*(4), 743–762.

Rudman, L. A., & Kilianski, S. E. (2000). Implicit and explicit attitudes toward female authority. *Personality and Social Psychology Bulletin, 26*(11), 1315–1328).

Rudolph, F. (1962). *The American college and university: A history.* New York: Knopf.

Runciman, W. G. (1966). *Relative deprivation and social justice: A study of attitudes to social inequality in twentieth-century England.* Berkeley: University of California Press.

Russell, D. E. H. (1988). Pornography and rape: A causal model. *Political Psychology, 9,* 41–73.

Russell, K., Wilson, M., & Hall, R. (1992). *The color complex: The politics of skin color among African Americans.* New York: Harcourt Brace Jovanovich.

Russell, M. J., Switz, G. M., & Thompson, K. (1980). Olfactory influences on the human menstrual cycle. *Pharmacology, Biochemistry & Behavior, 13,* 737–738.

Russell, S. (1995, Fall). Citizen Payne. *Northwestern Perspectives,* pp. 14–18.

Russo, N. F., Amaro, H., & Winter, M. (1987). The use of inpatient mental health services by Hispanic women. *Psychology of Women Quarterly, 11*(4), 427–441.

Saadawi, N. (1998). The question that no one would answer. In M. C. Ward (Ed.), *A sounding of women: Autobiographies from unexpected places* (pp. 174–178). Boston: Allyn & Bacon.

Sadker, M., & Sadker, D. (1985). Sexism in the schoolroom of the 80's. *Psychology Today, 19,* 54–57.

Sadker, M., & Sadker, D. (1994). *Failing at fairness: How America's schools cheat girls.* New York: Charles Scribner's Sons.

Saffron, L. (1998). Raising children in an age of diversity–advantages of having a lesbian mother. *Journal of Lesbian Studies, 2*(4), 35–47.

Safire, W. (Ed.). (1992). *Lend me your ears: Great speeches in history.* New York: Norton.

Saladin d'Anglure, B. (1988). Penser le feminin chamanique ou le tiers-sex des chamanes inuit. *Recherches Amerindiennes au Québec, 18,* 19–50.

Saldich, A. R. (2000, March 15). Board of contributors: Bearing witness for a better workplace. Palo Alto Weekly, Online Edition. **www.service.com/paw/morgue/spectrum/ 2000_Mar_15.BOARD15.htm**

Salguero, C., & McCusker, W. R. (1996). Symptom expression in inner-city Latinas: Psychopathology or help seeking? In B. J. R. Leadbetter & N. Way (Eds.), *Urban girls: Resisting stereotypes, creating identities* (pp. 328–336). New York: New York University Press.

Same-sex Dutch couples gain marriage and adoption rights (2001, December 20). *New York Times,* International, p. 8.

Sanday, P. R. (1981). *Female power and male dominance: On the origins of sexual inequality.* Cambridge: Cambridge University Press.

Sanders, J. L., Hakky, U. M., & Brizzolara, M. M. (1985). Personal space amongst Arabs and Americans. *International Journal of Psychology, 20,* 13–17.

Saris, R. N., & Johnston-Robledo, I. (2000). Poor women are still shut out of mainstream psy-chology. *Psychology of Women Quarterly, 24*(3), 233–235.

Sasson, J. P. (1992). *Princess: A true story of life behind the veil in Saudi Arabia.* New York: Avon.

Savicki, V., Kelley, M., & Lingenfelter, D. (1996a). Gender and group composition in small task groups using computer-mediated communication. *Computers in Human Behavior, 12*(2), 209–224.

Savicki, V., Kelley, M., & Lingenfelter, D. (1996b). Gender, group composition, and task type in small task groups using computer-mediated communication. *Computers in Human Behavior, 12*(4), 549–565.

Savicki, V., & Kelley, M. (2000). Computer-mediated communication: Gender and group composition. *Cyberpsychology & Behavior, 3*(5), 817–826.

Schafer, S. (2001, July 25). When violence at home comes to work. *Washington Post,* pp. E1, E12.

Schauben, L. J., & Frazier, P. A. (1995). Vicarious trauma: The effects on female counselors of working with sexual violence survivors. *Psychology of Women Quarterly, 19*(1), 49–64.

Schein, V. E. (2001). A global look at psychological barriers to women's progress in management. *Journal of Social Issues, 57*(4), 675–688.

Schiff, W., & Oldak, R. (1990). Accuracy of judging time to arrival: *Effects of modality, trajectory, and gender. Journal of Experimental Psychology, Human Perception and Performance, 16,* 303–316.

Schilit, R., Lie, G., & Montagne, M. (1990). Substance use as a correlate of violence in intimate lesbian relationships. *Journal of Homosexuality, 19*(3), 51–65.

Schlaug, G., Jancke, L., Huang, Y., Staiger, J. F., & Steinmetz, H. (1995). Increased corpus callosum size in musicians. *Neuropsychologia, 33,* 1047–1055.

Schneider, H. (2000, April 14). Egyptian women given faster route to divorce. *Washington Post,* pp. 16, A17.

Schneider, J. W., & Hacker, S. W. (1973). Sex role imagery and use of generic "man" in introductory texts: A case in the sociology of sociology. *American Sociology, 8,* 12–18.

Schnittker, J., Freesse, J., & Powell, B. (2003). Who are feminists and what do they believe? The role of generations. *American Sociological Review, 68*(4), 607–622.

Schoenberger, K. (1989, May 18). Korea's "Henyo" divers: Master of the sea—but second class on land. *Los Angeles Times,* pp. 1, 12–13.

Schooler, D., Ward, L. M., Merriwether, A., & Caruthers, A. (2004). Who's that girl: Television's role in the body image development of young White and Black women. *Psychology of Women Quarterly, 28*(1), 38–47.

Schreurs, K. M. G., & Buunk, B. P. (1996). Closeness, autonomy, equity, and relationship satisfaction in lesbian couples. *Psychology of Women Quarterly, 20*(4), 577–592.

Schulz, J. J., & Schulz, L. (1999). The darkest of ages: Afghan women under the Taliban. *Peace and Conflict: Journal of Peace Psychology, 5*(3), 237–254.

Schuman, M. (2001, May 29). On an Indonesian isle, there's a way to avoid the arranged marriage. *The Wall Street Journal,* pp. A1, A12.

Schwartz, I. M. (1993). Affective reactions of American and Swedish women to their first premarital coitus: A cross-cultural comparison. *Journal of Sex Research, 30*(1), 18–26.

Sczesny, S. (2003). A closer look beneath the surface: Various facets of the think-manager-think-male stereotype. *Sex Roles, 49*(7–8), 353–363.

Sears, D. O. (1986). College sophomores in the laboratory: Influence of a narrow data base on psychology's view of human nature. *Journal of Personality and Social Psychology, 51,* 515–530.

Sedikides, C., Oliver, M. B., & Campbell, W. K. (1994). Perceived benefits and costs of romantic relationships for women and men: Implications for exchange theory. *Personal Relationships, 1,* 5–21.

Serafica, F. C., Weng, A., & Kim, H. K. (2000). Friendships and social networks among Asian American women. In J. L. Chin (Ed.). *Relationships among Asian American women* (pp. 151–175). Washington, DC: American Psychological Association.

Serbin, L. A., Powlishta, K. K., & Gulko, J. (1993). The development of sex typing in middle childhood. *Monographs of the Society for Research in Child Development, 58*(2, Serial No. 232).

Seshadri, S., Zornberg, G. L., Derby, L. E., Myers, M. W., Jick, H., & Drachman, D. A. (2001, March). Postmenopausal estrogen replacement therapy and the risk of Alzheimer disease. *Archives of Neurology, 58,* 435–440.

Sexy clothing a factor in rape cases, psychiatrists say. (1991, November 25). *Tucson Citizen,* p. 6B.

Shaked, R. (2001, August). *Sexual harassment: A revolution in social norms—The Israeli experience.* Paper presented at the 27th annual conference of the International Federation of University Women, Ottawa, Canada.

Shange, N. (1976). *for colored girls who have considered suicide/when the rainbow is enuf.* New York: Macmillan.

Shange, N. (1982). *Sassafras, Cypress & Indigo.* New York: St. Martin's.

Shapiro-Baruch, A. (1995). The dismissal of female clients' reports of medication side effects: A first hand account. *Women & Therapy, 16*(1), 113–127.

Sharpe, P. A. (1995). Older women and health services: Moving toward empowerment. *Women & Health, 22*(3), 9–23.

Shaver, L. D. (1997). The dilemma of Oklahoma Native American women elders: Traditional roles and sociocultural roles. In H. S. Noor Al-Deen (Ed.), *Cross-cultural communication and aging in the United States* (pp. 161–178). Mahwah, NJ: Lawrence Erlbaum Associates, Inc.

She, H. (2000). The interplay of a biology teacher's beliefs, teaching practices and gender-based student-teacher classroom interaction. *Educational Research, 42*(1), 100–111.

Sheehan, N. W., & Donorfio, L. M. (1999). Efforts to create meaning in the relationship between aging mothers and their caregiving daughters: A qualitative study of caregiving. *Journal of Aging Studies, 13*(2), 161–176.

Shields, S. A. (1995). The role of emotion, beliefs and values in gender development. In N. Eisenberg (Ed.), *Social development* (pp. 212–232). Thousand Oaks, CA: Sage.

Shields, S. A. (1975). Functionalism, Darwinism and the psychology of women: A study in social myth. *American Psychologist, 30*(7), 739–754.

Shipley, A. (1997, July 6). Playing field levels at Texas. *Washington Post,* pp. A1, A6–A7.

Shostak, M. (1981). *Nisa: The life and words of a !Kung woman.* New York: Vintage.

Shucard, D. W., Shucard, J. L., & Thomas, D. G. (1987). Sex differences in electrophysiological activity in infancy: Possible implications for language development. In S. U. Philips, S. Steels, & C. Tanz (Eds.), *Language, gender, and sex in comparative perspective* (pp. 278–295). Cambridge: Cambridge University Press.

Shulman, P. (2000, June). The girl who loved math. *Discover Magazine.* Obtained from **www.findarticles.com.**

Sigelman, C. K., Thomas, D. B., Sigelman, L., & Ribich, F. D. (1986). Gender, physical attractiveness, and electability: An experimental investigation of voter bias. *Journal of Applied Social Psychology, 16*(3), 229–248.

Signorella, M. L., Bigler, R. S., & Liben, L. S. (1993). Developmental differences in children's gender schemata about others: A meta-analytic review. *Developmental Review, 20,* 147–183.

Signorielli, N., & Bacue, A. (1999). Recognition and respect: A content analysis of prime-time television characters across three decades. *Sex Roles, 40*(7–8), 527–544.

Signorielli, N., McLeod, D., & Healy, E. (1994). Gender stereotypes in MTV commercials: The beat goes on. *Journal of Broadcasting and Electronic Media, 38*(1), 91–101.

Sijuwade, P. O. (1991). Sex differences in perception of aging among the Nigerian elderly. *Social Behavior and Personality, 19*(4), 289–296.

Silber, C. (1992, September–October). A 1,000-year-old secret. *Ms.,* pp. 58–60.

Silberschmidt, M., & Rasch, V. (2001). Adolescent girls, illegal abortions and "sugar-daddies" in Dar es Salaam: Vulnerable victims and active social agents. *Social Science & Medicine, 52*(12), 1815–1826.

Silva, C. P. da (1988). A mulher na comunidade matematica Brasileira, de 1879 a 1979 [Women in the Brazilian mathematical community from 1879 to 1979]. *Quipu* [Mexico], *5*(2), 277–289.

Silverman, C. (2000). Macedonian and Bulgarian Muslim Romani women: Power, politics, and creativity in ritual. *Roma Rights, 1* [online] **www.errc.org/rr_nr1_2000/noteb2.shtml**

Silverman, J. G., Raj. A., Mucci, L. A., & Hathaway, J. E. (2001). Dating violence against adolescent girls and associated substance use, unhealthy weight control, sexual risk behavior, pregnancy, and suicidality. *Journal of the American Medical Association, 286*(5), 572–579.

Silverstein, L. B. (1996). Fathering is a feminist issue. *Psychology of Women Quarterly, 20* (1), 3–38.

Simmons, R. (2002). *Odd girl out: The hidden culture of aggression in girls.* New York: Harcourt.

Simoni-Wastila, L. (2000). The use of abusable prescription drugs: The role of gender. *Journal of Women's Health & Gender-Based Medicine, 9*(3), 289–297.

Siskind, T. G., & Kearns, S. P. (1997). Gender bias in the evaluation of female faculty at the Citadel: A qualitative analysis. *Sex Roles, 37*(7/8), 495–525.

Six, B., & Eckes, T. (1991). A closer look at the complex structure of sex stereotypes. *Journal of Personality and Social Psychology, 17,* 200–207.

Skaalvik, S., & Skaalvik, E. M. (2004). Gender differences in math and verbal self-concept, performance expectations, and motivation. *Sex Roles, 50* (3/4), 241–252.

Skinner, P. H., & Shelton, R. L. (1985). *Speech, language, and hearing: Normal processes and disorders* (2nd ed.). New York: Wiley.

Slaby, R. G., & Frey, K. S. (1975). Development of gender constancy and selective attention to same-sex models. *Child Development, 46,* 849–856.

Slavin, B. (2001, April 18). Women find ways to promote their liberation. *Washington Post,* p. 10A.

Sloane, E. (2002). *Biology of women* (4th ed.). Albany, NY: Delmar.

Smith, A., & Schneider, B. H. (2000). The inter-ethnic friendships of adolescent students: A Canadian study. *International Journal of Intercultural Relations. 24*(2), 247–258.

Smith, G. A., & McPhee, K. A. (1987). Performance on a coincidence timing task correlates with intelligence. *Intelligence, 11,* 161–167.

Smith, H. (2001). Practices of the 100 best companies. [online] **www.pbs.org/workfamily/resources_practices.htm**

Smith, J. E., Waldorf, V. A., & Trembath, D. L. (1990). "Single White male looking for thin, very attractive . . ." *Sex Roles, 23*(11/12), 675–685.

Smith, J. S. (1992). Women in charge: Politeness and directives in the speech of Japanese women. *Language in Society, 21*(1), 59–82.

Smith, P. B., & Bond, M. H. (1993). *Social psychology across cultures: Analysis and perspectives.* Boston: Allyn & Bacon.

Smith-Rosenberg, C. (1975). The female world of love and ritual: Relationships between women in nineteenth-century America. *Signs, 1,* 1–29.

Smoreda, Z. (1995). Power, gender stereotypes and perceptions of heterosexual couples. *British Journal of Social Psychology, 34,* 421–435.

Snow, J. T., & Harris, M. B. (1989). Disordered eating in Southwestern Pueblo Indians and Hispanics. *Journal of Adolescence, 12,* 329–336.

Sobal, J., & Stunkard, A. J. (1989). Socioeconomic status and obesity: A review of the literature. *Psychological Bulletin, 105,* 260–275.

Soet, J. E., Dudley, W. N., & Dilorio, C. (1999). The effects of ethnicity and perceived power on women's sexual behavior. *Psychology of Women Quarterly,* 23(4), 707–723.

Soh, C-H. S. (1993). Sexual equality, male superiority, and Korean women in politics: Changing gender relationships in a "patriarchal democracy." *Sex Roles, 28*(1/2), 73–90.

Solovay, S. (2000). *Tipping the scales of justice: Fighting weight-based discrimination.* New York: Prometheus Books.

Sommers, C. H. (2000). *The war against boys: How misguided feminism is harming our young men.* New York: Simon & Schuster.,

Sorenson, S. B., Siegel, J. M., Golding, J. M., & Stein, J. A. (1991). Repeated sexual victimization. *Violence and Victims, 6,* 299–308.

South, S. J., & Spitze, G. (1994). Housework in marital and non-marital households. *American Sociological Review, 59,* 327–347.

Southerland, D. (1990, May 27). Limited sexual revolution seen in China: Nationwide survey shows more liberal attitudes developing in conservative society. *Washington Post.*

Spartos, C. (2000, December 6–12). Sarafem nation. The Village Voice. [online] **www .villagevoice.com.issue/0049/spartos.php**

Spencer, S. J., Steele, C. M., & Quinn, D. M. (1999). Stereotype threat and women's math performance. *Journal of Experimental Social Psychology, 31*(1), 4–28.

Spender, D. (1989). *The writing or the sex?* New York: Pergamon.

Spigelman, M., & Schultz, K. (1981, June). *Attitudes toward obesity.* Paper presented at the annual convention of the Canadian Psychological Association, Toronto.

Sprecher, S., Hatfield, E., Cortese, A., Potapova, E., & Levitskaya, A. (1994). Token resistance to sexual intercourse and consent to unwanted sexual intercourse: College students' dating experiences in three countries. *Journal of Sex Research, 31*(2), 125–132.

Springer, S. P., & Deutsch, G. (1993). *Left brain, right brain* (3rd ed.). New York: W. H. Freeman.

Stanley, J. (1990, January 10). We need to know why women falter in math [letter to the editor]. *Chronicle of Higher Education,* p. B4.

Stark-Adamec, C., & Kimball, M. (1984). Science free of sexism: A guide to the conduct of non-sexist research. *Canadian Psychology, 25*(1), 23–34.

Starrels, M. E. (1994). Gender differences in parent–child relations. *Journal of Family Issues, 15* (1), 148–165.

Statistics Canada (1995). *Women in Canada: A statistical report.* Ottawa: Author.

Statistics Canada (2002). Family studies kit. [online] **http://www.statcan.ca/english/kits/ Family.pdf**

Statistics Canada (2004, April 16). Employment income groups (22) in constant (2000) dollars and sex (3) for population 15 years and over, for Canada, provinces, territories, census metropolitan areas and census agglomerations, 1995 and 2000—20% Sample Data. [online] **http://www12.statcan.ca/english/census01/ home/Index.cfm**

Stave, K. (2001, Summer). Let's talk about "Sex and the City." *Bust, 18,* pp. 40–43.

Steele, C. M. (1997). A threat in the air: How stereotypes shape intellectual identity and performance. *American Psychologist, 52,* 613–629.

Steil, J. M. (1995). Supermoms and second shifts: Marital inequality in the 1990s. In J. Freeman (Ed.), *Women: A feminist perspective* (5th ed., pp. 149–161). Mountain View, CA: Mayfield.

Steil, J. M., & Hillman, J. L. (1993). The perceived value of direct and indirect influence strategies: A cross-cultural comparison. *Psychology of Women Quarterly, 17*(4), 457–462.

Steil, J. M., & Weltman, K. (1992). Influence strategies at home and at work: A study of sixty dual career couples. *Journal of Social and Personal Relations, 9,* 65–88.

Steinberg, J. (2001, August 29). National briefing. Education: Support for gay rights. *New York Times,* p. 18.

Stepakoff, S. A. (2000). Mother–infant tactile communication at four months: Effects of infant gender, maternal ethnicity, and maternal depression. *Dissertation Abstracts International, 60*(11-B), 5793.

Stevenson, H. W., Chen, C., & Booth, J. (1990). Influences of schooling and urban–rural residence on gender differences in cognitive abilities and academic achievement. *Sex Roles, 23*(9/10), 535–551.

Stevenson, H. W., Chen, C., & Lee, S. (1993). Mathematics achievement of Chinese, Japanese, and American children: Ten years later. *Science, 259,* 53–58.

Stevenson, H. W., Chen, C., & Uttal, D. H. (1990). Beliefs and achievement: A study of Black, White, and Hispanic children. *Child Development, 60,* 508–523.

Stevenson, H. W., Lee, S., & Stigler, J. (1986, February 14). Mathematics achievement of Chinese, Japanese, and American children. *Science,* pp. 693–699.

Stier, H., & Tienda, M. (1993). Are men marginal to the family? Insights from Chicago's inner city. In J. C. Hood (Ed.), *Men, work, and family.* Newbury Park, CA: Sage.

Stockman, L. (2003, December). Ethical threads: Nicaraguan women's co-op offers altherna-tive to sweatshops—Fair Trade. *New Interna-tionalist.* [online] **http://www.findarticles.com/p/articles/mi_m0JQP/is_363/ai_111617786**

Stopes, M. (1918). *Married love.* London: A. C. Fifield.

Stoppard, J. M., & Gruchy, C. D. G. (1993). Gen-der, context, and expression of positive emo-tion. *Personality and Social Psychology Bul-letin, 19,* 143–150.

Storms, M. D. (1980). Theories of sexual orienta-tion. *Journal of Personality and Social Psy-chology, 38,* 783–792.

Strykowska, M. (1995). Women in management in Poland. *Women's Studies International Forum, 18*(1), 9–12.

Studies show women 50% more likely to die of heart attacks than men. (1998, April 2). *Roanoke Times,* p. A6.

Study: Depression in pregnancy common, harm-ful. (2001, August 3). *Roanoke Times,* p. A1.

Sugawara, S. (1996, May 1). Japanese women confront "sekuhara." *Washington Post,* pp. A1, A25.

Sun, L. H. (1993, February 16). A great leap back: Chinese women losing jobs, status as ancient ways subvert socialist ideal. *Washing-ton Post,* pp. A1, A24–25.

Swaab, D. F., Chung, W. C. J., Kruijver, F. P. M., Hofman, M. A., & Hestiantoro, A. (2003). Sex differences in the hypothalamus in the different stages of human life. *Neurobiology of Aging, 24* (Suppl 1), S1–S16.

Sweeney, J., & Bradbard, M. R. (1988). Mothers' and fathers' changing perceptions of their male and female infants over the course of pregnancy. *Journal of Genetic Psychology, 149*(3), 393–404.

Swim, J. K., Aikin, K. J., Hall, W. S., & Hunter, B. A. (1995). Sexism and racism: Old-fashioned and modern prejudices. *Journal of Personality and Social Psychology, 68*(2), 199–214.

Swim, J. K., Borgida, E., Maruyama, G., & Myers, D. G. (1989). Joan McKay versus John McKay: Do gender stereotypes bias evaluations? *Psychological Bulletin, 105,* 409–425.

Swim, J. K., Cohen, L. L., & Hyers, L. L. (1998). Experiencing everyday prejudice and discrim-ination. In J. K. Swim & C. Stangor (Eds.),

Prejudice: The target's perspective (pp. 37–60). San Diego: Academic Press.

Swim, J. K., & Hyers, L. L. (1999). Excuse me—What did you just say?!: Women's public and private responses to sexist remarks. *Journal of Experimental Social Psychology, 35*(1), 68–88.

Swim, J. K., Hyers, L. L., Cohen, L. L., & Fergu-son, M. J. (2001). Everyday sexism: Evidence for its incidence, nature, and psychological impact from three daily diary studies. *Journal of Social Issues, 57*(1), 31–53.

Swoboda, F. (1995, November 25). Law, educa-tion failing to break glass ceiling. *Washington Post,* pp. C1, C2.

Swoboda, Swoboda, F. & Joyce, A. (2000, March 10). 9–5 gives way to 24–7. *Washington Post,* p. E01.

Tajfel, H. (1981). *Human groups and social cate-gories.* Cambridge: Cambridge University Press.

Taliban publicly executes 2 Afghan women (2001, February 26). Feminist Daily News-wire. [online] **www.feminist.org/news/newsbyte/uswirestory.asp?id=5294**

Tang, C. S., Yik, M. S., Cheung, F. M. C., Choi, P. K. et al. (1995). How do Chinese college students define sexual harassment? *Journal of Interpersonal Violence, 10*(4), 503–515.

Tang, T. N., & Tang, C. S. (2001). Gender role in-ternalization, multiple roles, and Chinese women's mental health. *Psychology of Women Quarterly, 25*(3), 181–196.

Tangri, S., & Jenkins, S. (1986). Stability and change in role-innovation and life plans. *Sex Roles, 14,* 647–662.

Tannen, D. (1990). *You just don't understand: Women and men in conversation.* New York: Morrow.

Tanzania fails to enforce law against female geni-tal mutilation (2001, June 26). Afrol News. [online] **www.afrol.com/News2001/tan007_fgm.htm**

Tanzania Media Women's Association. (1994). How common is sexual harassment in Tanza-nia? In M. Davies (Ed.), *Women and violence: Realities and responses worldwide* (pp. 76–84). London: Zed Books.

Tasker, F., & Golombok, S. (1995). Adults raised as children in lesbian families. *American Journal of Orthopsychiatry, 65*(2), 203–215.

Taylor, J. M. (1996). Cultural stories: Latina and Portuguese daughters and mothers. In B. J. Leadbeater & N. Way (Eds.), *Urban girls: Re-sisting stereotypes, creating identities* (pp. 117–131). New York: New York University Press.

Taylor, J. M., Gilligan, C., & Sullivan, A. M. (1995). *Between voice and silence: Women and girls, race and relationship.* Cambridge, MA: Harvard University Press.

Taylor, S. E. (1981). A categorization approach to stereotyping. In D. L. Hamilton (Ed.), *Cognitive processes in stereotyping and intergroup behavior.* Hillsdale, NJ: Erlbaum (pp. 365–376).

Taylor, S. E., Klein, L. C., Lewis, B. P., Gruenewald, T. L., Gurung, R. A., & Updegraff, J. A. (2000). Biobehavioral responses to stress in females: Tend-and-befriend, not fight-or-flight. *Psychological Review, 107*(3), 411–429.

Tel, S. A. (1993). The effect of having women instructors as role models on perceptions of performance in chemistry. In *Contributions to the Seventh International Gender and Science and Technology Conference* (Vol. 1, pp. 168–176). Waterloo, Ontario: University of Waterloo.

Teo, P., & Mehta, K. (2001). Participating in the home: Widows cope in Singapore. *Journal of Aging Studies, 15*(2), 127–144.

Thibaut, J., & Kelley, H. (1959). *The social psychology of groups.* New York: Wiley.

Thomas, C. (1999, December 21). OK to hit a girl? Increase of females in high school contact sports brings problems, rewards. *USA Today,* pp. C1, C2.

Thomas, D. Q. (1994). In search of solutions: Women's police stations in Brazil. In M. Davies (Ed.), *Women and violence: Realities and responses worldwide* (pp. 32–43). London: Zed Books.

Thomas, V. G. (1989). Body-image satisfaction among Black women. *Journal of Social Psychology, 129*(1), 107–112.

Thompson (Woolley), H. B. (1903). *The mental traits of sex: An experimental investigation of the normal mind in men and women.* Chicago: University of Chicago Press.

Thompson, J. M. (1995). Silencing the self: Depressive symptomatology and close relationships. *Psychology of Women Quarterly, 19*(3), 337–353.

Thompson, S. D., & Walker, A. C. (2004). Satisfaction with parenting: A comparison between adolescent mothers and fathers. *Sex Roles, 50*(9/10), 677–688.

Thompson, S. H., Rafiroiu, A. C., & Sargent, R. G. (2003). Examining gender, racial, and age differences in weight concern among third, fifth, eighth, and eleventh graders. *Eating Behaviors, 3*(4), 307–323.

Thompson, T. L., & Zerbinos, E. (1995). Gender roles in animated cartoons: Has the picture changed in 20 years? *Sex Roles, 32*(9/10), 651–673.

Thornborrow, N. M., & Sheldon, M. B. (1995). Women in the labor force. In J. Freeman (Ed.), *Women: A feminist perspective* (pp. 197–219). Mountain View, CA: Mayfield.

Thorpe, K. J., Dragonas, T., & Golding, J. (1992). The effects of psychosocial factors on the emotional well-being of women during pregnancy: A cross-cultural study of Britain and Greece. *Journal of Reproductive and Infant Psychology, 10*(4), 191–204.

Tiedje, L. B., & Darling-Fisher, C. S. (1993). Factors that influence fathers' participation in child care. *Health Care for Women International, 14,* 99–107.

Tiefer, L. (1995). *Sex is not a natural act and other essays.* Boulder, CO: Westview.

Tien, L. (1994). Southeast Asian American refugee women. In L. Comas-Díaz & B. Greene (Eds.), *Women of color: Integrating ethnic and gender identities in psychotherapy* (pp. 479–503). New York: Guilford.

Tiffany, S. (1982). *Women, work, and motherhood.* Englewood Cliffs, NJ: Prentice-Hall.

Tiggemann, M., & Pennington, B. (1990). The development of gender differences in body-size dissatisfaction. *Australian Psychologist, 25*(3), 306–313.

Time U.S. children spend with their fathers, and what they do. (1999, June 10). News release, University of Michigan News and Information Services. [online] **http://www.gendercenter.org/fathertime.htm**

Tirodkar, M. A., & Jain, A. (2003). Food messages on African American television shows. *American Journal of Public Health, 93,* 439–441.

Tolman, D. L. (1999). Female adolescent sexuality in relational context: Beyond sexual decision making. In Johnson, N. G & Roberts, M. C. (Eds). *Beyond appearance: A new look at adolescent girls.* (pp. 227–246). Washington, DC, US: American Psychological Association.

Top, T. J. (1991). Sex bias in the evaluation of performance in the scientific, artistic, and literary professions: A review. *Sex Roles, 24*(1/2), 73–106.

Torkington, N. P. K. (1995). Black migrant women and health. *Women's Studies International Forum, 18* (2), 153–158.

Tougas, F., Brown, R., Beaton, A. M., & Joly, S. (1995). Neosexism: Plus ça change, plus c'est pareil. *Personality and Social Psychology Bulletin, 21,* 842–849.

Tougas, F., Dubé, L., & Veilleux, F. (1987). Privation relative et programmes d'action positive. *Revue Canadienne des sciences du comportement, 19,* 167–177.

Tougas, F., & Veilleux, F. (1988). The influence of identification, collective relative deprivation, and procedure of implementation on women's response to affirmative action: A causal modeling approach. *Canadian Journal of Behavioural Science, 20,* 16–29.

Tousignant, M. (1995, February 11). Helping Black students picture themselves as physicists. *Washington Post,* p. C3.

Travis, C. B. (1988). *Women and health psychology: Mental health issues.* Hillsdale, NJ: Erlbaum.

Trivers, R. L. (1972). Parental investment and sexual selection. In B. Campbell (Ed.), *Sexual selection and the descent of man, 1871–1971* (pp. 136–179). Chicago: Aldine.

Trueheart, C. (1993, February 27). Canada opens to new kind of refugee. *Washington Post,* p. A17.

Turell, S. C., Armsworth, M. W., & Gaa, J. P. (1990). Emotional responses to abortion: A critical review of the literature. *Women & Therapy, 9*(4), 49–68.

Turkle, S. & Papert, S. (1990). Epistemological pluralism: Styles and voices within the computer culture. *Signs, 16*(1), 128–157.

Udry, J. R. (2000). Biological limits of gender construction. *American Sociological Review, 65,* 443–457.

UNAIDS (2004). Global report on HIV/AIDS 2004. [online] **http://www.unaids.org/ NetTools/Misc/DocInfo.aspx?href=http% 3A%2F%2Fgva%2Ddoc%2Dowl %2FWEBcontent%2FDocuments%2Fpub %2FGlobal%2DReports%2FBangkok %2FTable%5Fcountryestimates %5FGlobalReport2004%5Fen%2Epdf**

Unger, R. (1979a). Sexism in teacher evaluation: The comparability of real life to laboratory analogs. *Academic Psychology Bulletin, 1,* 163–171.

Unger, R. (1979b). Toward a redefinition of sex and gender. *American Psychologist, 34,* 1085–1094.

Ungerleider, L. G., (1995). Functional brain imaging studies of cortical mechanisms for memory. *Science, 270,* 769–775.

United Nations. (1995). *The world's women 1995: Trends and statistics.* New York: Author.

United Nations. (2000). *The world's women 2000: Trends and statistics.* New York: Author.

United Nations (2001, May). Convention on the elimination of all forms of discrimination against women. [online] **www.un.org/ womenwatch/daw/cedaw/states.htm**

United Nations (2001, June). *Fact Sheet: Gender and HIV/AIDS.* Produced for the United Nations special session on HIV/AIDS, June 25–27. New York: Author.

United Nations Children's Emergency Fund (2002). UNICEF executive director targets violence against women. [online] **http://www .unicef.org/newsline/00pr17.htm**

United Nations Children's Fund (2000, May). Domestic violence against women and girls. *Innocenti Digest* No. 6. Florence, Italy: Innocenti Research Centre.

United Nations Development Program (2000). Overcoming human poverty: UNDP poverty report 2000. [online] **www.undp.org/poverty report**

United Nations Development Program (2004). *Human development report, 2004.* [online] **http://hdr.undp.org/statistics/**

United Nations Population Fund (2000). *Lives together, worlds apart: Men and women in a time of change.* New York: Author.

Uray, N., & Burnaz, S. (2003). An analysis of the portrayal of gender roles in Turkish television advertisements. [References]. *Sex Roles, 48*(1–2), 77–87.

U.S. Bureau of the Census (2000). *Statistical abstract of the United States* (120th Ed.). Washington, DC: Author.

U.S. Bureau of the Census (2000b). Poverty: 2000 Highlights. [online] **www.census.gov/ hhes/poverty/poverty00/pov00hi.htm**

U.S. Bureau of the Census (2001). Statistical Abstract of the United States, 2001. Section 12: Labor force, employment and earnings. [online] **http://www.census.gov/prod/ 2002pubs/01statab/labor.pdf**

U.S. Bureau of the Census (2003). Statistical Abstract of the United States, 2003. Section 12: Labor force, employment and earnings. [online] **http://www.census.gov/prod/ 2004pubs/03statab/labor.pdf**

U.S. Bureau of the Census (2004, May). Evidence from Census 2000 about earnings by detailed occupation for men and women. [online] **http://www.census.gov/prod/ 2004pubs/censr-15.pdf**

U.S. Department of Education, National Center for Education Statistics (2003). *Digest of Education Statistics, 2002.* [online] **http://nces .ed.gov/pubsearch/pubsinfo.asp?pubid =2003060**

U.S. Department of Health and Human Services. (1996a). *Physical activity and health: A report of the surgeon general.* Atlanta, GA:

Centers for Disease Control and Prevention, National Center for Chronic Disease Prevention and Health Promotion.

U.S. Department of Health and Human Services. (1996). *National household survey on drug abuse: Main findings 1994.* Rockville, MD: Author.

U.S. Department of Justice. (1994, July 10). Press release: Wives are the most frequent victims in family murders. Washington, DC: Author.

U.S. Department of Justice, Bureau of Justice Statistics. (1997). *Criminal victimization in the United States, 1994: A National Crime Victimization Survey report.* Washington, DC: Author.

U.S. Department of Justice, Federal Bureau of Investigation. (2001). *Crime in the United States 2001. Uniform crime reports.* Washington, DC: Author.

U.S. Department of Justice, Office of Justice Programs. (1995). *Violence against women: Estimates from the redesigned survey, August 1995.* Washington, DC: Author.

U.S. Department of Justice, Office of Justice Programs (2000). *Bureau of Justice Statistics Special Report: Intimate partner violence.* Washington DC: Author.

U.S. Department of Labor (2000). Women's share of the labor force to edge higher by 2008. [online] **http://www.bls.gov/opub/ted/2000/feb/wk3/art01.htm**

U.S. Department of Labor, (2003, September). Highlights of women's earnings in 2002. Bureau of Labor Statistics report number 972. [online] **http://www.bls.gov/cps/cpswom2002.pdf**

U.S. Department of Labor (2004). 20 leading occupations of employed women full-time wage and salary workers. [online] **http://www.dol.gov/wb/factsheets/20lead2003.htm**

U.S. Department of Labor (2004a). Nontraditional occupations for women in 2003. [online]. **http://www.dol.gov/wb/factsheets/nontra2003.htm**.

U.S. Department of Labor (2004b). *Women in the labor force: A databook.* Bureau of Labor Statistics report #973 [online] **http://www.bls.gov/cps/wlf-databook.pdf**.

U.S. Merit Systems Protection Board, (1996). Sexual harassment in the federal workplace: Trends, progress, continuing challenges. [online] **http://www.mspb.gov/studies/sexhar.pdf**

Urbaniak, G. C., & P. R. Kilmann. (2003). Physical attractiveness and the "nice guy paradox": Do nice guys really finish last? *Sex Roles, 49*(9/10), 413–426.

Van Den Bergh, N. (1999). Workplace problems and needs for lesbian and gay male employees: Implications for EAOS. *Employee Assistance Quarterly, 15*(1), 21–60.

Vance, E. B., & Wagner, N. N. (1976). Written descriptions of orgasm: A study of sex differences. *Archives of Sexual Behavior, 5,* 87–98.

Vandenberg, S. G. (1987). Sex differences in mental retardation and their implications for sex differences in ability. In J. M. Reinisch, L. A. Rosenblum, & S. A. Sanders (Eds.), *Masculinity/femininity: Basic perspectives* (pp. 157–171). New York: Oxford University Press.

van Eeden, C., & Wissing, M. (2000, July). *Gender and psychological well-being: Trends in South African findings.* Paper presented at the XXVIIth International Congress of Psychology, Stockholm, Sweden.

Vera Institute of Justice (2004, June 14). Case study: Specialized police services for women. [online] **http://www.vera.org/project/project1_10.asp?section_id=2&project_id=31&sub_section_id=6**

Vera, O. M. (1999). The mother–daughter relationship in the Mexian American culture: The daughter's perspective. *Dissertation Abstracts International, 60*(6-B), 3023.

Villarruel, A. M. (1998). Cultural influences on the sexual attitudes, beliefs, and norms of young Latina adolescents. *Journal of the Society of Pediatric Nurses, 3*(2), 69–80.

Vishnudevananda, S. (1970). *The complete illustrated book of yoga.* New York: Bell.

von Baeyer, C. L., Sherk, D. L., & Zanna, M. P. (1981). Impression management in the job interview: When the female applicant meets the male "chauvinist" interviewer. *Personality and Social Psychology Bulletin, 7,* 45–51.

Voyer, D. (1996). On the magnitude of laterality effects and sex differences in functional lateralities. *Laterality, 1,* 51–83.

Voyer, D., Voyer, S., & Bryden, P. (1995). Magnitude of sex differences in spatial abilities: A meta-analysis and consideration of critical variables. *Psychological Bulletin, 117,* 250–270.

Wagner, R. (1987). Changes in the friend network during the first year of single parenthood for Mexican American and Anglo women. *Journal of Divorce, 11*(2), 89–109.

Wainer, H., & Steinberg, L. (1992). Sex differences in performance on the mathematics section of the Scholastic Aptitude Test: A bidirectional validity study. *Harvard Educational Review, 62*(3), 323–336.

Waitzkin, H., Cabrera, A., Cabrera, E. A., Radlow, M., & Rodriguez, F. (1996). Patient–doctor communication in cross-national perspective: A study in Mexico. *Medical Care, 34*(7), 641–671.

Walcott, D. D., Pratt, H. D., & Patel, D. R. (2003). Adolescents and eating disorders: Gender, racial, ethnic, sociocultural, and socioeconomic issues. *Journal of Adolescent Research, 18*(3), 223–243.

Walker, A. (1984). Zora Neale Hurston: A cautionary tale and a partisan review. In A. Walker (Ed.), *In search of our mothers' gardens: Womanist prose* (pp. 83–92). San Diego: Harcourt Brace.

Walker, C. (2004, February 26). Vagina Monologues stirs up Cairo. *Women's e-news.* [online] **http://www.womensenews.org/article .cfm/dyn/aid/1727/context/archive**

Walker, K. (1994). Men, women, and friendship: What they say, what they do. *Gender and Society, 8,* 246–265.

Walker, L. E. A. (1979). *The battered woman.* New York: Harper & Row.

Walker, L. E. A. (1991). Post-traumatic stress disorder in women: Diagnosis and treatment of battered woman syndrome. *Psychotherapy, 28*(1), 21–29.

Walker, L. E. A. (1995). Racism and violence against women. In J. Adelman & G. Enguídanos (Eds.), *Racism in the lives of women* (pp. 239–250). New York: Harrington Park Press.

Walker, L. O., & Best, M. A. (1991). Well-being of mothers with infant children: A preliminary comparison of employed women and homemakers. *Women & Health, 17* (1), 71–89.

Wall, S. N., Frieze, I. H., Ferligoj, A., Jarosova, E., Pauknerova, D., Horvat, J., & Sarlija, N. (1999). Gender role and religion as predictors of attitude toward abortion in Croatia, Slovenia, the Czech Republic, and the United States. *Journal of Cross-Cultural Psychology, 30*(4), 443–465.

Wallich, P. (1996). Having it all. *Scientific American, 274*(3), 31.

Walsh, M. R. (1977). *Doctors wanted: No women need apply.* New Haven, CT: Yale University Press.

Walzer, S. (1995, December). Transition into motherhood: Pregnant daughters' responses to their mothers. *Families in Society, 76*(10), 596–603.

Wang, A. H-J. (2001). A cross-national invertistigation of gender differences in mean and variance of mathematics achievement of thirteen-year-old students from a social-psychological perspective. *Dissertation Abstracts International, 62*(2–A), 504.

Wang, N. (1995). Born Chinese and a woman in America. In J. Adleman & G. Enguídanos (Eds.), *Racism in the lives of women: Testimony, theory, and guides to antiracist practice* (pp. 97–110). New York: Harrington Park Press.

Ward, J. V. (1996). Raising resisters: The role of truth telling in the psychological development of African American girls. In B. J. R. Leadbeater & N. Way (Eds.), *Urban girls: Resisting stereotypes, creating identities* (pp. 85–99). New York: New York University Press.

Ward, M. C. (1999). *A world full of women.* (Second Ed.). Boston: Allyn & Bacon.

Warner, C. (1992). *A treasury of women's quotations.* Englewood Cliffs, NJ: Prentice-Hall.

Warren, C. W., Goldberg, H. I., Oge, L., & Pepion, D. (1990). Assessing the reproductive behavior of on- and off-reservation American Indian females: Characteristics of two groups in Montana. *Social Biology, 37,* 69–83.

Washbourn, P. (1977). *Becoming woman: The quest for wholeness in female experience.* New York: Harper & Row.

Watkins, P. L., & Lee, J. (1997). A feminist perspective on panic disorder and agoraphobia: Etiology and treatment. *Journal of Gender, Culture, and Health, 2*(1), 65–87.

Way, N. (1995). "Can't you see the courage, the strength that I have?": Listening to urban adolescent girls speak about their relationships. *Psychology of Women Quarterly, 19*(1), 107–128.

Way, N. (1996). Between experiences of betrayal and desire: Close friendships among urban adolescents. In B. J. Leadbeater & N. Way (Eds.), *Urban girls: Resisting stereotypes, creating identities.* New York: New York University Press.

Webb, J. (2001). (Secretary, International Mathematical Olympiad Advisory Board). Personal communication.

Weber, B. (1996, December 19). Chess's problematic endgame. *New York Times,* pp. B1, B10.

Wechsler, L. S., & Rubin, L. J. (2000, August). *Acculturation, self-silencing, and depression in Asian American college women.* Paper presented at the annual conference of the American Psychological Association, Washington, DC.

Weekend Edition (2001, May 20). Azizah: Interview with Tayyiba Taylor. Washington DC: National Public Radio.

Weis, D. L. (1985). The experience of pain during women's first sexual intercourse: Cultural mythology about female sexual initiation. *Archives of Sexual Behavior, 14,* 421–438.

Weiss, E. M., Kemmler, G., Deisenhammer, E. A., Fleischhacker, W. W., & Delazer, M. (2003). Sex differences in cognitive functions. *Personality and Individual Differences, 35*(4), 863–875.

Weissman, R. (2001, March/April). Women and tobacco. *The Network News,* National Women's Health Network, pp. 1, 4.

Weisstein, N. (1971). *Psychology constructs the female or, the fantasy life of the male psychologist.* Boston: New England Free Press.

Wekker, G. (1997). Mati-ism and Black lesbianism: Two idealtypical expressions of female homosexuality in Black communities of the diaspora. *Journal of Lesbian Studies, 1*(1), 11–24 (reprinted from *Journal of Homosexuality, 24* [1993]).

Weller, A., & Weller, L. (1992). Menstrual synchrony in female couples. *Psychoneuroendocrinology, 17,* 171–177.

Weller, A., & Weller, L. (1993). Menstrual synchrony between mothers and daughters and between roommates. *Physiology and Behavior, 53,* 943–949.

Weller, A., & Weller, L. (1995). Examination of menstrual synchrony among women basketball players. *Psychoneuroendocrinology, 20* (6), 613–622.

Weller, A., & Weller, L. (1997). Menstrual synchrony under optimal conditions: Bedouin families. *Journal of Comparative Psychology, 111*(2), 143–151.

Weller, L., Weller, A., & Roizman, S. (1999). Human menstural synchrony in families and among close friends: Examining the importance of mutual exposure. *Journal of Comparative Psychology, 113*(3), 261–268.

West, L., Anderson, J., & Duck, S. (1996). Crossing the barriers to friendships between men and women. In J. T. Wood (Ed.), *Gendered relationships* (pp. 111–127). Mountain View, CA: Mayfield.

West, M. S. (1995). Women faculty: Frozen in time. *Academe, 81*(4), 26–29.

Westkott, M. (1986). *The feminist legacy of Karen Horney.* New Haven, CT: Yale University Press.

Whalen, D. M., Bigner, J. J., & Barber, C. E. (2000). Grandmother role as experienced by lesbian women. *Journal of Women and Aging, 12*(3–4), 39–57.

Wheelwright, J. (1989). *Amazons and military maids: Women who dressed as men in pursuit of life, liberty and happiness.* London: Pandora.

Whipple, B., & Komisaruk, R. (1991). The G spot, orgasm, and female ejaculation: Are they related? In P. Kothari (Ed.), *Proceedings of the First International Conference on Orgasm* (pp. 227–237). Bombay, India: VRP.

Whipple, B., Ogden, G., & Komisaruk, B. R. (1992). Physiological correlates of imagery-induced orgasm in women. *Archives of Sexual Behavior, 21,* 121–133.

Whitaker, L., & Austin, E. (2001, June 24). Teaching good girls to be tough negotiators. *Roanoke Times,* Horizon section, pp. 1, 5.

White, D. G. (1985). *Ar'n't I a woman? Female slaves in the plantation South.* New York: Norton.

White, J. W. (1983). Sex and gender issues in aggression research. In R. G. Geen & E. I. Donnerstein (Eds.), *Aggression: Theoretical and empirical reviews* (pp. 1–26). New York: Academic Press.

White, J. W., & Koss, M. P. (1991). Courtship violence: Incidence in a national sample of higher education students. *Violence and Victims, 6,* 247–256.

White, J. W., & Kowalski, R. M. (1994). Deconstructing the myth of the nonaggressive woman: A feminist analysis. *Psychology of Women Quarterly, 18,* 487–508.

White, J. W., & Roufail, M. (1989). Gender and influence strategies of first and last resort. *Psychology of Women Quarterly, 13,* 175–189.

Whitehead, B. D., & Popenoe, D. (2001). The state of our unions: The social health of marriage in America, 2001. Produced by the National Marriage Project. [online] **http://marriage.rutgers.edu/about.htm**

Wiersma, U. J. (1990). Gender differences in job attribute preferences: Work–home role conflict and job level as mediating variables. *Journal of Occupational Psychology, 63,* 231–243.

Wikipedia, the Free Encyclopedia (2001). [online] **http://en.wikipedia.org/wiki/Riot_grrl**

Wilkinson, S., & Kitzinger, C. (1992). Theorizing heterosexuality. Special Issue. *Feminism & Psychology, 2*(3).

Williams, J. E., & Bennett, S. M. (1975). The definition of sex stereotypes via the adjective check list. *Sex Roles, 1,* 327–337.

Williams, J. E., & Best, D. L. (1982). *Measuring sex stereotypes: A thirty-nation study.* Beverly Hills, CA: Sage.

Williams, J. E., & Best, D. L. (1990). *Measuring sex stereotypes: A multination study* (revised edition). Newbury Park, CA: Sage.

Wilson, A. (1996). How we find ourselves: Identity development and two-spirit people. *Harvard Educational Review, 66*(2), 303–317.

Wilson, M., & Russell, K. (1996). *Divided sisters: Bridging the gap between Black women and White women.* New York: Doubleday Anchor.

Wilson, R. A. (1966). *Feminine forever.* New York: M. Evans.

Wilson, R. A., & Wilson, T. A. (1963). The fate of the nontreated postmenopausal woman: A plea for the maintenance of adequate estrogen from puberty to the grave. *Journal of the American Geriatric Society, 11,* 347–362.

Wingard, D. L., Kritz-Silverstein, D., & Barrett-Connor, E. (1992, February). Employment status and heart disease risk factors in middle-aged women: The Rancho Bernardo Study. *American Journal of Public Health, 82*(2), 215–219.

Winkvist, A., & Akhtar, H. Z. (2000). God should give daughters to rich families only: Attitudes towards childbearing among low-income women in Punjab, Pakistan. *Social Science and Medicine, 51*(1), 73–81.

Winter, D. G. (1988). The power motive in women—and men. *Journal of Personality and Social Psychology, 54*(3), 510–519.

Wirth, L. (1997). *Breaking through the glass ceiling: Women in management. Report for discussion at the Tripartite Meeting on Breaking through the Glass Ceiling: Women in Management.* Geneva: International Labour Office.

Wirth, L. (2001). *Breaking through the glass ceiling: Women in management.* Geneva: International Labour Office.

Witkin, H. A. (1949). Sex differences in perception. *Transactions of New York Academy of Science, 12*(1), 25.

Witkin, H. A., Lewis, H. B., Hertzman, M., Machover, K., Meissner, P. B., & Wagner, S. (1954). *Personality through perception.* New York: Wiley.

Witkowska, E., Eliasson, M., & Menckel, E. (2000, July). *Sexual harassment in Swedish schools: Developing an environmental model based on available data and models.* Paper presented at the International Congress of Psychology, Stockholm, Sweden.

Wolf, N. (1991). *The beauty myth.* New York: Morrow.

Women, Men, and Media. (1994). *Arriving on the scene. Women's growing presence in the news.* Washington, DC: Author.

Women in Management. (2001, December/January). Harassment cited for why women quit: 30% of female executives factor it in decision. *Newsletter 11*(2), p. 12.

Women's Bureau (2001). Nontraditional occupations for women in 2001. [online] **www.dol .gov/dol/wb/public/wb_pubs/nontra2000 .htm**

Women's Commission for Refugee Women and Children (2001). [online] **www.womens commission.org**

Women's Institute for a Secure Retirement (WISER) (2001). *Top 5 reasons why retirement is a challenge for women workers.* [online] **www.wiser.heinz.org/mainpage.html**

Women sexually assaulted under INS detention to be deported (2001, Fall). *Amnesty Now,* pp. 2–3.

Wood, J. T. (1996a). Gender, relationships, and communication. In J. T. Wood (Ed.), *Gendered relationships* (pp. 3–19). Mountain View, CA: Mayfield.

Wood, J. T. (1996b). She says/he says: Communication, caring, and conflict in heterosexual relationships. In J. T. Wood (Ed.), *Gendered relationships* (pp.149–162). Mountain View, CA: Mayfield.

Wood, J. T. (2001). *Gendered lives: Communication, gender and culture.* Belmont, CA: Wadsworth/Thompson Learning.

Wood, M. (2002, October 15). Lawsuit Will Eventually Topple Rule Barring Women from Ground Combat, Draft, Coughlin Says. University of Virginia School of Law—News and Events [online] **http://www.law.virginia .edu/home2002/html/news/2002_fall/ women_military.htm**

Wood, W., & Karten, S. J. (1986). Sex differences in interaction style as a product of perceived sex differences in competence. *Journal of Personality and Social Psychology, 50,* 341–347.

Worell, J., & Johnson, D. (2001). Therapy with women: Feminist frameworks. In. R. K. Unger (Ed.), *Handbook of the psychology of women and gender* (pp. 317–329). New York: John Wiley & Sons.

World Bank (2002). Global country data—Summary education profiles. [online] **http:// genderstats.worldbank.org/edstats/cd1.asp**

World Bank (2002a). GenderStats. Database of gender statistics. [online] **http://devdata .worldbank.org/genderstats/**

World Economic Forum (2003). Meet some Russian women leaders. [online] **http:// www.weforum.org/site/knowledgenaviga- tor.nsf/Content/Meet%20Some%20Rus- sian%20Women%20Leaders_2003?open &country_id=**

World Health Organization (2000). Suicide. [online] **www.who.int/mental_health/Topic _suicide/suicide1.html**

World Health Organization (2002). *World report on violence and health.* Geneva, Switzerland: Author. [online] **http://www.who.int/violence_injury_prevention/violence/world_report/en/**

World Health Organization (2003). *The world health report 2003.* [online] **http://www.who.int/whr/2003/en**

World Health Organization (2004). *Unsafe abortion—Global and regional estimates of the incidence of unsafe abortion and associated mortality in 2000* (4th edition). [online] **http://www.who.int/reproductive-health/publications/unsafe_abortion_estimates_04/index.html**

World Internet Project (2004, January 14). First release of findings from the UCLA Work Internet Project shows significant "digital gender gap" in many countries. [online] **http://www.ccp.ucla.edu/downloads/UCLA_World_Internet_Project.doc**

Wyatt, G. E. (1982). The sexual experience of Afro-American women: A middle-income sample. In M. Kirkpatrick (Ed.), *Women's sexual experience: Explorations of the dark continent* (pp. 17–39). New York: Plenum.

Wyatt, G. E. (1989). Reexamining factors predicting Afro-American and White American women's age at first coitus. *Archives of Sexual Behavior, 18,* 271–298.

Wyatt, G. E. (1992). The sociocultural context of African American and White American women's rape. *Journal of Social Issues, 48*(1), 77–92.

Wyatt, G. E., Guthrie, D., & Notgrass, C. (1992). Differential effects of women's child sexual abuse and subsequent sexual revictimization. *Journal of Consulting and Clinical Psychology, 60,* 167–173.

Wyatt, N. (2000). Information on sexual harassment: International perspectives. Pennsylvania State University, Delaware County.[online] **http://www.de.psu.edu/harassment/generalinfo/international.html**

Wyche, K. F. (2001). Sociocultural issues in counseling for women of color. In R. K. Unger (Ed.), *Handbook of the psychology of women and gender* (pp. 330–340). New York: John Wiley & Sons.

Xu, X. (1997). The prevalence and determination of wife abuse in urban China. *Journal of Comparative Family Studies, 28*(3), 280–303.

Yahr, P. (1988). Sexual differentiation of behavior in the context of developmental psychobiology. *Handbook of behavioral neurobiology* (pp. 197–243). New York: Plenum.

Yale 1st-year med class predominantly female. (1995, June 1). *Arizona Daily Star,* p. 4A.

Yamaguchi, M. (1998, September 29). Japanese women defy abusive relationships. *Cavalier Daily,* p. 2.

Yee, D. K., & Eccles, J. S. (1988). Parent perceptions and attributions for children's math achievement. *Sex Roles, 19*(5/6), 317–333.

Yesko, J. (1995, May–June). A leap of faith. *Women's Sports & Fitness,* p. 34.

Yeung, R. M. (2000). Acculturation: Its impact on Chinese-American women's relationship with their mothers. *Dissertation Abstracts International, 60*(8-B), 4262.

Yewchuk, C. R., & Schlosser, G. A. (1995). Characteristics of the parents of eminent Canadian women. *Roeper Review, 18*(1), 78–83.

Yi, K. Y. (1989, April). Symptoms of eating disorders among Asian-American college female students as a function of acculturation. *Dissertation Abstracts International, 50,* 10.

Yoder, J. D., Schleicher, T. L., & McDonald, T. W. (1998). Empowering token women leaders: The importance of organizationally legitimated credibility. *Psychology of Women Quarterly, 22,* 209–222.

Zafarullah, H. (2000). Through the brick wall and the glass ceiling: Women in the civil service in Bangladesh. *Gender, Work & Organization, 7*(3), 197–209.

Zayas, L., Torres, L., Malcolm, J., & DesRosiers, F. (1996). Clinicians' definitions of ethnically sensitive therapy. *Professional Psychology: Research and Practice, 27,* 78–82.

Zellman, G. L., & Goodchilds, J. D. (1983). Becoming sexual in adolescence. In E. R. Allgeier & N. B. McCormick (Eds.), *Changing boundaries: Gender roles and sexual behavior* (pp. 49–63). Mountain View, CA: Mayfield.

Zia, H. (2000, Winter). A great leap forward for girls. *Ford Foundation Report, 31*(1), 14–16.

Zucker, A. N., Harrell, Z. A., Miner-Rubino, K., Stewart, A. J., Pomerleau, C. S., & Boyd, C. J. (2001). Smoking in college women: The role of thinness pressures, media exposure, and critical consciousness. *Psychology of Women Quarterly, 25*(3), 233–241.

Zumwalt, R. L. (1992). *Wealth and rebellion: Elsie Clews Parsons, anthropologist and folklorist.* Urbana: University of Illinois Press.

Zwerner, J. (1982). A study of issues in sexuality counseling for women with spinal cord injuries. *Women & Therapy, 1*(3), 21–100.

PHOTO CREDITS

AUTHOR INDEX

SUBJECT INDEX